ALSO BY HARLAN LANE

AS AUTHOR
The Wild Boy of Aveyron

The Wild Boy of Burundi
(with Richard Pillard)

AS EDITOR
Recent Perspectives on American Sign Language
(François Grosjean, co-editor)

The Deaf Experience:
Classics in Language and Education
(Franklin Philip, translator)

WHEN THE MIND HEARS

A HISTORY

OF THE DEAF

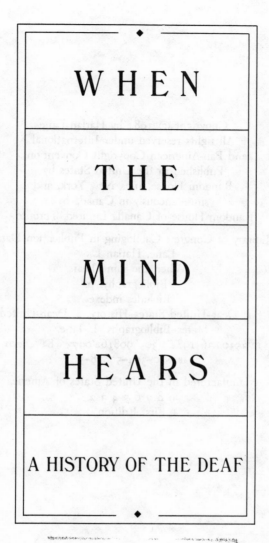

WHEN THE MIND HEARS

A HISTORY OF THE DEAF

HARLAN LANE

RANDOM HOUSE • NEW YORK

Library of Congress Cataloging in Publication Data
Lane, Harlan L⟨handwritten: Lawson, 1936–⟩
When the mind hears.
Bibliography: p.
Includes indexes.
1. Deaf–United States–History. 2. Deaf–United
States–Bibliography. I. Title.
HV2530.L36 1984   305'.908162'0973   83–43201
ISBN 0-394-50878-5

Manufactured in the United States of America
9 8 7 6 5 4 3 2
First Edition

for
FRANKLIN
PHILIP

What matters deafness of the ear, when
the mind hears. The one true deafness,
the incurable deafness, is that of the mind.

VICTOR HUGO TO FERDINAND BERTHIER,
November 25, 1845

CONTENTS

FOREWORD

On the face of it, people are quite afraid of human diversity and look to their social institutions to limit or eradicate it. As a psychologist I am interested in learning more about that fear, and as a psychologist of language, more about the role of language policy in catering to it. The history of relations between the society of hearing-speaking people and the community of deaf-signing people is an excellent case study in the motives and means at work when fear of diversity leads majorities to oppress minorities. The attempt to force assimilation, to claim biological insufficiency when assimilation fails, to indoctrinate minority children in majority values through the schools—all this and much more will be familiar to readers interested in the predicament of other minority communities. In short, *When the Mind Hears* is a study in the anatomy of prejudice.

The hearing loss of most members of the signing community has proven disastrous for them because it has played into the hands of those who seek to dispose of social problems by medicalizing them. The two million or so men and women who use manual language in the United States are not handicapped in the usual sense; theirs is largely a problem of overcoming language barriers, not a problem of disability. So say my deaf friends, and the evidence bears them out. Then why do we hearing people consider the deaf disabled, defective? Why do we and our institutions class them not with groups such as Spanish-speaking Americans but with groups such as blind Americans? Why indeed?

Using the medical model, our society is irresponsibly tearing many deaf children from the social fabric of the signing community in which their lives are interwoven and casting them willy-nilly into "mainstream" schools, as if pretending that they spoke would make it so. Some hearing educators reply that proximity is the first step in integration, and integration—making others like ourselves—is a self-evident good. When no provision is made in "mainstreaming" for the language barrier, however, this proximity proves, in the words of a deaf educator, as productive as that between a dog and its fleas. The mainstreaming movement is proceeding with near total disregard of the wishes of the signing community, which has always been at odds with its hearing benefactors—otologists, audiologists, speech pathologists, special educators. As long as this establishment clings to the medical model, it cannot take the next step forward with the signing community, which is to supplant that model.

Thus it has become necessary for a student of language to tell the history of the deaf minority; hearing students of the deaf have been proceeding on the premise that there is no minority and hence no minority history to tell. Until recently, no deaf person had written a history of the deaf community either—bitter testimony to the effectiveness of the establishment in inculcating the medical model of deafness in deaf children.*

I expect there are many people, hearing and deaf, particularly outside the signing community, who will find my interpretation of the record unpalatable. Some reject the view that the signing community is foremost a linguistic minority; others contend that the first priority of minorities, sign-language, spoken-language, or otherwise, should be assimilation. The proper relations between a minority and the society in which it is embedded are generally the subject of heated dispute, and the proper relation between the signing community and hearing society has been the subject of an impassioned debate for over two hundred years. These readers and others with strongly held views at odds with those of this history may be tempted to dismiss the history for its strongly held views, preferring what they would choose to call a more impartial account, a statement of the hard facts.

A history cannot be written, however, without a point of view. Nor even, if that were possible, should it be. A history is bound to be an interpretation because, for one thing, it makes selections at every turn among an infinity of facts. It defines its domain, excluding some periods, nations, individuals, including others. Within the domain, the documentation is incomplete, and of those facts well documented the historian will cite some and not others,

*The National Association of the Deaf has published *Deaf Heritage: A Narrative History of Deaf America*, by Jack R. Gannon.

according to their significance. That is, the historian has a vantage point and he will arrange and subordinate his selected facts and describe them in a way that allows him to develop his interpretation.

Thus the history of a language community has some things in common with a grammar of that community's language. Both are theories that attempt to account in insightful ways for a selection of facts, a selection motivated by the nature of the theory itself. There can be many histories of the signing community as there can be many grammars of American Sign Language, and we can choose among them. Theories are, of course, social artifacts, and the same cultural forces that so long delayed the linguistic description of American Sign Language have also delayed the history of the community that uses it. Just as hearing people assumed, and taught the deaf, that the deaf community had no language of its own but at best a manual variant of spoken language, so they assumed, and taught the deaf, that they had no history in their own right but only at best a chapter in hearing history (generally entitled "Educating the Deaf").

Even if we could write history as documentation, we should not. If there is truth to Hegel's claim that "people and governments have never learned anything from history," this should motivate the historian who wants to have an impact on human affairs, as I do, to write in a way that commands general attention. If his subject, moreover, turns on sustained outrages against fundamental human values, as mine does, is he to deny his humanity and pretend indifference?

Since a history, then, must have a point of view and should have a point of view, the reader might like to have mine clearly posted, as follows. With the recent evidence from linguistics that American Sign Language is a natural language, the signing community is revealed to be a linguistic minority, and this history interprets the record of their struggle in that light.

The one hundred fifty years from the founding of the education of the signing community to the abandonment of that minority education—from mid-Enlightenment to 1900—seemed to me a coherent interval (to use Barbara Tuchman's term) to study. In fact, nothing fundamental has changed in these matters since 1900 in most of the Western world, although there have been some recent stirrings here and there.* Furthermore, I have chosen to examine that interval, during which use of the language of the deaf made possible their education, from the vantage point and in the person of the central figure in the history of the deaf, Laurent Clerc.

When the distinguished chairman of the drama department at Gallaudet College, Gil Eastman, and I wished to present, to a symposium of the National Association of the Deaf, a brief historical sketch of the American

*See chapter 11 and my *Recent Perspectives on American Sign Language* (with François Grosjean; Hillsdale, N.J.: Lawrence Erlbaum Associates, 1980).

deaf community (in English and American Sign Language concurrently), we began: "My name is Laurent Clerc"; and so I begin here. Clerc was the intellectual leader of the French and then the American deaf communities; he knew most of the important figures in my "coherent interval" personally or at one remove and he was the prime mover in that history. To learn what Clerc's experiences and views were I consulted his published articles, addresses, diary, and autobiographical sketch, his book with Jean Massieu, the Clerc Papers at Yale University, the Gallaudet Papers at the Library of Congress, and numerous documents by others describing or quoting his opinions. Often I have been able to let Clerc speak for himself by taking sentences and paragraphs from these various sources (identified in the notes). When that was not possible, the views of Clerc's contemporaries served as my guide (where there was no reason to believe Clerc would have seen things otherwise). Where the facts are known, I have remained faithful to the facts, and I have indicated in the notes when I was obliged to give rein to my imagination.*

I have dared to speak in Clerc's name in order to present the views of the deaf themselves as clearly and cogently as possible. What are those views? They are stated throughout this history but epitomized by the words of Robert P. McGregor, deaf orator, writer, school principal, and first president of the National Association of the Deaf:

"By whom, then, are signs proscribed? By a few educators of the deaf whose boast is that they do not understand signs and do not want to; by a few philanthropists who are otherwise ignorant of the language; by parents who do not understand the requisites to the happiness of their deaf children and are inspired with false fears by the educators and philanthropists.

"These few have banded together and, backed up by unlimited wealth, send forth men and women who travel all over the country from Maine to California the year round, insidiously creating and fostering everywhere a false, a forced, an artificial sentiment against signs. They also have access to the public press and, making use of impecunious and sensational writers, seek to make what is old appear new and convince the uninitiated that what is white is black. And worst of all they ignore the deaf themselves in their senseless and mischievous propaganda against signs. Professing to have no object in view but the benefit of the deaf, they exhibit an utter contempt for the opinions, the wishes, the desires of the deaf!

"And why should we not be consulted in a matter of such vital interest to us? This is a question that no man has yet answered satisfactorily.

---

*As in psychological research, the evidence marshaled by my theoretical perspective is open to independent inspection. Some 1,200 reference notes give the sources for specific facts and claims; the 2,000-odd sources are listed in the bibliography; and the appended guide (a counterpart to the method section of a psychological study) will aid the student of deaf history in gaining access to these sources among others.

"The utmost extreme to which tyranny can go when its mailed hand descends upon a conquered people is the proscription of their national language, and with the utmost rigor several generations are required to eradicate it. But all the attempts to suppress signs, wherever tried, have most signally failed. After a hundred years of proscription in Germany and Austria, they still flourish, and will continue to flourish to the end of time.

"What heinous crime have the deaf been guilty of that their language should be proscribed?"

PART ONE

LAURENT

CLERC'S

STORY

LAURENT CLERC
(PAINTING BY JOHN CARLIN)

ONE

MY NEW FAMILY

My name is Laurent Clerc. I am eighty-three years old. My hair is white, my skin wrinkled and scarred, my posture crooked; I shuffle when I walk. Undoubtedly my life will soon end in this time and place: 1869, Hartford, Connecticut. I spend most of my day sitting alone at my dining room window, looking at my orchard and remembering.[1] I also read the paper and occasionally friends come to visit. I know what's going on. Important people, distinguished gentlemen, are repudiating the cause to which I have devoted my life. Endowed with the sacred trust of my people's welfare, they seek, without consulting us, to prevent our worship, marriage, and procreation, to stultify our education, and to banish our mother tongue simply because our way and our language are different from theirs.[2] As I write, America licks its nearly fatal wounds; the enslavement of colored people has been ended, and the Union has begun the Reconstruction. Yet how should we rejoice who remain imperiled? The disease of intolerance itself is unchecked and threatens to invade other limbs of the body politic.

Every creature, every work of God, is admirably made; perhaps what we find faulty in its kind turns to our advantage without our knowing it. One day the sun shines on my orchard, another it does not. The orchard has fruitful trees and unfruitful; even in the same species there are different varieties—everything is variable and inconstant. And we ourselves: we vary in our forms and functions, in our hearts and minds. I do not know, as you do not know, why this should be so. We can only thank God for the rich diversity of His creation and hope that in the future world the reason for it may be explained to us all.[3]

Meanwhile—language must come once again to my aid. It has always been my weapon to fight evil, my vessel to fill minds thirsting for knowledge, my lure to solicit relief.* It must serve me grandly one last time and cast such a brilliant light on the history of present injustices that their perpetrators will cringe and their victims rally.

I am impelled by the present threat to the well-being, dignity, and freedom of my people to tell our story, one that I have lived almost from its beginning: how we gathered in France and in other European lands and then in America; how our language† spread throughout Europe and crossed the Atlantic; the great struggle to create schools for us, in which it was my lot to play a leading role. It is a story of builders: of an abbé rejected by the Church who established the education of an entire class rejected by society; of a deaf shepherd who achieved international acclaim by personifying what such an outcast class can achieve through education; of a frail New England pastor who channeled the love of a little deaf girl into a mighty force that has created the first college in the world for that class. It is also a tale of destroyers: of a zealous physician who put mock science ahead of true humanity; of a haughty nobleman who imposed his will on the deaf, knowing, he believed, what was best for them but knowing, in fact, none of them; of a professional reformer who has sought to recast entire classes of society in his own image.

The story has never been told. I will tell it all, and the forces of darkness will be revealed for what they are. I do not mean to say I shall relate all the facts; indeed, what interest would such an inventory have, even if all the facts were known? But I will tell the true story, how it really was, for I have seen much of it unfold with my own eyes; I have been a witness and a shaper of events.

My own story and my people's became one seven decades ago, when I was twelve years old. King Louis XVI had been guillotined four years before,‡ Robespierre's head had fallen in its turn a year after that, and the nightmare of the Terror he directed was beginning to fade.§ As my boyhood drew to a close, my prospects, like those of the new nation that proclaimed the fraternity of all its citizens, were uncertain, for I was starting a new life: my uncle had brought me to the capital to place me in the National Institution for Deaf-Mutes (my father could not accompany me because of his

*Aid for the deaf.
†French Sign Language.
‡January 21, 1793.
§The Reign of Terror, 1793–1794, during the French Revolution.

duties as mayor of our village, La Balme, on the sunny banks of the Rhône).

I am profoundly deaf. When I was about a year old, I was left home alone for a few moments, in a chair by the fire; I fell and badly burned my face (the scar remains and inspired my name sign, two fingers brushed against the right cheek). My family believed it was this accident that deprived me of my hearing and my sense of smell, too; but I may have been born that way.

At first my parents tried to undo my deafness. A certain doctor in Lyon had a cure and my mother took me there; he said he could make me hear if I called at his office twice a day for a fortnight. This we did and he injected I know not what liquids into my ears but without effect. At the end of the fortnight I returned home with my mother, still as deaf as I was before.[4]

My mother was a devout Catholic and I would often accompany her when she went to the church perched high on the cliff overlooking La Balme. Secreted within the cliff are magnificent and labyrinthine grottos, and in the giant archway at the opening lies an oratory, a chapel to which pilgrims traveled as early as the fourteenth century and which my mother and I visited from time to time. I was not supposed to go beyond the chapel, into the cavernous halls and dank recesses of the grottos themselves. But a deaf boy could not go to school and, like the village idiot, could not be instructed either in any useful occupation, so I was left to myself and I ventured where foaming rapids and strange concretions struck delicious terror in my mind: there was an avenging monk, I recall, and a pork-butcher covered in gore. Sometimes I sought out the more tranquil setting of the banks of the Rhône, where I spent hours watching the muddy river glide off to distant places beyond Lyon. Occasionally I drove my mother's turkeys to the field or her cows to pasture or my father's horse to the watering place.

My brother and sisters communicated with me in "home sign," gestures that were scarcely more than pantomime but had become abbreviated with use. I had the impression that my mother wanted to learn these signs but never could, while my father, who could learn anything, did not care to. He was the king's *notaire,** as was my maternal grandfather—thus were the careful keeping of records and the love of history bred into me. My father, who had offices in three villages, was a man more respected than liked, but he was elected mayor all the same. In his middle age he was encumbered with a deaf son and he was offended: it was inconvenient, untidy, embarrassing, and it implied that he was guilty of something.[5]

I could not know what reasoning or events lay behind his decision to send me to Paris. The fame of the Institution for Deaf-Mutes would have reached even La Balme, and it is possible that my father was not displeased

*The *notaire* draws up deeds and wills and keeps other civil records.

to have the opportunity of helping me while also discharging his burden. In any case, when I was twelve, a tawny-haired, gangly slip of a youth, I made the week's journey with my uncle to Paris. The bustle of the city, the imposing façade of the school, the long waiting alone in anterooms, my uncle's tearful farewell—all these frightened me terribly at first. Fortunately, I did not have to face as well the renowned head of the school, the abbé Sicard. The Directory, which then ruled in France, had recently ordered him deported, along with two of their own number and many politicians and journalists, for sympathy with the deposed monarchy, and he was in hiding to avoid the perils of an involuntary trip to the jungles of French Guiana.[6] I was received, instead, by a young deaf man, twenty-five at the time, Jean Massieu, who had been appointed Abbé Sicard's chief teaching assistant by Louis XVI.

Massieu had flowing brown locks and long sideburns, which emphasized his oblong face. His eyes and lips traced thin horizontal lines there, where his large flat nose extended from a broad forehead down toward a jutting chin. He wore, as I soon discovered was his custom, a bizarre outfit he had bought at auction and over it a gray riding coat that reached his ankles. The coat had two large deep pockets, filled with books and chalk and watches —Massieu had a passion for watches.[7] Jean Massieu would become my teacher, then my colleague, and my lifelong friend, but he appears in my memory after the passage of all these years as he did on that first day, like an icon: full face, calm, radiating a saintly aura, a childlike candor; loving, inviting. Jean Massieu—who had to wait until he was twenty to learn the mysteries of the Sacrament, as there was none to educate him before the abbé Sicard; Jean Massieu—who consecrated his life to the disinherited and died penniless himself.

I will tell you more about my teacher, Massieu; and about his teacher, the abbé Sicard, some thirty years older than he; and about Sicard's teacher, thirty years older again, "the father of the deaf," as he is called, the abbé de l'Epée. But let me begin this unfolding as I experienced it, with the product of their labors, or rather the temple devoted to them, the National Institution for Deaf-Mutes, where I would spend the next twenty years of my life. It was the first public school for the deaf in the history of the world and the inspiration and model for hundreds that would soon follow. Created by Epée and Sicard, it created in turn educated leaders among the deaf, instilling in us pride in our language and ourselves, and an elevated vision of what we could become.

Everything about the institution was grand, all the more so to a twelve-year-old boy from the provinces. Situated on the plateau of the Montagne Sainte-Geneviève, on the rue Saint-Jacques next to the Luxembourg Palace and gardens,* it had gardens of its own that occupied several acres, alleys

*In the Latin Quarter, on Paris's Left Bank.

Institut National de Jeunes Sourds de Paris

NATIONAL INSTITUTION FOR THE DEAF (PARIS, 1898)

lined with linden trees where we pupils played. The school building was shaped like an H, embracing a large courtyard in front and a spacious terrace overlooking the gardens behind. The façade was sculpted limestone and the two stories, each with more than a dozen lofty windows spaced a yard or so apart, were topped by a steep slate roof with little mansard windows and jutting chimneys.[8] It had been built by the Fathers of the Oratory,* in the seventeenth century, on the ruins of a refuge constructed in the thirteenth by the monks of the nearby church of Saint-Jacques-du-Haut-Pas—the first in a chain of refuges that served one of the most traveled pilgrimages in Christendom, from Paris to Santiago de Compostela in Spain, where a miracle had placed the body of the apostle. For over a century, the Oratorians trained the priests of the diocese of Paris there, and those destined for the provinces as well, until church property was abolished by the Revolution and the seminary was seized by the new Republic, to be turned over to the abbé Sicard for our school in 1794.[9] In the cobblestone court stood an elm tree of breathtaking size: reputedly planted in 1600 by the duke of Sully,† it had attained over 150 feet by the time I arrived and was known as the plume of Mount Sainte-Geneviève. It took six of us pupils, holding hands, to reach around it. By now, it must take seven or eight.

Once the formalities of my admission were completed I was led by way of a stately sweeping staircase of stone and wrought iron to the second-floor sleeping quarters, a long rectangular room, airy and light, with rows of windows on each side (overlooking the street and the gardens) and windows wide open at each end. Formerly each window had illuminated a monk's cell; the partitions had now been removed to create a spacious dormitory. Plain stone columns marched single file down the middle of the room, separating two rows of beds, some fifty in all, each covered with a counterpane and each bearing a sign at its foot giving the name of its tenant. A small chest stood alongside. All of these things were made in the school, the beds and chests in the woodshop, and the signs in the printshop.[10] The linen was woven by the twenty young women who were quartered across the rue Saint-Jacques, and tutored separately by Abbé Sicard's associate, the abbé Salvan.

My bed was last in the row, hence immediately next to the large, luxurious one, surrounded by curtains, in which slept the *surveillant,* ‡ an elderly deaf man who had studied for a time under the abbé de l'Epée, the abbé Sicard's predecessor. At the opposite end of the hall, in a smaller bed without curtains, slept the monitor, a senior student. The room was feebly lit at night by six oil lamps deployed between the two ends of the hall, and

---

*An order established during the Counter-Reformation.
†Finance minister to Henry IV.
‡Supervisor.

feebly warmed on winter mornings by a pot-bellied stove. It would be my sleeping quarters for years to come.

In the morning we were awakened at five o'clock by a drum roll (the sound woke a few, the vibrations, others, and the ensuing tumult, everyone).[11] The fifty of us ran helter-skelter into the washroom, where fifty watercocks protruded above a long leaden trough and fifty towels were suspended from a rod that ran the length of the trough, above the cocks. The monitor opened the large tap in the corner, one of the pupils pumped, a stream of cold water flowed into our hands, and we made our toilettes so, over the trough. Each of us then replaced his toilet articles in his pigeonhole (a box in a large dresser in the middle of the room) and went into one of the stalls containing a *chaise percée.** Finally, we returned to make our beds and stand beside them waiting for inspection.

So began all the days of my youth; it did not take me long to discover that "institution" meant regularity, regulation, regimentation. Each detail of everyday life was prescribed by written rules enshrined in a decree with seventy-nine articles issued by the Ministry of the Interior, which governed welfare establishments such as my school was considered to be. All orders to the staff were given in writing and special instructions were carried by a servant to the parties concerned. Pupils were not permitted to correspond with anyone except a parent, and even these letters passed through the hands of the director.[12]

It seemed that I had exchanged the fields and grottos of La Balme for the confines of a monastery. So much I had lost. What had I gained? The answer lay in the amazing flurries of signing all around me, although I understood little more than tantalizing snatches at first. After inspection, one of the students stepped forward, the rest of us kneeled, our eyes fixed on him while he recited the morning prayer.[13] His right hand, index finger pointing upward, swept in a horizontal arc across his chest (OUR); then he placed his two hands on his hips and lowered them obliquely so they came together over his stomach (FATHER); he raised them together to eye level and separated them describing an arc (HEAVEN); then he brought them together again, plunging the right hand into the partially open left (IN). He held his hands out, palm up, and pulled them toward him (WE-WANT), pointed to the sky (YOUR), struck his left index finger with his right a couple times (NAME), then touched his forehead with his open hand and swept it away from his body in an arc while inclining his head (SANCTIFY); WE-WANT YOUR SOULS REIGN PROVIDENCE COME-DOWN-TO-US; WE-WANT YOUR WORD DONE, HEAVEN, EARTH, SAME. . . . As I watched him run mechanically through this incantation, which my mother had long ago tried to explain to me in elaborate pantomime, I had my first idea about the nature of language (my life

*Night-commode.

would prove to be largely concerned with such ideas): I realized that the same notion could be expressed in different sign languages; or rather, as I would say now, I realized there was a difference between the home signs I used with my family and the sign language in use among the deaf in Paris. And I knew then, too, that I would learn this new language and that these people, this society of the deaf, would be my new family.

Just about the time I was making this discovery, a deaf Frenchman, Pierre Desloges, described it in a book that I came to read years later. He explained that when deaf children have no friends, when they are in an asylum or isolated in the countryside as I was, their signing is usually limited and concerns mainly physical wants. "But things are quite different for the deaf who live in a great city, in Paris for example, which could be justly called the epitome of all the marvels of the universe. In such a theater our ideas develop and when the isolated deaf man arrives he learns to polish and organize his signing, which was formerly without order and linkage. Dealing with his comrades he quickly learns the supposedly difficult art of portraying all his thoughts, even the most abstract. I ought to be believed," Desloges went on, "as this is what happened to me."[14] And to me, dear reader, to me. When I left La Balme for the City of Light,* I came out from a cave in which the shadows of meanings had flickered, cryptic and ominous, on the gray walls; I came out into the bright day of true communication, where meanings were as plain as the hand in front of your face, where a message was no sooner expressed than understood."

After prayer we regularly filed downstairs to our classrooms, but on my first day I was taken to the tailoring shop to be outfitted by one of the older boys. Our clothing and shoes were made in the institution. I was issued a blue cotton blouse, pants in blue velour, a sweater, and a beret. That was the inside uniform. For formal occasions such as the abbé Sicard's public exercises and our walks into town, we wore an outside uniform consisting of a shirt, pants, a jacket and a dark-blue peaked cap with red braid. And in winter an overcoat. New clothes in which to begin a new life.

At seven, breakfast—for the pupils, a thin soup—was served in the ground-floor dining hall, which had been the monks' refectory. This room was nearly as large and airy as the dormitory just above it: in the middle of the flagstone floor were three long tables of red-and-yellow marble beneath which, on a narrow wooden shelf, were arranged a napkin and a silver mug for each boy. At either end of the hall were three rows of tables set crosswise to ours, reserved for the deaf staff. (The hearing faculty had their meals in their homes, off the school grounds. The director dined in his own suite of rooms on the ground floor behind the chapel; they opened onto a private terrace in a corner of the gardens, and were decorated in ornate wood paneling carved by pupils at the school.)

*Paris, "Ville Lumière."

During the twenty years that were to pass before I left on my mission to America, the staff became nearly as numerous as the pupils, many of whom stayed on, as I did, to serve the deaf society. Even when I arrived, there were cooks and assistants and gardeners and the concierge and the masters of the shops and the business manager and his assistant, and the *surveillants,* and the deaf professors and *répétiteurs.* * And Père Antoine, an old deaf man, one of the kitchen staff, who was with the school for so long that his very existence came to tell part of its story. The abbé de l'Epée had bequeathed him to the abbé Sicard and he would live to see three more directors fired or forced to resign. For the twenty years I knew him at Saint-Jacques (as we called our school) he was always old, but always the same; time seemed to have no further sway over his body. I imagine him still, with his big round head topped with a little visored cap, his short jacket and pants of olive velour, his canvas smock, his back bent with age, arms dangling at his sides as he walked with measured strides. When he died it was a major project to discover his family name so that it could be properly inscribed on the mortuary register; I do not even know whether the project succeeded.

Père Antoine had never learned reading or writing or enough religion to receive first communion, but he had a good memory, he knew how to calculate, and he was unusually adept with mechanical things. He had managed to get money enough to buy a watch; none of the pupils had such an article and there was no clock in the institution, so they were constantly coming to him to know the time of day. He was, at first, willing to tell them, for it gave him an opportunity to gratify his vanity by showing the watch; but after a time he got tired of the annoyance and set his wits to work to get rid of the trouble. At length, an idea struck him. The clock on the church of Saint-Jacques was in full view of the school but it had not been maintained and no longer told time. Père Antoine studied the mechanism of his watch until he understood it: then, secretly, in his leisure moments, he managed to repair the old church clock. Thereafter, he referred the pupils to it when they asked him the time, and kept his watch to himself. Later he became the timekeeper for the church and it was said that he set the clock by his own gait, so regular and measured was his pace. He was extremely punctual. The last day of the month he infallibly appeared at the vestry to collect his salary. If by chance it was not prepared, he went away fuming. On the other hand, when he was ill and hadn't wound up the clock for a month, he refused his salary. Stubborn as a Breton and economical as an Auvergnat, he earned only eight francs a month but managed to save more than two hundred; it was his treasure and he would not have entrusted it to anyone. Still, he wasn't stingy, for he sometimes lent money to the pupils.

Time, perhaps charmed by his attentions, ignored him for many decades,

*Teaching assistants.

but in his last days it took him almost an hour to get from his room to the kitchen. Finally, his legs were too stiff to manage the stairs and he had to be carried. The staff would fetch him down in the morning and place him where he could catch some rays of the sun and greet passersby. Lunch was brought to him, and in the evening, they would take him up again to his room. It was on one of these days that a robber slipped into his room and stole his cache of francs, the savings of a lifetime. When Père Antoine discovered the loss, he was inconsolable, and though the staff calmed him by saying that the school had made good his loss and the money was deposited with the school treasurer, the old man never really believed it. He became somber, no longer took an interest in anything, and one morning the porters found him dead in his bed. Thus ended, after more than eighty years, the life of a contemporary of the abbé de l'Epée. The pupils and administrators accompanied his body to the cemetery, not only out of respect for him, I think, but also because they felt they were interring a way of life for the deaf. For Père Antoine had been born too soon and could only witness the progress that followed the abbé de l'Epée's discovery of a way to educate the deaf. My new family, profiting from that progress, could make me as lettered as my father, as Christian as my mother.[15]

My first class was taught by Jean Massieu. Standing before us, he withdrew a watch, checked the hour, took out a piece of chalk and wrote a student's name on the blackboard; the student promptly stood up. Then Massieu wrote my name on the blackboard; though I could neither read nor write, I could recognize my name and, following the example of the first student, I, too, stood up. Massieu beamed approval. "THAT'S YOUR NAME," he signed, pointing to the board, then to me, and executing a sign I understood at once to be NAME. "THAT'S HIS NAME," he signed, engaging the other student. Then he wrote *Jean Massieu* on the board and signed "THAT'S MY NAME." Then he wrote *chaise* on the board, pulled a chair to the front of the room, and signed "THAT'S ITS NAME." By noon I had learned the written names in French of chairs and pens and scissors and a few other objects. I had also learned their signs. Sometimes Massieu sketched an object, or he might point to it, or sign or write its name, and in every case we would variously be expected to fetch it, or sign it, or sketch it ourselves. I also learned his name sign, which consisted of a flick of the wrist near the head, as if to raise long hair, and I acquired my own, the stroke on the right cheek, where my scar lies. My new name.[16]

After the morning classes, lunch lasted half an hour and consisted of a vegetable, bread, and wine.[17] A half hour's play in the gardens and back to class. Newcomers like me were presently introduced to the alphabet as the stock of letters making up the names we had learned. We also learned a handshape to go with each letter, so we could spell French words on our hands as well as with chalk on the board. To these two ways of rendering

French to the eye, a third was added: most common French words, and even prefixes and suffixes, were assigned particular gestures. A precise sequence of gestures stood for a sequence of French words so, as with fingerspelling, we had to know French as well as the gestures to understand the message. Quite different from this manual French was the primary language of my new family, which had a vocabulary and a grammar all its own. But that language, French Sign Language, we were never formally taught. I simply acquired it from the older pupils and from the deaf faculty, who used it in the classroom much as any teacher of a foreign language might use the native language of his pupils to teach them another tongue.

Learning to fingerspell, and to read, write, and sign French nouns, took up most of the formal instruction of the first year. The curriculum for the second level centered on French verbs; adverbs, adjectives, prepositions and pronouns were also taught and we started to learn our catechism. The emphasis at the third level was French syntax, although there was some mathematics, more catechism, and confession, and we were required to give original definitions and descriptions; only at the fourth level were we finally given books and instructed in history and geography, and prepared for Communion. It generally took five years to complete the four levels.[18] Language and religion supplanted other fields of instruction in the curriculum more than we would allow nowadays but this is not surprising: the abbé Sicard (like his predecessor, the abbé de l'Epée) was both grammarian and priest; he labored to educate the impoverished deaf in order to save their immortal souls.

If salvation was the goal of our instruction in letters, self-sufficiency was the goal of our instruction in trades. We spent the early morning and late afternoon in the workshops in small groups. I have mentioned printing, carpentry, clothing- and shoe-making shops; there were also shops for design, engraving, and mosaic work.[19] I chose to work in the print shop, which produced on its three presses the school's learning materials as well as two scholarly journals.[20]

In the evening, from six-thirty to seven-thirty we studied under supervision; then to supper: a vegetable, wine, and boiled or roast meat. On Thursdays and Sundays there was also dessert.

At the end of the meal, weather permitting, some fifty students flowed out of the dining room and into the adjoining gardens for recreation. The pupils in each year played together and I rapidly came to know my classmates, at first relying on mime to communicate with them, then increasingly using our sign language.[21] Most were there on government scholarships: to obtain one of these, you had to come from a desperately poor family, not uncommon among the deaf, or to have your application supported by some notable—this was a great hurdle—or, preferably, both (Abbé Sicard was quite candid in later years in urging destitute parents to secure a noble sponsor, of whom the most distinguished was Napoleon's wife, Joséphine.) There was Joseph Desruez, son of a health officer in a military hospital who had died in an epidemic, leaving a widow and two children, both deaf. There was Pierre de Rodouan, whose father had been the king's prosecutor in the department of the Meuse before the Revolution, then a health officer in a military hospital in Metz, where he died, leaving a widow and four children. Louis Ferdinand Monteilh's father had been the king's prosecutor in Angoulême, but lost all his possessions and three of his children in the Revolution. Louis learned to engrave semiprecious stones, of which he gave several to Francis I, Emperor of Austria, when he visited our school during the allied occupation of Paris in 1814.* Guillaume-Pierre Rabeau had been wounded during the Vendée uprisings† when a band of robbers broke into his house to steal grain; they killed his mother and brother and deafened him. He went on to become an excellent typographer, employed, as many of our graduates were, in the Imperial Printing Office, whose director was a friend of the abbé Sicard and a fellow member of the Society of Observers of Man.‡

I have mentioned that there were also female pupils in the early years. They were, however, housed and schooled apart; we had few opportunities to meet and none to converse. Nevertheless, in my heart I came to know one of them. She was a golden-haired blue-eyed beauty my own age, and the white muslin robe with an open neckline that was the girls' uniform revealed much of her early womanhood. Little black slippers—like the dress, made at the school—graced her dainty feet. One day in chapel I stared so intently at the back of her head, at the risk of my immortal soul and a mundane thrashing, that she finally accorded me a demure glance, one that chastised and inflamed me at the same time. At each successive encounter, our eyes lingered longer, her mock reproof faded, my frustration grew. I was enthralled.

Let priests and pastors call me licentious if they will, I say candidly it is a great error to violate nature by segregating deaf men and women. Many pupils at Saint-Jacques were effectively incarcerated for years on end because they were orphans or because their families lacked the money or the desire to pay for their travel home. Is it any wonder that some, men and women alike, were led to commit unnatural acts?

Confined at the school until graduation at sixteen, my first love was confined forever thereafter when she entered the House of Refuge for Indigent Deaf and Dumb Girls, just down the rue Saint-Jacques from our school. I think the only moment of freedom she ever knew was on the afternoon of graduation day when she walked the block from the one institution to the other. I stood at the window nearest my bed in the vacant dormitory,

*The victory of this, the sixth, coalition against Napoleon led to his abdication.
†A royalist revolt in the first year of the new Republic.
‡The first anthropological society.

staring down into the courtyard until she appeared, her hair and dress shimmering pennons of gold and white that fluttered as she waved to me in the summer's haze. I watched immobilized by grief, hands dumbly at my side, as she turned, glided past Sully's elm and through the gate, and was eclipsed by the high wall.

A few years ago, I wrote to the director of the House of Refuge and decried the practice of entombing young women in their flower. Why could they not be placed in respectable families as seamstresses, cooks, or servants? He answered, "—for fear of their being exposed to danger or seduction. Everything is well arranged for them here: good order, cleanliness, facilities for air, exercise, amusements, religious instruction, morning and evening prayers. Thanks to an excellent matron, they form a family, if not quite happy, at least peaceable and edifying. . . . These unfortunate women tolerate celibacy without pain. They are not much disposed to loving in the ordinary sense of the word, and this is perhaps not so bad in their position since they thus avoid the greatest spiritual suffering."[22]

The same hearing tyranny that cloistered my beloved still seeks today to prevent deaf women from childbearing, even marriage. The same hearing tyranny that allowed most deaf children then to live and die in ignorance attempts today to deny the deaf as a class the opportunity for an education. The same hearing tyranny that then despised our language, distorting it to conform to French, as did even the well-meaning abbés, or condemning it entirely in favor of grunts and grimaces, now seeks to drive it not only from our schoolrooms and our dormitories but from our lives. You see, the bitterness of my early years is with me still, seven decades later. Indeed, now it burns with a bluer flame, fortified by the knowledge of who I am: a member of the society of the deaf.

Nothing was more important to the emergence of that self-knowledge than my first act of defiance, for how is a boy to learn who he really is without discarding who he is not? Significantly, the issue was speech. Epée and Sicard had the wisdom to see that the deaf as a class could never be educated orally, but still they pandered to the public enchantment with talking deaf-mutes. Thus, sometimes, instead of recreation after supper, I and a few other promising pupils were assigned to the abbé Margaron for articulation lessons. We learned to articulate pretty well all the letters of the alphabet and many words of one or two syllables. But I had great difficulty with the distinction between *da* and *ta, de* and *te, do* and *to,* and so on. The abbé would pull his chair up to my stool so close that our knees were touching and I could see the fine network of veins on his bulbous red-blue nose. He held my left hand firmly to his voice box and my right hand on my own throat, and glowered down at me through beady, rheumy eyes. Then his warm garlic-laden breath would wash over my head and fill my nostrils to suffocating.

"*Daaa,*" he wailed, exposing the wet pink cavern of his mouth, his tongue obscenely writhing on its floor, barely contained by the picket fence of little brown-and-yellow teeth.

"Taaa," he exploded and the glistening pendant of tissue in the back of his mouth flicked toward the roof, opening the floodgates to the miasma that rose from the roiling contents of his stomach below.

"Taaa, daaa, teee, deee," he made me screech again and again, but contort my face as I would, fighting back the tears, search as I would desperately, in a panic, for the place in my mouth *accurately* to put my tongue, convulse as I would my breathing—I succeeded no better. One day he became so impatient he gave me a violent blow on the chin; I bit my tongue and dissolved in tears—the awful boundless grief of childhood, the careening through anguish of a frightened boy who had drunk more than his fill of disgust and frustration and knew he could not follow this false route any longer. It seemed to me that all the evils of my old life—the incomprehension of strangers, loneliness, the unpredictability of the world around me— were arrayed against me in that moment. I turned my back on them and walked away, toward my new family. I have never spoken again.[23]

TWO

THE SHEPHERD

AND THE SYMBOL

•

It was Jean Massieu who gave me the courage to walk away from the abbé Margaron. Not by anything he said, but by his example. For, through him, I was coming to realize that I did not have to be a hearing person *manqué*. In my new family, loneliness and incomprehension were already slipping away. Massieu, who never spoke, was the head of that family by rank, by seniority (he had joined the abbé Sicard more than a dozen years before I came to the school), and by common consent: he was the first deaf teacher ever and a symbol worldwide of what a deaf man could achieve through education—more than that, a symbol of the power of education to create a new, egalitarian society in the wake of the destruction of the old aristocracy. Princes traveled to see and philosophers to interrogate the deaf scholar who had begun life as a shepherd. In 1805, the pope himself, Pius VII, visited our school and gave Massieu a copy of *The Lives of the Popes,* from which he was to communicate a selection in sign language—to me! I was twenty then, and trembling before the august father of the Church and his entourage of several hundred. His Holiness, seated on a throne that had been placed on the dais of the assembly hall and specially bedecked for this occasion, opened his book, indicated a page at random, and Massieu began signing the text in the system of manual French developed by the abbé de l'Epée and then the abbé Sicard.[1] I wrote the text on the blackboard. The

JEAN MASSIEU

pope questioned Massieu in writing about such matters as the definition of "hell" and he answered (while I transcribed), "Hell is the eternal torment of the wicked, a limitless torrent of fire that God uses to punish those who die offending Him."[2]

Deaf people had, of course, been educated before Jean Massieu. A noble family has a son deafened by disease. The family hires a private tutor, often a distinguished man of letters, who labors to maintain, perhaps restore, the boy's deteriorating speech, and to expand his knowledge of literature, history, the sciences. The boy makes admirable progress, a philosopher notes it in his journal, or the tutor publishes it in a book or in letters. The tutor goes on to other endeavors; the boy generally does not, but in any case such a youth could never attain the status of a symbol for deaf people because he is not truly deaf, he belongs to the hearing world.

Massieu was truly deaf. He had five deaf brothers and sisters and was signing by the time he was one year old. But I will let him tell his story in his own words, as he related it in sign language to the Society of Observers of Man in 1800.[3] In some ways it is the story of all deaf children everywhere. When he tells of his isolation, I remember my own; his needless fears, his frustrated desires—those were mine, too.

"I was born at Semens," Massieu told the society, "in the Cadillac district of the canton of Saint-Macaire in the department of the Gironde. My father died in January 1791; my mother is still living. There were six deaf-mutes in our family, three boys and three girls. . . . Until the age of thirteen years and nine months, I remained at home without ever receiving any education. I was totally unlettered. I expressed my ideas by manual signs or gestures. At that time the signs I used to express my ideas to my family were quite different from the signs of educated deaf-mutes. Strangers did not understand us when we expressed our ideas with signs, but the neighbors did. I saw cattle, horses, donkeys, pigs, dogs, cats, vegetables, houses, fields, grape-vines, and after seeing all these things, I remembered them well.

"Before my education, when I was a child, I did not know how to read or write. I wanted to read and write. I often saw boys and girls going to school; I wanted to follow them and I was very envious of them. With tears in my eyes I asked my father for permission to go to school. I took a book and opened it upside-down to show my ignorance; I put it under my arm as if to leave for school, but my father refused to give me this permission, signing that I could never learn anything, for I was a deaf-mute. Then I wept. . . . In desperation I put my fingers to my ears and impatiently asked my father to unclog them. He answered that there was no remedy. I was disconsolate.

"I left my father's house and went to school without telling him. I presented myself to the teacher and asked him with gestures to teach me to read and write. He sternly refused and sent me away. This made me cry a great deal but did not discourage me. I often thought about reading and writing. I was twelve at the time. I tried on my own to form the letters of the alphabet with a quill pen.

"When I was a child, my father made me pray morning and evening with gestures: I got on my knees, clasped my hands, and moved my lips, imitating speaking people when they prayed to God. Today I know there is a God, the creator of heaven and earth. But as a child I worshiped the sky, not God. I did not see God, I saw the sky. . . .

"Children my own age would not play with me; they looked down on me; I was like a dog. I passed the time alone, playing with a top or a mallet and ball, or walking on stilts. I did know how to count before my education; my fingers had taught me. I did not know numbers; I counted on my fingers, and when the count went beyond ten I made notches on a stick.

"When I was a child my parents sometimes had me watch over their flock of sheep, and sometimes people happening by took pity and gave me a little money. One day a passerby took a liking to me and invited me to his house to eat and drink. Later when he went to Bordeaux, he spoke about me to Abbé Sicard, who agreed to take charge of my education. This man wrote to my father, who showed me the letter, but I couldn't read it. My relatives and neighbors told me its contents: they informed me that I would be going to Bordeaux; they thought the reason was to learn to be a cooper. My father told me the reason was to learn to read and write. I made my way with him to the city. On our arrival I found the houses very beautiful. We went to visit the abbé Sicard, whom I found extremely thin.*

"I began my education tracing the letters of the alphabet with my fingers. Within several days I could write a few words. In a space of three months I knew how to write many words; in six months, I knew how to write some sentences. In one year's time I wrote fairly well. In a year and some months I wrote even better and gave good answers to questions. I had been with Abbé Sicard three and a half years when I left with him for Paris. In four years I became like people who hear and speak."[4]

Massieu addressed the society again, a week after presenting his autobiography. This time he answered questions from the floor while Sicard served as interpreter, and the secretary recorded the exchanges.

—Before your education began, what did you make of people who moved their lips in each other's presence?

—I thought they were expressing ideas.

—Why did you think that?

—Because I remembered that someone had spoken to my father about me and that he had threatened to punish me.

*The corpulent abbé Sicard was in the audience.

—So you thought that lip movements were a way to communicate ideas?

—Yes.

—Why didn't you move *your* lips to communicate *your* thoughts?

—Because I hadn't looked enough at the lips of people speaking and I was told that the noises I made were disagreeable. Since I had been told that my infirmity was in my ears, I took some brandy and poured it into my ears and stopped them up with cotton.

—Did you know what hearing was?

—Yes.

—How did you learn that?

—One of my hearing relatives who lived in our house had told me that she "saw with her ears" someone whom she could not see with her eyes when he came to see my father. Hearing people "see with their ears" when someone is walking about at night. Nightwalkers have a gait that is different for different people and hearing people can tell whose step it is and this identifies them.

—What were you thinking about while your father made you remain on your knees?

—About the sky.

—What were you trying to accomplish by praying to the sky?

—To make the night come down to earth so the plants I had planted would grow and so the sick would be restored to health.

—Were your prayers in ideas, words, feelings?

—It was my heart that prayed. I did not yet understand words or their meaning.

—What did you feel in your heart?

—Joy, when I found the plants and fruits growing; grief, when I saw them damaged by the hail and when my sick relatives remained sick.

With these words Massieu made many signs expressing anger. It seems that once, when his mother was ill, he used to go out every evening and pray to a particular star, which he had selected for its beauty, entreating it to bring about her recovery. Finding that she became worse, however, he was enraged and threw stones at the star.

—Were you cursing the sky?

—Yes.

—Why?

—Because I thought that I could not get at it to give it a thrashing, to kill it for causing all those disasters and for not healing my sick relatives.

—Weren't you afraid of provoking it and of being punished?

—I didn't then know my good teacher Sicard and I didn't know that it was merely the sky. It was only after a year of education that I was afraid of being punished by it.

—Did you imagine that this sky had a shape or form?

—My father had shown me a large statue in the church near our home. It represented an old man with a long beard and in his hand he held a globe. I thought he lived above the sun.

—Did you know who had made the cow or the horse or other animals?

—No, but I was very curious to see a birth. I often went and hid in a ditch to see the sky descend to earth to make things grow. I wanted very much to see it.

—What did you think when Abbé Sicard first had you trace words with the letters of the alphabet?

—I thought that words were images of the objects I saw around me. I memorized words with great enthusiasm. When I read the word "God" and had written it in chalk on the blackboard, I thought that God caused death and I was afraid of death.

Many uneducated deaf youths frame for themselves fanciful explanations of such striking events as illness and death, birth, and growth, the changing of the seasons; thus, the wind is blown from a great bellows, the rain pours down through small holes in the sky, snow is ground out like flour from a celestial mill, thunder and lightning are the discharges of cannon, the stars are candles lighted every evening.[5] Jean Massieu, however, retained such fancies and apprehensions after he became an adult. He was not stupid, he was unsophisticated; it is a great error to confuse the two, and never more so than with the deaf. In fact, Massieu was in many ways a genius. Jean-Marc Itard, the physician who, in 1800, brought the Wild Boy of Aveyron to our school to begin his education, wrote that Massieu was "a deep thinker and a keen observer with a prodigious memory, full of insights with flashes of brilliance."[6] His answers to questions were sometimes incorrect grammatically, for he did not slavishly observe the rules of French, but they were always in conformity with sound logic. When it happened that he did not know a word, Massieu invented one by following the principles of analogy, and his slight errors paled before the originality of his thoughts, the coloring of his fancies, the justness of his comparisons, and the brilliance of his metaphors. His answers to the deepest questions took the form of short artful blends of description and definition, given without the least hesitation. They seemed to flow spontaneously. Thus Sicard said of Massieu, "It was enough to strike the stone with the steel, and immediately the spark would issue."

A member of the British Parliament asked him: "What is hope?"

—Hope is the blossom of happiness.

—What is time?

—A line that has two ends, a path that begins in the cradle and ends in the tomb.

"What is intelligence?" Sicard asked him at a public demonstration.

"It is the power of the mind to move in the straight line of truth," he wrote on the board, "to distinguish the right from the wrong, the necessary from the superfluous, to see clearly and precisely. It is the force, courage, and vigor of the mind."

And all this was in manual or written French, Massieu's second language. In his primary language, the French Sign Language in use by the deaf community, Massieu was a fluent signer with animated expression and great vivacity.

At the same time, this man, whose only homes had been a farm and an institution, whose only teachers had been his parents and an eccentric abbé, was in many ways a child. He had a childish passion for watches, as I mentioned, and for seals and gilded keys. Likewise, he bought books throughout Paris, carried them in his pockets, under his arms and in his hands, and presented them for inspection at the slightest opportunity. He bought elaborate outfits at auctions and wore them to school, to the vast amusement of the pupils. I confess I was not above mocking him on occasion. Since he was guileless, Massieu consulted us pupils in matters of taste, shared his anxieties with us, even, I believe, feared to displease us. We found these unworldly ways laughable, but also lovable.[7]

"Massieu lived alone," wrote Itard, "without desire or ambition." But Massieu did have one burning desire, an overwhelming ambition, that preempted all other concerns and explains in part his naïveté: to promote the education of the deaf. Most of what we know about Jean Massieu can be summed up by these simple, noble words: he was a teacher.

He was, first, Sicard's teacher. He taught him the elements of sign language, as Sicard freely acknowledged. And he taught Sicard respect for the deaf. In his earliest writings, the abbé described the deaf man as "a being who is a total nullity in society, a living automaton. . . . Before we lift the shroud that envelops his mind, he does not even have primitive animal instincts."[8] But after some years of collaborating with Massieu, Sicard wrote: "The deaf man is not all that destitute. . . . He brings a communicative spirit to his teacher's lessons which . . . lights up his face . . . and gives his gestures all the shapes they require to designate objects. . . . Direct from his home and without any lessons he is not less eloquent than a hearing child."[9]

Massieu was my teacher as well as Sicard's, and later he was the teacher of Thomas Gallaudet, who came from America to learn how to educate the deaf. Massieu was a teacher in the larger sense as well; he seized every opportunity to campaign for the education of the deaf. He appeared with Sicard at the Ecole Normale* and demonstrated Sicard's method by using it to teach a deaf pupil to write the names of a few objects sketched on the board.[10] He was the star attraction at Sicard's thrice-weekly demonstration

*National Teacher Training College.

classes and monthly public exercises, which helped to protect the school through the tumultuous period of the Revolution and inspired other European nations to found similar schools. Indeed, I suspect the government would not have taken the school under its protection were it not for Massieu. Sicard was appointed director in 1790 largely on the strength of Massieu's performance, and when the Committee on Mendicancy received Sicard's plea for government funding, its favorable recommendation to the Legislative Assembly the following year cited Massieu's accomplishments: "He understands all our ideas and can express all his own. He knows all the intricacies of grammar and even of metaphysics perfectly. He is thoroughly familiar with the rules of mathematics, celestial mechanics, and geography. He has a knowledge of religion from the beginning of the world to the era of the death of the founder of that religion. He knows the principles of the Constitution and his mind has grasped them with all the more eagerness as it was never corrupted by any of our old beliefs."[11]

Massieu was a loyal friend and only remembered friends' kindnesses. He would brush off taunts, though he could be brusque when stung.[12] His loyalty to Sicard was deep and unwavering: "We are two bars forged together," Massieu wrote of their friendship. For thirty years he regularly gave the better part of his salary to Sicard for safekeeping and when Sicard lost it all to his creditors, Massieu forgave him.

Massieu's loyalty to Sicard and to the education of the deaf—the two were inextricable then—led him repeatedly to rescue Sicard from trouble with the political authorities; this young deaf man had access to very high places, such was his renown. Once he saved Sicard's life; both the abbé and Massieu often told the story, which took place five years before I came to the school, just as the monarchy was overthrown in France.

Two weeks after Louis XVI was suspended from office, sixty armed citizens stormed into the Celestine cloister, where the Institution for Deaf-Mutes was temporarily lodged, and seized Sicard as he was preparing his lessons. The Revolutionary Commune had ordered his arrest, along with that of many other priests who had failed to take the oath of civil allegiance, which was required by the legislature but prohibited by the pope—both on pain of dismissal from office.[13] Thus began Sicard's flirtation with death, in which he would be drawn into the bloody vortex of the September Massacre.*

Led at saber point through the streets to the city hall, the abbé was arraigned before the Executive Council, stripped of personal effects, including his breviary, which was minutely searched for counterrevolutionary notes, and locked up in the basement with a crowd of people from all social classes.[14] The following morning Massieu arrived and gave his teacher a

*September 2–7, 1792.

copy of the petition he was going to present to the Legislative Assembly:

"The deaf-mute pupils of the abbé Sicard have come here to implore the return of their father, their friend, and their teacher who is in prison; he has wronged no one, he has aided many, he has taught us to love the Revolution and the sacred principles of liberty and equality, he loves all men, good and evil." (Sicard later had this petition published, but saw fit to infantilize the language, consistent with his early conception of deaf people: ". . . He has killed no one; he has stolen nothing; he is not a bad citizen. . . . Without him we would be animals . . ." and so on.)[15]

The Assembly was greatly moved when its secretary read Massieu's appeal, and ordered the minister of the interior to show cause for Sicard's arrest. Directly, Massieu went to visit Sicard in prison. "Then I received the first visit of this precious pupil whom I named my heir," Sicard wrote. "What a meeting! Massieu in the arms of his father, his teacher, his friend . . . Massieu . . . his soul afire, joined to mine, our two hearts beating against each other. This miserable youth had gone without food and sleep every day that his teacher was endangered. . . . What signs his hands let fly! . . . What a scene the other prisoners witnessed! Who could have not been touched by it?"[16]

But days passed while the Assembly's order was ignored. The prosecutor of the Revolutionary Commune arrived and announced that the Assembly had ordered the deportation of all priests who had refused the oath of civil allegiance. He took their names, including Sicard's, who added the title, "instructor of deaf-mutes." Presently, the clergy were herded off as promised, but Sicard was left behind. A day later two dozen more prisoners arrived, and their visitors reported that the priests had been sent not into exile but to the abbey of Saint-Germain-des-Prés, to await execution.

On Sunday, September 2, the news came that Verdun was about to surrender to the Prussians, who were marching toward Paris with the aim of restoring the monarchy to power.* Tocsin and cannon sounded the alarm throughout the capital. Volunteers massed to leave for the front and rumors circulated that their departure was to be the signal for prisoners to stage an uprising. In the midst of the general agitation and uncertainty, soldiers entered the prison to lead Sicard and the others to the abbey of Saint-Germain.

The prisoners naturally pleaded for carriages to protect them from the mobs en route, and Sicard and five others were placed in the first. Word spread that the procession winding over the Pont Neuf and up the rue Dauphine contained traitors and foreign agents. The soldiers maliciously kept the doors of the carriages open, and by the time they reached the Buci Crossing, Sicard and all of his companions were bloody from saber strokes.

*The Prussian army was turned back at Valmy, in Champagne Province.

The courtyard of the abbey overflowed with an armed mob, which surrounded the carriages on their arrival. One of Sicard's group leaped out and his throat was cut; a second tried to slip out and escape in the tumult; the cutthroats fell on him and more blood flowed. A third was seized and swallowed up by the mob as the carriage approached the main door. The fourth was struck by a sword as he dashed into the building. Somehow Sicard, cowering in the back of the carriage, was overlooked, and the crowd turned its wrath on the second wagon.

Sicard slipped into a room in the abbey where an administrative committee was in session and begged for their protection. Soon there was pounding on the door; voices demanding the prisoner echoed through the room. Sicard gave his watch to one of the commissioners with instructions to give it to the first deaf-mute who inquired after him—that would be Massieu, who treasured watches—and knelt to commend his soul to God. The doors opened and the crowd flooded in: "There's the bastard we're after!" Several men lunged for Sicard, daggers drawn. Then suddenly one of the mob strode in front of him, turned to the assassins, and bared his chest: "Here is the breast you must penetrate first," he cried, "to reach the father of the deaf." It was a watchmaker from the rue des Petits-Augustins, named Monnot. There was a moment's hesitation. Sicard climbed onto a windowsill and addressed the crowd milling below in the courtyard: "My friends, I am innocent. Will you have me put to death without hearing me?" "You must die like the others!" was the reply. "Listen to who I am and what I do and then decide my fate! I instruct those who are born deaf and mute. Since there are many more of these unfortunate children among the poor than the rich, I belong more to you than to the rich." Now a voice cried, "We must spare Sicard. He is too useful to kill. He hasn't the time to be a conspirator."

"Spare Sicard! Spare Sicard," chanted the crowd and the cutthroats waiting behind him rushed forward and embraced him, offering to lead him home in triumph.

Sicard, to the astonishment of all, refused. He thanked the gathering but preferred to remain where he was until released officially. The crowd returned to the slaughter in the courtyard. Bodies were everywhere and the cobblestones were red with blood. The main prison had been emptied and its occupants were being stuck like pigs. As dusk fell, lamps were set out so the public could bear witness.

The concierge offered Sicard hospitality but he preferred a closet adjacent to the committee room, where he spent the night listening to the pleas and death cries of the victims in the courtyard outside and the applause of the witnesses. By dawn more than a thousand corpses filled the prison yards of Paris; about a fourth of these were priests.

In the morning Sicard received word that he would be executed at four o'clock. He sent word to a deputy of the Legislative Assembly, imploring him to come quickly and accompany him from the abbey directly to the Assembly. The Assembly was no longer in session, but a secretary in the hall carried the message to the deputy, who approached the president, who went before the Committee on Public Instruction, which ordered the Commune to release Sicard. The Commune received the message at six o'clock, two hours past the deadline, but a downpour had delayed Sicard's execution. At seven o'clock, a municipal officer, wearing the tricolor to fend off the waiting crowd of public executioners, led Sicard from the abbey.

Accompanied by the watchmaker Monnot, Sicard went at once to the Legislative Assembly. "All hearts awaited me there," he later wrote, "and general applause welcomed me. All the deputies wished to embrace me; tears flowed from all eyes when, inspired only by the finest sentiments, I gave a speech to thank my liberators."[17]

Within hours, Massieu was in his arms again, weak from hunger and sleeplessness, but reunited with his benefactor. It was September 4, ten days after Sicard's arrest. Once freed, Sicard thought it prudent not to resume office immediately and he took refuge in the home of another watchmaker, a M. Lacombe, who, at great personal risk, had been searching for the imprisoned abbé everywhere. Has the coincidence struck you? One watchmaker shields Sicard from the assassin's dagger, another hides him. I have since wondered if their actions were not prompted by affection for Massieu; perhaps my friend's passion for watches was not so childish after all.[18]

A year later Sicard was again denounced, imprisoned briefly, and released.[19] Then, in the summer of 1797, just before I arrived at the National Institution for Deaf-Mutes, the Directory launched a campaign against conservatives and Catholics.[20] Sicard, who had not been discreet about his sympathies for the deposed monarchy and who was editor of a politico-religious newspaper, the *Religious Annals*, which supported the authority of the pope over the national government when these conflicted, was banished to Guiana. As I have told, he fled instead into hiding in the outskirts of Paris.[21]

The months passed. The abbé used the time to write two books: one a general grammar,[22] the other a detailed account of how he had trained Massieu;[23] this was the second book ever to explain how to educate the deaf, preceded only by the treatise on the subject by Sicard's mentor, the abbé de l'Epée,[24] and it was to have a great influence. Fruitless efforts by friends to secure his release from exile led Sicard to publish a disclaimer in a revolutionary newspaper, affirming in effect that he believed what circumstances required him to believe and that he had not—this was a lie—written the articles for which he was banished.[25] "For me," he wrote, "all authority exercised by the powers that be is by that very fact legitimate. Thus, by the same faith that I was a royalist [I am now], since the proclamation of the Republic, a zealous republican."

In the end, however, it was Massieu who once again rescued his beloved teacher—Massieu and the playwright Jean Nicolas Bouilly.[26] Massieu's first efforts to secure Sicard's release from banishment failed. He wrote a petition and sent it to several authorities but to no effect. He went to the home of General Bonaparte, victorious commander of the French forces in Italy, with a petition in hand; he was not admitted, though a servant came to the school some days later to collect the document.[27] Meanwhile, however, Bouilly had written a drama called The Abbé de l'Epée in the hope of drawing attention to Sicard's plight.[28] The play was presented in December of 1799 at the National Theater,[29] a month after the general succeeded in a coup d'état[30] and suppressed the Directory.[31] Napoleon Bonaparte and Joséphine attended the second performance.[32] During the fifth act,[33] when the abbé de l'Epée says, "The other pupils that I left in Paris suffer greatly from my absence," several men of letters, friends of Sicard's, who were seated in the gallery facing Bonaparte's box,[34] rose and shouted, "We want Sicard released," or words to that effect. Many in the audience joined the chant: "Release Sicard, release Sicard." Napoleon appeared to take notice of the outburst.

Then Massieu conceived another plan to reinstate Sicard: a friendly legislator who knew Joseph Bonaparte, Napoleon's brother, would invite Joseph to dinner and Massieu and Sicard would visit afterward and appeal for his intervention with the first consul. It came to pass as hoped. Massieu pleaded for Sicard's reappointment, Joseph was moved by Massieu's petition and agreed to intervene, Massieu put an arm around each of these two great men (as he recounted), and the three of them cried together.[35] Less than a month later Napoleon ordered Sicard returned to the directorship of the National Institution after twenty-eight months in retreat.[36]

Sicard arranged for his return to take place with great pomp.[37] At eleven in the morning we were all gathered in the assembly hall, boys and girls alike, seated on benches facing the dais. I was somewhat impatient—this was to be my first glimpse of the famous Abbé Sicard—but Massieu seemed unable to wait even a second longer. He strode back and forth through the spectators' gallery, his head bowed, his eyes staring, his breathing shallow. The gallery was jammed: with men of letters, including the author of The Abbé de l'Epée, with beautiful women evidently from high society, and with the public at large. Suddenly Sicard appeared, moving briskly down the center aisle, the front of his black redingote splashed with decorations, the back billowing behind him. He had on black stockings and black shoes with buckles. He was much less grand than I had expected, rather short and fat, and he carried himself somewhat awkwardly, with his head tilted forward and to one side. His gray wig was long, flowing, and parted in the middle, which only seemed to accentuate a rather square face seated on a short neck. His large dark eyes and ample nose bespoke his Mediterranean origins, and deep lines were etched from his nose to the corners of a full mouth over a receding chin. He held his arms out in front of him when he walked, like a priest in a pulpit.[38] Massieu virtually leaped into them and they embraced warmly. Then he led Sicard by the hand into the middle of the gallery, where we rushed to join him. Some kissed his hands and knees; many were reduced to tears. As Massieu had arranged, I went to the blackboard and wrote an homage to Napoleon; another student told of our travails without our "father." Money for the school had stopped coming, meat had been dropped completely from our menu, and the rooms, never well heated, were now really quite cold. The government, as devoutly anticlerical as ever, had ordered an end to religious exercises and we were not even supposed to pray or make the sign of the cross.[39] Another student put a flowered crown on Sicard's head while Massieu wrote out a lesson on the blackboard. To express thanks to Bouilly, the students made a bust of the abbé de l'Epée and later delivered it to the playwright's home.[40] He afterward told us that when he described to Napoleon the moving return of Sicard to our institution, the first consul thanked him for his play, since it gave him the occasion to return Sicard to his pupils.[41] That was the first and last kindness the emperor ever extended to Sicard. Although the abbé had in common with his famous student a certain childlike naïveté, the calling of a teacher, and a strong claim on the love of humanitarians, he also had three failings, utterly alien to Massieu, that angered Napoleon: hypocrisy, guile, and vanity. But if Massieu knew of these flaws in his teacher, he was too loyal ever to speak of them in the half century of our friendship, which only death could dissolve.

THREE

HIGH THEATER

As you may have gathered from Sicard's window-ledge oration in the abbey of Saint-Germain, from his dramatic refusal of freedom in imitation of Saint Paul, from his headlong rush, once released, to gather the consolations and applause of the Legislative Assembly, from his outspoken papism, which led to his banishment, and from his dramatic ceremonial return to our institution—life with Sicard was high theater!

He loved center stage. In retrospect this is apparent from his first steps in French intellectual life. Roch-Ambroise Sicard was born in the south of France, during the reign of Louis XV, in 1742.[1] He studied for the priesthood, which was one of the more popular alternatives in that era to a life in commerce or the manual trades (Sicard had not the slightest talent for either), and he took his vows in the Congregation of Christian Doctrine, as the abbé de l'Epée had done before him.[2] He was ordained at twenty-eight and assigned to the cathedral in Bordeaux, where he eventually came to the attention of the archbishop, Champion de Cicé. When, on one of his trips to Paris, the archbishop had occasion to visit the school of the abbé de l'Epée, he decided to leave his mark on his own diocese by creating a similar school in Bordeaux, and he chose Sicard to direct it.[3]

Forty-three years old at the time, Sicard went to the capital to learn a new career, spending about a year attending Epée's classes and public exercises

ABBÉ ROCH-AMBROISE SICARD

with numerous other disciples from throughout Europe. I suspect Sicard realized from the outset that his new school for the deaf, the second to be founded in Europe, would attract public attention, and that "external" duties would thus command most of his time. Therefore, he kept up a steady correspondence, during his stay in Paris, with his friend Jean Saint-Sernin, who directed a boarding school in Bordeaux; he tried to interest him in leaving that secure post for a more uncertain one as his collaborator, and he described at length the "methodical signs" Epée had chosen to correspond to French words. On returning to Bordeaux he managed, with the archbishop's help, to press Saint-Sernin into service,[4] and while the experienced teacher provided the daily instruction in the new school, Sicard presented the fruits of that instruction in Sunday exercises at the museum and described its rationale in several published papers.[5] Although Sicard was officially director, he spent little time in the school itself—instead, he became vicar general of Condom and canon of Bordeaux—and thus he was long unaware of Massieu's remarkable progress under Saint-Sernin's tutelage.[6] So much for the legend that Sicard was Massieu's first teacher and instructed him with methods he learned from Epée. In fact, Epée's methods, imported to Bordeaux, simply did not work, and it fell to Saint-Sernin to improvise solutions in the classroom. All the weight of Epée's instruction was on vocabulary. Saint-Sernin added a concern for the ordering of words in the sentence and the rules of agreement among them. According to one of his best pupils, François Gard, who went on to become a teacher himself, it was Saint-Sernin who invented the system of numbering the parts of speech in a sentence, so that the deaf pupil could learn numerical formulae for transforming French sentences and could more easily detect his omissions.[7] Sicard credited himself with this invention, however, in his *Course of Instruction for a Congenitally Deaf Person* (namely, Massieu); it seems to be one of the few features of his method that has survived.[8]

In 1789, about three years after the Bordeaux school had opened, the abbé de l'Epée died and the Commune of Paris, a precursor of the body that would so cruelly persecute Sicard three years later, appointed the abbé Masse as temporary director of the school; he had been with Epée for nearly a decade and was the master's choice for successor.[9] Sicard, however, published a memoir announcing his own candidacy for the position. In it he stated that there were only four suitable contenders in France to succeed Epée. He mentioned the abbé Masse, Abbé Antoine Salvan, who had worked with Epée and now directed a private school for the deaf in Auvergne, and, of course, himself, and proposed a public contest judged by distinguished scholars, in which each candidate would display his best student and explain his methods of instruction.* Sicard was

*Sicard's fourth contender, the abbé Deschamps, director of a school for the deaf in Orléans, was mortally ill.

staking everything on Massieu and on his own abilities as an orator.

The contest took place as Sicard had proposed, and he won the day, one might say by default.[10] The abbé Masse refused to participate, contending that he was already the legal director, since Epée had chosen him as his successor; the abbé Salvan, whom I later came to know at the school, was a timid man and let it be known he would gladly accept the post of assistant director.[11] Louis XVI confirmed Sicard's appointment in April 1790.

When the abbé Sicard took over, he found his mentor's school in desperate straits. A little over a decade earlier the king had taken the school under his protection and ordered funds to be provided, but his orders had not been executed, and in Epée's declining years there had not been sufficient food or fuel for him and his pupils.[12] Twenty deaf children had been returned to their families on his death, but forty-five remained and the abbé Masse had spent most of his time seeking funds to feed and shelter them. The Commune of Paris had backed his appeal with a petition to the National Assembly to sponsor the school: "The deaf-mutes who were the adopted children of the abbé de l'Epée," they argued, "will thus be those of the Nation, and the Nation will do for them, for reasons of justice and social welfare, what the abbé de l'Epée had been inspired to do."[13] The petition had had no immediate effect, however; the school remained short of funds even for the necessities of life.

Sicard responded characteristically to this predicament: a few months after his appointment, he appeared before the Committee on Mendicancy of the Assembly with four of his students, including Massieu.[14] The committee was so impressed that it recommended he address the entire Assembly, and a week later Massieu presented a petition asking the Assembly to watch over the deaf and assure their welfare.[15] The Assembly agreed to place the school under its protection and ordered its committee to prepare a report and decree. In the fall Sicard took up residence with his pupils in the largely uninhabitable buildings of the Celestine monastery, on the Right Bank, next to the armory,[16] though it was not until the following year that the Assembly finally voted on the bill, declaring the school a national establishment, providing twenty-four scholarships and salaries for ten staff members, and placing the school officially in the Celestine monastery, along with the school for the blind.

These successful appearances with Massieu and other pupils, first in Bordeaux, then before the National Assembly in Paris, confirmed Sicard in a practice that would be the hallmark of his career: when he died, his successor at the French Academy asked rhetorically in his acceptance speech, "Who here has not witnessed the abbé Sicard's naïve satisfaction as he unfolded his theories to the general public, taking delight in showing off his pupils to the gathered throng?"[17] There were performances the third Monday of every month in the assembly hall of our school, once it had moved to Saint-Jacques,[18] as well as special exhibitions: for the pope, as I described;[19] for the archbishop of Paris a year later;[20] for the duchess of Angoulême; for Francis I, emperor of Austria; and, after I left Paris to come to Hartford, for the dukes of Gloucester and Angoulême and the duchess of Berry.[21] Moreover, Sicard took Massieu, me, and another pupil to London in 1815 for a dozen exhibitions, including one before Parliament, and thus it was through Sicard's love of theater that I came to America, for it was in London that I first met Reverend Thomas Gallaudet—but that is another story.[22]

A typical demonstration at Saint-Jacques started at noon and ended at four. The semicircular benches of the assembly hall would be filled to overflowing with some three to four hundred spectators.[23] The first rows were occupied by pupils of the school; just behind them were the elegantly dressed women and distinguished-looking gentlemen whose carriages attended in the adjacent courtyard; at the back sat the parents of the deaf pupils, often with the deaf or hearing brothers and sisters of my classmates. One of these demonstrations in particular comes to mind, the first time the abbé Sicard tested me before an audience; I must have been thirteen or fourteen.

The stage was bare except for a bust of the abbé de l'Epée. Since many came early to get good seats, the crowd awaited Sicard's arrival for quite a while, some engaged in significant glances, others in animated conversation. Finally, the abbé entered and the teachers and *répétiteurs* rose in greeting. He made his way to the stage, where Massieu joined him.

"I have been waiting," the abbé announced, "to introduce you to a new subject, almost an infant, a little savage, a block of unchiseled marble, or rather a statue, yet to be animated and endowed with intellect. . . ." (Not long before Sicard began teaching the deaf, a leading philosopher, the abbé de Condillac, had published his *Treatise on the Sensations,* in which he imagined a statue that he brought to life progressively, endowing it with each of our senses in turn. Sicard thought the tale was partly realized before his very eyes: he portrayed deaf-mutes as living statues whose senses he would open one by one. We rarely judge our own behavior more severely than does the public, and thus Sicard was increasingly confirmed in this absurd opinion of the deaf by the steady flow of spectators and the double file of carriages on both sides of the courtyard, which attested to the high rank of his admirers.)

"This child has received no instruction," Sicard continued. "I am as yet ignorant of his capacity, and his future prospects will be decided by the experiment I am about to conduct. I shall begin with one of my elementary lessons, and you will at once judge of my system and its effects."

Massieu then suspended a key, a hat, and spectacles from three nails placed over the blackboard; he drew a sketch of each object just beneath it. A boy of about five was brought into the room; taken from the arms of his mother, he was carried onto the stage and up to the board. He gazed at the objects for some time with an air of utter indifference while three hundred faces regarded him expectantly. Sicard showed signs of distress. Just as the audience and instructor began to doubt the youth's capacity and to despair of his salvation, the boy clapped a hand to his head and with a smile pointed to the hat drawn on the board.

"Enough," cried the abbé. "This child may be snatched from the abyss of night, from the cheerless impermeable solitude in which thousands of his unhappy brothers are doomed to suffer."

This experiment happily concluded and its subject carted off, the abbé signaled Massieu to demonstrate how the names of articles were first impressed on the mind and memory of the pupil—one of the introductory lessons to reading and writing. Massieu drew the letters of the word *clef* (key) on top of the sketch of the key but conforming to its outlines, so that the name had the shape of the object. These characters, thus united with the sketch, Sicard explained, were left for the pupil to study as an alternate sign of the thing they described; when the letters were firmly imprinted on memory, the line drawing was erased and the letters alone remained as the symbol or representation of the object. In the next stage, the letters were printed normally and the written word bore the full burden of signifying.

"I have shown you the foot of the ladder," the abbé Sicard continued. "I will now take you to the top. I will thank any gentleman for a book or newspaper; we will exercise the talents of this young man, Massieu." Someone in the audience furnished the day's *Gazette*. The abbé signaled me to come onstage and sign the text of an advertisement.

"Clerc will dictate the passage to Massieu, who will show you that he is able not merely to comprehend the ideas, but to repeat the exact words appearing in the paper."

I then communicated the passage in manual French while Massieu wrote it on the blackboard. He made only one error, writing *arrondissement** for *département.* † I spotted the slip and signed NATION. He then wrote *république.* But before I could prompt further, he wrote *département.*

"I will now ask him," the abbé explained while writing on the board, "to define two words. What is the difference between your word *arrondissement* and the word *département?*"

Massieu replied on the blackboard: "An *arrondissement* comprehends several communes, governed by a mayor; a *département* is a new province, part of the empire, under the dominion of a prefect."

"You use the word 'government,'" the abbé pursued. "What does it mean?"

---

*Municipal district.
†An administrative subdivision of France (there are at present one hundred).

"It is the power placed at the head of the community," Massieu replied, "to maintain its existence by providing for its wants and defending it against harm." Then, appearing dissatisfied, he added: "It is one man, or several, acting as the soul of the body politic and serving as the guide, the prompter, and the defender of the members."

The audience was obviously pleased and impressed. "Ask him any question," Sicard continued, "and I engage that his answer shall be prompt, clear, and correct."

"Ask him what is music," a gentleman in the audience called out.

Massieu shook his head when the question was put to him. He wrote on the board: "It is extremely difficult if not impossible for a deaf person to answer the question satisfactorily; our conceptions of music must be very imperfect. I can only say I conceive it to be an agreeable sensation excited by the voice or the sound of instruments."

"Speaking of music," said Sicard, "you no doubt recall the answer of the blind man Saunderson* when asked to what he could liken the color of scarlet; he replied, 'To the sound of a trumpet.' When I asked Massieu his conception of the sound of a trumpet, he answered: 'I can explain my ideas of the sound of a trumpet only by comparing it to the florid and effulgent rays which irradiate and adorn the horizon after the setting of the sun.' Each of you, ladies and gentlemen, entering this humble home of the poor deaf-mutes, must have come with sad reflections indeed on their present state and unhappy future. You must have had a thousand conjectures on the means employed to communicate with such singular pupils, who cannot hear and therefore know not how to speak. But although they may be deaf, they are not blind, and what we cannot cause to enter by the main door, to use the vivid metaphor of the abbé de l'Epée, we can send in through the window. If they do not have sound, voice, and spoken language, they have nonetheless light, facial expression, color, movement. They will therefore express their thoughts with gestures. The language of the deaf-mute will be the action of the oratorical art carried to the highest, essentially poetic and picturesque, painting what it sees, embellishing what it paints, a kind of exteriorized imagination and gesticulated etymology."

"Now the model precedes the copy," continued Sicard, who was fond of using analogies, "and thought is the model, speech the copy. Gesture is simply an adjective of speech. The first man was born with the ability to articulate sounds; he gave this gift to his child, who in turn gave it to his family, and language was born. But let it not be thought that there is some similarity between objects and the words that designate them; language is purely conventional. We can perhaps define thought as the attentiveness of the mind and divide this act, apparently so simple, into the initiation of

*Nicholas Saunderson (1682–1739) was professor of mathematics at Cambridge University.

thought, or reflection, and the use of thought, or judgment, just as we look in order to see and listen in order to hear. In the first moment of this rapid operation, the mind is purely passive, but it is active in the second. If we may hypothetically divide such an instantaneous point, these are two states of the same being: one is the doorkeeper of the other and alerts his master, or as Plato puts it more nobly, one is God, by virtue of thought, the other animal, by virtue of sensing, which recalls this beautiful definition of man, the mind served by the senses. . . ."[24]

Here Sicard broke off his harangue to ask the assembly, especially the women, to excuse him for finding it necessary to go back to metaphysical principles in order to explain his art. The apology was hardly necessary, as few of the audience were paying attention to his discourse; they were looking at each other or, occasionally, at my classmates in the first rows, who were engaged, hands flying, in a host of discussions.

"Speech does not communicate thought," the abbé went on. "Purely external, speech folds it in on itself, as it were, like an echo, so that it becomes strengthened. Thus the miserable being who is without hearing and voice, reduced to natural signs, living almost in isolation, does not enjoy this precious advantage—unless genius comes to his aid and helps him to perfect his signs, raising them to the dignity of written language, which alone can replace speech. Let us then put into action this difficult art of leading the deaf-mute from his natural signs to instructed ones, that is, from their primitive order to conventional form. We begin with a classification of all nomenclature. We proceed to notions of being and of objects, develop the origin of adjectives, of the verb *to be*, and of pronouns. Next comes the theory of the proposition. . . ."

And so on and so on. If I were to try and reconstruct faithfully all the epistemological nonsense, all the incoherence, all the digressions, all the naïve effusions over his achievements that made the spectators smile—if I were to try and reproduce all that, it would test your patience and mine. And still I could not do justice to his high-blown style (in a Gascony accent, I am told). Suffice it to say that his name was enshrined forever in the French lexicon when it acquired the verb *sicardiser*, meaning to pontificate or discourse for hours. Some of the public thought, indeed, that Sicard was a charlatan and that the deaf could not be taught anything useful. But his age, his simplicity, candor, and basic goodwill, and above all the cause for which he labored will excuse him in the eyes of history as they did in the eyes of most of his contemporaries.[25]

The demonstration concluded with questions to Massieu from the audience, which Sicard translated.

—What is God?

—The necessary Being, the sun of eternity, the mechanist of nature, the eye of justice, the watchmaker of the universe, the soul of the universe.

(You understand that these questions were a kind of test of our intelligence, and if they particularly dwelt on abstractions, it was because hearing people were under the misapprehension that the deaf could deal only with concrete things.)

—What is the difference between desire and hope?

—Desire is a tree in leaf, hope is a tree in bloom, enjoyment is a tree with fruit.

The abbé then turned to me. "How do you answer, Clerc?"

I said: "Desire is a tendency of the heart; hope is a trust of the mind."

Of Massieu he asked: "What is gratitude?"

"Gratitude," Massieu signed, looking deeply into Sicard's eyes, "is the memory of the heart."

Perhaps I should have more gratitude; I certainly was grateful for the abbé Sicard at the time. But this long life has hardened me: I now see benevolent clergy in a harsher, less flattering light. There is no gainsaying that we, the deaf, paid a price for these spectacles enacted for the idle and curious public; that preposterous and cruel things were said about us to our faces; that the reason for our accomplishments was always the genius of some hearing person; that, in short, we were treated like the wise horse who at his master's orders taps his foot on the public square as many times as the town clock shows hours. Massieu was wrong: bitterness can also dwell in the memory of the heart.

The *coup de théâtre*, as the French say, was always Sicard's friend: it saved him from the cutthroats' knives in the abbey of Saint-Germain; it incited Napoleon to release him from exile; it won him the post in Paris, the support of the government, and innumerable titles, domestic and foreign, which he amassed with the same childlike simplicity and satisfaction as Massieu collected watches. In 1795 he was appointed to the section on grammar in the French Institute when it was founded;[26] it was reorganized a few years later and he was assigned to the section on literature, later known as the French Academy.[27] (He helped lay the groundwork for the Academy's famous dictionary of the French language, which is still in progress.)[28] After the Reign of Terror, with Robespierre fallen, the Convention created the Ecole Normale, and staffed it with leading intellects of the time; Sicard was selected to teach in the department of grammar.[29] He was a member of administrative boards[30] overseeing the institution for the deaf,[31] the institution for the blind,[32] and all asylums in Paris collectively. The students and staff of the school for the blind came to Saint-Jacques annually to join in our celebration of Sicard's saint's day.[33]

The last such celebration I attended began in the early morning, when a group of us fired a cannon in the gardens to herald the day of Saint-Roch. At nine o'clock a parade of musicians arrived, boys and girls hand in hand, two by two—the blind children come to join the festivities. We rushed to meet them and guide them to the chapel. Some had learned to read finger-spelling in their hands and a few old friends became reacquainted. The girls in white linen with blue caps and belts, the boys in gray uniforms with high-collared jackets and blue cuffs, filed into the chapel in pairs and sepa-rated, girls to the benches on the right, boys to the left. The staffs of the schools and scores of visitors, including alumni, were present. The priest began the divine office, and from time to time the band went into motion. When the priest raised the host, a blind woman stood and sang an air.

From the chapel the cortège proceeded to the assembly hall, where the hero of the day received them, seated on the stage next to a curtain grasped by two pupils who, at the signal, tugged the veil, revealing a large bust of the abbé de l'Epée with the inscription: "Offered to the abbé Sicard by his children, the deaf." Then the children filed past Sicard, the blind guided by the deaf, each wishing him long life in his own language, some proffering the communal gifts of flowers, paintings, vases, and the like. Sicard rose and invited the assembly to a family banquet. It was now three o'clock. As the audience filed out, the blind choir sang, "Where is life better than in the bosom of your family?" Dinner was gay and animated; after dessert Massieu toasted the health of the royal family and Valentin Haüy, teacher of the blind. A blind girl then offered a toast to Epée and Sicard.

At five o'clock, when the assembly had dispersed into the courtyard and gardens, a beautiful blue globe was seen to rise gently from the bushes, climb over the trees, and soar into the sky above the Montagne Sainte-Geneviève: the deaf had launched a balloon to celebrate Sicard's day. With nightfall, the blind assembled in the court and marched away to a roll of drums, and then the deaf unleashed a dazzling fireworks: firecrackers and roman candles, those that exploded once and lit the night sky, and those that endlessly multiplied as they hurtled toward earth, tricolor, multicolor, blazing red, a crescendo of color at the end, and then we went to bed.

Sicard's honors were not limited to membership in scholarly societies and charitable boards. He was also a member of the Grammatical Society,[34] of the Academic Society of Sciences, and of the First Spanish Patriotic Society.[35] When Napoleon was exiled to Elba in 1814, and the Bourbon monarchy was restored to the throne, Sicard received the Legion of Honor, which he had long coveted but which Napoleon had withheld,[36] as well as the title of Honorary Canon of the Cathedral of Notre Dame, which the emperor had likewise refused to ratify.[37] Louis XVIII awarded him the order of Saint-Michel.[38] He received the order of Vasa,[39] presented by the king of Sweden,* and when the allied Prussian, Austrian, and Russian forces invaded, expelling Napoleon, Sicard met the czar, who awarded him the Order of Saint Vladimir.[40] If we smiled to see Massieu in class garbed in a riding outfit,

*Charles XIV (1763–1844), king of Sweden and Norway and French revolutionary general.

pockets bulging with books and watches, we laughed at the roly-poly Sicard bedecked with all the medals and ribbons and sashes that came with his various honors.

The abbé Sicard's naïveté about appearances—his theatricality, his love of titles—was a cause for mirth; his naïveté about power and money, however, were much graver matters: the former cost him years in exile, the latter robbed him of the peace of his old age. Perhaps it is unreasonable to expect a clergyman to sympathize with the anticlerical and antiroyalist Revolution, but many clergy, realizing the futility of resisting the tide, slipped below the surface, as it were, into less agitated waters; not Sicard, who thrashed about indiscreetly for years. As I have told, he refused to take the oath acknowledging the civil constitution of the clergy[41] and undertook to edit the *Religious Annals*;[42] he repeatedly had Massieu define God and His attributes at public exercises; and he himself discoursed on the immortality of the soul in public lectures. He struggled openly against the Revolutionary innovation of using the egalitarian *tu* form in addressing others and he managed to have it banished from the Ecole Normale. He kept up a brisk correspondence with the royal government in exile and he was naïve enough to believe that Napoleon was unaware of it.[43] Napoleon also knew of his correspondence with the duke of Enghien, whom he soon had shot for counterrevolutionary activity.*[44] Thus, the emperor detested the director of our new school, never gave him an audience, withheld honors from him, and would never visit Saint-Jacques.[45] You can imagine Sicard's childish glee, which I witnessed, when the Allied Powers entered Paris and Napoleon was escorted to Elba. The invading princes were *célestes,* the king of Prussia *excellent,* the emperor of Austria *très-bon.* His strongest praise was reserved for the czar, however, whose name he could not utter without the adjective *adorable.*[46] As soon as the French monarchy was restored in 1814, he went to see the new king to congratulate His Majesty on his happy return—and to secure the awards hitherto denied him. And, when Napoleon returned? When Napoleon quit Elba to return to France and seize power again in the spring of 1815,[47] Sicard quit France to go to England, with Massieu and me. Bonaparte had his minister of the interior call us back from London, but by the time we reached Paris he had fought and lost at Waterloo and his new reign was over.

The remaining few years of Sicard's life were his declining years.[48] At just this time he found himself in serious financial difficulties for having cosigned bad debts. To pay his creditors, he was reduced to abject poverty. He sold his carriage and his furniture, and somehow let go the 30,000 francs that Massieu had saved from his salary and deposited with him for safekeeping.[49] After a few years, he managed to pay off these debts, foolishly contracted, only to fall into new ones.[50]

*The Bourbon-Condé duke of Enghien was executed March 20, 1804.

Pure heroes exist in fiction but not in fact. No useful purpose will be served by idealizing this naïve, egotistical, and utterly devoted teacher of the deaf. It is ironic that the man who was to "restore the deaf to society," as hearing people are fond of putting it, flapped about in that society like a beached fish, in and out of exile, in and out of prison, in and out of solvency. Ironic that our adoptive father, who was to sophisticate us children of nature, was as naïve as a child and imprinted that naïveté on his children, notably Massieu. Ironic that our grammarian overlooked the grammar of sign language, thinking its grammar would have to be supplied by French.[51]

A year before his death, when his behavior had become infantile, word spread that Sicard would soon resign; he published a denial in the newspaper: only death would remove him from his post.[52] Death obliged on May 11, 1822. All the bells of the city tolled for hours and his body was on display in the cathedral of Notre Dame. How he would have loved to be there![53]

FOUR

A TALE BASED ON FACT

About a decade after the death of the abbé de l'Epée, as the nineteenth century dawned, Jean Nicolas Bouilly's dramatic tribute to "the father of the deaf" burst upon the Paris stage to wild applause: it ran for more than one hundred performances, making it the second-greatest dramatic success of the era.* I have already told how the play focused attention on the plight of the deaf and secured the freedom of the abbé Sicard. The reasons for the play's success are not difficult to discern. More than a eulogy, or a paean to Epée's character and acts, Bouilly's play is an allegory suited to an age of enlightenment and revolution: the abducted and dispossessed young count is every *misérable* disinherited by fate and society from all the advantages of social life; his savior, the abbé de l'Epée, is every wise and humble teacher who restores his pupil to his rightful heritage. And although Bouilly took some dramatic liberties with the facts, transforming the "despoiler of the young count" into an "evil uncle" named Darlemont, and inventing a lawyer, Franval, who would aid Epée, he accurately portrayed the abbé and his celebrated pupil, whose real name was Joseph, count of Solar (if you shared Epée's convictions as to his identity). Thus we have *"The abbé de l'Epée:* founder of the institution for deaf-mutes, age sixty-six. —He main-

*The first was the *Marriage of Figaro.*

ABBÉ CHARLES-MICHEL DE L'EPÉE

tains a simple, patriarchal character with a penetrating gaze that nothing escapes; while genius and goodness, with a tone of good society and amiable manners, are displayed by turns; but above all, gentle, unaffected piety and an unbounded trust in God. He is firm without arrogance in his treatment of the man who wronged his pupil, and he shows a perfect knowledge of nature." And *"The young count, pupil of the abbé de l'Epée* [he is called Théodore in the play]: born deaf and dumb, the only scion of a noble family; age eighteen.—He shows great intelligence, and extreme sensibility; unreserved confidence in his tutor and a quiet, modest demeanor. His glance is quick and penetrating, always accompanied by a gesture signifying that he understands or sees or wishes something to be explained. But the continual proof of his deafness is a happy, amiable smile when people about him are moved to commiseration by his affliction and misfortunes."

In Act I, Bouilly first entertains his audience with an irrelevant subplot of unrequited love. The son of the evil uncle, childhood companion of the deaf boy, seeks the hand of the lawyer's sister, but his father is opposed. Then the scene changes and Epée enters with young "Théodore," who is agitated: after wandering through several cities in search of his home, they have come upon one the boy recognizes, Toulouse. Just before the first-act curtain, Théodore identifies his house—in real life, the home of the count of Solar.[1] It is the most famous scene in the play; a painting of it by Ponce Camus, a pupil of David, contributed, along with the play, to making the deaf a *cause célèbre.* [2]

EPEE *(Brown coat, with black waistcoat, knee-breeches and stockings; white hair, cut round, and curling slightly at the ends; small cap, white collar, clerical hat; gray cloth gaiters with small black buttons; shoes covered with dust, a knotted stick in his hand)* By this sudden agitation, this change depicted in his face, I can no longer doubt that he recognizes his surroundings.

(THEODORE signs more expressively that he remembers the spot)

EPEE Can it be that we have finally come to the end of our long and painful search?

(The boy advances several steps toward the door, utters a cry, and returns breathless to the arms of EPEE)

EPEE What a piercing cry! He scarcely breathes. I have never seen him so agitated.

(THEODORE makes rapid signs announcing that he has found his father's home. He lays his hands one over the other, building up as it were, and joins them together with straightened fingers in the form of a roof—then designates with his right hand the height of a child, about two feet high)

EPEE *(Pointing to the mansion)* Yes, 'tis there he was born. The dwelling

that saw our birth, the beloved scene of our childhood, never loses its
power over us.

> (THEODORE *makes signs expressing gratitude to* EPEE, *whose hand he*
> *kisses.* EPEE *signs that it is not he whom the boy must thank, but God*
> *alone, who has directed their search.* THEODORE *immediately falls on*
> *one knee and expresses by signs that he is entreating heaven to shed*
> *blessings on his benefactor.* EPEE *bends with uncovered head, and the*
> *man and the boy pray together. They rise and fall into each others'*
> *arms)*

Act II tells the story of the abduction and dispossession of the deaf boy.
It takes place in the home of the young lawyer, where his sister declares her
love for the son of the evil Darlemont. A letter from Darlemont arrives,
asking Franval's help in discouraging the romance. Then Epée enters, en-
treats the lawyer's assistance, and tells Bouilly's version of the Solar story.
As the curtain falls, Franval accepts the commission to restore Théodore to
his rightful inheritance.

What had happened, in fact, was this. About the time Massieu was born
and Louis XVI took the throne—on September 2, 1773, to be exact—a
tradesman from Séchelles, in Picardy,* came to the château of Bicêtre on
the outskirts of Paris, accompanied by a twelve-year-old boy who was deaf
and mute. The boy had been found abandoned on the road from Séchelles
to Péronne and a police lieutenant in the former city ordered him brought
to the château, which served at the time as an asylum for the insane, for
the retarded, for the epileptic, and for lost children.[3] The boy had pale skin,
blond hair, and blue eyes. He had a sweet countenance, in which were read
sadness and intelligence; when he wished to communicate, he could infuse
his visage with a thousand images and emotions. He was issued the gray cap
and gown of the institution and left to wander its corridors, not understanding and not understood, prey to the madness and cruelty of the hearing
children and adults imprisoned along with him, for nearly two years.

The boy's fortunes changed for the better when he fell gravely ill and was
transported from the Bicêtre asylum to the Hôtel Dieu, a hospital in the
center of Paris, in June 1775.[4] There he received the love and care of a nun,
Mother Saint-Antoine, who presented him to the abbé de l'Epée during one
of the priest's pastoral visits. Epée recounted in a letter what the unnamed
deaf boy told him at the Hôtel Dieu: "He gave me to understand that he
was from an honest and wealthy family; that his father limped and had died;
that his widowed mother had four children, two sisters older than he and
one younger; that his mother wore ribbons, beautiful clothes and a watch;
that she lived in a large house; that they had servants and he himself was

*A former province in the north of France.

always waited upon; that the house had a large garden and a gardener to cultivate it; that the garden yielded much fruit, which was preserved for the winter; that one day he was told to mount a horse with a horseman; that the rider obliged him to wear a mask over his face and that, after leading him far away, very far away, the horseman abandoned him."[5]

The very evening of his encounter with the boy, the abbé told his story at a *salon*, which was by chance also attended by the head of the national police for the Paris area.[6] It sounded to him as if a crime had been committed; a few days later all police brigades throughout the land received a printed notice with the boy's description, his story, and the order to conduct appropriate investigations.

When the few leads produced by the police circular proved false, Epée chose a name for the boy, Joseph, removed him from the hospital, and placed him with twenty-six of his deaf pupils in the pension of M. Chevreau. The false leads put Epée on his guard, so much so that he was disinclined to trust the letter from Mme. de Hauteserre that the police transmitted to him in June 1776. She was in the habit, she explained, of spending some eight months of the year in Toulouse. In 1773 she had rented an apartment overlooking a vast garden from the widowed countess of Solar. The countess had a daughter of fourteen and a deaf son of twelve, highly intelligent, with blond hair, blue-gray eyes, a thin face, a large mouth, crooked teeth and an anomaly, an extra tooth. He had been led away, in August of 1773, by a retainer of the countess, supposedly to take the waters at Barèges* to treat his deafness. He had never been seen again. His mother had died two years later and his sister was in a convent in Toulouse.

The description fit "Joseph" exceedingly well and the differences could be explained by the care given him. His face was no longer thin and his teeth had straightened out once the extra tooth had been pulled—by order of Mother Saint-Antoine. Still, deceived before and with other leads linking the boy to Picardy and even to Liège, in Belgium, Epée chose to await a signal from Providence. It came at one of his public exercises, which were held in the handsome and spacious home located at number 14 rue des Moulins that Epée shared with his brother, an architect like their father.[7]

I have a word to say about these exercises, which were largely responsible for spreading the news throughout Europe that the deaf were educable. The public exercises at first followed the morning lessons that the abbé's pupils, including Joseph, received at his home from 7:00 until noon on Tuesday and Friday of every week;[8] but soon after they began, in 1771, the crowds seeking admission became so large that the abbé was obliged to add another session in the evening. At the head of the program in my hand for July 2, 1772, I read: "Because the assembly hall can hold only one hundred people,

*A spa in the Pyrenees.

spectators are kindly requested not to remain more than two hours."

One set of exercises concerned the sacrament of baptism. Epée asked in manual French, "Why is baptism called the portal of the sacraments?" and the pupils responded in written French, as well as in Latin, Italian, and Spanish.[9] In another exercise nine pupils responded in four languages to questions about baptism and penitence. Why several languages? Epée answered this question himself: to show the world that the deaf could be educated following his method, whatever their national language, and to give the students practice in rearranging their thoughts to correspond to a different grammar.

Still another exercise added German and English to the languages in which eleven pupils responded to questions about the Eucharist. It ended with an oral debate between two pupils on the definition of philosophy (Epée stated openly that they were coached on the arguments beforehand). In the final exercises, described in Epée's 1776 book, *Instruction of Deaf-Mutes by Means of Methodical Signs,* the same eleven pupils responded in seven languages to questions concerning penitence; one of these students was Jean-François Deydier, who would later accompany Solar in his wanderings. Another, Louis-Clément de la Pujade, opened the session with an oral discourse in Latin.

Epée had at least two motives for such displays, which continued until the last few years of his life: he was enlightening his society, as were the Encyclopedists, and, fearing that the education of the deaf as a social class might end when his own labors ended, he hoped, by drawing public attention to his work, to see it sponsored by sovereigns worldwide.

If you consider the deplorable state to which the deaf were reduced before Epée, you will understand the public wonderment and admiration at his accomplishment. Uneducated and believed ineducable, those who were deaf at birth or deafened before learning French were hidden away out of shame, or abandoned by the roadside like the count of Solar, or secreted in some institution, or simply left to vegetate. Even those with a natural gift for some trade rarely were taken as apprentices, out of prejudice and fear. That the deaf should discourse in written, much less spoken, French and other languages appeared truly miraculous.

Leading figures of the Enlightenment came to see the miracle. Etienne Bonnot de Condillac came; the philosopher's philosopher, who profoundly influenced all the French intellectuals of his time with his empiricist theories, Condillac wrote about what he saw at Epée's school in two of his books and was much impressed with sign language, which he thought far less prone to ambiguity than oral language.[10] The English philosopher James Burnett, Lord Monboddo, also attended,[11] as did the papal nuncio,[12] the archbishop of Tours,[13] and John Quincy Adams.[14] Catherine II, empress of Russia, sent her ambassador with an offer of money; the abbé de l'Epée

THE ABBÉ DE L'EPÉE WITH PUPILS AND VISITORS

responded that he did not want money but a deaf-mute pupil from Russia instead.

The Holy Roman Emperor, Joseph II, brother of Queen Marie-Antoinette, visited her at the palace of Versailles in April 1777 and with her traveled incognito as the count of Falkenstein to see Epée's miracle,[15] attending the classes on the rue des Moulins and Epée's sign-language mass for his deaf pupils at the church of Saint-Roch.[16]

As he had with the czarina, Epée refused gifts from the emperor; he asked instead for a disciple to aid in the perpetuation of his work. From his vast empire, which included most of Western Europe, except France and Spain, the emperor chose the abbé Storck and sent him to Epée bearing a diamond-encrusted snuffbox and a letter that began: "Dear Reverend Father —but no, I will say My Dear Abbé, for I love everyone who serves his neighbor and loves him with so much unselfishness." He begged Epée to "receive" the abbé Storck and to "impart to him your method, which you employ with so much success."[17] Storck eventually returned to Vienna to found the first Austrian school for the deaf.

It was at the public exercise two months after the emperor's visit that Providence gave the sign concerning Joseph that Epée awaited. As the abbé was standing for a moment amidst a group of his pupils, a lady in the audience singled out the mysterious boy with her finger and remarked audibly, "Why, it's the count of Solar!"

When questioned, Mlle. Debierre, for that was the lady's name, recounted that she had served as companion to the boy's great-aunt and great-uncle when they visited Paris on summer holidays. Alas, they were dead and could not confirm the identification, but their former maid was not and could. The maid was summoned, and she and the boy tearfully embraced. Of course she recognized her poor little Joseph, the very image of his father. Was it by another act of Providence that the unwitting Epée had given the boy his true name?

So Epée did not, as Bouilly pretends, spend three years waiting for the boy's mind to open but rather one year for his own mind to open and accept fully his pupil's story, confirmed by that of Mme. de Hauteserre. Joseph, count of Solar, had cousins and grandparents in the city of Clermont-en-Beauvoisis;* the abbé asked the king's permission to take the boy there. In Clermont, Joseph was recognized by twenty-eight people, including his maternal grandfather, whose emotion at seeing his grandson, whom he thought dead of smallpox at Barèges, can well be imagined. With one exception, all aspects of Joseph's story were confirmed, even to the detail that his father limped; he had indeed contracted gout in his last years. The exception: Joseph said he had three sisters; the count of Solar had only one. But it

---

*In the department of Oise, 77 km north of Paris.

transpired that his sister had two close friends who often came to visit and who loved him dearly, as a brother. The error and clarification seemed to confirm his story more than if he had made the distinction in the first place. If any doubts remained, two scars would remove them. The cousin asked if Joseph recalled a mark on his father's face. Indeed the boy did and he traced on his own face the mark of a scar that his father had acquired in an explosion. Several relatives, his wet-nurse, and his schoolteacher knew that the young count of Solar had a birthmark "in the place," as the abbé referred to it, "where we sit down." Indeed, his father had said, "If ever my son is lost, he can be recognized by his birthmark." And so he was!

In Act III of his play, Bouilly wins the audience's loyalty to the deaf boy by confirming his identity as the young count and by displaying his ability to reason as other men do, a feat then considered miraculous. The abbé enters with "Théodore." He wears a nut-colored greatcoat, white waistcoat, gray breeches, colored stockings, small boots in buskin fashion, colored cravat, loosely tied; his hair is slightly powdered; he throws off his round hat on entering, and thus shows all the expression of his face. Franval's mother recognizes him. Playing to the public interest in the newfound means of communicating with the deaf, Bouilly then has the lawyer's sister, Clémence, express wonderment that a deaf child can "understand everything, express everything." Epée answers, "Ask him anything you wish," and the following scene ensues, in which Bouilly's abbé is forced to communicate with "Théodore" in a drawn-out, awkward pantomime. In fact, Epée and Solar no doubt communicated in French Sign Language but Bouilly preferred something more understandable to his hearing audience.

CLEMENCE   Who is *(EPEE signs the question to the count by throwing both hands forward, the fingers straight and the nails toward the floor; then with the forefinger of the right hand he describes a half-circle from the right to the left)* in your opinion *(EPEE raises the fingers of his right hand to his forehead and keeps them there an instant, then points to the count with his right forefinger)* the greatest living man *(EPEE raises his right hand three times, then both hands as high as possible, brings them down on each shoulder, over the breast to his waist; he expresses "living" by breathing once with great force and touching the pulse at each wrist)* in France? *(EPEE raises both hands above his head, and points all around. These signs must be very distinct, but quick, and so as not to interrupt the scene)*

EPEE   *(Taking the paper on which the boy has written, and presenting it to CLEMENCE)*   You see, first, that he has written your question with precision. . . .

CLEMENCE   *(Reading)*   Question—Who is, in your opinion, the greatest living man in France? Answer—Nature names Buffon; science indicates d'Alembert; feeling and truth claim Jean-Jacques Rousseau; wit and taste point to Voltaire; but genius and humanity proclaim Epée. I prefer him to all the others.

> (THEODORE *makes several signs, expressing a balance by raising and lowering each hand in turn; then raising his right hand as high as possible and pointing to* EPEE *with the forefinger, then falls upon* EPEE's *breast and presses him in his arms)*

EPEE *(With emotion, which he endeavors to repress)* You must pardon him this mistake—it is the enthusiasm of gratitude. *(He embraces* THEODORE *again)*

Act IV is devoted to confronting the despoiling uncle. In the dress of "a rich financier, wig round and powdered," he soliloquizes: "What have I to fear? . . . In any case, what intelligence could be given by a deaf-mute?" Epée enters and informs him that his ward is still alive and that God has placed him in safe hands. The uncle denies all, though Epée affirms that "he who for sixty years has studied nature, deciphered every movement, every emotion, easily reads the heart of man. I needed but a single glance to unravel what is going on in yours." Even when his son enters and recognizes "Théodore" as his cousin, Darlemont remains steadfast in his refusal to confess and the curtain falls.

In the real-life story, the villain was no evil uncle but the countess's retainer, who was unmasked when the king's prosecutor ordered an inquiry in Toulouse to determine the identity of the person who, according to Mme. de Hauteserre's letter, had led the young count off, supposedly to take the waters at Barèges but in fact to the outskirts of Séchelles. It proved to be a young law student, Cazeaux by name, amiable, handsome, witty, who served as secretary to the countess and was utterly devoted to her. He had been seen leaving Toulouse in the summer of 1773 with the young count mounted in front of him. He had returned seven months later, alone, and had taken up residence with the countess, reporting that her son had died from smallpox in nearby Charlas, Cazeaux's native city, and was buried in the Cazeaux family tomb. The countess had left the matter there; it was widely known that she viewed her deaf son as an embarrassment and a burden. The lovers had moved to a suburb and had had a child, which they gave up for adoption. The countess had died shortly thereafter.

Cazeaux's story should have been easy to verify. If the young count of Solar had really died and Joseph was not he, there must be a death certificate in Charlas, and, indeed, when the registers of that parish for early 1774 were searched, the death certificate was found. But it was highly irregular: neither the family name nor the Christian name of the deceased was given. There were interpolations, blank spaces, and no signatures from witnesses. The words *Comte de Solar* appeared to have been added at a later date. Cazeaux was ordered arrested and brought to Paris. An angry mob accompanied by the Toulouse police broke into his home. He was tied up and thrown into jail. The next morning, irons attached to his hands and feet, chains around his body, he was placed in a wagon for the trip to the capital. On arriving, he was cast into an *oubliette,* a cell constructed six centuries earlier below the level of the Seine, where only the waters of the river, and not a ray of light, infiltrated.

The prima facie case against Cazeaux (and the case Bouilly built against Darlemont) was compelling. There was the agreement between the date on which the young count left his family on a supposedly innocent trip and the discovery of the deaf waif. There were the similar ages and afflictions of the purportedly dead count and the living orphan. There was the resemblance of the orphan to the noble family and his recognition by the family servant. And just as his cousin recognizes the count in the play, so, too, in real life, did Joseph's childhood companion, his sister, Caroline, recognize him. She was brought to Paris from her convent in Toulouse. Curiously, she was uncertain about the boy's identity at first but when she conversed with him at length in some form of manual communication, and when he reminded her of various details of family life, she acknowledged him as her brother. Why did Caroline's ability to communicate with Joseph in an idiosyncratic home sign not convince her from the start that he was her brother? In any event, it certainly convinced Epée.

In Act V of Bouilly's play, the servant who had taken the boy away and abandoned him confesses that he did so at the uncle's instigation and then signed a false death certificate. The lawyer prepares a complaint against Darlemont; he asks Epée to sign it and testify as necessary. It is then that Epée recites the lines that brought the audience to its feet clamoring for the release of Sicard: "Théodore is not the only one to whom I owe my care; my other pupils whom I left in Paris suffer much from my absence." Meanwhile, the count's cousin has gone off with the servant to extract his father's confession in the face of overwhelming evidence, and he succeeds. The count is reinstated in his rights. He offers half his fortune, in friendship, to the cousin, who asks how he can ever forget the dastardly acts of his father. Epée replies:

EPEE   If Mlle. Clémence would help you—by sharing your fate?
FRANVAL   *(To* EPEE*)* It is plain that nothing escapes your penetration. *(*EPEE *signs to* THEODORE, *expressing marriage by twice joining his hands together, and pointing to the finger for the wedding ring. The count joins the hands of the young lovers, pressing them both together on his heart)*
CLEMENCE   Happy moment, which I was far from expecting!
COUSIN   My happiness can be felt, but not expressed.
FRANVAL   My joy can only be equaled by my astonishment. *(To* EPEE*)* Benevolent man, how proud must you be of your pupil! Compare what he

is at this moment with what he was when first presented to you, and then enjoy your work.

EPEE *(Looking at the count and those around him)* At length I behold him restored to his home, crowned with the sacred name of his forefathers, and already surrounded by people whom he has rendered happy. O Providence! I have nothing more to desire in the world; and when I put off this mortal body, I shall be able to say, "Let me sleep in peace; I have finished my work."

The end. Of the play, but not the real-life story, for Cazeaux steadfastly refused to confess to abandoning his charge at Séchelles or anywhere else. Indeed, he maintained he could prove that the abbé's pupil was an imposter and not the count of Solar: He had set out from Toulouse with the count before many witnesses on September 4, 1773, whereas Epée's pupil had been brought two days before then to Bicêtre and had been found abandoned in Picardy a month before that! The bishop of Comminges, who had come to console Cazeaux in his cell, proposed to secure the services of the leading solicitor of the time, Eli de Beaumont.

It was a glamorous case to undertake: suspicions of intrigue in a noble family, accusations based on the declarations of a deaf-mute, the gravity of the crime imputed to Cazeaux, the name of the abbé de l'Epée and that of the duke of Penthièvre (a relative of the king who had agreed to sponsor Joseph's education)—all these made the affair the talk of Paris. Eli de Beaumont's briefs were awaited by the bench and the public at large with as much interest as the latest theatrical success or government proclamation. They were announced a week in advance and circulated, freshly printed, among the privileged classes, by whom they were read, debated, approved or criticized; when the lawyer had proved his case in the eyes of this privileged elite, he had half-proved it in the eyes of the bench.

Epée did not consider that the case of his protégé was lost, however. The law allowed a priest to appear before the bar in defense of those called *miserabiles personae,* and the deaf boy he had named Joseph certainly belonged to this category. He undertook to represent Joseph himself, to be the adversary of Eli de Beaumont and the bishop of Comminges despite the priestly soutane that he wore in this the sixty-sixth year of his life. The reasons why are to be found in his youth.

Charles-Michel de l'Epée was born into a wealthy family—his father was an architect in the king's service—at Versailles in 1712, near the end of the reign of the Sun King, Louis XIV.[18] He completed his schooling at seventeen and presented himself for the priesthood.[19] Then came the first sign of the independent spirit that would shape the rest of his life, including his conduct in the Solar affair. On admittance to the first degree of priesthood, he was required to sign an oath abjuring the heretical teachings of Jansenism. Perhaps Epée believed in tolerating all sects since God tolerated them; more likely he had some positive sympathy with the doctrine of Cornelius Jansen, which emphasized predestination, denied free will, and attacked the Jesuits and the new casuistry. In any case, he refused to subscribe to an oath that would ensure a division within the church.[20]

Because the young Epée was unyielding in this matter, he was told he could never take holy vows, and was given a deaconhood. Blocked in his religious pursuits, he took up legal studies and four years later was admitted to the Paris bar.[21] Whether he was repelled by the chicanery of the law courts, as his eulogist, my friend Bébian, contended,[22] I do not know, but it is certain that three years later he returned to his religious calling. A lenient bishop gave him a small canonry in his diocese in Troyes, and two years later he was ordained a priest.[23] However, his protector died not long after, and Epée was prohibited not only from administering the sacraments but even from pastoral counseling. He lost his canonry, which the new bishop of Troyes gave to one of his friends.

We know little of Epée's activities for the next quarter century. We know that he settled in Paris, that he continued to wear clerical garb, that he lived on a modest allowance from his family, that he often visited the poorer quarters, and that he encountered two deaf women on one such visit, which led him, in the fifth decade of his life, to take up the education of this class of outcasts with unparalleled perserverance and self-abnegation.

Yet this knowledge is enough for us to discern the central principle of Epée's conduct. He who had inherited so much formed in his youth an abiding commitment to the disinherited. Why? Because he feared for his soul. "Saints are created through great struggle," he told a fellow priest, preacher to the king, who was to give his funeral oration.[24] "God has done everything for my welfare and I have done nothing in return for the excellence of His grace." Thus Epée reasoned: I am prohibited from leading the hearing to know God; I will lead the deaf to know Him. I am prohibited from teaching those who speak to sing His praises; I will teach the deaf to sign them. The state has deserted me through intolerance;* I will repatriate an entire class of the abandoned as useful citizens. No one will aid me; then I will do it myself. If God is with me, if He gives me the love of my brothers, if His word communicates to me a spark of His creative light, I will overcome all obstacles, I will compensate for the weakness of the senses, I will give men to nature, Christians to the Gospel, citizens to the nation, and saints to eternity.

Epée was consumed by the burning desire to do good as others are consumed by the burning desire of their passions. In either case, strong emotion

*The Crown had made the papal bull against Jansenism a state law.

does not favor clear reasoning, and this may account in part for Epée's next steps in behalf of his protégé Joseph. Departing from the convention of addressing his brief to the judges, Epée addressed it instead to the lawyer of his adversary. If my pupil was already in Bicêtre when Cazeaux left the Solar residence with his charge, he argued, this does not mean that my pupil is not the count of Solar but rather that the boy with Cazeaux was not. In fact, after Joseph was abandoned in Picardy a month earlier, the countess of Solar and Cazeaux must have hired a stand-in. It was, then, the substitute whom Cazeaux buried in Charlas.

It is easy to imagine how vulnerable this argument was to Eli de Beaumont's acerbic wit. How was the stand-in obtained? Who took the real Joseph off to Séchelles? Why wasn't his carriage seen? How was he paid? Where is he now? How was the false Joseph induced to contract smallpox and hold his tongue? How were the priests at Charlas and Barèges bought off?

The barrister hired to plead Cazeaux's case in court was the widely acclaimed Tronson de Coudray[25] (who, fourteen years later, would defend Marie-Antoinette in the same courtroom), and he did so—the magistrates of the high court before him, a thousand spectators behind—with eloquence and cunning. It all came down to this, he said. If the youth who was in Bicêtre when Cazeaux left Toulouse with his charge was the real count, as Epée claimed, and not a fake, then the accused must have replaced one deaf youth with another deaf youth nearly his twin, shipped the one off to Picardy, and stuck by the other until he decided to die of smallpox. Even the most accomplished storytellers cannot make us suspend our disbelief of such baby-switches merely to have us enjoy their story. Would the abbé de l'Epée succeed and have the court take a man's life? Would the court indeed tolerate the abbé's leading a witness with a secret language, unintelligible to the judges, the accused and his defenders, when a man's life was at stake?

The court ordered Cazeaux released while the inquiry proceeded and Joseph was taken to Toulouse to confront various witnesses in the presence of the judges.[26] A veritable cortège accompanied him there: not the abbé de l'Epée, who had gout and could not travel so far, but his *maître de pension*, M. Chevreau, and Joseph's classmate Deydier, also Caroline de Solar and her guardian, and judges and officers of the court. Some days later, Cazeaux and another court officer took the same route. On the one hand, Joseph failed to recognize various places and people including, initially, Cazeaux himself; with some prompting he signed that he thought he had seen him at his mother's home. On the other hand, the Solars' maid and gardener and a neighbor all recognized Joseph confidently as the young count, as did his schoolteacher and Mme. de Hautesserre, called to the scene. The company adjourned to Charlas, where farmers, shopowners, and town gossips affirmed in one voice that the boy before them was not the one Cazeaux had brought to Charlas six years earlier. Nor did Joseph recognize any of them. Then there must have been two deaf boys and, given the dozens of times Joseph was identified as the count in Paris, Clermont, and Toulouse, it must have been the imposter who was buried in Charlas. All proceeded to the cemetery and gathered round the grave: judges, lawyers, witnesses, doctors, principals to the drama. Behind them no doubt the entire population of the town, restrained by a few gendarmes.

If the tomb was empty, it would prove Cazeaux had kidnapped Joseph, given him to an unidentified accomplice to release in Picardy, simulated Joseph's death and burial, and somehow disposed of the stand-in. If, however, the tomb contained the remains of a small boy, then the borrowed child died *chez* Cazeaux, who remained no less guilty of kidnapping and abandoning Joseph. The gravediggers uncovered the tomb little by little and removed the skeleton of a child some eight to ten years old. Boy or girl? The doctors could not say, for the pubic bones were missing. The skull was studied. Doctor Gares announced to the hushed spectators that an indentation in the left half of the upper jaw testified to the existence of an extra tooth. The earth was sifted, a tooth was found, and it fit perfectly in the indentation. The extra tooth of the count of Solar!

The proper conclusion seemed, if anything, more elusive than before. It was agreed that everyone would go back to Paris and reflect. The high court reflected for two years and then issued its verdict: Cazeaux was innocent of abandoning the count of Solar; and the abbé de l'Epée's pupil was indeed the count and should be restored to his rights![27]

The verdict, like the case it decided, was full of contradictions. If Epée's protégé was the count of Solar, then there had been a baby switch after all, and Cazeaux was guilty of fraud if not murder. If, on the other hand, Cazeaux was innocent of any crime, then the child he had cared for was the count, and Epée's pupil in Paris at the time could not be he.

Why release Cazeaux? Because there was no direct evidence he had committed a crime. But then why reinstate Joseph as count of Solar? Because of the many identifications, yes, but also because the abbé de l'Epée's affiliation with the boy placed a halo around him, such was Epée's prestige. Did the abbé wish a nationwide search conducted by the gendarmerie? Why, it must be done at once. Permission from the king to move an entourage to Clermont? Granted. A sponsor for the boy? The king's relative himself shall do it. This respect for the abbé, born of his piety and his charity, but especially born of wonderment at his restoration of the deaf to society, Bouilly highlighted in his creation of the role. Indeed, in postrevolutionary, anticlerical France, Bouilly found it inopportune to mention the substance and goal of Epée's instruction of the deaf, which was the Christian religion. Not a word of the Gospel, much less of Jesus Christ, appears in the play. Epée is transformed instead into a deist, a disciple of Jean-Jacques Rousseau, worshiping the Supreme Being and nature, opening the hearts and minds of his pupils to the world around them.

The abbé de l'Epée began teaching the deaf, seeking, as he put it, "to reach heaven by trying at least to lead others there," in the 1760s, some twenty-five years after his exclusion from the priesthood.[28] The chance encounter that launched him on this career is legendary; the few details we have are from his own pen. It took place, he tells us, on the rue des Fossés-Saint-Victor, in the home of a poor widow who had deaf twin daughters.* He had gone there on some commission or other, discovered the girls were deaf, learned from their mother that they had been receiving religious instruction from a Father Vanin, who used engravings to explain the lives of the saints, and who had died some time before.[29] Imagine the scene: a wretchedly poor quarter of Paris, a narrow winding street paved in cobblestone, a bleak courtyard with refuse piled against vestiges of the ancient walls, a steep, worn stair that leads to a small dimly lit room. The naked walls and ceilings are black with soot from the hearth; jagged scars show where they have shed flakes of whitewash applied by earlier generations long dead. A large rough-hewn table occupies most of the room; three pallets of straw have been pushed under it to clear a narrow passage around it. On the table, a basin and an extinguished candle. Beside it, two young women sit on stools. Some fifteen years old, they wear identical long dresses of solid-colored dark wool, *fichus*,† and frilly muslin bonnets. Their lips are still, their eyes averted, their faces haggard; two young deaf women, sisters in misfortune. Understand what this meant: the deaf cannot go to school; cannot read or write; have few friends. With hearing parents, conversation at home is sparse, kept to essentials. These women cannot have a real trade but neither can they marry; they are useless to themselves and a heavy burden to indigent parents. Sadly, they endure an idle and uniform existence, condemned to grow old in a long childhood. When the father dies, the family becomes poorer still; the two young women do needlepoint to put bread on the table. But if their lives are wretched, at least their souls will be saved: thanks to a kindly priest, Father Vanin, who comes from time to time with his engravings of the saints, they will soon take their first communion. And then the priest comes no more.

Now: enter the abbé de l'Epée in a flowing black soutane; fifty black buttons climb from the hem over an ample belly up to his throat to disappear under a little black dicky fringed in white. Rather patriarchal in manner, Epée, in his late fifties, has a full round face, a penetrating regard. He smiles affably. "Good day, ladies."

The young women do not hear him enter, continue sewing, do not re-

---

*The *fossés* were ditches that ran along the old city walls constructed in the twelfth century.
†A triangular scarf worn over the shoulders and crossed in a loose knot at the breast.

spond. Epée, so the legend has it, attributes this to an excess of feminine reserve and sits down to await their mother's return. Why has Epée gone there? I imagine he has been making rounds of the poor to offer such modest help and consolation as he can, to put his life to some Christian use despite the Church's strictures. When the mother returns she explains everything. The crowning affliction is that her children will never take communion after all. Epée tells us his response: "Believing these two children would live and die in ignorance of their religion if I did not attempt some means of instructing them, I told . . . the mother she might send them daily to my house."[30]

So began the education of the deaf worldwide; so began the long journey of repatriation for this class of outcasts, a journey that has not yet ended. When all the deaf and dumb are educated, there will never be another Darlemont in the world.

But how to instruct these women in the faith? It appeared impossible. Since the women were deaf twins, they were almost surely deaf at birth and in any event before they could learn French. As Epée was keenly aware, Saint Paul had said, *"ex auditu fidem"* ("Faith comes through hearing") and Saint Augustine said of the deaf, *"Quod vitium ipsum impedit fidem"* ("This impairment prevents faith").[31] It could not be done. To learn the faith one needed a language, which was to say, speech; his pupils had none.

Why didn't Epée realize that the signing of the deaf might be the expression of a language of their own, with its own vocabulary and syntax? Why did Sicard miss this fact as well? It was not that the deaf were without this language at the time; it develops wherever deaf people congregate and was all around Epée if he could only have listened to it. The deaf author Pierre Desloges told us that all the deaf of Paris were using sign language. Likewise, one of the delegates to the National Convention,* arguing that the government had been duped into spending too much money on our school, stated: "Before the abbé de l'Epée, the deaf were not such wise theologians, but they communicated their thoughts easily enough among themselves and with others close to them. . . . The deaf-mutes that I have known had quite their own sign language grammar long before the abbé de l'Epée established his school."[32] It seems to me that the deaf twins whom Epée was to teach may well have known French Sign Language if they were able to circulate among other deaf people. And the deaf children that Epée would soon gather in his school certainly knew the language. Excuse me if I insist overmuch on the priority of French Sign Language: I do so because hearing people are fond of perpetuating the myth that the abbé de l'Epée was the inventor of the sign language of the deaf. It is not so. The language of the deaf is transmitted each time a deaf mother holds her baby to

*The revolutionary congress.

her breast and signs to it; no hearing person has anything to do with this.

It no more occurred to Epée, however, than it did to the saints that the congenitally deaf could perfectly well learn the faith, or anything else for that matter, through their own language of signs. For hearing people had long concluded that those born deaf could only gesticulate and pantomime. Thus Condillac affirmed that the deaf had no abstract ideas and no memory, for these required symbols, that is, language[33]—though once he had acquired a little more familiarity with the deaf, at Epée's school, he changed his opinion.[34] After his death, however, his disciple, Destutt de Tracy, resurrected the old myth: "Without artificial signs and perhaps without spoken signs, there are no abstract ideas, and without abstract ideas, no deductions." Therefore, even after education, the deaf "have a much more limited ability to think than we do."[35]

Fortunately, Epée's independence of spirit kept him from adopting the prevailing views uncritically. "Faith comes through hearing," said Saint Paul. Well, perhaps: many people received their faith through the preaching of ministers, but many also by reading, and Saint John had said, "These are written that you may believe that Jesus is the Christ, the Son of God."[36] The deaf could come to Him through the written word. Epée recalled a precept from his early training in philosophy at the college* of Four Nations at Versailles: ideas and speech sounds have no more natural and immediate relation than ideas and written characters.[37] So he would give the deaf a language by associating their ideas with written French words.

Of course if a written word can stand for an idea as well as a spoken word can, the same may be said of a signed word. If it is arbitrary how we clothe our ideas to make them visible, then they are equally well dressed in the movements of the hands, body, and face that constitute the sign languages of the deaf. But Epée failed to reach this conclusion from his premise. Instead he reasoned, I will teach them the printed word for bread, *pain,* by showing them a piece of bread. I will show them the word "saint" and a picture of one. But how will I teach them the word "God," or "duty," or indeed any abstract word when I cannot evoke the associated idea by pointing? Explanations in French would be useless, since the sisters do not know the meanings of the words as yet. How was I taught abstract words in Latin? By explanations in my native language. Then I must learn the signs that they use natively, without instruction. These Epée broadly called the language of the deaf, although he thought they lacked a grammar and could not be used directly for education.

"Every deaf-mute sent to us already has a language," Epée wrote. "He is thoroughly in the habit of using it, and understands others who do. With it he expresses his needs, desires, doubts, pains, and so on, and makes no

*High school.

mistake when others express themselves likewise. We want to instruct him and therefore to teach him French. What is the shortest and easiest method? Isn't it to express ourselves in his language? By adopting his language and making it conform to clear rules* will we not be able to conduct his instruction as we wish?"[38]

When I was in Paris some years ago, I visited a former director of the school that Sicard had founded in Bordeaux. Professor Valade-Gabel showed me six volumes of Epée's handwritten notebooks, which he had obtained at auction, each one nearly four hundred pages long.[39] They contained texts recited by his deaf pupils at the public exercises, notes concerning the pupils and the pensions in which they were placed, some letters, and more than two thousand pages of Christian doctrine explained in question-and-answer format, apparently written beginning in 1764. Also included was the first act of a little play, performed, it seems, in one of Epée's public exercises. On the left-hand side of the page is the text of scene one, and on the right, not quite a translation in French Sign Language, but a list of the basic signs that would allow Epée to explain the meanings of the French sentences to his pupils (although he did not live among his pupils, it is evident that Epée knew something of the syntax of French Sign Language and its vocabulary).

By comparing the record of the two languages in the play, one sees immediately some of the difficulties Epée confronted when he decided to teach his first two pupils written French by means of the signs they already knew. Here is a sample from the very beginning of the play:

Saprice (a priest) and Nicéphore (his friend)

NICEPHORE Good day, my friend
Saprice; how are you?   HOW FEEL?

SAPRICE I am well.   GOOD.

NICEPHORE Did you have a   TRIP GOOD (or)
good trip?   BAD?

SAPRICE Good enough.   SO-SO.

NICEPHORE I was very worried   WORRIED-MUCH
about you.   ABOUT YOU.

SAPRICE Is that really true?   I DOUBT.

NICEPHORE Could you doubt   TRUE, TRUE.
that?

*I.e., the grammar of French.

Sentences in French Sign Language have fewer words than their French translations; they can dispense with articles, many prepositions, and other words of grammar that French requires because it cannot express relations spatially the way gestures can; and the order of the words is different from that of French. All of these differences could only confirm Epée in his prejudice that sign was not a true language that he could use to instruct his pupils. He thought, however, that he could convert it into one by inventing signs for the French words and word endings that had no direct counterparts and by using all these signs in the French word order. Once the pupil learned all the new signs and the French word that went with each, he could sign any written French sentence presented (as Massieu did for the pope) and could write any French sentence that had been signed in this way (as I did on the same occasion). Whether either party understood what the sentences were about was another matter.

To give you a sample of Epée's method, here is what he says about how to endow verbs in French Sign Language with the tenses of French: "We get our pupil to take note of the eight different tenses of the indicative mode in French; we write them down in a horizontal order with their respective names. To express something past, our pupil used to move his hand negligently toward his shoulder. We tell him he must move it just once for the imperfect, twice for the perfect, and three times for the past perfect. . . ."

When it came to nouns, all our signs that referred to objects and events had to have a sign of gender attached as in French. "We raise our hand to our hat for the masculine," Epée explained, "and to our ear, where a woman's bonnet ends, for the feminine." So we cannot speak of an armchair, a tomcat, or a bench (all masculine in French) without putting a hat on them, and every door and dish must have a bonnet in front of it.[40]

Then came the problem of French words for which there were no signs. Of course the deaf could express these ideas in their own language but in different ways. This would not do for signing French in the air; a unique sign or series of signs was needed for each French word. Epée followed Condillac's precept here: analysis. But the analysis was not conceptual, it was based on Latin etymology. For example, "intelligence" was not analyzed as, say, "can" + "know" but rather as "read" + "inside" because of its Latin roots, *legere*, to read, and *intus*, within. Once Epée started putting his Latin to use in this way, he could not stop. Even French words that had a perfectly good counterpart in sign were analyzed; thus, "satisfy" became "make + enough," "introduce," "lead + into," and so on.[41]

Finally Epée confronted the problem of suffixes and prefixes; these are alien to sign languages, which achieve the same ends by other means. For example, in American Sign Language, the difference between "wanted" and "unwanted" is, roughly, the difference between the sign for "want" moving toward the signer or away from him. But to transcribe the English word with invented signs, a sign would be needed for "un-," a second for "want," and a third for "-ed." Here is how Epée's pupils were to sign the word "unintelligibility": "The first sign announces an internal activity. The second represents the activity of someone who reads internally, that is who understands what is said to him. The third declares that this arrangement is possible. Doesn't that give the word 'intelligible'? But with a fourth sign transforming this adjective into an abstract quality, isn't 'intelligibility' the result? Finally, by a fifth sign, adding negation, do we not have the entire word 'unintelligibility'?"[42]

In this system, which Epée called methodical signing, even the simplest sentence took on enormous complexity. One example: a line from Racine, "To the smallest of the birds, He gives their crumbs," required forty-eight signs from Epée's pupils. "Gives" alone required five signs: those for verb, present, third person, singular, and "give."[43] To the deaf pupil accustomed to expressing such an idea in five or six signs in a different order, the sentence in methodical signs lacked unity, was full of distractions, was far too long for a single unit of meaning, and, in the end, was unintelligible. This did not prevent Epée's pupils from signing French sentences given a text and, conversely, from writing perfect French given a sentence in manual French; it just prevented them from understanding those sentences—they had to be explained in French Sign Language. For the same reasons, the fact that Epée's pupils could write French sentences from signed dictation did not mean they could construct any on their own; they could not, and hence Epée never asked them to. "Of course they can't," he wrote to Sicard. "Don't hope that they can ever express their ideas in writing. Our language is not theirs; theirs is sign language. Let it suffice that they know how to translate ours with theirs, as we translate foreign languages ourselves, without knowing how to think or express ourselves in that language."[44]

The basic progress of Epée's instruction was this. The pupil would first learn the manual alphabet, one handshape for each letter in French, so he could fingerspell French words. Next he would learn to write these letters and then to write out the conjugation of a verb, for example, "to carry." To provide him with a few nouns, Epée began with some twenty parts of the body that could be singled out by pointing, and he associated with each the French name of that part written on a card. The pupil would learn to spell those names with letter cutouts. Next he was taught the methodical signs for the persons and tenses of the verb he had conjugated, as well as a few signs for articles and prepositions. Now he could write his first sentence in French in response to dictation in methodical signs. From here on in, the lists of nouns and verbs and methodical signs grew.[45]

I confess that I learned this system of methodical signing from Sicard just as Epée's pupils had from the master, and I espoused it for some years, even after coming to America with Gallaudet. Thus we would first express some thought in American (or French) Sign Language; for example, "Try to understand me," which requires two signs, appropriately placed and carried out, that we can label TRY and UNDERSTAND-ME. Then, using the same sign language, we would teach and explain the ten methodical signs so the student could express the thought in manual English: "try" + second person + plural + imperative + "to" + "under" + "stand" + infinitive + "I" + accusative. Finally we would write the corresponding sentence in English words on the board: "Try to understand me." It took the genius of Sicard's disciple and successor, Roch-Ambroise Bébian, to help us realize that all this was a needless encumbrance on our instruction, that the labor involved in teaching the ten methodical signs was the very labor required to teach the corresponding English sentence. There was no need for the intermediate step of manual English. And so increasingly we presented the idea in American Sign Language and then turned at once to the written language. By the 1830s methodical signs had disappeared on both sides of the Atlantic.[46]

And so it had to be. Mangling the language of the deaf to make it conform to oral language, or disbarring it entirely, as distinguished gentlemen are urging us to do now, are two forms of the same crime. The failure to use the primary language of the deaf child shrouds instruction in a haze through which meanings and feelings can be only dimly perceived.

Thus the two sisters and all those who would come after them became copyists thanks to Epée's manual French and educated thanks to his use of French Sign Language.[47] The best of them also became renowned performers. While I was at Saint-Jacques, I knew four of Epée's pupils then living in Paris, and we often spoke of him. They were M. de Seine, a sculptor; M. Paul Grégoire, a portrait painter; M. Didier, a grocer, married to a hearing and speaking woman; and M. Roussel, a journeyman printer during the first Revolution,[48] who occupied a minor office in the treasury department during Napoleon's reign as first consul. They were among the first educated deaf; they all looked very intelligent old men and they had good handwriting, but their knowledge of French was limited; we conversed at length in sign language.[49]

Still, it was the abbé de l'Epée, son of the king's architect, who first turned to the poor, despised, illiterate deaf and said, "Teach me." And this act of humility gained him everlasting glory. It is his true title to our gratitude, for in becoming the student of his pupils, in seeking to learn their signs, he equipped himself to educate them and to found the education of the deaf. For this reason, the deaf everywhere have always excused him for failing to see that the sign language of the French deaf community was a complete language in its own right, not merely a collection of signs, and did not need to be made to "conform to clear rules"—French word order and word endings, to be transformed into "manual French"—in order to serve as the vehicle for instructing the deaf.

As the numbers of Epée's pupils grew, so did the numbers of his disciples and then the number of satellite schools that the disciples opened in their native lands. The first of these was in France, at Angers, founded by Charlotte Blouin in 1777. Among French schools, Sicard's came next at Bordeaux, a decade later.[50] The number of French institutions grew rapidly in Sicard's lifetime, reaching twenty-one; now there are fifty-four, with more than two thousand pupils.[51]

A decade before Epée's death, his disciple Delo returned to Amsterdam to open the first Dutch school. The abbé Storck, the disciple whom the emperor Joseph II had sent to Paris so that a school might be established in Vienna, trained there the Russian director sent by Catherine II, as well as the founders of some German schools. Storck's successor, Joseph May, taught many more directors, among them the founder of Danish education for the deaf, P. A. Castberg. Several German princes, however, followed the example of Joseph II and sent directly to Paris teachers who then founded schools for the deaf in their countries. So arose the institutions at Karlsruhe and Prague during Epée's career, and at Munich, Waitzen, Freising, and Linz during Sicard's.[52] The abbé Sylvestri returned to Rome to found his school five years before Epée died; it soon sent teachers to Poland, Naples, and Malta.[53] In the year of Epée's death, Michel de Tarente returned to the Italian city of the same name to open a school, and the following year Henri Guyot did likewise in Groningen, Holland. Three years later, Gosse established a school in Tournai, Belgium, and Hemeling one in the German state of Württemberg. Dangulo and J. M. d'Aléa founded the first Spanish school in Madrid in 1805 and I. R. Ulrich established one in Zurich four years later.[54] At about this time Per Avon Borg saw Bouilly's play and decided to follow in Epée's path. Within a few years he had founded a school on Epée's methods not only in his native Sweden but also in Portugal.[55]

And so it progressed: in his lifetime, Epée directly caused the founding of a dozen schools throughout Europe. Sicard's lifetime saw that number grow fivefold. From our institution alone came deaf mathematicians, chemists, painters, sculptors, lithographers, engravers, printers, poets, sailors and soldiers, men of letters, and, especially, deaf teachers of the deaf, who traveled throughout France and Europe to teach their brothers and sisters.[56] Nowadays there are more than two hundred schools throughout the world founded by Epée's disciples, twenty-eight of them—including a college for the deaf—in America. And there are more than five hundred deaf teachers of the deaf in Europe and America.[57]

The year that Epée died, 1789, was a year of momentous endings and beginnings for all the hearing and the deaf. On the ninth of July the Constituent Assembly was formed in France to create a constitution for the financially bankrupt kingdom. Louis XVI called his troops to his defense in

Paris, but on the fourteenth of July several thousands of Parisians and soldiers in revolt stormed the old fortress prison of La Bastille, symbol of royal power. The king yielded, removing his troops to the provinces and agreeing to replace the white cockade of the Bourbons with the red, white, and blue one of the Revolution. These concessions, a sign of weakness, fueled the peasant revolt in the countryside; a popular militia formed and the nobility began to flee. In the night of August fourth, the Assembly voted an end to the privilege of the clergy and the nobility, an end to feudal rights. On the twenty-sixth they voted the Declaration of the Rights of Man. In October, the revolutionaries went to Versailles "to get some bread"; they killed the king's guards and obliged the royal family to return to Paris, to the Tuileries; the Constituent Assembly followed. As the year ended, the French government was under the control of the revolutionaries.

Epée's failing strength coincided with that of the monarchy; his decline had begun toward the end of the Solar trial, which had consumed so much of the energy and time of the seventh decade of his life. By December of 1789, he was dying, rich in acclaim and gratitude, poor in worldly goods. The man who gave the deaf his genius, his heart, and his labor had not withheld his funds. He had inherited a modest income from his father, the equivalent of some $3,000 a year.[58] With this he paid the pensions of all his pupils, the salaries of his assistants, and the expenses of his home and the school within. In the terrible winter of 1788, when the rivers were frozen, transport blocked, bread in short supply, when the people were dying of famine and cold (thus hastening the advent of revolution)—in that cruel winter, Epée was almost destitute. His soutane was worn, he ate little, and he stopped buying wood for his fire. Legend has it that some of his pupils gathered in his lodgings, set the fire themselves, and would not leave until he promised to shepherd his failing strength and provide for his basic needs. "My children," he was wont to say thereafter, "I have cheated you of a hundred écus."*

Those "children" gathered around his deathbed, joined by a delegation from the National Assembly, chief among them Monseigneur Champion de Cicé, who had sent Sicard to him. He was there to tell Epée that his most fervent wish, the certain continuation of his school, was assured: the Assembly would be asked to take the school under its protection. The parish priest from the Church of Saint-Roch, where Epée had said mass for his deaf pupils, administered the last rites. Then Epée blessed his pupils in sign for the last time. He was buried in the crypt of Saint-Roch, where rest other great benefactors of humanity: the philosopher Diderot, the playwright Corneille, the creator of the French garden, Le Nôtre. . . .[59]

There is an epilogue to the Solar affair. Neither Cazeaux nor Caroline

---

*Approximately fifteen dollars.

Solar was pleased with the ruling of the tribunal. If Joseph was in fact the count of Solar he must have been kidnapped and replaced with a stand-in; the guilty could be none other than Cazeaux. As for Caroline, she was to lose half her inheritance to a deaf-mute who, on mature reflection, she doubted was her brother after all!

In 1791 they joined together to appeal the judgment. Conditions had changed in the decade since it was handed down. Epée was dead. The archbishop who had denied him the priesthood now denied Sicard permission to present evidence in behalf of the count of Solar. The duke of Penthièvre had lost all his influence in the Revolution. The high tribunal had been abolished and six district courts established for Paris instead. The second district court gave a definitive judgment in 1792, one that went largely unnoticed at the height of the Revolution: Epée's pupil Joseph was not the count of Solar and was forever proscribed from using that name or laying claim to any rights or goods of the family.

Joseph inclined to fate: without protectors, without funds, at a time when noble titles were more an onus than a blessing, he abandoned the society that abandoned him and disappeared into the army. According to the legend of hearing people, he died on the battlefield when he could not hear the bugle of retreat. Cazeaux and Caroline de Solar were married. A lawyer for the prosecution in the original trial, full of remorse, left them a small fortune and a house in the countryside, where they lived happily ever after. However, Tronson de Coudray, the eloquent barrister who had successfully defended Cazeaux, became the friend of Jean Nicolas Bouilly and when the Solar affair was over they often used to speak about it; Bouilly gave him before all others a draft of *The Abbé de l'Epée* to read. "As I pleaded the case," he told Bouilly, "I came to realize that Joseph was indeed the scion of a noble family. The conclusion of the appellate court was false. The true story of the count of Solar is in your play."[60]

FIVE

THE SECRET

There stands opposed to the true history of my people, whose modern era began when the abbé de l'Epée discovered how to educate us through sign language, quite another history. It is a record of the efforts of hearing people to supplant the language of the deaf with their language, to replace signs with speech. It calls itself the history of the deaf—yet it is an account not of my people but of our hearing benefactors, who affirm that the only proper route for elevating the deaf is oral instruction. It is a false history, for I state now, and shall soon show, that although it spans three centuries and a dozen nations, not one person born deaf has ever permanently supplanted his sign with speech. Yet even as Jacob Pereire, the leading oralist of the last century, challenged the great Epée, so repeatedly in my own lifetime have the oralists attempted to deny Epée's legacy. So they do today, these hearing benefactors who address the deaf in speech and rejoice not in our true education but in a feeble echo of their own utterances. Thus it is necessary to consider this alternative route that the deaf are urged to follow, to see where it has come from, where it has arrived—and where it promises to lead us if we choose it.

Never has this false history been presented with more authority and completeness than in the two volumes of *The Education of the Congenitally Deaf*, written by one of the great intellects and philanthropists in France,

Baron Joseph Marie De Gérando, chairman of the governing board of our school, which solicited the work soon after the abbé Sicard's death.[1] Dozens of hearing authors are cited in the work of this brilliant man who never taught a deaf person anything, and scores of hearing authors in turn have since cited him, and criticized each other's citations, and cited conflicting views, until all this citing of hearing people has become, for hearing people, the history of deaf people. Worse, deaf children have been led by hearing teachers to learn this so-called history, and to revere its heroes, who are, not surprisingly, other hearing teachers.

Baron De Gérando's story of the education of the deaf presents the march of history and the steady evolution of method: a parade of noble hearing scholars filing past in the dress of many lands and ages—sixteenth-century Spain, seventeenth-century England, eighteenth-century France—each following in the footsteps of those who have gone before, all selflessly toiling to repair the wrongs of nature. But it is all myth: there is no history here, nor march, nor method. It is an account only of hearing people of high culture who attempted to give ignorant deaf children not culture but sham speech, some lipreading, perhaps written language in close association with speech, perhaps fingerspelling, that is, oral language written in the air. It is the illusion only of a march, as one generation cites the nonhistory of the generation before, the mere reiteration of prejudice. Now, I say, let those in this parade stand down who did not really educate the deaf, who merely made early mention of the deaf or who report hearsay and fantasy.

Most histories begin with the Venerable Bede. He tells us in his *Ecclesiastical History*[2] that Bishop John of Hagulstat in Northumberland took hold of the tongue of a mute in A.D. 685, made over it the sign of the cross, and ordered him to draw his tongue back and to speak, "Yea, yea, and forthwith the ligaments of his tongue were loosened . . . and the Bishop then asked him to say 'A,' and he said 'A,' and to say 'B,' and he said 'B,' etc. . . . and he made him speak long sentences which he did." Let Bishop John of Hagulstat stand down and with him the Venerable Bede, and all those who have tried to perform this miracle since, and especially all those who have lied and said they have succeeded. Next cited is Rudolph Bauer, alias Agricola, professor at Heidelberg,[3] who merely mentioned in 1528 that he heard of a deaf man who could write. Let him stand down. Let Jérôme Cardan, physician, astrologer, gambler, withdraw: he simply affirmed that those born deaf could be taught to read without speech;[4] he never tried. Let John Wilkins, secretary of the Royal Society, step to the side,[5] and with him Kenelm Digby,[6] intimate of the English court: interested in all manner of things, they make mention of the astonishing achievements of a seventeenth-century Spaniard, Juan Pablo Bonet,[7] in teaching the deaf to speak but they do not tell how, much less repeat the feat. Let Juan Pablo Bonet step aside; he wrote the first book on teaching speech to the deaf, it is true, but he probably stole the method and he never tried it himself.[8]

Look at what is happening to the march of this history, how its ranks are growing thin! There are many other authorities cited in the hearing history of the deaf who never educated them: the Scot George Dalgarno, who published a book on the subject but preferred teaching the hearing at Oxford;[9] the Belgian Francis Van Helmont, who wandered about Europe with a caravan of Bohemian gypsies in search of the universal language of man, whose characters would immediately be understood by the deaf;[10] the Englishman George Sibscota, who in 1670 published the *Deaf and Dumb Man's Discourse*, which he stole from a Dutch physician and translated;[11] and his contemporary John Bulwer,[12] who wrote three books about the deaf and never taught a deaf man. Let us order the plagiarists to stand down— they only give the illusion of a parade by making the same marcher appear at intervals in different uniforms. Shall we likewise order out of the ranks those who unwittingly duplicated what went before, not having bothered to read earlier works? Then our parade is over; out of all the pages and citations, we can retain the names of only two men in the history of the education of the deaf who had the genius to originate and the commitment to act: the abbé de l'Epée is one, and, as I shall prove to you, Pedro Ponce de León, a sixteenth-century Benedictine monk from the monastery of San Salvador at Oña in Spain, is the other.

Neither history, nor march, nor method, if by method we mean a reasoned procedure that generally succeeds. How do you teach speech to those who never spoke? These hearing histories tell us: be patient; use every device you can think of. All of the methods across the ages come down to this: some observations on how we make various speech sounds, some homilies on which sounds to teach first, and some prejudices on what the deaf child should do meanwhile with his hands (hold the teacher's throat, his jaw, his tongue, or his mirror).

Patience instead of method. A day, a week, a year count for nothing in the struggle to twist your tongue around a vowel. So much diligence is required, in fact, to make the slightest progress in articulation with the truly deaf that many writers—Epée, for example, and Dalgarno—recommend the choice of a teacher whose mind is not too active. Monks like Ponce de León also make good teachers, for they have much time and patience in worldly matters such as tongue position.

If the history of oral education of the deaf reveals nary a principle for making a successful pupil, it reveals many for making a successful teacher. Principle first: the rich need your help as well as the poor and the rich can pay for it; the history of oralism is aglitter with bejeweled aristocracy. Second, teach a few carefully chosen pupils. When a teacher depends for his income on contented parents, he must select pupils with favorable characteristics: the greater their intelligence, their age at which some hearing was

JACOB RODRIGUES PEREIRE AND MARIE MAROIS
(PAINTING BY LENEPVEU)

lost, and their hearing remaining, the better. Deny your pupils' unique qualities: only teachers vary in intelligence; there are no degrees of deafness nor
diverse ages at which it begins—none worth noting. Disregard your pupils'
earlier teachers, and exaggerate your own accomplishments: one of your
pupils can sing, another can recite the Gospel according to Mark, a third
can imitate tongues he has never heard or seen uttered before. Teach few
but give the impression of teaching many. Learn your pupil's sign language:
pantomime is exhausting, and you can no more abstain from signing when
instructing a deaf person than you can abstain from speaking when instructing a blind person. Deny using sign language, however; your pupil is supposed to be communicating in speech. Be patient—you will be at it for
years: ideally, you should live in your pupil's home, or have him live in yours
at his expense. Swear your pupils to secrecy; permit no one to observe you;
the more you make your method a secret, the more people will believe in
its power. Hire relatives. You must publish: intimate that you have a
method; acknowledge your illustrious predecessors in this art, for that adds
substance to the profession, but state that your method is wholly original
and their works came into your hands after your book went to press. Obtain
testimonials from your pupils—they will surely comply—and from other
practitioners, who may require you to reciprocate.

Am I fair to the oralists? The greatest demutiser of them all, celebrated
by scientists and kings, the oralist who provoked Epée into publishing, was
Jacob Rodrigues Pereire. Listen to his story as told by his pupils and biographers, my contemporaries, and decide if I am fair.[13] Let Marie Marois speak
first; she was his most accomplished pupil in the eyes of many, including her
own: she signed her letters "Marie Marois, former deaf-mute." I met her
in her old age at her home in Orléans, and she regaled me—in sign—with
her memories, which predated the Revolution.

When Joseph II, Holy Roman Emperor, came to Paris in 1777 disguised
as the count of Falkenstein, and visited Epée's school, he also asked to meet
Pereire and his best pupil, and she was presented.[14] Marie was twenty-eight
then, her skin was fair and smooth; she wore a magnificent burgundy gown
for the occasion and her hair was bedecked with feathers. She had memorized a rather cunning tribute to the emperor, which she recited aloud:
"Monsieur le Comte, the fullness of my joy today has seemingly retied the
strings that once held my tongue immobile until art loosened them. The
more my heart swells with this happiness, sire, the less my mouth can express it." This was expression enough for Joseph II to give Pereire a vase
and a rhinoceros horn.

At that time, Marie was a masterful lipreader, a skill she had acquired on
her own (the priest at the church in Orléans said she had been very ugly
and had practiced lipreading with a mirror so she could know what men said
about her).[15] It proved impossible for her, however, to follow what the Holy

Roman Emperor said and at times Pereire repeated his words by rapid fingerspelling. Although the emperor was the brother of the French queen, his parents were Austrian and his French may have been heavily accented. Even the best lipreader requires a native speaker within a few meters in a good light who moves his lips broadly, slowly, and deliberately. If the speaker turns his head, addresses someone else, reads aloud, or has an accent, it is usually hopeless.

Marie Marois was born deaf in 1749. Like Pereire's other accomplished pupils, she had residual hearing: she could distinguish some sounds and perhaps thirty words with the aid of an ear trumpet.[16] Unlike them, she was quite poor, an orphan. She was given into Pereire's charge by the count of Saint-Florentin, on whose land she was born, near Orléans.[17]

Marie was only seven at the time of her presentation to Pereire but she still remembered the day—or remembered, in any event, her account of it, given so many times. She was taken first to the count's château and outfitted for the visit in a lovely lacy dress; then she was brought by coach to the royal palace at Versailles, where she was provided with a deaf companion her own age, who became a lifelong friend, Mlle. Le Rat de Magnitot. Her friend's uncle led the two little girls to a magnificent anteroom, where they were left rather uncomfortably, their legs dangling over the edge of spindly chairs, to wait for the count and their new teacher, who were expected any minute. The minutes stretched to an hour but even that was not enough time for Marie to take in the wonder of her new friend and the splendors of the chamber in which they waited: the walls and ceiling of carved mahogany with countless thousands of painted fleurs-de-lis in the interstices of the woodwork; the gold and crystal chandelier; the table topped in marble, with intricately carved molding and legs, flourishes of gilt, curlecues and arabesques; the two exquisite porcelain vases with handles in the shape of dragons with wings. Morning sunlight was streaming through the windows, and sparks everywhere glittered at edges of gilt and glass.

Marie sensed someone enter the room behind them and pause, but she continued whispering in sign to her friend. Pereire had to circle around in front of them, where he appeared abruptly, smiling. "Good day, ladies," he signed. The lighthearted flourish of his greeting was a welcome note, for his appearance was somber and forbidding. He wore black breeches with striped leggings and a waistcoat under a long coat, cut away in front with tails behind, a high collar, and a wig. He appeared about forty, with a dark and pocked complexion, an eagle-beaked nose, a broad, high forehead that ruled over wide eyes, full of fire and expression, and prominent cheeks and jaw. Scarcely was there time to sort out curiosity, apprehension, and wonderment before the count arrived and the party set out for Pereire's home in Paris, where Marie would spend the next twenty-two years.

She had so many splendid memories. Each New Year's Day, Pereire would bring her to visit the count of Saint-Florentin at the royal palace. When she was nine and a half, she recited this New Year's greeting: "My tongue, which owes to you the use of speech, will never cease to utter my wishes for your prosperity. Let the heavens deign to answer these prayers and fill your life with grace abundant as you have filled mine with your generosity."[18] As a child, she was introduced to the king of Poland and to Louis XVI, then the Dauphin.* When she was in her twenties, the king of Sweden asked to meet Pereire and his pupils and she was presented along with Mlle. Le Rat and one other woman.[19] Each of the three pupils paid the king a little compliment aloud. This was followed by question and answer, with Pereire repeating the king's questions on his fingers since the other deaf pupils could not lipread. Next, each pupil read aloud from a book opened at random and finally each presented the king with a written compliment in her own hand. According to Pereire's friend La Condamine,† who had arranged the audience, the king found that of all the sights of Paris and Versailles the most striking was the performance of Pereire's pupils.

When she came to Pereire, Marie Marois was mute, a signer. In the course of her years with him she came to speak fluently, to compose letters correctly, to read easily. The naturalist Georges Buffon[20] and the philosopher Jean-Jacques Rousseau[21] monitored her progress over the years. Her priest at Orléans told how she confessed: "She spoke, I listened. She looked at me, I answered her slowly and from the movement of my lips she didn't miss a syllable of what I said."[22]

How did she learn to speak? Pereire was a tireless teacher; extremely animated, he strode back and forth and circled around his pupils, manually arranged their speech organs. He gave frequent short lessons, made use of a special finger alphabet. He was a fluent signer: he used sign to give instructions, to explain words, and to converse with his pupils until they could converse orally or in writing, which he preferred.[23] But how did he actually teach and what was his hand alphabet? Near the time of his death, a few years before Epée published his definitive work, Pereire made Marie Marois the repository of his secret method and swore her to reveal it only to his son, Isaac, who was then a child. It was to be his legacy.[24] She refused to reveal it to Epée, who she believed had stolen some of Pereire's ideas, and to Sicard she said, "You are the last man on earth to whom I would give the legacy that my teacher confided in me."[25]

When I met her, all that was in the past. After Pereire's death, Marie Marois returned to Orléans. She had a pension from the duchess of Penthièvre until the Revolution; thereafter, she lived in poverty with her sister. All she could find for employment was repairing and cleaning fine lace,

*Heir to the throne.
†Charles de la Condamine (1701–1774), French mathematician.

which had returned to vogue under the Empire. She had little use for speech.[26] Marie Marois had always been a dependent: first of Pereire, then of the duchess, finally of her sister. When her sister died, she was utterly alone. Mercifully, death came to her rescue in 1829. I was quite shocked when Massieu sent me the news in Hartford; Marie Marois had long since slipped from my mind, the kindly gray-haired old woman who could not be hearing and would not be deaf.

The first recorded sign of the interest in the deaf that would sustain Pereire through a teaching career of forty-four years came when he was a youth of nineteen. He wrote to thank the president of the academy of letters at Bordeaux (to which Sicard would later belong), who had sent him as promised a list of works to read on the education of the deaf. His correspondent told him about the book published in 1620 by his countryman Juan Pablo Bonet,[27] about an English grammar written by William Holder fifty years later,[28] and about Johann Conrad Amman's book on teaching the deaf published in Amsterdam three decades after that.[29] (Pereire later translated Amman's work from its original Latin into French. He also knew Hebrew, Portuguese, Spanish, and Italian. In later years he was given the title of interpreter to the king.)[30]

What could have compelled a man to take up so young the specialized and difficult calling of teacher of the deaf? Persecution, and love. Pereire's parents were Marranos, that is, Spanish Jews who nominally converted to Christianity but continued to hold Judaic beliefs and customs. The word is an old Spanish one, meaning "swine";[31] the practice of false conversion dates as far back as the seventh century, when all the Jews of Spain were ordered baptized under pain of banishment. Pereire's ancestors had fled Spain to Portugal, but persecution of the Jews followed and those who secretly pursued their religion became a small closed society. Thus Abraham Rodrigues Pereire and Abigail Rebecca Pereire were wed, although cousins, and when they removed to Spain, they became New Christians, taking the names Jean and Lenor. Their son, Jacob Rodrigues Pereire, who was born in the marquisate of Berlanga, in the Spanish Estramadura in 1715, just as Louis XV ascended the French throne, was baptized Francesco-Antonio.[32] The Inquisition, however, renewed its ruthless campaign against the Marranos—during the half-century reign of Philip V, over 1,500 people were burned alive for the crime of Judaism—and as New Christians, the Pereires were suspect. Fearing for their lives, the family returned to Portugal. But in Portugal there was no refuge either; and after Pereire's father died, his mother, now a widow with several children, was arraigned for heresy. Somehow the family managed to escape again. Finally, in 1741, they reached safety in France, in Bordeaux, where a large colony of Marranos was allowed to live openly and enjoy full rights on payment to the crown of 110,000 *livres* (renewable at each royal succession). There, seven years after receiving the list of books on demutizing the deaf, Pereire opened a little school and set to work to teach speech to his first deaf pupil—his sister. Thus persecution may have been responsible twice over for Pereire's calling. First, it may have led to the consanguineous marriage of his parents and thus the deafness of his sister; as many as one child in ten from such marriages is likely to be born deaf. Second, and more important, it taught Pereire, and his parents and grandparents, a pattern of survival: to be in a minority is painful and dangerous; try to be like the majority. His father had given him an artificial name so his name would resemble accepted names and he could live a better life. He spent much of that life giving hard-of-hearing pupils artificial speech so their way of communicating would resemble the accepted way. It is only in the last few years of his life that we find Pereire reaffirming his Judaism, negotiating with the government, for example, to establish the first Jewish cemetery in France. At the same time, he had stopped trying to convert signers into speakers.

Pereire's second pupil was brought to him during a business visit to La Rochelle, just north of Bordeaux on the western coast. His name was Aaron Beaumarin, apprentice tailor, age thirteen; he was born profoundly deaf.[33] In one hundred lessons extending over a year, Pereire taught him to articulate all the basic speech sounds plus several words and common phrases such as "hat," "madame," and "What do you want?" When he was displayed at the Jesuit school in 1745 no one in the audience was more interested than M. Azy d'Etavigny, a prosperous businessman[34] of La Rochelle whose son, born deaf,[35] had been treated by the leading physicians and surgeons of Europe to no effect. At the time he was sixteen and attending school in a Benedictine abbey in Normandy,[36] where he had been for two or three years. Before that, he had spent eight years in the abbey of Saint-Jean at Amiens, and had been taught with a half dozen other deaf children by a deaf old monk.

Thus it appears that the first recorded teacher of the deaf in France, and the man surely responsible in part for Azy d'Etavigny's achievements, which would soon bring so much credit to Pereire, was a deaf man himself. His name was Etienne Defaye,[37] and he was born deaf of a noble family in 1670.[38] At the age of five he became a pupil at the abbey of Saint-Jean; eventually he served as architect for the monastery buildings and as sculptor of the stalls in the abbey with their faces of canonized saints against a background of fleurs-de-lis. According to a contemporary, he knew arithmetic, geometry, mechanics, design, architecture, and secular and sacred history.[39] He wrote a two-volume catalogue of the abbey's museum and its cabinets of medals, illustrated by his own drawings; but his greatest service was no doubt to the deaf pupils in his charge, including Azy d'Etavigny.

When this deaf youth's father heard Pereire's pupil speak, he determined, not to put his son in Pereire's charge, daunted perhaps by the cost or fearful of entrusting his education to a Jew, but to obtain a copy of Amman's treatise, which Pereire had no doubt mentioned. He sent it to the prior of the abbey in Normandy where his son was attending school, with the request that it be used to make his son speak.

After a year, the prior reported no significant progress and urged M. d'Etavigny to enter into a contract with Pereire. This he became resigned to do, but at least he would take precautions: he required the teacher to leave his family and closet himself with the boy at the abbey, to work alongside the prior (who would try to uncover the method), to teach the boy a fixed number of words in a fixed time in return for a fixed payment. No teacher of the deaf since has ever had such a stringent and unfavorable contract.[40]

Pereire, however, went to the abbey, where he found an intelligent eighteen-year-old who could read, write, and sign, but not speak; in eight days he had the boy saying "mama" and "papa" and in a month, fifty words. In four months Pereire's pupil had made so much progress that the prior convened the Royal Academy of Letters at Caen (of which he was a member) to bear witness.[41] Pereire addressed the academy at length without revealing anything about the nature or origins of his ideas, which he called a secret. He attributed them, however, to his ignorance of science (which would have made the obstacles seem greater) and to "the conversation and affection of a deaf woman who first awoke these ideas in me." Was Pereire, then, impelled, like so many pioneers, by the love of a woman or was he simply speaking of fraternal ties to his sister?

Next the young Azy d'Etavigny spoke, addressing the bishop, protector of the academy: *"Mon-sei-gneur, je vous sou-hai-te le bon-jour."* ("Good day, Sire.") The bishop wrote: "Father Cazeaux is good" (Cazeaux was the prior). The pupil answered, smiling: *"Ou-i."* Then the bishop wrote, "Father Cazeaux is bad," and Azy answered, frowning, *"Non."* Then he was asked by gesture the name for a sword, a shirt, a hat; *"E-pée; che-mi-se; cha-peau,"* he replied correctly.[42]

Pereire received the approval and encouragement of the academy and several national newspapers carried the story. The pupil continued to make progress until, after eleven months, according to a written testimonial,[43] he spoke 1,300 words that he understood, and many sentences. His speech was, however, influenced by the grammar of his sign language: he put all verbs in the infinitive and transposed word order. Shortly before the contract with Pereire was completed, Azy d'Etavigny's father withdrew him from the abbey in Normandy and Pereire moved to Paris,[44] where his reputation had preceded him. Six months later, however, the father wrote to him proposing a second contract. Without Pereire's attendance on the youth, his son's speech had greatly regressed. This is, alas, one of the hallmarks of the oral education of those born profoundly deaf: it must be sustained indefinitely or the speech degenerates. Early in 1748, Pereire returned to the school in Normandy, this time with his brother, to resume Azy d'Etavigny's training. "I can only employ this method myself," he wrote to a prospective client at about that time, "and I can be assisted only by my brother or sister for it is a secret I think I ought to keep entirely within my family and in any case cannot be easily divulged in the abstract."[45]

A year later, Pereire took his pupil to Paris to live,[46] and within a month had arranged to display him not before some provincial academy but before the most prestigious scholarly body in the land, counterpart to the Royal Society in Britain, the Academy of Sciences.[47] In the memoir given at the presentation, he stated that Azy d'Etavigny had learned to speak distinctly but slowly, could answer questions on ordinary topics put to him in writing or fingerspelling and pose his own, recite from memory the Our Father and other prayers and the Ten Commandments, and respond intelligently to several questions from catechism. He knew some grammar, arithmetic, geography, and history. Pereire told little about his method but did mention that it included sign language and a Spanish manual alphabet (the one in Bonet's book), which he had augmented and perfected.

The academy appointed a commission to evaluate the pupil and make a report: a professor of surgery and author of a treatise on the human voice; a physicist who had used Amman's book with some success in motivating a deaf youth; and, notably, Georges Buffon, who was then writing his monumental *Natural History of Man*, in which he would insert praise of Pereire and his method.[48] A month later,[49] at a meeting convened by the president of the academy, the duke of Chaulnes, the commission gave their report; it appeared in several newspapers just as Buffon's latest volume, hailing Pereire's achievement, came from the printers. All told, the news that the deaf were being made to speak, arriving in the middle of the Enlightenment, caused rather a stir.

One of the central questions of the Enlightenment was "What makes us human?" and one of the accepted answers had been, ever since Aristotle and then Descartes, "Language." "All that man has ever thought, wanted, done, or will do," one eighteenth-century philosopher lyricized, "depends on the movement of a breath of air, for if this divine breath had not inspired us, and floated like a charm on our lips, we would all still be running wild in the forests."[50] Deaf children and wild children were, however, an embarrassment for this definition of man, since the deaf were thought to have no language and feral children were invariably mute (that is one reason why the Society of Observers of Man took an active interest in Massieu and in the Wild Boy of Aveyron). Now Pereire had shown, in the eyes of his contemporaries, that the deaf could be "demutized" and thus brought into the human family. No wonder the Academy of Sciences would urge the dissemination of Pereire's methods.

The academy's report began by acknowledging that "this curious and useful art" did not begin with Pereire; Wallis in England and Amman in Holland had practiced it with success a century earlier, as did Ramirez de Carrion[51] and Pietro di Castro in Spain before them. The commissioners confirmed Pereire's claims for Azy. They added that the boy spoke loudly or softly as well, and that he intoned questions, answers, and prayers appropriately. However, his pronunciation was slow and guttural, as if issuing from the bottom of his chest, and he did not link his syllables sufficiently. Pereire asked for grace on this point, noting that the boy's speech organs had been inactive for sixteen years and there had not been enough time since to give them back their flexibility.

Some insight into the social condition of the deaf just a decade before the abbé de l'Epée founded the education of this class of pariahs may be had from the commissioners' hopes for the dissemination of Pereire's method: that the congenitally deaf might come not only to pronounce and read all sorts of words and to understand those designating visible things, but also to acquire the abstract and general notions that they lack, to relate to others in society, and to reason and act like people who have lost their hearing after reaching the age of reason.

In sum, the commission found that the art of teaching the mute to read and speak as Pereire practiced it was ingenious, very much in the public interest, and worthy of the strongest encouragement. With such acclamation, Pereire began to see his fondest hopes realized, to receive a subvention* for life from the king, to open a school and live comfortably in Paris, to leave a substantial legacy to his family so they would never again be obliged to wander over the face of Europe. Six months later, he and his pupil Azy d'Etavigny were presented to the king by one of his favorites, the duke of Chaulnes.

Pereire's brother David has left a precious record of the audience in a letter to their mother in Bordeaux. "Let God be blessed for the marvelous ways in which he treats Jacob! I wrote you yesterday to tell you of our trip to court, where we arrived at eleven in the morning.† We found the duke of Chaulnes in his apartment. He received us as cordially as ever and . . . leaving us in his room, he explained that he was going to see the Dauphin and then the king, and we should wait for his return. . . .

"Just as we entered the [king's] anteroom, the court was leaving the table. There was a great confusion of Knights of the Holy Ghost,‡ pages and servants and the Dauphin prepared to go for the ladies at Versailles; but he decided to wait to see the mute. Finally, at four-thirty, the duke came to

*Subsidy.
†This was January 7, 1750, at the château of Choisy-sur-Seine, one of Louis XV's favorite residences.
‡The chivalrous Ordre du Saint-Esprit was founded by Henri III and dissolved after the Revolution.

tell us that the king was coming. At which the confusion increased: 'The King! The King!' A column of the Knights of the Holy Ghost appeared and the king called, 'Chaulnes! Chaulnes! Chaulnes!' The duke ploughed through the crowd to speak with him and then, preceding the king, he approached us and said: 'M. Pereire, His Majesty grants leave to M. d'Etavigny to speak to him.' "

I imagine d'Etavigny's emotion at this moment. He had begun by addressing an old deaf monk in an abbey outside of Amiens in sign. Now he was addressing in speech the richest and most powerful man in the world. For this brief moment Azy was the representative of all the disinherited deaf of France, nay, of the world, for all eyes were on France, where the intellectual revolution called the Enlightenment was taking place. He must have been terrified. He said: "Sire, I am deeply appreciative of the honor of appearing before Your Majesty."

"The king was quite pleased and smiled," David Pereire wrote. "The duke said to him: 'He is afraid.' And Jacob said: 'It is not surprising, since all of Europe trembles before His Majesty.' Whereupon the king's hat slipped from his hand. Since Jacob and d'Etavigny were immediately in front of the king, both leaped for it and Jacob had the honor of returning it to him, one knee on the ground. The king never spoke to Jacob but always to the duke of Chaulnes and to other lords. Because of the crowd and the noisy confusion, you could not understand his words, but his gestures and beneficent expression made clear the pleasure that he felt. The duke told Jacob to have d'Etavigny read, and the mute read from Jacob's hand what Jacob read from a book."

Why have Etavigny read from fingerspelling rather than from the book directly? No doubt because Pereire's manual alphabet included handshapes for each of the vowel and consonant sounds of French, so he could present the words in their phonetic spelling and the youth would not have to know the vagaries of French spelling in order to pronounce the words correctly.

"Next, several questions posed by the duke were executed by Jacob. [Of Pereire's pupils, only Marie Marois was good at lipreading, and this was not part of his program, so questions had to be put in sign, fingerspelling, or writing.] From time to time, the king would take a walk around the room, speaking first with this person, then that one, finally returning to listen to the mute. The duke, leaning against a large table, spoke with the king. His Majesty spoke and laughed, pushed him against the table, and, placing both hands on his paunch, made him rock backward; then he came back to the mute. The duke told him what d'Etavigny was doing and that he knew how to recite prayers. The king told him to recite the Our Father, which he did best of all. After more than a half hour, His Majesty left and many knights leaving and following the king said: 'M. Pereire, I congratulate you. It's marvelous. It's marvelous. The king is full of admiration.' The duke was thoroughly delighted and said, 'Adieu. We will speak further in Paris.' And there you have, Madame, the end of our visit."[52]

Not quite. They were called back the next day so that the ladies of the court, whom the Dauphin had fetched from Versailles too late to catch the performance, might see the marvel of the talking mute. A few days later, the king sent Pereire an award of 800 *livres*[*] to express his pleasure. But the duke had hoped Pereire might secure the creation of a normal school to ensure the perpetuation of his art and its dissemination throughout the kingdom, or that a chair might be created for him at the Royal College where he could train disciples. Neither plan was realized. On the contrary, some years later Pereire would see his rival, the abbé de l'Epée, open the first public school for the deaf and enjoy the king's support. The duke was, however, able to render Pereire a service of another kind: six months after the audience, he gave him what Pereire called "the most splendid gift of my life," the charge of his godson, Saboureux de Fontenay.

Pereire would receive a few more pupils in the next ten years—De Gérando estimates he taught about a dozen during his career—but none would prove as brilliant as Saboureux, who became his outspoken exponent and even took part in a debate with the abbé de l'Epée on the merits of their respective conceptions of educating the deaf.

Saboureux was born in the same city as Epée, and for the same reason —the king's court was at Versailles. His father was a colonel in the Royal Guards. His hearing loss was congenital and at age seven we find him in school in the south of France,[53] receiving some additional instruction from a M. Lucas, a builder in the employ of the king. He had learned the manual alphabet, reading, writing, and arithmetic over some three to four years, before his godfather called him to Versailles and entrusted him to Pereire. Saboureux was twelve when he joined Azy d'Etavigny in Pereire's home. Here is what transpired in Saboureux's own words:

"M. Pereire, finding I was nearly thirteen, went about teaching me, consistent with the way a child learns French, common words and phrases, such as 'Open the window. Shut the window. Open the door. Close the door. Light the fire. Put out the fire. Get a log. Set the table. Give me some bread.' Once he saw that I was sufficiently well versed in everyday dialogues, which we fingerspelled with his enlarged and improved Spanish manual alphabet, he shunned the use of gestures. This was to get me accustomed to language, to rid me of my habitual use of my own signs, to train me in understanding sentences, to enable me to carry out all sorts of things consistent with my understanding of the language expressing the request, and to answer both easy and difficult questions. So that I might produce thoughts by myself, he had me describe everyday occurrences, to report what was said,

[*]I.e., francs; approximately $150.

to talk, to converse, to reason, to argue with people about various things that came to mind, to write letters to friends, to write back to people, and so on. In this way I reached a clear and automatic understanding of the meaning of pronouns, conjugations, adverbs, prepositions, conjunctions, and other parts of speech, of which M. Pereire then presented a goodly number of striking examples to get me to produce still others."

In merely two and a half months, Saboureux was ready to appear before the Royal Academy of Sciences,[54] which appointed the same commission that had evaluated Azy d'Etavigny. They found that Saboureux pronounced distinctly all the sounds of French, understood many common expressions and instructions in writing, read aloud with the intermediary of his teacher's manual alphabet, and recited the Our Father. In sum, their report of the year preceding on Azy d'Etavigny was confirmed.

A few months later the king awarded Pereire an annual stipend of 800 *livres* for life. Pereire was thirty-six; he had an assured income and two successful and brilliant pupils; Chaulnes, Buffon, and La Condamine were his friends, Diderot and Rousseau would soon become so. He had invented a calculating machine approved by the Academy of Sciences and was writing a memoir on sail power soon to win its approbation. He continued to work with Saboureux, as the pupil's autobiography describes:

"M. Pereire and my uncle enjoyed taking me to see experiments in physics, collections of scientific curiosities and so on, to visit different houses and to take walks in the country. Their main purpose was to familiarize me with everyday French, with giving appropriate answers to people's questions, and with social customs. I took frequent advantage of my leisure time to go by myself into the houses where I knew that friends would be glad to chat and instruct me. With company I began to get the idea of figurative speech, of the elegance of expressions, of the adornment of discourse. . . . Finally, when I had sufficient background knowledge of grammar, Christian doctrine and the Bible, around the fourth year of my instruction, the duke of Chaulnes, my godfather and protector, who for the first three years of my instruction tested me and taught me, did me the honor of asking me to write compositions. Then M. Pereire and my uncle had me write out notebooks on subjects they had selected; they got me to identify faulty French and other mistakes in these notebooks and had me correct them. This was the way that, thanks to the Creator of all men's minds, I managed to acquire a ready understanding of French and to express myself with ease in writing."[55]

Saboureux spent five years under Pereire's tutelage, then continued his education on his own: to French and Latin he added a command of Hebrew and Syriac and studied Arabic; he improved the elegance of his writing through "diligent reading of books written in sublime and lofty style"; he read widely on the nature of language, published his autobiography and a memoir on meteorology, and undertook the education of a deaf woman in

the city of Rennes.[56] "I scarcely remember being a deaf-mute," he wrote
a friend. Epée thought Saboureux did great credit to his teacher;[57] so did
Diderot,[58] who called him his friend.

Many wise and diligent people have tried to discover Pereire's secret of
successful teaching so that the legacy he wanted to leave for his family
might be left for all mankind. After his death in 1780, the sources available
were the letters of his pupils, his addresses to the Caen and Paris academies
and their reports, his family papers, and one further memoir he wrote himself attacking a plagiarist named Ernaud, who appropriated a student of
Pereire's and then presented him to the Academy as his own, under another
name.[59] Since Pereire would not reveal his methods, he had difficulty proving they were different from Ernaud's.

From these documents, Baron De Gérando concluded that Pereire's secret was his manual alphabet. Speaking of that alphabet, Pereire stated that
"each handshape designates simultaneously the position and movement of
the speech organs suitable to produce the sound and also the letter or letters
that normal writing requires to represent this very sound."[60] Thus, for example, there might have been a handshape for the single sound in French
which is variously written s (soupe), ç (façon), ti (nation); a constant position
of the articulators corresponds to that handshape. It appears that Pereire
took Bonet's manual alphabet and added his own set of handshapes, each
corresponding to one sound (there were thirty), plus shapes for numbers and
punctuation. Then, Saboureux explains, when Pereire spoke to him, he
would accompany his articulation with this phonetic fingerspelling designating sounds, much as one hearing person addressing another accompanies his
visible articulation with the sounds themselves.[61]

It is hard to believe that all the fuss over secrecy and the master's accomplishments boil down to a set of handshapes. A leading German oralist,
Samuel Heinicke, thought that Pereire's secret was to use pupils who were
not profoundly deaf and to obscure the fact (or minimize its importance).
The distinction between those born deaf and those accidentally deafened
"after the age of reason" was quite obvious to people then and had been
since the Romans, whose law made separate provisions for these two classes.
But the distinction—one of degree—between profound deafness and partial
hearing-loss was less clear. Pereire himself tells us that Marie Marois and
Saboureux de Fontenay were only hard of hearing: how much did that
facilitate their acquiring speech and the pillars of their education, reading
and writing?

A cynical kindred suggestion is that the secret of success is to use other
people's pupils: how formative were the eight years d'Etavigny spent as a
pupil of the deaf Defaye, learning through the medium of his primary language, and the further years he spent studying at the abbey in Normandy?
And those years M. Lucas devoted to Saboureux's education—how crucial

were they? This, too, is a feature of oralism: there is scarcely a pupil displayed to the credit of one teacher and method who has not first been taught by another.

Edouard Séguin, who was the first to show that you could educate the mentally retarded, speculates in his biography of Pereire, published in 1847, that his secret had come from his desire to touch and be touched by a deaf woman—she "who first awoke these ideas" in him—and that it reposed in the discovery that touch could be a channel of communication. And indeed, Pereire had said that when we are cradled in our mother's arms and take the first step in learning to speak, we feel the vibrations of her bosom.[62] The more a child is deaf, the more apt he will be to detect those effects of the voice. Put your hand in front of your mouth, he wrote, and notice that syllables can differ as much in touch as in sound.

In Pereire's time there was a great interest in the senses, the key to understanding man. "All our knowledge comes from the senses," affirmed Condillac. But touch had a special and formerly underrated role: "No sooner is touch trained, than it becomes the teacher of the other senses," Condillac argued. "By themselves, the eyes would only have sensations of light and color. Touch teaches them to estimate sizes, shapes and distances. And they are taught so quickly that they seem to see without having learned."[63] And Georges Buffon wrote: "We can acquire real and complete knowledge only through touch; this sense corrects all the others, whose impressions would only be illusions . . . if touch did not teach us to judge."[64] Likewise when Jean-Jacques Rousseau, who was a friend and neighbor of Pereire in the rue des Plâtrières, wrote his epochal work on education, *Emile,* he was much influenced by Pereire's experiments with touch. Rousseau's was a broader program than Pereire's: he applied to every sense the kind of training Pereire gave just to touch, and the philosopher would extend sensory education to all children, not just the deaf. But the sense of touch was pivotal: it is the one that best informs us, that we use most often, that gives us immediately the knowledge we need to survive, Rousseau argued. Moreover, touch can substitute for sight and for hearing. Saboureux de Fontenay also suggested that touch could be used with the blind as well as the deaf—a suggestion repeated by Epée and carried out by Valentin Haüy, the great champion of the blind and founder of the school, merged with ours until just before I arrived in Paris, that would make them literate and self-supporting. Haüy attended Epée's demonstrations in the 1780s and this may have given him the germ of his idea to print with raised characters, a system replaced a few years ago by the compact alphabet of raised dots invented by a teacher at his school, Louis Braille.[65]

Place your hand on the body of a cello, Rousseau said. Can you not tell whether the sound is low or high, whether it comes from the A string or the C string, just by the vibrations? "Let the senses be trained in these differences. I have no doubt that with time one could become sensitive enough to be able to hear an entire melody with the fingers." Thus you could communicate music, or speech, to the deaf through touch.[66] But still, how did Pereire produce the miracle, the talking mute? I maintain the question, rather, is—did he do so at all? Pereire could not, of course, teach real speech to a deaf-mute; real speech is never taught, it is acquired natively at an early age and remains fluent for a lifetime. Did he at least endow his pupils with sham speech, whatever its flaws and fluency? It appears not. Marie Marois has us understand that she let the skill fall into disuse, having retreated from Pereire's home into another cocoon, where a few intimates could sign with her. Saboureux de Fontenay apparently never spoke after he left Pereire; there is no mention of it in his autobiography. A linguist who met with him when he was thirty found "not a trace of his speech lessons," and when Saboureux undertook to become a teacher of the deaf himself he gave further evidence that speech was not crucial in his eyes.[67] Moreover, we have the testimony of an eyewitness, the publisher of Pierre Desloges's book *Observations of a Deaf-Mute*, who reports that those of Pereire's students who spoke the best, spoke quite poorly. Their articulation was forced, slow, broken, and painful to hear, for you sensed how painful it was to execute. Saboureux de Fontenay agrees with him. "In fact," he says, "all mutes express the same repugnance to speech."[68]

Perhaps Pereire had no particular secret at all. Like those of many other oralists, his method was empirical, a fine word meaning catch-as-catch-can. He took students who showed promise and had some prior education, used the senses available to them, communicated effectively in their native sign, to which he added fingerspelling and writing, and worked tirelessly at his task. Pereire's best friend, Olinde Rodrigues (they married sisters), wrote to Marie Marois after Pereire's death and asked her to reveal his method. She then wrote to Pereire's son Isaac, and here is the formula she gave: "Your relative seems to think this is a matter that can be revealed in conversation and correspondence. But a lot of time, work, and study are required, in addition to a well-disposed young child whom I might teach in his presence extensively. Moreover, I would need one of my friends whose knowledge complements mine."[69] Some years later, after Pereire's son Isaac had died, his widow again demanded the secret for the master's grandchildren. Marie Marois responded that she was old, and scarcely remembered anything: "The best I can remember of his method, he could convey it to his children only in person, by applying it to some pupil with whom he would progressively develop it."[70] As Pereire's family was still unsatisfied, one of the grandchildren dragged Marie Marois to Paris on her dying legs, but all she could do was hug each member of the family and go back to Orléans. Pereire had labored for forty-four years. For fifteen, his son tried half-heartedly to recover his heritage, then died. For another fifteen his grandson tried, equally without success.

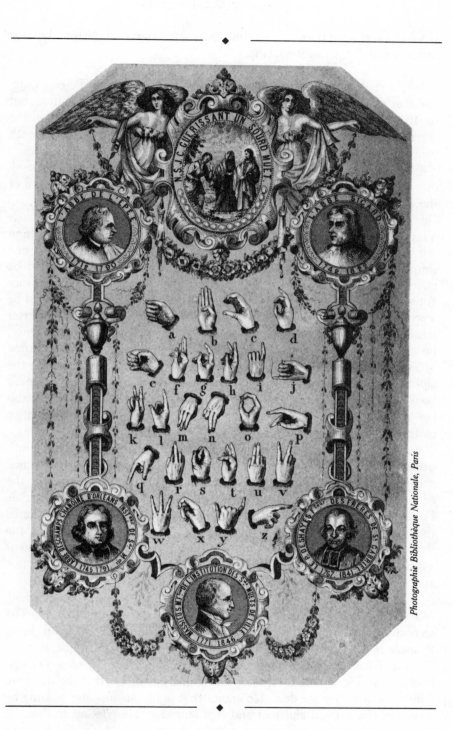

THE MANUAL ALPHABET

Doesn't it seem that the secret was this: there was no secret. The strongbox was locked precisely because it was empty.[71]

I believe that there was a secret of quite another kind in Pereire's life, one that concerned the women he loved and the origins of his method, but for that we need to return to his Spanish roots, to Juan Pablo Bonet in the seventeenth century, and earlier—to Pedro Ponce de León in the sixteenth century and the first efforts to teach the deaf.

Primarily Juan Pablo Bonet was a philologist; incidentally, he was a soldier—in the king's secret service and the service of the captain-general of the army, Bernardino Hernandez de Velasco, the constable of Castile; accidentally, he became concerned with the education of a deaf boy—de Velasco's younger brother, Luis. In his pioneering book he presents himself as the inventor of the art of teaching the deaf to speak and offers one simple, novel idea, which was also Pereire's a century later: it would be easier to learn to read if each speech sound was represented by one invariant visible shape. That shape could be a hand configuration or it could be a written letter, provided that we remember that the name of the letter must generally be "reduced" to discover its constant sound value. Hence, he called his book *Reductions of the Letters of the Alphabet and Method of Teaching Deaf-Mutes to Speak*. To illustrate, the first consonant in the alphabet is called "bee" but its sound value is the reduced "b." Bonet's book contains twenty-one drawings, each showing a letter from the Castilian alphabet with an accompanying handshape, often somewhat evocative of the letter in form.

Bonet's handshapes are used to this day by all the deaf throughout continental Europe and the Americas as a way of spelling rapidly without pencil and paper. They are Pereire's one contribution to the true history of the deaf. For Pereire taught them to his pupils, among them Saboureux de Fontenay. Saboureux pressed a copy of Bonet's book on Epée, who claimed that he undertook to learn enough Spanish to read it. Epée taught the manual alphabet to his pupils and disciples, including Sicard, and thus it spread throughout Europe.[72] Sicard taught it to his pupils, including me, and I brought it to America.

There is a great deal of pedantic nonsense in the first part of Bonet's book —a whole chapter is devoted to the etymology of the word "letter." The second part of the book is supposedly about teaching the deaf and dumb to speak but actually only the first seven chapters are on this topic, the rest being a course in Spanish grammar—to be taught, I note, by means of sign language. In the section on speech, Bonet first establishes that the mute are dumb because they are deaf. He argues that sight can supplant hearing by means of the manual alphabet and sign language. He goes on to describe the positions of the vocal organs in pronouncing each "reduced" letter of the Castilian alphabet and explains that teaching these positions requires great patience and good lighting, and can be aided by a leather or paper tongue. The last chapter on teaching the deaf to speak is concerned with their combining letters to make syllables and words. Lipreading Bonet left to his pupils' own ingenuity, as Pereire did later on.

All things considered, the book is just a simple and practical treatise on phonetics[73] written in the hope that it would be useful to the constable and his brother. Even the handshapes of the manual alphabet were not Bonet's. They appear in a book of prayers written thirty years before Bonet's manual, by a Franciscan monk, Melchor Yebra,[74] who attributed them to Saint Bonaventure. For each letter of the alphabet there was a prayer, and a person who was too ill to recite the prayer or even its first word or letter could indicate his selection by forming the proper handshape.

It was a twist of fate that called Bonet's book to the attention of scholars throughout Europe and made it the foundation for all further efforts to make the deaf speak, the base on which rest the three pillars of oral education: Pereire, in the Romance-speaking countries, Amman in the German-speaking nations, Wallis in the British Isles. Here is what happened. Three years after the book appeared, King Charles I of England, then Prince of Wales, went to Madrid to seek the hand of the Infanta, the daughter of the Spanish king. With its vast overseas territories, Spain was then the most powerful nation in all Europe; it was also the most exciting and fashionable: court life was glittering and animated by plays, masques, pantomimes —and talking deaf-mutes! The Prince of Wales conversed with one, the brother of a Spanish dignitary, the constable of Castile.

Now in the prince's party was the man who would tell the world of this astonishing event: Kenelm Digby, the nephew of the English ambassador. Young Digby was destined for a colorful career: this odd and gifted man, this "ornament of England,"[75] appears everywhere in the period in which England emerged from medievalism—in contemporary letters, religion, medicine, court life, privateering, navigation, embryology, botany, mathematics, cookery, diplomacy. A contemporary historian called him "a compleat chevalier. He had so graceful elocution and noble address that had he been dropt out of the clouds in any part of the world he would have made himself respected." To which the Jesuits added, "True, but then he must not stay there above six weeks."

Some years after his visit to Spain, Digby was imprisoned by Parliament for actively taking the king's side during the English Civil War; when King Charles I was beheaded, Digby was banished to France, where he wrote several religious and quasi-scientific books, including one on curing wounds —by rubbing a sympathetic powder on the weapon causing the wound, not on the wound itself! He was the best known of the English scientists to whom the French increasingly turned, a friend of Descartes and well received by other French philosophers. When he returned to England upon restoration of the monarchy in 1660, he became a founding member of the Royal Society, an intimate of its secretary, Robert Boyle, who ushered in the new chemistry, and of members such as the Oxford mathematician John Wallis, who claimed he founded oral education of the deaf in England.

The most successful of the books Digby published from his exile in France was *Two Treatises*, written to prove the soul is immortal. It went through eight editions in Paris, London, and Frankfurt, and contains experimental results, citations of authorities, anecdotes from Digby's vast career, and impassioned religious exhortation. It also contains an account of his meeting twenty years before with Luis de Velasco, thirteen years old at the time, the talking mute brother of the constable of Castile:

"A noble man of great quality that I knew in Spaine, the younger brother of the Constable of Castile . . . was born deafe, [so] that if a gun were shot off close by his eare he could not heare it, and consequently he was dumbe, for, not being able to heare the sound of words, he could neither imitate nor understand them. The loveliness of his face, and especially the exceeding life and spiritfullness of his eyes, and the comeliness of his person and the whole composure of his body throughout were pregnant signes of a well-tempered mind within. And, therefore, all that knew him lamented much the want of means to cultivate and to imbue it with the notions which it seemed to be capable of. . . .

"At last there was a Priest who undertooke the teaching him to understand others when they spoke, and to speak himself that others might understand him, for which attempt at first he was laughed at, yet after some years he was looked upon as if he had wrought a miracle. In a word, after strange patience, constancie and paines, he brought the young lord to speak as distinctly as any man whatsoever, and to understand so perfectly what others said that he would not lose a word in a whole dayes conversation. They who have curiosity to see by what steps the master proceeds in teaching him may satisfy it by a booke which he himself hath writ in Spanish upon that subject to instruct others how to teach deafe and dumbe persons to speak."[76]

Digby goes on to state that the priest "who by his booke and art, occasioned this discourse" was still alive and in the service of another deaf nobleman, Emmanuel Philibert Amedée, prince of Carignan, who was sixteen years old when Digby's book appeared. He was of royal blood: his mother was the Infanta; his father was Prince Thomas of Savoy, a member of the royal family and of the dynasty that ruled Savoy, Piedmont, Sicily, Sardinia, and Italy in various eras; he headed the Spanish armies for five years and no doubt that is when he heard of a celebrated Spanish teacher of the deaf and engaged him to tutor his son. The teacher was not Bonet, however, but a man named Ramirez de Carrion, as several sources confirm;[77] we owe to one of them a rather unflattering account of his methods:

"After trying everything, [the prince's family] turned him over to a man who promised to make him speak and understand provided he be given so much authority over him for many years that the family would not even know what became of him. The truth is he behaved toward him like a dog trainer would or like those people who for money display trained animals that surprise you with their skill and obedience and seem to understand and explain by signs all that their master tells them. He used hunger, bastinado [beatings on the soles of the feet with a stick], deprivation of light, and reward commensurate with performance. Such was his success that the boy came to grasp everything from the movements of the lips and a few gestures, to understand everything, to read, write, and even speak, although with considerable difficulty. The boy applied himself with so much determination, intelligence, and insight, profiting from all the cruel lessons he received, that he possessed several languages, some sciences, and history perfectly. He became a good politician, even to the point of being consulted on affairs of state, and was a public figure in Turin more for his ability than his birth. There he had his little court and conducted himself with dignity all his long life, which should be considered a wonder."[78]

Nine years after Bonet's book appeared, Ramirez de Carrion published a work describing two thousand secrets of nature collected from various sources and arranged in the form of aphorisms;[79] there he discusses his secret method of teaching the deaf to speak and names the pupils with whom he practiced this art. Foremost was the marquis of Priego,[80] whose education had been cut short, but who could read and write and govern. Next he mentions Luis de Velasco, the brother of the constable of Castile, Bonet's employer: in four years he taught him to read, write, speak, and converse with such success he was in the habit of saying "I am not dumb, only deaf."[81]

Now if you have followed my story so far, you know this cast of characters: Pereire, who studied and followed Bonet's book, the first on educating the deaf; Bonet, who wrote the book to be useful to the constable and his deaf brother, Luis; Digby, who reported Luis's accomplishment far and wide; Ramirez de Carrion, who taught Luis, as well as the prince of Carignan, and his own employer, the marquis of Priego. But what is Ramirez de Carrion's secret method of making the mute speak? And who really taught Luis, he or Bonet? Did Bonet take credit for his contemporary's pupil? Dear reader, I pray you are not quite full of this potpourri of polymaths and mutes, for I must serve you more if we are to answer these questions and thus trace the origins of this remarkable endeavor, to teach the deaf to speak. We need the testimony first of Pietro di Castro, a Jewish physician of Avignon who lived in Italy,[82] and who wrote a medical treatise in which he confirmed that Ramirez de Carrion taught the marquis of Priego, the marquis of Fresno (Luis de Velasco), and the son of Prince Thomas of Savoy (the prince of

Carignan). (Their teacher was not a priest, however, so Digby had erred in that detail.) Di Castro learned the teacher's rare secret "partly by conversation with the inventor himself, and partly by cogitating with extraordinary perseverance, and I [will] make a separate discourse on it."[83] That discourse came into the hands of the abbé de l'Epée and later was published.

The treatment consists first of drastic purgatives, if di Castro is to be believed. "Next the back of the skull is shaven over an area equal to the palm and twice daily, especially in the evening, the following salve is applied: spirits, saltpeter, or purified niter, oil of bitter almonds and naphtha in specific proportions." Once this has taken effect and the head has been well cleaned, you may speak to the patient's bald spot "and, amazing result, the deaf-mute hears the voice distinctly that he could not perceive at all by ear."

Di Castro goes on to give Ramirez de Carrion's method:

"If the deaf-mute does not know how to read, he must first be taught the alphabet; and every letter of it should be repeated several times until he can pronounce it; and then he is to proceed to acquire a knowledge of the mode of pronunciation, and thus he must persevere daily, until from the pronunciation of letters he attains to that of words, and common domestic objects are to be shown him that he may learn their names; and finally several words are to be spoken in a row, so that he may be able to join them in proper order in discourse."[84]

The first part of this secret treatment is based on much the same principle as Pereire's subsequent and more practical suggestion that if you speak to the back of the mute's hand, some syllables can be distinguished rather well. The second part is highly reminiscent of the approach described in vastly more detail by Bonet. This is not surprising, since di Castro got it from Ramirez de Carrion, who spent three years instructing Luis de Velasco, we are now convinced, under Bonet's very eyes. Not only do we find Bonet's alphabetical method in Ramirez de Carrion's work but also the latter's publisher reports that he taught the letters by the sounds they stood for, not by their names—what Bonet called reduction of the letters—and he employed the very manual alphabet that Bonet describes, Melchor Yebra's![85]

In sum, it seems likely that Luis's extraordinary performance, which Digby saw and later described, was the fruit of Ramirez de Carrion's efforts, not Bonet's.[86] Was it then Ramirez de Carrion's method that Bonet published, and Pereire, Wallis, and Amman adopted? I think not. When Ramirez de Carrion came to the house of de Velasco, possibly at Bonet's invitation, he found a family with a long history of grappling with deafness, no doubt because of intermarriage. Two of Luis's great-uncles and three great-aunts were deaf and had been taught to speak by the first person of record who ever educated the deaf, Pedro Ponce de León—a priest whose achievements in the late 1500s were celebrated in Spain and, of course, in the de Velasco family. Thus the evidence indicates that Ramirez de Carrion's true secret was not the shaved pate, but the source of his method, Bonet, to whom he never alludes, and Bonet's secret was that he never taught a deaf person, he merely plagiarized the methods of his predecessor, to whom he never alludes, Pedro Ponce de León.[87]

It is claimed nowadays that oralism restores the deaf to society—meaning to hearing people. The inventor of the art, however, had little use for speech or society: he spent most of his life, the better part of the sixteenth century, in silence and prayer in a monastery. Pedro Ponce de León was born about the same time his namesake began his quest for the fountain of youth in Florida and Hernando Cortez began the conquest of the Aztecs. He came from an old and noble Spanish family in the town of Sahagún, province of León. He went to the University of Salamanca, then entered the Benedictine monastery of his hometown, a center of political and religious life, one of the most famous in Spain. A few years later he was transferred to the order's monastery of San Salvador at Oña,* where he spent the rest of his life. Much of that life was devoted to educating the deaf, as he himself reported in a document discovered long afterward in the archives at Oña by a Spanish historian, a contemporary of Pereire's, named Feijóo. "I have pupils who were deaf and dumb from birth," Ponce wrote, "sons of great lords and of notable people, whom I have taught to speak, read, write, and reckon; to pray, to assist at the Mass, to know the doctrines of Christianity, and to confess themselves by speech. Some of them learned Latin and some, taught Latin and Greek, learned to understand Italian. One of the latter was ordained and held office and emolument in the Church, and performed the service of the Canonic Hours; he and others learned to read and understand natural philosophy and astrology. . . . Some were able historians of Spanish and foreign history. Even better, they manifested, by using them, the intellectual faculties that Aristotle denied they could possess."[88]

One of the monks at Oña wrote a life of Saint Benedict in which he bore witness to Ponce's achievements, some thirty years before Bonet's book, adding that Ponce had written a book about it, and that one of his pupils was the deaf son of the governor of Aragon.[89] Further confirmation comes from the record of Ponce's death at the monastery in 1584, which tells of his "universal renown" for teaching the deaf to speak. No wonder: it had formerly been believed that speech, which distinguishes man from the beasts, was exclusively the gift of human nature, an instinct. Moreover, Aristotle had said that, of all the senses, hearing contributes the most to intelligence and knowledge—by accident, since sound is contingently the vehicle of thought. This was alleged to prove, opposite to its import, that

---

*Near the city of Burgos, one of the ancient capitals of Castile, in the northern province of Burgos.

the deaf were incapable of intellectual instruction (which is what Ponce had in mind when he said that his pupils demonstrated abilities that Aristotle denied they could possess). Finally, the physicians claimed that dumbness was not, as Aristotle had affirmed, a mere result of deafness, but rather was caused along with deafness by a lesion of the brain where the lingual and auditory nerves arise, and this was taken as conclusive evidence that a deaf person could not be taught to articulate. Now Ponce had shown that all these beliefs about the deaf—religious, philosophical, medical—were false.[90]

The first hint of Ponce's method comes from the king's physician, Ponce's friend,[91] who recorded that the monk made the deaf speak by first teaching them the written names of visible objects, then "by prompting the movements of the tongue that correspond to the letters." Another contemporary stated that Ponce taught about a dozen deaf pupils to speak and that their relatives were instructed to communicate with them by fingerspelling.[92] The hand alphabet Ponce taught was probably the one by his contemporary Melchor Yebra, published posthumously, for the two men had close relations with the Spanish court. The king's historian was an eyewitness to Ponce's method: he reported that the monk taught with signs and writing and his pupils responded orally. One day, he asked Ponce how he taught speech and the monk requested one of his deaf pupils to reply aloud to the question: "I would have Your Grace know that when I was a child and knew nothing, like a stone, I began first by copying the writing samples my master gave me and then writing all the Spanish words in my own notebook. Next, with the aid of God, I devoted myself to analyzing these words and pronouncing them with great effort, although this made me drool a lot. Then I began to read histories, so that in ten years I read the histories of the whole world, and then I learned Latin."[93]

This was Pedro de Velasco speaking, the deaf brother of the constable of Castile. Thus, two generations before Ramirez de Carrion educated the deaf brother of one constable, Ponce had educated the deaf brother of another —his grandfather.[94] And now the reason for teaching speech comes to light. It was not primarily religion. Canon law did hold that the deaf were ineligible to celebrate the mass because they were unable to speak the words of the Eucharist required for the mystery of transubstantiation to take place. But Pedro de Velasco, and his deaf brother, Francisco, both taught by Ponce, were not destined for the priesthood, and religious instruction could be more easily conducted in sign. Nor did Ponce teach speech because he thought it was required to cultivate the mind. Ponce—indeed all Spain— knew of the king's deaf painter, Juan Fernandez Navarette,[95] called the Spanish Titian after his teacher. Navarette signed fluently, read, wrote, was well versed in history and theology, and never spoke: he was known as El Mudo, the mute. No, Ponce taught speech to one generation of de Velascos, and Ramirez de Carrion to another, because a mute was not a person at law, and if the fortune and noble title of the de Velascos passed by the rule of firstborn to a boy who was deaf-mute, the family would lose all.

Deaf-mutes have always been thus confused with another class of the dumb, the retarded; under Roman law they were given a curator. It was not until the twelfth century that they were allowed to marry: Pope Innocent III decreed that they could do so if they showed by sign that they understood the meaning of the ceremony. However, those who were deaf only but could speak—who had established their credentials in the eyes of the hearing society and knew their oral language—have always been regarded as persons at law. The division of the deaf into two classes based on speech is a legal device aimed at making a more important distinction. Those deaf who could speak were generally raised in hearing families and deafened after acquiring the national oral language and some education. In short, they belonged to society, though they had a disability. But those who could not speak were generally outcasts, considered uneducated and ineducable, and outside the privileges and obligations of the law.[96] Thus Pedro de Velasco and his brother, Francisco, and their grandnephew, Luis, could under Spanish law hold a fief, head the family, and control its fortunes if they were deaf only, but if they were deaf and dumb they could do none of these.[97]

There is no evidence that Ponce de León ever taught any disciple the art that he had discovered. Surely, however, Bonet's employer, Constable Bernardino, would have consulted older relatives and family records to discover Ponce's successful methods and communicate them to Bonet to aid his brother, Luis. Moreover, Bonet had also served Bernardino's father, the fifth constable, Juan, until he died, four years after the birth of his deaf son, Luis. Surely Juan would also have asked those deaf aunts and uncles still alive how they had been taught by Ponce.

Indeed Bonet himself states that he was moved to write his book by the immense labor of Juan's wife "in seeking out all possible remedies to supply the defect in her son, making inquiries of different persons, sparing no expense in order that so noble a gentleman might not be left unaided."[98] It seems likely that Luis's mother, then, would have obtained the manuscript of Ponce's book (mentioned by his fellow monk) from the monastery of Oña, and given it to Bonet to arrange the instruction of her son. Then Bonet could have published the book, under his own name, which explains the lack of any reference to Ponce, and have hired Ramirez de Carrion to follow its procedures in instructing Luis. Of course it is possible that Ponce's book could not be found, as De Gérando was unable to find it two centuries later, and that his method was passed to Bonet by the family. In either case, the method of teaching the deaf in Bonet's book is consistent with what is known of Ponce's method, including the use of Yebra's manual alphabet.[99]

Bonet's book, and Digby's twenty years later, propagated Ponce's method throughout Europe; Pietro di Castro obtained it through Ramirez de Carrion and spread it in Italy; Phillip Sachs played a similar role in Germany.[100] In France we know that the greatest oralist of all time, Pereire, had studied Bonet's book when but a lad of nineteen, inspired by the conversation and affection of a deaf woman. More than this, a friend of Pereire's who wrote a sketch of his work and life[101] reports that he often heard Pereire credit Ponce's achievements directly with having launched him on his career; he had read about them in the work of Feijóo.[102]

But I believe there is a more direct link between Ponce and Pereire, which does not pass through Bonet or Feijóo: Pereire's deaf love. As I mentioned earlier, Pereire was born in the marquisate of Berlanga. Now, Juan de Velasco, the father of Ponce's pupils, was by marriage the marquis of Berlanga. Surely Pereire had heard of him and of his deaf children, taught by Ponce, and deaf great-grandchildren, taught by Ramirez de Carrion. He may even have known personally the marquis's great-great-grandson Pedro, who became the Spanish ambassador to England. If deafness was still to be found in the house of de Velasco at this time, the deaf woman who inspired Pereire with conversation and affection may well have been a relative of Ponce's pupils, and not Pereire's sister after all. For if she was his sister, why did he not say so? But if the mysterious lady was a de Velasco, she could have given Pereire more than affection, she could have given him a de Velasco legacy, the oral education of the deaf. Even further, might she not have given Pereire the secret manuscript of Ponce de León?

Pereire's last words on his art, in the final year of his life, 1780, occurred in a conversation with Pierre Desloges, the deaf man whose book I quoted earlier on the sophisticated sign language used in Paris. In the book's preface, the publisher claims it is the first ever by a deaf author, which enraged Saboureux de Fontenay, Pereire's renowned pupil, since he felt his several memoirs all had priority to this title.[103] He had yet another complaint with Desloges, whose book aimed to defend sign language against an attack by a disciple of Pereire, the abbé Deschamps (who, a few years later, would offer his credentials in competition with Sicard to become the director of our school, on Epée's death). Saboureux considered that Desloges's book was also aimed at him, he wrote to the author, since "I was the first to have declared war on the practice of conversing with gestural signs."[104] Therefore, the hearing deaf man (hearing in all but audition) invited the signing mute to chat with the master of oralism; the conversation was conducted in writing.[105] First, allow Pierre Desloges to introduce himself as he did to the editors of a leading journal that published a review of his book:

"There never was a writer in a situation comparable to mine: a deaf-mute from the age of seven, abandoned to myself, and without any instruction since that time, knowing only how to read and to write a little; come to Paris at the age of twenty-one, taken into apprenticeship against the wishes and advice of my parents, who considered me incapable of learning anything; obliged to seek work for my existence, without aid, without protection, without resources; reduced twice to the poorhouse for lack of employment; obliged to struggle incessantly against poverty, against the prejudices, set opinions, insults, and scoffings of my parents, friends, neighbors, and companions, who called me an animal, an imbecile, a fool pretending to more spirit and reasoning power than they but destined someday to be placed in confinement."[106]

When Pereire met Desloges, he was astonished to discover that a deaf man could become so educated without speech, through sign language and reading, but he acknowledged that even the most confirmed oralist must rely extensively on sign in teaching the deaf.

"Nothing could be more natural than your unreserved total approval of signs," Pereire told Desloges in writing, "since in your condition it would be almost impossible to find another way to explain yourself and to understand others. Undoubtedly, signs are essential for instructing not only the deaf but everyone and without them nothing could be taught or learned. Moreover, the virtuous abbé de l'Epée surely deserves great credit for having put order into signing, etc. But . . . there is a misunderstanding in the debate between the abbé de l'Epée and the abbé Deschamps. Could one learn anything in childhood without the aid of signs? Would it even be possible to express our great passions by speech alone? One gesture speaks a thousand times more and better than the most forceful language. To sum it all up, from what I see, the abbés are debating each other without understanding each other. . . . Deschamps believes as I do that signs are appropriate, useful, even essential, but you must not conclude from that that signs are the only means of instructing the deaf and mute. That would be the case if there were only deaf people in the world."

Pereire was right about Deschamps and sign language; he did use it, much as Sicard did, to explain grammar, vocabulary, and the fields of knowledge he taught his pupils, which were, in the order he taught them, God, the stars, the earth, water, plants, animals, and man. Indeed, when the abbé de l'Epée was visiting Orléans he had explained his method at length to Deschamps, who subsequently opened his small private school for the deaf. But Deschamps's ties to the signing tradition stopped there. He believed with some philosophers that speech had a privileged status as the vehicle for thought, and with the founder of the Germanic tradition of oralism, Johann Conrad Amman, that "voice is a living emanation of the spirit that God breathed into man when He created him a living soul."[107] In fact, Deschamps included a translation of Amman's treatise in his own book on educating the deaf, published the same year as Desloges's rebuttal.[108] In the book, he also assails sign language, praises Pereire effusively—"Immortality is his"—claims to follow in his footsteps, and appends a manual alphabet he received from him, after inventing a bizarre one of his own that involved movements of the arms and legs.

Deschamps's lengthy railing against sign boils down to a few basic claims, which Desloges refuted. Gestures are vague and equivocal, he said; for example, we easily understand by the spoken word "God" the ultimate being who created everything and unites all perfections. But in sign we point to the sky, where the All-Powerful lives. Who can assure us that the deaf-mute does not take the sky to be God himself, will not pray to it, and attribute to it the perfections that are God's? I can reassure you about that, replied Desloges. When I want to designate the Supreme Being, I point to the heavens with adoration and respect, which makes my intention so clear even the abbé Deschamps would understand. When I want to designate the sky, I make the same gesture without these accessories. Thus there is no vagueness about these terms in sign language.

Signs are concrete, Deschamps argued, hence severely limited. "Could we with sign language paint all our various thoughts, develop our minds, teach others, cultivate social habits, destroy prejudices?" "Yes," Desloges replied: "Everything can be said in sign. . . . There are deaf-mutes from birth, workers in Paris, who know neither reading nor writing, and who never went to the lessons of the abbé de l'Epée but who were so well instructed in religion, solely through the medium of sign, that they were judged worthy of the sacraments of the church, even of the Eucharist and of marriage. There is no event in Paris, in France, and in the four corners of the world that is not a topic of our conversations. We express ourselves on all topics with as much orderliness, precision, and speed as if we enjoyed the faculties of speech and hearing."[109]

Signs are arbitrary, Deschamps said, a private code that is difficult to learn: "Who is such a devoted humanitarian," he asked, "that he can stomach the inevitable disgust in studying sign?"[110] Desloges replied first that the abbé exaggerated the difficulty—six weeks are sufficient to master the essentials. He further denied that sign is arbitrary: our language paints the proper idea of things and not the arbitrary names given them by spoken language.[111] Here I disagree with my brother, who confused expressive gesture with sign, as did Pereire and even Sicard. It is true that a deaf man will weave pantomime into his narrative, as a speaker weaves gesture into his speech; no doubt it is even more important for the deaf person, as Desloges's account of signing "God" illustrates. But sign language is not pantomime: most signs do not paint or portray so faithfully that you can guess their meaning. To serve as an instrument of facile communication signs must be rapid and easy to execute, and these requirements cannot be met by pantomime. Take an obvious example: if you were to mime "shoes" you would surely reach for your feet but the sign for "shoes" cannot be that long and awkward; instead the two fists are tapped together on their sides.

De Gérando understood this and contrasted the signs of our language, which he called "reduced," with the little skits in pantomime described in the dictionaries of Epée[112] and Sicard.[113]

You may judge for yourself how pictorial sign language really is. Here is a sentence—what am I saying? The edge of my right hand sweeps downward past my left, half closed, palm down. Then I close my right hand, and with the thumb pointing up I graze my cheek from top to bottom, back to front, repeatedly. Next I extend my two hands in front of me, palm down, and lower them abruptly. In the final sign I close my right hand, palm up, extend it and open it. I doubt you can tell from this description, or from observing me as I execute it, that these signs, which can be labeled in English BREAD, DAILY, TODAY, GIVE, are inflected in signed movement appropriately to yield the sentence in English translation "Give us this day our daily bread."[114]

The deaf derive from signs but few ideas, said Deschamps. "Reduced almost entirely to an animal existence, they have only their passions for a guide." How then, he asked, can we count on the deaf as Christians and citizens, when their language is so limited? But it is not limited, replied Desloges, as your own book reveals, since you repeatedly use sign to teach. For example, you say, "When we come to the conjugation of verbs, there are a thousand things to explain: person, number, tenses. . . . It is true that here I turn to signs to make myself understood."[115] Indeed you must. The way to teach someone a language is to learn his. Like a traveler in a strange land, Epée realized that to teach the natives his own tongue he had first to learn theirs.

The greatest obstacles to learning speech, wrote Deschamps, are the bad faith and ready discouragement of the pupils! They hate my placing my fingers in their mouths as much as they despise placing theirs in mine. Only the promise of reward, great friendliness, and adroit signing can keep them at it. "It is impossible to give an idea of the patience required." For once the adversaries agreed. Since that is so, concluded Desloges, why not adopt an easier and faster method, which has been practiced for so long and with so much success, the sign method of the abbé de l'Epée?

Actually, the abbé de l'Epée was not at all opposed to the congenitally deaf learning to speak their second language as well as read and write it, and, indeed, his pupils spoke at his public exercises, as we have seen. Shortly after he began those exercises, he asserted in a letter to a friend that it is neither hard nor painful to teach the deaf how to arrange their speech organs: three or four lessons following Bonet's method are sufficient.[116] The rest is practice, and that requires someone who lives with the pupil.[117] A dozen years later Epée still held the same opinion: "To teach deaf and dumb persons to speak is an enterprise that does not require great talent but much patience."[118]

Let there be no misunderstanding, however: as charmed as Epée was to hear his pupils speak, he would never allow French—spoken, fingerspelled, or written—to become the vehicle for their basic instruction. That would be to rest all on the very faculty the deaf lack, to take one of the ends of instruction as its means. When this course is followed, it takes so long to build the language skills in French that education is postponed indefinitely. If Pereire requires twelve to fifteen months, as he claims, to teach rudimentary speech to children living in his home, Epée argued, how much longer would it take me to do likewise with pupils coming to my school twice a week? Proportionately, it would take me seven years. And what would they know? Some words whose meanings were incompletely understood, and a few familiar expressions.[119] "I have sixty pupils," Epée wrote. "If I give each only ten minutes of speech instruction—for these lessons must be individual—it would take ten hours. What human being could survive that repeatedly? And how could I educate my pupils, which is my primary concern?"[120] And Abbé Sicard, who followed in Epée's footsteps in the matter of speech as well as sign, when asked why Massieu, his most intelligent student, did not speak, answered: "He might well come to speak if I had the time to teach him but it requires so much painful labor and the deaf set so little value on it and use it so rarely, that I believe it is more useful to perfect their intelligence employing methodical signs instead."[121]

That concern is no more met by using French fingerspelled than by using it orally, as Epée explained. The beginning student is preoccupied with interpreting the handshapes as letters, so the fingerspelling does not convey meanings. Furthermore, since the means for teaching the pupil the second language is in the language itself, the method is as unworkable as teaching a beginner German by giving him a German text. Finally, fingerspelling is ordinarily much slower than signing, and since it portrays nothing, students generally find it boring.[122] Epée acknowledged that Saboureux de Fontenay, whom he had met on several occasions, had become quite erudite under Pereire's instruction and that Pereire relied heavily on fingerspelling. Still, Epée argued, you can make considerable progress even though starting with a defective method—and much of Saboureux's instruction came through reading.[123] Moreover, he complained, Pereire keeps his method a secret, so it is hard to know how he really educated Saboureux.

The rivalry between Pereire and Epée dated almost from the opening of Epée's school on the rue des Moulins in the early 1760s. First, Pereire's pupil, Saboureux, assailed education of the deaf with sign language in his autobiography, published in a major journal in 1765. He asserted that when Father Vanin instructed him with gesticulations and signs, he gave him only concrete, physical and mechanistic ideas about religion: God the father was a venerable old man in the sky, the Holy Ghost a dove surrounded by light, the Devil a hideous monster living beneath the earth. Moreover, Saboureux affirmed, pupils taught by this method simply memorize the signs for every word and word ending, thus signing or writing sentences like a trained animal, without understanding them. Clearly, Saboureux failed to distinguish between the sign language of the deaf and Epée's system of manual French. Saboureux went on to explain and defend fingerspelling, which is "as convenient and quick as speech itself and as expressive as good writing."[124]

Not long after this sally, which Epée took as a personal attack, he invited Pereire to his school to see its injustice for himself. Pereire provided a letter, which Epée started translating into manual French while a deaf pupil transcribed his sign accurately in writing. "That's quite enough, sir," Pereire interrupted. "I would never have believed it. So have you, then, as many signs as the Chinese have characters?"[125] Epée felt his point had been made, although he saw in the Chinese characters more arbitrariness than in signs. But the gravest flaw in Pereire's analogy eluded both hearing teachers: as long as methodical signs stand for the words of spoken language, they are like characters; but the French Sign Language of the deaf does not stand for anything else—the signs *are* the language and thus the counterpart not of Chinese characters but of Chinese (or French, or English) utterances.

The next volley was fired by Epée, who, as we have seen, made light of oralism in his published letters in the early 1770s. In response, Saboureux set to work on a book defending oralism, affirming that signs could give only concrete sensory ideas to the deaf, and mocking signers. He submitted a chapter to Epée, in which the kindly old abbé could read this description of himself and his pupils: "They are gesticulators who agitate their eyes, their heads, their arms, et cetera. Their signs are like gestures in a pantomime comedy, like those used farcically by the mutes of the seraglio* for the amusement of the sultan."[126]

The abbé de l'Epée's first book, in 1776, was published partly to refute these claims. In the second part of the book he republished the programs of his four public exercises with the accompanying letters critical of oralists, theologians, and other unbelievers in the efficacy of sign. The first part of the book, however, was devoted about equally to a positive statement of his own method, on the one hand, and to the attack on Pereire, speech teaching, and fingerspelling that I have described.

Pereire was beside himself. "My method has been slandered as unjustly and inappropriately as humanly possible," he wrote to the editor of a Parisian newspaper. And speaking of Epée's book, he continued, "It is truly a shame that such a work of piety and goodwill, which could be useful at least to the destitute deaf, who are the most numerous and hence most deserving of our commiseration, is so badly marred. I would have thought it the product of base jealousy and a wish to see me destroyed were it not for the

---

*Residence at Constantinople of the Ottoman sultans, where mutes served as guards.

universally recognized virtue of the author."[127] Pereire went on to promise a rebuttal, while Saboureux was already at work on one.[128]

But the master demutizer was isolated, old, and dying. After forty-four years of labor—ten years of preparatory studies, thirty-four years of practice —after success, setbacks, plagiarism, and criticism borne in silence, he received word that Louis XVI had given his protection—and his money—to his rival's school. A Catholic always wins over a Jew, he thought. I have clergy on my side (the prior who taught d'Etavigny, Father Vanin, and Mlle. Le Rat's uncle, also an abbé) but the philosophers support the apostate. During the Enlightenment, it was more important that Epée was ordained by Condillac, head of a secular religion called metaphysics, than that he was not ordained by Bishop Bossuet. Pereire copied the king's decree longhand. Then he put it away and never said a word about the deaf again.

Thus, the language of the deaf emerged victorious from its first major battle in the new era brought about by the abbé de l'Epée. Pereire stopped teaching speech, his pupils stopped using it, and when they died nothing was left behind—nothing, that is, except a moral lesson that most continue to ignore.

The forces of oralism, however, waged the battle against signing on two other European fronts, in the German- and the English-speaking countries. Johann Conrad Amman in Holland and John Wallis in England belonged to Bonet's epoch, the seventeenth century, each was guided by his book, and each had a prominent follower in the next century, the Prussian Samuel Heinicke in the first case, the Scot Thomas Braidwood in the second. There was no Epée in Germany or Great Britain to show the route the deaf must follow to achieve true education, and oralists in those lands were able to gain a monopoly on the instruction of the deaf as Pereire could not in France. Their efforts not only stultified the society and education of the deaf throughout much of Europe but also provided a springboard for the oralist assault begun recently in America by that great "benefactor" Samuel Gridley Howe and his associate, Horace Mann.

The "German system" these oralists urge upon us now began at the dawn of the eighteenth century with Amman, the perpetrator of a particularly evil and self-serving thesis I call the God's breath flimflam: "The breath of life resides in the voice, transmitting enlightenment through it," Amman wrote. "The voice is the interpreter of our hearts and expresses its affections and desires. . . . The voice is a living emanation of that spirit that God breathed into man when he created him a living soul."[129]

What arrogance! What drivel! Am I, then, not a living soul? Did God, then, not breath his spirit into me? No, indeed, according to Amman: "What stupidity we find in most of these unfortunate deaf! How little they differ from animals!"[130]

I am not reading you the ravings of some deranged religious fanatic whom humanity has ignored. I am quoting from the Latin text of a Swiss doctor of medicine, a text translated twice into German, once into French, once into English, the text considered the origin of the German oralist movement, the text Deschamps published alongside his own attack on Epée.

"I will state some preliminary axioms of indisputable truth," Amman went on, "by which it will be shown from the nature of God that creatures formed in God's image ought of necessity to be able to speak and in this respect resemble their Creator."[131]

Are not my hands in His image as well? Are they not the interpreter of my heart, do they not express its affections and desires? When I raise them in silent prayer to Him, does He not understand? "How inadequate and defective is the language of gesture and signs which the deaf must use. How little do they comprehend, even superficially, those things that concern the health of the body, the improvement of the mind, or their moral duties!" I will let you judge who is moral here and who is not. The deification of speech: Why, O God, why must we deaf slay this false god, this hideous monster of self-love, over and over again, in each of its disguises, in each generation, in each land? "Faith comes by hearing," said the theologians (but not Our Savior), and Epée showed them wrong. "Speech is the exclusive instrument of thought," said the philosophers (but not Aristotle), and Massieu showed them wrong. "No acts shall be legal except in words," said the jurists (but not the law), and my pupil Berthier showed them wrong.

How did Amman become the vessel for such slander? After getting his degree from the University of Basel at the age of eighteen, he moved to Amsterdam, a city much to his liking for its charm and literary clubs. Here he encountered a wealthy businessman from Haarlem who induced him to come live in his home and instruct his daughter. "I taught Esther Kolard (a young maiden of great promise who was born deaf) not only to read but also to speak readily."[132] This took him twelve months, he relates in his book published at the close of the seventeenth century. After four years he had six pupils—all from wealthy families. If they ever erect a statue to an oralist, it must have its hands outstretched and the motto in bas relief "Money and patience." Witness Amman: "I have often been amused," he wrote, "by those who complain that I ask too great a fee . . . whereas they do not know that I am put to immense and incredible labor for a year or so in giving instruction to a single deaf-mute. . . . The patience necessary to the practice of my method is all but miraculous."[133]

Amman was solidly in the oralist tradition of remaining silent on the sources of his ideas, but his method is much like that preached by Bonet, except that it puts all the emphasis on restoring articulation, whatever the cost in education. Speech was God's gift to man, its loss a proof of man's fall, its restoration redemption. What price was too great for that? When

Amman revised his book, he published a letter from the distinguished English scientist John Wallis, who implied that their methods were so similar it was almost as if Amman had consulted *his* method, published nearly fifty years before. In fairness to Amman I should note that he and Wallis each might have independently plagiarized Bonet (that is, Ponce). Amman hastened to affirm his prior ignorance of Wallis, Bonet, Ponce, and the rest, although he must not have frequented the literary circles that attracted him to Amsterdam if he had never heard of Wallis's published work or Bonet's book, or Digby's account of Luis de Velasco, or any of at least a half dozen books that cited Ponce's amazing discovery.[134]

Amman died without leaving a school, disciples, or pupils, but his book became the foundation of German education of the deaf[135] in the hands of Samuel Heinicke, who launched institutional education of the deaf in Germany.

"The method which I now pursue," Heinicke wrote to Epée, "was never known to anyone besides myself and my son. The invention and arrangement of it cost me incredible labor and pains: I am not inclined to let others have the benefit of it for nothing."[136] He offered, however, to disclose something of it if Epée would go to Leipzig and live on the spot with him for half a year. Epée answered: what I can teach in two weeks, I will not spend six months to learn.

Of what does Heinicke's method consist? Heinicke himself is obscure on all points except the terms of sale. When the abbé Storck, whom Joseph II had sent to study under Epée, asked Heinicke if he could attend his lessons, the German oralist agreed—provided the Viennese would pay him 36,000 francs. Heinicke's letters to Epée make it clear that his emphasis was on speech, to which, as did Amman, he attributed special powers. He was much opposed to sign, believing that its use unfitted the mind for later thought through speech. Nevertheless, he used gestural communication with his pupils and taught reading, writing, and the manual alphabet. We would think him a straightforward exponent of Amman and Pereire were it not for his insistence that he had his own secret method, which "corresponds in no way with the mode adopted by Pereire, Deschamps, and others of note."[137] As Amman said of Bonet so Heinicke said of Amman: his predecessor's books came into his hands after his own method had crystallized, so the similarities reflect the confluence of great minds rather than an intellectual debt.

In one way, however, Heinicke resembled his rival, Epée: he founded a school for the deaf poor when he was getting on, in his fifties—though unlike Epée he waited for royal sponsorship before he began. Frederick Augustus, prince of Saxony, invited him to Leipzig for this purpose, and the first public school for the deaf in Germany opened, with nine pupils under Heinicke's direction, in 1778—the same year Louis XVI sponsored Epée's school. It was a remarkable achievement for a man who had begun as a farm boy and at twenty-one was a private soldier in the bodyguard of the prince. Later, he spent a year at the university in Jena, then moved to Hamburg and employment as a teacher and secretary, then Eppendorf and the duties of choirmaster. While a soldier he had given lessons to a deaf-mute boy. Then he taught the deaf son of a miller and announced in the newspapers that in six weeks he had taught the boy to respond in writing to all questions put to him. Presently three other pupils came to study. Finally he was called to Leipzig, and his fifth and last career. According to De Gérando, Heinicke was prolific and the first to write textbooks for the deaf. He had a quick temper, was easily irritated, and had brusque manners, all of which showed in his relations with his pupils and his rivals.[138]

When Samuel Heinicke died, shortly after Epée, the carefully guarded secret of his method came to light in a well-protected will. Here is what Storck was asked to pay 36,000 francs for: "Sight and touch are not enough to learn the vowels; a third sense must be brought into play." Namely, taste. Heinicke prescribed pure water for *ie*, sugar water for *o*, olive oil for *ou*, absinthe for *e*, vinegar for *a*. What this cuisine would do, Heinicke explained, was "fix" the vowels, giving the pupil a guide more intimate and hence more enduring than vision.[139] Even this ludicrous facet of his method seems not to have been original. Saboureux had published Heinicke's great secret before the oralist taught his first pupil. "Easily discriminable tastes," Saboureux wrote in his autobiographical letter, "can represent the sounds of letters and we can put them in the mouth as a means of getting ideas into the mind."[140]

Various German governments sent teachers to train with Heinicke at Leipzig. Charles Frederick, duke of Baden, for example, sent a young priest named Hemeling to him (as well as to Sicard and to Storck), and on Hemeling's return he opened a deaf school in the capital, Karlsruhe.[141] Five years later, Heinicke's first son-in-law, Eschke, founded a deaf school in Berlin.[142] When the master died, his widow and Eschke succeeded him at Leipzig, to be succeeded in turn by Heinicke's second son-in-law, Petschke, who was replaced by his third son-in-law, Reich—whose son-in-law is the current director. Thus, because nearly all schools for the deaf in Germany* proceeded directly or indirectly from this clan (Storck's school in Vienna and a few in Bavaria were the exceptions), the Germans came to believe they had developed a German method to rival the French, though in fact they were merely promulgating part of the method of a sixteenth-century Spanish monk.

What we know of John Wallis, generally considered the first English writer in the education of the deaf, will hardly endear him more to the

*I.e., German-speaking states.

reader, or to history, than Samuel Heinicke. I should hasten to say that there is little doubt of his intelligence: he was a founding member of the Royal Society, he was professor of geometry and keeper of the archives at Oxford, and he published a grammar, thirty years after Bonet's, with a preface on phonetics.[143] However, Wallis's contemporary, the Oxford historian Anthony Wood, described him as "a liver by rapine," "a liver by perjury," and "a taker and breaker of oaths, who could at any time make black white and white black."[144] Another contemporary historian said of him, he is "a most ill-natured man, an egregious liar and backbiter, a flatterer and a fawner . . . a person of real worth [who need not] be beholden to any man for fame yet so extremely greedy of glory that he steals feathers from others to adorn his own cap . . . puts down their notions in his notebook, and then prints it without owning the authors."[145]

It was natural for Wallis to apply the section on phonetics in his grammar to the education of the deaf; he had read Digby's book, which appeared shortly before his own, with its account of the education of Luis de Velasco. Eight years after his own publication, he wrote to Robert Boyle, secretary of the newly founded Royal Society, to announce that he was teaching a deaf and dumb person to speak and understand language.[146] In a second letter, he described the education of his pupil, Daniel Whaley, son of the mayor of Northampton, who had become deaf at age five.[147] Whaley appeared before the Royal Society and pronounced distinctly various words put by the Fellows, who were consumed with a desire to conduct experimental philosophy. They concluded by applauding Wallis's achievement, which led to an audience with King Charles II.[148] The fact that Whaley had some residual hearing, according to Wallis, and was recovering speech, not learning it for the first time, dampened no one's enthusiasm.

Whaley stayed with Wallis for one year, in which time, according to his teacher, he read most of the English Bible, acquired enough speech to communicate on everyday matters, and learned how to write letters. "And in the presence of many forraigners (who out of curiosity have come to see him) hath oft-times not only read English and Latin to them, but pronounced the most difficult words of their languages (even Polish itself) which they could propose to him." As word of Wallis's feat spread, he was approached by Admiral Popham and Lady Wharton: they were alarmed at how much their son Alexander, born deaf, had regressed when three years' tuition under a distinguished divine and member of the Royal Society, William Holder, had ended with his teacher's removal to some remote post. Now the boy could still write a little but he could no longer speak save for his name and a few words. Popham *père* was brother-in-law to the Earl of Oxford, and Wallis was quite prepared to undertake the boy's education; he shortly restored some of his lost speech. An addendum to his letter to the Royal Society concerning Whaley also alludes to Popham—with no reference to Holder, I need scarcely add.

Holder had fallen a little behind in his reading but, when he came across Wallis's letter eight years after publication, he dispatched a complaint to the society: the title of first English teacher of the deaf belonged to him, as Wallis well knew.[149] Wallis answered Holder's claim of precedence with an angry rebuttal impugning his truthfulness.[150] His contemporaries nevertheless judged Wallis the plagiarist,[151] and the Royal Society reelected Holder to its council the following year.[152] There is reason to suspect that Wallis was also guided by Ponce's methods, as Bonet described them, and made no mention of it—especially when we recall that Digby's account of the talking mutes in Spain appeared in four London editions in the decades Wallis was teaching the deaf. In addition, Digby was a fellow member of the Royal Society and well known to Wallis, who had dedicated a book of letters on mathematics to him.[153]

Wallis's instruction, in any event, had no enduring result; the Popham boy stopped speaking once again—because he couldn't endure his teacher's morose and pedantic personality, a contemporary at Oxford said. The famous philosopher Thomas Hobbes knew Wallis well and had this to say about his method: he who can make a deaf man hear deserves to be honored and enriched; he who can make him speak only a few words deserves nothing; but he who brags of this and cannot do it deserves to be whipped.[154] Actually, it is quite common for deaf students who once spoke to relearn some speech and then lose it again, as both Popham and Whaley did. Wallis explained why: the deaf speaker, unable to correct himself, needs constant correction from someone else. Thus, Wallis stopped teaching articulation to the deaf and taught only written language to the two other deaf pupils in his career. Teaching speech to the deaf is easy, he wrote; one need only display the positions of the speech organs as I did in my book.[155] But no permanent progress can be had in this way, he warned; the speech will deteriorate. So the emphasis must be on written language, but only as a means to an end, the intellectual development of the deaf child. For each grammatical category, words must be taught in logical groupings (in contrast with learning one's native language), and Wallis also sets down a progression for teaching the parts of speech. His account does not go much beyond these rudiments, but when we put them side by side with an earlier and more extensive work on the education of the deaf by the Scot George Dalgarno, whom Wallis knew at Oxford, it appears they originated with Wallis's predecessor, whom he never credits.[156] (Incidentally, Wallis's brother-in-law was Daniel Defoe, author of *Robinson Crusoe.* Defoe used the letter I am describing as the basis for a book, *The Life and Adventures of Mr. Duncan Campbell,* which enhanced the fame of his relative.[157] In the book, Campbell was born deaf and educated by a clergyman who knew Wallis. The manual alphabet Wallis used, which he also took from Dalgarno, is shown without identifying its true source. In real life, Campbell was a charlatan who preyed on London, pretending to be deaf and dumb and able to tell fortunes.)[158]

Wallis's description of his method ends by affirming that the deaf are extremely able in expressing their thoughts by signs and that the hearing must learn this language of the deaf in order to teach them their own by showing them which words correspond to which signs. The instructor would first write a few clear, simple sentences and then explain them by signs to give his pupils an understanding of simple propositions.[159] "Sign language has the same role in Wallis's system," De Gérando wrote, "as history shows us it has generally had for teachers of the deaf, as it will always have, as it must necessarily have—an appropriate auxiliary to instruction for explaining fundamental ideas."[160]

In view of the evidence that Wallis was a plagiarist, abandoned speech teaching, and used sign, it is astonishing that the whole precarious edifice of British oralism cites him as its keystone. The most successful oralist of them all, the British counterpart to Pereire, whose clan has dominated education of the deaf in Britain right up to the present day, studied Wallis's letters to the Royal Society a century after they appeared in its *Proceedings*, and was inspired to seek his fortune as a teacher of the deaf. His name was Thomas Braidwood and he was engaged in teaching mathematics at a little school in Edinburgh[161] when an eminent merchant from Leith brought him his son, Charles Shirreff, to educate; the boy had become deaf when he was three years old. This was 1760 and about the same time that Epée took *his* first pupils; both men were also entering this career in their late forties, and both found it necessary to learn sign language to communicate with their students. But the similarities stop there. Braidwood, as did Amman and Heinicke, confused the gift of speech with the gift of reason, and he taught primarily rich, hard-of-hearing pupils.

Over the course of a few years, Braidwood taught Shirreff, then fifteen, to speak again, and to read and write. Lord Monboddo visited and stated that Braidwood had taught the boy to speak and write good English. "But it is surprising what labors it costs him to teach and his scholars to learn." First, it was difficult to get them to make any sound at all—they only breathed strongly or croaked, which reminded Monboddo of the wild girl of Sogny,* whom he had studied in France. Next, to teach the pupils the letters, Braidwood was obliged to use many distortions and grimaces, and to place and move the pupils' speech organs properly "while the scholars themselves labor so much and bestow such pains and attention that I am really surprised that, with all the desire they have to learn, which is very great, they

*A teenager, she was captured in Champagne Province in 1731, after spending some years in the wild with a companion.

should be able to tolerate the drudgery."[162] Shirreff chose a profession that made few demands on the speaking skill so painfully restored: he became a successful painter of miniatures.[163] One writer who knew him well disputed the claim that he ever did recover much speech: "More than a hundred inhabitants of Cambridge would acknowledge," he wrote, "that they could never understand a single sentence of Mr. Shirreff's."[164]

The progress, real or imagined, that he made with Shirreff encouraged Braidwood to accept a second pupil, John Douglas, born deaf, the son of a London physician. Shortly thereafter he placed a letter in *Scots Magazine* advertising that Douglas, then thirteen, had made remarkable gains in speech in just four months "owing chiefly to the superior skill which Mr. Braidwood has acquired by experience."[165] A year and a half later, a second advertisement stated that Braidwood had several deaf pupils, and would welcome more. He could also correct stuttering and other speech impediments in hearing children.[166] In another two years he announced in the same way that he had been obliged to refuse more than thirty pupils, since he "can teach only a few at the same time, which of necessity renders the expense of this kind of education greater than some parents can afford."[167] He asked the nobility and gentry to consider creating a fund to encourage his invention; without such assistance only a few could benefit, and "this valuable art will probably die with him."

Braidwood's fame grew in Britain, but when Samuel Johnson and James Boswell put his school on their itinerary while exploring the Western Islands of Scotland they insured his reputation throughout the Continent. "The improvement of Braidwood's pupils is wonderful," Johnson wrote. They read, write, and speak; when addressed directly and distinctly they lipread so well "it is an expression scarcely figurative to say they hear with the eye."[168]

By the time of Pereire's death in 1780, Thomas Braidwood's school had grown to twenty pupils and had become the primary place for speech correction in Europe; several pupils were hearing but had speech impediments. One visitor reported that pupils learned simple written words first, with their meaning and pronunciation, then lipreading. Their speech was slow and harsh, although he met one angelic creature of about thirteen who looked him through and through with her piercing eyes and conversed with him fluently. She read and wrote well and showed her understanding of what she wrote by paraphrase.[169] For example, the pupil read the proverb "He becometh poor that dealeth with a slack hand, but the hand of the diligent maketh rich." This means, she wrote, "He returneth indigent that distributeth with an untight hand, but the hand of the industrious createth wealth." Dr. Johnson was also much impressed by this type of exercise. Another visitor, an Edinburgh historian, found that the pupils spoke distinctly but slowly. The manual alphabet was used; the period of instruction was three to six years. The female pupils were taught needlework and those from the lower classes learned to become domestic servants. The boys were given a general education unless they returned for an additional year of training in trades—tailoring or shoemaking. There were some pupils from America.[170] The school was obliged to refuse over one hundred applications from the parents of deaf children who could not afford the fee, although some poor deaf pupils were accepted free.

Thomas Braidwood's school in Edinburgh spawned many more throughout the British Isles and even one in America, all forming a tight-knit monopoly. Once again, the principle of secrecy imposed, as it did for Pereire and Heinicke, the necessity of hiring relatives to manage the growing business. First, Braidwood's school moved to Hackney, near London, at about the time Epée published his final work. Son John and his mother ran the school until John's death, when his wife took control.[171] John's eldest son, also named John, accepted an invitation to reopen the Edinburgh school "on his own terms," according to a former pupil, but "took little interest in the instruction," and left abruptly after a year for America.[172] It was conjectured that he misused school funds, but the school secretary denied this. He was succeeded by Robert Kinniburgh, an evangelical minister, who was sent to the Braidwood academy at Hackney for training, then placed under a substantial bond never to enable anyone else to teach the deaf. After three years, however, he was allowed to take private pupils of his own, provided that he pay half the sum received to Braidwood.[173] It was about this time that Kinniburgh refused to reveal the secret of Braidwood's craft to Thomas Gallaudet, who had come from America to learn how to teach the deaf. It is a happy irony that Kinniburgh's refusal sent Thomas to the abbé Sicard in Paris, and thus was indirectly the cause of my coming to America, and with me the method of the abbé de l'Epée. While the second John Braidwood was in America teaching some deaf children, the family arranged for John's brother, Thomas (named after his grandfather), to open a school in Birmingham.[174] He directed the school for a decade, but when he died his successor, recruited from Switzerland, was a proponent of Epée's methods and he abolished oralism.

To their schools in Hackney, Birmingham, Edinburgh, and America, the Braidwood clan would add yet one more.[175] The parents of a deaf boy attending a Braidwood school, dismayed by the cost of his tuition, organized a school for the indigent deaf in Bermondsey, under the direction of a local minister, John Townsend.[176] So synonymous with deaf education had the name Braidwood become that when Joseph Watson, Thomas Braidwood's nephew, offered to instruct the pupils, they hired him, and after about two decades the school moved to London, where Joseph's son, Thomas Watson, took charge.[177] Townsend, meanwhile, traveled all over England seeking funds for the school; there was no legislative or governmental provision for

educating British deaf citizens—even now it is left to the vagaries of voluntary charity, and to exploitation by profit-seekers. All in all, the Braidwood
monopoly on British education of the deaf lasted from the opening of
Epée's school until the death of Sicard.

There are several indications that the Braidwood clan soon became aware
of the sterility of efforts to inculcate speech, as had John Wallis before
them. Indeed, the report of the Edinburgh school the year of Sicard's death
affirmed: "Signs are the only language the deaf can comprehend and they
must be taught by its means."[178] And several anecdotes concerning famous
Braidwood pupils confirm that, whatever lasting benefits the school imparted, speech was not one of them. According to a British newspaper, when
Lady Melville was expecting the visit of Lord Seaforth, governor of Barbados
and a former Braidwood pupil, she was careful to invite a friend who could
"converse with the fingers" so the nobleman would have someone to talk
to.[179] A writer attending a dinner party at Hackney with the famous English
member of Parliament Charles Fox and his deaf son—"the very image of
his father, having come for the occasion from Braidwood's academy"—
recounted that Fox "confined his attention almost entirely to the boy, conversing with him by the fingers; and their eyes glistened as they looked at
each other. Talleyrand remarked to me, 'How strange it is to dine in company with the first orator in England and see him talk with his fingers!' "
[180] Likewise, Braidwood's nephew, Joseph Watson, had a celebrated deaf
pupil who became a barrister; it was said that a stranger might exchange
several sentences with this gentleman, John William Lowe, before discovering he was totally deaf. Yet Lowe confided in my friend Harvey Peet that
he used sign with his family and writing with strangers. We are reminded
of Saboureux de Fontenay.[181]

The first American deaf child to receive a regular course of instruction
was Charles Green, whose father, Francis Green, a loyalist Boston merchant
banished to England during the American Revolution, sent him to Braidwood's academy in early 1780, when he was eight years old. The boy could
not speak, read, or write when he went, but when his father visited about
a year later, he spoke intelligibly. In another year and a half, he had progressed in writing, mathematics, drawing, and speech. I fancy he was a
rather intelligent little boy: when his father asked him why he used sign with
a fellow pupil who happened by, he answered: "He is deaf."

Francis Green was so impressed with his son's progress that he became
a lifelong advocate of deaf education, the first in America. Following his
visits to the Braidwood school, he sent a letter to the first health officer of
New York describing his son's accomplishments and urging the citizens of
New York to provide likewise for the education of their deaf children. Some
years later the letter was published and read at the first public meeting
advocating the establishment of a school for the deaf in New York.[182]

Charles Green was joined at Braidwood's school by three other pupils from America, John, Thomas, and Mary Bolling, the children, born deaf, of Major Thomas Bolling of Cobbs, Virginia, and his cousin, Elizabeth Gray. The major had a fourth child, William, who was hearing and had this to say about his brothers and sister when they returned from Edinburgh in 1783: "John died about three months after his return. Thomas's acquirements were most extraordinary. He was a ready penman of nice* discriminating judgment, of scrupulous integrity. In all his transactions, his intelligence and tact in communication were such as to attract the attention and entertain and amuse every company in which he associated, with the manners of a most finished gentleman. His articulation was so perfect that his family and friends and the servants understood him in conversation and reading aloud. My sister's acquirements were equal to his though her voice was not so pleasant, yet she was cheerful, intelligent, entertaining and industrious."[183] It was this William Bolling who, decades later, sponsored John Braidwood in America and hired him to teach his two deaf children, William and Mary.[184]

In the same year that the Bolling children returned to America, Charles's father, Francis Green, published a book in London whose title was the Latin motto of Braidwood's academy: *Vox Oculis Subjecta* (the voice governed by the eye). As he had done in his letter to New York, he urged the development in England of a public institution to be supported by public subscription.[185] He stated that the king was ready to contribute one hundred pounds a year (at Braidwood's exorbitant rates that would have paid the tuition of one pupil!), and gave some hints as to Braidwood's secret method, describing an instrument—"a small round piece of silver, a few inches long, the size of a tobacco pipe, flattened at one end, with a ball as large as a marble at the other"—to aid in placing the pupil's tongue in the right positions. But the Braidwoods did not take kindly to Green's plan for extending their methods to the poor, and he was disgusted: "Far from allowing the world at large the knowledge of their advances or the benefit of their improvements, they have rather, like Pereire and Heinicke, desired to keep them in obscurity and mystery and, like the Jewish Talmudists who dealt in secret writings, to allow no one to be professed practical conjurers but the Sanhedrin themselves."[186]

Francis Green eventually returned to North America, settling in Halifax, where he became high sheriff and remarried. His son joined him after graduating from Braidwood's academy. Whether it was the Braidwoods' secrecy that was responsible or the regression of his son's speech after he left the academy I cannot say, but Green soon abandoned oralism in favor of the education of the deaf through sign language. He visited the abbé Sicard on

*I.e., exacting.

two occasions and worked with Reverend Townsend to break the Braidwood monopoly with the school for the indigent deaf at Bermondsey. He published an English translation of some of the abbé de l'Epée's letters and all of his final book, *The True Manner of Educating Those Born Deaf*, and publicly criticized Braidwood's secrecy. In his autobiography, he calls his earlier 240-page book on Braidwood's academy a hasty pamphlet and makes no mention of the academy itself. Even after his son Charles died tragically in a hunting accident, the father labored on, appealing to New England clergy in a Boston newspaper to conduct a census of the deaf "showing a sufficient number to warrant establishment of an American school for the deaf." Alas, he died in 1808, nine years before Thomas Gallaudet and I would make his dream come true.

Nowadays, we have the word of such august authorities as Mr. Horace Mann that while the American deaf sign, in Europe the deaf learn to speak, that there are hardly any mutes there, that "substantially in all cases" deaf children can thus be restored to society. We are told by other wealthy benefactors of the deaf that oral instruction is the oldest and best established of methods for educating the deaf, that Pereire's pupils were taught so well they had their teacher's accent in French, that Heinicke's school was an acclaimed success, that the one absolute requirement of oral instruction is that teacher and pupil must never use sign, that oralism gives the deaf ready intercourse with the rest of society, discourages deaf congregation and intermarriage, helps the deaf read in English while cultivating their minds, and aids in making us "as precisely as possible like other people."[187]

History, however, true history, gives us a different understanding of oralism. In fact, the oralist tradition is a story of greed, plagiarism, secrecy, trickery—but not education. Its aim is speech. In the course of pursuing that evanescent goal, a few deaf scions of wealthy noblemen were also, almost fortuitously, educated. Nothing has come down to us from this tradition except one more reason to distrust those who style themselves our benefactors for their own gain. One man, a silent monk in the mid-sixteenth century, had an idea: the deaf could be taught a simulacrum of speech and thus could circumvent a law that whimsically deprived them of their birthright. One man, one idea, an idea that was, as far as can be determined, plagiarized by Bonet, exploited by Ramirez de Carrion, expounded by Digby, copied by Pereire, Amman, and Wallis; and Pereire begat Deschamps; Amman begat Heinicke; Wallis begat Braidwood. One idea: plagiarized, published, translated, rationalized, propounded, cited, footnoted, cross-referenced, capitalized—but still, the same idea. This is the final dirty secret of the history of oralism: it is not a history at all. Should we now refuse to recognize this fact, and instead follow the exhortations of Mr. Horace Mann, we will but relive past mistakes, condemning the friends of the deaf to sterile efforts and the deaf themselves to lives of ignorance, poverty, and isolation.

SIX

SUCCESS AND FAILURE

The oralist movement that had begun in the sixteenth century with Ponce de León ended late in the eighteenth with the deaths of its major proponents, Pereire, Heinicke, and Braidwood—or so it seemed. As I arrived at Saint-Jacques, signing communities were evolving and thriving not only in Paris and the provinces but, as Napoleon's empire spread, throughout Europe. Carlos IV of Spain founded a school in Madrid modeled on our own. The first Swiss school was also formed on the French model. One of Sicard's disciples had founded the deaf school in Genoa and now another grew up in Siena. Epée had long ago sent down roots in Austria but now similar schools were founded in Saxony and Prussia. As far as I know it was the *principle* of educating the deaf by sign, and methodical sign in particular, that was universally adopted, not the French signs themselves; the Prussians, for example, had their own sign language that could be used for instruction and modified to sign German.

Each new school for the deaf was like a planet that revolved around the sun—Saint-Jacques—yet had its own satellites, for each attracted not only deaf pupils, faculty, and staff, but also deaf adults in the community. In the nurturing atmosphere of each of these planets there evolved in time a fully developed deaf society, lettered and cultivated through the medium of its manual language. I will tell you about the fruition of the one I know best.

To describe French signing society in its maturity is to introduce its lumi-
naries, first and foremost Ferdinand Berthier. Nearly twenty years younger
than I, Berthier came to our school from Mâcon in 1811. He was born deaf
of hearing parents; his father was a doctor. He was my most gifted student
and remained to rise rapidly through the teaching ranks: monitor at sixteen,
teaching assistant at twenty-one, professor at twenty-six; nowadays, he is
dean of the professors. During his long and continuing career he has published numerous articles and books recording the struggle and advancing the
welfare of the deaf.[1]

From the start, Berthier was intent on making a name for himself. "I
want to be a genius like Clerc," he said to a professor. "What must I do?"[2]
Even as a young man, he revealed rare intelligence and aptitude for the
ways of society. I cannot say he is handsome—he has a large head and
forehead poised on a small body—but he has good taste, is witty, elegant, and
humble, and always wears a smile.[3] Berthier loves languages—he knows
French, Latin, and Greek, but he naturally prefers his own sign language
above all these. "How few men," he wrote, "have deeply studied the immense resources hidden in this universal idiom, so clear, so positive, so
reliable."[4] Berthier is a living argument for his cause. His wide knowledge,
refined use of language, and sincere and lively style have won him many
readers and won the deaf many friends. He is a prolific writer: his works
include voluminous biographies of Epée and Sicard, a book explaining the
Napoleonic Code to the deaf, and numerous encyclopedia entries and newspaper articles.

Berthier's teaching and administrative duties at our school and his scholarly research and writing would have filled the life of the average man to
overflowing, but he has been equally active socially and politically on behalf
of the deaf. It was Berthier who built a bridge from the citadel of sign on
the rue Saint-Jacques to the larger and more diffuse signing society in Paris,
one that counts, among its more successful members, writers, publishers,
painters—some with works on display at the Louvre—artisans, and businessmen. To enhance the lives of these adult deaf people through legal reform,
education, and fund-raising, Berthier created the first known social organization of the deaf.[5] He was also vice-president of our first welfare organization
and he is a member of literary and historical societies.[6] For several decades
he has addressed a stream of letters to the legislature protesting laws unfair
to the deaf. When I visited Paris in 1846, Berthier was working on his
monumental biography of Epée while serving as dean of the faculty at the
Paris school. Nationally, events were under way that would lead to universal
suffrage and the declaration of the Second Republic. Sixty-nine years after
Pierre Desloges wrote, "There is no event in Paris, in France, and in the
four corners of the world, that is not a topic of our conversations," the
French deaf were finally enfranchised. The deaf of Paris looked to my friend

FERDINAND BERTHIER

ROCH-AMBROISE BÉBIAN

and pupil Ferdinand Berthier, nominated him for the National Assembly, and pursued a vigorous campaign in his behalf. They also petitioned the provisional government to choose the instructors and administrators at the national school for the deaf by suffrage of those concerned and not by political fealty. Neither undertaking was successful but both reflect Berthier's high status in his community. When Napoleon III visited our school, Berthier gave the official welcome. Later, he was awarded the Legion of Honor—never before conferred on any deaf person (an annual pension is attached).[7]

Another leading deaf professor with a gift for the arts was Pierre Pélissier: in 1844 he published a collection of poems that were elegant, harmonious, and very well received. I do not mean poems in French Sign Language, quite a beautiful art-form for those who know the language but one that is transmitted *viva mano,* not written. I mean poems in French that contained rhyme, rhythm, and meter. Pélissier was as fluent in French as he was in French Sign Language, and a skillful poet in both languages; yet he was totally deaf from early childhood. He came to our school from Toulouse, where great efforts were made, unsuccessfully, to teach him to speak, and he spent most of his life on the rue Saint-Jacques, where he died six years ago. Despite his early training and work as a French poet, Pélissier hated oralism and loved sign. He found speech of little or no value and did not hesitate to say so.[8] About a decade ago Pélissier published the first pronouncing sign dictionary of sign language. Unlike Epée's and Sicard's dictionaries, it recorded the "reduced signs" actually used by the deaf and did so with pictures so that the execution of the sign could be imagined. Pélissier's name will go down in history for this achievement alone.[9]

Last I will single out from this intellectual circle of the deaf in the rue Saint-Jacques Claudius Forestier. Seven years younger than Berthier, Forestier was born profoundly deaf, and has several deaf brothers and sisters, one of whom he raised himself. He was the angel of the school, his behavior marked by sweetness and sound judgment.[10] For a long time he studied to become a professor while he held the title of aspirant. But though he had an indisputable right to the first opening available, he was passed over several times in favor of hearing professors. With his hopes repeatedly dashed on the rocks of prejudice and finally shattered, in 1833 Forestier left the school that had been his intellectual cradle and became director of a deaf school at Lyon.[11] I stopped by there about twenty years ago, when I was in nearby La Balme visiting my family. Forestier introduced me to the staff, all of whom were deaf, and took me at length through his gardens, for he is an accomplished cultivator of flowers and vegetables. Forestier has written an extensive course of instruction for the deaf[12] and three other books, including a sacred history. He was also the first vice-president of the national welfare society for the deaf and remains our ardent and outspoken champion to this day.

One of the most important forces in the development of signing society in Paris and elsewhere as our current century progressed was, however, a hearing man, a true martyr for the cause of the deaf and, I am proud to say, my student and friend. In the declining years of the abbé Sicard, Roch-Ambroise Bébian rose like the sun partially dispelling the clouds. For the deaf, he holds a place next to the abbé de l'Epée.[13]

Bébian was born in Pointe-à-Pitre, Guadeloupe, the year Epée died.[14] When eleven he was sent to Paris to be educated under his godfather, the abbé Sicard. He was lodged in the home of one of the hearing teachers,* went to the Lycée Charlemagne, and won several prizes. Then he came to our school and started attending my classes regularly; we became friends. Over the years, I helped Bébian develop a power and fluency of expression in sign language that no hearing teacher has rivaled before or since. I pride myself on my ability to tell a hearing signer from a deaf one, but Bébian would have escaped detection.[15]

Bébian worked his way up through the ranks: first, monitor; next, teaching assistant. At this point we almost lost him, for his father thought it undignified for him to remain in such menial posts and wanted to call him home. Sicard then had a position created just for him—he was to supervise the study-hall supervisors. Bébian was "outstanding and has best understood the spirit of my method," he told the board. "He must be kept at all costs."[16] The ministry agreed, and Bébian was made censor of studies, responsible for discipline and good order. He was a godsend in this role, for he was the only one in the administration who could communicate fluently with the pupils.

At about this time Bébian published an essay on the deaf and their language and the prize-winning eulogy of the abbé de l'Epée in which he criticized Epée's system of methodical signs.[17] This very fervor on behalf of the deaf was too great for him to temper his remarks when he saw injustice or error, and frequently brought him into conflict with the administrative board. While Sicard was active he protected his protégé, but in the abbé's failing years Bébian's indiscretions cost him his job. I have mentioned earlier the disarray at the school, in instruction and in finances, as its director became feeble. Bébian could not tolerate the abuses he saw daily, the disorder of the program, the malfeasance of the board, and he complained repeatedly. His candor was initially annoying and ultimately intolerable. On the day the board expected the visit of the duchess of Berry, Bébian, who had been sent away expressly, appeared and offered her some pupils' works. She complained that she had not met any pupils during her visit. "If the

*Jean-Baptiste Jauffret, who later became head of the czarina's school for the deaf in St. Petersburg.

deaf do not appear before your Royal Highness," he said, "it is because they are unclothed. For four months now they have been unable to go on walks for lack of clothing and shoes." Two days later Bébian was forced to resign.[18]

The National Institution for the Deaf, the flagship for deaf schools throughout Europe, was beginning to drift as if cut loose from its moorings in a fog.[19] While it had been Epée's and then Sicard's little school, a certain orderliness and uniformity prevailed; now the institution had grown to nearly two hundred people all told, while the director's health had declined. The administrative board bemoaned the lack of any curriculum: students moved from one teacher to the next with each passing year but their education did not progress, since each teacher had his own agenda and methods that neither built on what had preceded nor set the stage for what followed. A common textbook was needed, but where could one be found? Neither Epée's book nor Sicard's provides an instructional method, they concluded: the first is an explanation of methodical signs, the second a "philosophical novel." The methods actually followed under their leadership had never been written down; a matter of tradition, they were taught by apprenticeship. So the board turned to the one hearing man in France who could write a teaching manual, the man who had just been fired, Bébian.[20]

Bébian wrote a superb manual.[21] For Sicard's pompous metaphysical processes he substituted a course that was natural, simple, direct. He arranged the stages of learning the French language and the subjects of instruction in an orderly progression, so each difficulty overcome was a stepping-stone. He imparted life to every French sentence with just the right sentences in French Sign Language. "There is no more sure, direct and effective way to initiate the deaf into our written language than with sign language," Bébian wrote.[22] The administrative board applauded Bébian's work, but I wonder how sincerely, for five years elapsed before it was published and it appeared the same year as De Gérando's monumental history of educating the deaf, which ends opposed to using sign language.

When Bébian finished his manual, the board suggested that he write a book to accompany it containing a statement of the rules of French Sign Language and a description of the signs required to explain each example in the manual. To describe the signs, Bébian felt the need of a writing system for our language—which, in any case, would be one of the most beautiful gifts that anyone could give the deaf world. It puzzles me that linguists are prepared to develop alphabets for the unwritten languages of Africa, but not for a language of their fellow countrymen. Bébian assigned characters he invented to the distinctive hand movements, shapes, and positions of our language, and added some for facial expression, where needed for clarity of ideas. He named his method "mimography" and published it with a few illustrations, but he did not make it a working companion to his manual and it did not receive much attention.[23]

The disarray in organization and the discord on method at Saint-Jacques led Bébian to take another major step: in 1826 he founded a journal in which he criticized abuses with characteristic candor.[24] He also sought alternative ways to educate the deaf because our school was frankly foundering: he revised his manual for use at home by parents of deaf children,[25] and he opened his own little school, Boulevard Montparnasse.

Eight years after Sicard's death, a group of deaf professors, including Berthier, formed an audacious plan to save our school by putting the case for reinstating Bébian before the new king, Louis-Philippe, who was a descendant of the duke of Penthièvre and had known Sicard and even Epée.[26] The plan failed, and I always suspected that De Gérando deflected the king's wishes (he was by now a powerful figure in the Ministry of the Interior), arranging instead to offer Bébian a post in the provinces; he succeeded the recently deceased director of the deaf school at Rouen. This separation from his home and work of so many years, at a time when the National Institution needed him so desperately, did not suit Bébian at all. With the sole purpose of rescuing our ship, he published an extensive attack on the mismanagement of the school by its board and succession of new directors, an attack and a set of positive proposals that were met with stony silence.[27] Frustrated, his life's work a failure and his health failing as well, Bébian returned with his wife and son to Pointe-à-Pitre and opened a little school for the deaf there. Soon after, his son died, and then he did, at the age of forty-five. On that day, three decades ago, I lost a comrade, but all the deaf lost an innovator, a spokesman, and one of the rare hearing persons whom we could truly call our friend.

Bébian understood that many of the faults attributed to sign language, such as prolixity, were actually faults of Epée's and Sicard's invented sign system. He was the first instructor to use French Sign Language itself and he based his method of teaching French and his manual on it. Moreover, in virtually every book he wrote and in his journal, he lashed out at manual French, showing how it distorted our language and rendered it unmanageable. Perhaps the elaborate scaffolding on sign language erected by Epée and Sicard was already beginning to crumble under its own weight, but to Bébian goes the credit for tearing it down. When he began his work, manual French was used in teaching throughout France and in many foreign institutions.[28] Within a decade he caused it to be banished from the Paris school and two decades of his labor caused it to be expelled from Bordeaux, Lyon, Toulouse, Rodez, Nancy, finally from deaf schools everywhere, including, as I have told, America,[29] much to the joy of the deaf faculty and pupils.[30] The year Bébian died, the annual report of the New York Institution described methodical signs as "wholly discarded."[31]

Forestier's resignation and Bébian's dismissal and exile, however, were not isolated reversals of the fortunes of the French deaf. In fact, the abbé Sicard's death allowed the forces of oralism to wage a new campaign on the rue Saint-Jacques itself, a campaign to undermine the mature deaf society I have just described.

The surface issue in this renewed struggle for the soul of the deaf was who should succeed Sicard as head of the National Institution for the Deaf, but the deeper question was whether benevolence confers authority on the bene-factor. The natural choice to succeed Sicard was Jean Massieu, fifty, at the height of his career, a symbol throughout Europe and America of the edu-cated deaf, extolled in scores of books and articles. Jean Massieu, Sicard's teacher, mine, Gallaudet's; teacher of countless deaf pupils in the thirty years he had labored at Sicard's side. Jean Massieu, author of a vocabulary and a grammar, campaigner for the cause of the deaf, spokesman. Massieu's pupils directed schools for the deaf in Lyon, Limoges, Besançon, Geneva, Cambray, Hartford, Mexico City. Now the parent of all these principals would direct the parent school. He was the logical choice for the administra-tive board to make and he was the sentimental choice: he had earned the post and he deserved it.

Years before, when Massieu was asked if a deaf man could understand an abstract concept such as gratitude, he answered yes, and gave this oft-repeated definition: gratitude is the memory of the heart. Ironically, the concept proved too abstract for the hearing, not the deaf: the administrative board did not choose Massieu. Instead it forced him to resign, to leave his home, his school, his friends, his colleagues, his pupils. He returned to the plot of land near Bordeaux where the passerby had found him as a boy tending his flock.

I saw Massieu again, about a decade after these events, when I visited France in 1835. He had been recalled from forced retirement after a year, to second the abbé Perrier, director of a small school for the deaf in Rodez, the capital of Aveyron. He was then fifty-one years old. Soon after his arrival, he was struck with the beauty and charm of a young lady of eighteen who could hear and speak and who was employed in the establishment, and it was not long before he married her. When the abbé Perrier went to Paris to direct the National Institution, Massieu became director of the Rodez school. He and his wife had one son when they moved from Rodez to Lille, a large city just south of the Belgian border, where they established the first school for the deaf in the north of France, just two years before my visit. There were about thirty pupils. Massieu was principal and his wife matron; they had lost their son but Mme. Massieu was nursing a daughter. I found Massieu quite different from what I had known him to be. He was rather gray, but polite, social, sensible, much respected and happy as could be. No doubt he was indebted to his kind wife for his total alteration.

That was our last meeting. The next few years saw his health and lucidity decline, much as Sicard's had done toward the end, and he finally ceded place to the Brothers of Saint-Gabriel, who ever since have managed the school he founded. He bid a final goodbye to the land and the people he loved so well in his seventy-fourth year, just as I was embarking once more for France, in the summer of 1846.[32]

The leader of the new oralist campaign that led to Massieu's ousting was Jean-Marc Itard, tutor of the Wild Boy of Aveyron; his fellow perpetrator and friend, the more dogmatic of the pair, was Baron Joseph Marie De Gérando, who became head of our school's administrative board in 1814, a dozen years before he wrote his famous "history." Why did two would-be benefactors of the deaf mount a campaign to impose oralism on the deaf, starting in the very sanctuary of sign language, a campaign to oblige all of us to relive in this century the proven errors of the past? Why would intelligent hearing people such as these, willing students of history's lessons, devote vast effort and money to a program detested by the deaf and doomed to certain failure? The question is important because now, here in America, men of similar benevolence and erudition seek to repeat the effort yet again. Its answer lies in the motives and means of benevolence embodied in the lives of these two Frenchmen. First, Dr. Itard.

It was a day like any other at Saint-Jacques when my schoolmate, the son of General Gazan, slipped while rushing toward dinner down the sweeping marble staircase of the Oratorians, tumbled most of a flight, and lay motionless on the bottom few steps. Massieu was sent for, then Sicard. There was much hand-wringing and then I was singled out from the pupils huddled on the periphery of the scene; Massieu's hands swooped and darted, beating an urgent staccato in the air: "Run, Clerc. Val-de-Grâce. Bring a doctor!"

Massieu had just sent me on an historic mission. It would transform the life of the young medical student I was about to encounter and launch him on a career that would earn him these titles: the first speech and hearing specialist; founder of otology; the father of oral education of the deaf in modern times; inventor of educational devices; father of the education of idiots.

Val-de-Grâce is a military hospital in a former Benedictine abbey, five breathless minutes up the rue Saint-Jacques. I ran with all the ferocity and self-importance of youth, charged across the cobblestone courtyard of the abbey, and hurtled into a vast hall, lined with beds on both sides—there must have been a hundred. At one of these a young medical student was changing bandages. He read the alarm in my eyes, the urgency in my heaving chest, and the reason in my pantomime and sprinted back with me to the school. Jean-Marc Itard, surgeon second class, twenty-five years old, pronounced his new patient's leg broken and proceeded to bandage it. Gazan revived and was carried back up the stairs to bed. Sicard ushered the young physician into his apartment, and their lifelong friendship began. As it turned out, it was to be a propitious occasion for Itard, but a disastrous one for the deaf.

By one of those bizarre coincidences that make one wonder if history is thumbing its nose at us, the very day of Gazan's accident another youth of about his age was involved in another signal encounter that would concern Itard, the deaf, and countless children everywhere. As Gazan slipped down the staircase of Saint-Jacques, the Wild Boy of Aveyron slipped through the doorway of the cottage belonging to the dyer Vidal, in the village of Saint-Sernin, in the south of France.[33]

The wild boy had been glimpsed occasionally in the three years prior as he fled naked through the woods called La Bassine. Peasants in that mountainous region sometimes lay in wait and saw him searching for acorns and roots, or, in the fields on the edge of the forest, digging up potatoes and turnips. Twice he was captured. The first time he was tied to a post and left on display in the village of Lacaune; either a kindly hand or his ferocious struggling loosened his bonds during the night and he escaped into the forest. On the second occasion, fifteen months later, in the summer of 1799, he was entrusted to the care of an old widow in the same village. This devoted guardian, one of her contemporaries recounted, dressed him in a sort of gown to hide his nakedness and offered him various foods, including raw and cooked meat, which he always refused. He did accept nuts and potatoes, sniffing them before putting them into his mouth. When not eating or sleeping, he prowled from door to door and window to window seeking to escape. After eight days he succeeded.

This time the wild boy did not return to the forest. Climbing the nearby mountains he gained a broad plateau in the department of Aveyron. Through the autumn and into a particularly cold winter he wandered over this elevated and sparsely populated region, sometimes entering farmhouses, where he was fed. When given potatoes, he threw them into the coals of the hearth, retrieving and eating them only a few minutes later. During the day he was seen swimming and drinking in streams, climbing trees, running at great speed on all fours, digging for roots and bulbs in the fields; and when the wind blew from the south he turned toward the sky and rendered up deep cries and great bursts of laughter. Finally, working his way down the mountain along the course of the Lavergne and Vernoubre rivers, he arrived on the outskirts of the village of Saint-Sernin. Encouraged perhaps by the treatment he had received from the farmers on the plateau, urged on perhaps by hunger, he approached the workshop of the dyer Vidal. It was seven o'clock in the morning, January 8, 1800. The boy stepped across the threshold into a new life, and into a new era in the education of man.

The wild boy had more than age and a moment in history in common with my fellow pupil Gazan. He was mute, and he appeared also, to the government official summoned to Vidal's home, to be deaf: the boy sat impassively by the fire and seemed to be unaware of the commissioner's questioning. But the similarities between the wild boy and my friend stopped there. When he was brought to our school one sweltering August day, I beheld an animal sitting on the ground in a pool of his own urine, rocking back and forth ceaselessly, his eyes staring wildly, then darting aimlessly. He growled and snapped at the pupils who came too near, and tore at the sack of cloth that had been belted around him. He had a round face with dark eyes deep-set beneath a huge head of snarled hair, which he matted with wads of saliva. His nose was long and pointed. His thin lips revealed large yellow teeth when he burst into intemperate bouts of laughter, seemingly without provocation. He was covered from head to foot with scars of all shapes and sizes. The largest was a two-inch gash across his voice box, the trace of an attempted infanticide, it was believed. There was a scar over one eyebrow, scars on each cheek, one on his chin, several on his arms and legs—and his entire body was covered with blisters from smallpox.

The look on Sicard's face when he came into the courtyard to greet his new and celebrated pupil was yet another spectacle. Since Sicard had presented the uneducated deaf as savages, what could be more appropriate than to send this savage to Sicard? Still, the abbé's face caved in at the sight of the creature; I don't know what he was expecting. Commands were given, and the youth was promptly bundled off to a little locked room under the eaves.

In the days that followed, a stream of visitors made their way up the Oratorians' staircase to that room to see the Wild Boy of Aveyron, as he was titled by the papers, which carried major stories every day. The first to come were distinguished scientists from the newly founded Society of Observers of Man.[34] Under the banner "Know thyself!" this impressive gathering had joined the previous December in a comparative study of man in "all the different scenes of his life." Now, within weeks, a seemingly ideal experiment on the nature of man had fallen into its lap—a young man who had been isolated since early childhood from all the social influences to which we are normally subjected and who could thus reveal which of our ideas, abilities, and desires we owe to society and which to our biological nature.[35]

How many of our innumerable discriminations, concepts, tastes, skills, fears, and desires would the savage from Aveyron lack? When Massieu was questioned about his own life, he revealed that he had observed, compared, judged, remembered, and so on without articulate language, but then he had sign language. Would the wild boy, who had no language at all, still give evidence of having lived more than an animal existence?

The wild boy—*homo ferus*, as Linnaeus classed such children—was as interesting for what he might become as for what he was. If our most human trait was not our appearance (wild boys and Hottentots did not look like Parisians), nor our language (wild boys had none), nor our upright gait (wild boys would run on all fours), it might be, Rousseau argued, our ability

LE DOCTEUR ITARD

Bienfaiteur de l'Inst: Roy: des Sourds-muets.

DR. JEAN-MARC ITARD

to change: man is able to leave the state of nature and in collective life to become educated. The wild boy certainly did not fit Rousseau's description of the noble savage any more than Massieu was Condillac's statue incarnate, but the boy might still prove to be perfectible, just as Massieu had been, and to justify the deep optimistic belief in human potentiality that motivated many of the reforms of the French Revolution.

Itard was among the first to visit the boy, not only because Sicard asked him to as a physician, but especially because he was a keenly ambitious young man from the provinces who intended to seize this opportunity to make his mark on the world. He had been born twenty-six years before in southern France, the son of a master carpenter.[36] He studied the classics, then science, and at age nineteen took a job at a Marseilles bank. I would never have found him treating soldiers at Val-de-Grâce if the National Convention had not decided to draft 300,000 citizens the summer of his employment. It feared invasion by the growing monarchist coalition that had begun by attacking Verdun at the time of the king's imprisonment, Sicard's arrest, and the September Massacre. To avoid the draft, Itard turned to a friend of the family who directed a military hospital, and presently, although he had never before set foot in a hospital or opened a medical book, he found himself with the rank of health officer. Assigned next to the headquarters of the Army of Italy with the rank of surgeon third class, Itard was responsible for public health at some encampments. (Another energetic young man was making a meteoric rise to fame in the same theater of war: artillery captain, then brigadier general in the Army of Italy—Napoleon Bonaparte.)

Eighteen months later, the doctor who would become Napoleon's surgeon-general, Dominique Larrey, arrived from Paris to head the medical corps of an expedition to Corsica. Before embarcation, Larrey offered courses in anatomy and pathology, which Itard followed diligently. When the expedition was canceled, Larrey returned to the military hospital in Paris, Val-de-Grâce, and Itard followed soon after. Over the next three years preceding our encounter, he took courses in medicine, especially with the physician who directed the asylum for the insane at La Salpêtrière, Philippe Pinel, and he successfully presented a thesis to the faculty of medicine, securing a promotion to surgeon second class.

During his studies, Itard also read the philosopher Condillac, who inspired Pinel and indeed almost every other French thinker of that time; so when he went up to see the wild boy, he went expecting Condillac's statue —or at least a version of it, in which socialization, language, judgment, and so on had been stripped away by prolonged isolation, leaving a kind of *tabula rasa* on which the message of humanity would have to be written anew. What he saw was a caged animal, a filthy naked urchin who stared blankly out the window or blankly at him, cringing.

Itard descended from the attic mopping his forehead and affirmed that the boy was only what he had to be: what could you expect of an adolescent separated since early childhood from others of his species, he asked rhetorically. "His intelligence would be concerned with his few needs," he later wrote, "and because of isolation, it would lack all the simple and compound ideas that we receive through education and that combine in so many ways with the help of language."[37]

The naturalist Pierre-Joseph Bonnaterre, who had examined the wild boy in Aveyron, had ended his essay on the savage saying that we may expect every success from his instruction with Sicard, "that philosopher-teacher who has worked such miracles in this kind of education and we may hope that . . . he will one day become the rival of Massieu."[38] In fact, Sicard had not the least idea what to do with a child who actually fit his fanciful description of the deaf before instruction: "a being isolated in nature, incapable of communicating with other men, reduced to a condition of stupor."[39] Here was no docile city child with a hearing loss who was fluent in sign and could be initiated into the mysteries of the Supreme Being and the even more recondite mysteries of Sicard's metaphysics. Hence Sicard preferred Pinel's diagnosis to Itard's; the first psychiatrist examined the boy and concluded that he was not retarded because he had been left in the wilds; rather, he had been left in the wilds because he was retarded. Still, if Itard wanted to try to fashion the wild boy into a Massieu, on his own responsibility of course . . . When Itard accepted his proposal, Sicard, on the last day of the year 1800, appointed him resident physician with one of the highest salaries in the school, and a free apartment and board.[40]

Itard set to work, then, as the new century began. "Dare I confess that I have set myself both of these two great undertakings," Itard wrote. First, "to deduce from what the wild boy lacks the hitherto uncalculated sum of knowledge and ideas which man owes to his education."[41] In fact, Itard's report and that of Bonnaterre abound in examples of sensory and intellectual skills that the boy lacked, apparently because of his lack of socialization. He was living proof, it appears, of Condillac's precept that all knowledge comes from experience, and living refutation of Rousseau's conception of man in nature as a "noble savage." Initially, Victor—as Itard named him—rejected clothing even in the coldest weather; did not hesitate to put his hand in the fire; reached alike for painted objects, three-dimensional objects, and virtual objects in a mirror; did not sneeze or weep; did not respond to loud noises; recognized edible food not by sight but by smell; had no emotional ties or sexual expression; did not communicate; and so on. Itard concluded that sensitivity is proportional to civilization.

Itard's second great undertaking was "to bring to bear all the resources of . . . present knowledge in order to develop the boy physically and morally." It was to be an experimental verification of Condillac's theories.

Itard set down five principal aims for his training program, and organized

ABC

SAVAGE OF AVEYRON.

Photographie Bibliothèque Nationale, Paris

THE WILD BOY OF AVEYRON
(ENGRAVING BY JAMES CUNDEE)

his first report on Victor accordingly: to interest the wild boy in social life by rendering it more pleasant for him than the one he was then leading; to awaken his nervous sensibility; to extend the range of his ideas by giving him new needs and by increasing his social contacts; to lead him to the use of speech by imitation (Itard was convinced that the pupil was not deaf: if he responded to the sound of nuts cracked and not to the commissioner's questions, it was because the first had significance for him and the second did not); and to make him exercise the simplest mental operations. The methods that Itard worked out to teach Victor to speak and understand speech he later attempted to apply to the semi-deaf;[42] more felicitously, his disciple, Edouard Séguin, would soon apply his entire training program to the mentally retarded, to the astonishment of all Europe.

Aiming to make the boy's life in society less stressful than it had been since his capture, Itard took Victor into his apartment at Saint-Jacques and charged the housekeeper, Mme. Guérin, with his daily care. In those spacious and beautifully decorated quarters, which contrasted starkly with the dormitory in which we pupils lived, he roamed freely. The first room in Itard's private suite was Mme. Guérin's, with a painted bed, a stately armchair, a walnut table, silver candlesticks on the mantelpiece, and framed prints on the wall. One door led to a small kitchen, another to a sparsely furnished bedroom for Victor, which he always kept punctiliously neat. The boy ate with the Guérins, and sometimes with Itard, in a private dining room with a beechwood table and four cane and cherrywood chairs. Mme. Guérin treated him kindly and gave in to his tastes and inclinations "with all the patience of a mother and the intelligence of an enlightened teacher." He was put to bed at dusk, provided with his favorite foods, allowed his indolence, and taken on frequent walks.

In order to awaken the boy's "nervous sensibility by the most energetic stimulation," Itard administered very hot baths daily, lasting two or three hours; he also clothed, bedded, and housed the boy warmly; and he gave him dry rubs of the spine and lumbar region (although he soon discontinued the latter when he found it aroused him physically as well as mentally). Three months of this treatment, which also included provoking joy and anger on occasion, resulted in a "general excitement of all the senses." The boy would test the bath with his finger and refuse to get in if it were cool. He removed potatoes from the fire with a spoon and squeezed them to judge how well cooked they were. He dropped burning paper before the flame could reach his fingers. He liked to stroke velvet.

Itard had less success with his third aim. He tried to give the wild boy new needs, but the toys and sweets, most of the foods and beverages we love, did not interest him at all. What did interest him was freedom: when taken to the countryside he would try to escape, so his teacher restricted his outings to the gardens of our school.

That Victor could hear but not speak was a puzzle to us pupils, for we knew the two faculties went together. Massieu attributed Victor's mutism to his having forgotten how to speak during all those solitary years in the forest, which is, I suppose, what Itard meant when he wrote that "complete absence of exercise renders our organs unfit for their functions."[43] But despite this obstacle to Victor's acquiring speech by normal means, Itard hoped that substitute means could bring it about, specifically, inducements to imitation. He chose the word for water, *eau,* as his first target, since Victor could both hear and produce this simple sound* and since water was the boy's preferred drink. But "even when his thirst was most intense, it was in vain that I held a glass of water in front of him, repeatedly crying *eau, eau.* When I gave the glass to someone next to him who pronounced the same word, and when I asked for it back in the same way, the poor child, tormented on all sides, waved his arms around the glass almost convulsively, producing a kind of hiss but not articulating any sound." Switching to milk and the word *lait*† produced some result: Itard heard his efforts rewarded after four days when Victor pronounced the word *lait,* "distinctly, though rather crudely, it is true; and he repeated it almost immediately." According to Itard's report, Victor also picked up Madame Guérin's habit of saying "O Dieu!" ("O God!"), and when her twelve-year-old daughter Julie was around, he would say "li, li." Despite these good signs, however, it was clear that if Victor was to learn French by imitation, at this rate it would take several years!

Itard now undertook his final aim in the initial period of instruction, training at least some of the essential higher mental operations, with a view to preparing Victor to acquire more formal education in various branches of knowledge. He would have preferred to teach concepts orally, by dialogues with his student, just as Condillac had done with the prince of Parma. But Victor was, for the present at least, like a deaf-mute, indistinguishable in this from the rest of us, and so it was that Itard adopted the method of Sicard, beginning as Sicard had done by teaching the written names of familiar objects.

After many false starts, blind alleys, moments of despair, threats, imprecations, and ruses, Victor came to distinguish the metal letters that Itard had fashioned, to arrange them into a few simple words, and even to make them spell *lait* when he wanted some milk.

After a year of untiring efforts by teacher and pupil, De Gérando could write: "In a very short time, Citizen Itard has obtained extraordinary success. . . . Each day the child aquires some new expression; they are, it is true, only those that have some immediate relation to his needs, but such are the

---

*Pronounced as is the first syllable of the English "open."
†Pronounced like "let" without a *t.*

only terms that it is permissible for a philosopher to teach him. At last, here he is not only able to communicate with us, here he is in possession of our conventional signs. . . . He has broken through the barriers that separated him from our society; we are now on common ground."[44]

This first phase of Itard's work with Victor made him famous. He opened a private medical practice, taking an additional apartment for it in the heart of the city; the Russian ambassador brought him a ring in the name of his sovereign and tried unsuccessfully to induce him to carry on his work in St. Petersburg, as Joseph II had tried to win Epée to Vienna three decades before.

In the second phase of training Victor, which lasted for another four and a half years, Itard aimed at further developing the boy's senses, intellect, and emotions. Previously he had been content merely to observe the first increases in broadened sensitivity and discrimination that the sense of hearing gained as part of Victor's general rehabilitation. Now he undertook to train Victor's hearing explicitly by requiring increasingly fine discriminations, much as he had done to teach visual distinctions among the letters of the alphabet. He began by providing student and teacher alike with a drum, a bell, a shovel, and a stick. Itard struck his drum; Victor did likewise. Then the boy was blindfolded. If the teacher hit the hoop, the rim, or the body of the drum, the pupil followed suit. If the teacher struck the clock's bell or the fire shovel, the pupil did likewise.

Edging his way toward the discrimination of vowel sounds, Itard next took up the tones of a wind instrument and then different voice intonations. He no longer required imitation but only that Victor raise his hand when he heard a sound, and the pupil learned this readily, as much to his teacher's delight as to his own. Itard took up next "the five vowels." *A* was assigned to the thumb, *E* to the index finger and so on, and Victor was to raise the finger corresponding to the vowel uttered by his teacher. Itard reports that the first vowel Victor distinguished clearly was *O*. Next *A* seems to have come into focus, reliably distinguished from the others. The remaining three vowels were more refractory. Removing the blindfold, putting it back on, striking the boy's fingers when he made a mistake, persisting doggedly or, on the contrary, spacing out the lessons—none of these availed. The pupil became increasingly rowdy and the teacher lost heart. "How thoroughly did I regret ever having known this child, and fully condemn the sterile and inhuman curiosity of the men who first snatched him away from his innocent and happy life!

"Nevertheless this series of experiments on the sense of hearing was not altogether useless. Victor owes to it the fact that he can hear several one-syllable words distinctly and, above all, can distinguish quite precisely those intonations of language that express reproach, anger, sadness, contempt, and friendship, even when these various emotions are not accompanied by facial expression or by the natural pantomime that is their outward expression."

As for the other senses, Victor practiced distinguishing letters by sight, shapes by touch (blindfolded), and foods by taste. He learned the written names of many more things through little treasure hunts around Itard's apartment, then progressed to their qualities, fetching the *little* book, the *large* nail, and so on. Next came the verbs: "Touch the key," Itard wrote on the board, and Victor would touch the key. "Cut the cup," Itard wrote in a mistaken permutation and the boy promptly smashed his cup on the floor. As Victor came to understand and construct more and more sentences, his means of producing them by assembling metal letters became unwieldy and Itard taught him to form letters with chalk.

Although Victor showed no flair for distinguishing speech sounds by ear, Itard still hoped to teach him to speak by using methods designed for the deaf. He borrowed Sicard's copies of Bonet and Amman, read Epée's treatise on speech, and set to work. He had taught Victor to imitate his movements as a preliminary for teaching writing, so he aimed to teach articulation in the same way, beginning with gross facial expressions. Thus we have teacher and pupil seated opposite each other, grimacing, protruding their tongues, dropping their jaws, much as the abbé Margaron and I had done, but Itard found that "all I could obtain from this long series of exercises was a few unformed monosyllables, sometimes shrill, sometimes deep."[45] Finally, Itard abandoned Victor to mutism.

What to my mind is unforgivable is that Itard, blocked in restoring Victor's spoken language, failed to allow him the only other facile means of communication, the only other natural language of man (transmitted from mother to child), sign language. In compelling the youth to return to society, Itard contracted the obligation to give him the essential skill for surviving in society—communication. Itard's preference for restoring the boy to speaking society is understandable as he himself was a hearing person; when he concluded that this was impossible, however, it was inexcusable to exclude the boy from signing society as well. In this he was like those hearing parents who are so bitter about their children's inability to participate in their oral society that they refuse to let them participate in the deaf society either. Then, like Victor, the deaf child is reduced to gesticulating a few simple needs to his caretakers, and his mind shrivels and dies.

It probably would not have cost Itard any effort to have Victor acquire sign. The boy was living, after all, in the midst of a signing society and might have acquired French Sign Language much as I did, the more so as gesturing was his preferred mode of communication. But Victor was prevented from associating with us; he was imprisoned in Itard's apartment—scene of his lessons and his life.

How could Victor learn to be with people, to play, to do chores, how could he refine and temper his emotions without social experience and without communication? He could not. In the end, Victor always preferred the open country to the company of others. One night he slipped out of his prison into the gardens and woke half the staff shrieking at the moon while splashing about in the fountain. On another occasion, Victor and Itard were invited to the château of Mme. Récamier, who presided at one of the great *salons* of the day. Members of the English parliament and of the French government, actors, poets, scientists, and a future king were assembled for dinner. Victor was placed next to the hostess, presumably to show that even a child of nature would be dazzled by her beauty. His education had advanced far enough that he wore clothes, took his place, and waited to be served. But after gorging himself with his hands, he slipped out, during a discussion of Voltaire's atheism, tore off his garments, climbed a tree, and leapt, stark naked, from one tree to the next, the length of the avenue that approached the château. The women gaped and fanned themselves, the men urged all to stand back, the gardener tempted Victor down with fruit, and someone lamented that Rousseau had not lived to see this proof that society is kinder to man than nature is.

Discouraged by the boy's lack of progress, Itard spent less and less time with him. Finally, in 1810, De Gérando decided it would be better to be rid of him, and the ministry arranged to pay Mme. Guérin one hundred fifty francs a year to lodge the boy in her home down the street from the school.[46] When a member of the Society of Observers of Man went to visit him there in 1817, he found him "fearful, half-wild, still unable to speak despite all the efforts that were made."[47] Victor of Aveyron died in that house, in his forties, in the year 1828.[48]

In the years he tended and taught the savage, Itard, the resident physician in our school, had little time left for us, though two illnesses ending in death and three fatal accidents among my schoolmates had given him as many irresistible opportunities to examine the ears of cadavers. "I derived nothing from this," Itard wrote, "except the old finding that the ears of the deaf are free from visible lesions."[49] Now that he had abandoned the wild boy, he was able to turn his attention to his medical experiments. Without information about a lesion associated with deafness, he had no rational guide for treatment; nonetheless, he took it for granted that he should proceed. He started by applying electricity to the ears of some pupils, since an Italian surgeon had recently found that a frog's leg would contract if touched with charged metal.[50] Itard thought there was some analogy between the paralysis of the hearing organ and the paralysis of a limb. He also placed leeches on the necks of some of the pupils in the hope that local bleeding would help somehow. Six students had their eardrums pierced, but the operation was painful and fruitless, and he desisted. Not soon enough for Christian Dietz, who died following this treatment. At first, however, his ears discharged some foreign matter and he reportedly recovered some hearing and with it some speech, which led Itard to think the deaf ear might be blocked up rather than paralyzed.

It was known that the postmaster at Versailles, M. Guyot, had cured his own hearing loss by inserting a probe in his Eustachian tube, which leads from the throat to the ear, and "flushing out the lymphatic excrement."[51] The method had been widely tried by physicians and abandoned as impracticable and ineffective. Itard made improvements, or rather, he had them made by pupils working in the carpentry shop; for example, a metal headband was added to hold the probe still despite the patient's agitated movements. Then, over a period of eleven months, one hundred twenty pupils, almost every last one in the school save for some two dozen who would not be subdued, were subjected to the treatments. Let me tell you what it was like. The band was wrapped around my forehead so that a clamp hung in front of my mouth. A long silver probe was pushed into my nose and turned and worked back and forth until it penetrated my Eustachian tube; the pain was intense and I am not ashamed to say that I cried. The end of the probe was then attached to a syringe leading to a jar with a flexible bottom containing irrigating fluid. When the liquid surged into my head I became dizzy and nauseated. After some minutes of this, the probe was removed and I was dismissed. Throughout, Itard never addressed a single word to me, since he knew no sign. After each of these treatments—there were eight—I had headaches, dizziness, and fever; my friend Berthier developed an ear inflammation and pus, to Itard's delight. What was accomplished? Why, nothing at all. Not one pupil derived any benefit. Nevertheless Itard came to be the world's authority on catheterizing the ear and published several articles about it; the silver shaft of pain now carries his name, the *sonde d'Itard*.

The reason Itard took delight in Berthier's infection was that a M. Merle, a self-styled naturalist doctor, had applied a treatment to all twenty-six pupils at the Bordeaux school and two were reportedly cured who had first developed severe pain and running liquid from their ears. Itard hastened to write to the inventor and obtain a quantity of the secret brew, which he dispensed into the ears of a dozen pupils without effect. The doctor responded to Itard's complaint by explaining that the potion lost its power if left standing. Itard offered to buy the recipe and prepare it himself, but the inventor said only the government could compensate him properly. When M. Merle died not long after, however, Itard obtained the prescription from his wife: ground wild ginger, 8 grams; roses of Provence, 1 pinch; wild horseradish, 4 grams; glasswort, 1 pinch; boil in white wine, reduce to half volume, strain, and add: sea salt, 8 grams. He prepared this concoction himself and put it in the ears of every pupil in the school who was not born deaf, a few drops a day for two weeks—without effect.[52]

A humbler man might have agreed at this point with the count of Noailles, a member of our administrative board, who said: "You wish to unstop the ears of the deaf but God does not." Itard said no such thing; if all of these methods were failures, then more extreme methods were called for. When Claudius Forestier was a lad of thirteen, he was subjected to a regime of daily purgatives, and his outer ear was covered with a bandage soaked in a blistering agent. Within a few days, his ear lost all its skin, oozed pus, and was excruciatingly painful. When it scabbed, Itard reapplied the bandage and the wound reopened. Then Itard repeated the cycle and applied caustic soda to the skin behind Forestier's ear. All of this was to no avail, no more for Forestier than for thirty other pupils on whom it was tried.

In desperation Itard tried fracturing the skull of a few pupils, striking the area just behind the ear with a hammer. With a dozen pupils he applied a white-hot metal button behind the ear, which led to pus and a scab in about a week. Yet another of Itard's treatments was to thread a string through a pupil's neck with a seton needle, which caused a suppurating wound that supposedly allowed "feculent humors" to dry up. In addition, several of the pupils in the school were badly scarred from his use of the moxa, an old Chinese remedy that involved burning a cylinder of dried leaves of the mugwort plant applied to the skin from the back of the neck to the chin. The moxa had fallen into disrepute by the time Itard was a medical student because it was so painful, generally fruitless, and sometimes fatal. But Itard was prompted to try it on a dozen of my schoolmates because one of Napoleon's military doctors had recently reported a cure of deafness by this means.[53]

It was all a miserable failure. "Medicine does not work on the dead," Itard concluded, "and as far as I am concerned the ear is dead in the deaf-mute. There is nothing for science to do about it."[54] There may be those people—hearing, no doubt—who admire Itard's determination at our expense. To me it seems like a crazed abuse of power, so dangerous and painful were the treatments, so slight the benefits. We were clearly not Itard's brothers but his raw materials. His successor as resident physician at our school, Prosper Ménière, said it outright: "The deaf believe that they are our equals in all respects. We should be generous and not destroy that illusion. But whatever they believe, deafness is an infirmity and we should repair it whether the person who has it is disturbed by it or not."[55] Will the day ever come when it will be unnecessary to affirm the immorality and danger of such a view? Hear it, then: the deaf are the equal of any man (perhaps better than some, for there has never been a deaf man who put out the ears of the hearing whether they wished it or not). Deafness is an infirmity for some, a source of strength for others, simply a condition of existence for most. It is my condition. I am what I am. I have done what I saw my duty to be. I have no wish to be anyone else or anything else, and I never have.

In this I am by no means unique. Of course, there are deaf people who view deafness as an infirmity and a calamity. They are generally hearing people who lost their hearing as adults. Their distress arises more from the necessity of changing their life against their will and habit—and in the first place acquiring another language—than it does from a failure to hear sounds. I have seen Frenchmen obliged to settle in America who responded with the same distress when they found their cherished tongue useless and had to learn another. Yet God made men adaptive; the best are capable of graceful change.

Here is what John Kitto, the English Bible commentator who lost his hearing when he was twelve, says about having it restored: "They poured into my tortured ears various infusions hot and cold; they bled me, they blistered me, leeched me, physicked me; and at last they gave it up as a bad case. . . . I have not sought any relief. . . . It had become a habit to me, a part of my physical nature: I have learned to acquiesce in it and to mold my habits of life accordingly. I cannot pretend to any permanent regret in connection with the absence of vocal or other sounds."[56]

Massieu tried to explain all this to Itard (in writing, of course, since Itard knew no sign). Itard said, Deafness is a disease: you would not choose it, although you may be reconciled to it. Massieu said, Poverty is a disease by the same logic; in fact you could live well without sound, as without means, if only society saw no disgrace and threat in this, if only it gave deaf children and poor children access to education and thus a chance to be what they can be. Itard said, But deafness stands in the way of education and admission into society. Massieu said, The failure to use sign was the obstacle to education and there always was a *deaf* society.

It was hopeless. Their shared language (written French) merely allowed the two men the illusion they were communicating. Massieu had no idea what it was like to be hearing and to fear the world of deafness, and Itard had no idea what it was like to be deaf and to fear the world of hearing. Asked, about a decade later, to write the entry on deafness for the major medical dictionary of the time, Itard described us as "civilized men on the outside, barbaric and ignorant as a savage on the inside; indeed, the savage is superior if he has a spoken language, however limited."[57]

In this same entry and in his *Treatise on Diseases of the Ear*, also published in 1821, which was the first and final word in that specialty for many years, Itard explains that we deaf are emotionally as well as intellectually primitive.[58] He says we are impassive (yet I burn with rage at this slander). He says we are as credulous as savages, because the poor children entrusted to his care have limitless belief in his medicine "and turn to me for health and life even in their gravest illness." He says that before education we cannot love and after it we cannot love deeply or know gratitude. Witness how little they love Sicard, he wrote; I wonder if this lonely bachelor also meant, Witness how little they love me. He says we are less sensitive than others; we accept surgical pain calmly and do not react to many medicines, such as purgatives. We have few friends. We cannot feel sadness or melancholy (yet all this makes me very sad and melancholic).[59]

Itard knew nothing of the deaf because he had lived among us only nominally.[60] In his incomprehension he believed the deaf had a "frightful predicament," and if he could not solve it with medicine, perhaps he could solve it with training. Might not the methods he developed to exercise Victor's sense organs, long inactive through isolation, be applied with more success to those of the hard-of-hearing, long inactive through disuse?[61]

Previously, Itard had seen only two ways to try to transform a deaf man into a hearing one and both were failures. The first was medicine. The second was training in speech, which is "always painful, slow, and defective and yields no useful exchanges. . . . The deaf man cannot increase, develop, and clarify his ideas in this way, his education is unaffected, he is still a deaf-mute."[62] Now, however, Itard thought he saw a third way to restore speech—by restoring hearing, through the exercise of the deaf man's ears. He took it for granted that when hearing was restored, speech would be, too. When the cataracts had been removed from a patient born blind, had not the man come to see shapes, colors, and depth in a few weeks without instruction?* Likewise, when the deaf boy of Chartres abruptly acquired hearing,† didn't he soon acquire speech on his own?[63]

Like all those before him who had tried to teach the deaf speech, Itard worked long hours with just a handful of pupils who were predisposed to profit. He drew six from among the ten percent at our school who could discern vowels and a few consonants but nothing more. He began by improving their ability to detect sound rapidly and reliably. Originally, he had a church bell installed in their classroom, and he taught his pupils to respond to successively softer notes, which he obtained either by striking the bell with different objects or by seating the pupils farther away. Itard next employed the vibrating bell of a clock and, placing his students in a row in a long corridor, he gradually withdrew the source of sound, marking on the wall the point at which it became inaudible for each child. In this way he recorded the relative standing of each of his pupils and his day-to-day progress.

Another series of exercises concerned the perception of rhythm: Itard dragged out Victor's old drum and tapped out a few simple marches for his pupils, "as often poorly as well," he adds modestly. (His selections were apparently good ones, since he reports that his six pupils took to beating them out together in the classroom while awaiting his arrival.) Progressing

---

*In a celebrated case reported by the British surgeon William Chesselden (1688–1752).
†At the age of twenty-three; the case was reported to the French Academy of Sciences in 1702.

toward speech discriminations, Itard next taught his pupils to distinguish high and low notes on the flute. They reached a point where they perfectly distinguished the re and la of the musical scale, but they still could not distinguish among the vowels. The teacher wrote the "five vowels" on a blackboard, then placed himself behind the children and pronounced them while his pupils were to point to the corresponding transcription: with practice they mastered the task.

Distinguishing the consonants proved much more difficult for his pupils and Itard says frankly that he had to use a thousand and one different devices, tailoring his instruction to each individual student. This necessity led him to reduce the group from six to three pupils and to give an hour's lesson daily to each. After a year, or about a thousand hours of instruction, Itard's hard-of-hearing pupils could reliably recognize all the vowels and consonants as they occurred in various simple words, and the best could understand sentences spoken directly and slowly. Yet certain confusions persisted and, most disappointing of all, the pupils spoke no better than before all this training. There were many speech sounds they heard distinctly that they could not utter distinctly. Itard attributed this to the same causes as in Victor's case: the ability to imitate wanes with age; and speech organs that have remained long inactive require physiological training just as ears do.

So in the end Itard set to work to teach speech directly. He developed a careful progression of sounds to be taught, from the highly contrastive to the very similar, from the easily articulated to the more difficult, from the simple to the complex. Moreover, he brought vision and touch into play; he took up, he said, where Pereire's pioneering work left off, in the tradition of Bonet, Wallis, and Amman.

Soon his pupils were able to read words and simple sentences "more or less intelligibly," and, in 1808, Itard could parade them past the Faculty of Medicine, which had high praise for their performance.[64] Itard found to his dismay, however, that they would never speak of their own accord, nor could they respond fluently to questions he was sure they understood. Despite his efforts, they were no more educated nor able to be educated orally than when he began, since they rarely used their speech and they could not hear what was said around them or even to them unless it was addressed to each directly, loudly, slowly.[65]

What was responsible for this failure, coming on the heels of that with Victor and with the medical treatment of deafness? An unwise undertaking? An unsuitable technique? A poor choice of pupils? Not in Itard's eyes. Like so many oralists since, he put the blame for his failure on the language of the deaf. The deaf man has an unreasonable attachment to that language, he argued, and will always use it in preference to that of the hearing if he is permitted to get away with it. If he is allowed to sign he will have rare occasion to speak.[66] When he is forced to speak, he does what everyone does who is trying to speak a foreign language he is learning: he thinks in his own language, constructs sentences in his own language, and then translates them slowly into the foreign tongue. That is why a pupil would work the answer to a question over on his fingers before stammering a reply.

It is interesting that French was a foreign language for these almost-hearing pupils: even though it was the language proffered at their mother's breast, it was alien from the start if they were born hard-of-hearing, or rapidly became so if they lost their hearing later. In either case, thoughts sprang first to their hands, not to their lips. It is for reasons like this that we say sign language is the primary language of nearly all the deaf, whatever their hearing loss. Epée and Sicard called it their "natural language." But Itard could not hear nature's voice, or rather, he could not read her hands, and he arrived at a quite different conclusion. I should have isolated my pupils, he thought, as I isolated Victor. If, in addition, I could prevent them from signing among themselves, then "they would be obliged to fall back exclusively on speech to express their needs and all their thoughts."[67]

Jean-Marc Itard was the physician to the deaf who never learned a sign during his forty years among them at the institution founded by Epée. Itard was the tutor who isolated the mutely gesticulating wild boy for four years rather than allow him to learn sign language. Itard was the founder of oral education who trained pupils in hearing and speech during three years without ever employing signs. Itard was the zealot who lamented that he could not perfect his pupils' speech because he lacked authority to isolate them. How significant, then, that Jean-Marc Itard was also, finally, an apostate from the oralist camp: he came to believe that the education of hard-of-hearing children as well as those profoundly deaf should be—must be—conducted in sign language. No other means allows their full development, he wrote in his *Treatise*, sixteen years after the beginning of his labors; none other is so analogous with the education of the hearing child in speech; none other can offer as sign does full, facile, continual communication between the pupil and his teachers and between the pupil and his schoolmates.

What caused this about-face on the language of the deaf? I will let Itard give you his scientific reasons, but there is a personal one he does not reveal: his pupil, Eugène Allibert. Every great hearing teacher of the deaf is standing in front of a deaf man. As Pereire stood in front of Saboureux, as Sicard stood in front of Massieu, as Gallaudet stood in front of me, so Itard stood in front of and was guided by Allibert. They made a strange couple, the lonely, austere, and taciturn bachelor and the sunny, loquacious boy. Allibert had been raised in a hearing foster family; the other pupils who received Itard's physiological training lived in the signing society of our school. Thus the comparison between his progress and the others' was a kind of experiment, which the Academy of Medicine evaluated in 1818. "One might have thought that the nurture provided by the hearing family, its interest in and influence over its foster child, would have yielded a better result than education by signs in the institution for deaf-mutes. The contrary happened: his spoken conversation seemed to us more limited, more narrow than that of the other child."[68] Indeed, many years later Allibert wrote to the academy that, despite the five years of intensive effort Itard lavished on him, despite his own strenuous efforts to speak, which turned his hair to gray when he was only eighteen, and despite his residual hearing (he perceived noises and vowels), he could not be understood orally except by his relatives and he could not understand an oral address.[69]

From his inauspicious beginning under Itard, Allibert went on to a brilliant and rapid scholarly success and became a professor at our school a few years ago. That success began only after he left the oralist cocoon in which Itard had enveloped him and devoted himself to an education in sign language. And they both knew it. Itard allowed him to go daily to our school for explanations in sign language of the French texts he was studying and not comprehending under the oral method. Finally, his French was sufficient for him to explain to Itard, as well as to embody, the reasons for educating the deaf in their own language. Itard was grateful for Allibert's friendship and guidance to his dying day, and remembered him in his will.[70]

A decade after his experiments with Allibert and the others, Itard wrote that he had favored oralism at first because he had seen children who had recovered a little speech, such as Allibert, or who had retained some speech after recently becoming deaf, go on to lose that speech gradually as they lived in the signing society. He had believed that exclusion of sign and instruction in speech would slow the steady erosion of their oral skills. But the sacrifices were too great, even for this special group of pupils. A well-trained teacher and an indefatigable speech therapist were needed nearly full-time for just one hard-of-hearing pupil, and even then the process was long, painful, and uncertain of success.[71] Moreover, these pupils have quite imperfect hearing, so there are oral "difficulties, blockages and misunderstandings from which sign language is exempt. . . . It is absolutely impossible to educate these children exclusively by means of speech."[72] If oral instruction was impossible for the hard-of-hearing, it was unthinkable for the truly deaf.[73]

Even when the hard-of-hearing child has a teacher all to himself, that teacher must address him slowly and directly. When the teacher stops speaking, the pupil's education stops, Itard wrote. The deaf-mute instructed and raised in a signing society, however, sees both the signs addressed to him and also all the conversations among the deaf within view. This indirect communication is instructive because "a large and seasoned institution of deaf-mutes, bringing together individuals of diverse ages and degrees of education, represents a genuine society, with its own language. This language is endowed with its own acquired ideas and traditions and it is capable, like spoken language, of communicating all intended meanings, directly or indirectly." In sum, Itard became convinced that the deaf child absorbs knowledge from the signing society around him. He had seen children develop all sorts of knowledge and skills that were not being taught in class.

If the deaf man is to communicate with the educated men of other times and places he must learn a written language. This, says Itard, requires education using sign language. "Reading can be taught orally and with writing but this is rare and difficult, or in sign language, which is the natural language of those born deaf, whatever the degree of their hearing loss." Once the deaf man is able to tap the inexhaustible supply of knowledge in books, he can draw off all that he lacks to complete his education. Itard then cites me as proof of his claim.[74] I am flattered to be singled out and I trust I will not be accused of immodesty when I confirm Itard's view: sign language and diligence gave me the gift of reading, which has ever been a source of pleasure and illumination.

Itard continued to believe that the hard-of-hearing who could profit from articulation training should have it, but if anyone had suggested to him even before his change of heart that all or nearly all pupils, whatever their degree of deafness, should receive articulation training, he would have considered the proposal wildly impractical: "The language of the deaf-mute is in his hands, as his hearing is in his eyes; to want to give him another language is to act directly counter to the laws of nature, and against the least contested principles of physiology and sound metaphysics. If we are proposing another means of communication, it is not at all for this class of [true] deaf-mutes but for another group of pupils which is quite distinct and which, strictly speaking, should no more be classed with the deaf than the nearsighted with the blind."[75]

So all pupils had to be educated in sign but a small group could profit by ancillary articulation training. Just what Epée and Sicard thought. Even when it came to teaching speech, however, sign was necessary. In the first place, great speech teachers, from Ponce to Wallis to Pereire, have always relied on it. Indeed, how could you teach a pupil if you couldn't communicate with him? You might start with pantomime, but its awkwardness and slowness in daily lessons soon leads the teacher to adopt his pupil's system of manual communication. In the second place, the great aid to understanding a spoken sentence is not the imperfect ears of the pupil nor his eyes but his cultivation. Itard compared the ability to lipread of two pupils, one born hard-of-hearing, the other recently become so. The latter, with less experience lipreading but a more complete education, was much the better. "This experiment convinced me," Itard wrote, "that when you teach the partially deaf, speech must hinge on education and not education hinge on speech as I had first planned."[76]

What of Itard's earlier belief that his hard-of-hearing pupils had to be isolated from sign because they were apparently thinking in sign, moving their hands before they spoke, then corrupting their French by importing ways of saying things in sign? Itard rescinded that judgment, perhaps because he came to know some of the more advanced students, for whom reading and writing were directly connected with ideas and feelings. Deaf people agree that there are no speech movements or signs that mediate between the written page and the idea in the fluent reader. The beginner, however, signs while he reads out the words in the text in order to remember them better, much as a hearing child, learning to read, moves his lips.[77]

Thus it became quite clear to Itard in the last decade of his life that classroom instruction could be intelligible only in sign, that the pupils derive much of their education from the signing society around them, that sign is the necessary vehicle for learning how to read, and finally that the one pupil in ten who can learn some speech and lipreading also requires an education in sign. It would be pointless after all to isolate these pupils, since "all the advantages I have cited would be lost while nothing would be gained. We cannot delude ourselves that such pupils left on their own with only speech as a means of communicating would use it for their mutual relations. They would create their own sign language. Thus it is not necessary to isolate this group, since sign language is as profitable for them as it is indispensable."[78]

So Itard came to see a great institution for the deaf for what it really is, a society with a language of its own. He even imagined what society would have been like if it had developed so that men expressed their ideas and emotions by moving their limbs and faces rather than their tongues. In such a society, vision would be the main source of learning, and hearing and deaf people would be perfectly on a par. Writing might have been invented sooner, he decided, for it is easier to imagine representing signs than drawing sounds. Once this was accomplished, mankind would have embarked just as promptly on the glorious career that written language made possible. Suppose everyone in that society were deaf; apart from lacking a few ideas concerning sound, people there would be what speech and hearing have made them in our society. Man realizes his potentialities by dint of his genius, not by the suppleness of his organs.[79]

If hearing really matters so little, why are deaf people at such a disadvantage? Why obviously, Itard answers, "because our language is not visual but spoken, which deprives the deaf-mute of the first and most powerful means of perfecting the human species, the commerce of his equals."[80] If you want to know how much the equal of a hearing person a deaf man can be, make everything equal. Let him be born and live among his own kind.

Our school approximated this ideal, but only in part. It was run by hearing people, not the deaf. For a long time, instruction was given in manual French, which is no one's language. Few pupils had learned French Sign Language natively, from their parents, or had grown up surrounded by friends who also used that language. Nevertheless, there was certainly a larger, older, and more integrated deaf society by the time Itard published these thoughts in his *Treatise* than there had been two decades earlier, when he (and I) first came to Saint-Jacques. A pupil arriving at this later time had more signed lessons and more signed conversations with pupils already educated than I had had. Itard concluded that this growth and evolution of the signing society had made instruction easier and more effective. To prove his point he cited differences between Massieu and me:

"At that time, Massieu was a dazzling phenomenon in the midst of his unfortunate companions, who remained well behind him, still at the first stages of their education: nowadays, he is nothing more than a highly distinguished student. Instruction, powerfully assisted by tradition, has more rapidly developed and civilized his companions; one among them has equaled him, and several have come close and would have surpassed him had they not so promptly left the institution. . . .

"Let us contrast Massieu . . . with Clerc, this student whom I said was his equal in instruction but who, having come quite recently to the institution, ought to have profited by all the advantages that a more advanced civilization can offer. Massieu, a profound thinker, gifted with a genius for observation and a prodigious memory, favored by the particular attention of his celebrated teacher, benefiting from an extensive education, seems nevertheless to have developed incompletely; his ways, habits, and expressions have a certain strangeness that leaves a considerable gap between him and society. Uninterested in all that motivates that society, inept at conducting its affairs, he lives alone, without desires and ambition. When he writes, we can judge even better what is lacking in his mentality: his style fits him to a tee; it is choppy, unconventional, disorderly, without transition but swarming with apt thought and flashes of brilliance.

"Clerc," Itard continues, "with a less encompassing and towering intelligence, trained as much by the institution as by any teacher, presents a picture of much more uniform development. He is entirely a man of the world. He likes social life, and often seeks it out, and he is singled out for his polite manners and his perfect understanding of social custom and interests. He likes to be well groomed, appreciates luxury and all our contrived needs, and is not insensitive to the goads of ambition. It is ambition that snatched him from the Paris institution, where he had a worthy and comfortable existence, and led him across the seas to seek his fortune."[81]

* * *

Institut Royal de France.
Acad.ⁱᵉ des Inscript et Belles lettres. (Histoire de la Philosophie.)

LE BARON DE GÉRANDO,
(Joseph-Marie.)

Pair de France, Conseiller d'État, Commandeur de la Légion d'honneur,
Professeur à la Faculté de droit de Paris, Secrétaire de la société d'encouragem.ᵗ
pour l'industrie nationale et de la société pour l'Instruction élémentaire.

Né à Lyon, le 29 Février 1772, élu en 1804.

BARON JOSEPH-MARIE DE GÉRANDO

Although Jean-Marc Itard, then, had taken up the torch of oralism early in this century that Pereire had relinquished late in the eighteenth, by the time of the publication of his *Treatise* in 1821 he had radically changed his views; thus, when the abbé Sicard died a year later, it fell entirely to Baron De Gérando to champion the oralist cause at Saint-Jacques. If only he had read Itard's mature work as well as he had read the early papers! But he did not, and so it was De Gérando who came to symbolize the oppression of the deaf as Jean Massieu symbolized their enlightenment.

Joseph Marie, Baron De Gérando, philosopher, administrator, historian, and philanthropist, conducted philanthropy the way generals wage war: it was organized, it was imposed by force, it was self-righteous. He conducted it in external affairs, where the "beneficiaries" called it imperialism, and he conducted it in internal affairs, where the "beneficiaries" called it paternalism. These are two sides of the same coin.

In 1806 De Gérando was sent to Milan to reorganize the administration of Lombardy, then under French dominion. Next he went to Genoa to help bring the government of the Ligurian Republic under French rule. Two years later Napoleon sent him to Florence to help rule Tuscany. As the Arno, the Tiber, the Sègre, the Weser became French rivers, De Gérando was responsible for imparting French administration to the new territories. When Napoleon incorporated the states of the Holy See into France and removed the pope by force, Catholic De Gérando accepted responsibility, despite scruples, for instituting the new French order; he was charged with Roman education, health, monuments, arts, bridges, and roads. When Napoleon conquered the vast northeast region of Spain called Catalonia and converted it into two French states, De Gérando went to administer them. He returned from Spain to witness the fall of the Napoleonic empire and the restoration of the Bourbon monarchy in France. Somehow, he kept his post—in effect, deputy minister of the interior—under this new regime, as he did when Napoleon returned and placed him in charge of the defense of the eastern states. I am reminded of Sicard's candid avowal that he was a royalist under the king and a republican under the republic.

In a career devoted to bringing the new French order to the conquered nations of Europe, De Gérando made time for bringing it as well to the uncivilized peoples of Africa and the South Pacific. He looked down from even loftier heights on these nations, so dissimilar from the French, and, faced with their evident barbarity, he was even more organized, forceful, self-righteous. (In fairness to De Gérando, it should be said that his views were of a piece with those of most French intellectuals, who knew nothing firsthand of these remote societies and were equally disdainful of them.)[82] And as for the deaf: "The deaf-mute is also a savage," he wrote.

De Gérando had no humility, no doubts about his own culture and language. He believed that the various societies existing reflected stages in human development, culminating with Western Europe. Philanthropy guided by science could raise the retarded savage to the level of his European brother. "What more touching purpose than to . . . meet again these ancestors separated by a long exile from the rest of the common family, than to extend the hand by which they will raise themselves to a more happy state." What more noble activity than to go among them, "always well received, well treated, living proof of our happiness, our wealth, our superiority. . . . Perhaps they will call us to their midst to show them the road that can lead them to our condition. What joy! What conquest!"[83] Clearly, the "love of man" in this philanthropy is self-love.

De Gérando's philanthropy to the poor was equally flawed by his arrogance. "Let the rich man know the dignity with which he is invested," De Gérando wrote in his *Visitor to the Poor*. "The rich must exercise a personal, immediate, individual patronage. . . . That man on the hangman's scaffold was our brother and might have been good. He was poor."[84] And further: "It is necessary to the good order of society that the poorer classes should learn to behold the more prosperous conditions without a feeling of bitterness and to respect the distance which Providence has established between the different ranks in society. This is absolutely necessary to the repose of those who belong to the least favored conditions" (and, I might add, also soothing to members of the privileged classes). "The poor on many accounts are like children. They have want of foresight and are ignorant. They easily allow themselves to be carried away. They need to be supported, restrained, directed; they need more than a benefactor, they need an instructor."[85]

In all, De Gérando spent fifty years doing good and wrote twenty-five volumes to teach others to do what he did so perfectly himself. He opened a home for fallen women, in his words, "a place of refuge and repentance where they are snatched from chaos, accustomed to work, reconciled with their families, put back on the road to honesty." He founded a society for industrial training and another for elementary instruction. He gave a normal course for primary school teachers and wrote a two-volume work on self-education. He was one of the founders of the first savings bank. He adopted the seven orphaned children of his wife's sister and the five his brother bequeathed him on his death.

Clearly the man was possessed by the desire to engage in benevolence, but of a certain kind. I have sought its sources in the details of his life and the traits of his character. He came from a comfortable home in Lyon—his father was an architect. His parents initially thought him dull but when he entered the college of the Oratorians he did well in his studies. At one point in those years De Gérando became seriously ill and wrote in his diary: "God, save this life and I will devote it to doing good." When he recovered, he began to study for holy orders.

He was to become a soldier instead, first in the service of his native city when it took up arms in open rebellion against the soldiers of the new republic, and then, when the insurrection was put down (with the political agility he would reveal again later in life), in the ranks of the republican cavalry. Over the next few years he narrowly escaped death on several occasions, left the army surreptitiously to work for a wealthy relative by day while pursuing an arduous program of study by night, and finally, under a general amnesty, returned to his unit stationed near the German border. He was a simple soldier when he decided to enter a competition announced in the newspapers by the French Institute, offering five hectograms of gold for the best essay on "the influence of symbols on the development of ideas."

In his essay De Gérando accepted Condillac's principle that ideas arise from sensations, but he argued that the mind also embodies an active principle triggered by sensations, one that is not symbolic in itself but uses symbols. To Condillac's aphorism "To think is to sense" he opposed his own: "Thought is to the mind what action is to a body." Imagine the judges' surprise when the authors of the essays were disclosed and the winner proved to be a young soldier. The all-powerful Institute had him released from the army and brought to Paris, where Lucien Bonaparte gave him a post in the Ministry of the Interior so that he could support himself and his new wife while continuing to do philosophy. The minister of finance put his château at his disposal and there he expanded his essay into a four-volume treatise, followed two years later by a vast comparative history of philosophical systems, which served as a model for his later history of systems for educating the deaf. Bonaparte's successor at the Interior made it a condition of his appointment that De Gérando would be his second in command, and thus began his long and distinguished administrative career.

For much of that career, De Gérando was a member of the state council (the highest administrative body in the land), the Chamber of Peers,* the French Institute, and the faculty of law. Yet he was an inarticulate man, timid and reserved. He withdrew inside himself after his closest friend died and further yet after his wife died, quite young. In his diary, he pledged "to serve her through the children and, in doing good, become worthy of her, prepare to join her, take care of her through those who still suffer."

What is the wellspring, then, of De Gérando's indefatigable benevolence toward his family, his country, his continent? Is it a well-intentioned desire to leave something of permanent value as the trace of a life whose precariousness was reaffirmed at every turn—in short, a desire to escape mortality? Or is the man's sententiousness a mask for a hesitant, shy youth trembling within, as bravado often disguises fear?

Baron De Gérando extended the same well-meaning paternalism that he

---

*The upper house of the French legislature from 1814 to 1848.

had brought to conquered lands, to uncivilized peoples, and to the poor, to us, the deaf: we were his savages, his conquered people. "The deaf man scarcely knows anything other than his own physical well-being or illness," he wrote in his essay on symbols and thought prepared the same year as his guide to studying savages.[86] The deaf man does not reflect on his own destiny. He has no sense of duty. He has little control over his attention. He seems to be unaware that he can direct his own actions. And on and on. We have heard such rantings before: they remind us of Sicard's before he met Massieu, of Itard's before he knew Allibert. But De Gérando was at too many removes from the deaf for him to be befriended by even one, and he was too persuaded that the deaf have no language to learn ours and communicate with us directly. "The deaf-mute shows us an interesting phenomenon," he wrote, "human society in its infancy, the first communications that our ancestors were able to have among themselves. . . . With only the beginnings of a language, the deaf have only limited intellectual abilities."[87]

De Gérando's biographers say that, as a high school student in his native Lyon, he made friends with a deaf boy and "learned to create a language to reach him."[88] I strongly suspect the boy's parents were hearing, that he did not belong to the deaf community, that he had only recently become deaf. This would explain why De Gérando thought the deaf have just the beginnings of a language, why he argued that a hearing man is heir to a symbolic system shaped by successive generations whereas a deaf man is reduced to his own individual resources. He thought the language of the deaf was invented anew each time it was needed: he knew about pantomime and perhaps even home sign but not about the French Sign Language! No wonder that in his history of the deaf, he called our language "impoverished, made of disjointed scraps," and concluded that we could not be educated by its means.

In the last days of his life De Gérando reflected on the deaf he had known, on his history of their education, and on his decades of service as head of the administrative board at Saint-Jacques, and he wrote in his diary, "Let it be said that they loved me as a father." To his dying day he did not understand that his paternalism demeaned us. He did not understand that, though it was well-intentioned, it was self-defeating because it prolonged our inequality by promoting it. In the end its "beneficiaries" could not love him. There were no deaf at his funeral, no poor, no fallen women, no savages, no Italians or Catalonians. His eulogy was written several times by wealthy benefactors such as he—a peer, a baroness, a member of the Institute. If only he could have come to know us, a little of our language, then he could have helped Massieu shepherd the growing, evolving signing society into a golden age, an empire of the exiled deaf, a land of Pélissiers and Forestiers and Berthiers, yes, and Clercs—of poets and writers and painters and sculptors and teachers and craftsmen—a model for the world, the culmination of the vision that was given to Epée. Instead he closed the gates of Saint-Jacques behind Massieu, behind Bébian, and tried to subdue the signing society within the walls by force alone.[89] Here is what happened; this was the struggle.

As we have seen, at Sicard's death, the administrative board wanted to end the disorder of teaching methods: they commissioned Bébian's *Manual*, which was to provide a uniform, graduated curriculum, and they sought a suitable director. A post occupied by two abbés successively could only be filled by another. Besides, Sicard had written to the abbé Gondelin, second in command at the Bordeaux school: "With death near, I bequeath the souls of my children to your religion, their bodies to your care, their minds to your teachings. Promise me you will fulfill this noble task and I will die in peace."[90] So Gondelin came to Paris but he lasted only six months. Then the abbé Beulé appeared briefly and withdrew, and the school drifted, leaderless, for nearly two years.[91] The administrative board wanted to hear speech but speech could only be heard in Itard's infirmary. The hearing faculty wanted to use methodical sign but the deaf faculty and pupils, encouraged by Bébian, clung to French Sign Language.[92] De Gérando was then charged with preparing a comprehensive review of methods of educating the deaf and, since the robes counted more than the man, another abbé was finally called to direct the school: the abbé Perrier, vicar-general in the city of Cahors, founder of a deaf school in Aveyron. But Perrier, too, was unequal to the task; after four years he was replaced by the abbé Borel, who, although he knew nothing of the deaf, was about to found a little school for them in Normandy.

At this moment De Gérando's survey of deaf education appeared. He had seen correctly that the signs deaf people used were not depictions as in pantomime but brief symbolic movements. He called these signs "reduced" and concluded falsely that they were therefore degenerate, imprecise, and useless for education. He urged that schools use instead fingerspelling, writing, and speaking when possible; sign language was to be banned. Faculty meetings were held to seek agreement on this innovation, but of course Berthier and the other deaf faculty refused to agree, preferring to use Bébian's *Manual*. De Gérando then announced that Saint-Jacques would meet its responsibility for worldwide leadership by gathering and disseminating information on educating the deaf, and he appointed his nephew, Edouard Morel, to edit and publish a series of circulars.[93] The first, dated 1827, simply announced De Gérando's wish as a reality: no more deaf faculty! Each class has a hearing teacher with a deaf teaching assistant; there is a new emphasis on lipreading and articulation. It had never happened. The abbé Borel took no interest in instruction and was overwhelmed by all the contention. Perhaps because he lacked the authority to enforce De

Gérando's will, perhaps for general incompetence, he was discharged.[94] Nine years without leadership, nine years of disarray, but the worst was yet to come.

In his efforts to convert a school of the deaf into a school of the hearing, De Gérando found few allies in the institution founded by Epée and nourished by Sicard, an institution where two-thirds of the professors were deaf and all the instruction in sign. So he gathered a group of outsiders and installed them as the "academic board" of the institution,[95] although they knew no more about the deaf than did the administrative board. To make matters worse, the Ministry of the Interior was even further from understanding the deaf and their education than either board: our school had come under the ministry's division of stud farms, then that of fine arts, then that of welfare and insane asylums. Repeated appeals to assign Saint-Jacques to the Ministry of Education were unsuccessful. For the government, it was (and is) an asylum first and an educational institution second. Had not its directors all been men of the cloth, acting out of Christian charity?

Discouraged by the repeated failures of the latest men of the cloth, who knew nothing of education, the administrative board now hired as director a layman who knew nothing of the deaf. His name was Désiré Ordinaire and on the face of it he was just the man to bring about the transformation (indeed annihilation) of the deaf society that De Gérando desired. Ordinaire was born shortly before Epée's death, became a doctor, taught natural history at the university in Besançon, was appointed its dean, then became rector of the University of Strasbourg at the German border, in Alsace. Shortly thereafter he left under a cloud: some say he was fired; if so, I don't know the reason. Ordinaire's brother was a member of the recently formed academic board at Saint-Jacques: perhaps De Gérando had known him from his days in Alsace or perhaps he was simply well disposed toward him since he did love that region and its people so much (his wife was Alsatian). In any case, it seems that the brother and De Gérando hatched a plan. Désiré Ordinaire would quit his retirement and go on a fact-finding tour of the deaf schools in Germany and Switzerland—which were then, as we shall see, gripped by a resurgence of oralism. He would send glowing accounts of what they were achieving to the administrative board at Saint-Jacques, which would naturally recommend him to the ministry to accomplish the same oralist revolution in Paris.[96] It transpired as planned. Edouard Morel even published Ordinaire's reports from Germany in the third circular from Saint-Jacques, accompanied by rather fulsome praise of the man as well as the system.[97]

Meanwhile Itard, though he no longer believed the deaf could be educated orally, had been advocating supplementary training in articulation for the hard-of-hearing. Itard sent his plea in three memoirs to the administrative board, which requested funds from the ministry to hire an articulation teacher. The ministry in turn asked the Academy of Medicine—the same that had evaluated Azy d'Etavigny eight years before—to evaluate Itard's recommendations. After studying Itard's reports and observing "physiological training of hearing and speech" in action with a new group of deaf-mutes, the academy concluded that combined education, sign and speech, "is possible in the case of one-tenth of the children admitted into the institution for deaf-mutes," that oral instruction is accelerated and facilitated by sign education, and that sign language is incomplete and truncated but "indispensable in all cases of early or congenital deafness, however slight."[98] The government followed the academy's advice and gave funds for an articulation class: one professor, Jean-Jacques Valade-Gabel, taught one hour of speech daily to those who seemed to profit.[99] Thus the "combined method" began.

As soon as he became director, Ordinaire advanced a cunning two-step scheme to elevate spoken French from a complement for a few to the universal principle of education for all. De Gérando had correctly seen that the deaf professors were the great obstacle, for even if all the hearing teachers taught orally, the students would still receive much instruction in sign from the deaf faculty. Therefore, in step one Ordinaire ordered that students would no longer move from teacher to teacher as they went from year to year; instead, an entering class would stay with one professor for its entire six-year term.[100] This meant an end to the problem of articulating the curriculum in successive years and it also meant that students assigned to a deaf professor could get no oral French education at all. Then, in step two, he ordered that all students must get *some* oral education. Logically, then, the deaf teachers must be supplanted by hearing teachers. Berthier and four other professors, supported by Bébian, protested to the administrative board, but of course they were ignored, since Ordinaire was carrying out the will of the board.

In an effort to win support for his program, Ordinaire conducted demonstrations that were reportedly painful to behold. First, the few hesitant and gauche signs that he had learned the night before were greeted with open mirth by the pupils. Worse, the children appeared one after the other on the stage and performed little oral exercises under Ordinaire's direction that had in fact been memorized before, as all the pupils knew. Their responses to apparently impromptu questions, "By the way . . . ," had likewise been rehearsed. The youngest pupils might have been pleased by the applause of the duped audience but the oldest pupils knew better, as did the faculty.[101] At one demonstration that Bébian describes, several students spoke so unintelligibly that the director had to repeat their words for the audience. Then came four who spoke rather well—but all had arrived at the school with fluent speech, having lost their hearing between six and eleven years of age. Finally, three pupils demonstrated they could lipread by writing from dictation on a blackboard; one of the three, unfortunately, skipped a sentence and wrote its successor before it had been uttered.[102]

Despite Ordinaire's demonstration and orders, both the deaf and the hearing faculty continued to teach exclusively in sign. De Gérando then decided on drastic action in behalf of the deaf: he drew up a thirty-article decree spelling out the new regime for Saint-Jacques, he had the board and then the ministry approve it, and he had it sent to every professor.[103] The provisions were so unrealistic they were laughable, but this was no laughing matter. Article 8 said that each professor must teach articulation, thus dispensing with deaf teachers. Article 13 said that every professor would teach every lesson first orally, then in writing. Article 14 said that all pupils must communicate among themselves and with their teachers, whether in class or play periods or on walks or in the workshops, by means of spoken French alone or by writing on little slates. What role would the deaf professors play? Articles 26 and 27 said that there could be special classes for composition, sign language, and other matters taught by auxiliary professors, who could be deaf. Of course it didn't work. There was no way to get the pupils to write laboriously in French what they could say in a flash in their primary language—especially when in the garden! Nor were the hearing professors prepared to teach everything twice—or even once—in French when the pupils were clearly uncomprehending. Only men separated by an abyss from the deaf could ever imagine such a regime might succeed; De Gérando and his board were such men.

The effort to impose speech by force was a gross error that lasted all of three days! Resistance to the invasion of oralism was universal: pupils and teachers, hearing and deaf, banded together, determined to block the introduction of a principle that would replace education by drills in articulation and grammar.[104] The only person in the school who would teach speech after that was Ordinaire; his course was a complement to the regular instruction and he required it of all first- and second-year students. Berthier's pupils who were taking this course were asked if they wanted to learn to speak. Only a few said yes, and they were hard-of-hearing.[105] Still, it was a touching sight to see the stooped, gray-haired former rector of the University of Strasbourg exhorting his deaf pupils to contort their mouths in various ways. It was apparently a touching scene to hear as well, for the director had a speech defect, according to Bébian.[106]

The deaf faculty appealed their demotion to the ministry, were reinstated provisionally, and resumed teaching in sign. It became a matter of record that the pupils spoke in class but a matter of fact and general knowledge that they did not.[107] The reasons for this continued failure were that most students made little progress in lipreading and intelligible speech, so it was impractical to teach orally, while teaching in the written mode was equally unintelligible unless the written language was explained in sign. Therefore sign remained the vehicle for instruction in all subjects, including composition.[108] Finally, De Gérando himself acknowledged that French Sign Language, the primary language of all the pupils and the native language of many, was the principal means of instruction at the school.[109] Ordinaire made one last attempt, in 1836, to get the hearing faculty to do some instruction orally. Only one professor tried to obey, Léon Vaïsse. It was, likewise, proving fruitless to teach articulation to all entering students. The circular issued that year acknowledged the failure, stating that oral French had been reduced to a complement of instruction for the few. Ordinaire resigned. The academic board was dissolved.[110]

The oralist coup had for all purposes ended, although the occasional death rattle could still be heard. In the year that Ordinaire resigned, one of Itard's successors as resident physician, Alexandre Blanchet, launched a program to educate the deaf in ordinary hearing schools. Over the next decade a dozen schools tried it, primarily with students who had some speech and hearing, while Blanchet published and proselytized, finally convincing the Ministry of the Interior to issue a circular envisioning the universal inclusion of deaf children in the public schools. The outcry from oralists abroad who believed no such thing possible and the dismal failure of the experiment at home shortly led the ministry to withdraw its endorsement. A commission of the French Institute visiting two integrated schools found they had disintegrated rapidly: alongside of the deaf, and by the force of the same arguments, there were the semi-deaf, the blind, stammerers, and imbeciles—but no ordinary children.[111] By the time of Blanchet's death two years ago, nothing was left of this attempt to make the deaf hearing by fiat.[112]

In the failing years of the Blanchet plan for placing deaf children in the public day schools, its author also urged on the government a major reform of the residential schools for the deaf, with the same oralist goals in view. On the pretext that he had improved the speech and hearing of some pupils at the Paris school by exposing them to organ music five hours a week, Blanchet proposed that the semi-mute and semi-deaf pupils be separated from the rest of the signing community in order to receive special oral instruction, presumably at his hands. The government asked the opinion of the Academy of Medicine and its physicians engaged in a prolonged and impassioned debate on an issue entirely outside their competence—the relative merits for the deaf of speech and sign.[113]

Berthier warned the academy against miscasting the social issues of the deaf community as a medical problem in words that should go down in history and be repeated by generations to come: "The topic that concerns you, gentlemen, rather than an ordinary medical issue is, above all, a lofty question of humanity and civilization which requires deep reflection, not only by doctors but by teachers, philosophers and scholars."[114]

The academy seemed to agree on only one point: this had all been tried by Itard twenty-five years earlier. His prime student, Allibert, wrote to plead: "This action language of ours, so clear, so expressive, so accurate a reflection of our feelings and thoughts—is it not part of our very nature? No human power can take away from us what God has given us. . . . It is as essential for our minds as air is for our respiration."[115]

Two other reversions to oralism were equally brief. The government ordered merged with Saint-Jacques a private oral class for the deaf taught by a hard-of-hearing student of Ordinaire's named Benjamin Dubois. The class was soon terminated, however.[116] A dramatic artist named Fourcade gave instruction in elocution to the nuns and pupils at the Bordeaux school— until he was dismissed summarily.[117] Under Ordinaire's successor—neither a man of the cloth nor an educator but a politician—education in our school continued in French Sign Language. The present director, Léon Vaïsse, signs superlatively; he is now committed to sign language instruction and highly critical of what he saw in Germany, where he retraced Ordinaire's steps. He has, however, started up the articulation class again as a complement to the education of the hard-of-hearing pupils.[118]

In the end even De Gérando learned the lesson of his failed experiment, though it was a costly experiment for the deaf. Like Itard, he came around, with kind words for Bébian's reforms and for sign language, "whose richness of expression and eloquence we have learned to appreciate," he wrote shortly before he died.[119]

And what of Itard? He had been one of the most successful physicians of his time and yet he failed to find a medical treatment for deafness, he failed to find a way of producing speech in even that fraction of the deaf who had once spoken or had retained some hearing. Of course he knew this and died a bitter, disappointed, isolated old man. He wrote in his will: "The sad inescapable circumstances of man's existence are to suffer and to die."[120]

If only those who now urge oralism on the deaf in America, who—ignoring Berthier's counsel—would treat our social difference as a medical infirmity, who class us with defectives, idiots, and the insane, who would block our marriages and regulate the lives of our children, who refuse to listen to our own will—if only they would learn from Itard's failures, from De Gérando's failures.

But surely, you will say, the mentally ill are ill, and the deaf are deaf. Yet what do these words mean? Did you know it was enough to be an albino to be interned in the asylum for the mentally ill at La Salpêtrière, or an epileptic, or even, in some cases, a foundling? And the deaf: am I truly ill because I do not speak your language, or because I am more exposed than you to the danger of a runaway horse approaching from behind? There was a station on the Underground Railroad in the street where I now live, and I have learned the terrible stories of those who passed through it. (Harriet

Beecher Stowe is from Hartford, you know.) Yet certain doctors said these black people were suffering from an illness that led them to slip away and flee north. This illness had a name, drapetomania; a symptom, willful flight; and a cure, published a few years ago in a medical journal: "If any one or more of them are inclined to raise their heads to a level with their master or overseer, humanity and their own good require that they should be punished until they fall into that submissive state which was intended for them to occupy. . . . They have only to be kept in that state and treated like children to prevent and cure them from running away."[121]

Clearly, it is the doctors who warrant our concern here, not the patients! It is the hearing who are deaf, not I.

SEVEN

FORTUNE AND MISFORTUNE

The events that led to the founding of the education of the deaf in the New World began in 1805, a dozen years before my arrival here, when a beautiful and gifted child named Alice was born into the family of a leading New England physician, Mason Cogswell. At about the same time, the Cogswells' neighbor, Thomas Gallaudet, who was to become my lifelong collaborator and friend, was graduated from Yale, while I, on the other side of the Atlantic, was graduated from the National Institution for Deaf-Mutes. Two years later, Alice contracted spotted fever and became deaf, and the abbé Sicard promoted me to the post of Massieu's teaching assistant. At the end of Alice's first decade, while her mind lay dormant in silence, her father received an honorary M.D.; her neighbor Gallaudet was appointed tutor at Yale; and I, twenty-five, yearned for my own opportunity for greatness. Unaware as yet of Alice or Mason or Thomas, I thought that my opportunity lay—in the passion of youth I believed it exclusively lay—in the frozen wastes of Russia.

About the time of my graduation, the princess Maria Feodorovna, mother of Czar Alexander I and the protector of science, arts, and welfare in Russia, had founded a school for the deaf in the Palace of Paulowsky, their summer residence, and appointed as director a Polish priest, a certain Abbé Sigmund, trained in Epée's methods at the Vienna school under the abbé

Storck. There is evidence that this early solicitude for the Russian deaf was not entirely disinterested. First, Alexander's own hearing was impaired; he had been deaf in his left ear since early childhood, which was why he always turned his head in conversation, and with age he began to lose hearing in his right ear as well.[1] Second, the czar had no recognized heirs, but he had, in fact, a deaf son, Count Machwitz, who was sent to Paris and became my pupil. I was told he was the natural son of the czar but he could well have been the rightful heir to the throne.[2] In any event, the dowager empress took a keen interest in the education of the deaf and wrote a letter to Abbé Sicard, praising the abbé Sigmund for teaching her deaf subjects to calculate, write, and even read aloud intelligibly, but criticizing him for failing to give them ideas of God and religion. She asked Sicard if he would train a replacement, preferably someone whose native language was Russian, and inquired what other qualifications he would like his latest disciple to have.[3] In response, the abbé Sicard sent her a copy of his recently published *Theory of Signs*, which concerned none of these matters, and a letter proposing a friend of his, Jean-Baptiste Jauffret, as her new director. Since Jauffret knew little of the deaf or sign language, I was to accompany him as his *éminence grise*, much as Massieu had originally served Sicard.[4]

Some months later Sicard called me to his office to tell me that the empress had agreed to his proposition (elation!) but had provided funds for only one person (despair!). That person must, of course, be M. Jauffret. It did not occur to me to ask why, if only one person could go, it had to be an incompetent hearing man rather than a competent deaf one, and I was beside myself. How could I know that I was destined for other, greater things?

It was not long after this that I received my first American pupil, a harbinger of what was to come. Until Thomas Gallaudet and I opened the first school for the deaf in the United States, most American deaf had no school to go to or, like little Alice Cogswell, were mascots in hearing schools; only a very few from rich families, like Charles Green and the three Bolling children, were sent to schools for the deaf in Europe. One of these privileged few, a cousin of the Bollings' and, like them, descended from the Indian princess Pocahontas, was sent to Saint-Jacques and to me. His name was John St. George Randolph, and the uncle who adopted him at his father's death was the famous Senator John Randolph from Virginia. A friend and supporter of James Monroe, the senator had asked the future president, who was then on his way to the Court of Saint James's, to place his nephew in a school for the deaf in England. Monroe had the fourteen-year-old boy enrolled in the Braidwood academy, but after St. George had made little progress in two years (and none in acquiring speech), he was sent to the abbé Sicard instead.[5]

He was one of the handsomest young men I ever saw, with flashing black

eyes and dark curls. Since he had some knowledge of English, he made rapid
progress in French and in a few months achieved a creditable standing in
his class. The two ambitions of a Virginia boy, he explained to me, were to
be a good orator and a good shot on the wing. He thought the first was
foreclosed when he was born deaf but, though he was too deaf to hear the
whirr of a partridge's wings and unable to utter a command to a pointer,
he had once killed five partridges and a hare with a total of eight shots. He
spent his Sundays with the American consul in Paris and hunted on the
consul's estate in the Loire Valley. When the consul was recalled in 1814,
he took St. George Randolph with him.

I will anticipate my visit, some years later, to the Pennsylvania Institution
for the Deaf, in order to tell you what I learned there about St. George's
fate after his return to the United States: he had become a patient at the
Philadelphia Hospital for the Insane. I hastened to visit him there and
obtained permission to take him for a walk. As we strolled down Walnut
Street talking of old times, I asked gently what had happened to give him
such trouble. At first he would not tell me, but on my urging he said that
a year after his return from France he had made the acquaintance of a
beautiful young lady, daughter of wealthy parents in Virginia, that he had
succeeded in gaining her affection and in obtaining her promise of marriage,
but that afterward she had changed her mind and refused to ratify the
engagement on the plea that he was deaf and dumb. The broken engagement was, St. George said in the French idiom, a "thunderbolt," and when
he learned that another had married his beloved, he was overwhelmed with
so much sorrow that he became deranged.

Soon after our conversation, he was placed in the Maryland hospital at
Baltimore and remained there for twenty-five years. You must not conclude
that he was very ill; I do not think so. Since none of the patients knew our
language, he was isolated; since none of the doctors knew it, no one was
competent to judge the quality of his mind; with the passing of years he
increasingly adjusted to his bizarre situation and no doubt seemed increasingly bizarre himself. Finally, a good Christian from Charlottesville
managed to get him out of the institution and into his home. St. George
had a horse, attended church with his guardian, read extensively in English
and French, and was something of a local celebrity, with many tales to tell
of his famous uncle and the politics of the day. He died a few years ago,
the last of the Randolphs, and is buried in the churchyard at Charlottesville,
in an unmarked grave. His life would have worked out differently, had he
stayed among the deaf.[6]

In the year that St. George returned to America, Thomas Gallaudet was
graduated from Andover and gave Alice her first lessons, Alice was enrolled
in Lydia Sigourney's new school, and the Allies invaded Paris, dispatching
Napoleon to administer the Mediterranean island of Elba and restoring the

Bourbon monarchy. Since the final coalition against Napoleon had also included England, where the Bourbons had taken refuge, Sicard could now contemplate a trip to London in search of fame and funds to mollify his creditors. "I will go and spend at least a month there, maybe two," Sicard wrote to a friend during the celebration of the Allied entry into Paris. "I will take Massieu and another pupil who surpasses him. We will put on some public demonstrations. I am assured that what would be found wanting in Paris will be warmly received in London. I hope to gain the wherewithal to alleviate some part of my present troubles."[7]

He was to make the journey ahead of schedule. Acting on signs of public dissatisfaction with the monarchy, Napoleon left Elba for France with a thousand soldiers, only eleven months after his fall. From the first to the twentieth of March, he sped from village to village, right to Notre Dame, spurred onward by general acclaim. "I will follow all your advice," Sicard wrote to Baron De Gérando as Napoleon was in mid-course toward Paris. "I have given away all the medals from royalty and the crosses and the honoraria, I have returned unopened the little package bearing the seal of the adorable princess."*[8] In the following weeks (while, in Hartford, Mason Cogswell convened a meeting to found the first American school for the deaf and Thomas Gallaudet agreed to go to Europe to learn how to educate them), Louis XVIII fled to Ghent, and the abbé Sicard fled to London with Massieu, me, and a young pupil, Goddard, in tow.

We arrived at the end of May 1815.[9] The Argyle Room, at Little Argyle and Oxford streets, was reserved, and handbills were printed announcing a series of six lecture demonstrations, during the second and third weeks of June.[10] The public response was overwhelming. The prestigious *Quarterly Review* said: "That the deaf and dumb who have never been taught to utter articulate sounds may acquire a perfect command of a system of written and manual signs is certain. . . . The quickness and intelligence displayed by the pupils who accompanied the abbé Sicard . . . must remove the doubts of the most skeptical."[11]

A large and distinguished audience—including the duchess of Wellington, the duke of Orléans,† and members of both houses of Parliament— pressed into the lecture hall at every exhibition, so a second series of six lectures and finally even a third were announced.[12] A secretary transcribed the proceedings at these exhibitions, mainly pompous lectures by Sicard and questions from the audience addressed to Massieu and me designed to test the niceness of our discrimination and to display that of the questioner.[13]

The ambassador of Austria asked me what difference I found between the

---

*Probably the daughter of Louis XVI, the duchess of Angoulême.
†Later King Louis-Philippe.

abbé de l'Epée and the abbé Sicard. I replied that the former invented the method of instructing us but left much to be done; the latter had greatly improved the work. "Had there been no Abbé de l'Epée there would have been no Abbé Sicard; let honor, glory, and eternal gratitude therefore be awarded these friends of humanity."[14] A certain marquise asked if the deaf and dumb were unhappy. I replied: "He who never had anything has never lost anything; and he who never lost anything has no loss to regret. Consequently, the deaf and dumb who have never spoken have never lost either hearing or speech, and therefore cannot lament either the one or the other. And he who has nothing to lament cannot be unhappy; consequently, the deaf and dumb are not unhappy. Besides, it is a great consolation for them to be able to replace hearing by writing and speech by signs."[15]

Massieu's *bons mots* flowed more readily from his hands than ever I recall.[16] Some were simply literal translations from our language which struck hearing people who did not know it as marvelously insightful. Others were the product of Massieu's own genius.

—What is eternity?

—A day without yesterday or tomorrow, a line that has no end.

—What is a difficulty?

—A possibility with an obstacle.

Sir James Mackintosh asked the wily and treacherous question: "Does God reason?"

—Man reasons because he doubts; he deliberates, he decides. God is omniscient; He never doubts; therefore, He never reasons.

"What difference do you find between English women and French women?" we were asked. I answered candidly: "The English ladies are in general tall, handsome, well-shaped. The beauty of their complexion is particularly remarkable. But I beg their pardon for saying that, in general, they are somewhat deficient when it comes to deportment and elegance. If their shape and the regularity of their features are often preferable to those of Parisian ladies, still how inferior they are with respect to carriage and taste in dressing." Q: "You seem frank." A: "It's the privilege of a man of nature." (Massieu and I shook with laughter over that later.) Q: "Would you object to marrying an English lady?" A: "As much an English as a French one." Q: "Why so?" A: "Because I am not rich enough to support a wife and children."[17] Happily my fortunes were to improve.

You may wonder why three educated deaf Frenchmen were the object of such great curiosity and astonishment in London when there were several schools for the deaf in England and the largest of them in that very city on the Old Kent Road. I suspect the reason was this: unfortunately for the English deaf, Britain had never been part of the Napoleonic empire; thus the abbé de l'Epée's methods had never taken root there, and despite the growing infiltration of sign into the British schools, most instruction, under the sway of the Braidwoods, was still provided in English.

A group of us went to visit the asylum directed by Dr. Joseph Watson, who told Abbé Sicard that speech was peculiarly useful for the deaf poor, because they were placed in factories and speech enabled them to communicate more readily with their masters. Sicard allowed this motive of convenience but argued that when it came to opening the minds of the deaf with the aim of giving them the same rank in society they would have had were they not deprived of hearing and speech, his own experience showed that nothing could replace the natural language of the deaf, the language of signs, "of which all languages spoken or written are no more to them than translations."[18] After this exchange, we went into the dining room, where I noticed some pupils signing and engaged them in conversation in pantomime and sign. Presently one hundred fifty faces were beaming at me with expressions of surprise and pleasure; Dr. Watson assured us that the pupils were never allowed to sign in class.

Soon after, at the close of one of our public lectures, Mr. Gallaudet was introduced to me for the first time by Abbé Sicard. He explained that he had come to England from America in order to learn from the Braidwood family their method of educating the deaf, so that he might found the first school for the deaf in his native land. So far, he had found the Braidwoods secretive and unaccommodating, and he feared for the success of his mission.

Gallaudet was not bathed in light when he entered the room; I saw no harbinger of the great events to come, only a tentative, self-effacing man, dressed mainly in black, who said little. His eyes said a great deal more: candor, humility, determination, excitement, fatigue—their very message when we met nearly a year later in a Paris café, for we earnestly invited him to come to Paris, assuring him that he would be welcome to visit our school and attend our daily lessons.[19]

During the course of our lectures, an order issued by Napoleon's minister of the interior recalled us peremptorily to Paris, but it reached us after Waterloo, and Louis XVIII was returned to the Tuileries by the time we regained the capital.[20] In the months that followed, I was promoted to instructor of the senior class,[21] but I was increasingly restive at Saint-Jacques. For one thing, despite the promotion, I continued to receive the same salary—five hundred francs annually, equivalent to the cost of sending a pupil to Saint-Jacques for one year (I had never received a raise in nine years of teaching at Saint-Jacques!)—and my protest to the administrative board went unheeded.[22] The London trip and its accolades had reinforced my desire to travel, and increasingly I resented the loss of the Russian opportunity. Even the food at our school had grown particularly distasteful, after changes in the kitchen staff.[23]

Such was my position when, after six futile months in Edinburgh,

Yrs truly,
Thomas H. Gallaudet

The Reverend Thomas Hopkins Gallaudet

entreating the instruction there that he had been refused in London, Thomas Gallaudet left by way of London for Paris, where he arrived in mid-February 1816.[24] After his death, I found among Thomas's papers the torn remnant of a paper tablecloth (of the kind used in many French cafés) on which he had conducted his first conversation, in broken French, with Jean Massieu.[25] Thomas begins by apologizing for arriving late: he had to go to church in town. He thanks Sicard and Massieu "in the name of the poor deaf-mutes of America." He asks for private lessons and proposes seventy francs a month payment; "I would offer more but my expenses are paid by charitable contributions." Massieu agrees: "Clerc and I will take turns giving you lessons." Apparently the lessons began on the spot, for Thomas has listed nearly a dozen tenses for several French auxiliary verbs, and next to each appears a little notation of the appropriate methodical sign. Massieu worries in writing that it will be difficult to rework all this for English grammar and they make a date to start Thomas's private instruction a few days later.

I have found such a record of *my* first meeting with Thomas, too.[26] We discussed our families in English—mine broken; I had taken a few lessons before going to London.[27] I said: "I have one brother and two sisters but they are not deaf." Thomas asked if I read the Bible ("I know it by heart, since Sicard is a priest," I answered in French), and I asked if the Americans loved Napoleon ("We do not know much of the politics of Europe," he answered). "There is a great deal of wickedness in this city," Thomas told me. "Particularly among the women. I am very sorry to see so many fine young girls going to destruction." We discussed Sicard's age and the trades of the deaf and dumb. I taught Thomas a few signs (GOOD, BETTER, BEST; MAN, WOMAN, FRIEND). I tried to explain the difference between French Sign Language and manual French but I didn't do it very well; the former I called "natural," the latter "conventional." That could hardly be helpful, since all societies' languages are natural and they all involve conventions. Much of our conversation at that meeting and the many to follow, however, concerned life in America and especially the people and events in Hartford that had led up to our fateful encounter.

I have thought so often about those events, how easily history might have veered onto another course, that I scarcely remember which scenes in my memory I witnessed myself, which ones Thomas described, and which I reconstructed later, living among these people. If the personages in my story seem more lifelike for that, so much the better. I will let them speak for themselves in the scenes I witnessed and those I did not, so certain am I now of the principles of their characters and the circumstances of their lives. First, Mason Cogswell, the man to whom redounds inestimable credit for organizing the first philanthropic institution in the United States, our school for the deaf. Like Epée, when Mason was personally touched by deafness,

DR. MASON FITCH COGSWELL

he understood at once the great social issue that transcended his own concerns, and he acted upon that understanding.

MASON COGSWELL'S HOME, HARTFORD, CONNECTICUT, 1807. A large company is assembled at the Cogswells' dinner table. Sunlight pours through the windows facing Prospect Street and suffuses the dark wood table, chairs, and wainscotting with a warm glow. Stripes of sunlight lie across the embroidered white tablecloth and glimmer on burnished pewterware. On the table are the remains of several roast chickens, baked peppers, pudding, blackberry pies, tankards of cider, and pieces of maple sugar—all from the Cogswell property. Beaming at the assembly from the head of the table is Mason Fitch Cogswell, forty-six, a tall, thin, handsome man with close-cut thick brown hair tinged with gray, a high forehead, and large brown eyes with a penetrating gaze. He wears a high-necked frilly white shirt, a long waistcoat, and knee breeches, silk stockings, white-top boots. This is decidedly old-fashioned, the dress of his father's generation, but Mason Fitch Cogswell is old school, courtly, mild mannered, the beloved physician of Hartford, easy, gracious. He might often be seen on Village Street or on Main, striding briskly to the next of a dozen daily calls, the skirts of his long overcoat flying in the wind. At this moment he is holding his wife's hand under the table and, by cocking his head to one side, pretending to give his full attention to the Reverend Nathan Strong on his left, who is reading from his eulogy to the Reverend James Cogswell, Mason's father, deceased some three months past in his eighty-eighth year.

Mary Cogswell, the daughter of Colonel William Ledyard, who was treacherously slain with his own sword in the act of surrendering to the British at Groton, is widely admired in Hartford society for her good common sense, calm judgment, and propriety.[28] Because she is a woman, her major sphere of influence is her home, and there she excels in her devotion to others and in gracefulness, which helps to make the Cogswell house a center of culture and refined life.

On her right sits the Cogswells' neighbor, Peter Gallaudet, a diminutive merchant who had moved to Hartford from Philadelphia some seven years before with eight children; he now has twelve and his wife, at his side, looks appropriately exhausted. As his name suggests, Peter Gallaudet's heritage is French. His grandfather, Pierre Elisée Gallaudet, a doctor, left La Rochelle in the early 1690s in the great exodus of French Protestants caused by the revocation of the Edict of Nantes; he became founder of New Rochelle in New York. No less distinguished, Peter has served in the Continental Army, and acted as secretary to George Washington.[29] Like Mason Cogswell, he is old school. Moreover, at the age of thirty-seven, having lived without religion, he had made a public profession of faith, and as a result there is more Bible-reading in the family and prayer and churchgoing and exhortation to goodness than is typical of Protestant homes.

While his son Thomas and I were together in Europe, Peter Gallaudet moved his family to New York, then Philadelphia, and they finally settled in Washington, where he took a job with the Treasury Department, and founded the Washington Manual Labor School and Male Orphan Asylum. Those who believe, as I do, that nurture as well as blood make the man will not be surprised that Thomas, eldest of his twelve children, often sought out as a young man for guidance and comfort by his brothers and sisters, was destined to become the pastor of a flock and the principal of a school.[30]

At the foot of the table, next to Mrs. Gallaudet, a woman of clear intellect and deep piety, we find one of Mason Cogswell's intellectual friends, probably Joel Barlow, a fellow member of the Hartford Wits—America's first literary coterie, which gained its name from attempting to cure the current taste for bombast with large doses of bitter satire. Then come two medical students (at this time there was no medical school in the state—that of Yale College would not open for another five years, when they offered Mason the chair of surgery—and licensing required two years with a reputable physician after college, or three years if the student had not attended college) and, finally, the circle is completed by the Reverend Nathan Strong, a large man whose thick gray hair flows down over his shoulders. He has keen eyes and lips thinly drawn under a hooked nose.

Strong was one of the best-known divines in the country. A scholar, he had published his sermons, several theology books, and an evangelical magazine. His language was forcible and plain, his general tenor as a preacher solemn and evangelical. The principles of his religion were robustly Calvinistic: original sin, eternal election, justification by faith alone, the necessity of special grace in conversion, the saint's perseverance in holiness unto eternal life.[31] When he died, the year of my arrival in America, it was said that there were more communicants at the sacramental table of his Center Church than at any other in the whole state;[32] they included the Cogswells, the Gallaudets, and indeed all the first families of Hartford.

It would be hard to overestimate the importance of the meetinghouse, as the church was called, in the life of a New England town, more important even than the church in a French village. A town might lack a center or a tavern but it surely had its place of worship and this was its point of reckoning. The meetinghouse was also the town hall, and it was the center of social life. No doubt this arose because every dispute or division among the Puritan settlers gave rise to a new town, which was at once a unit of civil and religious organization. The first duty of a new settlement was to organize a church on a plan called Puritan. The adults affirmed the experience that made them professing Christians, they chose or simply recognized someone suitable to be pastor, and they covenanted to hold the faith, obey divine law, and observe the ordinances they legislated. Center Church was, as its full name affirmed, Hartford's First Church of Christ.

Nowadays the puritanical strain in New England has been diluted by

immigration and democratization, but when I came to Connecticut its aus-
terity, mortification, and asceticism were astonishing to one from a nation
where the needs of this life and those of the next had had a millennium in
which to come to terms. New Englanders were intelligent and industrious,
yes, but also with rare exceptions (Mason was one; I'll explain why later)
they wore penitential scowls and were sadly alike in dress, manners, and
pursuits. Their daughters and wives were cheerless, self-effacing. Their food
was boiled or roasted but not prepared; sauces would have been a wicked
indulgence, no doubt. They drank little wine but much rum. Education
meant divinity, law, medicine. To enjoy works of the imagination was considered an idle waste of time, somewhat sinful. They built their churches
on the same model as their barns. They worked hard on their stony soil and
read hard in their stony books of doctrine. Here is a stanza from their
favorite hymn:

> *Conceived in sin, O woeful state!*
> *Before we draw our breath,*
> *The first young pulse begins to beat*
> *Iniquity and death.*[33]

No deaf man has lived who has not encountered hypocrisy, but that of
these latter-day Puritans knew no bounds. Reverend Strong, for example,
engaged extensively in the distillery business while preaching temperance.
When his firm failed, the minister shut himself up in his house to avoid the
sheriff, who sought to serve him a writ, but on Sundays, when no writ could
be served, he sallied forth to preach before his congregation. It was said of
him that when in the pulpit it seemed he ought never to leave it and when
out of it that he ought never to go into it.[34] One of his characteristically
pointed remarks concerned a fellow divine, Reverend Flint, pastor of Hartford's Second Church of Christ, which had split off from Strong's congregation some decades earlier. At a church meeting someone had suggested that
it was hardly fitting for Strong, their pastor, to be engaged in the manufacture and sale of liquor. "Oh," said Strong, "we are all congregationalists in
the business working together. Brother Perkins here grows the grain, I distill
it, and Brother Flint drinks it."

Now, as Reverend Strong draws his eulogy sonorously to a close, Mason
nods his head and speaks. "My father's was a life of afflictions," he says.
"Some Christians fear for their salvation because their lives were blessed
with ease"—his eyes say he is speaking of his own fears—"but my father
had suffered so much at Christ's bidding that he dared believe in his election to eternal grace." It is true. James Cogswell had suffered greatly during
his long life. A member of the fourth generation of Cogswells in New
England, he had experienced religion when he was fifteen, a youth in Say-

brook, and was considered a very promising young man—a scholar, a good logician, a graceful speaker. When Canterbury Parish asked the president of Yale to recommend a minister, he said he knew none better than James. And indeed, at first the parish found him amiable, dignified in the pulpit, conciliatory in private, and they voted a call to settle him. He married Alice Fitch, descended from the famous hero of the Pequot war, James Mason, and took two pupils into his family, Naphthali Daggett and Benedict Arnold. (The former became president of Yale College, the latter, the brilliant Revolutionary general and then infamous traitor. The astonishing influence of the clergy in New England to this day is in good part explained by this practice of taking promising young men into their homes and fitting them for college.)

Alas, presently it became clear that James favored centralized church government, did not insist on the personal experience of conversion, and allowed unconverted sons and daughters of parishioners into the church; a segment of the congregation, a majority, walked out.[35] In the end, the Separatist movement was crushed in Canterbury as elsewhere, but James's congregation was greatly reduced and, unable to pay his salary, dismissed him.

Some Yale alumni put James up for the presidency of the college, but he was not selected, and the following year he was called to Scotland Parish, in Windham County, to replace their pastor, recently deceased.[36] In less than three months his wife, Alice, died in her forties, and her daughter followed her, only twenty-three. Then the youngest child, Septimus, died, age four. That left the oldest son, James, who was to become a surgeon in the Revolutionary Army; the second son, Sam, at Yale; and Mason at home. Mason's father, though suffering from headaches, luminous flashes, and loss of temper, troubled by his tendency to tell jokes and stories, harassed in money matters (the diminishing height of his woodpile was an accurate gauge of the diminishing love of his parishioners), and alarmed by the growth of infidelity, antifederalism, and the course of the revolution in France, nevertheless soon remarried. Martha Devotion, the widow of his predecessor at Scotland Parish, had a son in local politics and three daughters. One daughter, also named Martha, was married to Governor Huntington*—of course he was just a lawyer in those days—and Mason was sent off to Norwich to live with his family and be fitted for Yale.

It had to be Yale: it was nearby, Mason's father and two brothers had gone there, President Daggett was a friend of the family, and the school was an orthodox expression of religion in education. It was organized on the lines of the Trinity; three professors: divinity, mathematics, philosophy. Three

*Samuel Huntington, signer of the Declaration of Independence and governor of Connecticut, 1786–1796.

tutors. Three principles: industry, frugality, rectitude. Three shabby buildings on a barren common that the students called the Brick Prison. Mason
entered at fifteen and graduated valedictorian and youngest member of his
class in 1780.

When he left Yale, Mason joined his brother James at Stamford, where
he was examining surgeon of volunteers,[37] then went with him to New York
to pursue his training in surgery at Soldiers' Hospital. But a new set of
misfortunes soon befell the family. Mason's brother Sam lost his son to some
childhood disease,[38] and then died himself in an accident.[39] Two years later
his brother James died. The Reverend James Cogswell had now lost a wife
and four children, and only Mason remained. The next few years brought
still other bereavements. Mason's adoptive sister, James's stepdaughter, died
and the governor was not long in following her. The loss of her daughter
and son-in-law was too much for Martha Devotion to bear and James found
himself a widower again. He married a third time after a suitable delay—
one of his parishioners—and continued to preach despite failing voice and
a dwindling congregation that found his obstinacy and ill-temper offensive.
Of course he was ill-tempered; they would not hire an assistant for him in
his declining years, they would not allow him to retire with provision, finally
they would not even pay him. In the end, his last remaining son brought
him to Hartford to die. Mason reported that, on his father's last day, he
asked him, "Do you know me, father?" There was no response. Then the
son asked: "Do you know the Lord Jesus Christ?" The aged face brightened
with confidence, even joy, and the father replied: "I do know Him: He is
my God and my Savior."[40]

I found among Mason Cogswell's papers a diary he kept of a month's trip
from New York to Scotland Parish, where he joined his father's Thanksgiving Day table.[41] Along the way the reader encounters many of the important figures in Mason's life, who would also shape Alice's and my own, and
the diary reveals the kindness, sensitivity, and urbanity of its twenty-seven-
year-old author, so it takes its place in my narrative here. The first two pages
are missing and the third page starts "went to bed and slept luxuriously after
supping plenteously on sweetmeats and cream pompion pie,* and bridal
kisses." Evidently, he had been at a wedding.

Then comes a date, "Friday, 14th"—it was in fact November 14, 1788,
the bitter cold winter in which, across the Atlantic, Epée went without a
fire in his room so he could clothe the poor deaf in his charge: "Slept late
in the morning on account of the wedding—made several morning calls—
wished the bride more joy—got my horse shod and set out for Norwalk
where I made a cousinly visit." The next day, "Rode to Greenfield," he says,
"and breakfasted with Mr. Dwight." This is Timothy Dwight, the famous

*Pumpkin pie.

"pastor of Greenfield Hill" and grandson of the leading New England preacher Jonathan Edwards; he was soon to become president of Yale College, where we later met. "Stayed much longer than I had intended." It was well known that the charms of Dwight's conversation, like those of the Ancient Mariner, could hold even a wedding guest fast. Still, before the day is too advanced, Mason has been ferried across the Housatonic: "The last part of the ride," he says, "was solitary, as it was evening; but it was the better calculated for reflection."

The next morning, at New Haven, he attends divine service and "in the afternoon my old place of worship, the Chapel, was honored with my presence—where I was highly entertained with a sermon from Dr. Edwards, from these words: 'In the day thou eatest thereof, thou shalt surely die.' The discourse was accompanied with good music." Mason was a great music-lover, played the flute, and had led a church choir in Stamford, before moving to New York. "Spent the evening at Dr. Stiles's" (the current president of Yale).

Mason spends "Monday, 17th" visiting old friends, and on Tuesday he sets out for Hartford with a former schoolmate. There were no steamboats in those days, of course, no railroads, not even the Hartford Turnpike—so called from its turnstile of pikes every ten miles to ensure payment of the ten-cent toll—and the two young riders must make their way through North Haven and thence to Wallingford, where they spend the night. The next day they breakfast at Durham, dine at Middletown, and head due north along the Connecticut River Valley, some twenty miles across at Hartford, with its great fields of corn and tobacco. They reach Hartford about sunset. At the time it had about three hundred houses and some three thousand inhabitants, but it was a much more bustling center than these numbers imply, since it was the gateway to the upper Connecticut River Valley— flat-bottomed scows carried trade as far north as the Canadian border—and a staging and supply center for immigrants pushing westward.

"As soon as our horses were attended, we repaired to Col. Wadsworth's," Mason writes. Jeremiah Wadsworth was the richest and most influential man in Hartford, indeed in all of Connecticut. As a young businessman he had profited vastly by the trade with the West Indies, but his real wealth was acquired in his capacity as commissary-general of the Continental Army and of the French auxiliary army. Most Revolutionary officers were bankrupt, owing to the bankruptcy of the Continental treasury after the war, but Jeremiah had gone to France and presented his accounts to a government that could pay. His house occupied a full block between Prospect Street, where the Cogswells and Gallaudets later lived, and Main Street, the principal thoroughfare of Hartford, the site now of the Wadsworth Atheneum, America's first art museum.

In the diary, Mason describes Daniel Wadsworth, Colonel Wadsworth's son, a lifelong semi-invalid and dilettante who later became a member of the committee sponsoring Gallaudet's trip to Europe. "He is a strange youth. With his pockets full of money he had rather at any time sit down at home betwixt his two sisters and by some new act of tenderness call forth their affection toward him than to be in the *best* and most *fashionable* company at the gaming table, or at any place where he can spend his money in an *honorable* and *polite* way." Mason's underlining makes clear he is speaking tongue-in-cheek of fashion. " 'Tis true as it is strange, and furthermore he is warmly attached to the principles of virtue and morality, and really he is not ashamed of his God."

Mason arrives at his father's house in Scotland Parish two days later, at sunset. "The tear of pleasure glittered" in James Cogswell's eye as he embraced his son, and when the time for evening worship comes, the "old gentleman," as the journal tells us, "prayed with unusual fervency and affection."

After spending Thanksgiving and a few days following with his father, Mason rides to Norwich. "At about half past eight, I arrived at Gov. Huntington's, my former home, and the manner in which I was welcomed made it as much so as ever." Samuel Huntington was a man with swarthy complexion, a vivid and penetrating eye, moderate, circumspect, never angry or unkind, who put more emphasis on comfort and convenience in his home, to hear Mason tell it, than on splendor. The Huntingtons' warm hospitality had made their house a center of attraction for young people in Norwich —games in the parlor, dancing till curfew, and so on. I think it was this atmosphere during his formative years that gave Mason an uncommon measure of humanity for the son of an ascetic, cheerless New England preacher.

Mason's ten miles' ride that morning is not an excuse from Sunday worship and he "attended divine service both A.M. and P.M. and heard two metaphysical discourses from Mr. King; on the whole was well pleased with them—thought, however, he was a little out of his latitude." In the evening he makes a call at the home of Mr. Ward Woodbridge—a successful merchant who would also become a member of Gallaudet's sponsoring committee—where the two daughters of the household are as glad to see him as he is to see them and "paid more attention to me than to all the other gentlemen in the room."

I come now to the last two pages of the diary, which are torn. I can make out a social hour, a farewell at Colonel Wadsworth's, and the fact that Mason has been lodged the night at Reverend Strong's, where he "attended to Mrs. Strong's case" and had a long and friendly conversation—about settling in Hartford. The next day he makes his way to New Haven, and the last day, now mid-December, finds him again at Timothy Dwight's. There, he is "in the midst of a smiling circle" full of "cheerful and instructive" talk. There are four young ladies under Mr. Dwight's tuition: "the expression of each was uncommonly fine—a loveliness of disposition, a benevolence of heart, and a sprightliness of thought were discernible in every eye."[42]

The diary ends with this gracious appreciation of womanhood. Mason was not a disinterested observer, his journey being in some measure a quest for a companion, but it was ten years before he would meet the woman with whom he would share his life and love to his last day.[43] By the time of the dinner, they had been married seven years and had four children. I imagine Mary Cogswell signaling the Negro servant Lydia to bring the three eldest so they might be presented to the company. Lydia, sometimes called Lyd, was the daughter of an African tribal chieftain, and she had been a slave. Mason had met her at the boardinghouse where he lived when he moved to Hartford in 1789, and had cured her of lockjaw after several doctors had given up. When she died, after thirty years with the family, she left Mason's children the money she had saved and her heavy silver watch chain.[44]

The oldest Cogswell child, Mary, is only six, but her large dark-brown eyes are surely fixed on the company with the frankness and directness always to be found in her gaze. Later, she grew tall and dignified and became the mother of three young men herself. Two years younger is gentle Elizabeth, who seemed to live for the comfort and happiness of those she loved. With strangers she was always calm and reserved, with friends she was all enthusiasm and feeling. And finally, but two years old at the time, comes smiling, intelligent, animated Alice, such a child as the poet had in mind when he wrote, "heaven lies about us in our infancy."

The only son in the family, named after his father, is less than a year old and remains in the nursery; laughter-loving Catherine will come four years later.[45] Now here's a curious fact: I have outlived them all, parents and children, all but the last. I have watched the young grow into adults—or, rather, we shared those years, became friends, they learned my language, moved in my deaf circle, and suddenly they *were* adults. I have seen childhood reserve mature into studiousness and decline into self-absorption; childhood playfulness become youthful gaiety and then inconsequence; soft, fleshy skin draw firm then loosen again into pleats and jowls. Six times I have watched the gravediggers hollowing out a space in the loam and clay of the Connecticut River Valley and a Cogswell lowered into the ground. I am the record-keeper, the witness, though at one time I was also a participant. If my life has not yet ended, it must be—for no reason at all, or so I can tell this story.

Mason sat with Reverend Strong at many a deathbed. He also delivered many a baby; he was considered the best obstetrician in the state. Physician and minister were the two key professionals in every New England town, and Hartford, though larger than most, with four thousand inhabitants, was no exception. Thus Mason was widely known among the citizenry for his sympathy with the sick, and among the members of his profession for his skill. Said a colleague: "He performed all the great operations with inimitable dexterity and a coolness nothing could disturb."[46] Fellow surgeons marveled at his neatness and dispatch (I suppose accuracy was taken for granted). One reported his amputating a leg at the thigh in forty seconds.

In 1810 the Connecticut Medical Society conferred on Mason an honorary M.D. and two years later elected him its president; he was reelected ten times in succession. That same year Yale offered him the chair of obstetrics and surgery at its new school of medicine, but by then Mason had decided to found a school of his own, for deaf children, and felt he must stay in Hartford.[47] Some years after I arrived, Yale, too, awarded Mason the M.D.

At the dinner, as I imagine it, after the children have gone, Joel Barlow presents Mason with a gift: bound proofs of a collection of poems called The Echo, to which Mason was a contributor, the last publication, I believe, of the Hartford Wits.

The writing of the collection had begun, according to the preface, in "a moment of literary sportiveness at a time when pedantry, affectation and bombast pervaded most of the pieces published in the gazettes." The first piece, a parody of an inflated description of a thunderstorm, was originally published in 1791 in the American Mercury, which had been founded by Barlow only seven years before.[48] It caused a stir and the authors realized that they could aim their shafts at more worthy targets: what the preface calls "the hideous morality of revolutionary madness" spawned in France. Jefferson was called, as I remember, "the great sire of stories past belief" and his literary and scientific interests roundly ridiculed.[49] There were a score of pieces in all; when the Mercury became too democratic for the authors' tastes they published in the Courant instead.[50]

In addition to Barlow, the original four Wits included a physician, an aide to General George Washington, and a justice of the supreme court.[51] Mason was counted among the "Later Wits," who joined after the War of Independence. The president of Yale, Timothy Dwight, and his brother Theodore, a publisher, were in their number, as were a future governor and two linguists.[52]

The Wits have held my attention because I find in them the key to much of Mason Cogswell's character.[53] They were the minority to which he belonged—a rich, powerful minority to be sure, but one that was well on the way to being overwhelmed by the time I arrived. Of Puritan ancestry and rearing, with all the Puritan's earnest devotion to intellect, they exercised learned or genteel professions. They were fond of good food and drink, the arts, politics. Of course, they were conservative. That is, Federalist. They wanted a strong central government, encouragement of commerce, attention to the needs of merchants and landholders, and a well-ordered society. They distrusted the capacity of most people to govern themselves except through the guidance and authority of the superior classes, and their paternalism extended to the deaf, who were inferior in their eyes because of their poverty, lack of education, and lack of hearing.

It was not long after the dinner I have imagined that the light in Alice Cogswell's beautiful hazel eyes flickered and nearly went out. When she recovered from the spotted fever, her father said, she could not hear her mother's sobs, nor his prayers at her bedside, nor her sisters playing outside her window. For a little while her speech persisted: "Mommy cry," she said, and "ol' Lyd."[54] But then, as the vivid landscape in her window paled with the coming of winter, and all the riot of color drained out of the trees with the running sap, so her speech was drawn off and she was shrouded in silence.

"I cried, 'My God, why hast Thou forsaken me?'" Mason said. "And Reverend Strong reproved me: 'Are you then blameless?' And I thought, 'No, but what have I done to deserve such condemnation from my Maker?' I cried, too, from rage at my own impotence; I had liberated so many other children from illness and could do nothing for my own."

"I awoke one morning," Alice told me years later, "remarked the utter stillness and fell back to sleep. A long time passed; occasionally, I would half-awaken and see in a dense fog a jumbled form in the doorway or, as if through muslin, my mother's familiar face hovering over me. Always there was quiet. My father had a chaise drawn by the family horse, 'old Bob.' One day I saw them approach from my window but though the wheels turned they did not squeal, the carriage advanced without a rattle, old Bob's hooves struck the ground silently and steam rose from his nostrils when he whinnied—again, without a sound. I think it was then I realized, vaguely, that nothing seemed to sound anymore. I was a child of two and a half—I did not understand what that might mean. I simply accepted it. Time passed, I recovered, but my speech and hearing did not." Of the following months she recalled little except the various tortures to which she was subjected by doctors, including her father. They poured salt water into her ears, and oil of cream. They bled her, leeched her, physicked her, and finally gave way to despair. Some years later they brought her an ear trumpet, with which she could hear the church bell but little more.[55]

The worst was yet to come. It became painfully evident to Mason (and to the Gallaudets, for their son Theodore was Alice's age) that Alice's mind was not developing normally. Although she was in the midst of a highly cultivated society she understood little that went on around her. Her two older sisters learned the signs she gradually developed and introduced a few of their own. Mason and Mary learned some, too, and made awkward efforts at expressive pantomime; they no doubt brought the art to new heights among the normally stolid Puritans but at such a cost of energy and devotion that only the most essential messages (and the most insignificant ones) were communicated.

THE GALLAUDET GARDEN, 1813. Theodore Gallaudet, eight, comes running around the side of the house (he's the fox) with brother Edward and three Cogswells—Mason, Alice, and Elizabeth, six, eight, and ten (the hounds)—in hot pursuit.[56] Thomas Hopkins Gallaudet, home from studies at Andover Theological Seminary, stands under an elm tree watching Alice. What he beholds is a disabled hearing child, not a healthy deaf one, a child who needs a new language in which to learn about the world, grasp the thoughts of others and share her own. Not yet understanding such matters, the young theology student decides to teach her to spell H-A-T.

Thomas was not tall—five and a half feet—and there was something frail, even womanly, about his bearing. He had a placid oval face with darkish complexion and expressive dark gray eyes that rolled at you over his spectacles. His nose was straight, his lips large, and his teeth and gums visible when he spoke. His voice was soft and his manner unprepossessing.[57] But what a gift he had for communication! He had a natural talent for pantomime, and could convey even complex ideas by facial expression alone. Once when Colonel John Trumbull* was visiting the American Asylum, Thomas asked him to select any historical event that would make a striking canvas and offered to communicate it solely by expression and posture to a pupil, admittedly one who was particularly apt. This pupil—George Loring, I think it was, who went on to become a deaf educator himself—was not only intelligent but expressive. The play of his features showed clearly whether he was following at each moment or not.

Trumbull said: "Tell him that Brutus (Lucius Junius) condemned his two sons to death for resisting his authority and violating his orders." Now it was understood that the chosen event could come from any portion of history, sacred or profane, ancient or modern, but must be previously known to the pupil, as it was in this case. Gallaudet folded his arms to keep himself from signing and gazed eastward while undulating his head, as if looking across and beyond the Atlantic Ocean, to denote that the event happened on the Eastern Continent. This took the subject out of the range of American history, at least. Then he rolled his eyes upward and backward and leaned his head backward, as if looking far back in time past to denote that the event was of quite ancient date. He then conveyed the aquiline nose of the Romans by stretching and centering the remarkably supple muscles of his face.

By his countenance, attitude, and manner he conveyed an individual of high authority, commanding others whom he expected to obey him. Then

*(1756–1843), distinguished portrait painter (called "Colonel" Trumbull by his contemporaries).

ALICE COGSWELL AND THOMAS HOPKINS GALLAUDET
(STATUE BY DANIEL CHESTER FRENCH)

he appeared to be giving an order to many persons and threatening punishment to those who might resist—even the punishment of death. Next, to indicate a lapse of time, he portrayed sleeping during the night and waking in the morning, several times over. Then he looked with deep interest and surprise as if at a single person brought before him and his face showed fury at the violation of his order. Then looking at another guilty person near him, he denoted two offenders.

Exhibiting grave deliberation, then hesitation accompanied with strong conflicting emotions—he knows not what to feel or what to do. Looking at one of the persons and then the other as a father would look—he is a distressed parent. His bearing alternated repeatedly between the inflexible commander and the loving father. At length, the father yields, and the stern principle of justice as expressed in his countenance and manner prevails. His look and action denote the passing of the sentence of death on the offenders and ordering them away to execution. The pupil had been impatient for some time to show he understood; given leave, he wrote on his slate a complete account of the story of Brutus and his two sons.

Gallaudet repeated this feat on several occasions: on one, he was Noah building his ark; on another, Abraham sacrificing his son; on a third, Washington entering Trenton. And so on. So gifted was he at facial expression that he contrived a facespelling alphabet to replace the fingerspelled alphabet: *a* was denoted by awe, *b* by boldness, *c* by curiosity, *d* by despair, and so forth. Despair, eagerness, awe, and fear spelled *deaf*. [58]

Now Thomas's skills developed with experience, but they were augured the day he decided to teach Alice to write *H-A-T*. I imagine him dressed as New England men did early in this century: the tall stovepipe hat had replaced the broad brim and men wore tighter-fitting clothes with pantaloons instead of breeches, a frilled shirtfront, and a black long-tailed coat. Hats are playthings for children and I can easily picture Alice, wearing a full ruffled dress, long blond curls surrounding her cherubic face, holding Thomas's hat, trying it on, while Thomas fetches a stick to write the letters in the dirt.

Where does the magic of belief in youth, of love for youth, of thorough and undying sympathy with the hearts of youth that Thomas had, where does it come from, how is it nourished? He whom Thomas admired most possessed it, too: "a little child shall lead them." Thomas had a spirit purified by physical weakness and delicacy of health. He had a distrust of self and a full trust in God. He came from a home in which piety and study were valued. So much so, indeed, that he spent only two years in preparing for college before entering the sophomore class at Yale. He was to graduate with highest honors before he was eighteen, the youngest in his class,[59] and was one of six to give a commencement oration, which I found among his papers. It is written in the clear, well-rounded hand he retained all his life, and was carefully enveloped in a cover of marble paper secured with a pink-and-white ribbon—neatness and order he retained lifelong as well. Its title is equally reflective of his character: "The Increase in Luxury in Connecticut and Its Destructive Consequences."[60]

In the autumn following graduation, Thomas entered upon the study of law in the firm of the Honorable Chauncy Goodrich, who later became mayor of Hartford and deputy-governor, but I suspect he was uninspired, for at the close of his first year there he resigned and returned to Yale.[61] For the next two years, he read English literature and wrote; he kept a little notebook of "Prayers, Meditations, and Reflections" that makes it clear he was much preoccupied with personal religion: with skepticism, temptation, and the struggle for faith. His New Year's resolutions for 1808 included: to pray morning, noon, and night in private; to be kinder to his parents and brothers and sisters; to be less indolent, less self-indulgent with food and drink. His Master's oration, delivered in the fall of 1808, *On Ambition as a Motive in Education*, spurned the love of praise in favor of Christian humility.[62] Shortly after delivering it, he accepted a position as tutor at Yale.

The struggles within Thomas's Puritan soul became increasingly acute: "I know that I am walking in the way that leads to eternal perdition," he wrote at the end of 1808; and the following spring, with health and spirits enfeebled: "If He should see fit to restore me to health and strength of body and a capability of studying, I will devote myself to the ministry of the Gospel."

The fall of 1810 arrived without the improvement of health and spirits he so dearly desired, and Thomas decided to pursue some trade that would keep him in the open air and prove less demanding for his eyes and his mind: he became a Yankee trader. It was the heyday of the tin peddler with his pack filled with tinware, pins, needles, scissors, combs, children's books, cotton stuffs. As many as thirty might originate in a single town and fan out over the South and West. Thomas accepted a commission from a New York commercial house and traveled through Ohio and Kentucky on horseback. He returned in much improved health, and, determined to start a career in business, he took a job as a clerk.[63]

It soon became apparent, however, that Thomas was no more suited to business than to law, and we find him next, in 1812, enrolled at Andover Theological Seminary. He wants to preach and to spend his life in the service of his fellow man, but the specific field of endeavor is unknown. Then, midway through his two-year course, the man and the cause meet as Thomas scratches the letters *H-A-T* on the ground while Alice looks on in puzzlement. To show that the two go together, he places the hat on the ground next to the word and points to them alternately over and over while imitating the action of donning his hat. Alice seems to understand. To test her, Thomas rubs out the letters with his shoe and scratches them again a few feet away. Alice picks up the hat and places it on its new label.

Thomas runs, overjoyed, to the Cogswell home to announce his success.

Whether Thomas really taught Alice anything on this occasion does not matter. What does is that he began to take a consuming interest in deafness, and induced Mason to enroll Alice in the school to be opened by the poetess Lydia Huntley Sigourney.[64]

HARTFORD, 1814. ALICE AT LYDIA SIGOURNEY'S SCHOOL. In front of the class, a diminutive lady with flaxen curls, only twenty-three but on her way to becoming the most popular poetess in America ever. Her first published work, written in 1815, was entitled *Moral Pieces in Prose and Verse;* the last was a book of "educational remembrances," *Letters of Life,* which came out after her death four years ago: between the two she wrote two thousand contributions to periodicals and fifty volumes of verse, essays, travel pieces, fiction. She was flattered by Poe and patronized by Whittier; she was translated into many languages, met Queen Victoria, received gifts from the rulers of Prussia and France. Oh, she had her critics: Jane Carlyle* described her visitor as "beplastered with rouge and pomatum—bare-necked at an age which left certainty far behind—with long ringlets that never grew where they hung . . . all glistening in black satin as if she were an apothecary's *puff* for black sticking plaster and staring her eyes out to give them animation."[65] Asked to write an entry on her for *Female Poets of America,* Horace Greeley complained to the editor: "I shall try to plaster over Mrs. Sigourney but you know how bad the job is. As it won't do to say a word of her *real* history, how will it be possible to say anything?"[66]

I will come to her real history. Now the dozen or so girls in the class are bent over their composition books; Alice carries hers up to Lydia, flags her attention, and hands her the book, signing TEACH-ME. Once when she did this, her teacher responded with a "poetic effusion," as she liked to call her verses.[67] (Alice called them SHORT-LINES.) The poem is addressed to a friend whom she had intended to meet after school but . . .

> Slate and books and maps appear,
> And many a dear one cries,
> "Please tell us whence that river sprang,
> And where these mountains rise,
> And when that blind, old monarch reign'd,
> And who was king before,
> And stay a little after five,
> And tell us something more."
> And then our darling Alice comes,
> And who unmov'd can view

*English woman of letters (1801–1866), wife of Thomas Carlyle.

The glance of that imploring eye,
"Oh! teach me something, too. . . ."

Alice's book is open to an alphabetical list of words . . . congress, constitution, cotton, Cuba . . . that have come up during the history lessons. Lydia places a chair for Alice next to her desk facing the pupils—she will first conduct the weekly examination, a favorite exercise with the class. "KING EAT STUPID TOO-MUCH EELS, WHO?" Alice signs and all hands go up. "Nancy?" "Which king ate too many eels—Henry II!" "Very good." And so on. "If only you could have seen the play of naïveté, irony, and love that would radiate from Alice's beautiful eyes on these occasions," Lydia once told me.

After Alice had tested the other students, her teacher tested *her* by pointing to words in her composition book for Alice to define. This she would do with descriptions, definitions, or little stories—historical, biographical, scriptural—that she had learned related to each word. Her recitation was a mixture of her own home sign, pantomime, and fingerspelling with the two-handed British manual alphabet, which she had learned I know not where. The other pupils (all hearing) had learned the alphabet and many of her signs, and they would translate her answers as she went along (which no doubt aided the teacher as well). This is all quite charming as a supplement to education, which it was for the hearing children, but it was no substitute for the education that Alice needed. Lydia said Alice was a genius in perceptiveness, imagination, intellect, and the desire for knowledge. So she must have been to learn much under these circumstances.

Perhaps six months after school began, in the winter of 1815, Alice produced her first literary effort—at least, the first I can find. The pupils were writing letters to the teacher and Alice would not be satisfied until she, too, could be Lydia's correspondent. Her topics for this letter were the illumination on the return of peace,* Lydia's lack of family, and her lessons in history and geography. (As she wrote, Napoleon was leaving Elba for Paris and Sicard, Massieu, and I were leaving Paris for London.)

"The world—all peace.—Now am I glad.—Many candles in windows.—
Shine bright on snow.—Houses most beautiful.—Friends at my home
that night, and one baby.
"Sorry is Alice—you have no brother—no sister.—My sisters, three,—my
brothers, one.—They are beautiful.—Sorry am I you never had any.—
My father and my mother.—Much I love all.
"Girls, fifteen in school.—You teach.—You write, and give letters.—

---

*When the Senate formally ended the War of 1812, by ratifying the Treaty of Ghent in 1815, a relieved populace placed candles in their windows.

Cleopatra I learn—great queen face very handsome—say to maid,—
bring basket—figs—asp bite arm—swell—die.
"Xerxes, proud king—very many soldiers—go to fight Greeks—come
back creeping—many men killed.
"Zones, five;—one warm, all people faint; two very cold—two half hot,
half cold—temperate."[68]

The "Sweet Singer of Hartford," as Lydia was called, was fascinated—
even obsessed—with the blind, the deaf, and the dumb as subjects of poetry and objects of charity. She corresponded with Dr. Samuel Gridley
Howe, head of the institution for the blind in Boston, and contributed to
the keep of Julia Brace, a deaf, dumb, and blind girl who spent her adult
life at our school. She wrote a poem, "The Marriage of the Deaf and
Dumb," beginning "No word! no sound! But yet a solemn rite /
Proceedeth through the festive lighted hall,"[69] and another called "Prayers of the Deaf and Dumb."[70]

In Lydia's posthumous Letters of Life there is this poem about Alice,
whose "look of bliss" is offered as the answer to a question put to Massieu
and me in London: Are the deaf and dumb unhappy? Lydia's reply, addressed to Alice:[71]

> Oh, could the kind inquirer gaze
> Upon thy brow with gladness fraught,
> Its smile, like inspiration's rays,
> Would give the answer to his thought.
>
> And could he see thy sportive grace
> Soft blending with submission due,
> And note thy bosom's tenderness
> To every just emotion true;
>
> Or, when some new idea glows
> On the pure altar of the mind,
> Behold the exulting tear that flows,
> In silent ecstasy refined;
>
> Thine active life, thy look of bliss,
> The sparkling of thy magic eye,
> Would all his skeptic doubts dismiss
> And bid him lay his pity by . . .

I suppose lavish sentimentality may be excused a poetess who lived in an
age that valued it so highly, but what I do not excuse is her idealizing the
condition of the deaf. Placing them above all other men (or Alice above all

other women) in purity and beauty sets the deaf apart as surely as a refusal to communicate with them.

Lydia's critics did not see an innocent foible in her preposterously romantic descriptions of her childhood, her family, and herself, but rather thought it self-serving hypocrisy; I feel the same about her "effusions" on the deaf. Let me explain. The facts were that the "court of shorn velvet intersected by two paved avenues" at the house where Lydia claimed to have grown up was perhaps twelve feet in length and she was the daughter of the gardener, not the owner, and never occupied the "suites of rooms" she glowingly described. The fact was that the image promulgated of a loving wife nestled by the family hearth, pouring forth her effusions in a moment's respite from a mother's labors, was false. There was no love between her and her desiccated merchant husband and she despised his daughters by a prior marriage. In vain she repeatedly asked him for a separation. He upbraided her in a letter I have seen for "her lust of praise, which like the appetite of the cormorant is not to be satisfied," for her "apparently unconquerable passion of displaying herself."[72] Her only son, Andrew, turned violently against her before dying of consumption.

These terrible realities—low birth, unhappy marriage, frustrated motherhood—drove her to new heights of fantasizing. Lydia loved Alice partly because the child's isolation corresponded to her own. Turned in on herself, forswearing men and the world, feasting on her own sensibility, the poetess tried desperately to represent that isolation yielded richness of inner experience for Alice and for herself. The deaf and dumb, like the dead, commune directly with God, needing no language. Their isolation is ennobling, like that of the poetess.[73] This is self-love in disguise, and *that* is using deaf people for one's own ends. Beware the myth of nobility as you beware the myth of deviance. Deaf Joseph, who was really the wronged count of Solar all along—youth, purity, honesty, nobility personified. To arouse sympathy, he must be a pure victim of injustice; hence he must be pure. Deaf Alice, "a tear of exquisite feeling glistening in her eye," because her "peculiar misfortune opened for her new avenues to tenderness and sympathy"[74] —so said Lydia. Where in literature are the deaf seen truly, with deafness just one condition of their lives, acting in concert with deaf and hearing people, not living as isolates?

Mason had not stood idly by until the opportunity afforded by Lydia Sigourney's school presented itself in the fall of 1814. Concerned with his daughter's slowed development he had, three years earlier, conceived some grand designs befitting a loving parent, a great physician, and a New England Puritan.

Mason loved books; he had probably the best personal library in the state and it was his practice to spend several hours every evening quietly reading.

He obtained a copy of Francis Green's description of Braidwood's academy in Edinburgh, published in London in 1783. He also bought the translation of Epée's major work, which Green had prepared after his change of heart in favor of sign and published in London in 1801, the *Method of Educating the Deaf and Dumb Confirmed by Long Experience.*[75] Both works held the promise of restoring speech where it had been lost and Epée's opened the astonishing vista of an alternate means of communicating with, and hence educating, the deaf. To his everlasting glory, Mason's first instinct was not to hire a teacher to educate Alice following one or another scheme, but rather, like Epée, to seek a social solution, to help the deaf as a class. He saw at once that the great challenge was not to make Alice speak but to find a way to educate all the Alices of the new nation.

He had little doubt that there was a social need, although it might be difficult to determine its character and dimensions. The deaf were scattered and outcast, not highly visible. Alice had no deaf friends. Yet he had heard of the Gilbert family in Hebron, with a dozen or so children, half of them deaf and dumb. Sylvester Gilbert was a lawyer and the town clerk, and had served with Samuel Huntington on the second electoral college from Connecticut.[76] There must be other such families.

In June 1811—Alice was not quite six—Mason wrote to Reverend Abel Flint, the bibulous pastor of the other Congregational church in Hartford, asking him to persuade the General Association of Congregational ministers in Connecticut, of which he was the treasurer, to conduct a census of the deaf. "How many there are . . . of what age, of what sex, whether they were born so or became so by disease . . . I make this request in behalf of Mr. Gilbert and myself."[77] The association agreed to make the necessary inquiries before their next annual meeting.[78]

Then, two months before the meeting of the association, Mason happened on a remarkably timely notice in the evening newspaper. The errant grandson of Thomas Braidwood, who had fled his post as director of Braidwood's academy in Edinburgh as his creditors closed in, was now in Washington and was planning to pursue his profession of instructing the deaf. Unaware of Braidwood's unsavory past, Mason saw an act of Providence in his coming to America just as the need for a special instructor to create a school was becoming apparent. He wrote to him the next morning.

"You may be surprised to receive the address of a stranger, who has no other knowledge of you except what he obtained from a paragraph in the *National Intelligencer.* . . . I have a daughter, who belongs to the class of unfortunate beings which has claimed so much of your solicitude and attention. . . . Since her sickness I have felt the importance of establishing a school for the instruction of the deaf and dumb. . . . Allow me, Sir, to inquire if you have determined on the favored spot which shall be the theater of your future labors? Or whether you intend visiting the various

States, before you fix upon any place in which to commence your benevolent work?"[79]

Meanwhile, however, Colonel William Bolling, of Goochland County, Virginia, whose brothers and sister had attended Braidwood's academy with Francis Green's son Charles, had likewise learned of John Braidwood's arrival in Washington and had written at once to invite him to his home with a view also to aiding him in his future plans. Colonel Bolling had a deaf son and a deaf daughter and was loath to send them overseas. Braidwood went to Bolling Hall, described the American branch of the family enterprise that he would soon open in Baltimore, invited Colonel Bolling to join the other sponsoring parents, and received a six-hundred-dollar deposit toward the tuition of the colonel's son. They parted with the understanding that Braidwood would keep the colonel informed on the progress of the school and let him know when to bring his son to Baltimore, presumably the first of July. Soon after, Mason's letter arrived, but by then Braidwood, as Colonel Bolling later testified, was on a spending and drinking spree, moving in high style from Washington to Baltimore to Philadelphia until the colonel's deposit ran out (there were no other sponsoring parents—that was a lie) and a substantial debt was incurred. Braidwood fled to New York, where he was pursued, arrested for debt, and put in jail. Thus Mason (fortunately for Alice and all the American deaf) received no reply to his letter.[80]

The General Association met in June and heard the census results: eighty-four deaf and dumb had been counted in Connecticut. Mason then estimated that there must be some four hundred in New England and two thousand in the United States. Of course, only a much smaller number were of school age and fewer yet could attend a school in Hartford, even if the costs were subsidized. Still, an American asylum for the deaf was clearly needed!

I do not know why Mason let several years pass before acting decisively on this information but, for one thing, the opinion that there might be enough deaf people in the United States to warrant opening a school was widely considered extravagant. Few people could recall having met more than one or two deaf people, and it strained credulity to hear talk of thousands. For another, I suspect Mason was waiting for Thomas to finish theological seminary. Among Thomas's papers are letters from Andover schoolmates adverting to his interest in the deaf.[81] And among Mason's I found a letter from a wealthy parent of a deaf child to whom Gallaudet had written while in seminary, asking whether the father would contribute to sending someone abroad to learn methods of educating the deaf.[82] Thomas was graduated from Andover just as Alice was enrolled in Lydia Sigourney's new school, in the fall of 1814. In the ensuing winter, Thomas devoted much of his time to instructing Alice.

The following spring, Mason assembled a group of sponsors in his home. First, General Nathaniel Terry, a prominent Hartford citizen, later mayor, who (gossip had it) was so quick-tempered he could fell a man to earth without stopping to think, but was often accompanied on the street by a flock of children, who knew only the sunny side of his nature.[83] Then there was Terry's brother-in-law, Daniel Wadsworth, since his father's death, Connecticut's sole millionaire. A fragile man with an exaggerated dread of drafts, he arrived at the meeting, Thomas told me, in a big yellow coach in which he had installed a stove and a smokestack.[84] Only five people in Hartford were rich enough to have coaches and three of them were at this meeting: Terry, and Wadsworth, and the merchant Ward Woodbridge.[85] There were four other prominent businessmen, as well as Reverend Strong, who opened the meeting with a prayer, and Thomas and Mason. After considerable discussion, the group agreed to seek a competent person who would be sent overseas to learn European methods of educating the deaf, thence to return to direct a school they would found in Hartford. "If it is our duty to instill divine truth in the minds of children as soon as they are able to receive it; if we are bound by the injunction of Christ to convey the glad news of salvation to every creature under heaven, then we fail to obey this injunction if we neglect to make His name known to the poor deaf and dumb."[86]

Mason Cogswell and Ward Woodbridge were appointed a committee to find a suitable teacher and to raise subscriptions to meet the expense of the trip. Gallaudet was everyone's first choice and within a week he formally assented.[87] Sufficient funds were as quickly raised. Three weeks later, Thomas was packed and ready to go; equipped with a few letters of introduction, he planned to spend some weeks, or months if need be, observing methods of instruction at the London Asylum for the Deaf and Dumb, directed by Joseph Watson, Braidwood's nephew. Thomas made his way to New York and obtained passage on the *Mexico* (destination, Liverpool).

Bad weather delayed the ship's departure and Thomas made several valuable contacts among the passengers that yielded letters of introduction "of the very first value, to friends of respectability in Liverpool and London."[88] He also met a man and his deaf son, "who had been deaf for ten years and converses principally with his fingers using nearly our alphabet." All these contacts and letters "dropped into my hands without seeking," Thomas wrote. " 'Trust in the Lord with all thine heart and lean not to thine own understanding.' "

Five days and the ship had not budged from port. Thomas had a presentiment of difficulties to come: "I have such a constant conception of the mutability and uncertainty of earthly things," he wrote in a letter to Mason, "that I go forward resolved, with God's help, to do my duty, yet, all the while deeming it not a very improbable event that for some mysterious tho' wise purpose, He may perhaps cast a deep, tho' I trust only temporary, shade over our favorite undertaking."

Thomas also wrote to nine-year-old Alice: "In a few days I shall go into the ship. If God keeps me from all danger, I shall be in England in a few weeks. You must not forget what you told me you would do every morning and evening. Pray to God that he will keep me alive and safe and bring me back again to Hartford. Pray to him to blot out all your past sins, all that you have done wrong, all that you have thought wrong, all that you have felt wrong. . . . I hope when I come back to teach you much about the Bible, and about God, and Christ, and the world where we shall all be after we die. I hope God will keep you alive till I come back but if He should take your soul into the other world, I pray him to receive you into heaven, where you may be always good and happy."[89]

A month later, Thomas was in Liverpool. There he visited the school for the blind and then made his way to London through the verdant June countryside. "It has a delicacy and grace," he wrote, "that surpasses anything of the kind in our country."[90] At Leicester, about mid-course, he visited a famous divine; in Birmingham he visited the school for the deaf. In a decade it would be directed by a disciple of the abbé de l'Epée, but when Thomas arrived it had only recently been opened with a grandson and namesake of Thomas Braidwood as instructor and twenty pupils.[91] Braidwood, whose brother was then in jail in New York, suggested that Gallaudet also visit the small Braidwood school at Hackney, near London, which had moved there from Edinburgh and was now run by his widowed mother.[92] The next day Thomas traveled to Oxford and the day after arrived in London.

It is said that Mr. Webster remarked while in London that his constant and predominant feeling was that of wonder at its enormous extent: fourteen thousand streets, two hundred thousand houses, fifteen hundred places of public worship, three millions of human beings—all crowded within the space of seven miles square.[93] Gallaudet was aghast at the poverty and vice: in a letter to Daniel Wadsworth he mused on the good that would have been done if part of the vast sum expended on Saint Paul's needless expanse had been devoted instead to the relief of the thirty thousand beggars thronging the city streets.[94]

THE CITY TAVERN, LONDON, THE SECOND MONDAY IN JULY 1815. The trustees of the London Asylum for the Deaf and Dumb, led by the Reverend John Townsend, have adjourned their meeting in the committee room and are mounting the sweeping staircase to the second-floor ballroom, where a meeting of the subscribers to the fund for the asylum awaits them to hear their report and to vote on the admission of new applicants.[95] Only sixteen charity cases can be taken but seventy-three applicants line the stairs. As the committee in velvet cloaks and ruffles press their advance, shabbily clad parents push their children in the way, imploring their attention. Those who can speak cry, "Sir, sir!" Those who cannot just wave the tickets that give the details of their circumstances and their claim on charity.

The doors to the ballroom open, revealing His Royal Highness, the duke of Gloucester, patron of the asylum, in the chair, flanked by the marquis of Buckingham, president, and Mr. Wilberforce and others, vice-presidents. The president proposes the health of the patron and speaks at length on the benefits conferred on the community—indeed, on all mankind—by the patronage of His Royal Highness to an institution such as this, where human beings are rescued from a condition too painful to contemplate. His Royal Highness, in returning thanks, contrasts the condition of the taught and the untaught deaf and dumb. Forty pupils are then presented who exhibit specimens of their writing, arithmetic, and speech, leaving no doubt, in the words of the president, that they have been raised by education from mere automata to the condition of intelligent, moral, and religious beings. On the bishop of Oxford's health being drunk, His Lordship congratulates the friends of humanity on participating in the refined pleasure of relieving such objects of compassion. The president describes the particulars of sixteen such objects in most affecting terms and the body votes the slate for admission. Contributions amounting to seven hundred pounds are received.

Thomas is there at Reverend Townsend's suggestion. The Friday before, he had gone to see him, armed with letters of introduction from fellow pastors in New York and Liverpool, to explain the reason for his voyage. "He expressed an active willingness to do everything in his power to promote my full access to the asylum but spoke of certain difficulties," Thomas wrote.[96] In particular Dr. Watson required assurances that Thomas would not use what he learned for profit in England, and that he would devote enough effort and time to do credit to Dr. Watson's name. At the tavern, Thomas sends in to the committee room a paper he has drawn up "setting forth the importance of a school for the deaf and dumb in New England," accompanied by numerous letters of recommendation from Hartford and London. Shortly, he has a response. "They appointed a [sub]committee to confer with the teacher, Mr. Watson," Thomas wrote to Mason the next day "and in a few days, I shall know the result. It will, I doubt not, be favorable."[97]

Since he kept a diary in London, Thomas himself can describe what followed his application to the London Asylum, beginning with his meeting the abbé Sicard, who was, quite fortuitously, in the capital at the same time.[98]

"Saturday, July 8th, I visited the secretary of the abbé Sicard, Mr. Sievrac, and introduced myself to him. He was in a room with the abbé and two of his pupils, Massieu and Clerc. Mr. Townsend made the secretary acquainted

with my object in visiting Europe and also showed him some of my credentials. He immediately said that every facility would be granted me at Paris,
that I could regularly attend the school of the deaf and dumb, and also see
the private instruction of the abbé who devotes a portion of his time to
those who wish to acquire his art, for the sake of using it in their country.
He afterwards introduced me to the abbé who confirmed all that his secretary had told me. It is the abbé's secretary who is his interpreter. From him,
I received a ticket which gives me gratuitous access to all the remaining
lectures of the abbé during his residence in London.

"Monday 10th, at two o'clock I went to the abbé Sicard's lecture in the
Argyle room. His lecture, which was in French, lasted more than an hour.
Afterward there was an exhibition of the talents and acquirements of his
pupils, Massieu and Clerc. Many questions were put to them by the company, which they answered with great dispatch and propriety [with chalk on
two large blackboards].[99] The bishop of London was present as were several
of the nobility, among whom was the duchess of Wellington. Among other
questions, the following was put [in French]: 'What is education?' Clerc
replied, 'Education is the care which is taken to cultivate the minds of
youths, to elevate their hearts and to give them the knowledge of the
sciences and of that which is necessary to teach them to conduct themselves
well in the world.'

"Wednesday, 26th. In the forenoon I went with the Reverend Mr. Townsend to the manufacturing establishment of the asylum for the deaf and
dumb, where I saw several of these unfortunates, in different apartments,
engaged in shoemaking, tailoring, and printing. We afterwards proceeded to
the asylum, where I was introduced to Dr. Watson. I spent a little while
in his school.

"His pupils, both male and female, were all in one large room and appeared to be industriously employed under the care of several assistants. Mr.
Townsend, Dr. Watson and myself afterward returned to the committee
room, where [Watson stated] some difficulties which stood in the way of my
having access to his school. These, so far as I could understand them, appeared to arise from the apprehension that I might not be willing to devote
the necessary time and patience to the acquisition of the art, and that some
of his pupils, or rather his assistants, might take offense at seeing a stranger
receive the benefits of the establishment in so much shorter a period of time
than had been required of them. He mentioned that four or five years was
the customary length of time which his students devoted to his school, and
that those who became qualified as instructors received their knowledge and
skill, not so much from any private instruction or lectures of his own, as
from taking charge of an uninstructed pupil and conducting him regularly
through the several stages of his improvement. And I rather inferred, from
what he said, that he thought it would be required of me to pursue this

course. He distinctly disclaimed any intention of receiving a pecuniary remuneration for any assistance which his school might afford me.

"On my part, I observed that my motive [was] benevolence and not individual gain or emolument; . . . that I was willing to place myself under his complete care and trust and discretion for six weeks or two months [so he could judge] the time it might be necessary for me to spend at his school; [but] that I wished for a conclusive answer to my request as soon as convenient, as my expenses were considerable and their increase was diminishing the fund in America which could afford relief . . . to the unfortunate deaf and dumb of which we had great numbers in our country.

"Friday, 28th. This morning I visited the asylum, and by Dr. Watson's invitation, spent an hour among his pupils. I was much gratified with the proficiency which many of them appeared to have made. Among other questions which I proposed to one of the boys who appeared to be about sixteen years of age, was the following: 'What do you think of the Son of God, Jesus Christ?' He wrote on his slate without the least hesitancy, 'I think his Son, Jesus Christ, is the friend of all penitential sinners ("and," this conjunction he omitted, but I inserted it and he assented to the correctness of so doing) and deserves to be adored and loved for his great kindness.'

. . . Before I left the Asylum I had a few minutes' conversation with Dr. Watson on the subject of my admission into his school. He alluded to Mr. Braidwood, grandson of the original teacher of the deaf and dumb at Edinburgh, being in America and suggested the expediency of his being some way or other employed in the asylum in Connecticut. To this suggestion, of course, I gave no assent. [Colonel Bolling had advanced John Braidwood another six hundred dollars to pay his way out of jail in New York, and in repayment Braidwood had agreed to move into his sponsor's Virginia home to tutor his two deaf children. By the time of Dr. Watson's suggestion to Gallaudet, however, Braidwood had fallen into his former ways. Under renewed threat of debtor's prison, he slipped off into the night, to reappear shortly in New York attempting once more to start a school.[100]]

"Friday, August 11th. This morning I received a [report from the] chairman of the subcommittee:

" 'Resolved, That after mature deliberation, taking into view the due discipline of the asylum, and the proper time required to qualify an effective instructor of the deaf and dumb: The auditors, in conjunction with Dr. Watson, beg to recommend the committee to allow Mr. Gallaudet to be received into the asylum for one month upon liking, with the view that on the expiration of that period he shall be engaged as an assistant for three years on the usual terms with power to Dr. Watson to release him from his engagement sooner if it should appear that Mr. Gallaudet is qualified before the end of that time.'

"During the day I consulted with three judicious friends [who] unanimously gave it as their opinion, that I ought not to accept such terms and advised me to make application to the Asylum for the Deaf and Dumb at Edinburgh.

"Saturday, 12th. I called on Mr. Parnell, one of the subcommittee, [and] informed him that I thought the conditions stated in the report placed me too much in the power of Dr. Watson inasmuch as the duty of an assistant, if I rightly understood it, was to conduct the pupils step by step through their several gradations of improvement, which of course would very much retard my progress in the art; for after having made myself fully acquainted with one stage of the progress I must still wait for the pupil before I could advance to the succeeding stage. . . . I observed that I thought it a very unequal bargain; . . . that perhaps I ought to possess some power of judging in my own case, as every motive, both of duty and interest, would constrain me to wish to be fully qualified before I return to my own country.

"Tuesday, 15th. Dr. Watson informed me that it is expected of his assistants, and would be of me, to be in the school from seven o'clock in the morning till eight in the evening and also with the pupils in their hours of recreation. He observed that the first employment of an assistant is to teach the pupils penmanship. This I remarked would be a part of the principal difficulty that I had anticipated and would serve to illustrate it. For it showed that I might be familiar both with the theory and practice of certain stages of his pupils' improvements and yet be detained from advancing until they also should become familiar with them. This I observed would be a useless sacrifice of time on my part."

Thomas felt himself not a little trapped. To stay three years under Watson, most of the time engaged in menial work, was unthinkable. To abandon his plan for training, undesirable. In a letter to Mason, he gave his evaluation:

"Dr. Watson, I must say, from the very first has conducted toward me with a cautious reserve that I did not expect, and suggested certain plans which I thought interfered a little with my right of private judgment, not to say with my feelings of delicacy and honor. For instance, he alluded to the Mr. Braidwood, who is now in America, and suggests the expediency of his being associated with me in the school at Hartford. On this I need make no remarks. He also urged quite strongly the scheme of my carrying one of his assistants to America with me. How could I do this? How could I at present (not having heard a word from you) pledge myself to bear the expenses of an assistant across the water, and also that he should be supported when he arrived here. Besides, I knew not the character or talents of his assistants, and a more formidable objection still was the fear lest my plans of instruction and government might clash with this assistant's. He would be wedded to Dr. Watson's mode.

"I should wish, and I yet hope, to combine the peculiar advantages of both the French and English modes of instruction. For there are considerable differences between them. Well, Dr. Watson saw that I was bent upon acquiring the art myself and of pursuing my own plans of conduct. He now began to talk of difficulties in the way of my admission into the institution. . . . He invited me, to be sure, to visit the school and look among the pupils. He promised to give me any information in his power and to solve if possible any difficulties I had found in his art. But although I feel thankful to him for these civilities yet he must have known that I never could think of visiting his school, day after day, in the character of a mere visitor. I should soon have rendered myself obnoxious to him and to his assistants by the ardor of my curiosity and the frequency of my intercourse with his pupils. No, I wanted a definite arrangement with him of some kind or other that would have enabled me for several months, perhaps more than a year, to have become familiar with the theory and practice of his art. I offered him a remuneration for any services of this kind, but he declined it.

"He always talked of the length of time that would be necessary to acquire his art and generally spoke of four or five years. He alluded also to the difficulty of introducing me into the school in any other character than that of an assistant and for any short period of time, inasmuch as doing otherwise would create disaffection among his assistants, who engage to stay with him five years. . . . If I comply with the subcommittee's report, I must bind myself to labor for Dr. Watson three whole years, be subject to his complete disposal of me during that time, have no hope of freedom unless he please (and all his feelings of interest would lead him to detain me in order to make his art appear as difficult and important as possible), and what is worse than all, be continually retarded and cramped in my progress, because I should be obliged to wait for the progress of the pupils whom I might instruct. Besides, when am I to avail myself of the abbé Sicard's kindness? During these years? No; Dr. Watson would not consent to this. Afterwards? Then four or five years must elapse from the time when I left you to my return. This is too monstrous a sacrifice of time and patience and money.

"Again, is it generous to place me thus absolutely at Dr. Watson's disposal to say when I am qualified? Shall I be treated like a mere apprentice, whom his master must chain by indentures lest he make his escape? Is no confidence to be placed in my own judgment and integrity? The more I think of this proposed arrangement the more I dislike it, and I already begin to look for some other way in which Providence may guide me to the accomplishment of my wishes. . . . I ought to have observed that a salary of 35 pounds per annum (with my board), for the first year and something more for the next is offered me, if I become Dr. Watson's assistant. This would be well earned in toiling for him from morning till night with only one-half day's recreation in the week allowed me!!! Think, my dear sir, what a wound my feelings have received in all this business. Think how we used to speak before I left you of the ready welcome and the cheerful assistance that I should receive here. Compare that with what has happened. You can easily fill up the picture. . . .

"I hope to leave London for Edinburgh next week. I shall have the best letters of introduction, and I hope Providence will see fit to smile upon my visit there. . . ."[101]

DUGALD STEWART'S HOUSE, EDINBURGH, SEPTEMBER 1815. The city has a breathtaking natural site—three rocky ledges suspended over deep ravines. From the center of the old town, on the slope of castle rock, rises the castle, nearly four hundred feet above the level of the sea. In its shadow stands a narrow old house of three stories. On the third floor, there is a book-lined study, with shelves reaching from floor to ceiling on all sides but one, where Dugald Stewart, the leader of Scottish philosophers, professor emeritus at the University of Edinburgh, sits with his back to the tall windows. Stewart has spent much of his career seeking the laws of consciousness that explain the nature and operation of the human mind. Perhaps for this reason, there is scant hair on the top of his head, but all his other features are generous to a fault: bushy eyebrows, a full nose, a deep-lined fleshy face, a double chin. They radiate dignity, modesty, intelligence, and kindness.[102]

The conversation opens with introductions: Gallaudet has read Stewart's account of a boy born blind and deaf.[103] He himself has examined a rather similar case, Julia Brace (who was eight years old and living in Glastonbury, not far from Hartford).[104]

The philosopher states that the subject of his essay, James Mitchell, had been born deaf and blind in 1795, the sixth of seven children.[105] His mother soon discovered that he did not turn toward light or awaken at a loud noise. Julia Brace, Thomas explains, lost her sight and hearing when she was four and a half, after a bout of typhus. For a short time, she retained the use of speech; "she continued to say prayers, utter the names of friends, ask for what she wanted, utter profanities when crossed, but by the time I saw her she spoke nothing more than two or three inarticulate sounds." The two men go on comparing the two deaf-blind children for a long time. Finally, Stewart asks Thomas what has brought him to Edinburgh. When he learns that Thomas seeks admission to Braidwood's academy, the philosopher launches into a scathing attack on oralism, "which should rank only a little higher than the art of training starlings and parrots." Stewart accuses Wallis of misleading his successors, such as Braidwood, calls the Scotsman's pupils much inferior to Sicard's, and claims that speech teachers are perfectly aware of the difference between vocalizing and education but persevere in teaching articulation because a credulous public takes that as the measure of their success. As the light falls and lamps are set out, Thomas reviews the frustrations he has endured in Edinburgh, as recorded in his diary:

"Monday, August 28th. I delivered [a letter] to J. F. Gordon Esq., one of the secretaries of the Asylum for the Deaf and Dumb, on whom I called and explained the object of my visit to Edinburgh. He took me into his school, where I spent a little while [with the principal, Mr. Kinniburgh]. He expressed the strongest wish to render me every assistance in his power, but observed that he was under bond to Mr. Thomas Braidwood, instructor of the deaf and dumb at Birmingham, not to communicate his art to any person for seven years, four of which had now expired. Tomorrow I expect to see him and Mr. Gordon again and converse with them on the subject. The result of this and some subsequent conversations, was that I had better write Mr. Braidwood to endeavor to persuade him to release the institution from the obligation of the bond.

"Monday, September 4th. I have this day written to Mr. Thomas Braidwood of Birmingham, soliciting his consent that Mr. Kinniburgh may communicate with me what he may see fit to do of his mode of instructing deaf-mutes. . . . It seems that Mr. Kinniburgh met with a disappointment somewhat similar to my own in *his* application to the London Asylum a few years ago, that he then applied to Mr. Braidwood, who made it a condition of instructing him that he should not communicate his art to any person for seven years. Sad monopoly of the resources of Charity!!!

"Saturday, September 16th. Today I received a letter from Mr. Braidwood. In it he declines giving a direct answer to my application until he has consulted with his mother, who also possesses the art, and is, as he observes, 'at an advanced age, still dependent upon her own emotions, in this so arduous an undertaking.' He further observes, 'Dr. Watson was instructed in this art by my grandfather and my father—and has reaped most of the advantages resulting from their genius and abilities—you will therefore not I trust accuse me of illiberality if in giving or withholding my consent in a circumstance of this nature, I should first take the advice of my friends— at the same time believe me my best wishes are for an arrangement which may enable you to accomplish your benevolent design.'

"Friday, September 22nd. I this day received a letter from Mr. Braidwood in which he says, 'I feel it my duty, with the concurring opinion of my friends, to give a decided negative to your request.' He afterwards assigns as the reason for this the circumstance of his brother's being in America and refers me to him, with the firm conviction that liberal encouragement on the part of my countrymen will be followed by the most strenuous exertions of his brother to deserve it."

Thomas next wrote to Farquhar Gordon, one of the secretaries of the asylum, giving him the substance of Thomas Braidwood's letter and inquiring whether the committee might not be induced to think that the bond had no bearing, in that in the original intention of the parties, it had no reference to a foreign country. On October 10, Mr. Gordon returned from the country and promised to consult the committee in due course.

While Thomas waited in suspense, Alice wrote him a letter which, reminding him of the goal he was striving for, helped to fend off discouragement. It also reflected the progress she was making in English, though it required a word of explanation from her father first.[106]

"As soon as I knew of Mr. Upson's* sailing I proposed to Alice to write you by him. She readily consented, but she was at a loss what to write. I told her to write the story Miss Huntley [later Mrs. Sigourney] related to her from Mr. Colt—the circumstances I will relate, that you may the better understand it: Mr. Peter Colt, from Patterson, was lately here on a visit; he told her [Mrs. Sigourney] something that had happened to him when he was a little boy. It seems he had a very thick head of white curled hair; a clergyman who was visiting his mamma took a fancy to it for the purpose of making himself a wig; his mamma refused at first, but after a little urging, 'talk long' as Alice calls it, she consented, and the hair was cut off and the wig made. You will observe that the conversation between his mamma and the preacher is somewhat in the form of a dialogue. Miss Huntley communicated the story to her by signs. Miss Huntley, as you will perceive by Alice's letter, is in Norwich, on a visit. The letter is all [Alice's] own, without any assistance or correction.

"My Dear Sir:—I remember story Miss Huntley was tell me. Old many years Mr. Colt little boy Name man Peter Colt very much curls little boy hair Oh! very beautiful mama lap little boy comb curl love to see O beautiful. Morning long man preacher coat black come bow ask mama give little boy hair make wigs very beautiful preacher give, mama no preacher yes oh yes talk long man say come back little boy sisors cut hair white hair curls all in heap make wig preacher am very much glad proud little—little boy head very cold mama tie handkerchief warm, tears no more mama very sorry. I hope my hair never cut make wigs—This morning study all in school away Geography all beautiful a school all very beautiful very still very good noise no—the Play no, Miss Huntley work and two go Norwich all school come not—me very sorry come back little while—O all very glad,—O beautiful—I love you very much—"

Thomas's diary goes on:

"October 25th. I have just received from Mr. Gordon the minutes of the committee with a decision on my application. 'Mr. Gordon had stated to

*A friend in the export business.

Mr. Gallaudet [that] there was an obstacle, and an insuperable one he feared, to complying with his request—four years ago Mr. Braidwood of London had entered into a Contract by which he agreed to instruct Mr. Kinniburgh *gratuitously* upon condition that he would not communicate the same directly or indirectly to any individual for the space of seven years . . . under the penalty of 1000 pounds sterling. [The committee finds] that from the terms of the bond it does not appear to them possible to comply with Mr. Gallaudet's request which they all deeply regret.' Our projects are often thwarted by Providence on account of our sins. Ah! if mine have contributed to these difficulties most deeply would I lament the injury which I have thus done the poor deaf and dumb. Can I make them any recompense? With God's blessing it will be in devoting myself more faithfully to their relief. I long to be surrounded with them in my native land; to be their instructor, their guide, their friend, their father. How much is yet to be done before this can be accomplished. . . ."

How strange it seems now that Gallaudet should have seen in these developments the thwarting of his projects rather than the accomplishment of the Lord's: clearly, events were leading him inexorably away from the British capital and toward the French. If Thomas had not been such a dyed-in-the-wool federalist, as were his sponsors, fearing what was French as revolutionary, he would have swum more effortlessly in the stream of history. Even now he hesitated to take the plunge across the Channel.

"November 10th. As the political state of France is apparently in a very unsettled state, and as the season of the year is considerably advanced, I have concluded to spend a few months in Edinburgh. . . . I shall attend the lectures of Dr. Brown on the Philosophy of the Human Mind. . . . I shall read the abbé Sicard's treatises on the instruction of deaf-mutes and endeavor also to acquire a greater familiarity with the French language than I now have. . . . And by the spring it will probably be determined what the state of France will be, so that I can decide with more safety than at present on the expediency of going thither or not.

"February 3rd. This day at one o'clock Mr. Kinniburgh had a public examination of his pupils in Corris' rooms, at which nearly seven hundred persons were present. His Grace the duke of Buccleuch was in the chair and near him others of the nobility and much of the clergy of the city. . . . Among other illustrations of the progress of the pupils I noticed the following. Someone was called upon to define thumb—The reply was 'The short strong finger answering to the other four.' [A student named Turner was asked to define 'believe, eternity, and anger.'] 'Believe is to give credit to. He who loves God and believes the gospel is a Christian. Eternal is everlasting—God is eternal—The world will not be eternal but have an end. I am lost of thinking about eternity. Anger is a great uneasiness which we feel whenever we receive any injury either real or imaginary. It is not right to be angry.' Some questions in Arithmetic were proposed to the pupils and answered. . . . The Lord's prayer was repeated by several of the pupils and also some lines of poetry. Several compositions were also read. . . . The definitions were good, the composition quite interesting and ingenious, the communication of signs very partial and imperfect, and the articulation not of such a kind as to lead me to form a very favorable idea of this branch of the instruction of the deaf and dumb."[107]

Thomas spent a fortnight, on his way to Paris, in the British capital, and there sought out the editor of the *Christian Observer*, the organ of evangelical Anglicans, which reported on benevolent reforms and the signs of the approaching millennium and was much admired among New England ministers. Thomas had a letter of introduction from the English writer Hannah More, a frequent contributor, dear to American evangelicals because of her moral fiction and her reforming zeal.[108] The editor was Zachary Macaulay, father of the great English historian; he had led in the formation of the Anti-Slavery Society, the Missionary Society, and the Society for the Suppression of Vice; and he and Thomas became close friends.[109] During the Sunday they spent together at his country home, Thomas described in detail his months of frustration in Britain and his fresh hopes for France. Not long after, Watson, Gordon, and Kinniburgh received a searing rebuke in the pages of the *Christian Observer:* "We are grieved and mortified to find that neither in London nor Edinburgh did Dr. Gallaudet meet with that encouragement which his benevolent purpose merited." Macaulay accused his compatriots of a "niggardly and exclusive spirit. . . . We should as soon have expected a churlish refusal of vaccine virus to our Trans-Atlantic brethren as a moment's doubt or hesitation in communicating to them the blessed art of making the dumb to speak and the deaf to hear."[110] J. F. Gordon cried "No fair!" in a later issue of the journal: the Scots "would have been glad to give Mr. Gallaudet the desired information," but for Kinniburgh's thousand-pound bond to Dr. Watson.[111] Not surprisingly, Watson then wrote to the journal to defend himself: he disclaimed all knowledge of any obligation and bond!—adding that you cannot become an instructor of the deaf and dumb by interning for a scant few months. To which Macaulay replied, Surely that is not the only way to acquire knowledge.[112]

On arriving in Paris, Thomas took a furnished room not far from our school, in the Faubourg Saint-Germain near the abbey where Sicard had been imprisoned some twenty years earlier. "I hire my room of the landlady," he wrote to Mason, "procure my breakfast from the porter who brings it to me after purchasing and cooking the articles that I need, have my room cleaned and bed made by his wife, and dine and sup at a restaurant in the neighborhood."[113] Thus snug in the City of Light, was Thomas comfortable and enthusiastic? Not a bit of it. "It is a lonely way of life. I am quite sick of it," he wrote after only a week. "There is no *domestic* comfort in it. But it's the way in which half Paris lives. . . . I daresay you are often thinking what a delightful excursion I must be making and what a rich feast of novelty I must have continually spread before me. It is far otherwise." Thomas abstained from "public amusements" entirely, and "were it not that I thought my usefulness might be diminished by my returning home ignorant of what all travellers speak of, I would not put myself out of the way to see one of the wonders of this wonderful city." The letter closes with a paragraph bemoaning the depravity of my countrymen: "You read it, my dear sir, you talk of it and of your own privileges in Connecticut but you don't *realize* these things—you cannot without being an eye-witness to them—Oh how this poor heathen people want the Bible and the Sabbath! Will my own country ever lose them through its corruption and vice? My heart bleeds at the possibility of this." Heathen people, indeed!

When Thomas first came to the rue Saint-Jacques he had every reason to expect a warm welcome; after all, Abbé Sicard had invited him. He was not disappointed: "The abbé promised me every facility and invited me to attend his public lecture on Saturday next," he recorded in his diary. Thomas much enjoyed the lecture and was struck by one of Massieu's *bons mots* in particular. Asked to define "insouciance," my friend and teacher replied in sign: "the neutral zone between like and dislike."

Thomas and Sicard agreed that he would attend the abbé three days a week for instruction. (Do I need to add that, although the abbé was in considerable financial difficulty, there was never any question of charging for this instruction.) In addition, he would attend the regular classes each day from 10:30 to 12:30, beginning with the lowest, taught by the abbé Huilard, and working his way up to mine. He described the school and his reactions in a letter to Alice.

"You have written to me that you want me to come back in one year. I want very much to go back to Hartford, and to begin to instruct you and the other deaf and dumb children. But I shall stay here some time. I do not know how long. I must learn all that Abbé Sicard can teach me. Then I shall be able to teach you in the best way.

"I have seen the abbé Sicard and Massieu and Clerc, two of his scholars. In the little book which I send you, you will see their pictures. When you write me again, tell me what you think of them.

"Do you think you can learn the French alphabet on the fingers? Try. Perhaps it will be the one that I shall use.

"The school for the Deaf and Dumb here is a very large building of stone. In front of it is a large yard, and behind it a fine garden. There are nearly ninety scholars, boys and girls. I have seen the lowest class several times. There are fifteen boys in it. The master is a Romish clergyman. He is more than fifty years old.

"In the room are a number of large blackboards, on which the scholars write with chalk. I wrote on these boards and talked with the boys. They understood me very well. One told me he was from the same country as I. But he was mistaken. He was from Guadeloupe, an island in the West Indies. Another said he was from the United States, from Georgia. They are taught about God and Jesus Christ, and some of them can read the Bible very well.

"Do you learn any new verses in the Bible and any hymns or psalms? And do you often think about God? Do you pray to Him to make you good, and to make you ready to go to Heaven when you die? Do not forget to do this every morning and evening. . . .

"You must write me long letters. I put your last letter into French and showed it to Clerc. He loved to read it. Do not be afraid to write. You write very well and you will improve by writing.

"Give my love to your Mama and Papa and all the family. I shall remember what you wished me in your last letter to give the deaf and dumb scholars—your love.

"P.S. All the streets in Paris are paved with round stone. It is not easy to walk fast. And when it rains the streets are very muddy. And there are no sidewalks. Everybody must take great care that the chaises and coaches do not run over them. I had rather live in Hartford than Paris.—You would be sorry to see the Sabbath kept so badly in Paris. Most of the shops are open, and people buy and sell goods. And the theaters are all open, and but few people go to church, particularly in the afternoon. How much we ought to be sorry for such a people, and to thank God that it is not so in Connecticut."[114]

After ten days or so, Thomas progressed to the next class, Massieu's. He sat next to Massieu while he taught some fifteen pupils the French names of objects and qualities, both physical and mental, the divisions of time, of the earth, of the waters, and the like, together with short sentences—all by signs. "This is very improving to me," Thomas wrote to Mason.[115] "I imitate all Massieu's pantomimes," (he means signing) "and watch the manner in which his pupils catch his ideas. . . . I have often thought how you would wish to see me making all sorts of gestures and faces. But I am now convinced of the utility of this language of pantomime to *a certain extent.*"

After lunch Thomas went to Massieu's room or mine for lessons in manual French.[116] After a few weeks, "I have already learned the signs of most of the tenses of the verbs in all their moods and in all their varieties, of the articles . . . of many adjectives, pronouns and prepositions." (Bébian's reforms were a decade away and we were still using Epée's methodical signs in the institution's classes.) "Don't be alarmed at this system of signs," he tried to reassure Mason. "A great deal of it is truly valuable and will very much accelerate the progress of my scholars."

As the weeks wore on, Thomas settled into a routine. Mornings, he spent attending our classes, afternoons receiving lessons in sign, evenings reading and studying French. On the weekend, he preached to an English-speaking congregation at the Chapel of the Oratory, thus initiating the services of the American Chapel in Paris. His fifteen sermons were afterward published in London and Hartford,[117] to the applause of, among others, the *Christian Observer*—"He appears to have drunk from the pure streams of Christianity"—and Hannah More: "Your discourses are of a very superior cast. . . . I was charmed and deeply affected with the sweet letter of my dear little dumb correspondent," she added.[118] Alice had written to More thanking her for her contribution to the school fund, and to Thomas with news from the home he so dearly missed:

"You 1 year come back do do do. Dr. Webster* said no no no you 3 year come back no. Me I am very much glad you give me letter O beautiful me very glad you my give letter. Miss Huntley I love you very much. Ago day my tooth ache my father pull out me very afraid. Me my book life of Washington me read O beautiful I love you my book.—Miss Huntley school none 3 months. . . . Next Monday yes school, very glad. I thank you my book to me given. O beautiful my book.—When you come back kiss you. Love give my deaf and Dumb school. I love you very much."[119]

Gallaudet's American collaborators had not been idle. The nine members of the sponsoring committee and fifty-four others had made contributions ranging from $8 to $100—$2,340 in all.[120] Daniel Wadsworth made a handsome gift; so did the children of Miss Lydia Huntley's school, and Governor John Cotton Smith. Then Mason and others petitioned the state government for an act of incorporation for "the Connecticut Asylum for the Education and Instruction of Deaf and Dumb Persons,"[121] and they held their first meeting, as required by charter, in the State House in Hartford.[122]

Knowing as yet little of the puritanical way of thought, I was puzzled and disappointed by Thomas's apparent indifference to the splendor that surrounded him in Paris. It was then, and remains now, the capital of the world: the treasures of art and science, the ornaments and needs of the intellectual and refined community of the world were in her keeping. One particularly glorious spring day, I called at Thomas's quarters and urged that our Saturday lesson in sign take place in the Tuileries. We strolled leisurely to the Seine, a glistening ribbon of royal blue in the late morning sun; we crossed at the Pont Neuf, which had vaulted its stately way past the Ile de la Cité for more than two centuries; and we proceeded along the quay near the Royal Palace: Louis XVIII was in residence and may have looked down on us as Louis XV may have looked down on Pereire and Azy d'Etavigny, come to the palace to appear before the Academy of Sciences. We entered

*Noah Webster (1758–1843), lexicographer and Hartford Wit.

the royal gardens and stood in the Place du Carrousel, where Napoleon had erected his arch of triumph, copied from Constantine's. Before us lay the vast prospect in which nature had been perfectly proportioned by art. We looked down the central avenue of the Tuileries: water jetted upward in a stream from two basins, one near, one far, and descended in a spray of silvery particles that scattered among the leaves of orange trees bordering the avenue. Our line of sight continued across the grand Place de la Concorde, constructed by Louis XV, and up the great avenue des Champs-Elysées to the crest, where work on the Arch of Triumph had already begun. The public buildings of Paris with their elegant beige façades and ornate balconies rose in the neighborhood, and in the foreground, marble gods and goddesses regarded us vacantly from their partially concealed places amidst the foliage.

In the middle of the garden were numerous dancing parties of Parisian young men and women. The dancers had joined hands to form a circle and were singing as the circle slowly turned. Shopkeepers and their wives, peasants in from the country, schoolchildren, an occasional redcoat (a remnant of the British occupation)—all these strolled by. I was reminded of the magnificent treasures that were displayed just behind me in the Louvre, but the knowledge that they had been plundered by the British, leaving long blank spaces of dirty blue walls, and the distracted and fatigued air of my pupil discouraged me from proposing a tour. Instead we retired to a little restaurant I knew on the Right Bank that specialized in the cuisine of my native region, *coq au vin*, potatoes Lyonnaise, and the like.

These efforts to bring Thomas to his senses were unsuccessful: after only two months in Paris, his homesickness was getting the better of him. "How much longer must I stay?" he asked me in frustration.[123] I answered that it would take him six months to gain a tolerably good knowledge of signs, and a year to be well qualified in the method of instruction. And then he did a most astonishing and momentous thing: he urged me to leave Paris and go with him to Hartford in Connecticut.[124] "You will be a living proof that what has been believed impossible—the education of those born deaf —is indeed possible," he argued. "You will teach sign language as a near-native, which I cannot. You can guide me in arranging the instruction, aid me in providing it, serve as a model for the pupils, and create enthusiasm for education among the uneducated deaf!" Whose head would not be turned by such a preacher! Yet—to leave my recently widowed mother, my friends, to abandon Massieu and break with Sicard—not to establish myself in a great capital such as London or St. Petersburg but in an Indian-infested frontier village in the New World! My hard-won French never to serve me again; my primitive English and pantomime initially my only means of communicating; no cafés, no galleries, palaces, gardens, fountains; no libraries, museums, no croissants, no cuisine, no tasteful clothes, no taste; no

Catholic church, no absolution from sin but only sanctimoniousness— No! No! No!

But you know already: we do not choose to make history, history chooses to make us. I was a teacher of the deaf, there was none in America. I was an educated man born deaf, there was none in America. I was the teacher of the senior class of the mother school for all deaf education. A hearing American had come to France to bring back enlightenment for my deaf brothers and sisters. I was his guide and his friend, now I must be his collaborator and his interlocutor. I told Thomas I would go if the abbé Sicard gave me leave for three years and if my mother approved. Thomas wrote to my master:

". . . I am fully sensible, Reverend Sir, that in asking you to part with so faithful and valuable a pupil, I solicit, on your part, a great sacrifice; and I should have but little hope of succeeding in my request, were I not satisfied that the interest of humanity in the western world will plead strongly with you in my behalf. To these interests, in Europe, your life and genius have been devoted, and I can assure you the pleasure which I should feel in transmitting, from your hands, so great a blessing to my countrymen would only be equaled by their gratitude in receiving it. They are by no means ignorant of your justly acquired reputation, and could I thus commence the establishment in New England for the the instruction of the deaf and dumb, under your auspices, the name of Sicard would be as dear to America as it now is to France. . . ."[125]

Before Abbé Sicard could refuse Thomas's request, I went to see him. At the end of our conversation, he gave me the sheet of paper on which it had taken place:[126]

"I am very grateful to you, my dear master," I began, "for the kindness which you have always shown me; I shall be still more obliged if you will please give me permission to go to America with Mr. Gallauted [sic]. This journey will be very advantageous to me in several respects: I shall have the pleasure of seeing that beautiful country, and of acquiring valuable knowledge; I shall be able to master the English language; I shall receive a salary of 2500 francs with board, lodging, washing, fires and lights [this was five times what I was earning];[127] after three years' engagement I shall be free to return to France with an award of 7500 francs.

"I dare think that you will consider this arrangement an honorable one and more advantageous than I shall be able to obtain if I continue here.— The day of departure is fixed for the beginning of July.—If you approve of my voyage across the ocean, I will leave the day after tomorrow, or Monday, for Lyon, to take leave of my relatives, and I will return in time to embark. Mr. Bébian might take advantage of my absence to obtain what he has for sometime been proposing to ask [a position as a teacher].

"You have secured many advantages to M. Jauffret [the Russian post], and to Mlle. Duler and to many others. I hope you will have the goodness to do as well for me."

"I can do without you," Abbé Sicard replied, "and I would be disposed to favor anything that would promote your welfare, even if you were essential to me, but you ask of me something which would cause your eternal misery.

"You have the happiness, as well as I and all your family, of being born in the Catholic, Apostolic, Roman religion and you wish to go to a country where this, the only true religion, the only one which leads to eternal salvation, is proscribed, forbidden. . . . You will be obliged to teach the children the Anglican religion, the Protestant religion, whose ministers are not true ministers. You know that all the considerations of fortune . . . ought not to outweigh the advantages of religion, which alone can assure us of eternal happiness. This is the only obstacle to your project. . . . You ought to tell [Mr. Gallaudet] that you feel obliged to be true to your religion, as he feels obliged to be true to his.—I will allow you to go and take advice of your family, but I forewarn you; I shall write to them and inform them of the danger, if they should permit you to follow out your project. You would lose your faith, you would embrace a false religion, instead of the true; and they will do what they may judge most suitable for you. But I must tell you that if they allow you the fatal liberty of going to a heretical country, where you would be forever lost, I shall forever deplore your fate, and forever regret the labor and the pains I have taken to make of you a good Christian and a good Catholic.

"As I feel obliged to write all this to your good mother, I hand back what you have written to me and what I have answered you, that you may send it to them and that they may decide, with full knowledge, on your temporal and eternal fate."

I thought that my mother would understand the necessity of my going as I did, and so I consented to Thomas's pleas to start making arrangements for the trip: the ship, the *Mary Augusta,* was due to leave Le Havre for New York in less than three weeks! I went home on the first of June; my mother was expecting me, having received a letter from Abbé Sicard the day before. She pleaded with me to stay in France, but to no purpose, for I told her that my resolution was taken. And so she gave her consent, though with much reluctance, and said she would pray to God every day for my safety through the intercession of the Holy Virgin. I bade her, my sisters and brothers and friends adieu and returned to Paris.

At Saint-Jacques I went again to see Sicard, whose first words were: "You are hastening me toward the grave. Give up this folly."

"I am really troubled, my dear master," I wrote. "It is painful, I assure you, to leave you; but we must take courage and pray to God to give us the needful strength. Alas, it is too late to give up the journey. My fare in the diligence was paid yesterday. I should lose 70 francs. I have ordered clothing for 300 francs."

"I will pay for the fare and the clothing."

"The tailor has already cut them out. This morning I called on M. Viscount de Montmorency;* he gave me the same approval as did M. De Gérando."

"Then it must be so."

"He required of me that I should remain faithful to my religion, to my country, to my king. I have promised this. I renew the promise more specially to you, my dear master, and I pray God to grant you the strength needed for this cruel parting. The viscount will give me letters to respectable clerics of his acquaintance in New York."

"Since M. de Montmorency will give you introductions to Catholic clergy, I yield; but my dear child, will you indeed be firm in the religion which I have taught you? Can I count on your promises in this respect? Can I rest easy on this essential point? Will you be faithful in the holy observances of our religion? Will you, among Protestants, have the opportunity for those holy observances? Will you know the festivals of our holy religion? Will you know when Lent comes, the Easter Season, the fasting days? How will you learn them? Will you dare to abstain from meat on the prescribed days, Friday and Saturday? Answer my questions frankly. Your father is no longer living; I am more than ever such a one to you; you must pardon my anxiety."[128]

I swore to the abbé that I would keep the faith, observe the holidays. The interview lasted a long time. I watched the sun descend behind the gardens of the institution, cast a few mournful rays through the French windows of the abbé's apartment, and set. "You will find me buried when you return," he said. I denied it. Had I dreamed that I would never again live in my native land, that I would marry in America, raise my children here, and die here, I doubt I would have left France. "This is not au revoir," my master said, "but adieu." And with a sigh of resignation, he took a fresh sheet of paper and wrote to the bishop of Boston:

"Sir, The extreme desire to procure for the unfortunate deaf-mutes [who are citizens] of the country in which you dwell and fulfill so worthily the mission of the holy apostles, the happiness of knowing our holy religion leads me to a sacrifice which would exceed human strength. I send to the United States the best taught of my pupils, a deaf-mute, whom my art has restored to society and to religion. [He has] the great talent of teaching, and he alone was accustomed to prepare the pupils . . . for their first communion and for confirmation. This good and interesting young man goes with an ecclesiastic belonging to the Anglican religion, but he shall be obliged to teach nothing

*Mathieu de Montmorency was a member of the administrative board at "Saint-Jacques."

contrary to the Catholic religion, he shall stop where that divine religion stops, he shall himself observe all its practices. . . .

"He carries with him the regrets of his pupils and of the whole establishment. He was its glory and honor. . . . To console myself for his departure, I love to think of him as the Apostle of the Deaf-Mutes of the New World. . . . He will make his confessions in writing on a large sheet of paper with a half margin; writing his faults on the right of the sheet, and the confessor will write his reproofs and his exhortations on the left. He is slightly acquainted with the English language, and as he learns anything with extreme ease, he will acquire it without assistance."[129]

Sicard then sent the following note of acquiescence to Gallaudet: "I give Clerc my approval with conditions he will explain to you. I hope, sir, that you will be pleased with me. It is with pleasure that I make the sacrifice you have asked of me."[130]

"Les jeux sont faits!" I exulted to Thomas the same evening. "The die is cast!" We discussed the terms of a contract, which was drawn up a few days later.[131] It provided that I would instruct the deaf for six hours each weekday, three hours on Saturday, and not at all on Sundays and on holidays. I would teach "grammar, language, arithmetic, the globe, geography, history; the Old Testament as contained in the Bible, and the New Testament including the life of Jesus Christ, the Acts of the Apostles, the Epistles of Saint Paul, Saint John, Saint Peter, and Saint Jude. He is not to be called upon to teach anything contrary to the Roman Catholic religion which he professes, and in which faith he desires to live and die. Mr. Gallaudet, as head of the institution, will take charge of all matters of religious teaching which may not be in accordance with this faith . . ." Mr. Gallaudet would defray all my traveling expenses from Paris to Hartford, and pay me an annual salary of 2,500 francs.

I went to say farewell to Massieu, my friend for twenty years. At first he was businesslike: if we can secure your post for Bébian, the school may yet be saved. If not . . . The administration now only coddles Sicard; they no longer listen to him. Then he stopped flailing his arms, his shoulders drooped as he reached into his huge patch pockets, his eyes became moist, and he handed me—a watch! I still have it.

When I went to say goodbye to my pupils, there took place a painful scene I have never forgotten. I will remember each of you, I said, my eyes brimming and my arms tingling, gooseflesh. Then Alexander Machwitz, tears in his eyes, took hold of me, signing with his free hand that I could not depart, that I must not, scolding me, asking why had I kept it a secret. I apologized as well as I could—I had thought it best to wait and be sure. "You don't care for us. You never cared for us. You are the false *sourd-muet,* everyone calls you fake!" And more ranting . . . In the end there was no reasoning with him, he would not release me. He held me fast, this thirteen-year-old boy, despite my struggles to disentangle myself. It was absurd, it was embarrassing, it was hurtful. I wanted to hurl at him the accumulated pain and fear of a dozen farewells, it is MY LIFE, MY FREEDOM, MY CHANCE! My rage exploded. I flung him to the ground, and ran away. When Sicard wrote to me in Hartford the following summer he mentioned that the incident had sent Machwitz to bed for many months. Then he and Massieu were drawn quite close, it seems, by their shared loss, and Machwitz recovered.[132]

Of course, I could not know this happy outcome at the time. Added to Sicard's protestations and my mother's reluctance, Machwitz's outburst made me waver. Then a second letter came from Alice, in response to Thomas's last from Edinburgh.[133] "Do you remember how I tried to make you understand why Christ died?" he had written her. "I hope you do not forget to pray to God every morning and evening." Alice's tender conscience—she was eleven and had little experience of religious exhortation—was more disturbed by Thomas's appeal than he had a right to expect. "I am very much afraid God think me very wicked and bad heart," she wrote. "I am not good heart. I wish good heart, so very want, not I am feeling bad, very sorry. All people men and women little wicked and very bad heart. I am very sorry. . . . God made me Deaf and Dumb. Perhaps me very bad, I hear not. Me perhaps blind and Deaf and Dumb I hope not." (She had been to see Julia Brace with Mason.) "God Jesus christ know best and God make all. I think every day all all all men and woman children and baby Beast dead and sick fever very many. God made me Deaf and Dumb I was a little child 2 year old Spotted fever. God make so Deaf and Dumb. I love very much God Jesus Christ all all all Best. God Jesus Christ very Beautiful. I don't know reading Holy bible. I am very sorry. Books all very many Best me think reading Best Holy Bible. I wish and very want read. I know and did not. I am very sorry."

This was what it was all about—what Epée struggled for, what Sicard had even lately affirmed as his great fear for my mission, the raison d'être for Thomas's odyssey—the saving of souls. Not the fraternity of man (which includes education), not justice, certainly not the needs of the state, nor even the temporal needs of the individual. And I grew ashamed. Epée had dared defy the Church, the courts, the accepted wisdom of his time. Massieu had snatched Sicard from the Reign of Terror and had addressed the National Assembly. Was I then to quail before my own noble calling, apostle to the deaf in the New World? And where was my faith in the deaf and in their desire to cast off the shroud of darkness that enveloped them? If I passed them the torch of language, would they not then prove able on their own to use it to illuminate their lives?

We made the day's journey to Le Havre in mid-June and while we waited to board our ship, Thomas wrote to Mason to announce the grand news of his return.[134] "Tomorrow I expect to sail from this port in the *Mary Augusta*, Capt. Hall, for New York in company with Mr. S.V.S. Wilder, Mr. Upson's particular friend, and a Mr. Clerc. . . . Yes, my dear friend, Providence has most kindly provided for my speedy and successful return by furnishing me with the most accomplished pupil of the abbé Sicard and one, too, who is not less recommended by the probity and sweetness of his character . . . than by his rare talents. He already understands a good deal of English, we shall work hard together on the passage in order that he may acquire more, and a few months in America will quite make him master of it."

The passport that I tendered at the head of the gangway asked all civil and military officers, friends and allies of France, to let pass one Laurent Clerc, thirty, 1 meter 73, chestnut hair, blue eyes, large nose, high forehead, average mouth, round chin, oval face, dark skin. Soon, the ship slipped her moorings and came about, the Channel wind violently flapping her vast expanse of sail.[135]

EIGHT

SPREADING THE WORD

♦

Owing to adverse winds and frequent calms, my voyage to America with Thomas Gallaudet was to last fifty-two days! We were only six passengers (Thomas, Mr. Wilder, me, and three other Frenchmen)—not counting various species of living animals for our daily nourishment, among them six pigs, several ducks and cocks and hens. There were also canaries to tickle the ears of the passengers by the agreeable sound of their singing. Ah well!

I take these details from a journal that Gallaudet suggested I keep "to exercise and perfect myself in the English language."[1] Whereas Thomas would correct my journal, I would correct his signing; he taught me about American ways, I explained French methods of instruction, and we worked together on an article he was preparing for Zachary Macaulay. My journal entry for a typical day:

"Wednesday, June 19, 1816: I awoke at five o'clock, and I fell asleep again immediately. I awoke again at seven o'clock, and I rose upon the spot, lest I should fall asleep again. I dressed myself, I washed my face and my hands. I combed my head. Afterwards I went to take the air upon deck, and at the same time to rinse my teeth. I soon went again into our cabin where my friends waited for me to breakfast. I sat at table between Mr. Wilder and one of our companions, and over against Mr. Gallaudet. We took off our hats and prayed to God. Our breakfast consisted of coffee, tea, butter,

LAURENT CLERC

(PAINTING BY CHARLES WILLSON PEALE)

buttered bread, cold meat, fish, radishes, cool eggs, cider and wine. I ate some of all. Mr. Wilder only never takes coffee, nor tea, nor meat. After our breakfast and our prayer, we all ascended upon deck. It was fair weather, the sun lighted the land, but the sea was a little agitated. I cast my eyes upon the ocean and admired God's works. By turns I walked, read, wrote, talked with Mr. Gallaudet and amused myself by fishing or by seeing others fish.

"At two o'clock, the steward gave us notice that the dinner was ready. We all descended into our cabin, and sat in our own places. After the benediction, we hastened all to the mess which covered the table. Our dinner was good enough and as good as is possible in a ship. We said Grace, rose from the table and went upon deck. The weather had changed and become cold. I soon went and threw myself all dressed on my bed. I took my book and whilst I read it, I fell asleep in spite of myself. At seven, Mr. Gallaudet came, awoke me and told me that supper waited for me. I was up in a trice; but I had no appetite. I drank only two bowls of tea with some buttered bread. I returned to bed as soon as I had prayed to God and wished my friends a good night, and I slept till the next day."

I find this note for June 26: "I talked a little with M. Wilder. He asked me if I should like to marry a deaf and dumb lady, handsome, young, virtuous, pious and amiable. I answered him that it would give me much pleasure but that a deaf and dumb gentleman and a lady suffering the same misfortune could not be companions for each other, and that consequently a lady endowed with the sense of hearing and with the gift of speech was and ought to be preferable and indispensable to a deaf and dumb person. Mr. Wilder replied nothing, but I am sure that he found my argument just."

You see what a poor opinion I sometimes had of myself then! (I hide neither the good nor the bad.) Happily, by the time I was ready to marry I knew better and chose a deaf wife (as most deaf people do), who has filled my heart with gladness to this day.

Later that morning: "I conversed a little with M. Gallaudet and told him that the speaker of the House of Commons in London was a man of mean parentage, and that nevertheless he was not a mean orator, and that he had made his way by his merits and talents; a wonderful, admirable and unusual event!!! Afterwards I translated from memory into English a passage out of *Paul et Virginie.* * Then I labored with M. Gallaudet on the method of figures which we employ, in France, to facilitate the progress of our deaf and dumb pupils in the construction of phrases and periods. Then we dined. Then I walked a little. Then, with the aid of my dictionary, I took a lesson in geography and learned to write in English the names of all the nations or states of Europe."

---

*A precursor of French Romanticism, this widely read tropical love story was first published in 1787 by Jacques Henri Bernardin de Saint-Pierre.

The following day: "M. Gallaudet and I took occasion to speak of London, and he asked me what I thought of the Houses of Peers and of Commons in England and of those of France, and if I had seen each one. I answered him that I had seen all; that I was at the English House of Peers when the Prince Regent came there to announce in a fine discourse the victory of Waterloo, the flight of the Emperor Napoleon and his second abdication of the Throne of France, and the future happiness and repose of all the nations of Europe; and that I was at the House of Commons when a member of that illustrious assembly proposed to raise a monument to the honor of the Hero of Waterloo (the Duke of Wellington). I questioned afterwards Mr. Gallaudet on our own houses of France. He told me that he had seen each one, with this difference, that when he was at the Chamber of Peers, there was nobody in it, and that when he was in that of Commons, there was a crowd. He found the exterior of the House fine and yet the interior finest. He praised the uniforms and regular manner in which the members were dressed. He did them the justice to acknowledge the dignity of their character and their talents. He admired the place, distinguished and raised in the middle of the House, where every orator can conveniently pronounce his discourse; but at the same time, he censured their motions of body and their gestures, and the manner in which they discoursed. He found that they made too much noise. He would wish that they would stand like statues. I rejected Mr. Gallaudet's argument and assured him that the manners of the French orators were much better than those of the English who, though celebrated by their wisdom and knowledge, made their discourse but little interesting, since they do not accompany it with some motion of the body to give some idea of the beauty of expression, and since they discourse with their head fixed and arms crossed. M. Gallaudet and I were going to continue to speak for and against, when one gave the sign of rising from table and that caused our debate to cease."

Thomas had come away from his experience with deaf education in Europe convinced of the superiority of the French product over the British one, although, like every hearing person, he had initially been biased toward speech and, like every federalist, against France. In thinking about his new views he took as his point of departure, as had Epée, the observation that there is no natural connection between a spoken word and the idea to which it refers.[2] From this claim of John Locke's, Epée deduced that written words could serve the deaf as spoken ones serve the hearing. The problem was to teach them written French and for this he designed methodical signs. Gallaudet's deduction, more than half a century later, was more insightful: manual signs can represent ideas just as well as they can represent written or spoken words. In his enthusiasm he went further: sign language is more significant than other kinds because it includes the changes in our bodies and countenances produced by the movements of the soul.

Thomas was now definitely opposed to speech for the deaf and rehearsed the reasons he proposed to state in the *Christian Observer*.[3] "The deaf never use speech among themselves or with others. I rarely heard it in all the schools I visited. I doubt whether one in a hundred, after six years' instruction, could make himself usefully understood or understand the continued discourse of a stranger."[4] I agreed, and added, It is not the natural language of the deaf and we find it irksome. He marshaled more arguments: It is a purely mechanical feat, and teaching it conveys not one new idea. It confuses the minds of the pupils by directing their attention to many things at once, something like the effort we should have to make to learn two languages at the same time. It involves immense labor and fatigue for instructor and pupils, as the syllables in words, their accents, the differences between pronunciation and writing, must all be clearly communicated—a task of tremendous difficulty and in most cases a hopeless one. It prevents the instructor from devoting his labors to more pupils and a more important part of education—the actual communication of knowledge, the unfolding of the human mind. It discourages the pupils, for they know they have another language at hand which is easy, rapid, and delightful. Besides, how much more beautiful is the silent language of the countenance, gestures, and the fingers than the harsh and discordant sounds of those who cannot regulate the tones of their voice.[5]

When Thomas's article later did appear in print it elicited a spirited (anonymous) reply. "Give the deaf what they accidentally lack and you remove the wall that separates them from the rest of society: they will be enlivened by conversation, instructed by history, enlightened and comforted by the records of eternal truth. We must give them a mother tongue, the language of the country where they reside. Now written language will not serve: it is arbitrary, external and unmeaning; speech we can see in others and feel in ourselves."[6]

This is the prototype of the oralist argument. First, the difference between us and the majority is labeled our lack: *we* lack English, *they* do not lack sign. Now add the God's breath notion: it is not enough to learn the written language of the majority, you must speak it as we do.

Thomas published a rebuttal in which he did not dispute the goal but the practicality of attaining it. The pain, labor, and expense of acquiring speech, he argued, are generally thrown away.[7] "Let one of these unfortunate individuals who has even attained the honor of reciting the Lord's Prayer in public (told it is the Lord's Prayer, we recognize something like it)—let him read a paragraph in a newspaper, and immediately his words cease to be intelligible." Moreover, the effort of acquiring speech, even if partially successful, usurps the place of a more useful pursuit, mental improvement.

In a sequel to this rebuttal a few months later, Thomas shifted the emphasis from attacking speech for the deaf to espousing sign.[8] Whatever language we teach the deaf, we must use their native language of sign as the medium of instruction, he affirmed. So sign is necessary; it is also peculiarly vivid: "My mind has been more agitated by a description of the day of judgment that I have seen my ingenious friend Mr. Clerc exhibit in his own native language of signs than by the loftiest flights of eloquence which are to be found in the pages of Massillon or Bossuet. He was the judge and I trembled before him. He was the accepted disciple of Christ, and I almost felt the rapture which the 'Come, ye blessed' will inspire. He was the impenitent sinner and I shuddered with horror at the yawning gulf beneath his feet."

These were uncomfortable times for the British oralists! First, Macaulay accused them of illiberality, then Gallaudet charged them with impracticality and downright ignorance. Next, John Arrowsmith, the hearing brother of one of Epée's pupils, published in London a second edition of Francis Green's translation of the abbé's final work and commented: "I am inclined to believe the first edition was suppressed. It is extraordinary that it should have entirely disappeared and there is not now a single copy to be found."[9] Arrowsmith seconded Thomas's rebuttal of the anonymous oralist in the *Christian Observer:* "So long as the deaf and dumb are taught utterance, the system of delusion will continue at their asylums which has been supported and upheld by the crafty and imposed on the credulous."[10] The prestigious *Quarterly Review,* reporting on Arrowsmith's book, agreed with him:

"Mr. Braidwood very successfully taught his pupils the use of a written and manual alphabet, and, through that natural medium, stored their minds with a large portion of various and useful information. In an evil hour, however, he clogged his plan with the unnecessary and cumbersome appendage of teaching them utterance. As might have been anticipated, 'the school' immediately fastened upon the appendage as containing the essence of the plan and, through the medium of their [articles in] encyclopedias, their annual reports and their harangues to periodical 'meetings of subscribers,' succeeded but too well in persuading the public that the science which they profess is a profitable and indispensable 'craft.' 'Observe,' they say, 'the progress which children make in our asylums where they are, invariably, taught to speak! Speech, therefore, must be the cause and instrument of the progress which has been made in instructing them.' Admirable logicians! Observe the progress which children make in establishments where they are, invariably, taught the art of carving wood—carving in wood must, therefore, be the efficient cause of their mental improvement."[11]

The problem with oralists, Thomas said, is that they are unacquainted with what they oppose so doggedly. He admitted candidly that he had had many false ideas about sign language before taking lessons from Massieu and me. He had been thinking about our fund-raising tour for the school: perhaps it would be wisest to start our lectures by dispelling such fallacies about sign before we explained its positive advantages for instructing the deaf. I no longer recall Thomas's list of fallacies, but here is mine.

Fallacy: sign language is pictorial. This error comes from confusing pantomime with sign language, a common confusion because signers do use a lot of pantomime. But the two are different: there are no ungrammatical pantomimes, only unsuccessful ones. A hearing person's sentences in sign, on the other hand, can be quite wrong if he is not fluent, even while they are quite clear. (Just as "I call myself Laurent Clerc" is incorrect but clear.) Indeed, if sign language were very pictorial it would be immediately understood and easy to learn; it is not.

You might think of a sign language as pantomime transformed into a secret code that makes it fast and easy. The users of the code agree, as it were, to use only a score of handshapes and a like number of hand movements in a limited number of combinations. That makes signs easy to spot, use, and remember but their meanings are not obvious and have to be learned. Something similar applies to spoken language. The users of the French code agree, as it were, to restrict their words to just a score of vowels and a like number of consonants in a limited number of combinations. That makes the form of the language easier even if the content is harder to divine.

Fallacy: sign language is universal. This error comes from the fallacy that it is pictorial. To communicate with the English deaf, I had to resort to pantomime and to my lowest-level signing (lots of pointing, simple, slow signs, and the like). Similarly, I expected to find deaf people who congregated in New York City using some kind of common parlance to socialize, worship, trade, and play and I did not expect to understand it from the start. (Thus, my travels took me to just the wrong places when it came to facile communication: instead of London or New York, I would have preferred Madrid or Copenhagen, or any of numerous other European cities where disciples of Epée and Sicard had already opened schools and had spread my sign language which, with some changes, became the language of the deaf community there.)

Fallacy: sign language is concrete. This error, too, comes from the fallacy that it is pictorial. It is a particularly foolish myth, however, since even pantomime can convey abstract ideas, such as love, reverence, death, by depicting their emblems—the heart, praying hands, rigor mortis. American Sign Language, like its French parent, abounds in signs for abstract ideas, such as LOVE, FAITH, BELIEF, TRUST, and many others, some of which are not easily expressed in English words, for example AMBULATORY-PERSON and HOLLOW-CARVED-OBJECT-WITH-RIM. Anyway, all languages use words that have concrete meanings to convey abstract ideas as well. You can still "sail" into trouble in the age of steam power, and Saint John wrote, "In the beginning was the Word . . . and the Word was made flesh and dwelt among us."

Fallacy: Sign language is primitive. This error is induced by word-for-word translations from a signed into a written language: the substitution yields a series of words that must violate the rules of the reader's language and makes the source appear primitive and ungrammatical. For example, the Latin for "A bear killed my father's geese; father shouldered his gun and went to look for it," is, word for word, "Bear father's geese my killed; gun shoulder leaned against and went so bear might search for." The American Sign Language version is: "Bear geese father his catch eat; gun shoulder-on, go-look-for bear." For a long time the French were fond of saying that not only sign language but also the spoken languages of our colonies were primitive and for the same reason. Both the deaf and the Africans share an oral tradition rather than a written one: parents teach their children by word of mouth (or hand), there are storytellers and folk tales, and much of the recording of history is done in the peoples' second language, French. As far as I know, all societies everywhere have complicated languages that take years to learn to use properly, and deaf societies are no exception.

Thomas gave one reason why signed languages are in some ways better than spoken ones—they reflect the movements of the soul—and I want to suggest another. More of what we talk about every day has to do with the things we see, touch, and encounter than with the sounds we hear, the odors we detect, or the tastes we savor. Life is, foremost, a visual experience that takes place in space, and a visual and spatial language can tell about it efficiently and gracefully. Sign language has no need for all the little prepositions of French or English that try, and often fail, to capture spatial arrangements—nearby, underneath, circling-in-the-neighborhood, and so on. We can put the signs for the things so related in the correct relationship and move them appropriately. So much is man a seeing animal moving in space that he often conceives nonspatial matters in spatial terms—thus enlarging boundlessly the world of experience that sign conveys well. For example, everyone knows the future is ahead of us, the present here, and the past behind, and it is easy for sign language to use this spatial understanding of time, among other means, to describe when events occur. One more example: French and English sentences get all twisted around themselves trying to say who did what to whom with what, and they need lots of pronouns to help keep track. In sign we designate points in space for the actors in our story and as the verb moves from point to point the actors do directly to each other in sign what French struggles to say they did. Sign language primitive? I never met a man who called a language primitive that he knew.[12]

After a voyage of more than seven weeks, the sailors at long last sighted land, and the passengers went on deck to observe our entry into the harbor. I had arrived in America! The date was August 9, 1816.[13] Suddenly, I was assailed by renewed doubts. What would the Americans waiting on the dock think of the deaf man with the awkward English? An educated deaf person must be something akin to a raree-show* for them.

I need not have doubted. Thomas and I stayed about ten days in New York, and his family and friends gave me a cordial welcome. One of the latter, who would become president of Columbia College, described our meeting in a letter:

"Mr. Clerc does not speak except by signs, by means of which we saw him and Mr. Gallaudet communicate with each other as expeditiously, almost, as we could do by words. With strangers he converses by writing. Mr. Gallaudet says that Mr. Clerc knew very little of English before they embarked together. You may judge yourself of his progress in it. My father saw him several days ago at the house of Mr. Gallaudet's father, and wrote upon a slate, 'I hope you are pleased with New York.' He wrote in reply, 'Yes— so well that soon I shall not regret France.' When he called the day before yesterday with Mr. Gallaudet to return my father's visit, my father wrote, 'I hope you continue to be pleased with this country.' He wrote, 'Yes— better and better,' and before my father could read his answer he reached out his hand for the slate and added: 'I meet with a good reception everywhere, and the kindest attentions are shown me.' I wrote: 'We are surprised at your progress in English, your method of learning must have something peculiar in it, or your industry must be very great.' He wrote: 'By dint of studying I have got some progress, but my friend, Mr. Gallaudet, has been my best methodic.' Before I had time to read his answer, he asked Mr. Gallaudet by signs whether he had not committed an error in the last word, and being told he had, he stepped up to me and rubbed out the two last letters. . . .

"I have not been able to learn how abstract ideas are communicated to the deaf and dumb, but as an example of the justness of their notions I give you the following definition of virtue which Mr. Clerc wrote verbatim and literatim, as you have it below, on my father's asking him what idea he had of virtue: 'It is the disposition or habit of the soul to do good, to avoid evil, and to observe what divine and human laws order and what reason dictates.' "[14]

Thomas wrote to Mason from New York: "We have been visited by and we have seen a great many persons, and all take a great interest in Clerc. He is so modest and easy in his manners and converses with such charm and propriety with all that it is a matter of general admiration."

But there was a cause for consternation, and just at the outset of our great undertaking! Thomas's letter goes on: "We have much to do to get our establishment on an eligible footing. Many here speak of the necessity of a similar establishment in New York. A great deal is said about Mr. Gard

*A cheap street show.

of Bordeaux. Setting aside all personal feeling, I do think it will be not a little discreditable to our country if some local and state feelings cannot be laid aside in the commencement of a project like ours."[15]

Do you recall François Gard, the best student of Saint-Sernin at Bordeaux? Many considered Gard superior to Massieu; Edouard Morel, who edited the fourth circular from Saint-Jacques in which Gard wrote a report, said he had "never yet seen work from the pen of a deaf-mute that compared with his." My friend Gard had entrusted the American consul to Bordeaux, William Lee, with a letter addressed "to the philanthropists of the United States," offering himself—and in English at that—as a teacher of the deaf and dumb,[16] "for humanity," he said, but went on to describe his family responsibilities and present salary, which were three times what mine had been.[17] I admit my reaction to Gard's proposition was not of the most charitable. He knew I had missed out on the Russian post and now had staked all on America, yet he went into competition with me, risking a collision that might sink us all, for surely funds could not be raised for two new schools simultaneously.

Consul Lee had returned to New York from his post in France just four days before Thomas and I reached the city, and had given Gard's letter to the New York surgeon general, Samuel Mitchill, "the Nestor of American science." Among many professional activities, Mitchill was a founder and editor of the *New York Medical Repository*, and in it he had published the letter that Francis Green, in his initial burst of enthusiasm, had written from the Braidwood school to the health officer of New York, urging a similar school in America.[18] Now, even as Thomas and I journeyed toward Hartford by way of New Haven, a meeting of concerned citizens was held at the home of the Reverend John Stanford, who once had assembled a class of deaf-mutes within the New York Alms House (administrative changes soon led to its dismantling).[19] There Mitchill read Green's and Gard's letters and affirmed the possibility of educating the deaf; a larger public meeting was called at Tammany Hall.[20]

Thomas and I, meanwhile, called upon Yale's distinguished president, Timothy Dwight, to seek his assistance in our effort to found what I was later to learn would be the first charitable institution in the United States. Why Dwight? Because the key to federalist philanthropy must be religion, and the crux of the religious argument must be the Christian's responsibility for benevolence; if Thomas and I were to travel about New England preaching the obligation and feasibility of educating the deaf, then Thomas wanted his doctrine clear and convincing. Furthermore, Dwight was no learned recluse; he was one of the three great New England revivalists (the others were his grandfather, Jonathan Edwards, and his pupil, Lyman Beecher) and actively engaged in social and moral issues.

Dwight's manner was grand and commanding (he was a large, robust man in his sixties) and he spoke, Thomas said, in an authoritative, deep, and melodious voice. (The democratic press, anxious to destroy a symbol it could not ignore, called him Pope Dwight.) He had been a Yale student at thirteen, a classmate of Reverend Strong's, a chaplain, a Yale tutor, a Hartford Wit, and the pastor at Greenfield Hill, where he ran a famous seminary (and was visited by Mason in his youth), before becoming president of the college.

"The basis of my appeal for the asylum," Thomas began, "is that religion consists in disinterested affection; if the first law of God given by Christ is to love the Lord, the second, 'like unto it,' is to 'love thy neighbor as thyself.' Matthew says, 'On these two commandments hang all the law and the prophets.' "

"Christ went further," Dwight replied. (I could not follow all of Thomas's signing at the time but I have reconstructed the gist from later conversations, sermons, and publications.) "Those who were undeserving, unworthy, abusive, criminal—for those Christ died out of love. 'He who dwelleth in this love dwelleth in God and God in him.' "

"Self-love, then—staking all on personal interest," Thomas went on, "is sinful, it is the opposite of benevolence."

"But when a man thinks of the public interest he also thinks of himself," Dwight argued. "More than that, we cannot know all of the public interest; we naturally know best the interest and happiness of those who are nearest, ourselves, our family, our neighborhood. This is the Christian meaning of 'Charity begins at home.' "

"That is indeed helpful," Thomas answered, "but I fear that my audience will want, even more than a local appeal, one that is businesslike, a return on their investment, and we shall presently be said to be selling grace like the Catholics, and made a mockery of."

"But you should know your Hopkins. What did they teach you at Andover?" Pope Dwight smiled for the first time. It was Samuel Hopkins* who, in Lyman Beecher's words, "made disinterested benevolence the core of New England theology." Dwight quoted him: "He who has a new heart and universal disinterested benevolence will be a friend to God and will be pleased with his infinitely benevolent character though he sees not the least evidence and has not a thought that God loves him and designs to save him."[21]

Some would contribute to our asylum, then, because they loved their neighbor, others because it showed that they and God were friends, still others in the hope of gaining an eternal reward, some on the grounds of practicality (for an educated deaf man is less of a burden on society than an ignorant one), and some out of a sense of civic duty. These motives seemed to cover just about anyone who would venture into the audience on our projected tour of fund-raising.

*(1721–1803); a leading theologian and disciple of Jonathan Edwards.

Thomas was right in worrying from the start that the thrifty Yankees would expect a return on their investment—even in charity. In those days, the town poor were farmed out to the lowest bidders, who served their charges scraps and leftovers from the family table. The Hartford Retreat for the Insane, which Mason would help to found, would take only paying patients, and even our own asylum rejected many pupils who could not pay tuition. Benevolence is not solid ground on which to erect an institution but it was the only ground available to Thomas and me. Eventually, as the American population grew and spread south and west, its politics changed from the aristocratic beliefs of Washington and Adams to the French democratic ideals that inspired Jefferson and Jackson: if the people were to participate in government they must be equipped for that responsibility. The state's responsibility for education extended to all its people, and schools for the deaf must be created. But this shift took many decades because it had to overcome the individualistic spirit: why should I be obliged to pay for another man's child?

From New Haven Thomas and I took the stage to Hartford. Although the day was fair, that summer had been the coldest in memory in New England. The crop of Indian corn had been destroyed in the ground; potatoes, hay, oats were in short supply, and the barren hills in the Connecticut River Valley contrasted starkly with the verdant banks of the Rhône still vivid in my memory. I entered the city, then, in a somber and remote frame of mind. But—how fair this city was! How stately its tree-lined avenues! How palatial its homes! I felt rather as Mark Twain did when he came to live in Hartford last year: "Of all the beautiful towns it has been my fortune to see," he wrote, "this is the chief. You do not know what beauty is if you have not been here."[22]

The Cogswell residence at 38 Prospect Street was three stories high (the third under a sloping roof), with five windows giving onto the street in front, another five onto the gardens and fields behind, and on this sunny day it was filled with light that seemed to bind the ample rooms, the porch, the terrace, and the sweep of the countryside into a single scene.[23] Mrs. Cogswell and her daughters, Mary and Elizabeth, young ladies of fifteen and thirteen, greeted us, and Alice was immediately sent for at Mrs. Sigourney's (she was then still Miss Lydia Huntley). Standing awkwardly in the parlor, anticipating Alice's arrival, I thought, She is what I have come for; for Alice and others like her, I have left everything familiar behind, and everything strange is ahead of me. Suddenly, she appeared. The room was still: all eyes were on us, and ours on each other. For one brief moment her open, ample gaze seemed to call to my soul to flow out toward her, to enter through her pupils and mingle with her own. Then reality jerked my head; I thought, Why, she's just a little girl, not a symbol, a little girl like any other, really. "HELLO," I signed. She laughed, her curls shaking, merriment dancing in her eyes. "DEAF YOU-ME-SAME," she signed. I understood. "Will you teach me many signs?" she asked. "What signs will you teach me?" It was my turn to laugh, out of joy. "I will teach you the sign for love." ("When I first met you in the parlor," Alice told me many months later, "I thought I had never seen such beautiful signs before. MY-HEART GLOW," she signed.)

The day after my arrival, Mason convened the directors of the asylum at the State House and before long I had made the acquaintance of the principal citizens of Hartford and their families, all of whom received and treated me so kindly I began to feel at home. But alas, before that feeling could take root, Mason, Thomas, and I were off on our fund-raising tour around the New England states. We began in Boston, armed with letters of introduction, including one from our governor to the governor of Massachusetts.[24] Mason wrote to his wife with word of our initial success: "Here I am in Ben Russell's office." Colonel Russell published the influential semiweekly the *Columbian Centinel* for more than forty years. It gave full coverage to our Boston appearances. "Since our arrival we have been incessantly engaged in delivering our letters, feeling the pulses of the rich and contriving the best possible way of picking their pockets genteelly. Matters, we think, are working up towards a favorable issue. Whatever impression Mr. Gallaudet and myself have made, Clerc is doing wonders—he makes them all stare—at the different offices, at private parties, at our lodgings, and even in the streets."[25]

On the day that Mason wrote, and again two days later, I appeared at the Boston Athenaeum and answered numerous questions put to me by a large company of gentlemen. On the second occasion I delivered an address through Thomas. I spoke of why I had come to America, of the abbé de l'Epée and the abbé Sicard, of my ignorance before my education and the needs of the deaf everywhere for schooling, of the fact that every European nation, however small, had a school for the deaf, but America had none. "If the deaf and dumb become happy," I concluded, "it will be your joy to see that it is the effect of your generosity and they will preserve the remembrance of it as long as they live, and your reward will be in heaven." (This, despite what Dwight had said.) The following day we had another exhibition for the ladies, and I appealed to the women to influence their men. "You have naturally great sensibility. If you remark among your husbands, relations or friends, some who may be insensible to this action of benevolence, I beg you to change them into better dispositions." More than one hundred generous donations were made to the institution: the largest, $500, was from the governor, and his example was followed by all classes in the community to the amount of several thousand dollars.

Mason returned to Hartford while Thomas and I went on to Salem, where I presented yet a third address. "A great variety of questions were put to Mr. Clerc," the *Gazette* reported, "to all of which he gave ready and pertinent answers, generally with the addition of some sensible remarks and sometimes with even metaphysical acuteness. Several hours were spent in the exercise of the faculties of the interesting stranger, to the great delight of the admiring assembly." We collected over $1,000 from two score subscribers.

Early in October we returned to Hartford and in a few days Mason, Thomas, and I went on to New Haven, where the legislature was in session.* We had an exhibition before the governor and both houses, and again I delivered an address and answered numerous questions. I appealed to the legislators to urge the establishment of the school, to set an example for other legislatures, and to the citizenry. I spoke of the thousands of deaf and dumb who needed their aid and of the representative few whom I had already met: Mr. Thomas Aspinwall of Roxbury, George Ropes of Salem, Alice Cogswell of Hartford, and a Mr. Jones of New Haven. "As soon as I beheld them my face became animated, I was as agitated as a traveler of sensibility would be on meeting all of a sudden in distant regions a colony of his countrymen. On their side, those deaf and dumb persons fixed their looks on me, and recognized me as one of themselves. An expression of surprise and pleasure enlivened all their features. I approached them. I made some signs and they answered me by signs. This communication caused a most delicious sensation in each of us. . . . But gentlemen, if the deaf and dumb are happy together, those who do not know how to read and write are not so with persons endowed with the sense of hearing and the use of speech because they cannot make themselves understood. Be then so good as to hasten their happiness. Your countrymen have been too negligent of the unfortunate class of deaf and dumb. I hope you will soon rival the benevolence of Europe."[26]

My eloquence was not, however, crowned with success, as Mason explained in a letter to Mary: "Nothing short of an immediate revelation would touch the hearts of the obdurate democrats, and ignorant and selfish federalists. The house, in the abundance of their liberality, granted $5,000. The council sent the bill back to them with $10,000. The house refused to concur and the bill falls to the ground between them. Thus all our hopes from the legislature, for the present, are blasted."[27]

"I pity the cold, cautious, calculating, captious, phlegmatic legislature of our state," Thomas wrote in a fury.[28]

Still, we were soon off to New York, by a novel means of transportation, the steamboat; it was a most delightful passage, "without the slightest accident," Mason wrote to Mary. We traveled about the city speaking to members of the committee that Dr. Mitchill had convened and found them unaware of our efforts, although Mason was convinced Mitchill knew about them.[29] Of course, these citizens were disinclined to contribute funds to our

*New Haven and Hartford were co-capitals at the time.

school until it became clearer whether New York was to have its own school or not.[30] So we were left at loose ends and went immediately to the state capital in hopes of catching the rich and great while the legislature was in session.

In Albany, De Witt Clinton, the mayor of New York City for the last dozen years and shortly to become governor, received us warmly and we persuaded him of our design to have but one institution, located at Hartford.[31] We had a splendid meeting at the capitol in the representatives' chamber, where had gathered virtually all the members of the legislature, a large number of leading citizens from Albany, and many strangers from all parts of the state. At Mason's suggestion, I emphasized the reasons for creating a single school: "As it will be large and the pupils numerous, there will be great emulation among them, and they will become better instructed." The *Albany Advertiser** gave an additional reason for a single school when it published my address: "Uniformity in the signs of thought, the language of the deaf and dumb, is of immense importance in extending their means of intercourse with each other. . . . This uniformity it will be difficult to preserve when the seminaries for the deaf and dumb are fairly numerous." I had thought of this argument only after my address, but I am pleased to see I thought of it at all. At that early point in my career, Epée and Sicard's belief that sign was everywhere the same still had great influence on me, and I might not have seen the danger of allowing several isolated signing societies to develop. I gave several reasons for choosing Hartford as the location for the single institution: its central location in the populous North, its healthful air, the low cost of living, and its distance from the largest cities, which often attract youth by various distractions and corrupt their manners (hardly a reason I would have given in France!).

The address was well received and the legislators plied me with questions, Thomas serving as translator. Q: "What is truth?" (This, I believe, was to establish if those born deaf can manage abstract ideas.) A: "It is the conformity of an action with its fact, of what we say with what we have seen, or heard, or learned." Q: "What is the difference in the manners and habits of the people of this country and those of the French people?" A: "Your manners and habits seem to me to be more regular and simple, and consequently more salutary. Those of the French, though less regular and less constant, are nevertheless more elegant and polite, but you improve more and more every day and I hope you will be quite equal to them in a few years."

We shortly began what Mason called our "begging tour" and by the end of the week we had collected in cash and promissory notes nearly $2,000.[32]

---

*Its editor was Theodore Dwight (1764–1846), member of Congress, Hartford Wit, and former editor of the Hartford *Courant.*

We returned to New York by steamboat and learned on arriving that Mitchill was pursuing Gard's offer and intended to call for a census of the city's deaf, and that John Braidwood was in town in a third attempt to start a deaf school of his own.[33] (The last Mason had heard of him he had been fired from Colonel Bolling's school at Cobb, had left debts at two Richmond taverns, and had grabbed the stage north.)[34] Mitchill's colleague Samuel Akerly went to see Braidwood and perhaps discouraged him; he reported that the Scot was obliged to leave New York because of improper conduct.[35] The next word we had of Braidwood was in the spring, when he had returned to Virginia "penniless, friendless, and scarcely decently clad," in the words of Colonel Bolling, who assisted him again—this time in opening a school in Manchester in conjunction with the Reverend John Kirkpatrick.[36] We decided not to remain in New York for Mitchill's meeting in about two weeks; for one thing, word had it that Consul Lee had left New York for Philadelphia and had circulated Gard's letter there.[37] We hoped to preempt yet a fourth attempt to open an asylum by proceeding there at once and raising a subscription.

In Philadelphia, I gave an address in Washington Hall. The meeting was crowded and I spoke of the nature of sign language, and of the abbé de l'Epée, who had communicated his system of instruction to disciples from throughout Europe, "so that all the European deaf and dumb owe their present happiness to him." I told how Sicard perfected his method and how the deaf in Europe were trained for professions and self-sufficiency—as teachers, administrators, painters, sculptors, engravers, workers in mosaic, printers, merchants.[38]

I was well received, but beginning the following week the Philadelphia papers carried a series of exchanges on the merits and demerits of a local school for the deaf, and Gard's letter was published.[39] This materially hindered our fund-raising, and our subscriptions—$1,700 in all—were not as great as we had anticipated. Our worst fears about the dispersion of effort thus confirmed, we agreed to return to New York to attempt again to head off the school there and raise a subscription of our own.[40]

Back in New York we made several calls attempting to interest leading citizens in the Hartford school and to persuade members of Mitchill's committee to end their independent course.[41] We decided not to attend Mitchill's next meeting ourselves for fear of appearing to exert undue influence, but we urged our friends to attend. Stanford and Akerly reported that there were forty-seven deaf and dumb in the city (four wards not yet heard from) and that thirty-four were between six and eighteen and could receive instruction. They went on to state falsely that the Braidwoods had invented the art of teaching speech and that their method had all the advantages of Epée's plus one more—conversation with the hearing. They proposed not to pursue François Gard's offer because they wished their pupils to speak.

Mitchill moved to form a committee of nine members to write a constitution and to petition the legislature and the city for funds to start a school for the deaf. Our friends opposed the motion, but the meeting decided in favor, and we took the steamer home to Hartford with only twenty-five donations in hand.

Ours had been a long campaign: five months, seven different cities, I don't know how many addresses! And, except for New York and Philadelphia, it had been successful. Many towns in Connecticut and Massachusetts followed the lead of their capital cities. The other New England states and a handful of Southern states responded to our published appeals. About $700 came from overseas (S.V.S. Wilder, Hannah More, Zachary Macaulay). In all, $12,000 was collected and the legislature of Connecticut finally provided us with $5,000 more. A school for the American deaf was no longer a dream, it was about to become a reality. And Alice Cogswell would be its first pupil.

Like all gestations, that of our new school was filled with joy and apprehension. It lasted only three months. A commodious house on Main Street (now the south half of the City Hotel, adjacent to the small building that had been occupied by Noah Webster when he wrote his famous spelling book) was secured. Announcements in the newspapers specified an annual charge of $200, which included the cost of instruction that Thomas and I would provide as well as "lodging, board, washing, continued superintendence of health, conduct, manners and morals, fuel, candles, stationery, and incidentals."[42] We had so much trouble finding a head for the domestic department to supervise all these ancillary matters that Thomas chose a day in February to invoke divine assistance and the several pastors of Hartford were invited to be present to conduct religious services.[43] This yielded, most improvidentially, as it turned out, the Reverend A. O. Stansbury and his lady. The notice went on to state that the term of instruction was three to six years and, I am sorry to say, that the school could not receive charity scholars except from the very few towns that had contributed to its resources.

Classes began on April 15. By the time of the opening ceremonies in Center Church the following Sunday, there were seven pupils for me to accompany.[44] Reverend Strong had died while we were in New York, and it was Thomas who preached to the crowded assembly. As he entered the pulpit I thought, It is two years exactly since he consented to go to Europe and learn to be a teacher of the deaf. A parent cries: "My child will live and die in ignorance" and a servant of Christ consents to learn in order to teach. The text of what must have been the first signed sermon in America was from Isaiah: "Then the eyes of the blind shall be opened and the ears of the deaf unstopped. Then shall the lame man leap as an hart and the tongue of the dumb sing." (Thomas said the passage referred to Christ's miracles then and to the diffusion of the Gospel now.)

Thomas spoke of the advantages likely to arise from a school for the deaf. The deaf child is a kind of experiment of nature and from its careful study we can learn much about the human mind in general—about innate ideas of God, about the faculties that do not require language and those that do, about original notions of right and wrong and the obligations of conscience. More immediately, our school would provide consolation to relatives and friends of the deaf. It is difficult to imagine the heartbreak of a mother who cannot truly communicate with her child, to explain an absence, a danger, to reassure it in times of illness, in brief, to explain the world. (And how the world's ways are mysterious and infuriating for the deaf youth, I recalled. And how my temper did rage when I could not fathom the wants of others nor tell them my own!)

Then Thomas came to it: the greatest advantage of educating the deaf accrues to the deaf themselves. "Must not each one of them in the language of thought sometimes say: 'What is it that makes me different from my fellow men? Why are they so much my superiors? What is the strange mode of communicating by which they understand each other with the rapidity of lightning, and which enlightens their faces with the brightest expressions of joy?' " (Images of the neighbors' children shunning me, of Massieu pleading with his father to go to school, of my first visit to the doctor, when my parents mysteriously allowed him to inflict great pain—these and a thousand others flickered on the screen of my mind.) " 'What are those mysterious characters over which they pore with such incessant delight and that seem to gladden the hours that pass by me so sad and cheerless? What mean the ten thousand customs which I witness in the private circles and public assemblies and which possess such mighty influence over the conduct and feelings of those around me. And the termination of life, the placing in the cold bosom of the earth those whom I have loved so long and so tenderly: how it makes me shudder! What is death? Why are my friends thus laid by and forgotten? Will they never revive from this strange slumber? Shall the grass always grow over them? Shall I see their faces no more forever? And must I also thus cease to move, and fall into an eternal sleep?' "

Thomas was a fine preacher and, whether in Paris or Albany or Hartford, always a popular one. Out of the pulpit he was an excellent conversationalist, with anecdotes from wide experience. He was tactful in winning others to his views; he would rather pray for them than reprove them; he never voted, so he could "secure the cooperation of all parties." Neither greatness nor favor nor rank could seduce or dazzle him. In the pulpit, his manner was earnest, his subject clear, his development compelling: the audience was borne along by a swelling tide.[45]

Thomas went on to say how the first school for the deaf in the Western world came to be founded in Hartford ("Here God saw fit to afflict an interesting child that her misfortune might move the feelings and rouse the efforts of her parents and friends") and why all the resources of the country should now be focused in this one school (uniformity of education and the training of teachers). He explained the rewards forthcoming for future exertions in behalf of these children, incorporating much from our discussion with President Dwight. "Do we participate in the Redeemer's spirit? Are we promoting the welfare of his kingdom? Does our benevolence toward men spring from love toward the Savior of our souls? Let us trust alone to his righteousness for acceptance with God. That this may be the sure foundation, to each one of us, of peace in this world and of happiness in the next, may God of his mercy grant! Amen."[46]

The Connecticut Asylum for the Education and Instruction of Deaf and Dumb Persons prospered, and by the time of President Monroe's visit in June we had twenty-one pupils.[47] I remember the occasion of the visit well, for it was my first meeting with a president and one I had heard much about (from St. George Randolph). In later years Henry Clay and Andrew Jackson also visited our school.[48]

The ostensible purpose of the newly elected President's tour of New England was to inspect national defenses. In New Haven he visited Eli Whitney's gun manufacture* and Yale College, then on to Middletown and the munitions works. At Hartford, his party was met by the first company of the governor's Horse Guard and a large concourse of citizens, who escorted it over the city bridge, ornamented with three lofty evergreen and laurel arches in imitation of the triumphal arches of Rome. The assembly stopped at Morgan's coffeehouse, where John Morgan, the senior alderman, gave a speech of welcome and the President reviewed the elegant line of troops drawn up on Main Street.[49] He was then hurried down Main Street to our school, where a high platform had been prepared, and here he took his seat, as on a throne. The President's appearance was quite unprepossessing: a small man with deep-set eyes and no forehead, he was dressed somewhat carelessly, all in plain black, bare-headed. "He hasn't got enough brains to hold his hat on!" said one federalist.

All around the platform were the spectators, on one side was Thomas, and on the other side, myself. Thomas invited the President to ask me a question, which he would interpret in the language of signs, much as the abbé Sicard had done with the duke of Wellington. I was to answer on a slate provided me. The President wrinkled his brow and became lost in thought and a very long time went by without his framing any question at all, so Thomas repeated his offer: "If Your Excellency will be so kind as to ask some question, I will repeat it on my fingers to Mr. Clerc, and he will write

*Shortly after inventing the cotton gin, Whitney built this firearms factory.

an answer on the slate, to show the manner and facility of conversing by sign." Still there was a long pause, and Thomas, seeming to fear that the President was going to sleep, roused him by repeating his offer a third time. At last the President seemed conscious, his eyes twinkled, his lips moved: "Ask him how—old he is" was the profound question. Of course, nowadays the American government does much more for the deaf, but I wonder if it does not still have this trifling image of our language and our minds: adequate perhaps to give our age or our names but inadequate for real conversation.[50]

The school the President visited was three stories high. From the rear there was a fine vista, cultivated country with houses here and there half-obscured by trees, bright patches of red or white in the sunlight. Closer in was the school garden, with lettuce, radishes, beets, beans, corn, cucumbers, and cabbages. No, it was not the stately seminary of the Oratorians, the vista did not include the rooftops of Paris and the Seine, and the gardens would have fit in one corner of those of Saint-Jacques. Yes, everything was scaled down in size and age, except the dreams of the new school's young directors.

All the asylum family lived and learned within.[51] (At first, our pupils had boarded out, but this put their health and comfort at the mercy of pecuniary interests and prevented the older students from socializing with the younger.) The morning assembled us to worship; the pupils then amused themselves until breakfast at seven, followed by study until nine, when half entered my classroom, the others, Thomas's. The lessons were written with chalk on large slates placed on easels. From twelve to two, cleanup, dinner, and free time, followed by an hour's writing instruction from Reverend Stansbury. From three to six came more classes, then a light snack, a walk or visit until nine, when all assembled for worship again and then our scholars retired.

Besides Alice, the initial class included George Loring, youngest of the group at age nine and perhaps the brightest—he had an astonishing memory for historical facts and dates. (I spoke of him earlier as the astute reader of Thomas's facial communication.) He came from a distinguished Boston family—an illness when he was two and a half had taken his hearing and the sight of one eye—and his father had contributed liberally to the asylum during our fund-raising campaign there. He was a pupil for over eight years, then became a teacher at our school, as did the friend he arrived with, Wilson Whiton.[52] The fourth pupil to join the class, as I recall, was Abigail Dillingham, from Lenox, Massachusetts. She was gifted at writing, drawing, and drafting and very industrious, and had a deaf sister who was admitted the following year.[53] Abigail also became a teacher of the deaf, in Pennsylvania. Do you remember Silvester Gilbert from nearby Hebron, with five deaf children? He had corresponded with Mason and joined his appeal for a census of the deaf. When the asylum opened he sent us fifty dollars as a contribution and his eldest daughter, Mary, as a pupil.[54] Gilbert's neighbor, a Mr. Backus, sent his son to the same class: Levi Backus went on to become an instructor of the deaf in New York State and has the distinction of having launched the silent press in America: in 1836 he started editing the Canajoharie (New York) *Radii*.[55] No less an authority than Horace Greeley* said in his magazine that Backus's "editorials are sententious and sensible, his selections judicious, and his journal every way respectable."[56] After a decade Levi's office burned down and he resumed publication in Fort Plain, New York, with the paper known thereafter as the *Radii and Phoenix*.

Parnel and Sophia Fowler came from a family of six children in Guilford; the other four were hearing, though a cousin was deaf. Alice became quite close to Sophia, who was then nineteen,[57] and to another pupil in that class, Eliza Boardman of Whitesborough, New York. Thomas and I, however, were to become even closer, for he married Sophia Fowler four years later —shortly after I wed Eliza. But more of that later.

Our pupils came that first year—at its end, we had thirty-one—from ten different states.[58] About half were male and their ages ranged from ten to fifty; the average pupil was in his early twenties. A little over half had been born deaf and another nine had lost their hearing before they were four, so roughly four out of five students had never spoken English to any degree. Nearly all had hearing parents and knew no other deaf people outside their family, which had increased their isolation and reliance on pantomime and home sign.[59] The average stay at the asylum was initially four years, though that varied. Later the minimum stay became four years, and then five.[60]

My duties kept me very busy indeed. I taught a class; I assisted Thomas, especially where planning instruction and sign language were concerned. I gave some of the religious instruction. And I gave lessons in sign language after hours to Reverend Stansbury, to new teachers as they joined us, and, later, to the many hearing teachers who came to the asylum to study with me and then return to their home states to teach the deaf. In these lessons and the classroom I used French Sign Language amended for American practices; for example, I had no signs for various articles of clothing and food unknown in France and these I took from my pupils. We also used methodical sign amended for English. Most English words had a simple French translation with its methodical sign, but where that was not the case we had to invent one. The other means of communication in the classroom were written English and the French Manual Alphabet (fingerspelling), used since Epée's time and originally taken from Bonet.

Gradually my sign language underwent expansion and modification in the hands of my American pupils. At first that caused me considerable distress;

*(1811–1872); founder of the New York *Tribune*.

I viewed it as a kind of corruption, one so extensive in fact that when I last saw Massieu he told me to stop talking like an Indian![61] But I have come to view it as a natural evolution. Here is how it occurs.

The isolated deaf-mute who comes to our asylum, as I came to the Paris school, brings with him a more or less abridged pantomime, the only skill of communication he has been able to develop in a world that cut him off from all natural languages. To indicate individual objects, he points them out if they happen to be present. Actions can be called to mind by literal imitation. If he means to recall the idea of writing, he actually seems to write. And the signs of the passions consist simply of the facial expressions that usually accompany them. The same is true for some of the simpler intellectual operations. When our isolated deaf child wants to indicate an absent object he tries to portray its form and exhibit its qualities or any characteristic circumstances that attend it. Thus a house may be represented by carrying the hands upward parallel to each other for the sides and then joining them at the top for a roof. An object with an irregular outline—for example an animal—can be indicated by a peculiar habit or motion: what can be easier than to imitate the motion of a fish swimming? The undulation of the sea, the rolling of a ship (with the bow represented by the joined hands), the waving of a tree, the action of flying, all these will illustrate descriptive pantomime.

The uses of objects provide another fertile source of description. A stable may be distinguished from other dwellings by having a horse enter it. The horse itself may be denoted by showing its use or by the act of mounting it. Common tools and items of furniture, things that we characteristically put our hands on, provide little problem. The mode of production or preparation may likewise be resorted to if it singularly indicates the target idea. Cloth may be called to mind by reference to weaving. The shoemaker, the carpenter, the bricklayer, and so on may be personified in their various employments. The deaf child may sharpen an imaginary razor, or wind an absent watch. The materials of which objects are composed furnish yet another source for pantomime. Tastes may be conveyed by facial expressions, colors by objects at hand: the lips for red, the bosom for white, the eyebrow for black. Moral qualities may be expressed by facial expression or by metaphor. Justice, for example, may be portrayed by the action of weighing, while the countenance assumes an expression of inquiry and candor. The divisions of time can be represented by positions of the sun. The seasons suggest descriptive signs: sprouting for spring, perspiration for summer, falling leaves for autumn, cold and snow for winter.

Now as others become more conversant with the pantomime of our deaf child, he finds that he can omit many of the auxiliary signs of description and still be understood. In all his conversation, he is continually on the watch to carry this process of retrenchment further: his eye is constantly on the face of the person he is addressing and he continues his descriptions no longer than is absolutely necessary for understanding. When the deaf child then arrives at our school, he finds that his abridged home sign is often unintelligible to the other pupils and their signing is often unintelligible to him. This at first slows down communication but is not an insuperable barrier since both parties can fall back on expanded pantomime of the sort I have described. By and large, the newcomer quickly succumbs to the pressure of the group and learns that, in using their signs rather than his own, he is readily understood. No doubt he finds the signing of the community easier, too, for it is not only concise but also regular. It uses only a small stock of handshapes and movements and displays these signs in space in predictable ways he comes to expect.

The newcomer also learns a great many new signs; some have been introduced by other pupils when they came, others have arisen in the course of life at the school, the greater part I introduced in the classroom and during extracurricular activities. Additional signs develop not based on resemblance or metaphor but primarily because they distinguish one person or place from another in the limited universe of the pupils. Their growing mastery of English provides yet another source of vocabulary growth: often the first letter of an English word, represented in the manual alphabet, is employed (with some appropriate movement) to represent the same idea the word does. The expanded vocabulary attained by all of these means is of the greatest importance for it allows new activity for the intellect. I use it to impart new ideas, to define English words, to explain English word order and endings, to secure discipline and teach religion. Thus it happens that deaf-mutes familiar with the language of our school can converse on subjects, even at a very early stage of their education, that are a sealed book to their less-favored counterparts at home. And thus it happens that the vocabulary I brought from France has been superseded, modified, and added to, leaving me a little behind the times.[62]

I trust it is clear that I did not actually teach sign language in class; newcomers learn it from the older students spontaneously. For many years I did teach methodical sign, the invented signs for spoken language words to be used in the English word order. But after Bébian's reform we abandoned methodical signs altogether and they are now simply an interesting monument to the ingenuity, perseverance, and classical education of Epée and Sicard.[63] Neither was it necessary, of course, to teach fingerspelling. That can be learned in an hour or two—every educated person should know how—and facility comes simply with practice.

Thus of the three forms of communication eventually used in the classroom—American Sign Language, written English, and fingerspelling—only written English required instruction. It demanded, however, the greater part of our efforts, which is not surprising since it was, in the first place, a foreign language quite unfamiliar to a majority of our students and, in the second place, organized along lines totally different from the language they did know, sign language. We always used English sentences, never mere lists of words, and we tried to tie those sentences into various themes and activities as an alternate description to the one appropriate in sign.[64]

In our very first lessons we presented tangible things and aimed to make the pupil notice his own sensations, observations, and feelings and to talk about them in sign. Daily and Sabbath worship was conducted in sign. Increasingly, we expressed these ideas in written English sentences as well, then asked the pupil to retranslate them into sign. As he progressed, the pupil would be called on at intervals to express his own ideas in written English and to translate the signed sentence of another. The topics moved away from firsthand experience to astronomy, geography, and, later, history, biography, and arithmetic.[65] Still, it must be admitted that language instruction always crowds out much of the arts and sciences, even when articulation is not taught (it crowds them out entirely when it is, as we have seen).

The one subject that was not neglected at our school, you may be sure, was religion.[66] The reason, of course, was that for Gallaudet as for Epée there was not a minute to lose in saving the pupils' souls, lest they be doomed to eternal torment by dying suddenly, unprepared. "O Almighty God," Thomas wrote in his diary, "Thou knowest my desire is to be devoted to Thy service and to be made the instrument of training up the deaf and dumb for heaven."[67] By his every act as much as by his preaching, Thomas taught Christian values: his benevolence was practical and universal and could be followed by everyone, every day, in some way or other. As did Epée, Massieu, and Sicard, he had about him a childlike air—a certain candor and lack of guile—and thus a singular aptitude for exciting the interest and winning the confidence of children.[68] Henry Barnard, the first U.S. Commissioner of Education—a post offered first to Thomas—said of him: "His religious life was his whole life. . . . His life was a living sermon." Not quite, alas, for temporal demands were made on him: he taught six hours a day, he corresponded, he received visitors, arranged exhibitions, taught teachers, wrote reports, appealed for funds, conducted services, fought with the board—and found it all distasteful and desperately tiring! His very modesty, courtesy, humility made him indisposed to assume and exercise authority, impaired his efficiency, and added greatly to his cares.[69]

In its second year, our school quite outgrew its quarters—we had passed the hundred mark—and we took a building down the street from Mason's home. The new site was used for all purposes except meals, which were still taken at the City Hotel, our little family marching to and fro.[70] Another signal event that year was the departure of Reverend Stansbury to head the rival institution in New York, which did the deaf a great disservice. It came about in this way. As we had prepared to open our school in Hartford the year before, Mitchill had convened a fifth meeting of his committee in Manhattan to consider a draft constitution for a New York school. He announced that, with another ward now reporting, there were sixty-six deaf and dumb in New York City, perhaps two-thirds of school age. Most of the people present agreed with our earlier arguments for a single institution and thought the Connecticut Asylum sufficient to receive these additional pupils: they voted to adjourn indefinitely. Mitchill and Akerly, however, saw themselves as president and secretary of a grand new institution and were not to be deterred. They prepared a list of organizers and directors, with the Honorable De Witt Clinton duplicitously heading the list, and they petitioned the New York Legislature for an act of incorporation. It was granted the very day our school opened its doors.[71] The directors then wrote to England to get themselves a Braidwood. How could it be otherwise? Mitchill and Akerly were both physicians who saw the deaf as disabled, and the task of education as obliterating their disability, or at least reducing it. Moreover, he who speaks of oralism and Braidwood speaks of money, and these gentlemen were not disinterested.

Meanwhile, Reverend Stansbury had dreams of glory. Why should he not be superintendent and principal of the new school? Never mind that he signed like a dead man, in a tiny box in front of his chest without a glint of facial expression, never mind that all he knew of a classroom was how to mix chalk and paste. "I wish you [would go and] see De Witt Clinton," he wrote to his brother in New York, "and know what are his ideas, as I understand a large subscription is to be taken up in New York for this asylum [yet] no persons are instructed as teachers, and when anything is said [here] on this head, the only reply is, that perhaps it may not be expedient to furnish New York with teachers, which might raise up a rival establishment."[72]

Around the time of our school's first anniversary, Stansbury was offered the position he so dearly sought, and asked our board to excuse him from his bond.[73] Although I thought he would prejudice the people in New York against our system by misrepresenting it, since he knew so little of it, and although I knew he was quite unqualified to be the principal of a school for the deaf, I could not brook hindering him, for such an action might be construed by history as similar to the Braidwoods'; and I said so to the board.[74] So, in the spring Stansbury moved to New York and the city authorities set aside a room in the almshouse for his class. Four young deaf-mutes were brought to him as day students, and all he could think to do with them was teach them the manual alphabet! Nevertheless, the enrollment grew steadily. When the long-awaited reply finally came from the Braidwoods, their proposal was deemed exorbitant and rejected. Instead, the committee hired Stansbury's daughter. There were twenty-four day scholars and nine residential pupils who were lodged and boarded in hired rooms—hired from Akerly!

The familiar story of oralism. It would have been funny if it had not been tragic, for the children.[75]

We not only changed quarters and superintendents in 1818, we also started hiring and training teachers. The first went on to become rather famous as a teacher of the deaf, an editor, and author of the most popular public school geography. His name was William Channing Woodbridge and his father had organized the first association of teachers in the United States.[76] A Yale graduate, Woodbridge had attended Princeton Theological Seminary with a view to becoming a foreign missionary, but Thomas urged him to consider a calling closer to hand, and he consented to visit the asylum. I still have the record of our conversation in Thomas's chamber.[77]

W: My father writes me that this is "enchanted ground," and that he is afraid I shall not judge correctly when there is so much to excite my feelings.

C: Your father, I believe, imagines that your task would be very hard; but when you see him again and inform him about our institution and tell him how much good you would do to these unfortunate beings, I am persuaded he would not urge you anymore to pursue the profession to which you intend to devote yourself.

W: My mother died eight years ago with joyful anticipation of future blessedness in the presence of God, saying, "I love my husband—I love my children, but I love my Savior more, and I long to be where he is." On her bed of death she charged me, "My son, be an apostolic preacher. Speak for your Savior, every day you live."—Must I not comply with this charge?

C: If your mother lived yet at this moment she would have no objection to the proposition we make to you; for you will do much good by restoring more than two thousand unfortunates to Society and Religion: it would be more agreeable to make our Savior known to them than to preach to those who have already an idea of religion.

W: It had been long my desire to teach those who had no other means of instruction, but when I think of the *millions* of idolators who have no teachers it becomes more important to spend my life in teaching them.

(Woodbridge pointed to the words "millions" and "two thousand" to contrast them.)

C: If you go on purpose to teach the *million idolators* you will not be able to teach them all, they all will not be very docile; and the good you will have done will be reduced to a few individuals; but if you teach the deaf and dumb they will be more docile, and you will have restored to the religion of our Savior more people in this country than elsewhere.

W: You are a good *lawyer* for the deaf and dumb but can you encourage me by mentioning any good effects of your religious instruction of the deaf and dumb?

C: I may assure you that if you decide to stay with us, you will serve the cause of Jesus Christ more perfectly; may God determine you; what satisfaction will you not experience when you see around you the numerous persons you will have rendered happy; Jesus Christ cured the deaf and dumb, the limping, the paralytic—preferably to others; you must imitate him and cure the deaf and dumb.

I am a bit startled to see how tailored to his disposition my arguments were but they were successful in persuading him. Woodbridge suffered from a frail constitution and nervous ailments, however, and, after only three years with us, sailed off to Europe in the hope of relief. When he came back, he resigned and spent his full time on a universal geography; later, he moved to Boston and took over the *American Journal of Education*, changing its name to the *Annals of Education*.[78]

When the asylum's enrollments had grown to fifty, and two more instructors were needed besides Woodbridge, Thomas, and me, Thomas applied to Yale, and Lewis Weld and Isaac Orr were recommended. Orr had an incredible amount of nervous energy, which he lavished on mechanical inventions and overwork in the schoolroom. This injured his health and, like Woodbridge, he retired early. Weld, however, began a long career at Hartford that led him to preeminence as a teacher of the deaf; he became head of the Pennsylvania school and then, with Thomas's retirement, head of our own school, which he ably defended against the attacks of the know-nothing New England aristocracy. Weld cut a tall commanding figure. His blue eyes sparkled with intelligence in a highly expressive face whose aquiline nose and firmly compressed lips intimated the resolve with which he pursued the interests of the deaf.

In time, deaf teachers who had begun as pupils at our school joined the ranks of the faculty. You know a bit about George Loring. George had wealth, influence, intelligence, and culture. He studied French with me and after nine months wrote it with near-perfect accuracy. He loved poetry. After sixteen years with us, eight as a pupil, eight more as a teacher, he went home, in part so a poor classmate might have his job. There he read for fifteen years, while serving as acknowledged head of the Boston deaf community. At the age of forty, he married a deaf woman but that happy union ended shockingly when he died three years later.[79]

Loring's friend Wilson Whiton is usually considered the first American deaf teacher, though as I recall he and Loring started teaching the same year.[80] Whiton, who was born deaf and entered our school when he was twelve, was the first student sponsored by another state and the third to arrive at the asylum. He is still at our school; his wife, Sybil, a former pupil, died a few years ago.

Edmund Booth, like Alice Cogswell, had been deafened by spotted fever. When he was sixteen a neighbor informed him about our school, and he went by stage from Springfield to Hartford over the protestations of his uncle and guardian, who wanted his labor on the family farm. His autobiography describes his arrival at our school: "The coach stopped at the front door and we emerged. A few small boys came around with curious looks; the nearest with bright eager face and quick eyes scanned me from head to foot, glanced at brother Charles who was talking and attending to the baggage, motioned to the next nearest boy and then to me, and said I was a 'new pupil.' I did not understand then but guessed and remembered these simple signs. We entered the hall and in a few minutes Mr. Gallaudet, the principal, came. In conversation with him, my brother informed him I could speak and on this hint he—Mr. G.—proceeded to ascertain the extent of my knowledge of words. The only word he selected was 'accumulate,' a word with which I was wholly unacquainted. Probably he so understood from my look, he being quick enough at reading looks. He then defined the word in signs as unintelligible to me as the word itself. . . . Charles and I went into the boys' and next the girls' sitting rooms. It was all new to me and to Charles it was amusing, the innumerable motions of arms and hands. After dinner he left and I was among strangers but knew I was at home."[81]

Booth was to be an excellent pupil, acquiring a very good command of English and French, and we asked him to stay on as a teacher, which he did for seven years. He resigned after a dispute over pay. Loring and Whiton had been hired at the scandalously low salary of $250 a year and Booth was told that hiring him at a higher salary, as he requested, would cause them to be dissatisfied. The sum was not enough to live on—board, fuel, washing, and traveling took up more than that amount—and all three were obliged to borrow. The salary increased yearly by $100 for four years and then $50 annually thereafter, but it was still far too low. When Lewis Weld succeeded Thomas he urged the board to increase Booth's salary but they replied that it would entail raising those of present and future deaf teachers as well—unthinkable! Besides, since Booth had been educated on charity he should be glad to offer some of his services gratis![82]

After resigning, Booth set out on a 1300-mile journey to the town of Anamosa, Iowa, where he joined a former pupil, later to become his wife, and took up farming. He was elected repeatedly to the office of county recorder but at mid-century he joined the Gold Rush past his door. The trek to California took six months and he stayed there five arduous, dangerous, lonely years,[83] finally earning enough to return—by way of the Panama Canal and the Mississippi River—and buy a local newspaper, the *Anamosa Eureka*, which he made into a strongly abolitionist paper. He is still the editor.

The second year of our school was a time not only of moving, hiring, and training but also of raising funds from the Congress. Either Thomas or I had to go to Washington, since one of us must remain in Hartford to teach; it was felt that I would be more effective, although I did not relish the prospect of exhibiting myself as a specimen before the representatives, especially in the role of soliciting aid. When I was introduced to Henry Clay in the House, however, he said he recognized me as one of two mutes he had seen signing in a Paris restaurant: he greeted me most cordially, gave me a seat by his side, interrupted the proceedings to introduce me to the members present, and suspended the session for a half hour so they could ascertain by free conversation (on paper) the ability of an educated deaf man to read and express his ideas. I repeated this performance some days later and then told the Speaker the object of my visit; he promised to assist me personally. Afterward, I visited the Senate chamber. The next day I went to the White House, where the French ambassador, to whom I had a letter of recommendation from the duc de Montmorency, introduced me to President Monroe. The President received me affably and bid me welcome to America. He said he remembered me from one of the abbé Sicard's demonstrations (not from Hartford!) and that he hoped I would receive great honor and much gratitude by doing good to the deaf and dumb.[84]

A year later, on the petition of our board, which argued that we had a national mission since we received pupils from ten states, and with the support of Henry Clay as promised, a bill passed awarding the school 23,000 acres of uninhabited land in Alabama; when all of it was finally sold it provided an endowment of nearly $300,000. One immediate result of the act was that the board could obtain credit to begin building on seven acres we had recently acquired, one-half mile west of the city. Another prompt result was that the state General Assembly approved our request to change the name of the school from the Connecticut Asylum to the American Asylum at Hartford. (The deaf at our school vigorously opposed the label "asylum" but the board would not listen: appeals for funds could not be based simply on the right of the deaf to an education.)[85]

About the same time our school changed its name and Eliza Boardman became my wife, I reminded Thomas and the board that my three-year contract would soon expire, that I had always planned to return to my native land. Moreover, I wished to present my wife to my family, and I had received a letter from the abbé Sicard—Massieu and Machwitz miss you so, I am destitute and need you, when are you coming back?[86] The board argued that the most important part of my task, the training of teachers, had just begun, that I was needed more in America than France. We reached a compromise: I would return to France for a year. If I returned to Hartford, a new three-year contract would apply at more than double my present salary and with six weeks annual vacation.[87]

This salary, $1,200 a year, was substantially greater than Thomas's, a point of embarrassment to me but he insisted he did not mind. All he asked was "that we may continue to labor together in doing good to the dear immortal souls by whom we are surrounded."[88] Dear Thomas, he always felt surrounded by our pupils, never followed or accompanied by them. He entered our profession poor and after thirteen years he left it poor. Money-making was to him no passion. Benevolence, reflection, friendship—these were his passions.[89]

Once I was back in France, my friends, family, and the abbé urged me to stay. I still have his note to Massieu; he was then eighty and failing rapidly, but his demonstrations went on. "Beg Clerc for me to come with us [to the lecture] and tell him it will give me extreme pleasure if he will leave us no more. . . . I will be delighted if he prefers our country. . . . Paris is the foremost city in the world."[90] Massieu, however, said he could not in good conscience paint a favorable picture of prospects at Saint-Jacques: De Gérando was then increasingly taking the reins, Itard was urging more training in speech, each teacher was proceeding independently of the others. On the other hand, letters came to me from Hartford with reminders of friendship and with enticements: the new buildings were almost finished, I would find magnificent facilities on my return.

In the end, then, I came back to Hartford, postponing a final decision for another three years. Alice described my return in a letter to the parents of a friend. I excerpt it here so you can see the progress she had made in four years at our school.

"You cannot imagine how I was glad at the arrival of Mr. Clerc. Every Hartford body is extremely happy to see him. He is fleshy, happy and healthy. He had made a great deals of travels in the part of Europe. When you come here you will undoubtedly feel glad to see him again. I suppose you have not heard of this, that the new Asylum is completely finished, and the deaf and dumb persons live already there now. I used to go to school nowadays, sometimes in a chaise when it rains. But I dine with the D. and D. every noon. It is a most delightful and cool place and has as fine a prospect as I ever saw or felt. When you are in this town I will show you the apartments of the new Asylum. In the highest storey it is a very large garret called the hall and has four arched windows. You will be delighted to view the prospect. The new Asylum has been dedicated about a few weeks ago. A great number of people assembled to hear Mr. Gallaudet's sermon, and a dedicatory hymn written by Mrs. Sigourney was sung."[91]

The dedication of our school's new home shortly after my return was a splendid event. A large audience was assembled on the spacious lawn in front of the handsome four-story brick building. Nature, too, had dedicated a new cycle of fertility and growth: the lawns were lush and green, the orchards in bloom, the gardens sprouting. The sun reflected in the windows dazzled the spectators and seemed to encircle Thomas with a halo as he preached: "For we know that if our earthly house of this tabernacle were dissolved, we have a building of God." The earthly building was designed by Daniel Wadsworth and contained accommodations for one hundred fifty pupils and others, several schoolrooms, and a chapel. How light, airy, and

American Asylum at Hartford for the Education
and Instruction of the Deaf and Dumb (1821)

grand it was! "Thou didst direct the attention of the benevolent to these children of suffering," Thomas intoned. It had begun with Alice—could it be just over four years ago? She seemed virtually a solitary instance then. Now she sat bright-eyed and alert surrounded by classmates. "Thou didst move the hand of charity to supply their wants." And made Thomas her neighbor—how extraordinary—and gave him a glimpse of the abbé Sicard and me in London, equally fortuitous. Chance is an illusion. "Thou didst provide the means of their instruction." Yes, even Epée's alienation from the Church now seemed full of purpose. And Braidwood's refusal. And Jauffret leaving me behind. "Thou didst touch the hearts of the wise and honorable with compassion towards them." And used me as a vessel, a vassal. The endless voyage, the torrent of language, cities with strange names, Albany, New Haven, Philadelphia; the nights when I was drained, so depleted from incessant novelty. That was over now; I thought, I am home. "We do now dedicate this whole institution to Thee." There on that lawn, on that rise, in that capital, my heart began to swell, my feet seemed scarcely planted on the ground: It is as grand as Saint-Jacques, I thought, and I have helped make it happen. "And to the Father, to the Son, and to the Holy Spirit, be rendered everlasting praises. Amen."[92]

Thomas and I were provided separate houses adjacent to the grounds of the institution; mine was the former Sigourney residence, with imposing columns and stately interior, which financial reverses had caused the family to relinquish a few years earlier.[93] Before long, shops were also erected at the school. Some of the earliest pupils had been grown men with trades, one a cutler, another a shoemaker, a third a cooper. They had asked to conduct their trades after school hours and had been given some facilities; when other pupils saw this and asked to be likewise engaged, the three tradesmen became teachers. Finally, it was decided to include this training in the curriculum, and the new shops were constructed.[94] Nowadays there is a tailor shop, one for cabinetry, which also trains carpenters, coopers, and carriage makers, and one for shoemaking, a trade suited to many pupils since it requires little capital.[95] Those students more gifted in letters or the arts can now go on to the National Deaf-Mute College, founded by Thomas's son Edward—but that comes a little later in my story. (After the new shops were built, were the deaf shop-masters paid a stipend for their services as instructors? Not a bit of it: they were replaced with hearing masters. But more of that later, as well.)

With our expanded facilities able to receive more pupils, Thomas set out on a tour of New England legislatures to recruit more of the uneducated deaf and obtain tuition for them. "How cheerless is their perpetual solitude!" Thomas preached in Burlington and Montpelier, Vermont. "How are they shorn off from the fellowship of man!" in Portland, Maine. "How ignorant are they of many of the common transactions of life!" in Concord,

New Hampshire. "We would make some of them capable of mechanical employments." Oh, listen ye thrifty Yankees! "Others shall be capable of holding respectable stations in private and public commerce! Those who have a genius and taste for such pursuits, shall be taught to cultivate the fine arts. We would introduce them to the delights of social intercourse, to the dignity of citizens, to the solace that may be drawn at the fountains of science and literature. . . ." It was, you see, now Thomas's turn to plead and he did it as well as I. If I had the advantage of illustrating the goal for which I implored aid, Thomas had the training of a preacher and the fluency in English of a native speaker. Massachusetts and then New Hampshire had started sponsoring pupils some years before.[96] Now Thomas induced each of the four Northern states to send commissioners to examine the asylum and negotiate terms for receiving their pupils. Soon after, Rhode Island followed suit, as did South Carolina and Georgia, following visits from Lewis Weld and a train of our pupils.[97] Connecticut waited ten years before making legislative provision for the deaf children of the state too poor to attend our school: a commission was appointed with authority to select not more than fifteen of them, which would have cost the state treasury about $3,000 a year. This sum, however, the assemblymen considered excessive, and a compromise was reached by which the governor could select as many children of indigent parents as could be kept at the asylum for a total of $2,000 a year.[98] (And there remains the level of state generosity in Connecticut to this day, forty years later!) Within a decade after my return from France, then, half of the states in the Union were sending their deaf pupils to the American Asylum.

This assembly of much of the deaf youth of America in one place, then to return to their several states, was one of the main forces that created a true society of the deaf throughout this vast land, with a single language serving to elevate its users and bind them together. There were three other forces at work. As state legislatures created additional schools for the deaf around the country modeled after ours—there are some thirty now—their principals were sent to Hartford for instruction.[99] They studied sign language with me and each paid $50 for this private course. Then, too, teachers for the new schools were recruited from our faculty and graduates. Later on, they were also recruited from other schools, but those schools had been established by Hartford graduates. There was, then, a fanning-out throughout America from Hartford in the nineteenth century as there was throughout Western Europe from Paris in the eighteenth. However, the ties are more closely knit here because there are no national frontiers and because more deaf teachers and pupils traveled to the center and then out again.

Surprisingly, considering its beginning, the foremost of the other schools that would spread the Hartford model and language was the New York Institution. Having found a Braidwood too expensive, they had decided to get a Braidwood book instead—Joseph Watson's. Stansbury tried to use it, but all he could get from his pupils were croaks (I assure you he was naïve enough to have tried it with the congenitally deaf). "Their utterance was harsh and indistinct," states a report from the New York Institution, "and led to a universal sentiment in favor of discontinuing the effort."[100] The school found its funds inadequate, so Dr. Akerly took a group of pupils to appear before the legislature in Albany; this yielded $10,000 and a percentage of the tax on the state lottery. A Mr. Horace Loofborrow was then hired; although he had been a schoolteacher for ten years, he had never received any instruction in sign or in educating the deaf. With four untrained teachers and many day scholars who hindered the progress of all the pupils, the situation was a fiasco.[101] Stansbury was obliged to resign and he shortly left the country: "It will be an emancipation to leave this institution," he wrote to a friend.

The first report from the school was printed before his resignation but it made no mention of speech. Pupils learned letters and words and expressed them by signs. There was, however, a lengthy appendix in which Akerly reported on various experiments conducted on his unwilling pupils, much in the manner of Itard, but with this difference: he made the most outlandish claims of cure. "After ten weeks' steady and laborious attention to these sixteen pupils, in which the physician has been assisted by his brother Dr. Benjamin A. Akerly, he concludes that six of them have improved in their hearing and may be learned to speak so well that hereafter they may be removed from the institution and taught like other children at an ordinary school." Continuing in the best oralist tradition, he implied that his services could be had full-time for a fee and stated that his patients should be prohibited from signing lest they remain mutes despite the improvement in their hearing.[102] The board of the institution, now headed by Akerly's friend Mitchill, hired Akerly to replace Stansbury and also to serve as physician and it promoted the willing but uninitiated Loofborrow to principal.[103] Loofborrow at least initiated a change in the mode of instruction. He and Akerly read Sicard avidly and tried to construct a method accordingly. But they were too proud to do as other schools did and send us teachers for training; when I visited the school in 1821 it was a shambles.[104] There was no system or method. The signs they employed were a combination of those used by the Plains Indians to communicate between tribes, those they had learned from some of our pupils, and those they had gathered from the works of Epée and Sicard. They thought their job was finished when they had legislated a sign for every English word that came up. No one knew sign language: the only way to learn that is from a living instructor.[105] I gave this frank appraisal to the New York State Senate when they wrote to me for my opinion of the school, which had requested an appropriation to construct a building. As a result, the senate made it a condition of the award that the superintendent of common schools conduct an inspection. This he did with two other gentlemen, visiting Hartford, New York, and Philadelphia. The superintendent found the New York product quite inferior to ours, and the Pennsylvania product our equal (not surprising, since I had organized the Pennsylvania school and Lewis Weld directed it).[106] He urged or instructed the New York board to get qualified people: there was an internal struggle; Akerly and Mitchill resigned. The new president of the board, James Milnor, offered one of our best teachers and my friend, Harvey Peet, the positions of principal and superintendent and went to Paris to obtain a deaf teacher from Saint-Jacques. Sicard had died, however, and De Gérando's puppet, the abbé Borel, proposed Léon Vaïsse, a hearing man, though, as I have told, a fluent signer.

Harvey Peet is today the intellectual leader of American teachers of the deaf. His textbooks are widely used and are now in their eighth or ninth editions.[107] His monograph on the history of educating the deaf is clear, incisive, comprehensive: it has been a great help to me. He is the author of two dozen other articles on every facet of deaf culture, language, and education. Peet had joined us in Hartford when he was graduated from Yale, five years after our school opened; in two years he had become steward (we abolished the title superintendent) as well as teacher; his wife became our matron.

The first thing you notice about Peet is his commanding presence: he has an athletic frame, a strong will, a high opinion of himself, and indomitable energy. In recent years his hair has turned white and rheumatism has dared to oppose him, yet his movements are still graceful, his signing a pleasure to observe, his manners courtly, and his humor abundant. A few years ago, he retired in favor of his eldest son, Isaac Lewis Peet, who has married a poet and former pupil at the New York school. Harvey Peet's two other sons are also teachers at the school, as was Thomas's son and namesake, Reverend Thomas Gallaudet.[108] Since I have witnessed the burial of so many founders of our profession, it is comforting to realize that I shall not witness Peet's. He will go only when he is good and ready and that will not be for some time yet.

The New York school thrived under Peet and Vaïsse.[109] In 1829 it was installed in excellent quarters on Fifth Avenue at Fiftieth Street, in those days about three miles from the thickly populated center of the city. The grounds took up five acres with a commanding prospect of the surrounding countryside. There were gardens and shops for tailoring, shoemaking, bookbinding, and cabinetry that supplied school needs and prepared pupils for trades.[110] Several more of our teachers joined Harvey Peet as enrollments at the New York school grew to more than five hundred. The first of these was F.A.P. Barnard, who recently became president of Columbia University.[111] Barnard wrote an account of how he, Peet, and Vaïsse did their share to bring about the uniformity in language and instruction that existed then, as now, among American schools for the deaf, and he described how Vaïsse introduced Bébian's reforms in the New York school.

Barnard went to New York with another of our hearing teachers, David Bartlett, a fellow Yale alumnus whom Reverend Flint had fitted for college and Thomas persuaded to join us. It was I who taught Bartlett American Sign Language, for which he showed great flair. His limbs are so lithe and his control of facial expression so complete that he is a master signer. He is a sympathetic friend of the deaf, a cheering influence, a pious man, and an earnest teacher. The deaf writer J. R. Burnet, now a teacher at the New York school, wrote this poem about Bartlett's manual language:

> When Bartlett stands to pray or teach, and all
> The eyes around drink in the thoughts that fall,
> Not from the breathing lips and tuneful tongue,
> But from the hand with graceful gesture flung,
> The feelings that burn deep in his own breast
> Ask not the aid of words to touch the rest,
> But from his speaking limbs and changing face,
> In all the thousand forms of motion's grace,
> Mind emanates in coruscations fraught
> With all the thousand varied shades of thought,
> That to each mind their own bright hues impart,
> And glow reflected back from every heart.[112]

Bartlett stayed with Peet for twenty years, then opened a private school for the deaf that took only young deaf children, ages four and a half to seven, with their hearing brothers and sisters where possible. In the classroom he used sign, written English, and fingerspelling. He succeeded in making his point: in those days most schools required pupils to be ten to twelve years old—a devastatingly long time to leave a deaf child in a hearing family without language. Nowadays pupils are taken some four years younger.[113] Not long ago Bartlett closed his school because of financial problems and rejoined us in Hartford, where his enthusiasm, warmth, and good humor continue unabated.[114]

Another of our Hartford teachers who went to New York, besides Peet, Barnard, and Bartlett, was Fisher Spofford. He hailed from an old Maine family, became deaf when he was three, and entered our school in its second year. Spofford was close friends with Whiton and Loring; he joined us as a teacher soon after they did and left with Loring for Boston, in part because of the abysmally poor pay at the asylum. He took lessons in portrait painting and, when he became proficient, practiced it for several years with considerable success. The invention of my countryman Louis Daguerre changed all that and Spofford laid aside his brush. He became a teacher at the New York school, where he remained until a hearing colleague, J. A. Cary, became superintendent of the Ohio Institution and persuaded him to join him there.

"Fisher Spofford constantly impressed on us," one former pupil told me, "that we were to regard him as a father. Deprived as we were of all the little attentions lavished on us at home, we were grateful for his show of concern. It was his delight to entertain us with short humorous stories which we were then to repeat. Seated on his high oaken chair, with his elbow on the writing board attached to the arm of the chair, resting his chin on his thumb, the forefinger on his Roman nose, his lustrous gray eyes would observe us go through the story. If we appreciated the finer points, he would rise and pat us on the back. He would tell magical stories of the Orient with graceful motions of his supple limbs; with a suite of compelling expressions of his countenance, he would transport us to glittering palaces, lead us through jewelled apartments, usher us into the presence of majestic princes, indoctrinate us into the secrets of the genii." Fisher Spofford's signing was extraordinary: it had a dignity, a grace, and a force all its own. As a lecturer in chapel, he would rivet the pupils' attention: he not only put his thought and feelings into graceful signs, he also acted them—he breathed them, as one student put it—and has thus acquired the sobriquet "the mute Garrick."

Last year, having come into an independent legacy, Spofford withdrew from the work of teaching to return to his friends and family in New England, and to gratify his love of drawing and painting.[115]

A few years ago I went to New York and gave an address at the laying of the cornerstone for a new school building on a thirty-seven-acre estate overlooking the Hudson, called Fanwood. The New York school had become by then the largest in the world, and had sent principals to Ohio, as I mentioned, to Michigan twice, to Tennessee, Texas, California, and Maryland. It has sent two professors to the National Deaf-Mute College and two teachers to our school in Hartford, and educated pupils throughout the Atlantic states. And all these people took my language with them.

The second Hartford satellite was located in Philadelphia; like the one in New York it disseminated education and the American Sign Language. I went there as principal and instructor of the first class, shortly after my return from France, in 1821, to get the program going, but the real beginning of the project was in the years when we were launching the American Asylum in Hartford. A humble dealer in crockeryware, a Portuguese Jew named David Seixas, who had a little shop on Market Street in Philadelphia, had started taking in the deaf-mute children who wandered the streets begging. Presently he was clothing and feeding five boys and six girls and learning their manual communication. Was his philanthropy born of natural empathy, or did David Seixas know something of the deaf because he was related to Gersham Seixas, "the patriot rabbi," who was a collaborator of Samuel Mitchill?[116]

About the time I left for France, in the spring of 1820, Seixas met with his rabbi and some prominent citizens and decided to call a public meeting to consider planning a Pennsylvania school for the deaf. The response to the call was gratifying, and in rapid succession a constitution was drawn up, a board of directors was elected, the board hired Seixas at an annual salary of $1,000, and the new principal began teaching the pupils in his home. That summer, Seixas came to study at Hartford and returned to Philadelphia urging a residential school. A house was procured in August, and a score of pupils moved in in the fall.

The opening of the new year found Seixas and six pupils in Harrisburg demonstrating their achievements to the governor and legislature, which proceeded to pass a bill sponsoring fifty indigent pupils at Seixas's school, for three years each, at $160 a year. Eventually the legislature would extend the term to six years and remove the limit on the number of pupils. But just as all seemed auspicious for Seixas and his charges, a great tragedy befell him. The mother of one of the pupils, it seems, had a dream that told of great harm coming to her fifteen-year-old daughter. She questioned the youth, Letitia, who said that Seixas had made physical advances and had offered her money and clothes. Seixas was called before the board and vigorously denied the charges, giving a different account of each event. He asked to be confronted by his accusers. By this time, the fall, Abigail Dillingham, and her hearing brother, Charles, had been hired as teachers and Charles served as interpreter for the proceedings. According to the minutes of the meeting, Letitia was nervous but affirmed her original accusation and denied Seixas's account. He waived the right to cross-examine her or her roommate, who confirmed her story. The matron agreed with Seixas that the children were storytellers and vindictive but the board voted by a narrow margin to dismiss him.[117]

It was at this juncture that the board asked the American Asylum to release me for six months to serve as principal and put the school on a sound footing.[118] During my stay we hired Abraham Hutton from Princeton, to whom I gave an intensive course in sign. Charles Dillingham had previously taken lessons from me in Hartford, and with his sister seconding that instruction, he became a fluent signer and teacher. When it was time for me to leave, I recommended that Charles take my place as instructor of the senior class. Mr. Hutton's hands "are still rather stiff," I wrote to the board, "but he is competent to take charge of the middle class." Abigail Dillingham was put at the head of the entering class.[119] When I left, Lewis Weld was called from Hartford to succeed me as principal; he remained in Philadelphia for eight years, until he returned to our school to succeed Thomas when he resigned. Hutton then took over the Pennsylvania school from Weld and is still in charge, married to the school, a graceful and fluent signer and a kind headmaster.[120] There is a staff of a dozen instructors now, about a fourth of them deaf, and about one hundred fifty pupils. All instruction is in American Sign Language, of course.

What happened to Seixas? The minority of the board that supported him brought his case before the legislature and he was acquitted. He started another school that survived for a while in competition with the Pennsylvania Institution, which he attacked from various platforms. The larger institution had more access to the ear of the legislature, however, and in the end Seixas gave it all up and moved west, a bitter man.

The deaf are frequently excellent artists, perhaps because our manual language encourages keen visual observation and subtle hand control. The only deaf man in all surviving Roman literature, Quintus Pedius, was mentioned by Pliny as among the most eminent painters of Rome.[121] I spoke earlier of the Spanish artist El Mudo, and I should mention the painter of the masterpiece "Last Moments of the abbé de l'Epée," and many other works, Frédéric Peyson, who entered the Paris school the year after I left with Thomas for America. Two of the most gifted American deaf artists were pupils at the Pennsylvania Institution when I was there: Albert Newsam and John Carlin.

Newsam was born deaf and his father, a boatman on the Ohio River, drowned soon after his birth. When he was about ten, he was taken to Philadelphia by a traveling deaf-mute who used him to solicit alms. In the spring of 1820 he was making a street sketch in chalk when the president of the board of the newly founded institution happened by, took him in charge, and enrolled him in the school. Nothing was known of his origins until a visitor from Steubenville, Ohio, elicited the keenest emotion in young Albert, who rapidly sketched the outlines of a house—the visitor's own! Then the youth drew an adjoining street and a particular house in it, which the visitor recalled had been occupied by a poor boatman, since drowned.[122]

When he was my pupil, Newsam behaved himself very well and gave me no trouble. He learned his lessons thoroughly, and out of school, instead of playing with his fellow pupils in the yard, he repaired upstairs and amused himself with drawing figures of domestic animals on the blackboard; I could tell that he would become a good designer or engraver.[123]

When Lewis Weld directed the school he developed Newsam's artistic talent, having him draw portraits on a large slate, and then he placed him with George Catlin, traveler and artist, especially known for his sketches of Indians. Next, when Newsam was seventeen, a handsome youth with thick black hair, an open regard, and a Roman nose, he was placed with Cephas Childs and Henry Inman, from whom he learned the art of drawing on stone for lithography, a process just introduced from France. He became justly celebrated as the most skillful and faithful portrait artist in lithography that this country has ever produced and assembled an unequaled collection of lithographic drawings and engravings, especially of Napoleon, whom he admired without bound. Newsam married a hearing woman, but the marriage was soon dissolved. I am inclined to blame the hearing woman, since I remember him as a gentle man, kindly disposed toward others, a strict teetotaler, an avid reader, and a graceful signer with a keen dislike of speech.

In his later years, Newsam was struck down by incurable paralysis. He took up drawing in bed with his left hand: "Some paint to live," he signed, "I live to paint." He became the prey of an imposter who, in the guise of friendship, obtained Newsam's art treasures for safekeeping and then sold them before the artist could discover his treachery. Albert Newsam died about five years ago.[124]

John Carlin, Newsam's classmate, was born deaf, as was his brother, and as a child was free to wander the streets of Philadelphia, since his father, a poor cobbler, could not make him understand the tasks that normally befall young children. When he was seven, he was one of the children taken in by Seixas and later trained at the Pennsylvania Institution. The school offered only five years' instruction, so Carlin, when a youth of twelve, became a housepainter and studied art and languages in his spare time.

Carlin's mother learned to fingerspell very skillfully; she enlarged her son's vocabulary and strongly encouraged his reading. The two of them and a devoted aunt would hold long conversations by fingerspelling; signs were not used and Carlin shunned the company of other deaf children. Later he was "enticed" (his word) into the company of the deaf and "spellbound" by their signing, but he found he totally neglected his English in their company (his "mental culture" as he called it) and he soon withdrew again.[125]

In the 1830s Carlin went to New York to study drawing, managed some business affairs well, and paid his way to Europe, where his talent came to the attention of Paul Delaroche,* who gave him lessons. He returned to America after three years, when his money ran out, and established a studio in New York. His patrons were generally among the higher class of Knickerbocker families but he did a portrait of me that is a good likeness. It was Carlin who encouraged Thomas's son Edward to found a college for the deaf, and he received its first Master of Arts, giving an oration in American Sign Language at the opening, as I did, in 1864.

John Carlin wrote poetry, a children's book, treatises on architecture, lectures on topics ranging from geology to Central Park, columns in many of the leading papers in the silent press. There he contended that oralism and fingerspelling were sufficient for the education of the deaf and for communication with them, though he does not speak at all nor lipread, and

*Hippolyte (also "Paul") Delaroche (1797–1856); French historical and portrait painter.

he married a deaf woman, a former pupil at the New York Institution.[126]

It is obvious that you can belong to the society of the deaf and still be able to hear: hearing children of deaf parents often choose to live among us, socialize and worship with deaf people, sometimes marry them. Hard-of-hearing people often do likewise, for they find the rewards of manual communication worth the effort to overcome the social barriers. It is equally true, though perhaps less obvious, that you can be deaf, even born deaf, and still resist membership in the deaf community. John Carlin is an example; he was born deaf, but he chose to be disabled among the hearing. He is a gifted painter, like deaf men before him, but he chose to write poetry in an oral language, practically unique among those who have never spoken one. Though unable to speak and read lips, he has consistently urged the teaching of speech and lipreading. Methodical signs he would tolerate, since they correspond to English, but American Sign Language he despises. He is, you see, a hearing person in everything but fact, and that fact has tortured him all his life, as witness these verses from his poem in the Philadelphia *Saturday Courier*:

> *I move—a silent exile on this earth;*
> *As in his dreary cell one doomed for life,*
> *My tongue is mute, and closed ear heedeth not;*
> *No gleam of hope this darken'd mind assures*
> *That the blest power of speech shall e'er be known.*
>
> *Murmuring gaily o'er their pebbly beds*
> *The limpid streamlets, as they onward flow*
> *Through verdant meadows and responding woodlands,*
> *Vocal with merry tones—I hear them not.*
>
> *The linnet's dulcet tone; the robin's strain;*
> *The whippowil's; the lightsome mock-bird's cry,*
> *When merrily from branch to branch they skip,*
> *Flap their blithe wings, and o'er the tranquil air*
> *Diffuse their melodies—I hear them not.*
>
> . . . .
>
> *O, Hope? How sweetly smileth Heavenly Hope*
> *On the sad, drooping soul and trembling heart!*
> *Bright as the morning star when night recedes,*
> *His genial smile this longing soul assures*
> *That when it leaves this sphere replete with woes,*
> *For Paradise replete with purest joys,*
> *My ears shall be unsealed, and I shall hear;*
> *My tongue shall be unbound, and I shall speak,*
> *And happy with the angels sing forever!*[127]

Any discussion of deaf poets must mention, in addition to John Burnet[128] and John Carlin, James Nack,[129] who entered the New York Institution just after becoming deaf at age nine and, shortly after graduating, wrote the first of many volumes of poetry. Here, too, comes the noted literary patriot Laura Redden, who lost her hearing at age eleven, attended the Missouri school for the deaf, then published poetry and journalism under the pseudonym Howard Glyndon. Her interviews with Lincoln, several famous generals, and elected officials whom she counted among her friends were widely read, as were her war poems. Recently, she returned from assignment as French correspondent of *The New York Times* and her poems and stories now appear in *Harper's*, the *Atlantic Monthly*, and other magazines.[130] Even more interesting, perhaps, because the author was deaf from early childhood, is the poetry of my fellow teacher at Saint-Jacques, Pierre Pélissier, whom I mentioned earlier as the author of the first pictorial vocabulary of our language.[131] Pélissier's poem "Ma Mère! Mon Dieu!" ("My Mother! My God!") was widely cited and even plagiarized, so that he had to bring suit against a hearing poet. Most interesting of all are the poems that deaf people compose in their native language, which exploit the patterning of shape and movement that is possible in sign. Alas, such poems, anecdotes, and stories are never written down and you must spend time among the deaf and know sign fluently if you want to sample poetry in motion.

A Kentucky senator's love for his deaf daughter led to the founding of the first school for the deaf west of the Alleghenies, under the direction of Centre College in Danville;[132] since it was to serve all of the West of the United States, it received substantial land grants under the administrations of John Quincy Adams and Martin Van Buren. The sponsors hired for principal someone representing himself as an educated deaf-mute, but he proved to be an imposter and was discharged for misconduct. Then, with as little perspicacity, they hired Mr. De Witt Clinton Mitchill, so named by a grateful father for the favors of an equally underhanded governor. He brought with him what he pleased to call the "New York method"; this was 1823 and it was merely Watson's method gone amok. (I neglected to mention earlier that when Stansbury hired his wife and daughter, and when Mitchill hired his friend Akerly, who hired his brother, Mitchill then hired his son, who served as instructor for a year before going to Danville.) The young Mitchill's arrival had been impatiently awaited, for a class of pupils had been idling five months with no one to instruct it but the steward. It was a bitter disappointment indeed to find after a few months' trial that Mitchill and his method were unsatisfactory.[133]

Finally, the board made a wise choice, selecting John A. Jacobs from the ranks of the students at Centre College, which he had entered at fourteen.[134] Jacobs mounted a white horse in Danville and rode for thirty days to Hartford, where he took private lessons from me at forty cents an hour, lived and roomed with the pupils (some his own age), and observed my classes and Thomas's for a year and a half. He was then nineteen. He got on the same white horse and rode back where he came from, carrying my warm letter of recommendation and considerable fluency in American Sign Language—and manual English.[135]

Every teacher has a "disciple more devout than the master," and Jacobs was mine. He learned methodical signs from me and when we abandoned them in Hartford, as Vaïsse did in New York and Weld in Philadelphia, Jacobs continued using them zealously in the original way. He reasoned that when a hearing person reads a sentence, each printed word evokes an idea only because it first triggers in the mind of the reader a spoken word, which is, in turn, coupled to the idea. What can the printed words trigger in the mind of a person born deaf as he reads a sentence? Why, the corresponding sequence of methodical signs, thought Jacobs. He reasoned that printed English could not trigger the reader's sign language, since sign has quite a different order from that of English. Harvey Peet countered that there is no necessary intermediary between printed words and ideas—you can get the idea of the whole sentence directly from the words themselves. He pointed to the case of Laura Bridgman, a deaf-blind inmate of the Perkins Institution, who knows no sign and yet can use words correctly. Neither Carlin, Spofford, nor I could find methodical signs in our minds as we read texts, but none of this impressed Jacobs. Sicard would have been proud of him but I was not. I wanted to say: Don't you see that making a deaf child sign like an English speaker and making him talk like one amount to the same thing? Embrace the language we taught you, American Sign Language; use it, use it to teach written English, but love it for itself. Now Jacobs is dying, and so am I, and I regret never having spoken my mind.[136]

One of our Hartford pupils launched the next school for the deaf in America—and of course brought his sign language with him. Mr. Colonel Smith had eleven pupils in his private school at Tallmadge, Ohio. Concurrently, an association of gentlemen in Cincinnati tried to establish the second school in the West and in 1821 sent the Reverend James Chute to Hartford for four months, but no support came from the legislature for another seven years. When it finally did, Horatio Hubbell was sent to me for a year and a half; I gave him private lessons in sign and he returned to found the statewide school in Columbus, which absorbed Smith's pupils.[137] All of Hubbell's teachers were former Hartford pupils.[138]

When he retired after two decades or so, his successor came from the New York school: J. Addison Cary, who was an impressive signer. Unfortunately, he died within a year, and was succeeded by Collins Stone, a Hartford teacher for nineteen years.[139] When Stone resigned six years ago to become our principal here at Hartford, another of our teachers replaced him.[140] The Ohio Institution sired, in turn, three more state schools, opening one after the other with Ohio-trained principals and teachers: Indiana, Illinois, and Tennessee.

The Ohio school was the first in the United States established on the principle that the state must defray the entire expense of providing a complete education for the deaf, a matter of plain and acknowledged duty. Last year the school occupied new quarters, the largest structure devoted to the deaf anywhere, housing some four hundred residents. The curriculum ranges from arithmetic to Latin (required for admission to Gallaudet College) and all instruction is in American Sign Language. About a third of the teachers are deaf. This seems to be the average: four out of twelve in Hartford and in New York, two out of seven in Philadelphia, one in three in Danville, a little higher in Virginia, two out of four.

I do want to say a word about Virginia before summing up this story of the dissemination of American Sign Language and the education of the deaf. F.A.P. Barnard went down there at the urging of Dr. L. Chamberlayne, the father of two deaf boys, the older a pupil at Hartford, and put on an exhibition in the state capitol. Then Samuel Gridley Howe of Boston's Perkins Institution for the Blind did likewise. The result was that the legislature created two schools, one for the deaf, one for the blind, and linked them, as had been tried for a while in Paris. Harvey Peet was offered the principal's post but when he declined it, another of our teachers accepted, Reverend J. D. Tyler, a kindhearted man and an open abolitionist, the son of the chief justice of Vermont.[141] When he went to Staunton, he took with him one of my pupils and dear friends, Job Turner, who was destined to become possibly the best known and most generally loved deaf man in America. Turner is descended from the rural folk of Cornwall and Hampshire, where his namesake, the great English landscape painter, was raised. He is fond of reading and skilled in English, though born deaf, and he mingles freely in general society. He will not speak or lipread but he is an excellent signer. He married a Hartford pupil and has two hearing children, who became a lawyer and a doctor but have now turned to teaching the deaf.[142]

Dr. Chamberlayne's second deaf son, Hartwell, who was a pupil at the Virginia School and then the New York school, knew John Braidwood's pupils at Manchester, where Colonel Bolling had joined the intemperate Scotsman with Reverend Kirkpatrick, after Braidwood had returned from New York and thrown himself on the colonel's mercy. Chamberlayne says the signs used by those pupils—Colonel Bolling's two children and three others—differed in some respects from those used now among the deaf in America, but not so materially as to prevent his talking freely with them. He thought the pupils not nearly so well educated as those he knew at Staunton and New York.[143]

Braidwood's irregularities became so frequent and irritating before a year of the arrangement with Reverend Kirkpatrick had ended that the clergy-man dissolved the connection and carried on the school alone—so reported Mason's correspondent in Virginia.[144] After another year, Kirkpatrick moved to another county and stopped taking deaf pupils. John Braidwood found a job as a bartender in Manchester, where he died a victim of the bottle, in 1820. With the closing of Kirkpatrick's Manchester school and the end of the abortive oral experiment in New York, the first attempts to introduce oralism in America had failed.[145]

On the other hand, we can look with pride and satisfaction at the nation-wide network of residential schools for the deaf that, by instructing them using their primary language, has raised them as a class to fuller participation in society. Our own school now has some two hundred pupils, with fifteen instructors, half of them deaf. I alone have taught more than one thousand five hundred pupils since I came to Hartford.[146] Then there were only Thomas and me; now there are one hundred thirty teachers in some thirty residential schools around the nation.[147] Yet there is so much more to be done: over half of all deaf children who should be in school are kept at home by ignorant, grasping, or fearful parents.[148]

In the Northeast, our pupils came to us to learn a profitable trade or profession and to become literate in English, bilingual. As the network spread south and west, increasing numbers came from the farms; they were already productive members of society. In no matter which region, they came to the residential school to find their place as deaf people among the deaf, to develop as individuals and citizens, then to return to their villages, towns, and cities to farm, to teach, to manufacture, to write, to paint, to preach, to publish, to defend the nation, and more.

Only residential institutions can provide all this; day schools cannot. The very forces that urge us now to repeat the folly of Amman, Heinicke, Wallis, and Braidwood also urge us to repeat the follies of Graser and Blanchet and Akerly. Oralism and day schools are a single enemy of the deaf, a means of dispersing us and submerging us in the larger culture and of imposing the language of the nation at the expense of our own. The New York school under Mitchill and the Philadelphia school under Seixas started as day schools; their directors were ignorant of the deaf. They soon changed to residential schools, for such mistakes cannot endure. But they can recur in another generation.

Only residential schools can provide the social contact necessary for the continued evolution of our language. Only residential schools can provide the bath of language and culture that allow the intellectual development of the child—especially the unfortunate child of hearing parents, whom nature has also cast into a second culture from which it is cut off. Only residential schools can ensure the transmission of deaf culture on a large scale, for most deaf youths learn nothing of their language and culture at home, find there no elaboration of what it means to be deaf, find there only a void. Only residential schools can provide the breadth of social contacts that allow a discriminating choice of a partner for life, only residential schools can be relied on to provide effective instruction in the pupil's primary language. Residential schools provide the noblest of careers for talented deaf men and women, Massieu's career and mine, the elevation of our companions in misfortune. Residential schools stand proud, imposing, before society. They say: America is made of many people. We are the deaf people: we have a language and a culture; we have a past, a present, and a future.

As each new residential school has opened it has drawn its teachers from the American Asylum or its satellites and it has spread the American Sign Language of the Deaf and the program of education that has been evolving and improving since 1760 and that I brought to these shores in 1816. Thousands of deaf citizens can justifiably say, "I was a pupil of the abbé de l'Epée"; hundreds of deaf and hearing teachers can say, "I am one of his disciples." And this is true north and south of the border, as well. The Quebec school was started by Ronald McDonald, whom I trained. The Mexican school was started by my schoolmate Edouard Huet, who also brought French Sign Language to Brazil, when he founded the national school there.[149]

A mother who cries, "My children will live and die in ignorance." A priest who answers, "I will learn their language and teach them." Three continents where countless pairs of hands weave messages in a perpetual salute.

NINE

CONCERNING WOMEN,

AND THE FURTHER PROGRESS

OF THE DEAF IN AMERICA

There have been many women in my life, fair and plain, hearing and deaf, but I have chosen four among them to record here, for their role in deaf history or for their closeness to me. The first, Alice Cogswell, qualifies on both counts. Then I will speak of Julia Brace, the deaf-blind girl whose flowering into womanhood has inspired people the world over by demonstrating that human potentiality lies in the plasticity of the mind and not in the mechanics of the senses. Third comes my own dear Eliza and our family, and finally the queen of the deaf, Sophia Fowler Gallaudet.

Never have I felt my limitations as a historian more keenly than at this moment. Having shown the falsity of the hearing history that styles itself a history of the deaf, shall I now, an old man who has spent all his youth and most of his adult years among men, write a history of women and the deaf? To this problem must be added another: I have been able to distill this history so far from a fund of documents written by friends of the deaf and by the deaf themselves—Bébian's journal, Berthier's biographies, the silent press. . . . But the record of the lives of women, their qualities and their acts, is very scant indeed. Many women have been kept in servitude by some relative; coarsely clad, faithful and diligent in labor, often skillful in household duties or farm work, they live and die knowing little of the outer world, and it records nothing of them. And yet, I cannot omit to speak of deaf women, and so I have determined to write about those of my own acquaintance and the men and issues that particularly concerned them.

Most of the letters Alice Cogswell wrote after she entered our school have been lost. Those that survive—her compositions printed in the annual reports, for example—are on sober and religious topics, gracefully discussed. After three years' instruction, she wrote: "What is hope? It is to aim the good thing with moderate wish and smile, but it is not a violent emotion. What is admiration? It is to elevate with sweet feeling to see the beautiful and elegant objects and it differs from wonder."[1] Some years later, Alice had occasion to write her reflections on death when a neighbor committed suicide; the closing lines move me for their imagery and portent of her own premature death:

"In my memory she moved like a blithe bird. She was full of life and buoyancy. All that saw her admired her, and all that knew, loved her. She was like a 'bright bud of promise,' but fading in the grave, and will 'bloom out in righteousness' in Heaven, forever and forever.

"My memory is now afresh, that her sunny ringlets always plaited before my eyes, and they won't perhaps be the less shining in the cold bed of Death. They may be the emblem of Eternity, which ever curl, and curl without end."[2]

In the happy and fruitful years after her schooling, a young woman in her twenties, Alice flourished. Her brothers and sisters married—the oldest of her sisters, as you will recall, married Lewis Weld[3]—and Alice, much loved by her nephews and nieces, visited them all—those who lived in New York and New Jersey as well as those who lived in Hartford. If not all her new relatives could sign, all her old ones did, so there was always an interpreter around, as well as the slate she kept handy.

With Alice thriving, Mason's mind was relieved of a great burden, but he did not abandon his concern for the unfortunate. He continued to care for the sick, to operate, to teach, and he launched a great new project, the Hartford Retreat for the Insane. In the year Alice was graduated from the asylum, 1824, the doors of the retreat were opened to patients. It was the first in Connecticut and one of the first in the nation. (Since it received no aid from the state, which like all others was content to imprison the insane with common criminals, the retreat had to charge high fees, and few of the thousand or so insane living in Connecticut could be accepted.)[4] As general overseer, Mason endeavored to make the institution worthy of its standing as a model, following the precepts of the new "mental medicine," whose leading proponent was Abbé Sicard's colleague in the Society of Observers of Man and Itard's mentor, Philippe Pinel, director of the Paris insane asylum. It called for good personal hygiene, exercise, and constructive labor from the patients and kindness and respect from the attendants.

On the threshold of his seventies, and of the third decade of this century,

Mason could look with satisfaction at the works of his lifetime. His children were well launched in their marital or professional careers. The Hartford school was highly successful and was emulated throughout the nation. The Retreat for the Insane was firmly established. It is almost as if he said, "Now I have done what I could do," and then he lay down. His mortal illness was short—five days—but long enough for all the city to be gripped by anxiety.[5] Late in the afternoon on the last two days, people gathered in knots on the sidewalk outside his house on Prospect Street, whispering among themselves. Some recounted how he had snatched them from death, others how he had eased their pain, saved their child, taught their son, pleaded their cause. Why were they there? There was nothing they wanted other than the privilege of bearing witness to the last earthly act of a great man. Catherine Beecher* came to the house and said: "We feel as orphans."[6]

The final night, quite late—neighbors and friends had gone home to rest —we gathered around Mason's bed. Two of his former pupils stayed by his side, though there was little they could do beyond summon us. Alice, her eyes wide with alarm, watched the agony of her sisters' faces, took in her mother's tears, observed the words of encouragement and peace consigning Mason to God's care, and now kept a silent, immobile vigil.

The next day we assembled in Mason's room again while neighbors arranged the funeral and prepared mourning clothes. We wept, but Alice, dry-eyed, moved among us with words of consolation. The following day, the Sabbath, Lewis Weld, who was staying with the Cogswells, sent for me early with the appalling information that Alice had gone berserk. As I rushed to the house I encountered the knots of neighbors and Reverend Strong's successor, Joel Hawes, who said and mimed, "God give you strength." Lewis spilled out the awful events of the previous night. He had been awakened by heartrending shrieks just at the hour his father-in-law had died the night before. Rushing down to Mason's room, he had found Elizabeth on the floor, apparently dead, his wife, Mary, struggling with a frantic and screaming Alice, and Mason's widow on the verge of fainting (as Elizabeth had done). Now, after a night of terror and distress, Alice was dozing; I took up my station at her bedside. Outside, the day was bleak and cold; a steel-gray sky glowered at barren trees and a sweep of bare fields covered in old, encrusted snow. They'll have a time digging the grave behind the church, I thought. The dim light insinuated itself into the room between the half-closed shutters. Alice's face was drawn, her sleep troubled; at one moment she awoke with a start. "ME-SICK. FATHER DEAD TAKE-CARE-OF-ME CAN'T." "But you have many fathers," I said. "Jesus is your father. The abbé de l'Epée is the father of the deaf. I love you like a father. So do Thomas and

---

*American educator and feminist (1800–1878), daughter of Lyman Beecher and sister of Harriet Beecher Stowe.

Lewis." We spoke of Jesus—his tenderness to little children, his pity for the sick and suffering, his compassion for his disciples when he left them.

In time, there were movements about the house as her father's body was taken away. "I am too sick to go to the grave," she said. "I must try to sleep." I dozed next to her and awoke to see her staring at the chink in the shutters: large flakes of snow drifted past it. "Cold, icy grave," she signed. I answered: "The snow reminds us of the white robes he will don in heaven." She smiled and slept.

Perhaps unwisely, I returned to my own family that night; Alice spent it moaning and shrieking. In the morning she did not recognize her family; the doctor was with her. Over the next few days, Catherine Beecher, Lydia Sigourney, and Thomas tried unsuccessfully to break through the wall she had erected. Sometimes she fancied she was already in heaven. "I hear David's harp!" she signed. There were short intervals of reason: once she reflected on her grief in a signed phrase of striking poetry; the English translation cannot do it justice: "Our two hearts had grown so close together they became one and can no longer be separated."

A few hours before her death, Thomas stood calmly, tenderly by her bed waiting; at last, he seemed to catch her eye. He made the sign of the wounded hand, emblem of our Savior. Alice signed, "PRAY"; and Thomas commended her soul to the Good Shepherd.

There is nowhere in France as desolate as the Connecticut River Valley in winter. The wind comes funneling in from the Sound and strips bare everything in its path in its rush north to Canada. The gray-shingled houses hunker down close to the ground, the trees resemble skeletons of giant travelers caught long ago in the snow. If you trudge through the fields as I did that day, punching holes in the earth's crust, the swirling crystals ice on your scalp and eyelids, you lose your vision and your sense of here, now. I withdrew to an inner hearth where Alice, insubstantial, also dwelled. Alice, we did it for you, I explained. Thomas, Mason, and I. (This was true: Eliza, Sophia, the others, came later.) We failed you. We spoke so little of the joys of this earth, so much of those in the kingdom of God, that only Mason's sturdy anchor firmly held you here. We administered the strong medicine of the Gospel, compounded for cynics, hypocrites, and sinners, to a child's soul that knew none of these, that hearing people had sheltered out of ignorance and love, that was too vulnerable. Now Alice was in a realm in which ideas were communicated without language, where there were no hearing and no deaf, where there were no barriers and no one was shunned or silenced. But that, I thought, would not excuse us. I followed my footsteps back to the house. Lydia wrote some obituary verse: "Joy! I am mute no more." And life, as it always does, went on.[7]

A few years before these events, Julia Brace was admitted to our school at age seventeen. She was to become the first educated deaf-blind person;

I know of only a half dozen more since then, of whom Samuel Gridley Howe's pupil Laura Bridgman is the most famous. (We shall learn more of Howe and Laura later in this history.) Thomas had visited Julia's home in Glastonbury just before going overseas; while abroad he discussed her case with the philosopher Dugald Stewart and sent back instructions that a tangible alphabet should be constructed out of wood, clay, or pins in a cushion, and Julia taught to read and spell. (Valentin Haüy had not yet invented raised print, nor Louis Braille his system of tangible dots.) Mason visited Julia's home for this purpose just before the asylum opened, and Alice accompanied him. "Miss Julia Brace blind and Deaf and Dumb very poor," Alice wrote. "She live in very little house very cold. She no frock. Me very sorry. Have yes me give one new frock her very much glad she for winter."[8]

Diderot's famous letter on the blind makes several allusions to the hypothetical case of a blind deaf-mute; in one place he remarks somewhat whimsically that if someone born in these circumstances should begin to philosophize concerning man according to the method of Descartes, he would place the seat of his soul at the tips of his fingers and after an effort of profound meditation, he would feel his fingers ache as much as we should do our heads. He also said that no communication could exist between such a person and ourselves and that he must remain in a state of imbecility. Julia Brace showed that he was wrong, that hearing and vision are not the only avenues to the mind. But how to teach true language through touch? Epée's plan was to have a polished steel alphabet constructed, if any such child should ever be found and brought to him, for which he advertised in the papers.

You might think it particularly obtuse to try and teach a deaf-blind girl to manipulate shapes that represent in a complicated way the component sounds in words she cannot hear, but it should be said in Thomas's defense that Julia had heard and spoken until her illness at four and a half. Still, letters could not penetrate the veil of darkness that surrounded her. In fact, the abbé Sicard did not think much of this way of proceeding. He wrote that he started out with the alphabet when he went to teach Massieu, but "what information, in reality, can the understanding possibly derive from a series of abstract characters arranged in a particular order by chance alone and to which nothing equivalent can be exhibited in Nature?" Sicard urged, instead, that our instruction be modeled not on the teaching of reading but on the child's natural acquisition of his mother tongue. He was right: it was sign, which Julia learned promptly and well once she joined the deaf in our school, that penetrated the veil and did so beautifully. How extraordinary that this language, destined for the eye and obeying, as it were, the eye's imperatives, could be equally grasped by Julia's opened palms passed ever so lightly over the hands of the signer. How little it seems to matter if the ear, the eye, or the palm receives the message!

Once Thomas had returned from Europe to Hartford, he sent Dugald Stewart a summary of Julia's case, as he promised he would. Here are the essentials:

Julia had no sight or hearing but like Stewart's pupil, James Mitchell, she seemed to have the most acute senses of smell and touch. For example, when Mason Cogswell and Thomas met her, she freely felt them, rubbing their hands with her own. (She had formerly been afraid of strangers, which her family traced to her dread of her physician, who had applied painful blisters to various parts of her body.) Then she put her hands to her nose as if still retaining on them the peculiarity of her visitors' smell. They conducted an experiment. They put their watches in her hands. As they did so, she rubbed their hands with one of her own, which she immediately applied to her nose in order to determine to whom the object belonged. Then each of them attempted to take back the other's watch. She invariably perceived the deception, would not suffer the wrong commutation, but returned to each his own watch.

If smell was particularly the sense of recognition for Julia, touch was the sense of exploration. When any new object was given to her, she first felt every part of it, moving the ends of her fingers over it with peculiar minuteness and delicacy. She then applied it to her upper lip, on which she rubbed it for some time as if there was the seat of a more nice sensibility of feeling.

The cases of Brace and Mitchell both led to the same conclusion: loss of some senses sharpens the acuteness of those remaining. These senses were entirely sufficient to allow Julia to go to any part of her home in Glastonbury without assistance. She even went into the yard with a basket for the purpose of gathering wood chips.

Her parents had reported to Thomas that Julia was solicitous of her brothers and sisters. She had several—all younger than herself. When they lived together at home, she sometimes washed their faces and hands; she would rock the infant in the cradle and feel its eyes to ascertain if it were sleeping, and if she found it crying she would sometimes give it sugar. The asylum, so rich in possibilities of communication and useful labor, rapidly supplanted the sterility (hardly the word, for it was a filthy hovel) of her parents' farmhouse, though before their death, they sometimes came to see her at our school, and she would visit them during vacations. Julia is deeply tied to her family in her affections, but separation from friends seems to weaken her attachment rapidly. Those who have made her presents of particular value —in her view—she is apt to remember and she shows pleasure on meeting them again, whereupon she generally refers to the gift with which they are associated. Her support comes from charitable donations dropped in an alms box at the front door of the asylum that is reserved specifically for her. This box she frequently hefts and she expresses pleasure when it shows an increase in weight, for she learned early that money is the means to satisfy many of her wants.

When Julia came to the asylum, I readily taught her my name sign. I let her feel the scar on my face. Thereafter, to greet her, I would touch her arm to get her attention, then brush her cheek lightly. She would do likewise when speaking to me. Thomas was the only one who wore spectacles; after he let her feel them and feel the sign made for them, which was also his name sign, she learned to use this sign as appropriate to him alone. Similarly, she learned the names of objects around her that concerned her. Soon, she could be sent to fetch an article of dress, her scissors, thimble, or anything of her own with as much assurance that she would understand and procure it as with anyone else. When she needed new clothing she could go to the matron, tell her what she wanted, ask her to go to the principal to get him to open her money box, take some money, and give it for the thing desired. If some girl's behavior should offend her, she would go with the offender to the matron, state the offense in strong terms of condemnation and say the steward or the principal must be called to inflict the appropriate punishment, specifying sometimes locking up, boxing ears, or thrashing.

Although she has spent nearly her entire life in our asylum, Julia's knowledge of the external world, acquired through signed communication and some firsthand experience, is considerable. On one occasion she asked to visit a family she knew who lived rather far from the asylum. When told that the road was too muddy, she asked how deep the mud was, whether the water ran along the gutters, and if the cows drank the water. Like all of us, she talks a great deal about the weather: will Miss P. be able to return to the asylum through the snow? Mr. W. must put on his high-top boots.

You may wonder how she tells time. At school, she is guided during the day by the regular succession of the pupils' activities. She anticipates the return of the seasons, holidays, and vacations, no doubt by her own observation and by talking with those around her. Julia rises in summer about four, in winter five o'clock; the earliest riser in the women's dormitory, she washes, dresses without assistance, brushes her hair before the looking glass, and makes her bed impeccably. She then goes down to the sitting room and waits until summoned for breakfast. Then comes one of her duties: she has for years washed and wiped the teaspoons used by the pupils at meals and tea, some 130 of them. Others on the kitchen staff collect them for her, except during vacation. Then it is her job, and on the very first morning of vacation she sets off around the hall without a word being said to her on the subject. Once she has cleaned and dried the spoons, she puts them in their proper place and changes the towels as often as cleanliness requires. If teaspoons from the steward's table become mixed with the others, she instantly detects the error and puts them to one side, though I wager you would not see the difference between the two sets of spoons.

In the morning, she sews, knits, or mends. Clothing has become the central concern of Julia's life. She had been sent to a little school for children where she learned to knit and now, at sixty-two, she sews or knits five or six hours a day, but if making anything for herself, she doubles her diligence, working with great perseverance until it is finished. Julia performs the entire work of knitting a stocking without assistance: shapes it properly, narrowing, widening, and so on. Matron reports that she has been known, on examining the knitting work of a little girl, to discover its defects with surprising readiness and, after condemning them roundly, to pull out the needles, unravel the work till she had removed all its imperfect parts, and then taking up the stitches, return the item to its owner finished. Though she needs some assistance in cutting elaborate patterns and in sewing the waist and sleeves, she makes her own clothes, threading her needle with her fingers and tongue. She wants her dresses fashionable, or rather like those of others, especially of the younger girls around her. Sometimes, matron assigns her some other task, for example, ironing. Then she goes to the ironing room, puts her flatirons to the fire, selects her own clothes from the mass belonging to more than one hundred people, and irons them to perfection.

Julia knows most if not all of the women in the institution and is well disposed to all of them, strongly attached to a few. Though she has seen forty-four entering classes come and go, she still takes particular interest when a new young girl is admitted, asks to meet her, wants to know who her instructor will be, inquires about her progress. She is, however, ill-disposed to male pupils and markedly averse to men; Thomas and I and one or two of the oldest teachers are the only exceptions. On Thanksgiving, when the boys are invited to the girls' sitting room and gallantly accompany them on a tour around the building, with parents in attendance, Julia will accept no man's arm.[9]

So far as I know, Julia has never been guilty of theft, falsehood, or wickedness. She is scrupulous about property—even a straight pin found in her work must be restored to its owner; she expects the same from others. Although she is very fond of money, she is perfectly trustworthy with that of others and is occasionally asked to deliver money from one person to another without the least apprehension. Even articles given to her she will not retain unless it is quite certain they were meant as a gift, not for inspection alone.

Whence this morality arises I do not know, but it does not arise from her belief in God, and this is an interesting finding for moral philosophy. Julia abstains from labor of any kind on Sabbath, but she also abstains from chapel, and I think she simply enjoys a day of rest wearing her finery. We tried an experiment: we called her attention to various objects and said Miss C. made that one, Mr. H. another and so on. The idea of making is familiar to her; she makes many things herself. Then we presented fruits, flowers, vegetables, stones and told her that neither this friend nor that acquaintance made any of them; neither men nor women made them. We hoped thus to arouse her curiosity and convey to her mind the idea of the Almighty Creator, but the attempt was not successful.

We do not know what her ideas of death are. Many deaths have occurred in the asylum during her residence and all deeply interested her. At the first, she examined the body carefully and finding it was incapable of movement and had ceased breathing, she was horrified. With each successive death she was less agitated. She makes the signs for weeping, for being sorry, perhaps for burying, and asks to see the corpse. She examines the graveclothes, feels the face and hands of the dead body with delicacy, makes the sign for being dead, says the friends are sorry, and so on. Sometimes she says the individual was good "and has gone up." I believe she has a conscious spiritual existence and assumes, therefore, that others do, too.

All of these observations about Julia further demonstrate how grievously wrong are the beliefs of hearing-sighted people with respect to the deaf-blind. In his great compendium of English common law, Blackstone wrote, "Such a man is looked upon as in the same state with an idiot . . . incapable of any understanding, as wanting all those senses which furnish the human mind with ideas."[10] How wonderfully Julia proves it is not so.

And yet—Julia's fate was in some ways little better than that of my long-ago love, the pupil of Abbé Salvan. For she was never taught a trade, and, disliking men, has never married. Unable to be self-sufficient, she has remained in her asylum all her life. She is now sixty-two. Perhaps she suffered a more cruel affliction than deafness and blindness in the parental ignorance that condemned her to live for years like a primitive animal at the bottom of the ocean; had her parents known sign language, had she been put in contact sooner with the world around her, she could have had a rich and fulfilling childhood and her life a happier unfolding.

But there are other, less melancholy fates for those such as Alice and Julia. Consider a happy, healthy deaf woman who bloomed with education into intelligent maturity, married a devoted and industrious deaf man, raised wonderful children, and lived happily ever after: my beloved wife, Eliza Boardman Clerc.[11] We have been married for half a century, and such is the sweet complementarity of our dispositions that we could remain together in tranquillity and joy for another fifty years. We have grown old together in uncanny synchrony. As my hair turned to gray, so did Liza's. As my wrinkles appeared, hers did, too. In recent years, my sleep grew light and short; Liza joins me for hot chocolate as the sun rises. We don't go out any more—we are both too old and too frail, and while I spend the day writing, Liza gracefully arranges its regime around me. It would gratify us both to go hand in hand to our Savior.

Gallaudet College Archives

ELIZA BOARDMAN CLERC (MRS. LAURENT CLERC)
AND DAUGHTER ELIZABETH
(PAINTING BY CHARLES WILLSON PEALE)

Liza came to Hartford, one of the first score of students, from the home of relatives in Whitesborough, New York. She was an orphan who had lost her hearing in early childhood. I confess at first I scarcely noticed her; those early months at the asylum were busy and breathless times. The months passed, summer vacation came and went, I knew who she was, of course, yet I had never really seen her. And then, one day, for no apparent reason, I was keenly aware of Eliza's presence, of her comely twenty-five years. Her gently oval face was a work of art of perfect symmetry: her hair parted in the middle, beautiful large eyes and arching eyebrows, a long slender nose, a small mouth with perfect lips turned slightly up at the corners, an intimation of dimples. Now when she came into the room each day I was a little short of breath, as when walking into the wind. Her signing had at first an endearing awkwardness or, rather, hesitancy. I found that I would call on her in class more and more frequently, which made her blush more crimson, and I braved the matron's glare to converse with Liza and her friends in the girls' sitting room. As the days passed, rumors spread; our lighthearted glances became soulful looks, full of vulnerability and affection. I was encouraged, no, I was divinely inspired. Finally, one day when I saw her from my study window picking berries with her classmates, the sun glinting in her chestnut hair, bending, rising, skipping along the path, I went out into the garden, brazenly summoned her to my side, and announced: "My intentions are honorable, Miss Boardman."

"Oh, yes, Mr. Clerc," she replied. "Oh, yes!"

Returning to my study I realized with awe the immensity of what was happening: I was in love, and my love was returned, but all the rest was obstacles. I was Catholic and Eliza was not. It would be, as far as I knew, the first deaf marriage in America and its symbolic meaning could weigh heavily on us. There had been successful deaf marriages in France, but here in America they were unfamiliar and some might disapprove. I was still a French citizen and wondered if I even had the right to marry in Connecticut. Would Eliza be happy to live with me in France, if I were to return there permanently?

When I came to Hartford, Congregationalism was the state religion. There were only a few other Catholics, mainly poor Irish, and no Catholic church. The Episcopal church, attended by many members of the board of the asylum, generously set aside seats for me and such pupils as wished to attend. There were no interpreters, but we could follow the different parts of the service in the prayerbook.[12] Abbé Sicard was truly hurt when, during my first visit to France, I told him of this, and worse, introduced my Protestant wife. "You are an apostate!" he cried. "My stipulations, your mother's entreaties were for naught!" He went on and on. My contract specifically prohibited my teaching contrary to my religion. Thomas was the worst sort of Protestant, evangelical: he sought to keep the Roman Church out of

America. (In that Sicard was right.) My kindness had allowed the Protestants to monopolize the education of the deaf in America! (Right, again.)[13] Yet I had no choice: it was not for some years that the first Catholic church was gathered in Connecticut. Hardly a reason to marry a non-Catholic, Sicard countered, but in truth, I was not an abbé and I did not feel doctrinal differences quite so strongly. Besides, I was in love.

When, two years earlier, I had joyfully brought the good news of my marriage proposal to Thomas, he, too, received it with gloom:[14] it will be most difficult for you, Clerc; people will disapprove; you will have deaf-mute children, increasing the number. I left the interview in a fury. Then we will not be married here at all, I decided. I wrote to Liza's guardian, asking if I might offer his ward my hand and if the wedding could take place among Eliza's family. She must have written home about me, for the response was prompt, warm, and positive. Come before the spring is too far advanced, he wrote, or the roads to Cohoes Falls will be impassable. Take a coach from Albany or Troy.

We were married by the rector of the Episcopal church at Troy and chaplain of the U.S. Senate, the Reverend Dr. Butler, whom I had met when Thomas and I were fund-raising in Albany. Friends also dating from that time who attended included Harmanus Bleecker and Theodore Sedgwick, distinguished law partners who held various government posts, and a few others. Lewis Weld was my best man and Reverend Butler's daughter and Eliza's cousin were bridesmaids.[15]

I thought a lot about what Thomas had said and about the furtive character of this wedding in rural New York far from my friends and colleagues. I believed in the rightness of what I was doing but—less than three years before, on shipboard, had I not told Mr. Wilder that I should marry a hearing woman? Now I know I was right to wed Eliza, and Thomas very very wrong, as he willingly acknowledged in later years. Healthy deaf people should always be encouraged to marry if they so desire, as most do, and they should marry other deaf people if they so desire, as most do. Hearing people —not deaf—have written a lot of arrant nonsense on this topic. At best it is born of ignorant superstition; at worst it is part of the same campaign that would deprive us of our language. I want to set the record straight.

Of the seventeen hundred pupils received since our asylum opened, only one hundred have deaf relatives, a smaller number, deaf parents.[16] It is hearing parents whose children populate our asylums, and if deaf people never again married and had children, the deaf population of the United States would not change perceptibly. The first reason for this is that half our pupils have acquired deafness: spotted fever alone, the disease that took Alice's hearing, is responsible for a fifth of these cases, scarlet fever for nearly one half; then come falls and inflammations.[17] Another ten percent of our pupils come from the marriage of blood relatives. Again, it is hearing people who are responsible; a minuscule number of these parents are deaf. Many of these kindred hearing parents have children who are retarded as well as deaf but not all do; remember the de Velascos, for example.[18]

As for the remaining deaf pupils who were born so, some nine out of ten have hearing parents.[19]

Thus, discouraging deaf marriage would not have any significant impact on the incidence of deafness. Now look at the reasons for encouraging it. It is what deaf people themselves desire: the uneducated deaf, the orally trained deaf, the deaf from our asylums, they all wish to marry and most wish to marry other deaf people. The reasons are not hard to find: facile communication; shared experience; the friends of the one more readily become the friends of the other. Deaf people know, too, that for these reasons such marriages are less subject to divorce. The chances of having a deaf child are small, one in ten, but if deaf parents should be blessed with one, is there anything to regret? Deafness does not entail wrongdoing, disgrace, physical suffering. Educated deaf people generally manage their affairs judiciously, bring up their children well, become useful and respectable members of the community—these are the words of our former director, William Turner, and he is right.[20]

As an old man who has followed the course of many marriages, hearing and deaf and mixed, my advice to the deaf is that given in Scripture: "Be ye not unequally yoked together." The chances of having a deaf child are not reduced if you take a hearing spouse, and deaf should marry deaf. Raise your children, hearing or deaf, well. Give them all the priceless heritage of your language and see that they add to it a command of written English. If God gives you a deaf child, make him wise, devout, strong, proud. He has a special mission: to serve as the vehicle of our language and culture, to sustain deaf society as an evolving variety of the human condition.

I presume to offer some advice to hearing parents as well. If a deaf child should come into your family, it is up to you whether the event becomes a tragedy or a source of great joy and instruction. At first you wonder at him, sympathize with him, do all you can to make him happy, rejoice to see that the infant seems more and more to appreciate what you do. He is constantly struggling to make his wishes known by various expressions of his face, by the signs and gestures that his own spontaneous feelings lead him to employ. If you have not experienced it, you cannot imagine the joy in witnessing the child's growing originality and skill in doing this, his graphic pantomime, his evident pleasure when he is understood, his rapid progress in this singular language, the development of his intellect, your pleasure (and that of the other children) in learning signs from him, in your newfound power to express to him increasingly subtle ideas and desires.[21] Parents! Seek out the deaf parents in your community. Ask their help in learning sign. Encourage your child to play with theirs so he may make more rapid progress in language. Not only will you and your child continue to grow as you continue to communicate but you yourself will gain much of great value, a second tongue, a second set of friends, a deeper insight into the variety and richness of the human condition.

Or will the advent of your deaf child be a tragedy? Will you quail before the onus of learning a second language? Will you deny his difference, pretend that there is nothing for you to learn, that you can raise him as you raised your other children? Will you heed the oralists, who say, "Your child is not deaf, he just cannot hear"; who use your increasing guilt to whip you into a frenzy of denial: force the child to speak, never sign, struggle, labor, persevere—or plead guilty![22] But having a deaf child is not a crime. Refusing to communicate with him is. That is an abuse of your child as surely as if you walled him up in an attic room. Hearing parents who prevent their deaf child from learning sign language from fluent users should have the child taken from them by the state, for their intolerance and ignorance are doing the child serious damage. I have taught nearly two thousand deaf children of deaf and hearing parents; the deaf parents are poorer, less well read, less traveled, engage in more menial trades—and yet, as a rule, their children do better in school and better in life.[23] Why? What is the difference? Deaf children of deaf parents grow up in a loving, communicative home. They arrive at our school with a store of knowledge, moral values, good habits. The deaf child of hearing parents generally grows up in cruel isolation, not so different from that of the Wild Boy of Aveyron. His parents have long ago reduced their messages to a few simple gestures; the child's mind atrophies. Lessons in lipreading hardly change the bleak picture, for the child can glean little from his parents' lips without prior knowledge of language and the world.[24] Parents! If your child cannot communicate—truly share his fears, love, needs, wonder, and ideas—in aural language and you *will* not communicate in visual language, then you have decided he will be truly deaf and blind, virtually without communication. And that is a tragedy.

Eliza and I had our first child: her dark eyes were as bright as diamonds. Soon after her arrival, while she was awake and lying quietly, I got down on my knees, sneaked up on her, and rang a little bell next to her ear. She turned around abruptly, laughing.[25] Then, forty-nine years ago, I was filled with joy: she would not face the struggle of so many deaf children. Now I feel differently. In any case, it is God's will, as it was that four of our six children (all hearing) would grow to adulthood: Elizabeth, now married, with a son of her own; Francis, rector of Saint John's Episcopal Church, who has two children; Charles, who died as a young man in New York; and Sarah, now Mrs. Henry Deming.[26]

Since Eliza and I were wed, several hundred deaf and dumb persons of both sexes here, in the United States of America, have married after leaving school, and are blessed with children, which is a great comfort for them in their old age! I wish the same could be said of my native land, but today there are hardly two dozen deaf women to be found thus happily situated. I learned why on the occasion of my last visit to France, in 1846. After spending the winter months with my sisters in Lyon, I stopped over in Paris on the way home and, of course, promptly repaired to Saint-Jacques, where I was able to visit the classes of the girls. As was true when I was a pupil there, they are shut up as in a cloister, and few gentlemen ever have access to them; nor are the teachers of the boys admitted to visit them. An exception was made in my favor. I owed it to the politeness of the director, who alone has the right of entering and giving permission to enter; and he gave me this permission, probably, on account of my being a stranger, visiting from a foreign land. It was the recreation hour when I called. The girls were in their garden, and on learning of my arrival, immediately left their amusements and crowded around me. Some believed they recognized me; others stood gazing; some inquired of others who I was and what I had come for. Their curiosity was soon satisfied, and they politely ushered me into their sitting-room upstairs. They numbered about sixty. Most of them were between the ages of ten and sixteen; all dressed alike in plain clothes, uniformity being rigorously enforced, as is the case elsewhere in boarding schools for young ladies. At two P.M. they were called out to their respective classes, which I attended by turns. Their teachers, with two of whom I had the honor of being acquainted, received me kindly. They were all ladies of fine talents, first-rate education, and extensive reading; but of rather too much self-confidence, for we have not yet seen or heard of their ever having produced any very remarkable female scholars. Their apology is that this is wholly owing to a want, on the part of their pupils, of an opportunity to practice their scholarship. This may be true in a certain sense; but why do they keep their pupils shut up like nuns in a convent, and thereby deprive them of the opportunity of practicing? Why do they not permit them to visit or to receive visits? Why do they never introduce them into the very society they themselves frequent? What inconsistency, therefore, between their excuse and their objections! They say that they fear there may be danger for these unfortunate girls should they go out, even when accompanied, in so large a city as Paris. This may be true. But if their pupils are taught self-respect and know to whom they may resort for protection, and have principles of morality imbued into their minds and the fear of God in their hearts, there will be no ground for the apprehensions of these good ladies, who, although unmarried, know very well how to conduct themselves in this world of wickedness, deception, and misery.

I remarked among these poor girls several who were very intelligent and who would become useful members of society, make excellent wives, and be good mothers, if they had ever a chance of being known; which, alas, will never happen as long as they continue to be cut off from society. I wish the lady professors of Saint-Jacques could see what a contrast there is between the present condition of their pupils and our own.

I shortly made this remark to Ferdinand Berthier, whom I visited in another wing of the school. Berthier had always taken an interest in the laws concerning deaf marriage and had several stories to tell me that bear on the subject of deaf women and their mistreatment in hearing society. One in particular stays with me.

The mayor of Gensac, a village in the southwest, had recently been called before the civil tribunal at the instance of a young deaf woman, Marguerite L., for refusing to marry her and a hearing man from her village. She was a churchgoer, a housekeeper, she cared for her father's cows, prepared her own clothing, but she had never been to school. M. le Maire, cold interpreter of the law, acknowledged all her good qualities but did not find in her the intelligence required by Chapter VI of the civil code, the section on marriage. At the tribunal, she was overawed by the pomp and circumstance; questioned by the president in a loud voice, she did not respond, for she was deaf. When Marguerite was asked in elaborate pantomime if she wanted to marry the groom, she cried out; when offered the court reporter instead, she pushed him aside. When asked to find her beloved in the audience she spotted him in half a minute and led him to the bench hand in hand. Nevertheless, the state's attorney could not find that she knew the "responsibilities and obligations of marriage." Her curé offered to serve as her interpreter, if given three months to familiarize himself with her pantomime. Permission refused. The tribunal then ruled against authorizing the marriage and ordered Marguerite to pay the costs of the hearing. The young woman rapidly apprehended this and was reduced to tears. Her fiancé intends to appeal. "The first village lout who presents himself is allowed to marry," Berthier stormed in my presence, "provided he says 'yes'; but a doctor's diploma is almost necessary for the deaf-mute who would marry."[27]

My last portrait of a woman is that of Sophia Gallaudet, Thomas's wife, the queen of the deaf. When he first saw her, as he told the story, we were in New Haven, fund-raising. Her parents, hardy farmers, had taken Sophia, then nineteen, and her sister Parnel, nine years older, both born deaf, to meet Thomas and secure admission to our school. "When I met the two sisters I was much impressed," Thomas recalled. "Both were of rare comeliness with jet-black hair and dark and enquiring eyes. I bowed with exaggerated courtliness and the high-spirited Sophia returned the greeting with a deep curtsy. The father explained that he hoped we would teach them to read, write, and cipher. They used a rapid and abbreviated form of signing among themselves but I responded in pantomime that we would do all that and more." They were the thirteenth and fourteenth pupils to enter the asylum.

SOPHIA FOWLER GALLAUDET (MRS. T. H. GALLAUDET)

Sophia's parents were from old New England stock, her mother descended from a member of the Hooker colony that founded Hartford, her father one of four sons of a pioneer settler who marched at the head of the Seventh Connecticut Regiment in response to the call of Lexington. He built his son and daughter-in-law a handsome mansion, where Sophia and her five brothers and sisters were born, and willed them one hundred acres on Moose Hill, a little in from the Sound, on the carriage road to New Haven.[28] Like Massieu, Sophia worked around the farm but longed to go to school; like him, she had a circle of people with whom to communicate, including her older sister, her deaf cousin, Ward, who lived across the road, and her hearing parents; and, like Massieu, when finally allowed a formal education, she progressed with lightning speed. I have come across one of Thomas's letters in which he boasts, "Eighteen months ago, Sophia knew not that there was a creator of the world and she felt no moral accountability to him. Now she understands the simple doctrines of the Gospel and of late gives such satisfactory evidence of hopeful piety to our pastor that he has admitted her to the communion of the church."[29]

As Sophia—vivacious, intelligent, attractive—progressed, so did Thomas's affections, but he kept them to himself for a year. When he proposed she was amazed:

—I have no knowledge of the world.

—You can travel and meet people.

—My education has just begun.

—I will help you continue it.

He was thirty-three, an "earnest Christian of wide and varied culture," she later told me, "travelled, accomplished, high-minded, accustomed to move in refined society. Is he doing it from pity," she asked, "or as a symbolic gesture?"

"Neither," I told her, "it is love." She had ample color, open generous eyes, rippling hair, graceful proportions, dignity, and poise. They were married soon after we moved into the new asylum, and went to Saratoga, where one takes the waters, on their wedding trip.

Hartford society fussed a little at first but soon accepted Sophia as they came to know her, and she created a society of her own in her home, for she developed a fluent command of written English and was a fund of general information; Thomas, too, had an active mind at home as at work, and table talk concerned affairs of the world and especially practical religion. Their marriage was marked by sweet accord of temper, taste, and views on instruction and child-rearing.[30] Sophia was loving, gentle, judicious. Thomas's somewhat more excitable disposition was mastered by self-discipline. Together they raised a large family, four sons and four daughters. The oldest, Thomas, is rector of an Episcopal church, Saint Ann's, which he founded for the deaf in New York; moreover, he has promoted services in sign language in churches throughout the United States. The second, Sophia, married a Southern military man and died recently. The third, Peter Wallace, is a businessman on Wall Street. Jane Hall is a teacher in a ladies' seminary, William Lewis, an inventor living in New Jersey, Catherine Fowler is married, living in New York. The daughter born the year Alice Cogswell died was named after her; she married a minister, editor of the *Sunday School Times* and close friend of the Gallaudets' last child, Edward Miner. Edward is president of the National Deaf-Mute College in Washington. Thus the oldest and the youngest sons carry the banner passed from their father.[31]

The same year that Alice and Mason Cogswell died, Thomas felt particularly exhausted, unwell, and overburdened. He petitioned the board for relief from daily instruction. Word had it that some of the faculty objected to a commensurate increase in their duties, the board did not accede to Thomas's request, and he resigned in April, effective October 1830.[32] Thus ended thirteen years at the head of our institution and at the helm of American education for the deaf. We had been so intimate, so harmonious, Thomas and I, so attached to each other, we had labored together so many years, that when he resigned in the same year I lost Alice and Mason, I was full of pain. I felt betrayed, though of course I never said so.

Thomas's activities in the next score of years were many and diverse. In particular, he published children's books, beginning with *A Child's Book of the Soul*, which went through many editions in many languages. Then came *The Child's Book of Repentance, The Child's Book on Natural Theology*, nine volumes of scriptural biography and much more.[33]

During his long retirement Thomas refused invitations to head the first normal school in Massachusetts, to teach philosophy of education at New York University, to serve as superintendent of common schools in Connecticut (the post then went to Henry Barnard), to direct the New England Asylum for the Blind (Samuel Gridley Howe became head instead), to found a teacher training school at Princeton. He experimented with educating the feebleminded, helped Catherine Beecher found her female seminary, planned an institution for chronic alcoholics, aided in founding normal schools (he served on a committee for this purpose with Noah Webster when the first teachers' convention was held the year he retired). For seven years Thomas directed religious services at the Hartford jail. He promoted religious education in the West and belonged to several evangelical societies. He also took on the post of chaplain at the Retreat for the Insane that Mason had founded. It would have warmed your heart, as it did mine, to see that truly good man moving with composure and kindness among the ranting, the spellbound, the hysterical, beaming reassurance and love. His chapel was a hallway, his pulpit an old desk, but his subject, ah, his subject was Christ's love, which he so masterfully unfolded to their bleary eyes that the patients listened attentively and with decorum.

In the fall of 1850 Thomas and I were honored by a large gathering of deaf people at the asylum at which each of us was presented with a silver pitcher and tray, the gift of those throughout the United States who had been educated at our school.[34] With two hundred visitors and the two hundred pupils enrolled, it was the largest deaf convocation up to that time, ever, anywhere. The participants' general appearance was of intelligence and respectability, industrious habits, comfortable circumstances. The event was the forerunner of conventions and associations of the deaf that have sprung up in the twenty years since—and the countless more sure to come. It was modeled on Berthier's Central Society of the Deaf, which counted members from diverse regions, schools, and professions and held annual banquets in honor of Epée, beginning in 1834. These meetings develop a special type of deaf leader—the organizer and platform orator. In Paris, Berthier, in Hartford, Thomas Brown, who, after five years as a pupil at our school and two as an assistant and carpentry instructor, had returned to his aging parents on their hundred-acre farm in Henniker, New Hampshire, and made it thrive; he was a hard worker, a good horseman, a reliable wheat grower, and a respected citizen, active in town affairs (he was sent to the state Democratic convention the year following the presentation, where he prepared several speeches).

Brown is the central figure in a little deaf settlement in Henniker. His father, Nahum, was a good example of deaf people in the era before schools who got along nicely on the land without formal education. He never learned to read but his hearing wife was his interpreter. They had two deaf children, Thomas and his sister, Persis. Thomas married one of the Smith sisters, former asylum pupils, from Chilmark, and their son, also deaf, became a teacher at the Michigan school. Persis wed a hearing carpenter of the village and their two sons, also deaf, went to our school, then returned home. Thus the deaf community at Henniker included at one time Thomas's father, sister, two nephews, son, and wife. There was also another deaf couple farming nearby. Later on, the two nephews acquired deaf wives and deaf children, so it was quite a community. The oldest nephew, William B. Swett, had a colorful career as a seafarer, general-purpose mechanic, writer, and artist before settling down in Henniker with a former pupil from the New York School.[35] They have two deaf daughters, Persis and Lucy.

Thomas's wife, Mary, was an amiable woman, industrious, kindhearted, called "an ornament to Society in Henniker." The same *History of Henniker County* calls Thomas "one of our most intelligent, upright, industrious and respectable citizens."[36] Mary came from another deaf community, on the island of Martha's Vineyard, where one in every hundred fifty people is deaf —over ten times the usual rate. In one island village with about five hundred inhabitants, one in every twenty-five is deaf. I believe all of the deaf people there are descendants of an English missionary who settled on the island in 1720.[37] Naturally, hearing children on the island, like the deaf, have long learned the indigenous sign language that developed there, a century before I ever brought French Sign Language to America. Consequently, most speakers on the island will use sign language when they are in a mixed group of hearing and deaf people; the fishermen use sign to communicate at a distance, and others use it in church, where audible speech would be disturbing. The hearing and deaf children also learn written English in school, and everyone gets along nicely in this bilingual community.

Thomas Brown towered above his brethren at the presentation-day ceremonies, his full reddish beard streaked with white; he had a mane of gray hair on a large head, and a slender but powerful frame. He was quiet, slow to arrive at an opinion, but set once there, practical, methodical, deliberate. He said that his spirit had sought vainly for rest until he found a way to express his gratitude to Thomas and me.

Then he thought of a testimonial, and when he had suggested it to his deaf friends, "the flame of love ran like a prairie fire through the hearts of the whole deaf-mute band, scattered though they were through the various parts of the country." A committee had been appointed and the necessary funds raised. Hundreds of visitors came from as far as Virginia for the ceremony. The procession made its way to Center Church, Reverend Hawes gave a prayer, Lewis Weld a welcome in sign and then in speech. Thereafter, all the proceedings were in sign language. Thomas Brown gave a welcoming address, Fischer Spofford, the oration of the day, George Loring presented Thomas with his pitcher, and Thomas gave a little speech. He said he saw the hand of Providence in Alice's privation, in its occurring to the daughter of Mason Cogswell, in Hartford, with him next door, the hand of Providence in his referrals in England, encounter with Sicard, studies with me, and in my agreeing to join him in his labors, in our successful fundraising. "Little did I think then, in Paris, that we should thus stand together before such a gathering of our pupils and those of kindred institutions." The very thought was running through my mind at the same time. I was presented my pitcher next, responded with a few words of gratitude, and was followed by Job Turner, who offered the closing prayer. On one side of my pitcher you see Thomas and me leaving France; the ship is at hand and beyond the waves you can see our future school (how reassuring that sight would have been for me had I been able to discern it at the time!). On the other side of the pitcher is engraved the interior of a schoolroom with pupils. On the front, the head of Sicard; around the neck are the coats of arms of the New England states.[38]

The governor attended the banquet after the presentation. There were toasts, addresses, resolutions. I was reminded of Berthier's story that at a Central Society banquet such as this one, Napoleon III, then president of the Second Republic, unexpectedly appeared with his suite in the midst of the assembly and bestowed on Berthier the rosette of the Legion of Honor.

Many of the guests stayed on at Hartford through Saturday until Sunday so they could enjoy a religious service in sign, which they badly miss when dispersed to their several communities. The scattered deaf need these gatherings vitally for many reasons in addition to religious worship: they inform, they initiate social action, they come to the aid of those in difficulty, they allow communication in our primary language—since it is not written, there is no vehicle other than reunions. Alumni reunions, religious, social, and literary associations, state and national conventions, all these should be encouraged, for they enlarge the mental life, enrich the social life, and reinforce the political life of our deaf society.

In the summer of 1851, my great friend and colleague Thomas Gallaudet took to his bed. He was never to leave it. His fatal disease was an aggravated form of dysentery. At times wracked by the most acute pain, he always endeavored to feel a perfect submission to the will of God. During the first part of the illness his mind was quite clear, and he wanted to know about everything transpiring at the school and in Hartford. Later on, he lapsed into a state of placid calm, his body became weaker, his consciousness diminished, and finally his gentle spirit passed away without a struggle. Sophia was fanning him, unaware until a few minutes afterward that his breathing had stopped.

A little while after Thomas's death, Brown convened a convention in Vermont to raise money for a monument.[39] I was elected president of the Gallaudet Monument Association. At the same time, a permanent society to honor Thomas, the New England Gallaudet Association, was proposed and William Chamberlain, a deaf journalist in the tradition of Edmund Booth, was charged with drafting a constitution (he later served as secretary). Jolly, tall, broad-shouldered, kindhearted Will Chamberlain was deafened at age five and is a skilled, self-taught lipreader.[40] He came to the asylum when he was ten, gave a star performance before the Massachusetts Legislature (he arranged a dozen words into two long sentences of startling complexity and aptness), graduated at fourteen, later edited, in succession, the *Marblehead Messenger*, the *Boston Owl* (a comic paper), and the *Gallaudet Guide and Deaf-Mute Companion* (the first monthly magazine for the deaf), and he recently launched the *National Deaf-Mute Gazette*. Equally adept as a carpenter and shoemaker, as well as printer, editor, and teacher, he continues to shine as a brilliant, witty debater and an entertaining conversationalist, active in social programs for the deaf.

Chamberlain, Brown, and others met in Henniker to draw up the constitution for the new association,[41] and the first deaf organization in America convened in March of 1854. Its second meeting was held two years later in Concord (it was at this meeting that Reverend Turner called Thomas

Brown "the mute Cincinnatus" for his readiness to drop his plough and hasten to the aid of his fellow deaf—a title which has clung to him ever since) and the third in Worcester, Massachusetts, two years after that.[42]

I want to describe an important issue that came up at the third meeting and was also discussed in the *American Annals of the Deaf* (our professional journal) in those years—the concept of a deaf commonwealth. Many years earlier, when the Congress had donated land in Alabama to our school, after my successful visit to Washington, I thought of selling the part of the land necessary to meet our operating expenses but using the rest as a headquarters for the deaf and dumb, a place to which they might migrate after completing their education. It didn't work out that way, but the idea came up again a little before the War, no doubt inspired by similar ideas then current for the accommodation of people of color.* One of our former pupils, John Flournoy, was a leader in the movement (as he was in the drive to establish a national deaf college). He proposed that the deaf petition Congress for a small slice of uncommitted western lands where they might migrate, the better to enjoy social intercourse, civil and religious privileges, and means of self-improvement. Our former director, William Turner, was an unconvincing opponent. He argued that deaf people would not migrate there, for it would mean breaking ties with parents and friends, and that even if they did, the community would soon become predominantly hearing, since their offspring would not generally be deaf. Flournoy had given as a further reason for the commonwealth that the deaf in America are barred from all manner of employment by social prejudice; Turner foolishly denied that, claiming instead that we were excluded only because our want of hearing and speech unfitted us for those posts. Edmund Booth wrote in from Iowa to raise some doubts (wouldn't the community be too small to support all the trades the deaf would want to exercise?) and to discuss the choice of site. He revealed that he and William Willard and a few other Hartford graduates had formed an association two decades earlier to purchase land out west so they might continue to live in proximity and enjoy the friendship formed at the asylum. They had voted in thirteen members, but then Willard became a teacher at Ohio, two more joined the faculty at Hartford, the rest scattered, and the project died. William Chamberlain spoke out in favor of a more modest plan than Flournoy's. A company of 200 to 300 deaf, with such hearing friends and relations as chose to join them, would go west, form a community governed by suitable laws, headed by able leaders. A township thirty-six miles square would cost $20,000. This would suffice for 140 farms at 160 acres each. A classmate of Chamberlain's joined the debate on his side and offered $5,000 toward the purchase of land.[43]

The concept of a deaf township was advanced independently in France,

---

*By 1860, more than 11,000 Negroes had been transported to Liberia by the American Colonization Society.

at the same time Booth and Willard made their proposal, by the senior deaf professor at the Nancy institution, C. J. Richardin. Suppose the government established a new city, he argued in his book on the education of the deaf, and all the deaf in the realm were invited to migrate there. No doubt they would be very happy there, for no one would communicate orally and everyone would understand every other person's language all the time. The citizens could engage in almost all the professions and arts; they could be, for example, mayors, teachers, judges, lawyers, businessmen, entertainers: in brief, they could do just about what hearing people do. "I am persuaded that in this town civilization would make great progress," he wrote, "that each deaf person would be pleased with his existence." Dr. Itard likewise thought that a deaf community would be successful, but he thought it impractical to arrange.[44] For Richardin this was no abstract matter; he yearned to belong to such a community. He warned his hearing readers, however, that they would not be happy there. It would be as awkward for you among us, he said, as it is for us now among you. You would be singled out. A deaf person seeing you come along would say: here comes one of those foreigners who speak. On entering his home, you would say to him abashedly, "I speak and hear," as we often must say, "I am deaf and mute." You would be forced to communicate in pantomime with the deaf who do not know your language, as we are obliged to do with the hearing who do not know ours. You would be bored at shows where the deaf would seem only to gesticulate and act confusedly, as we are bored at shows where there is only singing and little or no action.[45]

Dreams like Flournoy's, Richardin's, Willard's, and mine—and similar dreams of countless deaf persons—though unlikely now to become reality, are natural, and they are important, for they remind us of our dignity and they remind hearing people of how they have robbed us of it. (Not surprisingly, John Carlin joined the debate with the statement that he preferred the company of hearing people, and in any case, the scheme would never get launched, for "it is a well-known fact that the majority of deaf people show little decision of purpose in any enterprise whatever." Such slander from the lips of a deaf man is more destructive than from the lips of the hearing, for not everyone sees through Carlin's disguise; while he was at it, he ridiculed the Women's Rights Convention taking place at the same time as ours in Rutland, Vermont.)

Although the principal subject of my address to the New England Gallaudet Association was the proposal for a deaf township, I also informed them that I was dissolving the monument association. Its mission had been accomplished: money had been raised, Albert Newsam selected to design the monument, and John Carlin to prepare the four panels at the base. On one point I have, until now, maintained a discreet silence. In the bas relief that is the statue's most salient feature, Carlin represents Gallaudet in the act of teaching little deaf children. So far so good. What is he shown teaching them? Piety? Humility? No, the manual alphabet! Something any fool can learn in an hour, that no deaf man or woman or hearing friend of the deaf has contributed, least of all Thomas, something that is an emblem of oral language. It took John Carlin to think of that![46]

Not long after the dedication of the Gallaudet monument, a Washington philanthropist, Amos Kendall, wrote to Edward Miner Gallaudet at Harvey Peet's suggestion. Would he be interested in superintending the Columbian Institution for the Instruction of the Deaf and the Blind in Washington? There were several applicants, he said, and he alluded to Edward's youth (he was then twenty), but Peet had overcome that objection by noting that Sophia Gallaudet would aid and counsel her son.

At this time, Edward was just finishing his education at Trinity College while teaching at the asylum. The dream of a college for the deaf, the first in history, had fired his imagination; he had discussed it with many of us and had made a private commitment to bring it to reality.[47]

College preparatory classes, "high classes," modeled after Itard's "supplementary course" in Paris, had already been established. The one at our school opened at mid-century with William Turner as teacher; the need could no longer be ignored in a school that had graduated such students as Wilson Whiton, George Loring, Thomas Brown, and William Chamberlain. One year later, the New York school followed our example. Deaf pupils were then able to receive five years of elementary education, three years of secondary education, and three years in the high class—eleven years in all. The curriculum included English, history, geography, astronomy, mathematics, and languages. The following year John Carlin published an article in the *Annals* urging a national college with a particular mission to give more training to deaf teachers.[48]

Then came the momentous letter from Amos Kendall.

In his day, Amos Kendall was an astute journalist, businessman, and politician; he is old and ailing now, but his mind is as sharp as ever. He was postmaster general under President Jackson and the most influential member of his "kitchen cabinet." He served as propagandist for Jacksonian democracy, but this did not interfere with his becoming rich as business manager to Samuel Morse. When Morse had a telegraph line strung from the Library of Congress to Baltimore, it passed through Kendall's estate. Over that line the famous sentence "What hath God wrought" was transmitted in 1844.

Now Morse's wife was deaf—he used to speak with her by tapping out Morse code in her hands!—so Kendall had some acquaintance with deaf people, and when a certain P. H. Skinner appeared in Washington with five deaf children and solicited aid to open a school, Kendall offered to give him a house and two acres, helped him set up a board of directors, and entered a bill in Congress, rapidly passed, incorporating the Columbian Institution for the Deaf and Dumb and the Blind, and providing an allowance of $150 a year for each local child admitted. Skinner rented a house temporarily in the isolated northwest quadrant of the capital and gathered there a large number of poor deaf children.

Imagine Kendall's dismay, indeed horror, on learning from a friend, whose washerwoman had a son in the school, that the children were badly neglected and in miserable condition. Kendall got another board member and they rushed to the house. The door was locked and the children within could not open it, so Kendall and company broke it down. Inside they found a heart-sickening sight. Two children lay ill on a pallet moaning; it was clear they had been left unattended for days.[49] Kendall sued in orphan's court and obtained guardianship of the five children Skinner had brought from New York; the others were returned to their parents. Then he consulted the heads of various deaf schools in the East, and Harvey Peet, as I have told, suggested Thomas's son Edward to direct the new school.

Edward was a young man, twenty, full of fire and enthusiasm, when he and his mother met Amos Kendall in Washington in 1857. Kendall was seventy, frail, with white hair and side-whiskers but sparkling blue eyes. Edward told him of his dream, and Kendall agreed to help him achieve it in time.

The Columbian Institution opened in a house on Kendall's estate. The new school had five pupils, Edward as director, Sophia as matron, one instructor for the blind, and one for the deaf—James Denison, a former Hartford pupil, born deaf, who had taught one year at the Michigan school. Within a year, there were eighteen pupils, and Edward was ready to exhibit some to the Congress and then to request an additional appropriation, the technique that Thomas and I had raised to an art form nearly half a century earlier. Congress gave him an annual appropriation and Cupid added a brunette beauty for a wife, a college friend from Hartford. Two years later, Edward learned of the Washington Manual Labor School and Male Orphan Asylum, which had never been launched for lack of operating funds but had an endowment of $4,000. He asked that the society give over those funds to establish a national college of the deaf; the organization agreed.[50]

The following year found Edward with a new baby and a sick wife, the country in civil war, and his school used as a hospital by troops from Pennsylvania. Nevertheless, in 1864 Congress passed the law authorizing a National Deaf-Mute College. The president who unchained the slaves unlocked higher education for the deaf; it was one more way to emphasize national interest at a time of civil war. The college's doors opened as General Sherman began his march through Georgia to the sea.

The college has two divisions; a lower division for students who have not had access to the high classes at Hartford or New York, and an upper division for graduates of these three programs. Candidates for the upper division are examined in English, Latin, history, geography, physiology, natural philosophy, and mathematics through quadratic equations. They study geometry, Latin, rhetoric, chemistry, and mental science in the junior year and, in the senior year, history of English language and literature, Latin, astronomy, geology, political science, and moral science.[51]

There have been some superlative students in the few years since the college opened. Even in the first class, graduating this year, some students are paid correspondents of newspapers, one is a translator from French and German, one has invented and obtained a patent for an improvement in the microscope, one was offered a post as an editor.[52] Four new professors have joined the faculty as enrollments grew, and Frederick Law Olmsted was hired from Hartford to prepare a development plan for the hundred acres of the Kendall estate. There have been sadness and struggle, too. Edward's son and wife died in the same year. After a time, he took another wife, James Denison's sister. Then there was a prolonged battle in the House of Representatives: on the one side, Thaddeus Stevens, a friend of the deaf and an admirer of Sophia Gallaudet; on the other, Elihu Washburn, chairman of the Committee on Appropriations, who wished to see the institution dissolved and the deaf educated only in state schools. "Higher education of the deaf is a useless extravagance," he said.[53] History and justice were on the side of the deaf.

I am pleased to relate that I was at the inauguration of the national college, five years ago. It was a splendid event on the beautiful grounds of the Kendall estate. There were representatives from other colleges, including the president of the University of Pennsylvania. I gave a brief address, as did two of Thomas's sons and John Carlin, who received an honorary Master of Arts. Entering the third decade of his life, Edward had matured into a cultivated gentleman: in his cutaway suit, immaculate starched linen, and highly shined shoes he could be seen at art expositions, concerts, on Capitol Hill, or as he stood before me now, polite, poised, deferential yet determined. In his inaugural address, Edward pointed out that I was born while the abbé de l'Epée was still alive. He called me "a living monument of an age long past, a witness of events and men soon to be known only in the pages of history." It made me feel very old. I must have drifted off. I seemed to be witnessing a scene: a dimly lit room, a tearful mother and two daughters, a cherubic abbot, engravings of the saints scattered about on a table. The abbé looked up inquiringly as Edward placed a cowl around his neck. "This is Edward," I signed to Epée, "Thomas's son." My eyes filled with tears of frustration—there was so much to explain. My hands chattered names: Hartford, Mason, Alice, London, Edinburgh, Paris, Massieu, Sicard, Bordeaux. No one seemed to notice me, however. They acted as if I were not there.

"That," Eliza said when I told her of my reverie, "is because you are afraid of dying."

"No," I replied. "I am afraid of only two temporal things: that my history may die with me; and Samuel Gridley Howe."

"Then you must write your history," said Eliza, "and that may also take care of Samuel Gridley Howe."

After the ceremonies at Kendall Green, I sought out Sophia Gallaudet. I took her hands in mine and we old-timers stood there silently gazing at each other and into the past.

Forty years after entering the American Asylum and ten after Thomas's death, Sophia had started a new career as Edward's aide, and had become the representative woman of American deaf society. Teachers and pupils alike regard her with veneration and affection. Members of Congress have gone away impressed and charmed by her and thus disposed to aid any enterprise that would educate more like her. Thaddeus Stevens sent her a note last year from his deathbed, saying he hoped she had not forgotten him. (It was he who proposed the Fourteenth Amendment to the Constitution, guaranteeing all citizens equal protection under the laws.)[54] There in Washington, Sophia reigns still, though after nine years of service, at sixty-eight, even her enduring frame has begun to bend under her duties, and she has surrendered many of them.

We were a kind of marriage, too, Thomas and I. He was often the initiator and the negotiator, I the patient executor.[55] His early resignation and the passage of time made his death a little easier to bear when it came. It was always marginally expected, since Thomas was never totally well.[56] Lewis Weld succeeded Thomas on his resignation, as you know; he had married Mason's oldest daughter just a few years before. Shortly after Thomas's death, Lewis took a year's health leave and went to Europe, but he returned only to die in a few months. He was a firm, conscientious, and practical principal and a great friend to the deaf.[57] He was succeeded by William Wolcott Turner, who came to the asylum from Yale shortly after Weld did. Reverend Turner, an ordained minister, is a tall spare man with a fast sense of humor and a great love of music. He oversaw the expansion of the asylum in the forties and fifties and served as family guardian as well as teacher until he resigned about six years ago,[58] when our current principal, Collins Stone, succeeded him.

After forty-two years with the American Asylum and ten at the Paris school, more than half a century in which I saw dozens of institutions for the deaf spring up, it was time for me, too, to retire.[59] I had never been disabled by illness a single day. At the second meeting of the New England Gallaudet Association a petition was circulated by my former students asking the board of our asylum to grant me a comfortable retirement. It was signed by 143 of my pupils and accorded two years later. That was a little over a decade ago and only in the past few months have I begun to feel the years. Still, Eliza and I hope to welcome guests from around the nation to our golden wedding anniversary this coming June. We pray to God that He may allow us just a little more time, that I may add one conclusive chapter to this history, that we may say a few goodbyes at our anniversary, that we may prepare the continuation of our journey together.[60]

TEN

A DANGEROUS INCURSION

Indians sign. That's one reason I have always been interested in them. Moreover, they have a certain romance for a Frenchman: we don't have any aborigines of our own; reclusive peasants, troglodytes even, but no aborigines. I imagined I could communicate with an Indian, in pantomime if not sign, and I intended, when I came to America, to go out and find one when the moment was right.

Although sign is not a universal language, skillful signers can often communicate across language and cultural barriers, perhaps because they are also skilled at pantomime. Thus, when I was in London with Massieu and Sicard, I was able to converse with Dr. Watson's pupils.[1] Likewise, Gilbert Gamage, a pupil and then teacher at the New York school, accompanying its director, Harvey Peet, on a European tour, proved able to communicate several passages of Scripture to Forestier's pupils at Lyon. (The son of a poet, Gamage was known far and wide for the grace and graphic power of his pantomime. His classic presentation was "Christ Stilling the Tempest," which he performed for such distinguished observers as Henry Clay and the Prince of Wales.)

American Sign Language itself is unintelligible to strangers because, whatever basis a particular sign may have had in pantomime, it has undergone a species of abbreviation and regularization, so the movement is fluid and rapid, the handshapes are familiar, the locations are convenient. The meaning of the sign is further obscured for the stranger by the origins of many signs not in depiction but in metaphor. Thus, the beginning of one operation, piercing a wall for example, is taken for the idea of beginning in general; falling, for death; the balanced scales, for justice; straightforward speech, for truth; and, I could give countless other examples. Gamage, Peet, and I would not have been successful had we remained strictly in the bounds of our sign language, as a Frenchman speaking fluent French would not be understood in the United States. In this predicament speakers of sign do some of the same things as do speakers of oral languages. First, we engage in pantomime: we point, we imitate, we draw in the air, we enact with facial expression. Signers are generally better at this than talkers, for a properly told narrative in sign has pantomime interwoven. A second stratagem available to signers and speakers alike is to select words whose meaning the stranger might be able to guess. A French speaker looking for an inn might say *hôtel*, not the word he would use in France but one that an American might recognize. And I favor signs in such cases that depict contours, such as HOUSE, rather than embody metaphors, such as HOME (a compound whose roots are EAT and SLEEP). Finally, I try to unfurl many of my signs; at the cost of speed and gracefulness, I perform a throwback. For example, instead of simply closing my hand into a fist for MILK, I stoop to the appropriate height and pump my hands alternately while closing each into a fist at the bottom of its stroke.

These were the devices Thomas and I used in the celebrated case of the *Amistad* Africans. Portuguese slave hunters had abducted a large group of tribesmen from Sierra Leone and shipped them to Havana, the center of the illegal slave trade. There, more than fifty of the Africans were purchased by Spanish planters and placed on the Cuban schooner *Amistad* for shipment to a Caribbean plantation. The Africans seized the ship, killed two crew members, put the rest ashore, and ordered the owners to sail to Africa. The schooner was seized offshore by a United States brig, however, and the planters freed. The Africans were imprisoned in New Haven on charges of murder. Most of the nation's press and the President favored extraditing them to Cuba, but abolitionists raised money for defense counsel and the case went to trial in Hartford. Thomas and I served as interpreters in the pretrial proceedings until a suitable translator was found, and so learned the details of their origin, their abduction, and their trials at sea, where several had died. In the end, the court ruled that slaves escaping from bondage are free men and the Africans were returned to their homeland.[2]

Another occasion to test my pantomime arose not long after the asylum was founded, when Thomas visited the home in Cornwall, Connecticut, run by the American Board of Commissioners for Foreign Missions, where scores of heathens from the South Seas and from American Indian tribes were pursuing their education. He returned with Indians from three different tribes, as well as a Hawaiian, a Tahitian, and a Malay. We asked them many questions in manual language about their lives, their families, and the state of manners and morals in their respective communities. Not only were the Indians skilled at pantomime but many of our signs were so similar to theirs that they were immediately understood. American Sign Language TRUE, for example, is pronounced with the index finger moving straight forward from the mouth; the Indian sign was the same save that the movement was curved slightly upward. In HOUSE the two hands touching at the fingertips slide downward roughly tracing the outlines of a house; the Indian sign is the same but the movement is played backward, ending at the rooftop. The signs for eating, drinking, sleeping are readily imagined and much the same. So were the signs for "good," "death," "pretty," "theft," and more that I don't recall.[3] One of the group, Thomas Hooper, conversed with us and our pupils for an hour and was well understood. He gave an account of the customs and beliefs of his people and the disruption and suffering caused by the white man. As his narrative progressed, I felt a familiar stirring in my breast. I had set out to discover how universal sign was and was discovering another kinship. Like the deaf pupils who watched him in rapt attention, Thomas Hooper was an exile in his own land.

It would be some time before I found an opportunity to pursue this discovery and it happened in a most unexpected way. A few years ago, I began a lively correspondence with my schoolmate Edouard Huet, who, having opened the first school for the deaf in Brazil,[4] had been invited to Mexico to found a school there.[5] Some of Huet's pupils were from the Aztec nation and their families spoke Aztec. Huet, who wrote fluent French, Portuguese, and Spanish, took an interest in Aztecan history, customs, and language. His letters set me to thinking about the parallels between efforts to replace Aztec with Spanish, with the goal of absorbing the Indians, and efforts to replace sign with English, with the goal of absorbing the deaf.

For Queen Isabella, and countless imperialists since, language was "the perfect instrument of empire." Her colonies were to abandon their "crude barbaric tongues" in favor of Castilian so that they would become subject to God—and the Crown. As in the history of the deaf, those in power imposed their language on the subjugated, but the clergy, wanting a real rather than an apparent transformation of belief, learned to speak to the Indian in his native tongue. In this way the clergy came to realize the richness of the Indian's culture and the depth of his commitment to it, and so they tried to persuade the government that the only sure way to bring the Indian into the Christian way of life was to teach him with an understanding of his culture and through his primary language. The government, however, was bent on imposing Castilian directly.

The plan failed under the early viceroys, but the underlying forces for language replacement were still there, so a resurgence was inevitable. It came under Charles II, who ordered that the Indians learn Spanish and "other good habits of reasonable men"—this time for a practical reason (the same one urged on the signing community): the benefits it would bring in dealing with those in power. He demanded the most intense efforts of his Archbishop Loranza, whose edict on the extension of Castilian is a complete education on language and power. "The most learned and intelligent authors," reads the decree, "defend with very solid arguments not only the idea that the Indians ought to learn Castilian but also that they can be obliged to do so. [The king has repeatedly ordered] that the Indians be instructed in the dogmas of our religion in Castilian and be taught to read and write in this idiom which ought to be understood throughout his dominions and become the one and universal idiom there by virtue of its belonging to the monarchs and conquerors. This universal knowledge is necessary in order to facilitate the governing and the spiritual guidance of the Indians, in order that they may be understood by their superiors, conceive a love for the conquering nation, banish idolatry and be civilized for purposes of business and commerce; and in order that men might not be confounded by a great diversity of languages as in the Tower of Babel. . . . The natives' inclination to retain their own language impedes their will to learn another and foreign language, an inclination accentuated by the somewhat malicious desire to hide their actions from the Spaniards and not answer them directly when they believe they can be evasive."[6]

Despite all these efforts, Spanish remains the language of none but the elite in Mexico. In the first years after independence, the new leaders simply closed their eyes to the masses in the countryside, declaring that there were no Indians in Mexico. Now the Indians' existence is recognized, but the Mexican authorities say that teaching the natives in their own language contributes to the conservation of the native tongue, which may appeal to linguists and antiquarians but provides a persistent and serious obstacle to civilization and a national soul; if the state refuses to teach the Indian in his native tongue, he will find it necessary, they contend, to learn Spanish and he will forget his own language.[7]

Rarely are the reasons for proscribing a minority language stated as candidly as in the archbishop's edict. Instead the Indians—and the deaf—are told: the grammar of your language is primitive, its vocabulary is impoverished, its use is socially marginal, it is not written. A government bent on eliminating its subjects' "inferior" tongue is not satisfied if they merely learn the national language in addition to their own, and this reveals that the given objections to the native language are only a pretext for intolerance of the native culture. Likewise, those who start by attacking the language of the deaf usually end by attacking marriages among the deaf, residential schools, deaf organizations, and all the things dear to the deaf.[8] If our native language is allowed to survive, we are told, our social isolation will be aggravated: like the Indians, we are advised to forget our native tongue, not merely acquire a second one.

Fortunately, for the Mexicans, for the American Indians, for the deaf and numerous others, there are countervailing forces that perpetuate their languages. The first of these is the very human desire for the society of others like oneself. The clergy as well can be a positive force: they have proven so among the deaf as among the Indians. For the clergy are intent on religious education and they know, what lay authorities deny at every moment, that the only effective education takes place in the pupil's primary language.

A third force tending to sustain these languages, especially in the case of the deaf, is the great difficulty of mastering a second language—a difficulty compounded if the second language is utterly unrelated to one's own, and further compounded if it is orally based and yours is silent, manual. Nevertheless, in a nation such as ours, there is only one possible course that reconciles the need for national unity with the rewards of national diversity: it is to do all in our power, using the primary language of the deaf, to give them a command of a second language of broader communication, written English. The aim is not to relieve the deaf of the task of learning English (though they may never speak it), but to arrange for them to learn it, and much besides, through the medium of their own language. Then, should one pupil prove less skillful at languages than another (as some Englishmen despair of learning French), he will at least know something of his own culture, and that of his region, his nation, and the world.

This is precisely what we have been doing in the network of residential schools for the deaf. Until recently, I thought our gains were secure. New York affirmed: "The advocates of teaching the deaf and dumb to articulate are few. All efforts to accomplish it in the institutions for their instruction are now considered useless."[9] Likewise, Hartford: "It is comparatively a useless branch of the education of the deaf and dumb. In no case is it the source of any original knowledge to the mind of the pupil. In few cases does it succeed so as to answer any valuable end."[10] But now, perhaps because of the intense desire to restore the nation so recently rent by war, there is in this land a new wave of antipathy to sign language in favor of spoken English. Now, once again, we are told that if sign cannot be made into a version of English, then it must be replaced entirely by speech. And the wealth, power, and intolerance that nourished oralism in Europe from the constable of Castile to Louis XVI now nourishes it again in America as well, with one slight difference: the role of kings in European oralism is played here by wealthy businessmen. Once again my history is rife with fortunes spent on sham speech, squandered on the surface appearance of oral language rather than invested in the bedrock of intellectual development; the leading servants of the rich New Englanders pressing for replacement of sign by English have been the inseparable social reformers Horace Mann and Samuel Gridley Howe.

When I spoke, on the first page of my history, of the "distinguished gentlemen" who are "repudiating the cause to which I have devoted my life," when I charged them with heaping abuse on my mother tongue simply because it is different from theirs, I had in mind these two men. Mann is now dead; Howe continues to spew venom for them both, so let me begin with him and explain what kind of man he is.

A true social reformer is committed to a cause and suffers the struggle; such was Thomas Gallaudet. Howe has been committed to the struggle and well-nigh indifferent to the cause. He is combative by nature, his spirit rises in opposition, and he has found in reform a way of remaining contentious all his life.[11] He is proud, cantankerous, quick to take offense. His voluminous publications on all manner of reform are paternalistic, condescending, and in the face of opposition, vituperative and contemptuous.[12] After graduating from medical school, he became involved in the Greek war of independence, raising money and then fighting. On his return in 1831, he accepted an invitation to direct the newly founded New England Asylum for the Blind in Boston (later renamed the Perkins Institution after a benefactor).[13] Subsequently, when his friend Horace Mann bitterly attacked all education in Massachusetts (including the practice of sending the commonwealth's deaf children to Hartford) and the schoolmasters fought back, Howe decided to run for election to the Boston school committee, guide a model school, and reform from within. Once elected, he set out to teach the teachers a lesson. A holy war. In the end it became clear that the schools' deficiencies had been grossly exaggerated, and Howe was not re-elected.

Then Howe entered the legislature to lead the fight for reform of the care of the insane. He pushed through a bill to enlarge the asylum in Worcester, Massachusetts, that Mann had helped found a decade after Mason founded the Hartford Retreat. Howe was instrumental in founding the first American school for mental defectives; he became the superintendent of the Massachusetts School for Idiotic and Feebleminded Youth, which he initially housed at Perkins. He hired Itard's disciple Edouard Séguin, who first thought to apply to the feebleminded the methods Itard had developed with Victor and thus founded that special branch of education. But Howe and Séguin could not get along, and my compatriot left after three months. Howe was also involved in prison reform, state reform schools, and troop sanitation, and traveled to Greece to aid the Cretans in their revolt against the Turks. And beyond all this, the great cause of Howe's career was the abolition of slavery. Although he had come to a concern for abolition only gradually—"Those who favor the immediate emancipation of the slaves," he wrote in 1833, "are the greatest enemies of blacks and whites"—he eventually shipped people and arms into Kansas to keep it a slave-free state and backed John Brown's ill-fated raid on Harpers Ferry.

In recent years he has become secretary of the Massachusetts Board of State Charities and has spoken out vigorously on the care of the blind, the deaf, the criminal, the insane, the feebleminded, the poor, and others. Certainly I do not mean to disparage all these causes, from Greeks to slaves. I do mean to show that it is reform itself in which Howe believes, and striving for so many causes, he cannot inform himself about the specific features of any one of them. You would never know, for example, from the absolute authority of his opinions about the deaf, that he has never taught a deaf person, or from his pronounced views on sign language that he knows none. Even vital affairs of the blind escape his notice: Louis Braille's great discovery of reading by raised dots was made forty years ago but has yet to be introduced at Perkins. But then, Howe long ago lost whatever interest he had in that school's affairs.

It began differently. While Howe studied medicine in Boston, a fellow alumnus from Brown, John Fisher, did likewise in Paris and returned to America with a plan for the first school for the blind here, modeled after the one he had visited, created by Valentin Haüy.

In Haüy's school, boys and girls learned, ate, played, and worked together. Both blind and sighted children were admitted and all were treated as children and not invalids. Haüy did not frown on the union of two blind persons, and though he was widely criticized for this, under his administration some fourteen of his pupils eventually married and most had children of their own. Haüy had a lifelong preoccupation with mechanical details of type and printing. He developed a system of printing in raised letters that allowed him to teach his pupils to read, write, and do mathematics; manual arts and music completed the curriculum. It was six years after Haüy's death, about the time Fisher visited in 1828, that Louis Braille, a nineteen-year-old blind pupil there, perfected an earlier dot system into a simpler one based on a six-dot cell to denote the alphabet and numerals.

Fisher agreed to sponsor Howe's trip to Europe to examine the school for the blind himself. Howe found it secretive and inhospitable, but in any case he had not intended to stay and master the system. He frequented the salon of the Marquis de Lafayette and, contrary to the Marquis's advice—Lafayette told him to go home—accepted a mission to carry funds to Polish revolutionaries. He was caught, imprisoned in Berlin, expelled for life from Prussia, and thrown bodily over the French border at Metz, whence he returned to Boston. Crucially, however, he brought back with him two blind instructors: Edouard Trencheri, trained at Haüy's school, who would teach academic subjects, and an Edinburgh mechanic to teach the rest of the curriculum. Trencheri had a thorough knowledge of the sciences and rapidly learned English. The Scot I never met.[14] The school opened in 1832 with seven students and in six months Howe was ready to parade the pupils before the Massachusetts legislature.

It was about a decade later that Dr. Howe came down from Boston to confront our pupil Julia Brace, then thirty-four (she had been in our asylum for seventeen years), with his own deaf-blind pupil, then twelve, Laura Bridgman. Howe's knowledge of our success with Julia had led him to pursue Laura's education, though with quite different means. As Howe told the story, it had all begun four years earlier when a Dartmouth student visited the farmhouse of Daniel Bridgman, a selectman of Hanover. He found a pretty little girl in the kitchen, playing with a boot as if it were a doll: she had nice features but red hollows where her eyes should have been. The farmer explained that a three-month bout of scarlet fever when his daughter was two had left her without sight or hearing and with her smell and taste blunted.[15] The same epidemic had killed her two older sisters and brother. She had spent five months recovering in a darkened room, one year before she could walk unaided, two before she could sit up all day. The student made a report to the head of the medical department at Dartmouth, and some weeks later, Howe, who had traveled to the college for a meeting of a learned society, heard about the case. Early the next morning he made his way to the Bridgman farmhouse, where he found a child of seven "with a well-formed figure, a strongly marked, nervous, sanguine temperament, a large and beautifully shaped head, and the whole system in healthy action." He engaged her parents to send her to his institution.[16]

When Laura Bridgman arrived at Howe's school she had a certain amount of rudimentary signing, as deaf children from a hearing home always do. For example, she had a sign for each member of her family: drawing fingers down each side of her face designated her father (alluding to his whiskers), twirling her hand designated her mother (in imitation of a spinning wheel).[17]

After allowing Laura two weeks to become used to her new home, Howe began her instruction. He could not expect his pupil to learn language simply by joining the social group, as would have happened to her at Hartford; every newcomer at our school quickly learned sign, including Julia Brace, and this was not part of our instruction. At Perkins, however, Laura was—most unsuitably—in a community that used an oral language she could not hear (though she had once heard a little of it). Howe might have capitalized on her rudimentary signs to teach her sign language, but he knew none. He mistook her gesturing for sign language and thus believed the foolish but widespread claim that sign language can deal only with tangible things. Furthermore, Howe reasoned, there was no one to sign with Laura. Only one possibility remained—to teach written English in some tangible form that the people around Laura could produce. He began with raised letters but soon switched to fingerspelling.[18]

DR. SAMUEL GRIDLEY HOWE

LAURA BRIDGMAN

Much as Sicard had printed letters on sketches of objects to teach Massieu their French names, Howe placed raised letters on real objects so Laura could learn the association by touch. After a few trials with a pen, a key, and such, the labels were detached and Laura learned to select the object corresponding to a given label and vice versa. Next the words were sliced up and the letters placed side by side; finally the three letters might be scrambled and Laura had to arrange them. With a pool of letters, she could select those three or four that designated an object and thus obtain it. According to Howe, the idea came to her one day in a flash that this was a means of communication. To facilitate the process, she was first given metal letters and a peg board, but she readily learned the twenty-six handshapes in the manual alphabet and thereafter fingerspelled hand in hand with her interlocuters. This took three months; the next year was spent gratifying her eager inquiries for names of things and events. She could now communicate with those around her.[19]

Laura was taught words for physical attributes, such as "hard" and "soft," then those for moral attributes, "good" and "bad." Next she studied spatial prepositions, "on," "in," "under," and so on, and then verbs for concrete actions in the present tense, and then in other tenses and moods. Instruction in writing began at this point; it took a while before she realized that she could communicate with people she did not touch but once this insight came her enthusiasm and progress were great.[20] Laura learned to write on grooved paper, as did the other students. She could write home; her joy was unbounded!

As admirably as fingerspelling reopened Laura's mind, its achievements must not be exaggerated. At age nine, she had the vocabulary of a child of three. "How limited is the range of her thought," Howe wrote. "How infantile is she in the exercise of her intellect!"[21] After five years, Howe reported that Laura fingerspelled in her dreams and in daydreaming, and that she could read a little in raised print as well as in the manual alphabet.

Once Howe started writing about Laura in the Perkins reports and the newspapers, she entered the public domain and gave Howe the reputation he would need for the rest of his career as a social reformer. The reports were translated into several languages and read by thousands with interest and compassion. Charles Dickens, then the most noted author in English, visited Laura and included an account in his *American Notes.*[22] Thomas Carlyle likewise wrote about her. Two of the world's leading psychologists, G. Stanley Hall and Wilhelm Wündt, examined her case.[23] Howe became a celebrity and sought to put his new-won fame to use in other fields. It was at this time that he brought Laura to Hartford to meet our Julia Brace.

When the news was passed that Laura was in the office accompanied by Howe and Lydia Sigourney, many pupils and teachers came thronging round and filled the room and hall: I was among them. Howe was a tall, handsome man, nearly six feet, with a wealth of brown hair, a full beard, and elegant attire. Laura had removed her bonnet and cloak. She was slender and delicately formed with fine features and fair complexion; she wore a green ribbon bound over her eyes and gesticulated a good deal, but clearly was ignorant of sign language. Julia was eventually brought down and introduced. Laura was most affectionate, indeed embarrassingly so, for when Julia learned that Laura was a visitor, not a new pupil, and could not sign, she seemed to lose all interest, although she accepted a little present from Laura gracefully.

Howe proposed that Julia accompany them to the Perkins school in Boston, where she would learn reading and writing by the same means Laura had. I was opposed on the grounds that Julia, a grown woman, would be disoriented there with no one who knew her language, and besides, she already had greater skills in communication than Laura, albeit in our language. I was overruled by Julia, who, much pleased with the proposal, set about preparing her wardrobe. Thomas and matron were inclined to accede to her wishes and Howe's urging.

Alas, I was proven right. Once separated from all her friends, duties and familiar environment, Julia sat apathetically all day long. If left alone she slept. She was pleased with her all-too-infrequent lessons, and learned the letter names of a handful of objects, but it was surely impractical to ask this beleaguered middle-aged woman to start learning a new language under such circumstances. After a year, she asked to be returned to Hartford, where she promptly resumed her old and effective means of communication.

It is a measure of the sweetness of Julia's personality that the whole experience at Perkins left an excellent impression on her. It was a most affecting scene to see Laura grasp Julia's larger hand with her slender fingers and guide her forefinger along the outlines of a raised letter while with the other hand she felt the changes in her face to find a sign of understanding the lesson; the two women regarded each other as surely as if they could see, the teacher full of patient attention, the older pupil frowning in puzzlement. Julia frequently alluded to Laura's efforts and never fails to this day to ask after her if she learns that someone has come to the asylum from Boston. She returned to Hartford carrying a copy of *The Blind Child's First Lessons* and for a time she continued to manifest some interest in it. Even now she occasionally spells the names of a few common objects, while also making the signs for them. But she soon tires of the exercise and raises her hand upward signifying that she wishes to carry the book back to her room. Still, she attaches a value to it, as she does to all of her possessions, and does not like to have others handle it.

Is it best to educate those born deaf and blind among deaf people who see or hearing people who do not? Clearly, the former, for a child has no more urgent and imperative need than facile communication with a group, which allows its normal intellectual, social, and emotional development. Howe attributed Julia's failure to profit by his lessons, where Laura did, to the ravages of time: "She is past the age which nature destines for acquiring and storing up knowledge."[24] Itard invoked the same explanation for the same reason with Victor. Our current principal, Collins Stone, who doesn't know Laura, suspects she may be unusually intelligent, Julia less so.[25] That would explain why two other deaf-blind children, Oliver Caswell and Lucy Reed, who entered Perkins after Laura and were taught by the same methods, made negligible progress.[26] By accepting these children in a school for the blind, Howe condemned them to a life of solitary confinement.

You might think it wondrous that Howe never tried to teach his deaf-blind pupils to speak, especially as he now advocates this course so stridently for all the deaf, whose friends cannot hear them, whereas if Laura, Oliver, or Lucy had spoken they would have been in instant communication with all around them at Perkins. In fact, all had once spoken before contracting their illness and Laura on her own initiative developed distinct vocal names for each of her Perkins acquaintances. Howe did not teach speech because he realized what he has now forgotten, how difficult such a task is and how meager the results. "It would have been a most rude and imperfect language," he wrote then. "It would have been indeed a foolish attempt to do in a few years what it took the human race generations and ages to effect." Amen.[27]

Instead, Howe taught his pupils fingerspelling, not sign. I have given some reasons. He did not know any sign and he did not realize, therefore, that language can be manual as well as vocal. He thought sign concrete, and hence unfit for restoring his deaf-blind pupils to society at large—as if they ever had belonged to society at large or ever would. And as if Massieu, Berthier, and I—and countless deaf people since—had not learned sign language first, then written language second. But Howe's most fallacious bit of reasoning—surely a record in the history of hearing people educating the deaf—is his invoking the God's breath notion in support of—not speech, but fingerspelling! "As people rise out of savagedom and pass through barbarism, they follow the instinct or disposition to express themselves by audible signs. . . . All come to speak as a matter of course and speech is the crowning acquisition in human development." (Acquisition of language, yes, acquisition of speech, no.) "All adopt speech because it is the means contemplated by nature and for which they have organs specially fitted." (Not so. Speech is a tenant on land owned by breathing and eating.) "I knew that Laura must have this innate desire and disposition."[28] So he taught her the manual alphabet.

At the same time that he urged fingerspelling exclusively for all the deaf, Howe hastened to acknowledge that his proposal "has an important bearing on the whole subject of deaf-mute instruction of which I by no means pretend to be a competent judge."[29] Then why not ask one, such as Thomas, me, or indeed virtually any deaf person at all? We would have told him that fingerspelling is slow and taxes the mind, that it takes ten different handshapes, for example, to convey the single brief sign UNDERSTAND, that it exists in space but does not exploit the possibilities of space, that when deaf people are obliged to use it with speakers of English they present a peculiar telegraphic form of English that is neither oral language nor manual language. Nothing shows more clearly how bizarre is a sequential spelled language to someone whose language is visual than Laura's question why it mattered whether you spelled "cat" CAT or TAC or TCA.[30]

Samuel Howe's renown as an educator, thanks to Laura, was equaled if not excelled by that of his "blood brother in reform" Horace Mann. When Howe was a freshman at Brown University, Mann was a tutor there, having graduated, valedictorian, the year before. Mann took a liking to his bright, good-looking, and sociable pupil, and they became fast friends. After Howe's sophomore year, Mann left to enter the practice of law but remained a frequent visitor to Brown and eventually married the president's daughter. He ran successfully for the state house of representatives and then, following the sudden death of his first wife, moved to Boston and ran successfully for the state senate. As a senator he agitated in behalf of a bill to provide an insane asylum for the state at Worcester, then took an interest in education for the first time and guided a bill through to create a state board of education to gather information and initiate reform in the schools. The governor, who had been persuaded by Mann and friends to advocate the board in his address to the legislature, now proceeded to name Mann to it. In turn, some members of the board, particularly a wealthy manufacturer and philanthropist, Edmund Dwight, urged Mann to resign from the senate and assume the board's direction as secretary, and Mann agreed.

One of Mann's first aims in his new post was to establish a normal or model school for teacher training. In order to persuade a reluctant legislature, Mann secured Dwight's backing and announced that an anonymous benefactor would contribute $10,000 to a teachers' seminary if the state would match his grant. The plan worked and in 1839 the Lexington Normal School opened.[31] In the first group of pupils was Mary Swift, whom Mann sent on graduation to Howe at Perkins; Howe assigned her to teach Laura Bridgman. Shortly thereafter, Howe came to Mann's aid, to ward off legislative forces that wished to abolish the Board of Education. "How can I thank you enough for the interest you take in me," Mann wrote to Howe. "I have tried many times but I choke; I feel that if I have had any success, I have been mainly indebted to you for it. . . . If I love the cause, then how must I feel towards one to whom it is so much indebted?"[32]

Howe defended his embattled friend many more times and in later years raised funds for Mann, who found himself in financial straits. They helped fugitive slaves together, Howe supported Mann in his successful bid for Congress and unsuccessful bid for governor, and when Mann died, president of Antioch College, Howe took up a collection for a bronze statue to be placed opposite that of Daniel Webster in front of the Massachusetts State House. Never did this friendship have more profound repercussions, however, than when, in 1844, Horace Mann issued the famous Seventh Annual Report of his Board of Education, in which he unleashed a mighty barrage assailing American education in general and the practice of educating the deaf through sign language in particular.

Horace Mann never evinced any interest in the deaf before or after his Seventh Report. The extravagant claims made there for oral instruction of the deaf are but a sixtieth of its bulk, which concerns schoolhouses, books, apparatus, curriculum, classification, and teacher training; elementary, normal, and reform schools; homes for juvenile offenders and poor children, orphanages, prisons, hospitals for the insane, and general hospitals. How did Mann come to pronounce so vigorously on teaching the deaf, at the very head of his report, just this once in his career? Clearly, because Howe asked him to. Mann's praise of oralism was designed to support Howe in his effort to wrest the education of the Massachusetts deaf from Hartford and place it under his aegis at the Perkins Institution for the Blind.

It was the astonishing progress of Laura Bridgman that led Howe to take an interest in the deaf. In 1842 he ran successfully for the Massachusetts House; once there, Howe was appointed by the governor as chairman of the House Committee on Public Charitable Institutions, which counted among its many duties an annual inspection of our school at Hartford, where Massachusetts sent twenty-five pupils annually and paid about half of their tuition.

As chairman, Howe was well placed to open his campaign to move the Massachusetts deaf from Hartford to Perkins. In a report issued a year after his appointment, he acknowledged that our pupils seemed to be happy and well cared-for, and then presented three objections to the tutelage of Massachusetts deaf at the American Asylum—the arrangement for all New England deaf, you may recall, for some two decades.

First, Howe recommended that the deaf be taught only written English and not sign; he had formed the mistaken impression that we taught the pupils sign. He explained that sign, although necessary for instructing the deaf, would not serve for communicating with the rest of society, whereas a solid knowledge of written English would. Note that Howe did not then advocate teaching the deaf spoken English, which he called "a foolish attempt." His second objection to the current mode of instructing the deaf was that it admitted students too late in life, between ten and twelve. The real problem here, which Howe chose not to mention, was that the state would pay for only six years of schooling for the deaf, much less than for

HORACE MANN

the hearing, and if we were to teach the deaf children a trade in that time, then they had to enter school around twelve. His third objection was that "uneducated parents whose ideas of geography are vague" would prefer to send their child to the capital of their own state—Boston! (Actually, Hartford is much more centrally located.)

But all of this was a pretext for the bill Howe then introduced, which stipulated that henceforth all of the state's deaf would be sent to Perkins, directed by S. G. Howe. Two further arguments were adduced as a parting shot: Perkins had excess space that a cost-conscious legislature should assign, and Laura Bridgman's rehabilitation at Perkins proved "beyond question" that those who were merely deaf could be educated there. But the bill was defeated—it was too easy to refute Howe's objections and to see his real goal —though he did succeed in getting authority to experiment with two sighted deaf children who had once spoken and were too young to attend our school; they were taught fingerspelling, as was Laura, but little else, and they were transferred to Hartford when old enough.[33]

Thus Howe was still smarting from the defeat of his bill to gain control of the deaf—he is not a man to accept defeat gracefully—when in 1843 he made plans for his joint honeymoon trip with Horace Mann and Mann's second wife, Mary Peabody. It was Laura Bridgman who had brought Howe and his new bride, Julia Ward, together. The New York belle, eighteen years younger than Howe, then forty, was spending the season at a cottage near Boston with her sisters when Henry Wadsworth Longfellow and Charles Sumner, friends of her brother, came to call. The conversation touched on Laura and the party agreed on an outing to South Boston to see her. There Julia met Howe. Her father was a wealthy Wall Street banker, and Julia had received an elegant education that included courses in dance and music and lessons in Italian from Mozart's librettist. Since Mary Peabody was as privileged as Julia Ward—one of her sisters was a distinguished educator and reformer; another married Nathaniel Hawthorne—nothing could be more natural than for the newlyweds to honeymoon together in Europe, visiting the sights, spas—and schools.

In London, with Charles Dickens as guide, they visited prisons, hospitals, asylums. Mann disliked the city, and Howe had nothing good to say about Watson's school for the deaf. In Baden to take the waters with wealthy friends, Mann made a valiant effort to learn some German so he would not have to impose on his wife each time he wished to visit a German school; she found his attempts laughable but confessed that her own German was not very good either. To make matters more difficult, it was summer, Europe was resplendent, and the ladies insisted on vacationing.[34] Moreover, most schools were not in session and Mann had to content himself with touring empty buildings, speaking with administrators, and visiting museums. Then it developed that Howe, because of his escapade involving

Polish revolutionaries a decade earlier, could not go on the most crucial leg of the joint trip, the tour of schools and asylums in Prussia.[35] Thus the parties separated: Howe and his wife went on to Rome to spend the winter (she was pregnant, a daughter was born in Rome the following spring, and they did not return to America until the fall). Mann continued through Germany—his Seventh Report is full of admiration for the Germans, who "stand pre-eminent among the nations of Europe in regard to the quantity and quality of education." By the time he and his wife reached Holland and France on the return leg of the trip, they were suffering from fatigue and homesickness; they paid scant attention to schools there.[36] They returned to Boston, where Mann worked on his Seventh Report, which he presented to the legislature early in January. Here is what Mann wrote about the deaf:

"I have seen no [European] institutions for the blind equal to that under the care of Dr. Howe at South Boston, but in regard to the instruction of the Deaf and Dumb, I am constrained to express a very different opinion. The schools for this class, in Prussia, Saxony and Holland, seem to me decidedly superior to any in this country. The point of difference is fundamental. With us, the deaf and dumb are taught to converse by signs made with the fingers. There, incredible as it may seem, they are taught *to speak* with the lips and tongue. That a person, utterly deprived of the organs of hearing—who indeed never knew of the existence of voice or sound—should be able *to talk*, seems almost to transcend the limits of possibility. . . . But in the countries last named, it seems almost absurd to speak of the *Dumb*. There are hardly any dumb there; and the sense of hearing, when lost, is almost supplied by that of sight.

"It is a great blessing of a deaf-mute to be able to converse in the language of signs. But it is obvious that, as soon as he passes out of the circle of those who understand that language, he is as helpless and hopeless as ever. The power of uttering articulate sounds—of speaking as others speak,— alone restores him to society. That this can be done, and substantially in all cases, I have had abundant proof. . . .

"I often heard pupils, in the deaf and dumb schools of Prussia and Saxony, read with more distinctness of articulation and appropriateness of expression than is done by some of the children in our own schools who possess perfect organs of speech and a complement of senses. . . . In some of the cities which I visited, the pupils who had gone through with a course of instruction at the deaf and dumb school were employed as artisans or mechanics, earning a competent livelihood, mingling with other men, and speaking and conversing like them. In the city of Berlin, there was a deaf and dumb man, named Habermaass, who was so famed for his correct speaking, that strangers used to call to see him. These he would meet at the door, conduct into the house, and enjoy their surprise when he told them that he was Habermaass. . . .

"The German teachers of the deaf and dumb prohibit as far as possible, all intercourse by the artificial language of signs, in order to enforce upon the pupils the constant use of the voice. At a later period, however, all are taught to write.

"I found a class in the school for the deaf and dumb in Paris, which the instructor was endeavoring to teach to speak orally; but it is not certain that the experiment will succeed in the French language,—that language having so many similar sounds for different ideas. With the English language, however, a triumph over this great natural imperfection might undoubtedly be won; and it was an objective,—certainly with some of the trustees of the Perkins Institution for the Blind, when they petitioned the legislature last winter for power to incorporate upon that institution a department for the deaf and dumb,—to exchange the limited language of signs for the universal language of words, in the instruction of this class of children in our state. Had the members of the legislature seen and heard what I have now often seen and heard, but what I then knew of only by report, I cannot but believe that that application would have found a different fate."[37]

How did Horace Mann, who had never taught a deaf child or even entered a school for the deaf prior to his European journey, come to have such pronounced and erroneous opinions about the deaf and their language?

I have suggested that Samuel Gridley Howe had seen an opportunity in his influential friend's report on education in Europe to make the legislature regret and recant their refusal to let him educate the deaf of Massachusetts. If this is so, then Mann would have had to find some attribute of deaf education in Europe that was significantly different from the American method as practiced in Hartford, and there was one place in Europe where he could find such a thing—Germany. As we have seen, French values and practices had flooded the German-speaking lands in the wake of Napoleon's armies; alas for the deaf, with his defeat and the withdrawal of French forces, there had been a rejection of all things French, and an upsurge of national feeling, including pride in the German language. Thus the "French method" of encouraging and using sign language had fallen into keen disfavor three decades before Mann's visit, and the Germans had found it timely to exhume Heinicke.[38] Whereas sign language had been flourishing in the school Heinicke founded at Leipzig, with the oralist resurgence, his son-in-law Carl Reich took charge and banned both sign and, for good measure, fingerspelling. But of course when the primary language of his pupils was pushed out the door it reentered by the windows; speech continued to play only a secondary role. Then Reich went on the attack; sign was like a deadly microbe: once it has contaminated the atmosphere, the only choice is to burn all the scholarly apparatus. Graduated exercises in German grammar superseded a curriculum formerly devoted to teaching elementary geography, history, and the like. By the time of Sicard's death in 1822, sterile memorization of the byways of German sentence construction ruled the day.[39]

A second important focus of German oralism was to be found in the southwest, near the French border, where Victor Jäger, pastor at Gmünd, directed an institute for the deaf on oralist principles. In the new political climate, Jäger published a book attacking methodical sign and the manual alphabet that became the leading text for instructing the German deaf and remained so for over two decades.[40] The school at Gmünd trained professors and directors for the majority of the new schools opening at this time in the German-speaking world—at Frankfurt, in the Grand Duchy of Baden, at Basel, and elsewhere. As part of the effort to discourage the language, gatherings, and intermarriage of the deaf, large residential schools became the exception, many small day schools the rule.

The most influential teacher who rallied to the new emphasis on instruction in German was Moritz Hill. Hill had been trained at the Berlin school founded by Heinicke's son-in-law Eschke.[41] Then he was appointed director at a Prussian school in Weissenfels, near Heinicke's home, and from there he sent out books and disciples promoting oralism throughout Germany. In his lectures and books, however, he opposed the form that oralism took under Jäger, in Saxony, namely dry grammatical exercises. He advocated instead that deaf children learn speech as hearing children do, through constant daily use—as if, in short, they were not deaf. This was his (somewhat blind) application of the influential theories of Johann Pestalozzi, according to which a pupil should acquire instruction the way a child acquires knowledge from his mother, simply through normal, natural everyday contact.[42]

Instructing a deaf child as if he were not deaf generally suits his parents, if they are hearing, but it never suits his education. The "denial method" was carried to the point of absurdity by Johann Graser, who was asked to open a school for the deaf as a department of an ordinary school in Bavaria.[43] His plan was to give the children a few years of oral training to enable them to be incorporated right into the regular classes, and he published a manual for teachers in the village schools to allow them to instruct "the deaf bench" along with their hearing pupils. All you need do, Graser told the teachers, is speak more slowly and distinctly than if you had only hearing children in your class. Although attempted with Teutonic thoroughness by nearly one hundred schools, the plan failed because its goal was unattainable.

Moritz Hill watched the experiment carefully. "The hope that each deaf-mute could receive the necessary instruction at the local school in common with hearing children and without injury to the latter has been abandoned," he wrote in 1858.[44] Not only were the deaf children a burden to the teacher and thus an obstacle to the instruction of the other students, but also they made less progress than their counterparts in the residential schools and earnestly wished to return there.[45] Eventually, even Graser retrenched, advocating at least one school in each province exclusively for the deaf. As Itard had discovered in Paris, most deaf children cannot learn to address and lipread a teacher, and even a slight hearing loss obliges their instruction in sign language. Thus, although German teachers spent more time speaking in class and teaching their deaf pupils to speak than did teachers in other lands, by the time Mann arrived, it was simply not true that "the German teachers prohibit as far as possible all intercourse by the artificial language of signs."

I do not mean to say Mann lied. He was, however, certainly well disposed to find the German method superior to ours because this finding would aid a loyal friend and was consistent with his general beliefs about German education. He was, as well, unable to judge spoken German and naïve about the education of the deaf: if Howe could write two years earlier, "On the whole subject of deaf-mute instruction . . . I by no means pretend to be a competent judge," how much more true was this of Mann. He was, I believe, duped, taken in.[46]

Here is how it happens.

A traveler visits an articulatory school. A pupil is called up who became deaf at eight or ten. The pupil speaks distinctly or recites a familiar phrase, seems to understand the everyday requests made of him vocally. The traveler never thinks of testing the pupil's abilities or determining if he is the exception or the rule but forthwith, in a fit of enthusiasm, writes to friends at home that in Germany or England or wherever, the deaf and dumb from birth are taught to speak substantially in all cases like other men so that in these places it is almost absurd to talk of the dumb, and the faculty of hearing is supplied by the eye in reading on the lips.[47] Thus, Mann. Zeal and intelligence could not compensate for a lack of practical knowledge. Had he asked a teacher of the deaf, had he deigned to ask a deaf teacher such as I, here is what I would have said. There are four great traps; they concern the pupil, his interlocutor, the material, and the visitor. Every large institution has a few outstanding pupils who can be trotted out for the visitor. How representative is the pupil? At what age did he lose his hearing? There is a world of difference between a deaf-mute and a semi-mute, between instilling a knowledge of oral language in one who is deaf, and slowing the deterioration of oral skills in someone who once spoke, perhaps even on arriving at school. Is the pupil selected semi-deaf? Can he hear speech addressed to him directly in a loud voice?

Does the pupil communicate only with familiar people, the teacher perhaps, or another pupil? It generally happens that the pupils come to understand the teacher better than they understand anyone else, and vice versa. Thomas Gallaudet told me about a man who claimed he had trained his parrot to talk. Thomas couldn't tell what the parrot was saying unless the teacher gave him the model in advance, but he could tell that the longer the teacher worked with the parrot, the more his models sounded parrotlike.

Is the material rehearsed? Oral teachers generally have a few pupils prepared with common utterances for use with visitors: "Where do you come from?" and the like. Furthermore, if the question or the text is familiar to the visitor, it can easily appear more intelligible to him than it is. Visitors are often unwitting accomplices to this charade when they ask to hear the Lord's Prayer, or follow by eye the pupil's reading in some text.

Finally, it is folly for the visitor to undertake this evaluation unless he is perfectly fluent in the language or has an interpreter who is. How is he to detect faulty pronunciation, grammatical errors, or mistakes in writing in an unfamiliar orthography?

Horace Mann was misled more than once by his ignorance of these precautions. Not long after his report appeared, he joined Henry Barnard, commissioner of education in Connecticut, in organizing a meeting in Hartford of the American Institute of Instruction, where he called attention to a young man from New London who was present, who was born deaf and dumb, but whose father had succeeded in teaching him to speak, read, and write. Enoch Whipple, eighteen, was then presented to the assembly and truly he could articulate well and had an uncommon ability to read from the lips. His father, Jonathan, then gave an account of how he had taught the boy.

Fortunately, William Turner, who later became our director at Hartford, was there with me and during luncheon he questioned the father closely and experimented on the son. The result was that the young man gave prompt replies to questions made close to his ear in little more than an ordinary tone of voice, without seeing the mouth of the speaker, and was evidently neither deaf nor dumb. That afternoon the results were laid before the convention; further experiments proved that the boy was only semi-deaf. How much better he could once hear we were not told. The convention saw in a moment that this boy could hear any question put to him and answer intelligently from the sound of the voice; the father and boy, who were lions in the morning, were pretty small cubs by afternoon and they decamped without our knowing what became of them. The father deserves some credit for teaching his son some lipreading, but the case had no bearing on Mann's assertion that those born deaf can be taught to speak and lipread. Mann had been duped again.[48]

I need not pursue here the common-school controversy, triggered by Mann's Seventh Report, which raged for more that a year and led Howe to run for the Boston school committee; suffice it to say that Mann found little but evil in our common schools and nothing but good in the German ones, that Massachusetts schoolteachers took offense, that a great deal of ink was spilled on both sides, and that little changed in the end.

With regard to the deaf, Thomas Gallaudet was the first to respond, though he had retired from the field a dozen years before. He did not question Mann's motives, as I have, nor his ability to judge—by now you know Thomas would never do such a thing. He simply affirmed—how wise! —that articulation is only one part of education. There is also mental and moral development, knowledge of our social and civil institutions, arithmetic, grammar, geography, history, reading, writing, learning a trade, and all these cannot be taught without "that very distinct, intelligible, copious, and beautiful language of signs."[49] Thomas did not publish this reply; he showed it to us and he sent it to Mann.

Harvey Peet was less generous. We cannot let Mann's denunciation pass, he argued, for it is widely circulated from a man of high authority, it could mislead parents and legislators and impair our usefulness in the end. He struck back in the pages of the *North American Review*:[50] "We are persuaded that if we should spend a large portion of the period, scanty at best, allowed to each pupil attempting to teach him to articulate and to read on the lips, the cases of partial failure in the far more essential, yet easier, task of teaching the vocabulary and idioms of language would be much more numerous. Articulation has been excluded from the course of instruction after careful and mature deliberation and, in the New York Institution, after actual and patient experiment; not because the object was considered of little account but because the small degree of success usually attainable was judged to be a very inadequate compensation for that expenditure of time and labor which the teaching of articulation exacts—for the many wearisome hours that must be spent in adjusting and readjusting the positions of the vocal organs, in teaching the seven sounds of the letter *a*, the hundreds of elementary sounds, as Mr. Mann says, represented by only twenty-six letters, and the thousand capricious irregularities in the pronunciation of the same letters or combinations of letters.

"Unless Mr. Mann has something stronger in reserve we hardly think he will succeed in persuading many of the American teachers of the deaf to tie the hands of their pupils, compel them to articulate disagreeably, and read on the lips of those who will consent to sit or stand full in the light and speak slowly and distinctly."

Peet admonished teachers of the deaf to remember the disastrous experiment with oralism at the Paris institution under Ordinaire and concluded, "We see no present prospect that the teaching of articulation will be introduced into our institutions at all."

If only Peet had been right! But Mann's report was to prove the greatest threat to the education of the signing community that the deaf had yet encountered.

We now know, with access to Mann's papers after his death, that even his friend Howe—an ardent opponent of sign language—was aghast at Mann's remarks on the deaf, which he read on returning from Europe ten months after their publication. He thought the report's wild claims could not survive careful scrutiny and would likely hinder more than help his efforts to gain control of deaf education. How can you say, he asked Mann, that "it is almost absurd to speak of the dumb in Germany"? "Well," Mann replied, "if they have been taught to speak, even though it be only to name common articles of dress, furniture and animals and to give the names of friends, they can no longer with propriety be called dumb, can they?"

How do you defend your claim, Howe went on, that the American deaf are "helpless and hopeless"? "Are they not so," Mann replied, "when they leave the circle of those who understand the sign language—like an English- man who knows not a word of French in a company of Frenchmen who know not a word of English?" (Not at all, for the American deaf learn English and can communicate by writing with those who know no sign.) And as for your Berliner Habermaass—the one who, though deaf, spoke flawlessly—how did you judge that, Howe asked, since you scarcely know German? "The account of Habermaass," Mann replied, "I took from a book on the subject by Moritz Hill." Howe also disagreed with Mann's claim that the deaf can be taught to speak "substantially in all cases." He thought only half at most could succeed. (About half the pupils at Hartford were semi- mutes.) "As to the percentage, I said nothing about that," Mann answered. "I said a triumph might undoubtedly be won over this natural impediment but I did not say, nor mean to be understood to say, *in all cases.* Nor could it be inferred that it could be won in so large a proportion of cases as in the German language, for I spoke in the report of a difference between English and German."[51]

Not immune to the general conviction that there must be something in Mann's assertions concerning the German schools, even though his charac- terization of the deaf was so completely in error, and eager to learn whatever there was to be learned from the Germans and others, our board sent Lewis Weld on a comprehensive tour of European schools. He was joined, for part of the tour, by a German interpreter and by two professors from Saint- Jacques, Edouard Morel and Léon Vaïsse, who had returned from New York. At the same time, the New York school independently sent George Day, fluent in German and French, to study European methods. Seven years later, Peet went himself with two deaf teachers and his son, and seven years after that Day went again.[52] Each of these investigators visited about two dozen schools, some of them in common, and filed voluminous reports with precise locations, tests, and findings, all of which were lacking in the Mann report on the deaf.

In Great Britain, Weld found manual language plentiful in schools for the deaf; pupils signed among themselves, teachers used pantomime extensively intermingled with words from sign language, or the language itself if they knew it. The British two-handed manual alphabet was broadly in use. In most schools, articulation training was not attempted. However, at the London asylum, then directed by Joseph Watson's son Thomas, oral skills were a part of the regular course for all pupils. Nevertheless, few of the 280 pupils spoke intelligibly. The *Christian Examiner* likewise assailed the quality of the pupils' speech at the annual exhibitions.[53] Weld was told that pupils who do not acquire some speech are considered deficient in intellect! (Actually, the opposite is closer to the truth: pupils deafened later in life, who generally benefit more from articulation training, are also more likely to have other problems, the result of the same disease that attacked their hearing.) When Day visited the London asylum shortly after Weld, the principal assured him that the object was not to teach all scholars to speak, but only to teach them to lipread. A professor there told him that not more than one-fourth could learn speech. Interviewing the seniors at this school, Weld concluded that only about half of them could read English with understanding. In Kinniburgh's school at Edinburgh, where Thomas had sojourned nearly thirty years earlier, Weld learned that articulation training had been tried on all pupils originally, but too much time was lost and labor expended for too little result and at too great a cost in general education. Now, only ten of the seventy pupils were receiving that training in the school Braidwood had founded. Weld does recount two cases of congenitally deaf pupils who had received early, intense, and prolonged training in speech; he found one of them spoke rather intelligibly, the second less so. Weld's conclusions: the deaf are educated in sign but, because the teachers don't know the language well, the form of communication in the classroom is less evolved than in America, and the British deaf are less well educated than their American counterparts. Articulation training is not pursued, except in London, where it is given to a few.

Weld visited six schools in France and one each in Holland, Belgium, and Switzerland that were founded by disciples of Epée and Sicard. All education, including the teaching of French, was conducted in the pupils' primary language. At the "mother school" in Paris, Day found "evidence of real solid attainment: I have seen nothing superior, if indeed anything equal to it, in my visits to the other schools." There was no trace of Ordinaire's attempt to replace sign by French. De Gérando had just died; Itard had passed away a few years earlier. Vaïsse was spending a half hour daily giving articulatory training after school to one-fourth of the boys and one-third of the girls, mainly semi-mutes. Similar efforts were made at several of the other schools in this group. By the time Peet visited Saint-Jacques, seven years later, Vaïsse was associate director, and Jean-Jacques Valade-Gabel had come from Bordeaux to teach articulation in Paris. It remained a matter of an hour or so a day for semi-mutes, an extracurricular activity. There was a third hearing professor, Puybonnieux, and four deaf professors, including Berthier, Allibert, and Pélissier. In brief, the situation outside of Germany was much as within the United States, where education was conducted in sign and some supplementary articulatory training was given to semi-mutes.[54]

As for Germany, the American investigators found the departures from standard practice there highly unsatisfactory. To discount their carefully documented findings on the ground that they all came from signing schools (Day, in fact, no longer did) would be to do a great injustice to the sincerity and diligence of each. Here is what they discovered; you may judge for yourself.

The investigators found the German pupils' speech unintelligible. They were not alone in this: most German schoolteachers, clergymen, and people in other professions who were asked said, "We cannot understand the deaf and dumb." The graduates themselves reported that they could not use speech in everyday intercourse. The teachers were frequently obliged to repeat for the visitors what a pupil had said. In the most advanced class at Leipzig, pupils read by turns, at Dr. Day's request, a verse from the fourth chapter of Saint John. Out of eight scholars, three did not utter a single word intelligibly, two others uttered but one or two words so as to be understood, and the remaining three uttered from four to six words intelligibly. Day concluded: "The process is correctly called by German writers 'mechanical speaking': much time must be devoted to it, and with the greatest efforts only a defective utterance can reasonably be expected, even under the labors of the most experienced instructors." There was no evidence whatsoever—quite the contrary—for Mann's claim that he often heard deaf pupils read "with more distinctness of articulation and appropriateness of expression" than some of the hearing children in our own schools "who possess perfect organs of speech and a complement of the senses."

The teachers in German schools signed so much in class while speaking —no doubt to make themselves understood—that the pupils' abilities in lipreading alone could not be judged. Day found that a third of the advanced students appeared to understand, with the help of signs and frequent repetition, most of the instructor's utterances. Another third lost a considerable part, and the final third were quite at a loss to say what was going on. Indeed, when the teacher was asked to refrain from signing while speaking, Day found some two-thirds of the pupils did not know what the lesson was about. How can we reconcile the pupils' poor speech and lipreading with their teachers' enthusiasm for instruction using oral language? Edouard Morel makes a good point: When the teachers enumerate the advantages of oral language, they contemplate it abstractly or in relation to hearing children, not the deaf. Thus they may say that oral language is rapid, that it leaves the speaker and hearer free to see and act, that it can be successfully used under a wide variety of conditions—in the dark, across a field, around a corner, and so on. But none of these things is true when oral language is used by the deaf. The speaker must speak slowly; the listener must stay still when spoken to and fix his eye upon the speaker—he dare not compare utterance with facts by looking elsewhere; the speaker must be close at hand, well lit, and so forth. Mann was quite mistaken when he wrote of lipreading: "The sense of hearing is almost supplied by that of sight."

Not surprisingly, all investigators found that much time and therefore money was spent on the effort to provide whatever articulatory and lipreading skills could be inculcated. According to one German educator, oral exercises occupy half of the first year, a third of the second year, and a considerable part of all remaining years.[55] If a third of the time is lost on the average, then a pupil loses two of his six years of schooling. Moreover, the pupils find the exercises tedious and boring, but no more so than the teachers. "The teacher needs an infinite patience," Moritz Hill writes, and should remember "how difficult it must be for the deaf and dumb to learn and to practice something so opposed to his nature."[56]

Although the failure of German teachers to instill oral skills might be considered a mere misdemeanor, a wasteful imposition on the teachers and pupils, it becomes a serious crime when coupled with an educational system that is predicated on those very oral skills. There are several grave charges. First, all investigators found that a very large proportion of deaf children were screened out of the educational system for lack of oral skills. The German schools for the deaf rejected children who were truly deaf, preferring instead the hard-of-hearing who had some speech. Morel estimated that a tenth were rejected during admissions, a fifth after trial, and only a third of those remaining could be instructed orally. This amounts to sacrificing the education of three-fourths of the students in order to provide an oral education for one-fourth.[57] The Riehen school, at the Swiss-German border, for example, has admitted sixty-six pupils since its founding and dismissed nineteen for incapacity. To the north, the Pforzheim school has received two hundred and forty-nine pupils in the last two decades, fifty-two of whom have been dismissed, yet these were not indiscriminately admitted. (The principal has a list of all the deaf and dumb in the Grand Duchy of Baden and before admitting them he obtains exact information about their mental and physical capacities.) Because many of those pupils admitted, however, cannot speak and lipread sufficiently well, German schools have often taken a second measure: the pupils have been sorted into separate classes. At a typical school, "The first class contains children who have spoken, the half-deaf, and some born deaf who are exceptionally gifted. The second class contains the deaf of average intelligence. The third contains the intractable signers, the cretins and the idiots."[58] There is no doubt in my mind that I would have been put in the third class, since I proved an "intractable" signer. Likewise, Massieu, Berthier, Pélissier, and so on. In short, the oralist schools found themselves obliged to screen out the deaf, first at the door of the school, then at the door of the classroom. Such screening discriminates particularly against deaf families, for a congenitally deaf child would have to be a prodigy to learn in an oral school, whereas children from hearing families who have once spoken the language of the school have one less disadvantage. Since deaf families are usually poor, the screening helps to keep the poor entrenched in poverty and ignorance and provides education to the higher social classes.

The investigators found that oral instruction not only excluded many deaf from an education, but also poorly equipped for a career the deaf pupils who did graduate. Because most schools took the deaf child from his home around age seven or eight and instructed him for six years, the typical pupil graduated at fourteen, too young and unprepared to be self-sufficient. American schools pride themselves on teaching trades to all students, or preparing them for college. German schools do neither. Yet another grave consequence of the insistence on oral instruction is the virtual exclusion of deaf teachers, for teaching is a highly rewarding career that many of the educated deaf choose, a choice that has only the most favorable consequences for the teacher and student alike.

I have saved the most grievous effect of oralism found by the investigators for last. Since the pupils cannot understand much of what the teacher says, and since much of their time is spent on articulatory skills, they do not learn much; they are poorly educated. Edouard Morel, De Gérando's nephew and no friend of sign language at Saint-Jacques, returned from a visit to Pforzheim reporting that pupils in their sixth year of school could not do two-digit multiplication. Yet this should not excite surprise; arithmetic, which presents no great obstacle to us who explain it in the pupils' primary language, can be explained only with great difficulty to deaf pupils who are trying to glean it from their teacher's lips and ciphers on the board. Indeed, some German teachers said the deaf could not be taught arithmetic beyond simple enumeration, for their minds were not equal to the task.[59] Morel concluded his report: "The development of the [German] pupils' intellect is less remarkable than in the French schools; their ideas move in a narrower circle. I attribute this inferiority to the too restricted use of the mimic [sign] language." Here is Vaïsse (in a letter to Weld): "The general standing of the pupils when they have completed their course is far below that of your own." And Weld: "The mass of German pupils I believe to be not so well fitted to encounter the vicissitudes of life." And Day: "If it were necessary to specify the schools for the deaf and dumb in Germany in which the knowledge of the pupils, their compass of thought, and their power of expressing it in written language are decidedly superior to those of others, the schools in which natural signs are the most employed would instantly receive the preference. Still, the difference between the best German schools and our own in this respect is striking." Even a German educator of the deaf, Ludwig Haug, wrote: "I doubt whether the mass of our deaf pupils when they leave school are as far advanced in moral and intellectual education, in the command of language, and in general information as those of the best foreign institutions."

Because the draft of oralism was too bitter to swallow and rarely seemed to cure once ingested, the Germans after a few years diluted it: many schools started postponing oral instruction and returning to a curriculum surprisingly like the one they had had before, in which speech training was a complement to education, given to those who could profit by it. The final stage in the dilution of oralism arrived when German schools reintroduced sign language in class; out of class, the pupils had been using it all along.

"Of course!" Jäger now announced to a visitor to Gmünd about the time of Mann's tour. "Only an utter ignorance of all that pertains to the subject can venture the assertion that the deaf and dumb can be educated without the aid of pantomime."[60] Likewise, in Prussia experience had quite mellowed Hill's oralism; he now called doing without sign "unthinkable," "contrary to nature," "refusing to use the key that fits the lock."[61] It's easier to find these tergiversations amusing if you can forget how many lives they destroyed.

Weld returned from Europe convinced that Mann's claims were without basis, that we had nothing to gain and much to lose by replacing sign as the language of instruction. Nevertheless, he told me, he would recommend a more systematic and sustained effort than we had pursued so far to preserve the speech of semi-mutes. The Weld plan was to have each hearing teacher devote twenty to thirty minutes a day to teaching articulation and lipreading to semi-mutes; the deaf teachers would excuse the semi-mutes from their classes during this time—the children would go to an adjacent room where there was a hearing teacher. I was much opposed. History does not tolerate such subtle arrangements in social institutions, I told Weld. Itard never intended his intensive oral training of three semi-deaf pupils to be imposed on all the rest of the school, but the board and Ordinaire soon tried to do just that. This present accommodation would lead at least to demands for a distinct curriculum for the semi-mutes. The effort to make them talk would consume more and more of their time and eventually crowd out their true education. We must keep to sign, I told him, only sign, and students whose primary language is English and who wish to have their instruction in that language should go to a common school, seconded perhaps by lessons with a speech teacher. But we inevitably get these semi-mutes, Lewis argued, and we cannot refuse them. Moreover, the mothers want their children to speak—especially if they once heard them. Tell the mothers, I said, "Don't try to change your child, you are the adult, you bear the burden, you change. Here is a circle of signing pupils: no straining of attention, no groping in the dark, no demand for frequent repetition, no cold and imperfect appreciation of each speaker's meaning; instead, eloquence, poetry.

. . . Now here are the same semi-mutes conversing orally, straining to glimpse a few fleeting movements of the speaker's lips, speculating on their significance, requesting a repetition, frowning from the effort of attention."[62]

We have to make some concessions, Lewis said; the board will demand them. We have already given training in articulation; we can do it again. I disagreed, but the board voted to give the Weld plan a fair trial. It took a year to see, and ten years to accept, that it was a failure. Only the semi-mutes received some slight benefit from it whereas all pupils suffered from a great loss of instructional time. Weld's successor, William Turner, chose the obvious solution, which was Vaïsse's in Paris: he hired a special teacher to provide oral instruction after class to those semi-mutes who might profit from it.[63] The gains made under this arrangement were also modest,[64] and when Turner retired and Collins Stone became director, the articulation teacher was released.

I spoke earlier of the deaf journalist William Chamberlain, who helped to found the New England Gallaudet Association. He was the first pupil to receive articulation training under the new regime, instituted on Weld's return from Europe. Chamberlain had lost his hearing when he was five; his parents communicated with him by writing, and insisted that he speak. When he was eight, his father began to teach him lipreading and the youth practiced on his own with a mirror. "My first success in lipreading," he has written, "was like a glimpse down a long vista, of freedom from trammels; but, oh! the long tiresome, discouraging time I have had in getting as far toward that freedom as I have, which is by no means half-way, although it is certainly better than nothing." He came to Hartford at the age of twelve, while Lewis was in Europe. "I got the full benefit of the newly aroused enthusiasm in the matter. They were at me early and late and their efforts permanently benefitted me. . . . I am able to understand a public speaker as well as anyone else similarly situated, which is not saying a great deal. The public has had foisted upon it, at public gatherings and exhibitions, semi-mutes who, it was announced beforehand, would, after a speaker had concluded his remarks, prove how well they understood the motion of his lips by writing out a synopsis of his remarks. I can easily do the same, provided I have the privilege, as they had, of reading the manuscript in advance of its delivery. I have had more than one such job offered to me and declined them. . . . For public speaking, and rapidity of communication on ordinary occasions, commend me to the elastic, graceful, and comprehensive sign language."[65]

Another semi-mute pupil who received oral training at Hartford is James Flournoy, the writer from Georgia who advocated a colony in which citizens would be deaf and sign language the medium of communication. In a recent issue of the *National Deaf-Mute Gazette*, Flournoy recounts that he arrived at Hartford speaking and lipreading, having attended hearing schools in Georgia. He had lost his hearing in an illness when he was seven. Turner boarded Flournoy in his own family, instructed him largely in English, had him read aloud and so forth. "Oral instruction to one who cannot hear *readily,*" Flournoy writes, "without the sign method as the principal reliance, appears to me a poor resort. It will not make literary proficients—but mediocre scholars, while the improvement of speech to converse with the hearing world will not compensate for lettered defect. Mr. Gallaudet's and Mr. Clerc's wisdom, therefore, was the anchor of hope of our unfortunate people."[66]

As with Hartford, so with New York. Day had revealed Mann's assertions baseless, but Hartford was trying the Weld plan, and New York would follow suit. Two years later, their board reported: "The experiment was accordingly commenced with the greater portion of the pupils, though most of them evinced a decided repugnance to this exercise. After a patient trial of several weeks, further efforts were, with the greater number, abandoned as a perfectly useless waste of time." An oral class was then formed from the few who seemed to show some promise of gain but after a year it, too, was dropped as a failure.[67]

What did Horace Mann and Samuel Gridley Howe have to say with their views thus repudiated and their falsehoods revealed? Mann said not a word further concerning the deaf to the day he died ten years ago. If only Howe had followed Mann's example! The Massachusetts legislature had defeated his proposal to arrogate the education of the deaf, the Mann report had failed to recoup his loss, and hearing and deaf people alike had assailed the document and its author, Howe's friend. All this, smoldering in him for twenty years, burst into flame three years ago, seven years after Mann's death. By this time there were more than 13,000 deaf people in the United States, some two dozen residential schools, a tried and effective system of education, a longer period of schooling extending up to some eight years, and an earlier age of admission, as low as six at the New York school. There was a national college for the deaf, several high classes, and distinguished deaf Americans in countless walks of life. Nevertheless, "The deaf person's lack of an important sense," Howe wrote in a widely publicized report of the Massachusetts Board of State Charities, "not only prevents the entire and harmonious development of mind and character but it tends to give morbid growth in certain directions; as a plant checked in its direct upward growth grows askew. . . . We should, in providing for the instruction and training of these persons, have association among them as little as is possible. . . . There should be no attempts to build up permanent asylums. . . . A society has recently been formed here among the mutes for public religious worship in the sign language. Now such an association surely is not accord-

ing to sound sociological principles. . . . It promotes their segregation and
thus their formation into a special class . . . The constant object should be
to fashion them into the likeness of common men. . . . If our mutes educated at Hartford had been taught as well as children are taught in the
German schools, they might attend public worship in our churches." Having
calumniated our minds, our characters, and our associations, Howe goes on
to vilify our language: "The rudimentary and lower parts of language or
pantomime are open to mutes; but the higher and finer part, that is, speech,
is forever closed; and any substitute for it is at best imperfect."[68]

All of this is a prelude to "a plan for a change in our system of educating
mutes." This time, rather than naming Perkins directly as the proper alternative, Howe proposed that the governor name three commissioners for the
education of deaf-mutes, who in turn would have the authority to contract
with any organization within the state to educate the Massachusetts deaf.
He gave three arguments for withdrawing pupils from Hartford in favor of
some organization in Massachusetts: repatriation, dispersion, and economy.
The care of these "wards" would fall upon the citizens of our state, he
argues, which would be instructive and the children would be closer to
home. By dispersing the children as boarders in families, no more than two
to a family, the evils of congregation would be lessened. New buildings
would not be required to house them and thus their education would be
more economical. He toys with a fourth argument, concerning methods: the
attempt at oralism in American schools for the deaf admittedly failed, but
it could not get a fair trial because the principals were wedded to the old
ways. In a new school, oralism might succeed. This time Howe had strengthened his forces, maneuvered into position, and intended to win. It was his
third attempt; I must first describe his second.[69]

Around the time of Horace Mann's death, a committee of the Massachusetts legislature urged the creation of a Board of State Charities, after hearing testimony from Howe among others (he was there as a trustee of the
state reform school).[70] The committee specified that the governor and his
council (Governor Andrew was a friend of Howe's, as was at least one
member of the council) should appoint a board with the power to move
inmates from one institution to another. The governor backed the recommendation personally and it was passed in 1863. He then appointed as
secretary of the board Franklin Sanborn, one of Howe's oldest political
allies, a fellow backer of John Brown's raid on Harpers Ferry, and he appointed Howe chairman of the board.[71]

Howe was ready for his second major battle to gain control of the
deaf and now he had one very important ally, a Boston millionaire by the
name of Gardiner Greene Hubbard, whose second daughter, Mabel, then
twelve, had contracted scarlet fever when she was five and had become totally deaf.[72]

GARDINER GREENE HUBBARD

Mabel Hubbard

As children often do in these cases, Mabel had continued to speak after her illness and her mother determined to do everything in her power to preserve her speech. She kept her with her hearing sisters, had her play their games, go to dance school with them.[73] A teacher was hired to keep up her speech, teach her lipreading, and encourage her reading. Mabel's father obtained a copy of Mann's Seventh Report, then went to see Samuel Gridley Howe in South Boston. Howe urged him to prevent Mabel from associating with any other deaf children, to forbid her gesturing and even communicating in writing. If you want your daughter to be normal, he told Hubbard, you must speak to your daughter and she must speak to you. But Mabel's speech continued to deteriorate, so the Hubbards hired a full-time governess, Miss Mary True, the daughter of the minister in the Maine town where their summer home was located.[74] Miss True knew nothing of articulation, and at the outset Mabel could not read her lips. To make matters worse, the teacher often could not understand the child, and although Mabel had learned to read many printed words aloud, she did not know their meanings and there seemed to be no way to explain them. Mrs. Hubbard continued to spend several hours a day having Mabel name pictures and objects and recite the rhymes and hymns she knew before her illness. Miss True tried to explain the language of her books by translating it into Mabel's own idiosyncratic English. When the child had fathomed the meaning of the original phrase or sentence in this way, the translation was set aside. Though Mabel's speech is now unintelligible and Miss True left a year ago, Mabel is bright and diligent, and she continues to read and to receive intensive training from her mother. With all my heart I wish her a better fate than that of Pereire's pupil Marie Marois.[75]

Hubbard and his wife agreed with Howe that they should not settle for sending Mabel to the asylum in Hartford with other, mainly indigent, deaf children, who used a gross, material language of the hands. What did Gardiner Greene Hubbard know about manual activities, about hands? And thus, Howe and Hubbard, two people who knew nothing of our language, culture, and heritage, not only decided the fate of one deaf child but sought to decide the fate of many.

Together, they were powerful; Howe enjoyed a reputation as a reformer and was chairman of the Board of State Charities; Hubbard had business standing and high social caste. It seems he had somewhat more political finesse than Howe, too, because Howe's second attempt to seize control of the deaf was much more sophisticated than his first. Hubbard joined with Dr. Thomas Hill, the president of Harvard, and several others to petition the legislature for an act incorporating a school for the deaf. A friendly representative in the House introduced the bill, probably drawn by Hubbard. It provided that the state would give $5,000 a year to this school, which would board and educate thirty deaf pupils designated by the governor. The bill was referred to the legislature's Committee on Public Charitable Institutions, but Howe was no longer in the legislature and the bill encountered stiff opposition, particularly from one representative and member of the governor's council, Lewis Dudley, a lawyer who has a deaf daughter.[76]

Theresa Dudley was born deaf. When she was four, her parents brought her to Hartford to determine why she had never spoken; her mother refused to believe she was deaf. Turner took a music box and set it going just behind Theresa while she looked through the window at something going on outside. The child made no response to the music. He whistled loudly into her ear and she did not react. When he told the mother her daughter was indeed deaf, she became quite distressed, but he explained that, since a mute child must be either deaf or an idiot, she could be thankful her daughter was deprived of her hearing, not her intellect, and he introduced me and several of our pupils to show how much the deaf can do.[77] As a result of this visit, one of our graduates, and then one from the New York school, were engaged to teach Theresa sign at home; thus the Dudleys became acquainted with some deaf people, and when Theresa was nine and entered our school, she could already read and write. During her two years with us in Hartford, she made rapid progress, not only academically but also in learning some oral skills, which were taught through the medium of her primary language, sign. When she began to articulate she had to learn not the meanings of the words but how to pronounce them—just the reverse of Mabel Hubbard. She left Hartford with a good education and a good command of English. It is not surprising, then, that her father joined our director, Collins Stone, in denouncing before the committee the Howe-Hubbard initiative, which would take Massachusetts deaf children from Hartford and impose on them an exclusively oral education.

In the event, despite an appearance by Howe, in which he disinterred the Mann report, and despite Mary Swift Lamson's testimony on her education of Laura Bridgman without sign, the committee report was unfavorable to Howe and Hubbard. It praised the work at Hartford, saw no reason to change the practice of sending Massachusetts deaf pupils to our school, and called the instruction of the deaf orally "a theory of visionary enthusiasts which has been repeatedly tried and abandoned as impracticable."[78] As the national college opened its doors to higher education in sign language, Howe's second attempt to obtain control of the deaf was defeated.

Dudley, however, was interested in learning more from Mary Swift Lamson about how she taught Laura Bridgman and he arranged an appointment; in one of those coincidences that cannot occur in fiction, a certain Mrs. James Cushing came to see him just as he was setting out. She had a deaf daughter, had heard he did, too, and wanted to know what means he was using to educate her. They pursued their conversation on the way to Mary

Lamson's, where Dudley learned little of interest. Mrs. Cushing, however, was delighted to hear that, with proper training, her daughter Fanny might be made normal again, and she asked Mrs. Lamson to recommend a teacher. A few days later, Mary Lamson asked her fellow teacher of Laura Bridgman, Eliza Rogers, for a suggestion and Eliza recommended her sister, Harriet.[79]

Harriet Rogers had graduated from the Normal School and had taught in the common schools, but she had no idea how to go about teaching a deaf child; she only remembered, thanks to Mann, that in Germany the deaf learned to speak and sign was prohibited. She began by following her sister's example with Laura; she took Fanny Cushing to live with her and taught her fingerspelling.[80]

One day Mrs. Cushing took Harriet Rogers to Providence to meet a friend, the wife of a wealthy manufacturer and banker, Mrs. Henry Lippitt, who had a deaf daughter, Jeannie, then twelve, deafened at four years and three months by scarlet fever.[81] The Lippitts were unwilling to send their daughter to an asylum where she would learn to speak with her hands, so Jeannie had been left in silence for some time. Finally, they heard of "a man in Boston who had been abroad and had seen a deaf boy speak and understand" and they got in touch with Samuel Gridley Howe. According to Jeannie, Howe said "he had never heard or seen such a thing," but he urged Mrs. Lippitt to give her daughter an oral education.[82] So for over three years Mrs. Lippitt had been spending five hours daily with her daughter, practicing articulation. But despite all this effort, Jeannie had made little progress in speech. When the Hubbards visited her at Howe's suggestion, they came away discouraged at Mabel's prospects since Jeannie's articulation was "indistinct" and they "could hardly understand a word she said," although she could lipread rather well. Nevertheless, Mrs. Cushing told Harriet Rogers to forget fingerspelling and to try to make her daughter Fanny speak; Harriet agreed to try.

Howe, meanwhile, twenty years after the Mann report and its repudiation, had decided to make his third and final assault on the legislature. This time he would have Mabel, Fanny, and Jeannie to show that oral education was not a "theory of visionary enthusiasts." This time he and his partners would do as Mann did when lobbying for a state board of education: first, an anonymous philanthropist (Hubbard?) would offer a gift of money to found a deaf school if the legislature would incorporate it, and second, the governor would request the school himself in an address to the legislature. This time, no appropriation would be asked initially so there could be no objection concerning the cost.

Gardiner Hubbard had a further plan. He invited a group of six distinguished and influential friends to gather at Mary Lamson's home, meet Harriet Rogers, and see the progress she had made with Fanny Cushing.

President Hill of Harvard was a participant, as he had been in the last effort before the legislature. Also there were an eminent Boston clergyman, who had ridden with Hubbard through the South just before the Civil War,[83] and Lewis B. Monroe, an elocutionist who founded the School of Oratory at Boston University.[84] The group signed a testimonial, which Hubbard then published as an advertisement, stating that Harriet Rogers was about to open an oral school, had two pupils, and would welcome several more. *That* would show the legislature what was practical and what visionary! Despite the advertisement, seven months passed before Miss Rogers could assemble three more pupils and open her school in Chelmsford, Massachusetts, in June 1866—and even those had to be admitted with reduced tuition, since the school was private and hence relatively expensive.[85]

A few months before, Howe had fired the opening volley of his third assault on the legislature by attacking the existing mode of educating the deaf in his charity board's report. Collins Stone was the first to protest publicly. Stone comes from an old New England family: he traces his ancestry back six generations to a Puritan divine in the reign of Queen Elizabeth and four generations to the first pastor of Hartford's congregational church. After graduating from Yale, he studied for the ministry under Reverend Strong's famous successor, Joel Hawes. He is a modest, cheerful, religious man with good practical sense, great powers of concentration, and painstaking attention to detail. Short and stout, with red hair that has become white over the years, he is not a striking signer or orator, but when he speaks, he speaks carefully, from the heart as well as the mind.[86] After teaching at the American Asylum for twenty years, he went to the Ohio Institution as director, returning to Hartford to succeed William Turner six years ago.

"The fact that it is not possible to restore speech to the deaf and dumb to any considerable or useful degree," he wrote in our annual report, "that the processes by which it is attempted are tedious and exhausting, and that the results attained are unsatisfactory and transient in their character, is not fully understood."[87] The dispute does not concern the semi-deaf and semi-mute pupils that we occasionally receive, he explained. It concerns those who have never spoken and cannot distinguish speech by ear: they constitute ninety-five percent of our students currently. Stone reviews all the arguments against oralism—the time lost, the pupils excluded from schooling, the disagreeable contortions of voice and facial expression, the inability of graduates to use their speech in general society, the many teachers required and hence great cost, the early admission precluding training in trades, the postponement of religious instruction and impossibility of group religious worship, the necessity of acquiring elusive lipreading skills, the reduced comprehension of general education. He protests Howe's characterizing the deaf as "dependent classes" just because a part of the state taxes goes to subsidize their education. He contends that preventing a deaf child from signing isolates him more than any clique he may form with other signers. He exposes Howe's plan for boarding deaf pupils in hearing families for the wildly impractical scheme that it is. Stone defends the Deaf-Mute Christian Association of Boston against Howe's imprecations: it is composed of mutes who have been educated and are now respected and prosperous members of society. These men and women wish to enjoy intelligible social religious worship. Living in a community of hearing persons, laboring in the same workshops, mingling with them in social intercourse during the week, on the Sabbath they assemble by themselves for worship in the language with which they are most familiar, a language whose gracefulness, beauty and graphic power impresses every beholder. What harm is there in such an assembly to which a company of French- or Italian-born citizens gathered for a similar purpose would not also be exposed? If such weekly gatherings are "not according to sound sociological principles," they are in any case most commendable to the deaf and dumb and must exert a happy influence on their social and moral condition.

Having disposed of Howe's arguments based on the need for oralism—greater economy and greater dispersion in educating the deaf—Stone points out that Howe's last argument, repatriation, is a pretext: Howe's Perkins Institution for the Blind invites and receives blind children from all the other states in New England. Howe considers his institution sufficient to meet the wants of all these states and gives excellent reasons to show that it is in their interest to sustain but one school of this kind within the region.

Howe published a pamphlet rebutting Stone and defending the report of his board.[88] He said that the American Asylum never takes his suggestions, that it is not inconsistent to make mistakes, learn from them, and revise your ideas. In the light of all that has happened and will happen, he makes an astonishing denial: he says that Stone spent most of his rebuttal on the disadvantages of oralism, which is a false issue, since the board had not recommended the teaching of articulation. But here is what Howe originally said in his report: "The friends of the system of articulation . . . persist in efforts to obtain for the mutes of Massachusetts the benefit of what they believe to be a vastly better system of instruction. Some of the board share in this belief."[89]

Having now denied that the real issue is English versus sign, Howe appears to have forfeited his main argument, that existing schools are using an inappropriate method. To recoup his loss somewhat, he chastises Hartford for placing so little emphasis on fingerspelling. This revealed such a total unfamiliarity with education of the deaf that Dudley insisted Howe be dismissed from all his posts since he proved so ignorant of his task.[90] If only it had been done! If only Dudley had remained so steadfast in our cause!

Two more significant events occurred in the struggle that year, 1866. In the fall, Gardiner Greene Hubbard went with Thomas Talbot, Harriet Rogers's brother-in-law and a member of the governor's council, to see Governor Alexander Bullock. They planned to ask the legislature to grant a charter for a school for the deaf, and solicited the governor's support. He informed them that a certain John Clarke, a banker in Northampton, had had his attention called to the dispute and offered $50,000 to endow a school for the deaf in Massachusetts.[91] Governor Bullock must have asked after Howe: they were close friends from antislavery days and he, too, was one of the backers of the raid on Harpers Ferry. I fancy Hubbard told him that Howe had decided, after his failure to persuade the legislature in two earlier attempts, that it would be best for him to stay discreetly in the background. The governor said he would be pleased to oblige these gentlemen in their humanitarian request, and would support it in his annual address to the legislature the following January.[92]

"I confess," said the governor in his address, "I share the sympathetic yearnings of the people of Massachusetts towards these children of the state, detained by indissoluble chains in the domain of silence. This rigid grasp we may never relax; but over unseen wires, through the seemingly impassable gulf that separates them from their fellows, we may impart no small amount of abstract knowledge and culture." Such oratory! I suppose it may be excused in a governor's address but, really, nothing more is involved that the prosaic issue of educating people in their primary language. The governor goes on to ring the ancient chimes of benevolence, which sound so sweet to the benefactor's ears: "They are wards of the state. Then, as ours is the responsibility, be ours also the grateful labor." There is money in it for everyone: "Assured as I am, on substantial grounds, that legislative action in this direction will develop rich sources of private beneficence, I have the honor to recommend that initial steps be taken to provide for this class of dependents within our own commonwealth. Should this policy be adopted, I have every reason to believe that it would eventually result in a permanent decrease of the present annual expenditure for their support." So it was agreed that the grounds on which the campaign would be pursued were repatriation and economy. All parties knew that the latter claim was as false as the former: Hartford charged only half the true cost of educating each pupil because of the interest accrued annually from its endowment, obtained by selling the congressional gift of land in Alabama. Moreover, oral schools are inherently very expensive because a teacher can teach articulation to scarcely more than one pupil at a time, and general education to only a few because of the limits of lipreading.[93] John Clarke had to be persuaded that his offer of an endowment should be restricted to an oral school: but Harriet Rogers convinced him.[94]

The governor appointed a special joint committee to conduct hearings on his proposal; Lewis Dudley was the chairman for the house, which augured well for the interests of the deaf. The two members drawn from the governor's council, Talbot again and Francis Bird, augured ill, for both had contributed to Harriet Rogers's oral school and Bird, a political boss, was a lifelong friend of Howe's. Howe and Hubbard testified in favor of the governor's proposal, of course; two Hartford directors, Turner and Stone, testified against. Many deaf people attended, and David Bartlett from our school served as interpreter.

While the hearings were taking place, Howe and Hubbard conducted an intensive campaign, publishing pamphlets and giving demonstrations. The trials of oralism conducted by the American and New York schools were unfair, Hubbard contended in one publication: "A fair trial can only be made where sign is not allowed. The two cannot be carried on together for the language of signs is without doubt more attractive to the deaf-mute." It is a great wonder to me that all the oralists over the centuries who have bewailed that attraction see no message implicit in it. In the end Itard did. Hubbard's pamphlet closes with a most damaging admission; I suppose it had to be made, for the joint committee visited Harriet Rogers's school during the hearings and judged matters for themselves. "The articulation of most of the pupils is very imperfect," Hubbard wrote, "and almost as unintelligible to strangers as the sign language; perhaps to some signs seem preferable to the indistinct utterances of the pupils."[95] Howe published the third report of the Board of State Charities during the hearings.[96] In the section following the account concerning convicts at the state prison (they were going to try weekly lectures for their instruction), he affirmed that the board had high regard for the Hartford school but, "as the governor has said in his address, we should educate the deaf in their home state." Then, in the section "The Blind, the Deaf-Mutes, and the Idiots," he shook the dollar bait: "We have good authority for believing that benevolent persons stand ready to endow largely any such school that may be established by the legislature." He repeated the arguments for repatriation and dispersion of the deaf. He reported on a visit to Harriet Rogers's school, where he saw Roscoe Green, a cousin of Mary Lamson from Providence, deafened at age seven, and another pupil; both impressed him favorably—although Green could speak on arriving and his companion was not yet able to.[97] He acknowledged that any conclusions about Harriet Rogers's school would be premature, but he passed in review the achievements of Pereire, Braidwood, Watson, and Itard, and ended by urging the passage of the governor's request.

As part of the campaign, Hubbard arranged three receptions for the joint special committee and members of the legislature. The first was at the home of Mary Swift Lamson, within view of the State House: an exhibition of Harriet Rogers's pupils brought an attendance of some seventy persons. The opposition was not invited, but I was told that all the tricks used on Howe and Mann in Germany were employed: pupils were exhibited without an account of when they became deaf, the extent of their hearing loss, the years of training they received, their abilities when they entered the school. The audience did not spontaneously question pupils or test them.[98]

The second reception, attended by hundreds of ladies and gentlemen, state officials, members of the legislature and of the city government, clergymen, and teachers, was held in the no doubt spacious home of the former mayor, Josiah Quincy, Jr., within earshot of the chamber in which the legislature was debating Hubbard's bill. Mrs. Quincy was a friend of Mrs. Horace Mann and was most ready to extend her hospitality for such a worthy cause. Harriet Rogers and her pupils were placed on display. Roscoe Green and Jeannie Lippitt were seated about eight feet apart in the drawing room and held a conversation for all to witness about their common home city, school studies, the pleasures of vacation, and the like. The audience, including Lewis Dudley, came away mightily impressed. No one mentioned that these two young people, eighteen and fifteen, were semi-mutes, the beneficiaries of years of arduous parental training, that Roscoe had attended Miss Rogers's school less than a year and that Jeannie Lippitt had never attended it but had had private tutors. Then, according to a newspaper report, the other children spelled words and sentences, wrote them from dictation, counted numbers, did sums, and so on. I find it noteworthy that apparently none of them spoke.[99]

In another stratagem, Hubbard invited Lewis Dudley, his wife, and his deaf daughter to visit Harriet Rogers's school at Chelmsford. As Hubbard warned the visitor he might be, Dudley was unimpressed. His wife and Theresa remained several days, however, and Miss Rogers's assistant taught their daughter, then thirteen, to articulate a few words—an event that would prove momentous. On the father's return home a few days later, his daughter greeted him with a word of welcome. Dudley was touched but guarded in his hopes for speech in a congenitally deaf child. His wife was adamant: Theresa would be sent to Miss Rogers's school; even if she could not learn to speak very much, she might learn to lipread.[100]

The first speaker on behalf of the bill to incorporate the Clarke Institution for Deaf-Mutes, Gardiner Greene Hubbard, director, and to authorize the governor to send all the Massachusetts deaf to Clarke, was Samuel Gridley Howe. His first argument was repatriation: the deaf of Kentucky are educated in Kentucky, likewise Ohio, and so on for twenty-four states, why not Massachusetts? He affirmed, second, the need for dispersing the deaf, the evils of congregation, and third, the importance of earlier admission to school than was allowed at Hartford.

In his testimony, Hubbard addressed the issue of language. Semi-deaf and semi-mutes can be taught to articulate, he argued—his experience with his own daughter proved that. "Her articulation is, of course, very imperfect, but still it is preserved." Even some congenitally deaf can be taught. (Lewis

Dudley asked him in an aside, he later recounted, "Do you think, Mr. Hubbard, that Theresa can ever be taught to say 'father and 'mother'?" Mr. Hubbard certainly thought she could.)[101] Signs and the manual alphabet must be discarded, Hubbard said. True, many teachers are needed for a small group of pupils, but the cost can be offset by employing untrained females. It requires no art or skill to teach the deaf, just patience. But a little later in his testimony, Hubbard warned the committee, "When you visit the American Asylum, remember they have fifty years headstart on us at Chelmsford [and] teachers who have lifelong experience in the art of teaching this particular class of scholars; they know how to teach better than we do, and the instruction there cannot be compared with that at Chelmsford." Only a lawyer could be that inconsequent!

FAY (chairman for the senate): I understand you to say that some persons can be taught to articulate who were born deaf-mutes?

HUBBARD: Yes, sir; I know that is so. We do not have sufficient experience in this country to tell exactly how.

DUDLEY: Would you recommend teaching all congenital deaf-mutes or merely making a trial of them?

HUBBARD: I would recommend a trial.

DUDLEY: What would be the criterion by which to judge?

HUBBARD: Well, I should want to take a child of a little more than average capacity, I think, or one that had more than usual opportunities of being taught.

DUDLEY: Of being taught in what way?

HUBBARD: Of being taught by articulation . . .

DUDLEY: How do you determine with regard to children at the age of four years who have not had any instruction at all? What shall be the criterion whether you shall commence by articulation or by some other method?

HUBBARD: That might depend upon the circumstances of the case. If the child were of poor parents, I should not attempt articulation.

BIRD: Let it grow up in ignorance?

HUBBARD: No, sir. I should send it to Hartford.

Three semi-mutes addressed the committee. The first was George Homer, from a distinguished old Boston family, who became hard of hearing gradually at the age of ten but retained his ability to talk, entering the American Asylum at thirteen. Homer is one of the leaders of the Boston deaf community and played a major role in establishing the Boston Deaf-Mute Christian Association, which Howe had criticized so roundly. Nevertheless, now addressing the committee in sign with Professor Bartlett interpreting, he stated that he agreed with Dr. Howe's views. He does not like the idea of the deaf congregating and living together; it would be well to have deaf children board out and live in hearing families. He is in favor of articulation and recommends the experiment of an oral school. He is opposed to the over-extended use of signs. In response to the committee's questions, Mr. Homer said that he talks about as well now as when he went to Hartford some forty years ago. He can talk with his relatives but not with strangers. Professor Bartlett spoke the word "apple" close to Mr. Homer's ear and he repeated the word immediately.

The other two communications were letters from semi-mutes, read to the committee by Howe's friend on the charities board, Franklin Sanborn. The first came from "our friend Amos Smith," a Boston deaf man and American Asylum graduate, who said: "The man who succeeded so grandly with Laura is the man, I say, to engineer the education of our deaf-mutes."[102] In short, the letter is an encomium to Samuel Gridley Howe. Mr. Smith anticipated the question, if you are so opposed to the use of signs, why do you use them yourself? "I reply, that to use them is a bad practice. All chewers of the weed, all moderate and immoderate drinkers, admit their habits to be bad, but the habit has become strong in them and while they must indulge themselves, they caution others not to follow in their footsteps." The last communication, from William Chase, a semi-mute, stated that recently thirty indigent deaf children in Massachusetts did not even apply for admission to the American Asylum because of the limited state appropriation, and that the state has shamefully reduced the permissible length of stay there from eight to six years. If those evils could be corrected by creating a Massachusetts school, and if the vacancies then left at Hartford would be filled by other deaf waiting their turn, as he understood they would be, then he favored a local school.

Franklin Sanborn summarized for the committee the history of teaching speech. He told of Marie Marois reputedly learning Pereire's Gascon accent —but not that she never used her speech and lived and died a recluse. He told of an oral school established in Saxony as early as 1778—but not that Heinicke was a charlatan, rejected by his contemporaries and posterity. He quoted from Francis Green's first book, on the oral progress of his son Charles—but did not reveal Green's change of allegiance. And so on. Sanborn closed by reiterating Clarke's offer of $50,000 if the bill was passed. The first hearing ended with an oral question-and-answer between William Turner and William Chamberlain, the first to be taught articulation at our school; Turner's point was to illustrate that the American Asylum did everything possible to preserve the speech of semi-mutes.

At the second hearing, Howe repeated his charges that the deaf are wards of the state who suffer from the consequences of deafness, which include an adverse effect on the whole character. To support his claim that no particular training is needed to teach the deaf, and thus that the new school could economize by employing untrained teachers, Howe read a letter from a friend who had met Jonathan Whipple and his son Enoch and who was full of admiration for how the father taught his son to speak and lipread.

Mr. Sanborn then read a highly articulate letter of support from John Carlin, in which Carlin strongly criticized the education that enabled him to write that letter. "The pantomimic language, generally employed in the schoolroom as well as in the sitting room and elsewhere, is not a language of words in written order," he wrote. "It is simply a jargon of gestures, each gesture representing a word or action, and all the gestures are thrown together, utterly without regard to the grammatical order." Carlin believes that the deaf should be taught through writing and fingerspelling; he is undecided about the feasibility of teaching by articulation but he is convinced that all our present institutions are unsatisfactory. Turner mentioned that Carlin had applied a few months earlier for a teaching position at our school, which suggested he did not entirely condemn our method of education.

The chair pointed out to Howe that the deaf audience present seemed to have been following the progress of the hearings very well, thanks to Professor Bartlett. If he were not there and the deaf did not have a manual system to guide them, how would that have been possible? Howe replied that they might be able to read his lips, but in any case he would teach them sign language after teaching them English. The important thing was not to mix the two in the course of learning.

It was finally the turn of the opposition and Collins Stone began by recalling that Howe already had the idiotic and the blind under his care and had tried for thirty-five years to add the deaf. He had brought these issues before committees of the legislature for many years and had never yet persuaded them of his views. The professional educators of the deaf were quite familiar with these ideas, there was nothing new here. The first oralists believed that you could not teach an idea by a written word or a sign but only by vocal utterance. That was Heinicke's theory. Experience has shown that it amounts to nothing. It was also Braidwood's strategy, and all the schools in England and Scotland tried it and gave it up for the system of Epée. "It is quite evident that Englishmen will never copy anything that a Frenchman does unless there is a very good reason for it; but this system they did adopt." We have investigated this matter five times, Stone said, and reviewed the findings of Weld, Day, Peet, and others. We have found by experience that the time spent teaching the child articulation is better spent teaching him ideas and cultivating his mind. Did the committee realize that day after day could be spent on a single sound?

Stone assailed Howe and Hubbard's claim that no special qualifications were required to teach the deaf. Consider how hard it is to teach a foreign language even to a hearing person, he said. We think an effective teacher needs a general education, then special training, and then four years of apprentice teaching before he is properly qualified. The argument from economy was simply false. A separate oral school in Massachusetts would incur considerable additional expense to the commonwealth.

William Turner, the next to testify, attacked the argument for dispersion of the deaf. The failure of earlier attempts to integrate the deaf into the common schools made clear that they must be gathered together for their education, so congregation is in any case a necessity. But it is also desirable. Howe's analogy of the criminal becoming more lawless through contact with convicts has no application to the deaf. On the contrary, the deaf child becomes more socialized in a residential school: his manners, dress, neatness, appearance at table, courtesy, and respect are all improved by association. Turner also attacked the plan for an oral school. The vast majority of the deaf, who have never spoken, can never be taught to speak. Never has a parent brought such a child to our school with vocal language. No perseverance of the mother—and we know how anxious mothers are to have the little one speak—no amount of repetition of "mama," "papa," "good boy," "nice boy," has led the deaf and dumb child to communicate with his parents orally. It never has been done. It never will be done.

At the last session of the hearings, Howe poured venom once again on the deaf as a social class and raised the hoary specter of their proliferation —their numbers are growing, they are procreating. The result of allowing the deaf to associate in residential schools has been, gentlemen, deaf intermarriage! Now at Perkins the blind are better managed, the sexes strictly separated. "I favor and cultivate among my pupils the idea that the more society they have, the better, provided it be not among themselves. . . . I say, 'Hands off! Don't have any manner of acquaintance with each other.' "

Better managed? Tragic for the blind as well as the deaf, I say. Some years ago, Laura Bridgman's teacher, a Miss Wight, had a suitor who came to call frequently at Perkins and joined in the teacher's efforts to amuse and gratify her pupil. Laura mistook his kind words, the friendly pressure of his hand; when Miss Wight became aware of the misunderstanding, she felt obliged to tell Laura where matters really stood, that she might never have a suitor. For the blind in Howe's care are forbidden to mix, not to mention court, marry, or have children—heavens, no! Laura could make no more sense of this than I can. Why should Howe deprive her of a companion because scarlet fever had deprived her of her sight and hearing? Her trembling fingers piteously spelled out: "Am I not pretty?"[103]

BRANNING: You would discountenance association between deaf-mutes?

HOWE: Entirely; but, mind you, I would not discountenance association between them and other persons. I would endeavor to prevent the effects of their infirmity by bringing them into relations, as close as possible, with ordinary persons, so that their infirmity should be, so to speak, wiped out of sight.

Gardiner Hubbard had become more moderate. "We do not reject natural signs; and in addition to the manual alphabet and signs, we would teach them to read from the lips. We are not here recommending for an instant the teaching of congenital deaf-mutes articulation. It may be successful it may not be. We do not urge it. We do not pretend that it can be."[104]

A few minutes later, however, he denied that his school tolerated sign.

HUBBARD: We teach at Chelmsford without the use of signs. Signs are forbidden in school and out of school.

STONE: Are not signs used in school?

HUBBARD: Very little indeed, sir. Scarcely ever.

STONE: I understand that they converse with each other entirely by signs.

BARTLETT: You will find that these children play by signs. I have seen them.

Hubbard continued: "You may not be able, probably will not be able, to understand a single word that any one of the articulating scholars speaks; they may not be able to read a single word from your lips; and yet it is the beginning, we hope, of great things. . . . We propose to continue this school now at Chelmsford. . . . Then we propose to open another school in Boston, where other deaf-mutes may be taught, perhaps by the language of signs. . . . I am not wedded to the idea of teaching articulation to deaf-mutes; I doubt very much whether it can be taught to congenital deaf-mutes; but I do believe in teaching these young semi-mutes the English language."[105]

When Sanborn's turn came for closing remarks, he read a resolution from a group of deaf people in Boston whom Amos Smith had apparently marshaled the night before. They stated that they would like to see deaf children educated in the common schools as are other children in the neighborhood and that the views of the Board of State Charities as set forth in its reports "meet with our approbation." The legislation under discussion had in fact nothing to do with placing deaf children in the common schools, but that was perhaps as close as Sanborn could come to obtaining an endorsement of the Howe plan. What the legislation did concern was ending the practice of sending the state's deaf to Hartford and sending them instead to an oral school in Massachusetts. Sanborn concluded by repeating the arguments for repatriation and dispersion. He reaffirmed that association makes the deaf more deaf, the dumb more dumb, and encourages them to intermarry. He emphasized the importance of beginning the deaf child's education early, earlier than permitted at Hartford.

It was Mr. Dudley who found an apparent compromise, one that would serve the committee, the American Asylum, and the Howe forces; only the deaf would not be served. Why not begin the education of deaf children in several little schools scattered around Massachusetts (Dudley is from John Clarke's home town, Northampton); then, when they are graduated at the age of ten, they can go on to Hartford. Since the state would pay our asylum for only six years' tuition, we preferred to admit the pupils when they were ten or older, so Collins Stone said he would not object to an experimental preschool.

And so it was agreed. The report to the legislature was a great victory for the deaf in all respects but one. It did repudiate Howe's criticism of sign, and the arguments from repatriation, dispersion, and economy. It wisely recommended that Howe and Sanborn no longer have any sway over the deaf: our schooling should be under the board of education, for the care of the commonwealth extends exactly that far, as it does for the hearing. It went on to conclude that sign and fingerspelling are the most effective means of communicating with a large majority of the deaf and that those who are congenitally deaf or who lost their hearing in infancy cannot be taught with speech. "The fact that it has been adopted by so small a portion of the schools throughout the world seems a strong argument against its exclusive use in any school intended for all classes of deaf-mutes." Whatever evil there may be in the deaf congregating, it does not seem great enough to recommend the abandonment of large institutions or to counterbalance the advantages they offer. The committee recommended that the schooling of the deaf be started earlier and continue longer than at present, as it is with the hearing.

But the representatives did want Clarke's money, so in a seemingly innocent compromise, they allowed what proved to be a dangerous incursion. They recommended that Clarke's money be accepted and an institution created at Northampton—nowhere else—for the primary instruction of pupils too young to attend the American Asylum.

If only Collins Stone had done as Harvey Peet did in New York and had opened a primary department in Hartford for young deaf children, oralism could not have gained a foothold. I hold myself responsible, too, for if we had encouraged the founding of a state school in Massachusetts thirty years ago, as we finally did in New York and twenty-one other states, the Massachusetts school would have belonged to our family of residential schools, and this incursion of oralism would have been avoided. Of course, there is nothing wrong with teaching in English those few semi-mutes or semi-deaf who can speak and understand English fluently; but there is a vital distinction between these children and those who, deafened earlier or more profoundly, can communicate fluently only in sign. The distinction eludes those who are not intimately acquainted with all kinds of deaf people, and the forces seeking to obliterate the distinction, to replace sign, and to educate all deaf children in English—whatever their primary language—are powerful and relentless. You may think I am exaggerating, but you have not yet heard how this cancer has multiplied and now threatens the education, the language, and the association of my people throughout the land.

Despite the favorable committee report, the governor's support, and Clarke's money, the bill incorporating the Clarke school and allowing the governor to send pupils there at state expense encountered vigorous opposition in the legislature. Why should Massachusetts depart from the practice of the other New England states and its own practice for four decades in order to create a school with an unproven method destined only for semi-mutes? Just when it seemed the bill would be defeated, Lewis Dudley rose to make an impassioned appeal. (Was it at this point or later that Hubbard promised to rent Dudley's property in Northampton to house the new school?) Theresa had been well educated at Hartford, Dudley said. But now he had heard her voice. And he had heard Jeannie Lippitt and Roscoe Green, two deaf-mutes, converse. And then Mabel Hubbard could lipread and speak some. One day Theresa might speak as these children did. (I am told there was nary a dry eye in the chamber.)[106]

The bill chartering the Clarke school but allowing parents to send their children to Hartford if they preferred was passed in June 1867.[107] The incorporators met in Northampton and agreed to ask Miss Rogers to transport her school there from Chelmsford. With Mr. Clarke's endowment and some rooms rented from Lewis Dudley, the Clarke Institution opened in the fall.[108] The initial group of eight pupils grew to twenty in the first year, including a number of congenitally deaf young men and women. None of the board thought their words before the legislature had been binding. Thus Clarke was a residential school where the deaf congregated; they were not boarded out. The school attempted to teach orally not only English-speakers but also eleven congenitally deaf children and others whose primary language was sign. It took children of all ages in competition with Hartford, not just preschoolers. It prohibited all forms of manual language and certainly did not teach sign after teaching English. It charged the state more than double what had been paid to the American Asylum, clearly no economy. (True to Howe's promise, however, Clarke did hire unqualified females as teachers.)

Theresa Dudley was enrolled at Clarke and her father took a position on its board; they are there to this day. After some three weeks at the school, Theresa came home one day and said to her parents: "I can say Fanny." She had a pet bird by that name. "Saul of Tarsus was not more surprised by the voice from heaven than we were," Dudley has written. "Here was something from Providence! Here was a possibility for congenital deaf-mutes! Here was a lesson for a skeptic and such as I had been."[109]

I have it on authority that Theresa's speech is slurred and unpleasant; that she has poor control of her voice; that she cannot pronounce some of the vowels and consonants, and therefore cannot make herself understood when she has a conversation or reads aloud.[110] Yet Miss Rogers seems to have a different opinion: "Her progress has exceeded our most sanguine expectations."[111] Theresa's father's words at public exercises of the Clarke school explain these conflicting descriptions of her progress: "Probably there are persons here today who will go away disappointed. They will be able to understand but a part, perhaps but a small part, of what the pupils shall say; and there will be lurking in their inmost thought the query whether this institution hasn't undertaken the impossible; and whether a large amount of time, labor and money isn't half wasted here." But "a wooden leg," Dudley argues, "is a pitiful semblance of bone, nerve and muscle. . . . A glass eye is utterly useless for vision. . . . The poorest articulation pays in the increased self-respect and happiness of the pupil. Said a little girl who had been silent more than ten years and then broke out in speech: 'I am like other people now.' "112 This is a parent's fantasy, though no doubt well-meaning. Theresa's sham speech no more makes her like hearing people than indeed a blind person's glass eyes make him like sighted people. The father who communicates so fluently with the world around him loftily announces that "the poorest articulation pays in self-respect." It is the child who pays the terrible price for this "self-respect": if she can barely communicate orally and is not allowed to communicate manually, then she cannot communicate at all. No, for Theresa the way to self-respect, to intellectual and social development, and even to the normalcy her father so dearly desires for her is sign language and full participation in the deaf community.

Edward Miner Gallaudet followed the legislative hearings on the Clarke school as closely as he could from his position in Washington. They led him to make two major decisions. He would convene the Conference of Principals of Institutions for the Deaf to determine the proper role of articulation in the residential schools. And he would first draw his own conclusions about oralism from inspecting European schools personally. He left for Europe in the spring of 1867, by way of Hartford and Boston, while the legislature was still debating its committee's recommendations. In Boston Hubbard gave a reception in Edward's honor and invited his daughter Mabel and Jeannie Lippitt. Of course, Edward soon realized that the girls were semi-mutes whose wealthy parents had ensured extensive individual tutoring. They revealed nothing of what oral education might mean to the deaf as a class. In Europe, Edward visited sign schools, oral schools, and what he dubbed combined schools, in fourteen countries, omitting only Spain, Portugal, and Greece.113

In Paris he met Léon Vaisse and found that Saint-Jacques was following a plan of supplementary articulation training similar to the one Weld had introduced in Hartford in 1845. Vaisse had also developed a vocabulary of symbols, one for each French sound, which were drawn to have a schematic likeness with the positions of the articulators and thus recall them to the pupil. In short, he had developed a reduction of the letters of the alphabet, a special kind of phonetic script, and was enjoying some success with it in his articulation class.

Blanchet had died recently, with his project to educate mutes in the common schools a total failure, according to Professor Vaïsse. Edward thought, as Weld and Day had concluded before him, that "the true friends of the deaf and dumb [hope] that all future experiments in this direction may be abandoned."114

In Milan Edward visited the Royal Institution founded at the turn of the century and recently converted to a normal primary and secondary school for teaching the deaf, and he visited the Provincial school under Giulio Tarra. Both schools taught in sign language, tried articulation training with all, then abandoned it with those who could not profit—an estimated two-thirds.

At the London Institution, which I had visited about half a century before in company with Massieu and Sicard, the director, the Reverend J. H. Watson, a Braidwood relative, seemed slow, easygoing, and not very interested in the deaf. He affirmed that education was impossible to conduct without sign, that few pupils could lipread well enough to understand a public speaker. Articulation was tried with all—there were 350 pupils—but continued only for the few who profit. Edward found, however, that even the most advanced pupils could not lipread his speech.115

At the school in Leipzig founded by Heinicke, Edward was invited to examine two young men, former pupils, now teachers at the school, one a semi-mute, the other semi-deaf. He found that they signed with each other and with the director, and that they were poor lipreaders, unable to follow a speaker unless they knew the text beforehand. According to Edward's German-speaking companion, they were largely unintelligible.

In Weissenfels, the other leading German institution, Edward met with Moritz Hill, now sixty and at the head of his profession, an author of textbooks and technical articles and an experienced instructor. Hill is persuaded of the necessity of sign; naturally Edward found his a school on the combined plan. Referring to the claim that sign is banished in German schools, Hill said: "Such an idea must be attributed to malevolence or unpardonable levity." And further: "The moral life, the intellectual development of the deaf and dumb would be inhumanly hampered."

Edward returned to the United States convinced, first, that oral schools must fail to educate a large body of the deaf or, to avoid this unhappy result, must use sign language. In fact, the vast majority of schools use both languages, oral and manual. Which shall get the preference as the vehicle of instruction, the pupils' primary manual language, or their secondary oral one? Edward found that the schools using sign in class obtained as good results in articulation and lipreading as schools using speech, and they obtained better results in general education. Edward concluded that the right plan for a school to follow was the Weld plan. Articulation skills are an adornment, he wrote. They can never be the basis of instruction. But they are a highly desirable adornment. Could he win the American principals over to this combined position? He would try.

About a year ago, then, he wrote to all the principals "of the regular institutions of the United States" citing the increased interest of the public in the education of the deaf and the hostility in some quarters to current methods, and inviting them to meet at the National College to discuss the controversy. Fearing a confrontation that would prove fruitless, he did not invite Harriet Rogers or Hubbard, Howe, or Sanborn, but he encouraged three of the principals to pay a visit to the Clarke school prior to the meeting. At about this time, Howe issued another report of the Board of State Charities, reaffirming that "speech is the only form of language natural to man," boasting that the Clarke school had been opened on this principle, classing the deaf, as always, with the blind and the idiotic, urging that the Blanchet plan be tried in Boston, although admittedly it had proved a failure in Paris (because it let the deaf children in the school congregate, he said), preaching the German system for all schools educating the deaf, and claiming that Edward "has returned from Europe an advocate for teaching articulation to all deaf-mutes."[116]

In his opening address to the conference, Edward denied Howe's statement: "I am not to be claimed as a convert to the system of teaching the deaf and dumb by articulation."[117] He did see, however, two "incidental defects" in the American system of instructing the deaf and he believed his tour of schools abroad suggested some remedies. First, there was agreement that our pupils' abilities to read and write English on graduation are insufficient. He advocated as remedies elementary schools for the deaf, as for the hearing, more trained teachers, a graded series of textbooks, and less use of sign, more of written English, in the later years.

I have a word to say about his goal of fluency in English: it is not the only goal of education and the other goals must not be subordinated to it. Oral instruction was originally a method, a means to an end, namely, the intellectual and social development of the deaf child. Other means could contribute to that end as well, and the deaf teacher had a role to play. But the oral method proved so laborious and its results so meager that it encroached more and more on the child's education, and ultimately became the end itself, virtually displacing all other ends. Yet fluency in English—even if the end were attained—does not confer sound judgment, keen observation, an appreciation of life's comedy and tragedy, or sensitivity to human relationships. Our hearing benefactors emphasize the power of the English language to put the American deaf child in contact with the larger English-speaking community—they insist on the extensive power of language for the child. Deaf people, however, emphasize the power of sign language to put the deaf child in contact with his immediate circle, to allow him an intimate, effortless, and full exchange of thought and feeling—they cite the intensive power of language for the child. Thus the giver and the receiver have very different concerns. The hearing English-speakers are prepared to sacrifice the intensive power of language for the deaf child in the hope of procuring him greater extensive power through English. This is destructive; the majority take the intensive power of their language for granted, scarcely realizing its importance for their mental well-being. Deaf people know better, and generally resist this sacrifice of the intensive power of sign. We agree with Edward that schools that fail to teach deaf children to read and write English have a defect, but we believe the remedy does not and should not lie in less use of sign.

When we consider the promises of articulation teachers, Edward continued, when we remember the wonderful proofs they are able to give in exceptional and half-explained cases, when we recall the vulnerability of human nature to accept shams when the advantage is great, then the wonder that so many are deceived is abated. Yet our duty is to discover if there is anything in the German system worth borrowing. Weld and Day have said yes, there is, namely, a complement to the instruction designed for semi-mute and semi-deaf pupils and, Weld adds, for the exceptional pupil who is congenitally deaf. Vaïsse agreed: try teaching articulation with all, continue with those who profit. Peet agreed, so did Day ten years later. I have found convergence, Edward said. The Germans are moving toward much greater dependence on sign, as we are moving toward more complementary training in articulation.

Edward then introduced two resolutions, the first affirming that it is the duty of all schools to provide some training in articulation and lipreading to those pupils who can profit by it; the second affirming the consequent need for more instructors and urging boards of directors to provide the necessary funds. Alarmed, Collins Stone presented two further resolutions, the first affirming that, while it is desirable to give semi-mutes and semi-deaf this complement, "it is not profitable except in very rare cases to attempt to teach congenital mutes articulation"; the second stating the American system commends itself by experience as in the highest degree adapted to the needs of the deaf.

The heads of the Illinois, Iowa, and Wisconsin schools, who had just visited Clarke, were invited to report. The first, Phillip Gillett, had gone to Northampton by way of Boston. There, Gardiner Hubbard took him into his home and then, to be absolutely certain he was properly informed before addressing the Conference of Principals, accompanied him to Clarke and remained with him at the school for two days. Gillett reported first that Clarke's putative achievements had been published in several Illinois newspapers and had excited considerable public interest there.[118] He saw some good lipreading and word articulation at Clarke, but was unable to determine the personal histories of the pupils. He did see Theresa Dudley, a congenital mute, who after six months at Clarke is "able to engage in intelligent oral conversation." He was unsure "whether it will be wise to encourage the adoption of the method of articulation at all."

Benjamin Talbot, from Iowa, said he had supposed those born deaf could not learn to articulate but he had been mistaken. And not only Dudley, but also the younger children spoke. One class of twelve was exercised in counting.

GALLAUDET: Did you hear any exercise where words were in combination —sentences, or short expressions?

TALBOT: Yes, sir; there was a short sentence written out upon the board.

GALLAUDET: Did you hear anyone read from a printed book or card?

TALBOT: None, except Miss Dudley.

TURNER: She learned at the American Asylum, did she not?

TALBOT: I suppose she did. . . . Her articulation was quite intelligible, although it was labored. She had to work hard in trying to make some of the combinations that were necessary, but I found we could understand what she said better than she could understand what we said. I sat down and conversed with her, and she would repeat what I said to her. Sometimes she would fail to catch my words. The fault, however, was probably not hers, but mine. When the teacher repeated the word to her she understood it perfectly.

GALLAUDET: Did you hear different individuals of the school converse?

TALBOT: I heard no conversation in the school except Miss Dudley's.

There was a lengthy discussion of Theresa Dudley's case. Clearly, Stone said, Dudley does not prove the merits of an oral education since she did not receive one. Nothing conclusive, it seemed, could be reported from Clarke. Stone had also visited the school with some others and their impression was that the teachers often could understand the pupils, although they themselves could not.

Turner denied that our schools are defective in the level of English proficiency the students attain. Hartford pupils, he claimed, can write English as well as any Yale student can write Latin. Moreover, that is sufficient. Our society does not require people whose native language is not English to write English flawlessly—only understandably.

When it came time to vote, the resolutions introduced by Edward proved uncontroversial. After all, the public discussion prompted by Howe and others required some action, the call by the son of Thomas Gallaudet for what was in essence the Weld plan made it seem eminently conservative, and a request to the board for supplementary funds for this purpose meant that no present activity need be sacrificed. With slight amendment, Stone's resolutions reaffirming the present system for the majority of the deaf were also endorsed.[119]

Milligan rushed off to Wisconsin and Gillett to Illinois to open articulation classes. Michigan had already started, Maryland followed suit, then

Minnesota. Now, in the spring of 1869, there are eight new oral teachers, three in New York, two in Ohio, one in Illinois, one in Wisconsin, one in Iowa, one in Hartford.[120]

In New York City, a group of parents of deaf children have just incorporated, on the Clarke model, the Institution for Improved Instruction of Deaf-Mutes, with a teacher brought over from Vienna.[121]

In Boston, the Reverend Dexter King, who was a member of the legislative committee that held hearings on the Clarke school, asked the Boston School Board, of which he is also a member, to consider opening a day school for the deaf. He conducted a census of the city's deaf through the schools and counted fifty, of whom twenty-eight lived at home without instruction.[122] Next, he held a public exhibition with pupils from Hartford and Clarke. The board has ordered that the Boston School for Deaf-Mutes shall open in the fall; it will be a primary school whose graduates are to go into the board's regular grammar schools.[123]

In Cambridge, a certain Alexander Melville Bell, a distinguished British elocutionist, gave lectures last year based on his pamphlet *English Visible Speech for the Millions.*[124] He has invented a system of symbols, on the same principle as Vaïsse, and claims that his son, Alexander Graham Bell, has used them successfully in teaching speech to the deaf in a small school in London. Hubbard has given a reception for the father and hopes to bring the son to Clarke.

Must we not consider these developments ominous? During the Conference of Principals, Edward Gallaudet remarked that the question of whether or not to teach speech had been blown out of all proportion. After all, the issue should be a minor one, he argued; it affects a minority of the deaf and even for them it is not of vital interest. But Edward was sorely mistaken. The teaching of articulation is not just an issue that has mysteriously grown out of proportion. Whether a small group shall be allowed to speak, congregate, marry, proliferate, work, and act as free men and women or whether they shall conform to the majority, be fashioned, in Howe's words, "into the likeness of common men"—that is the issue. To fail to understand this, to see oralism as an issue only of methods, is to be baffled by all of the history of my people, to fail to see that history's most salient trait and organizing principle: intolerance of human diversity. I believe in variety. It is the great hope of this nation. I will not condemn it, as do the oralists and the racists. I will not restrict it, as do the free-state advocates. I will not disparage it or merely tolerate it. I will seek it out, encourage it, embrace it, treasure it just as nature treasures variety in her proliferation. I see in it great human and material wealth for our society and the necessary precursor to all favorable change.

Alas, the signs augur less tolerance of diversity in our land, not more; I see the signing community threatened. It is true that the deaf have taken enormous strides merely in my lifetime, which is but a parenthesis in the history of the deaf. Recently, the National College for Deaf-Mutes held its first graduation, and thirty-nine students are currently enrolled. I remember when grave doubts existed whether the congenitally deaf could be educated at all, beyond the most limited range. I remember when governments would not hear of educating the deaf as they do other children, and we had to rely on private charity. I remember when a deaf man was looked on as a creature highly deviant, a kind of monster whose disenthrallment was a philosophical experiment and not a practical necessity, when parents could be induced only with difficulty to allow their deaf child to remain in school three or four years. Now in America, as in Europe, there are scores of mature institutions educating the deaf in their primary language, there are elementary schools, secondary schools, and a national college that is becoming, in truth, an international college.

Still, the deaf are in grave danger. Powerful hearing people want to replace our language, to educate us in a foreign tongue, to prohibit our public worship, to disperse our gatherings, to ban our marriages—and why? Because we do not speak as they do. Will they have their way, until the deaf are scattered, isolated, and stupid everywhere? Or will the deaf continue to gather into associations, clubs, and schools that defend our rights, exalt our language, educate our children, inform our hearing friends and teach them sign? I cannot know, nor wish to, what the future holds. I only ask that this history of our struggle weigh in the balance.

◆

At the American School for the Deaf in Hartford there is a memorial to Laurent Clerc, a bronze bust atop a tall marble pedestal. The inscription reads: "Laurent Clerc, the Apostle of the Deaf-Mute of the New World. Born in La Balme, France, December 26, 1785. Landed at New York, August 9, 1816. Died at Hartford, July 18, 1869."[125]

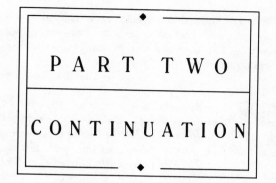

PART TWO

CONTINUATION

"Pure" (there is no such thing) oralism has not a leg to stand upon. It is a menace to the deaf mentally and morally, and robs them of the happiness and peace of mind God meant for them. . . . If I can do anything to combat this foolishness and this CRIME, please call on me.

—Isaac Goldberg, deaf chemist

The adult deaf . . . will say with one voice—and that voice not the artificial and mechanical voice of pure oralism—that signs are indispensable and the Combined System the only rational one to use. . . . The thousand or so members of the fraternity of which I am secretary would to a man agree with all I say.

—Francis P. Gibson, deaf director
National Fraternal Society of the Deaf

Probably I am personally acquainted with (or know about) more deaf adults than any other man in the United States. I have studied them, learned about their education, their daily lives and occupations, and in the entire list of the deaf whom I know, there is not a leading man, successful in the world and polished intellectually, who does not know and use the language of signs. Moreover I have never known a case where signs had a harmful effect. Instead, they have stimulated the mind, inspired the spirit, and developed the natural capabilities of the individual.

—Edwin A. Hodgson, deaf editor
President, National Convention of Deaf-Mutes

What heinous crime have the deaf been guilty of that their language should be proscribed?[1]

—Robert P. McGregor, deaf educator
First President, National Association of the Deaf

ELEVEN

THE DENIAL

My name is Harlan Lane; I am hearing. I am forty-six years old. I can detect the approach of white hair and wrinkled skin but they are still a comfortable distance away. I am a psychologist, concerned with that most human of activities, language, and a student of the sign language of the deaf. Like Clerc, I do not know why humankind is so various, and like him, I thank God for this rich diversity.

I propose to cheat death and complete Laurent Clerc's history for him, to tell how the forces of replacement, which he saw emerging but could not follow further, developed and, first in America and then Europe, ultimately triumphed over the deaf. I hope that the obvious importance of completing the story will excuse my impertinence in the eyes of the deaf, their well-meaning teachers, and the eternal Footman.

In the decades after his death, Clerc's worst fears were realized. The one oral day school he lamented spawned seventy by the turn of the century; a couple of oral residential schools grew to a dozen. Although Clerc knew only the occasional teacher of oral English across the land, supplementing the general education of a few semi-mutes, by 1900 most teachers of the deaf were speech teachers, and English skills had displaced general education as the central goal of schooling. In the vast network of schools that Clerc had created, two-thirds of the deaf pupils were now taught orally, by teachers speaking aloud in the classroom, and fully three-fourths were given instruction in speaking and lipreading.[2] In short the forces of replacement succeeded, and most of the deaf in America and Europe are, to this day, educated in the oral language of the national majority and not in their own primary language.

Samuel Gridley Howe died just a few years after Laurent Clerc. Old and ailing, with the battle for the Clarke school won, he passed the standard in his last years to younger and more vigorous allies, to Gardiner Greene Hubbard, and especially to the man who would emerge as the greatest champion of oralism for all time, Hubbard's son-in-law, Alexander Graham Bell.

Laurent Clerc was the leading figure in the development of the signing community and its language in the United States; the leading figure in its undoing was Alexander Graham Bell. Bell sought to banish the sign language; to disperse the deaf and discourage their socializing, organizing, publishing, and marriage; to have deaf children educated in and use exclusively the majority language. To this cause he devoted his great prestige, personal fortune and tireless efforts; thus he became, in the words of the first president of the National Association of the Deaf, "the most to be feared enemy of the American deaf, past and present."[3]

Clerc and Bell were opposed not only in the central cause to which they devoted their lives, in their historical roles, but in virtually every other way. Where Clerc found strength in human variety, Bell found weakness and danger. Where Clerc saw difference, Bell saw deviance; the one had a social model of atypical people, the other a medical model. For Clerc, deafness was, above all, a social disability; the great problem of the deaf was the hearing world in which they were a minority; he hoped for a day when hearing people of goodwill would remove the handicap by accepting deaf culture and language. For Bell, deafness was a physical handicap; if it could not be cured, it could be alleviated by covering its stigmata; hearing people of goodwill would aid the deaf in a denial of their particular language and culture, in "passing" as hearing people in a hearing world. Addressing a conference of speech teachers, Bell said of deaf children, "We should try ourselves to forget that they are deaf. We should teach *them* to forget that they are deaf."[4] Bell was infuriated with his mother, who was hard of hearing, and would not communicate with her for some months after she adverted to his fiancée's deafness and expressed "fears for your children."[5] Writing to his wife some years later, he said: "You cannot appreciate, as I do, what a blessing the miracle of lipreading is. It seems to me a greater wonder every day. When I am with you dear and speak to you fully by word of mouth, I often forget that you cannot hear. I never do so with mama. It seems so hard and cruel that she should be shut in all by herself, when it is possible to acquire the art of lipreading. Before I saw you, Mabel, and before I went to Boston, I acquiesced in my mother's affliction—for to her it is an affliction. . . ."[6]

While for Clerc the overriding purpose of education was personal fulfillment, for Bell it was integration with the hearing majority: "I admit . . . the ease with which a deaf child acquires this sign language and its perfect adaptability for the purpose of developing his mind; but after all, it is not the language of the millions of people among whom his lot in life is cast."[7] Clerc favored deaf teachers for the model they provided to the children, for their zeal, and for their own personal fulfillment, but Bell opposed them as an obstacle to integration. Clerc saw the signing community as an indigenous linguistic minority, and linguistic scholarship of the last few decades bears him out, for it has discovered many respects in which American Sign Language partakes of apparently universal properties of human language.[8] Bell viewed the deaf as one of the defective classes, among which he counted the blind and the mentally retarded. Clerc saw merit in congregation of the deaf—in couples, for compatibility; in schools, for mutual instruction by peers; in gatherings, for communal reflection and social action. Bell saw evil in marriage among the deaf, residential schools, and social organizations.

For Clerc, an immigrant and polyglot, bilingualism was a worthy goal for deaf and hearing alike. Every deaf person should learn to write at least essentials in the national language and the highly educated deaf, spokesmen for a community with no written language, should master that of the majority; he himself had done so. Bell, on the contrary, favored monolingualism for all Americans. Speaking to the National Education Association, he said, "Our population is recruited from all countries of the world and from this source another danger threatens the republic. It is important for the preservation of our national existence that the people of this country should speak one tongue."[9] Bell's opposition to all minority languages seems to confirm Clerc's fundamental belief that opposition to various sign languages was rooted in issues of national policy though it might appear on the surface as a parochial matter in deaf education.

The two leaders were equally opposed on the relative merits of signed and oral languages. Clerc naturally preferred sign, as did nearly all the deaf people he knew; it was, first, *their* language; it had in their eyes singular grace and expressiveness and was more successful than any other in communicating with the deaf. Bell saw dangers in just these merits: since it was the language of the deaf, it cut them off from the hearing; since it was so successful a mode of communication, the deaf thought in that language and laboriously translated their thought when using English. He acknowledged the grace of sign but thought it ideographic, imprecise, and concrete.[10] "I would urge the abolition of the sign language."[11] The overwhelming superiority of speech was patent: "To ask the value of speech . . . is like asking the value of life!"[12] "The adults who use sign represent our failures; let us have as few of them as we possibly can."[13] Bell's enthusiasm for spoken English led him early in his career to wildly overstate the possibility that deaf people could learn it: "All deaf-mutes can be taught intelligible speech," he wrote.[14]

Clerc's predecessors in the education of the deaf were Epée, Sicard, Massieu, his settings Paris and Hartford; Bell's predecessors were the Scots Dalgarno and Braidwood, his settings Edinburgh and Boston. In Boston, Howe and Hubbard won the struggle for the Clarke school, Fuller opened the Boston Day School for Deaf-Mutes, and Bell founded several oral schools of his own. Down to the present, Boston has remained largely faithful to this oral tradition.

Clerc was a man of letters, Bell a man of science. Inventor of the telephone, developer of the phonograph and airplane, founder of the journals *Science* and *National Geographic*, Bell believed that "science, adding to our knowledge, bringing us closer to God, is the highest of all things."[15] Clerc's most salient trait was humility, Bell's egoism. Bell had a keen sense of the importance of all his thoughts, however trivial, and recorded them in voluminous notebooks left for posterity.[16] As a young man, tall, slender, with jet-black hair brushed up from his forehead, with sparkling black eyes and a rich clear voice, Bell dominated social gatherings: he played the piano, recited Shakespeare, directed charades, sang Scottish songs—many found him a boor.[17] In a letter to Bell's betrothed, his father described him as "hot-headed but warm-hearted, sentimental, dreamy, self-absorbed, sincere, unselfish, ambitious to a fault, apt to let enthusiasm run away with judgment."[18] These last words are full of portent.

Clerc was a highly social man: witness the golden wedding anniversary he so looked forward to, when scores of deaf friends and former students, hearing and deaf, gathered in Hartford from all points of the compass.[19] Bell, despite his buffoonery, was essentially a solitary man. The propensity appeared in his youth, when he was inclined to long, lone musings on a hilltop near Edinburgh.[20] It developed in manhood, when he invariably worked alone long into the night, sleeping the following day. Bell spoke frankly of his sense of isolation and loneliness and equated it with the acute loneliness he imagined the deaf suffered.[21] To withdraw from his hectic Washington life, he would plead illness.[22] To his wife he wrote, "You my dear constitute the chief link between myself and the world outside."[23]

Clerc was passionately interested in the people he met: his writings are largely composed of sketches of people he knew, their traits, activities, and values, his reflections on them, their impact on others. There are two kinds of people in the world, a teacher of mine once said—those who love other people and those who love mankind. Bell belonged to the latter group. "You are always so thoughtful of others," he wrote to his wife, "whereas I somehow or other appear to be more interested in *things* than people, in people wholesale rather than in persons individual."[24] "How little you give me of your time and thoughts," she wrote to him, "how little willing you are to enter into little things which yet make up the sum of our lives."[25]

The women most important in Clerc's life were his wife, Eliza, and Sophia Gallaudet, who in later years was matron at the National Deaf-Mute College and, in a sense, mother to the deaf community. Both were educated in sign language, active in deaf affairs, light-hearted, outgoing, productive women. Bell grew up with a hard-of-hearing mother who played the piano and taught others to play, including her son, while resting her ear trumpet on the sounding board. Eliza Bell could not lipread and her son would fingerspell dinner conversations to her. She determined his conception of deafness in his formative years. It was reinforced when he married Gardiner Greene Hubbard's daughter, Mabel, who likewise had suffered a hearing loss in her youth; born hearing of a rich family, educated in English by her mother and tutors, Mabel was early made a symbol of the oralist movement. A beautiful, charming, intelligent woman, she traveled easily in hearing circles but had a phobia of the deaf. "I shrink from any reference to my disability," she wrote near the end of her life, "and won't be seen in public with another deaf person."[26] "I have striven in every way to have [my deafness] forgotten and to so completely be normal that I would pass as one. To have anything to do with other deaf people instantly brought this hard-concealed fact into evidence. So I have helped other things and people . . . anything, everything but the deaf. I would have no friends among them. . . . To say a child was deaf was enough to make me refuse to take any public notice of it. . . . Of all people, I hated [to meet] a teacher of the deaf. . . . Above all things I antagonized my husband's efforts to keep up his association with them."[27]

In the 1900 census, in which Bell had a hand, deaf citizens were asked how well they could speak and when they became deaf. Ninety percent of those who could not speak at all had become deaf before age five, while ninety percent of those who said they spoke well had lost their hearing after five.[28] The former group included Clerc's prime constituency, the latter Bell's. Clerc's archetype was the deaf child of deaf parents whose native language was American Sign Language; Bell's was the semi-mute or semi-deaf whose native tongue was English. Between these two camps lay the constituency of those deafened before learning English but with English-speaking parents. Clerc thought their natural tendency to congregate with other deaf and acquire American Sign Language should be encouraged; Bell wanted to win them to the camp of English-speakers but lacked an effective method of doing so. Since they had never acquired English as a native language, they could not, he acknowledged, learn to lipread spoken English. For the same reason, they rarely, if ever, succeeded in speaking intelligibly.

Clerc espoused the cause of the deaf by teaching, lecturing, and persuading. Once Bell had invented the telephone, at the age of twenty-nine, he increasingly shunned personal contact, and proselytized by founding journals and associations and hiring spokesmen. If Clerc, like Epée, can be called "the apostle of the poor," for most deaf families were, and continue to be, poor, Bell can be called the apostle of the rich, for his primary alliances were with wealthy hearing parents of children deafened by disease or accident.

As Clerc was enamored of the play of the hands, face, and body in communication, Bell admired the play of the tongue, larynx, and breath in speech. So deep and constant was Bell's preoccupation with voice from childhood on, that his invention of the telephone seems its logical and almost necessary culmination; he once said, indeed, that it seemed he had spent his life making things talk.[29] The first was the family dog, which quickly learned to growl for food. "I then attempted to manipulate his mouth," Bell wrote. "Taking his muzzle in my hand, I caused his lips to close and open a number of times in succession. . . . After a little practice I was able to make him say, with perfect distinctness, the word 'mama,' pronounced in the English way with the accent on the second syllable."[30] With practice and suitable manipulation of the lips he was able to get a reportedly intelligible "How are you, grandmama?" The dog's fame spread rapidly in Edinburgh.

When Aleck (as his family called him) was sixteen (about the time that Howe and Hubbard were launching their second campaign for an oral school in Massachusetts), he and his older brother, Melville, known as Melly, accepted their father's challenge to construct their own speaking machine, and they began by studying a book on the subject by Baron von Kempelen, who, in the prior century, had built a device to imitate the human voice. The brothers divided the labor: Aleck would make the tongue and mouth, Melly the throat, larynx, and lungs. To obtain some more guidance, they sacrificed their pet cat and also dissected a lamb's head. Melly's "throat" was a tin tube, his "larynx" two sheets of rubber meeting at an angle, and his "lungs" his very own—he simply blew through the tube. Aleck took impressions from a human skull and made a gutta-percha replica of the human mouth. He added soft rubber lips, cheeks, and a palate lowered by a lever to allow sound to enter a nasal tube. The "tongue" was made of six wooden sections, each of which could be raised or lowered to produce various consonants, and the whole was encased in rubber. After much experimenting the day arrived for an official trial: Aleck and Melly were jubilant when their device so convincingly cried "mama!" over and over again that a neighbor came to see "what can be the matter with the baby." From their father they won praise and a prize. What a contrast with Clerc's introduction to sham speech at about the same age!

The Bell family's interest in speech had begun two generations before Aleck, when grandfather Alexander Bell quit his trade of shoemaker, studied elocution, and joined the Royal Theatre in Edinburgh. With his rough-hewn Scottish features and burr, he appeared to acclaim in *Rob Roy* and was in the prompter's box for a production of Bouilly's *The Abbé de l'Epée*. The Bells had a daughter, Elizabeth, and two sons: David, who was born as the American Asylum opened, and Alexander Melville Bell (Aleck's father), called Melville, two years younger.

When grandfather Bell's earnings from the theater and the tavern he kept with his wife dwindled, he returned with his family to Saint Andrews, near Glasgow, where he had been born. There he established a school for teaching reading and correcting speech problems. With his commanding presence and expressive voice he was also in demand for public recitations. After some years he divorced his wife for cuckoldry and moved with his sons to London, where he taught speech and published several books, one on elocution, another on speech impediments, a third a version of the New Testament marked with symbols to indicate grouping and emphasis for preaching.[31]

Alexander Melville Bell grew into a handsome young man with dark eyes, luxuriant black hair, and a crystal-clear, finely modulated voice. When nineteen he went to Newfoundland to live with a friend of the family and recover from a bout of poor health; there he directed amateur theatricals, and treated stammerers. Then he crossed to England, at about the time that Howe and Mann did likewise, and in London taught speech three hours a day, assisting his father.

It was on a visit to Edinburgh that he met his wife-to-be. Her name was Eliza and it was love at first sight. "I found her very pretty, slim and delicate-looking—but she was deaf and could only hear with the aid of an ear tube. My sympathy was deeply excited," he later wrote, "she was so cheerful under her affliction."[32] Eliza had become hard-of-hearing at ten; she could get along with an ear trumpet and she could speak rather well. Melville's older brother, David, had married and settled in Dublin, teaching speech. Now Melville did likewise, securing Eliza's hand and a lectureship in elocution at the University of Edinburgh. There he remained for more than twenty years, publishing scores of works on elocution and speech correction; said a colleague: "He had an intense desire to remedy every defect of speech."[33]

One of Melville Bell's students and close friends witnessed his most important discovery, named Visible Speech, which he and his son Aleck would later bring to America.

"I happened to be at his house on the memorable night when, busy in his den, there flashed upon him the idea of a physiological alphabet which would furnish to the eye a complete guide to the production of any oral sound by showing in the very forms of the letter the position and action of the organs of speech which its production required. It was the end toward which years of thought and study had been bringing him, but all the same, it came upon him like a sudden revelation. . . . At times it looked as if, like

Archimedes, he might give vent to his emotions and shout 'Eureka.' "[34]

The same friend describes a private demonstration of Visible Speech in his home. "When Bell's sons had been sent away to another part of the house out of earshot, we gave Bell the most peculiar and difficult sounds we could think of, including words from the French and Gaelic, following these with inarticulate sounds, as of kissing, chuckling, etc. All these Bell wrote down in his Visible Speech alphabet, and his sons were then called in. I well remember our keen interest, and bye and bye, astonishment, as the lads—not yet thoroughly versed in the new alphabet—stood side by side looking earnestly at the paper their father had put in their hands, and slowly reproducing sound after sound just as we had uttered them. . . ."

With Visible Speech, Alexander Melville Bell aimed, as Bonet had two centuries earlier, to "reduce the value of the letters" so that for one symbol there would be one sound. Unlike Bonet's solution and that ultimately adopted by the International Phonetics Association, which were based on the familiar Roman alphabet but restricted the phonetic value of each letter, Bell's involved a new set of ten basic symbols referring to the tongue, the lips, the larynx, and the nasal passage. When these symbols were elaborated and combined, they told the speaker how to arrange his articulators to yield the corresponding speech sound. Bell's *Standard Elocutionist*, which appeared in 1860, united all his prior work, including a shorthand for writing Visible Speech. The book reportedly sold a quarter million copies and went through nearly two hundred editions.[35] Melville had become the dean of phonetics; Shaw saluted him in the preface to *Pygmalion*.

It was at about this time that Melville's son Aleck moved to London for a year, where his grandfather administered large doses of Shakespeare and phonetics to the teenager and polished Aleck's elocution and declamation. In these and other ways he impressed on the youth the power and primacy of speech. "In no higher respect has man been created in the image of his Maker," he wrote, much as Amman and Heinicke before him, "than in his adaptation for speech. . . . The Almighty fiat 'Let there be light' was not more wonderful in its results than the Creator endowing the clay, which he had taken from the ground, with the faculty of speech."[36]

On returning to Scotland Aleck took a job at a boarding school as a teacher of elocution and music. He wanted to become a pianist, for he had a marked talent and had received lessons from an excellent teacher, but his father urged him to consider phonetics. In preparation for entering the University of Edinburgh, he also studied Latin and Greek. Perhaps most significant, Aleck conducted his first experiments on speech, discovering the strongest frequencies in various vowels by the values of the tuning forks they would set in vibration. Upon the death of grandfather Bell, Melville moved to London to take over his practice, leaving his own in Edinburgh to his oldest son, Melly. Then Aleck's younger brother, Edward, died of tuberculosis and Aleck joined his father as an assistant. He enrolled in courses in anatomy at University College, where his father was professor of vocal physiology and lecturer in elocution, and then he matriculated at London University.[37]

While in Boston the joint legislative committee was holding hearings on the proposal for an oral school for the deaf, in London Alexander Melville Bell published the first edition of *Visible Speech: The Science of Universal Alphabetics*. From Dublin, his older brother, David, sent congratulations and a proposal to join him on an American lecture tour that would help to publicize his new work. The London practice was entrusted to Aleck.

Melville Bell arrived in Boston in time to read a scathing attack on Visible Speech in the latest issue of the *North American Review:* it pointed to flaws in the underlying analysis of speech articulation and claimed that the notation could be used only by trained phoneticians. Nevertheless, Harvard President Thomas Hill gave a reception for Bell, where Hubbard met him and urged him unsuccessfully to visit the newly opened Clarke school; he did accept an invitation from Hill to give six lectures at the Lowell Institute that fall. During those lectures, Melville Bell mentioned that his son was applying Visible Speech to the education of the deaf in a small London school under a Miss Susanna Hull. A schoolteacher named Sarah Fuller, who would soon direct the Boston Day School for Deaf-Mutes, was present at the lecture and wanted more details.

Susanna Hull had become interested in the deaf some five years earlier when she met a nine-year-old girl who had lost her hearing and some vision as the result of an illness when she was seven. Following a consultation with the Reverend Joseph Watson, director of the London Asylum, Hull taught the girl fingerspelling and restored some speech sounds. Soon she took on a second pupil, then a third, opening a little school in her father's residence. Two congenitally deaf sisters came along, whom she taught by writing and the manual alphabet. Next Hull sought advice on speech teaching from a leading British phonetician, who advised her to secure a copy of Melville Bell's *Visible Speech*. She found the symbol system too abstruse to use on her own, and applied to its inventor for assistance, with the result that she joined one of his classes then in progress and became conversant in the method. In the summer that Melville Bell left on his lecture tour of the United States, Hull hired his son to give speech lessons to her enlarged class of deaf pupils; this was the first of many such efforts to apply Visible Speech to the deaf.[38] Aleck had graduated from talking dogs and machines to talking children.

On returning to London, Melville Bell received a flattering letter from a member of the Hill-Hubbard circle, Lewis B. Monroe, the Boston elocutionist. He stated that "elocutionary studies have been unjustly neglected until your visit," and invited Bell to come to the United States again in the fall of the following year to give a series of twelve Lowell-endowed lectures on Shakespeare.[39] But tragedy struck the family in the ensuing months: Aleck's older brother, Melly, succumbed to the same disease as had his younger brother, Edward, tuberculosis.[40] Aleck, twenty-two, was slim and delicate; fearing to lose all his children, Melville recalled the years he himself had spent recovering his health in Newfoundland and decided to move the family to Canada, choosing Brantford, Ontario, where lived an old friend.

By the time of Melville Bell's second lecture series, in the fall of 1870, Sarah Fuller's school in Boston had been open a year, and she arranged for most of the Boston school board to call on him and urge him to give lessons in Visible Speech at her school. Melville declined, but as Hull, in London, had applied to the father and got the son, so Fuller, in Boston, arranged to hire Alexander Graham Bell, bringing him down from Canada for three months the following spring.

When Aleck arrived in Boston, he was taken to visit Lewis Monroe, who offered to help him repeat the experiments of Hermann von Helmholtz on synthesizing vowel sounds. Bell next met Sarah Fuller, who arranged lodging for him at her sister's home, where he soon spent hours every evening working with electrical equipment. During the day he taught Visible Speech to Fuller and her assistant, Mary True, Mabel Hubbard's former teacher, and gave demonstration lessons to some of their thirty pupils. Bell also began teaching Visible Speech to an evening class of deaf men. At an exhibition in June, children and adults alike showed they had learned to utter all of the English speech sounds written in Visible Speech. On his way home to Brantford for the summer, Bell stopped by Northampton, where he met Harriet Rogers and Lewis Dudley. He agreed to take Theresa Dudley into his private classes, which were projected for the following fall, and Lewis Dudley accompanied him to Hartford to visit the asylum.

Since Theresa Dudley was born deaf, it is not surprising to learn from Bell's correspondence that even after four years at Clarke her speech was "slurred and unpleasant, [she had] no voice control, some vowels and consonants [were] wrong. She could scarcely be understood."[41] Bell spent two or more hours every day with Theresa, who was now seventeen; he had three other pupils as well, but Theresa's fee paid most of his expenses, and after her father's moving appeal to the legislature in her behalf, a victory over her mutism would have symbolic value. After three months he exhibited his pupil: she had learned to read Visible Speech symbols, and the superintendent of schools was "mightily impressed."[42] At Christmas, Bell took Theresa home with him to Brantford, and on return to Boston, they continued their lessons until March, when he returned her to the Clarke school; Sarah Fuller then took the girl into her own home for a further program of private lessons. Bell remained at Clarke to give a series of lectures on Visible Speech, and there he met Gardiner Greene Hubbard, just returned from a stay in Germany, where he had taken his daughter Mabel in an effort to improve her speech.

From Clarke, Bell went to Hartford, where he spent two months at the invitation of the director, E. C. Stone, who had succeeded his father, Collins Stone, struck down by a locomotive. Bell taught Visible Speech to two teachers, gave a demonstration class for others, and provided all 250 pupils with some exercises in voice and Visible Speech. During his stay he continued to study sign language, which he had begun learning in Boston with some deaf adults, William Chamberlain in particular. At commencement he talked to the graduating class in sign.[43]

During the summer Sarah Fuller arranged for Bell to address the principals of deaf schools meeting in Flint, Michigan. Visible Speech, said Bell, could be used to correct speech defects and teach speech to the deaf; to teach literacy to adults, since it was a perfectly regular writing system; to make books for the blind less bulky, for the same reason; to allow missionaries to record unwritten tongues; and to enable phoneticians to record dying languages and dialects. He affirmed that Visible Speech had no part in the controversy between oral education, as at Clarke, and sign-language education, as at the Hartford school.[44] This address, also printed in the *American Annals*, helped to stir interest in Visible Speech, and trials were soon conducted by Harvey Peet's son and successor at the New York school, by Gallaudet at the Columbian Institution, and by several other principals.[45]

The following fall, at Sarah Fuller's urging, Bell moved from Brantford to Boston and sought out quarters for himself and his school, which he dubbed the Establishment for the Study of Vocal Physiology, and for the teacher-training school connected with it, in a once-fashionable neighborhood of brick townhouses a few streets from where I now write. Theresa Dudley enrolled for some more months of lessons, as did Jeannie Lippitt. Mabel Hubbard was supposed to come but did not. Sarah Fuller also obtained for Bell's new school a five-year-old boy, born deaf, who would prove his most lucrative and most lasting pupil. George Sanders had been receiving instruction for several weeks in Fuller's home when she was relieved of that heavy burden by George's father, a wealthy leather merchant, who contracted for his son to move into Bell's home along with his nurse.

In planning his course of instruction for young George, Bell took as his guide the educational theory then in vogue of Friedrich Froebel (the German creator of the kindergarten), which stressed learning by doing in pleasant surroundings. To this Bell added Dalgarno's advice that the deaf should be taught to read and write following the "mother method," that is, as hearing children learn speech. (I have never understood why the learning of a first language should be taken as a model for the learning of a second. Only in the former does the child begin knowing no language and invariably achieve fluency in a few years, whatever the adult intervention.) Bell made

Sanders's schoolroom a playroom and labeled most of the objects there, as well as items of tableware in the dining room. George's attempts at gestural communication were largely ignored and he was taught instead to find the card in his vocabulary pack that matched the label on the object he desired. To teach sentences, Bell and his assistant, Abbie Locke, tirelessly wrote sentences on the blackboards, which George learned to trace and act out. Later on he was taught to spell, with the teacher using a labeled glove designed by Dalgarno.[46]

Boston was then, as it is now, a major intellectual center and the home of several universities. Harvard's role in Bell's career I have already mentioned. At the recently opened Massachusetts Institute of Technology, Bell took courses in mechanics, electricity, and anatomy. Boston University was chartered in the year of his father's first American lectures and now Lewis Monroe was opening a School of Oratory there: Bell accepted the offer of a professorship, giving lectures on elocution, Visible Speech, and articulation training; he also started a second normal class for teachers and, since he had too few young pupils for practice teaching, began a class for deaf adults as well.[47] Sanders offered Bell free room and board in his home in Salem in return for instructing George there, and in the fall of 1873 Bell moved from Boston, commuting regularly. He would remain in Salem for two years.

No doubt the most important event for Bell that hectic fall occurred when Mabel Hubbard became his pupil. Some four years earlier, when Mabel was twelve, the time had come for her to enter school with her sisters. After a few months it became clear that an orally taught deaf child could not manage in an ordinary school. For one thing, although Mabel was renowned all her life for her expert lipreading skills, still she was unable to lipread sufficiently well a teacher addressing a class of hearing children. So her parents had removed her from school and, apparently convinced that Clarke could do little more for her skills, had taken her to an oral school for the deaf in Germany. According to one of Bell's biographers who had access to the Hubbard family papers, Mabel proved so superior to the other deaf pupils that she was finally enrolled in an ordinary day school, receiving speech lessons from a German instructor privately.[48] But when the Hubbards returned, after a stay of nearly three years, Mabel's voice was not much improved, and the following fall Miss True brought her to see Alexander Graham Bell at the Boston University School of Oratory.[49]

Mabel, almost sixteen, found Bell attractive, "tall and dark with jet-black hair and eyes but dressed badly and carelessly in an old-fashioned suit of black broadcloth." But he might help improve her speech, a highly desirable achievement, she said, in case she would want to marry a rich man and improve her position in society. Bell soon turned her over to his assistant, Abbie Locke.[50]

Mabel never took much interest in Visible Speech; shortly after their marriage, Bell complained "you have neither appreciated Visible Speech nor have encouraged me to work for its advancement."[51] Later, she claimed that she learned the system too late in life to derive any benefit from it but that it could do for the deaf child what lipreading does not—reveal the positions of hidden articulations.[52] In any case, the initial enthusiasm for Visible Speech faded rapidly. After a three-year trial at Clarke, Bell agreed it was not successful.[53] The American School (formerly, Asylum) found it "wearing and justified for only a few pupils: sign must still be the vehicle for education."[54] Bell acknowledged that progress in the Boston Day School had seemed much too slow for the effort expended on the symbols by teacher and pupils alike.[55] And Susanna Hull dropped Visible Speech in London, where it had first been tried with the deaf: "I would say what I have said of signs. . . . These symbols are of a nature to retard rather than advance speech."[56] When Bell conducted a survey of educational practices at deaf schools fifteen years after he introduced the system, he found it had generally been dropped.[57]

Not only was Visible Speech a failure, but Bell was also unsuccessful, it seems, in his other attempts at "making things talk." The underlying problem, says a leading textbook on educating the deaf, is that—right down to the present—"methods of teaching speech to the deaf in the United States have neither a theoretical nor a pragmatic base."[58] Bell's congenitally deaf pupils completely stymied his best efforts. George Sanders never learned to speak or lipread adequately; frustrated after nearly four years of tutoring him, and pressed by telephone matters, Bell turned him over to an assistant.[59] When George reached college age, Bell conceded that he might do best by enrolling at the National Deaf-Mute College, now renamed Gallaudet College in honor of Edward's father, where instruction was in sign. Likewise, we are told that Theresa Dudley learned to pronounce some Visible Speech symbols, but nowhere is it stated that she could speak intelligibly or lipread. It was Sarah Fuller's practice to keep pupils who had once heard and retained some speech separate from congenitally deaf children like Theresa, because the latter were so refractory.[60] The same is true of Harriet Rogers at the Clarke School, where an upper department was created for semi-mutes and a lower department for the rest. They even tried, as an experiment, shipping pupils born deaf off to the state residential schools—just as Hubbard said he would.[61] Bell himself opened a day school after he moved to Washington, and accepted four congenitally deaf pupils, only to close the school within a year. In later years he repeatedly urged that the congenitally deaf should not be taught orally because "speech is not clear to the eye and requires a knowledge of the language to unravel ambiguities."[62]

There is no evidence, however, that Bell had any greater success with his pupils who had once spoken. At a conference of principals of schools for the deaf, where several oral deaf were shown to prefer written communication, Bell affirmed that his wife "speaks more imperfectly than these gentlemen we have heard today" yet finds value in the skill.[63] On another occasion he defended her poor speech on the grounds that "the value of speech is in its intelligibility, not in its perfection"; if family and old friends understood Mabel's speech—that was good enough for him.[64]

There was one thing Bell could make speak beyond all doubt—the telephone. Six months after the first convention of articulation teachers Bell called a second, and there he delivered an address on methods of visualizing speech. He told how he had modified a device called the "manometric flame," invented by a Frenchman, Rudolph Koenig. A diaphragm is stretched over a hole in a gas pipe. The voice is carried to the diaphragm through a tube, and as the sound wave fluctuates in intensity, so does the diaphragm, imposing a corresponding fluctuation on the gas flame. To make the distinct pattern associated with each sound more visible, the flame is reflected in a set of revolving mirrors, where it appears as a broad band of light. Bell's idea was to attach a stylus to the diaphragm that would scratch a smoked drum, leaving a permanent trace that the deaf child could examine and match to the teacher's model—visible speech in a more literal sense than his father had ever envisioned. It then occurred to Bell that the best analysis of the sounds might be obtained by modeling the transmission of sound in the device on that in the ear. Indeed, why not use an ear itself—an otologist friend promptly provided him with one from a fresh cadaver. The sound waves moved the eardrum, which vibrated the tiny bones of the middle ear accordingly, and the attached stylus traced the pattern. Bell was struck by the fact that a membrane as light and thin as tissue paper could control the vibrations of much heavier bones. This meant that a larger membrane could vibrate an iron rod. Suppose the rod were magnetized and vibrated next to an electromagnetic coil; when the rod was out of the coil's magnetic field, the maximum current would flow in the coil, and the more the rod interrupted the lines of force, the less the current. Thus movements of the diaphragm would impose a corresponding undulating current in the line. At the other end of the line the arrangement would work backward, the current creating a field of varying force which would vibrate the rod accordingly, moving the diaphragm and creating sound, just as in a loudspeaker.

On March 10, 1876, Bell transmitted the first intelligible speech by telephone ("Mr. Watson—come here—I want to see you").[65] Two months later the Centennial Exhibition opened in Philadelphia. Bell's financial backers, the Hubbards and the Sanders, were determined to have the telephone displayed and to win recognition from the expert judges. Here is how they succeeded. The emperor of Brazil, Dom Pedro II, participated in opening the centennial and then paid a visit to Gallaudet College. He showed great interest in the work of the school, its president recounted, even sitting beside one of the students in the classroom and putting his arm around him, questioning him on his studies. As the visit came to an end, the emperor planted an ivy vine presented by Sophia Gallaudet. "Each of them advanced in years, each still youthful," wrote Professor Draper from the college, "each seemed to enter at once with kindred spirit into the emotions of the other. They were both of imposing but kindly presence, and most courteous in manner. It was like a meeting between sovereigns."[66] Dom Pedro went on to Boston, where he received a letter from Bell urging him to visit the Boston Day School for Deaf-Mutes. He accepted the invitation and there the two men met. Some days later they met again in Philadelphia when the judges, including the emperor, made their way around to Bell's exhibit. (Edward Miner Gallaudet was at the Centennial, too, with some hundred deaf students and teachers from the primary school and college in Washington.) Bell had set up a transmitter a hundred yards away in the northeast corner of the great main building. He invited the emperor to press the receiver against his ear while he withdrew to the transmitter. A moment later Dom Pedro leapt up and cried, "I hear, I hear!" As Bell's biographer describes it, the emperor "applied the little cylinder and repeated the words 'to be or not to be.'" (Here Bell had profited again from his work with the deaf, which had taught him that the most intelligible utterance is one the listener knows beforehand.) "Still declaiming Hamlet's soliloquy, [Bell] presently heard a pounding noise and saw Dom Pedro rushing toward him 'at a very un-emperor-like gait.' . . . Bell had scored what he reported to his parents as 'a glorious success.'"[67] In his desire to restore speech to the deaf, Bell had invented the one device that more than any other would prove their undoing, closing hosts of jobs to them, and depriving them of all the services and comforts that would be carried thereafter by an undulating current and no longer by a person.

But the telephone would not alienate Bell from the American deaf as much as this: Bell was a eugenicist. The term was introduced in 1883 by Darwin's cousin Sir Francis Galton, who began analyzing the pedigrees of famous men at about the time Bell began trying to make the deaf speak. A year before the invention of the telephone, Richard Dugdale published his famous study of the Jukes family, documenting a succession of criminals, paupers, and degenerates in one generation after another. Dugdale also pointed to environmental factors, but the study supported the popular view—especially appealing to wealthy Boston families in the Victorian era—that disease, pauperism, and immorality were largely the result of inheritance. Eugenicists hoped to improve society by selective breeding, which entailed, in turn, selective marriage, selective immigration, and selective sterilization.[68]

In his article "How to Improve the Race," published in 1914, Bell la-

MABEL HUBBARD BELL AND HUSBAND

ALEXANDER GRAHAM BELL

mented the constraints on eugenicists; no sheep breeder could ever improve his flock under such circumstances: "The weaklings are to be preserved and given special care," he wrote sarcastically. "In fact, all of the animals, including the poor little deformed lambs, are to be kept alive as long as possible. . . . We must not mutilate the animals nor do anything to them that is inconsistent with the humanitarian spirit of the age. . . . We are not permitted to select the individuals that should be mated together to improve the stock. . . . We may confidently assert that under such conditions no scientific breeder would undertake to improve the flock—it would not be possible." However, there is still hope, he said: individuals have intelligence and thus the power to improve the race by their actions; but they do not have the knowledge of how to proceed. Eugenicists, on the other hand, possess the knowledge but not the power. "What an opportunity!" Bell exulted. "Most of the disputed questions of human heredity can be settled by them, and their verdict will be acquiesced in by the general public."[69] To illustrate, Bell had this advice on the selection of a mate: "English, Irish, Scottish, German, Scandinavian, and Russian blood seems to mingle beneficially with the Anglo-Saxon American, apparently producing increased vigor in the offspring."[70]

After his early, glorious success in applied science, Bell devoted the rest of his life to projects of this kind, including stockbreeding. He looked into hereditary deafness in blue-eyed white cats, and with the purchase of a remote estate in Nova Scotia, he acquired a flock of sheep, which he endeavored for many years, and at great expense, to breed so that they would typically have six nipples and give birth to twins. The project failed but brought Bell into the American Breeders' Association as the eugenics movement entered its heyday; it thrived on a murky brew of Darwinism, racism, elitism, Mendelian genetics, and social reform.[71] When the Breeders' Association created a section on eugenics "to emphasize the value of superior blood and the menace to society of inferior blood," Bell agreed to serve.[72] His influence was great enough to have the name changed to the American Genetics Association and to propel his son-in-law into its presidency, and he contributed articles to the *American Breeders' Magazine* (renamed the *Journal of Heredity*). Skimming until I found Bell's "Saving the Six-nippled Breed," I passed such useful information as "There can be no question that the Nordic race is and has been a superior one," accompanied, to my relief, by the claim that antipathy to such racist pretensions is itself of evolutionary origin and survival value.[73] Bell and other eugenicists subscribed to Social Darwinism—because the fittest survive, those who have survived are fit, and those who have survived well (the rich) are particularly fit. This was not only naturally necessary but morally appropriate.

One result of the eugenics movement was sterilization laws. Another was racial restrictions on immigration, for if undesirables continued to pour into the population, the effect of selectively breeding superior people would be diluted. Before 1880—the year that Bell won the Volta Prize for inventing the telephone—some ten million Europeans had arrived from northern and western Europe. Then, as immigrants increasingly came from southern and eastern Europe, there was a call to reduce the tide. Bell's voice was clarion: "The only hope for a truly American race lies in the restriction of immigration."[74]

Bell took an active interest in census policy. He was responsible, in the 1900 census, for the collection and analysis of data on the blind and the deaf,[75] and he urged a new kind of census, "of equal if not of greater importance to the nation." Every American male between twenty and forty should submit every ten years to a fitness exam by the War Department. Certificates of fitness would be given to those with good health, physical strength and vigor, and freedom from defects disqualifying a man for military service. Certificates of unfitness would be given to the rest, including, presumably, the deaf. Certificates of fitness would have several uses: "Fathers and mothers of marriageable daughters, to say nothing of the daughters themselves, would be anxious to know whether a proposed suitor has or has not received a certificate . . . and, if the persons are disqualified, might demand to know the reason." The government would favor those certified fit in appointments and positions generally, and "salaries derived from appropriations of public money should be as much as possible expended upon healthy persons who are contributing to the production of the healthy and strong in the community." Since many educated deaf were employed in the civil service and in state-supported residential schools, such a plan would be particularly hard on the deaf.[76] In the same spirit as Bell's proposal, some eugenicists urged that those certified unfit be prevented from reproducing. For example, the Mississippi secretary of state urged the legislature to "enact laws compelling all male defectives and male deficients . . . to undergo vasectomy. The law should also include normal males who marry either deficients or defectives."[77]

Bell published a warning in 1920 that Americans were committing race suicide, for "children of foreign-born parents are increasing at a much greater rate than the children of native-born parents—and the position is sufficiently grave for serious consideration." As selective immigration laws had been only partially successful, he argued, restriction on marriage or child-bearing might be necessary: "It is now felt that the interests of the race demand that the best should marry and have large families and that any restrictions on reproduction should apply to the worst rather than the best."

Bell was opposed, however, to laws forbidding marriage of the deaf and other undesirables (as he called them). "This would not produce the desired improvement," he wrote, "for even were we to go to the extreme length of killing off the undesirables altogether, so that they could not propagate their kind . . . it would diminish the production of the undesirables without increasing the production of the desirables."[78]

Bell specifically engaged the issue of eugenics and the deaf beginning in the 1880s. Sign language and the residential schools were creating a deaf community, he warned, in which the deaf intermarried and reproduced, a situation fraught with danger to the rest of the society.[79] He sounded the alarm in a *Memoir Upon the Formation of a Deaf Variety of the Human Race*, presented to the National Academy of Sciences among other national organizations, and later printed for even wider dissemination. Reviewing enrollment records for two thousand pupils admitted to the American Asylum up to 1877, Bell found that two-thirds of them had at least one schoolmate with the same surname. He also examined six school reports listing deaf relatives and found that about thirty percent of pupils had them. If this were true for the whole country, he estimated that ten thousand deaf-mutes belonged to families containing more than one. Since there are, then, familial patterns of deafness, "It is to be feared that the intermarriage of such persons would be attended by calamitous results to their offspring." The congenitally deaf without deaf relatives also run a risk in marrying, as do the adventitiously deaf *with* deaf relatives, so all in all, Bell estimated, there were twenty thousand deaf "at risk."

Now, in fact, he argued, the records show that the deaf do intermarry: the American school reported that half its pupils' marriages were with another deaf person, while the average at five institutions was eighty percent. Only the Clarke school had a policy of "preventing such marriages as far as possible." When two congenitally deaf persons marry, Bell reasoned, and some of their children marry congenitally deaf, and then some of *theirs* do, and so on, the proportion of deaf children born of such marriages will increase from generation to generation until nearly all their children will be born deaf. These families "would then constitute a variety of the human race in which deafness would be the rule rather than the exception."

In his recommendations, Bell considered repressive and preventive measures. Under the first heading, a law prohibiting the deaf from marriage might only promote deaf children born out of wedlock. A law prohibiting just the congenitally deaf from marrying "would go a long way towards checking the evil," but it is difficult to prove whether a person was born deaf or not. "Legislation forbidding the intermarriage of persons belonging to families containing more than one deaf-mute would be more practical. This would cover the intermarriage of hearing parents belonging to such families," but more data are needed before we can justify the passage of such an act, he said.

Thus, for the present, Bell found that preventive measures must suffice. "We commence our efforts on behalf of the deaf-mute by changing his social environment." Residential schools should be closed and the deaf educated in small day schools. Coeducation with hearing children would be the ideal "but this is not practicable to any great extent." Sign language should be banished and deaf teachers shunned.[80]

The memoir received wide newspaper coverage. A story appeared in the *Washington Evening Star* that was telegraphed to all parts of the United States, stating that Bell had submitted a plan to Congress asking for laws restricting the marriage of deaf-mutes. A Bell apologist, biographer, and employee, Fred DeLand, gives this explanation: Bell's address was published by Congress among the memoirs of the Academy. An AP reporter saw it on a congressman's desk, thought it was a memorial (a petition), not a memoir, dealing with compulsory marriage laws, and wrote the story.[81]

Whatever Bell's intention, his actions led many to believe that there would be, or already were, laws prohibiting deaf marriage. Sir Francis Galton stated that Bell's memoir showed how easily a marked variety of mankind might be established permanently by a system of selection extending throughout two or three generations, and he concluded that legislative agencies "were sure to become aroused against unions that are likely to have hereditary effects harmful to the nation."[82] Proposals to segregate the congenitally deaf were made, as were counterproposals to allow them freedom as long as they did not reproduce.[83] A noted deaf author believed Bell had "brought before Congress a motion to prohibit marriages among the deaf. But his arguments were considered unsound."[84] At the World's Congress of the Deaf in 1893, a French delegate stated that in his country the deaf favored intermarriage, and he criticized the "erroneous theories of Professor Bell who would have a law passed preventing marriage between deaf-mutes."[85] A deaf Rochester couple felt constrained to announce in the local paper after the birth of their hearing child that neither parent was born mute and wished this stated "as the laws of the state forbid persons born mutes to be joined in marriage."[86] According to the rector of the All-Angels Mission to the Deaf in Baltimore at the time of Bell's memoir, news of it spread like wildfire among parents of the deaf, "their family physicians, and among surgeons generally throughout the world, and suggested to them a senseless and cruel procedure—the sterilization of children born deaf."[87] He came to know many deaf couples who were childless and unhappy as a result of having been sterilized in infancy; he laid the blame on Bell.

In 1907, at the eighth convention of the National Association of the Deaf, the president announced that Bell's committee on eugenics of the American Stockbreeders' Association was drafting a bill to restrict matrimony among: (1) persons mentally, morally, or physically defective; (2) criminals; (3) immature children; (4) people of plainly incompatible dispositions; (5) consumptives; (6) persons suffering from functional disorders; (7) the deaf and dumb. The bill was to be presented to the legislatures of all the states and the committee would disseminate scientific literature on the subject to pave the way for its passage.[88] The convention elected a committee to meet with Bell "in indignant protest against thus grouping the deaf with the outcast and unclean" and interfering with their happiness, but Bell protested he knew nothing about it and had always deprecated legislative interference with marriages of the deaf.[89]

A 1912 report from the eugenics section of the Breeders' Association, however, cites Bell's census of blind and deaf persons and lists a similar set of "socially unfit" classes, including the deaf, whose supply should, if possible, "be eliminated from the human stock."[90] The section drafted a model sterilization law to be applied to these classes; it was designed to satisfy the courts while purging the United States of its "burden of undesirable germplasm." By the time of World War I, sixteen states had such sterilization laws in force.[91]

Of the many rebuttals to Bell's *Memoir* by the deaf, I will mention three. William Chamberlain, who had taught Bell sign language, objected that "the persistence with which the memoir returns to legislative interference suggests the hearty support its author would give to such measures if they were passable." True, Bell equivocates on the subject, Chamberlin wrote, but the proposal should have been rejected right from the start; Bell's failure to do so created uncertainty among the deaf about their rights. The memoir recommends ending the employment of deaf teachers. Naturally the deaf resent an attempt to interfere with their employment. The memoir belittles the combined system of education, incorporating both sign and speech, and insists on "pure" oralism, but "the combined system takes all and educates them by means of such methods as are adapted to their individual cases. The oral system picks and chooses, rejecting a large percent of applicants as incapable or weak-minded who are simply average deaf people and who, sent to combined schools, turn out very well."[92]

Dudley George, a Gallaudet graduate and deaf teacher, affirmed at the World's Congress of the Deaf that deaf parents generally have hearing children: in the schools for the deaf it is a matter of remark if a pupil has a deaf parent but not if four have a hearing one. He pointed out that when the deaf marry the hearing, they may still have a deaf child. And if they have one, "they know how to raise it, where to find the schools that will train the head, hand and heart, elevating it to a condition equal to many hearing people and superior to uneducated hearing people."[93] Deaf marriages in which both partners are deaf are the happiest. Hearing persons willing to marry someone deaf are commonly inferior to their spouse morally, socially, or intellectually, or seek the alliance for reasons other than love.

F. L. Seliney, president of the Empire State Association of Deaf-Mutes, reported that over 2,000 admissions to schools for the deaf in New York State yielded only 18 students whose parents were deaf, less than one percent. Examining comparable data for all admissions to thirty-five institutions over more than half a century, he found 215 children with deaf parents, out of nearly 17,000 enrollments, an incidence of slightly more than one percent. Moreover, 83 of these had only one deaf parent, so the incidence attributable to deaf intermarriage is three-quarters of one percent. "The deaf do not understand why, since their marriages are the least among the circumstances producing deafness, they should be singled out as transgressors in chief and the demolition of their schools, association, and newspapers advocated."[94]

Seliney was right: the tables of data in Bell's memoir show that only one percent of the pupils in his sample had two deaf parents. Thus a total elimination of deaf intermarriages would have reduced the student population of the American School over more than fifty years by 25—that is, from 2,106 to 2,081. It is highly unlikely that Bell, a devotee of statistical analysis, was unaware of the trifling size of the issue over which so much controversy raged, so we may infer that he raised it for another reason. Bell's census data show, for example, that the disease which impaired his mother's hearing and his wife's, scarlet fever, was responsible for nearly ten times as many deaf pupils as all congenital causes.[95] Why not wage war on scarlet fever? Because the goal of this campaign was none other than the one he had pursued for many decades before the memoir: he aimed to break up the deaf community by banishing sign, residential schools, the silent press, deaf organizations, and other activities that led to their congregation. Bell invoked the specter of a deaf variety of human being mainly to add urgency to banishing sign and residential schools, and that is one reason why he preferred these so-called preventive measures to the direct repressive measure of interdicting deaf marriage.

This explanation of Bell's program simply drives our search for motives beneath the surface. Why should Bell have wished to eradicate sign, deaf schools, deaf teachers? He would have been baffled by the question. His family's lives were predicated on the deaf "passing" among the hearing, on assimilation, on denial. If there was indeed a large fellowship of the deaf with a common language, mutual aid and support, a common culture, organizations, newspapers, and so on, then a terrible crime had been committed when his mother and, to a lesser degree, his wife, were condemned to a life of solitude; then his family's focus on speech for three generations seemed more like an obsession.

What we have learned about heredity and the deaf in the hundred years since Bell's memoir supports the position of the deaf on this issue. One contemporary geneticist calls it a "serious misconception" that marriage between the deaf should be discouraged.[96] First of all, the vast majority of deaf children have hearing parents, for most deafness comes from adventitious causes such as contagious disease, and even most genetic deafness occurs in children of hearing parents. The reason for this is that a child who is deaf because he carries two recessive genes for deafness received one from each of his parents, which means they are hearing carriers of the gene. It follows that it would take thousands of years before preventing childbirth in the deaf would reduce the frequency of these recessive genes in the population, because most carriers are hearing, not deaf. Even if we could weed out these genes we might not want to: many genes have multiple effects, some of them salutary.[97]

There are in fact thirty to forty recessive genes that will cause deafness in a child who receives two *of the same kind*. Thus two parents, each of whom is congenitally deaf, will in all likelihood have a hearing child because they are probably carrying different pairs of recessive genes. There are, however, certain genes associated with deafness that are called dominant because possessing just one will make a person deaf; there are no carriers of the gene who are not deaf. But in this case it generally doesn't matter whether the deaf parent with the dominant gene marries a hearing or a deaf person, for each of his children will have a fifty-fifty chance of inheriting the dominant gene in any event.

There are, however, issues logically prior to the practical effect of interfering with deaf marriage. Bell presupposed, first, that deafness is a defect to be avoided rather than a characteristic of a variety of humankind; and he presupposed, second, that society's interest in avoiding that defect outweighed deaf people's interest in compatible marriage choice and childbearing. For someone who believed the Italians were adulterating the American racial stock, it was inconceivable that the deaf were not. This was so clear that Bell assumed that the outrage of the deaf and their friends must reflect some misunderstanding, and he welcomed an invitation to address the deaf directly at Gallaudet College. "It is the duty of every good man and every good woman," Bell told them, "to remember that children follow marriage, and I am sure there is no one among the deaf who desires to have his affliction handed down to his children. . . . I therefore hold before you as the ideal marriage, a marriage with a hearing person."[98] This amounted to urging the students to forgo marriage altogether, for nearly all the hearing people they knew who understood them and their kind had deaf relatives, and Bell enjoined them from those marriages as well, since they were as likely to transmit deafness as the students' preferred pairing with another deaf person.

Ironically, among those present for Bell's address was George Sanders, one of Bell's first students and the one who stayed with him the longest. Sanders did not view his deafness as an affliction nor did he think he would have to remain childless if he were to marry Lucy Swett, the young deaf woman who had captured his heart, one of Thomas Brown's relatives from Henniker, New Hampshire. "George will marry a deaf girl anyway," Lucy said. "Why not me?"[99]

Because of his keen commitment to assimilation of the deaf, Bell began a highly successful campaign in the year of his marriage, 1877, to develop small day schools for the deaf on the model of the Boston School for Deaf-Mutes, renamed the Horace Mann School in that year. Various plans for educating the deaf among the hearing had been tried before; Arrowsmith had described the failure of his deaf brother's education in the common schools in the preface to his translation of Epée,[100] and Blanchet's and Graser's enterprises of this kind had failed, but none of these experiments had the features Bell desired. He wanted to minimize contact among the deaf. Thus, ideally, each school should consist of just a few pupils—it should really be a class. And to maximize contact with the hearing, the class should meet in a hearing school; although total integration could not work, there should be common play and common instruction in a few select subjects, such as drawing.

Bell soon became involved with a plan to create day classes on a large scale in Wisconsin. The tide of immigration had brought there many Germans acquainted with the oralist movement of deaf education in Germany. A few encouraged a teacher of articulation for deaf-mutes to open a small private school, which grew from four pupils to seventeen the first year. It was both a boarding and a day school and was conducted initially in German. Several philanthropic German immigrants formed an association to sponsor indigent deaf children at the school, and they ultimately created a permanent organization called the Wisconsin Phonological Institute with over one hundred members. Next, the W.P.I. hired a public-school teacher and opened the Milwaukee Day School for Improved Education of Deaf-Mutes, which, according to the prospectus, would teach children "by the pure oral or German articulation method." The W.P.I. had a Department of Propaganda that published various pro-oral pamphlets, including Bell's *Memoir on the Formation of a Deaf Variety of the Human Race*, which helped to arouse public sentiment against the state residential school at Delavan. That pamphlet urged the adoption of the oral method in all schools for the deaf and the creation of day schools throughout the state. It included a draft law to that effect.

The W.P.I. then arranged an exhibition of the pupils from the first day school: in attendance were the governor, a committee of the legislature, the Milwaukee School Board and the Chamber of Commerce. Shortly thereafter, much as Governor Bullock had done in Massachusetts, Governor Smith called the attention of the legislature to the W.P.I. proposal, and the Milwaukee School Board prepared a bill giving itself the authority to establish day schools with state aid on the model of the Boston Day School for Deaf-Mutes. The bill, however, failed to pass the legislature in 1881 and again, despite intense lobbying, the following year.[101] In response, the W.P.I. called a meeting in the senate chambers to support integrating deaf-mute instruction in the public schools; it was held under the august auspices of the National Education Association, and three oralists spoke: the principal of the Nebraska school, Bell, and J. C. Gordon, soon to head the articulation department at Gallaudet. Also present were a number of experienced educators of the deaf who stopped off on return from a conference in Minnesota, most notable among them Bell's arch opponent, Edward Miner Gallaudet.

Bell urged the day-school plan because it would allow deaf children to mingle with their hearing peers, to live at home, and to escape the evils of sign language and hence to avoid intermarriage. In order to train teachers, a course in articulation would be added to the curriculum at the state normal school. All teachers could benefit by this, Bell said. Articulation should be taught in all schools, hearing and deaf; there was an urgent need to preserve the purity of the English tongue, which was degenerating as a result of the foreign influx.

Gallaudet took the rostrum to denounce widespread erroneous beliefs concerning the deaf: namely, all deaf children can learn speech; oral schools receive all pupils; the best oral results cannot be obtained where the sign language is employed; signs can be banished from schools for the deaf; orally educated deaf are more fully restored to society than manually educated deaf; sign language is an imperfect and crude means of conveying thought; and orally educated deaf will not associate with each other after graduation. The principal of the American School rose to stress this last observation: there is no point to forced dispersion of the deaf in small day schools, for as soon as they graduate, in Germany as in America, they congregate and intermarry. Bell moved that a section of the N.E.A. be created to deal with the education of the deaf, and the meeting was adjourned.[102]

A new governor proposed the day-school bill once again; Bell came from Washington and spent two weeks explaining and defending its provisions to the legislature. Before he left, he presented each lawmaker with a copy of an open letter strongly urging its passage. In an appeal to their hearts, he emphasized the numbers of deaf children not then in school; in an appeal to their pride, he said Wisconsin would be the first state in the nation to have a day-school plan. He cited the rights of motherhood: the deaf child should eat and sleep in his own home, under his mother's care. He warned of the dangers of deaf congregation at Delavan. He pointed to the success of oralism in the fatherland: "All the deaf-mutes of Germany are taught to speak" (shades of Horace Mann!). The legislature wavered but passed the law.[103]

Bell was called back to Madison some years later when the W.P.I. tried to amend the law to require the state to allow the formation of day classes (it had stopped authorizing them), to double the budgets of those classes, and to limit their size by law to four or five pupils. The amendment also provided that "for the purpose of obviating the tendency to the formation of a deaf variety of the human species, congenital deaf-mutes of the opposite sexes shall be kept apart as much as possible, and that marriage between them be discouraged on account of its liability, under the law of heredity, to result in deaf-mute offspring."[104] Bell went on strenuous speaking tours around the state in support of the amendment. By the turn of the century, Wisconsin had fifteen day schools for the deaf and Bell had proclaimed the Wisconsin system to be "the most important movement of the century for the benefit of the deaf."[105]

The next major day-school movement began in Chicago, where Bell offered advice, lobbied, drafted legislation, and made personal appearances. With his help, the local parents' association succeeded not only in winning state aid for day schools and in installing their man as superintendent, but also in ousting the principal of the state residential school, who was insufficiently oralist for their taste. Ironically, that was Philip Gillett, the first principal to take a strong oralist stand (at Gallaudet's Conference of Principals in 1867) and a consistent supporter of the movement. He was replaced by J. C. Gordon, who came from Gallaudet College and banished all classroom signing at the Illinois school. Gordon was also the first head of the N.E.A. section on Deaf, Blind and Feebleminded, created at Bell's instigation.[106] To honor Bell for his contribution to these developments, Chicago named an oral day school after him. The deaf community, however, opposed the bill, and when it passed, they opposed the school board's decision to make the day schools "pure oral."[107]

Over several decades, Bell aided many more such day-school programs: in Michigan, Maine, Connecticut, California. . . . He wrote letters, gave advice, made trips, hired educators to tour the states and lobby legislators and school principals.[108] The Michigan day-school law, which required Bell's energetic support for passage, went further than its predecessor in Wisconsin and specified: "The oral system shall be used exclusively but if, after nine months' trial, any child shall be unable to learn by the oral method, no further expense shall be incurred in the attempt to educate it."[109] Day classes continued to open around the nation. Bell believed that deaf children could now be transformed into hearing ones while quite young and, by the turn of the century, "special teaching would be a matter only of the first few years of life."[110] By 1913, there were seventy day schools—more than the number of residential schools—but their pupils constituted only thirteen percent of the deaf student population.[111]

The arguments of deaf leaders and educators against these day-school programs went largely unheeded. They protested the inadequate qualifications of the teachers, who were recruited without any specific training for or experience in educating the deaf. They decried the exclusion of sign from the classroom, which deprived most pupils of education in their primary language. Since no one at home and only a few pupils at school could use manual language, the children would be communicatively isolated. Unlike their counterparts at the state residential school, they could not learn from the older students. Tardiness and absenteeism would be higher in the day class. No trade could be taught there. Pupils with diverse abilities must be taught together because of the small enrollments. Eventually the pupils would go to the state residential school in any case to receive high school education, and there they would congregate, use sign, make deaf friends— all of which the day-school movement aimed to prevent. Because the deaf children could not make themselves intelligible to the hearing children and the hearing did not learn to sign, "the deaf of the day schools do not and cannot play with the hearing," one deaf writer explained. "When they leave they are drawn to the society of their own kind and the purpose of the day-school is defeated."[112] In the light of these arguments, it is doubtful whether the recent wave of de-institutionalization in the United States, which has swept the deaf out of their residential schools and the insane and retarded out of their asylums, will prove to have been of service to the deaf. Any activity that classes the deaf as defective members of the English-speaking community and misses the essential social and linguistic character of the deaf minority is liable to harm the very people it aims to help.

Bell placed assimilation into the hearing world above the mental development and professional training of the deaf. "If we have the mental condition of the child alone in view," Bell wrote, "without reference to language, no language will reach the mind like the language of signs."[113] But that could not be the main view because "the main object of the education of the deaf is to fit them to live in the world of hearing-speaking people."[114] When the conference of principals meeting in Minnesota placed on its agenda the question "What is the importance of speech to the deaf?" Bell was flabbergasted: "I am astonished. I am pained. To ask the value of speech? It is like asking the value of life! . . . What is the object of the education of the deaf and dumb if it is not to set them in communication with the world?"[115]

GALLAUDET: That is one object but a small part of it.

BELL: That is one object and the greatest of all objects.

Gallaudet and Bell would lock horns on this issue in testifying before the the British Royal Commission, in promoting professional organizations, and in addressing congressional committees on appropriations.

The Royal Commission was created by the Crown in 1884 about the time that Bell and Gallaudet debated in Madison; initially it was charged with investigating the education of the blind and feebleminded, but an influential barrister, member of Parliament, and father of a deaf girl, St. John Ackers, managed to have himself appointed to the commission and to have its scope enlarged. Something of a British Gardiner Greene Hubbard, Ackers had set out from England a decade earlier to discover for himself the best method of educating his daughter. He visited the Clarke school, the New York

Institution for the Improved Instruction of Deaf and Dumb (now the Lexington School), the American School, Bell's private school in Boston, and the Horace Mann School, and yet other schools in Washington and Philadelphia. Then he visited schools in Germany and France in company with a hired interpreter, and finally he visited many schools in Great Britain. In the end, he decided he would like his daughter to speak, although she had been deafened by fever at only a few months of age, and he hired a teacher from the Horace Mann School. Ackers became, in Gallaudet's terms, a rabid oralist (Edward had sat next to him at the congress of teachers of the deaf that met in Milan in 1880).[116] "I would entreat all interested in the success of the German system," Ackers wrote in the Clarke school report, "to unite together resolutely to refuse admission into their schools of any who can converse by signs."[117] Some years before joining the commission Ackers also published a pamphlet entitled *Deaf Not Dumb*. The chairman of the commission was hardly more impartial; a few months after it began its investigation, he opened a new wing of the Manchester school for the deaf with the claim that "if only the education of children were begun at an early age, in 99 cases out of 100 the deaf and dumb could be taught to speak by the oral system."[118] No one on the commission was an expert on teaching the deaf. In short, the coupling of deaf issues with those of the blind and feebleminded, ensuring a medical model, and the makeup of the commission left little doubt it would favor Bell's philosophy over Gallaudet's and Clerc's.[119]

Gallaudet and Bell were the key witnesses before the commission, the former invited as leader of the profession of teaching the deaf in the United States, the latter as the leading advocate of oralism, and probably the second most famous Briton alive. Although bitterly opposed in educational philosophy, the two had many traits in common. Each had a deaf mother and a highly successful father in whose work he followed. At twenty-seven, Gallaudet had been made president of the first college for the deaf in history; Bell had invented the telephone at twenty-nine. Gallaudet was ten years older than Bell and slimmer, but equally forceful and eloquent. Both were used to getting their own way. Relations between the two men were largely cordial until this time; over the next five years they deteriorated, and the last decade of the century was marked by their open warfare, in part over the issue of deaf teachers. Gallaudet's views placed him on a middle ground between Clerc and Bell. He had, after all, launched the movement that brought articulation training into the residential schools. He had coined the term "combined system" and aggressively espoused its cause—oral instruction for those who could profit, sign for the rest. But he was vigorously opposed to banishing sign. It was not that he wished to safeguard the signing community; like Bell, he opposed intermarriage of the deaf and even their organizations. It was rather that he believed education of the deaf in spoken language was impossible. "The great body of intelligent instructors," he wrote, ". . . are agreed that no error could be greater than to expect all deaf children to succeed in learning to speak. The supporters of pure oralism from the days of Heinicke to the present time have hugged this delusion to their hearts and, as a consequence, the education of hundreds and thousands of deaf children in Germany, France and Italy, who have been cruelly stretched on the Procrustean bed of a single method, has been more or less of a failure."[120]

Gallaudet went off to England not to gather knowledge, as his father did, but to impart it, not on behalf of the deaf in America but on behalf of those in Great Britain, not at the request of his countrymen, but at that of the British government. The headmasters of the three dozen schools for the deaf in England gave a magnificent dinner for him, "to atone," in the words of the toastmaster, "for their lack of hospitality to his father."[121] Gallaudet addressed the commission twice and answered their questions for ten hours. Bell appeared separately on four occasions, urging that all instruction of the deaf must be in speech, as in the German schools. He argued for dispersing the deaf ("decentralization"), for government certification of teachers, inspection of schools, and payment based on results, aid for apprenticing deaf students, and noninterference in teacher training.[122] All the issues on which Bell and the deaf were opposed were discussed: oralism, heredity, deaf association, day schools.

The report of the commission was called a victory by both sides. It begins by citing testimony in the four-volume transcript, including a statement that signs tend to isolate the deaf, with the result that they "are not at all competent witnesses as to which is the best system; those that have lived in cages all their lives are so much attached to the cage that they have no desire to fly outside. The children themselves may prefer the sign system as more natural to them and the parents of poor children are sometimes indifferent and careless."[123] This presumably explains the absence of deaf members on the commission. It came out in favor of a plan much like that adopted by Gallaudet's Conference of Principals in 1867: "All children should be, for the first year at least, instructed in the oral system"; those who cannot profit should then be taught manually. The first school for the deaf to open in England after the report adopted the combined system, although, according to Gallaudet, the directors were offered a private gift if it were made "pure oral."[124]

The developments that culminated in open warfare between Gallaudet and Bell and the division of the profession into two hostile camps began in this way. Shortly before the Royal Commission began hearings, the director of the Wisconsin Phonological Institute suggested to Bell a national organization for advocacy of oralism modeled after his own. Gallaudet proposed instead that the Convention of American Instructors of the Deaf create an oral section,[125] and so it came to pass. This did not satisfy Bell, however, since the balance of power in the organization was held by deaf teachers (who naturally opposed pure oralism and favored the combined system), so he urged a separate association of speech teachers, offering $25,000 to launch it. Sixty-two teachers, acting at his instigation, announced to the convention the formation of the American Association to Promote the Teaching of Speech to the Deaf. Bell was shortly elected president, and Hubbard vice-president.[126] This was, effectively, a revolt against Gallaudet's leadership and he hated to see the convention split into two camps. In retrospect, the split was inevitable from the opening of the convention, when Gallaudet, suave, courteous, dapper, took the podium and, looking down at his fierce, rumpled, and handsome opponent, said, "Deafness, once a calamity, has become through education little more than a serious inconvenience," and stopping to brush his bald pate, he added, "something like baldness in fly time."[127]

The speech association launched a series of annual summer meetings and began a long and active career expanding its membership (only a third were teachers), publishing, lobbying, and generally promoting pure oralism. With the $10,000 Bell had received with the Volta Prize for inventing the telephone he founded the Volta Laboratory. That laboratory improved on Edison's phonograph, among other inventions, and became rich. Thanks to the telephone, however, Bell was already a millionaire (in an era when there were few), so he sold his rights to the gramophone for $200,000, which he placed in trust for a bureau for the dissemination of the oralist literature that had grown out of his research on heredity. Three years after founding the A.A.P.T.S.D., Bell had a neoclassical building constructed in Washington, D.C., for this Volta Bureau, which eventually merged with the Association itself. The *Association Review* was renamed the *Volta Review*.[128]

The conflict between the two leaders and their organizations came to a head at a meeting of the convention in Flint, Michigan, in 1895. Gallaudet had been working to merge the two groups and had received what he thought was encouragement from Bell, especially when Bell announced the next head of the speech association would be the moderate Philip Gillett, who had been bumped by the Chicago parents' group.[129] But then Gillett urged postponement of the merger, which Gallaudet termed a "bootlicking surrender of his independence to Bell."

Convinced that reconciliation could never be achieved, Gallaudet went to the podium at Flint and delivered an address excoriating Bell. He charged that Bell and his collaborators "had worked with partisan spirit and purpose calculated to engender serious if not permanent antagonism in the profession." He charged Bell with trying to seize the space allocated to the convention at the Columbian Exposition and use it for the speech association. He charged Bell with working in the Conference of Principals to overthrow the combined system. He said that his own efforts to merge all teachers into one broad strong organization had failed because of "one man, outside the profession, to whom the promotion of speech teaching was of more interest than all things else concerning the deaf."[130]

Gallaudet concluded that the narrow platform of the speech association, its meager achievements, and Bell's express preference that it should be sustained by promoters rather than teachers justified "those who are merely teachers and not capitalists" in scorning the A.A.P.T.S.D.

According to one witness, it was the interpreter's starting at one end of a long platform and walking slowly to the other, while laboriously fingerspelling the full name of the speech association, that brought on the open clash between the two men. As the interpreter reached the end of the platform, everyone was smiling, there were some audible titters, and Bell was enraged —he was not used to being a laughingstock. The instant Gallaudet finished his paper, Bell was on his feet demanding to be heard. His temper had gotten the better of him and he raved. After a moment or two, the head of the Ontario school went up to the platform, lifted his hands, interrupting Bell, and signed, "Let us have peace." Then, turning to the crowded hall, he asked those present to join him in a request to Dr. Bell and Gallaudet to shake hands and forget their differences. For a long tense moment neither man moved; but at last they simultaneously stepped forward and the tips of their fingers met in a frigid handshake. That was the last time Bell ever attended a meeting of the convention and never again did the two men meet in amity.[131]

One of Gallaudet's most serious grievances was Bell's vocal opposition before the United States Congress to the establishment of a teacher-training department at Gallaudet College. Since the college's opening in mid-century, more than half its graduates had gone into the teaching profession. In addition, the New York, Pennsylvania, and Ohio schools, among others, also produced deaf teachers. It was deaf teachers who had founded the Florida school, the New Mexico school, the Kansas school, and numerous others— two dozen in all.[132] Many more taught in these schools and some had developed widely used teaching materials. Some had published learned articles and appeared on the international deaf stage, shaping the future of their profession worldwide.[133]

As the number of institutions for the deaf and the demand for deaf teachers grew, so too did the desire to found programs to train teachers. At mid-century there were only twelve schools for the deaf in the United States with 1,500 pupils, all taught manually, and 100 teachers, of whom nearly half were deaf. By the turn of the century, the American population had nearly doubled and there was a fivefold increase in deaf pupils and schools and a sixfold increase in instructors.[134] The Hartford, New York, Ohio, and Iowa schools among others served informally to train deaf teachers just as the Paris institution had trained Clerc. But in 1890, shortly after Bell had formed his speech association and in part as a response to it, Edward Miner Gallaudet placed an item of $5,000 in his annual budget request to Congress for the purpose of creating a formal teacher-training department in his school.

Gallaudet envisioned training sophisticated teachers who would be preferred as superintendents of the large residential schools and would therefore be in a position to dominate educational policy.[135] He informed Bell of his budget request and invited him to give an address to the department once founded; he understood Bell to have agreed. A few weeks later Gallaudet wrote in his diary: "I learned last night . . . that Graham Bell has asked for a hearing before the Appropriations Committee to [disapprove of] our normal school scheme. Shame!"[136] Gallaudet rushed to see Bell and discovered that he was exercised at the prospect of the college training deaf teachers —they could only impede the oralist movement. Gallaudet promised that he would admit only hearing students to the normal department, but Bell thought he might not keep his word, or the policy would be rescinded by his successors. Moreover, if Gallaudet succeeded in joining a national normal school to the deaf college, he would have created a citadel of the combined system right in the nation's capital. So Bell appeared before the House Appropriations Committee for thirty minutes to protest. He gave many reasons for his opposition. This is a proposal to train deaf teachers of the deaf, he said, but a teacher should be in possession of all his faculties. Moreover, the field for deaf teachers was diminishing. When he had come to America, nearly half of all teachers of the deaf were deaf themselves, whereas now, twenty years later, the fraction was one-quarter. This was because of increasing attention to articulation; deaf teachers cannot teach articulation, and sign comes into use. Finally, Gallaudet College could not admit both points of view in the training program, oral and manual, since oral advocates claimed that the teacher's mere knowledge of sign was detrimental because it tempted him to use sign instead of English.[137]

Despite Bell's testimony, the House committee approved Gallaudet's request and sent it to its counterpart in the Senate. "Bell was not satisfied with the muddle he had already made by meddling in affairs that did not concern him," Gallaudet fumed, "and he wrote letters to all the schools and institutions in the country that were so worded as to misguide those not informed and also contained several untruths that were untruths to his knowledge [concerning admissions of deaf students]."[138] The two men appeared before the Senate committee; each had two minutes. Bell presented a list of twenty-one schools opposed to the appropriation—oral schools, most of them day schools. He urged the committee to amend the measure to give Gallaudet $3,000 to open an articulation department. The legislators struck the appropriation entirely, but friends of the college on the conference committee put through the Bell amendment. Gallaudet took the money to hire an articulation teacher, then created the normal department anyway, securing six fellowships from his board. In the fall, seven hearing students entered for the one-year postgraduate course—including manual and oral methods of teaching the deaf. The college itself continued as before to prepare those deaf students who planned to pursue a career in teaching.[139]

Bell was dismayed, and his first response was to campaign for the creation of a counterpart oral department of teacher training: "The public agitation for an Oral Department at the National College should be continued. There is no harm in letting President Gallaudet have this idea that a fight is imminent in Congress, as the dread of a conflict that may injure the College and lead to a still further curtailment of his appropriations may operate as an element in inducing him to do better justice to oral work. Our program I think should be, first, public agitation concerning the relation of the National College to the oral schools of the country—public agitation *now;* second, private discussion to elaborate a practicable scheme to establish a separate school for the higher education of the deaf by the oral method."[140] On calmer reflection, Bell had the speech association back a normal department at the Clarke school, which had previously trained teachers primarily for its own needs.[141]

Gallaudet won the day, but Bell was right about the rise of oralism and the commensurate drop in opportunities for deaf teachers. The fraction of pupils taught with English as the vehicle rose from near zero in 1870 to half at the turn of the century to nearly all by World War I and ever since.[142] The fraction of deaf teachers fell from nearly half at mid-century, to one-quarter when Bell testified, to one-fifth by World War I, to an eighth in the 1960s.[143] And most of these were in the South, teaching manual trades in just a few schools. Things had indeed changed since the days of Laurent Clerc. At the Convention of American Instructors of the Deaf in 1890 there was this characteristic exchange:

DR. BURT: A teacher in a pure oral school who understands the sign language is out of place. . . . He might demoralize the school in a very short time. Only insofar as he would suppress his inclination to use sign could he be useful. . . .

CHAIR: I would like to hear from a deaf educator.

J. S. LONG: The Chinese women bind their babies' feet to make them small; the Flathead Indians bind their babies' heads to make them flat. And the people who prevent the sign language being used in the education of the deaf . . . are denying the deaf their free mental growth through natural expression of their ideas, and are in the same class of criminals.[144]

Modern studies in multilingual countries such as Canada show that excluding minority teachers and their language from the schools and thus attempting to force the assimilation of minority children carries heavy penalties. Educators become disciplinarians as they pursue the aggressive steps required to stop the child from using his or her primary language—grades are lowered, physical punishment is inflicted, friends are separated—and the school becomes a place of incarceration. An Alsatian student: "When I was in primary school it was forbidden to speak Alsatian both in and out of class. Children were punished if they were caught." An Arab student: "In my boarding school the nuns forced us to speak French to one another, even when we were playing. We had a special dog collar that every violator of the rule had to wear." A deaf student: "I resented having my lessons hurled at me. It seemed as if all the words, for which I never cared a tinker's damn, were invented for the sole purpose of harassing and tormenting me. . . . How I hated my teacher, my school, the whole creation."[145] In this kind of environment the minority pupil generally makes little progress and many drop out of school before graduating. As a result, educators and legislators in many countries have turned to some form of bilingual education, which, by providing some instruction in the pupil's primary language, implicitly reaffirms his or her linguistic and social identity. It encourages the development of two language repertories, and the evidence is that such children have a decided intellectual advantage over their monolingual peers.[146]

If benevolent authority is demeaning, misguided, and self-defeating, as Laurent Clerc contended so eloquently, if it is out of step with the morality of our nation, why is the education of the deaf one of the few social institutions that resist officially the fundamental principles of our society? It is easy to identify the reason. If the deaf community had major responsibility for the education of the deaf, they would overhaul it: the sign language would play a much larger role, and deaf teachers would be hired in much larger numbers, often instead of hearing teachers of lesser or equal qualifications. And what might happen then? Why, deaf students would have the freedom to choose the teaching profession and to emulate Jean Massieu. Deaf children would have role models, just as Clerc and countless others had Massieu as a model. Education might be enhanced, not only because of more ready communication between teacher and pupil, but also because deaf teachers can be expected to have a particularly sympathetic interest in the results of their teaching, to be particularly good at matching instruction to their pupils' abilities, to be particularly ready to spend time with them.

"We do not discuss deafness vicariously," a deaf teacher wrote recently, "but from direct experience. We are able to recreate scenes that actually occurred when we sought employment, when we pursued graduate work, when a salesman came into our homes. We teach students to develop a perspective and sense of reality about deafness. We are able to say and do things that will not have the same effect when coming from a hearing teacher. If students indulge in self-pity, for example, I say, 'Let's make a poster with the words I AM DEAF and I'll give you a cup and you can go out and beg.' If this came from a hearing person, their response might be, 'What the hell do you know about our problems?' I should not be here defending deaf teachers, I should be singing their praises. Beyond their duties in the classroom and the work they keep doing long after the bell has rung, they often act as parent substitutes because many deaf students are unable to satisfy their emotional needs at home, since their parents cannot communicate with them."[147]

There is, however, one serious argument against the deaf teacher to which the hearing majority clings and which we need to examine; it is Bell's argument: the deaf teacher generally cannot help the student learn oral language and will use sign with him instead.

I have just reasoned that this is not a choice for the majority community to make, that the deaf community must set its own priorities. But there is good reason to believe that, even if the deaf community embraced the oralist goal, even if the aim is above all to give the signing child a mastery of English, even then it is not appropriate to exclude deaf teachers. Here is the reason.

For the last hundred years or so, the general assumption has been that if the deaf child uses sign extensively, if deaf teachers using American Sign Language as the vehicle of instruction are employed, the child's acquisition of spoken and written English will be impaired—if only by reducing his opportunities to use them. However, the findings of recent research concerning the structure and processing of language invite us to take a fresh look at that assumption.[148] First we ask, Do the structures of manual and oral language have nothing in common, so that mastery of the one cannot facilitate mastery of the other? To the extent that language is a sensory and motor skill, manual and oral languages are quite different, but to the extent that language is a cognitive ability, they must be quite similar. Is most of understanding a sentence, be it lipread or heard, in the eye (or ear), or is most of understanding a sentence in the mind? Linguistic inquiry has shown us that manual language has principles of word formation and principles of sentence construction just as oral language does, and this has led us to a conception of language that is more abstract than speaking and listening, or signing and seeing sign.[149] So we answer that language is a capacity of the mind and thus the two languages have much in common despite the difference in the way they are transmitted. It seems as though man's biological capacity for language will out one way or the other, through the little articulators of the mouth or through the larger articulators of the hands and limbs.[150]

Now, recent psycholinguistic research has uncovered a parallel fact: much of the knowledge required to understand and produce a spoken or written sentence is not peculiar to the particular language in which the sentence is communicated. Alexander Graham Bell himself presaged these findings when he wrote: "Let speech teachers realize that intelligibility is almost entirely due to context."[151] He said, correctly, I believe, that there were three requisites to good lipreading. First, the child's eye must be trained to recognize the visible movements of the vocal organs. Second, he must know which words look alike, so that a given movement suggests a group of words from which he can make his choice, guided by context. Third, he must know the structure of the English language, which will assist him in verifying his choices made from inspection and context. But the fact that escaped Bell and subsequent oralist teachers is that the great guide in identifying a spoken word from context is the sense of the sentence, the meaning that the speaker is trying to convey and the listener to grasp.

Now, to interpret a sentence, to arrive at its sense, we depend not only on our knowledge of the meanings and structural roles of the words, we also depend on our knowledge about life—knowledge that is not specific to the particular language in which the sentence is communicated, knowledge that comes from general acculturation. Would a person commit an action like the one I understood? Can it even be done in principle? Would the person being talked about be likely to do it? Interpreting a spoken sentence requires us to bring this practical knowledge to bear alongside the grammatical possibilities and the word possibilities suggested by lipreading. So we start with the plan to teach the child to distinguish movements of the vocal organs and we end by finding that he needs a knowledge of everyday affairs—of human and physical relationships—before he can choose among the possibilities evoked by lipreading, and thus make sense of the sentence.

There is nearly universal agreement that if we should choose a language to give most deaf children a ready knowledge of life around them, manual language is the easiest and most effective—that is just why it is prohibited, because the child tends to use it at every opportunity. Virtually everyone, including Bell, agrees that spoken or written English is a poor choice of language to use with most deaf if the goal is rapid, facile communication to obtain intellectual development. So if using spoken or written English depends on a sensory and motor skill that needs practice, if understanding an English sentence is mainly a matter of visual or auditory discriminations and producing a sentence mainly a matter of moving the lips or the hand, then every opportunity to practice is sought, and deaf teachers can be less helpful than hearing ones in extending that practice, at least when it comes to speech. But if using spoken or written English depends on abstract linguistic abilities and practical knowledge, then the best classroom instruction may be provided by deaf and hearing teachers who use American Sign Language as the vehicle of instruction. This will give the deaf child the intellectual abilities that bear the burden of composing and comprehending a sentence—to which must be added, of course, a knowledge of the particulars of English.

Thus, the goal of leading the deaf child to a mastery of spoken and written English—only one goal among many—may best be realized through the child's preferred mode of manual communication. To the extent that the linguistic knowledge and the world knowledge required to communicate are more general than the particular language of communication, communicating in sign may significantly enhance communicating in English. And if that is so, then there is no reason to exclude deaf teachers even in this domain and every reason—moral, social, educational—to include them. Indeed, it is the hearing who must demonstrate their good faith and their capacity to work alongside the deaf teachers by working to acquire their language.

TWELVE

THE INCURABLE

DEAFNESS

None so deaf as those that will not hear.
—MATTHEW HENRY (1662–1714)

Incredible as it may seem, it took only a small clique of hearing educators and businessmen, late in the last century, to release a tidal wave of oralism that swept over Western Europe, drowning all its signing communities. In America, the submersion of sign language was nearly as complete for, although the European wave reached our shores attenuated, Alexander Graham Bell and his speech association had cleared the way for its progress from east to west.

Now, one hundred years later, the waters seem to be receding ever so slightly in a few American states, in Denmark and Sweden, in France, allowing a glimpse of a few tentative stirring of life: here, the hands of an interpreter are seen to move; there, a deaf actress signs; elsewhere, a teacher signs to his class. Still, nowhere are signing communities granted the status of other language minorities, nowhere are the deaf allowed an important influence in the education of deaf children, nowhere are the deaf enabled to graduate from high school in substantial numbers, nowhere does national policy implement what national ideals demand: self-fulfillment for the deaf as for all other citizens.

How were the signing communities of the Western world laid waste? By a conspiracy I will describe that pursued personal self-interest through a series of self-styled congresses. The first such meeting in the recrudescence of oralism was a gathering of a few directors of private schools for the deaf in France and some others who dubbed themselves the "World Congress for Improving the Welfare of Deaf-Mutes." It had been prompted by two Parisian railroad barons and financiers, Isaac and Eugène Pereire, son and grandson of Jacob Pereire, in an effort to secure at last their birthright, the recognition of their forebear as the savior of the deaf and the commercial exploitation of his miraculous but secret method.[1]

This uncanny resumption of the struggle between Pereire and Epée nearly a century after they were buried was precipitated by a coincidence. A relative of Eugène Pereire's wife, visiting friends in Geneva, learned of a Frenchman exiled there directing a small school for the deaf in a way few others were then conducted—without using the language of the deaf. Eugène Pereire corresponded with the director, Marius Magnat, and arranged to hire one of his teachers to open a small oral school for the deaf in a Paris suburb in 1873. The following year, Magnat came to Paris and Pereire gave him a sheaf of his grandfather's manuscripts and a copy of the biography by Edouard Séguin in the hope that Magnat would discover J. R. Pereire's famous secret method, the secret that Eugène's father, Isaac, had been unable to elicit from Marie Marois. Imagine Magnat's pleasure at finding in those yellowed pages the very method he had been using all along at his school in Geneva—or so he said. He hastened to inform Eugène Pereire, who, naturally, hired him to give a normal course explaining his technique.

On the same trip, Magnat met a government inspector of primary schools named Félix Hément, who had under his aegis a small class of deaf pupils in a parochial school for hearing children, all that remained of Blanchet's experiment. Hément introduced Magnat to the Brothers of Christian Schools, who taught the class and who agreed to have two of their order accompany Magnat back to Geneva to learn his methods, presumably with funding from Pereire; one of the brothers returned to Paris a convert to oralism and in turn converted the other brothers. When Magnat also returned with some of his pupils in tow, it was decided that, instead of training teachers, he would give a series of public lectures arranged by Hément. The public was astonished to learn, Magnat reports, that the "French method" of educating the deaf was not the silent method of Epée but the speaking method of Pereire.

The lectures were only one part of a carefully orchestrated plan "to erect a kind of monument to the memory of J. R. Pereire," in the words of one of his biographers, retained by his grandson. Much as in America Bell would shortly create the Association to Promote the Teaching of Speech to the Deaf, and as in England St. John Ackers had just formed the Society for Training Teachers of the Deaf and Diffusion of the German System, so Eugène Pereire established the J. R. Pereire Society to propagate the oral method. He secured as vice-president of his society a Paris city councilman,

Eugène Pereire

Photographie Bibliothèque Nationale, Paris

ISAAC PEREIRE

Eugène Rigault. Like its English-language counterparts, the society published a bulletin and offered normal courses; graduates were given a diploma and a cash award. Next Pereire opened a private oral school named after his grandfather and hired Magnat, his lecture series completed, as the director. Like Hubbard, Bell, and Ackers, Pereire was determined to provide an alternative to the national schools, in which the lower classes and manual language predominated. He knew that upper-class parents, rarely deaf themselves, wanted their deaf children to speak the same language they did, and that money was no object. Pereire also hired Inspector Hément to write a second, more concise, biography of his grandfather, establishing that Magnat was following in his footsteps and announcing the opening of the Pereire school (where Hément became a member of the advisory board).[2] Finally, Pereire arranged with Ernest La Rochelle of the national library to undertake a thorough scholarly analysis of his grandfather's life and works with the aim of writing a third biography and finally resolving the issue of a secret method, and he hired him as general agent of the Pereire Society.

There were only four other small oral schools in France at this time, and their directors, with the exception of Benjamin Dubois, who was deaf, were naturally intimates of the Pereire clique. Dubois's school, with some half-dozen pupils, was the oldest, although it had only recently been separated again from the National Institution. Then came the family school founded by Blanchet's assistant, Auguste Houdin, with a score of pupils, followed by that at Saint-Hippolyte-du-Fort. The directors of both schools were to be seen at the annual banquet given by the Pereire Society to honor its namesake. Lastly, Magnat's predecessor at Geneva, Jacques Hugentobler, had gone to Lyon to tutor the two deaf sons of the count of Monteynard, then opened his own school. A native of German-speaking Switzerland, he was an ardent oralist.[3] The private oral schools of Magnat, Houdin, and Hugentobler reestablished the class structure in the education of the deaf that it had once had in the time of Jacob Pereire but had lost in the rapid expansion of national and parochial schools.[4]

As part of the Universal Exposition of 1878, several congresses and lectures would be held in Paris: Hément and Magnat arranged to give a lecture with pupils from the Pereire school. A month before the opening of the exposition, however, Magnat received a circular from its directorate announcing a forthcoming congress on the blind, which inspired him to organize a sister meeting on the deaf. Of course, it was very late in the day to launch a new congress but the instructions for the meeting of the blind provided for three sections on "special topics" and Magnat asked the secretary-general to allocate them to him. His appeals were refused until Hément persuaded his superior in the Ministry of Public Instruction to intercede in their behalf. Even then, the help from the exposition was grudging and in the end Magnat sent out his own circular—to a select group.[5]

Hément and Magnat went to see the director of the national school for the deaf in Paris, Martin Etcheverry, and asked him to serve as president of their meeting. Etcheverry was in several ways the French counterpart of Edward Gallaudet. He believed in the combined system; he claimed that a large school must have sign language as the basis of instruction and that German schools circumvented this requirement by admitting students who were only partially deaf. He affirmed that many of the Paris students, trained in their primary (manual) language, were accomplished teachers, artists, craftsmen; and he reminded his visitors that the congress of German deaf had recently reaffirmed—even in that land—the necessity of sign language in deaf education.[6] When he learned, moreover, that the Pereire Society was arranging this rump meeting for self-serving purposes, he refused to have anything to do with it. It is puzzling that Magnat and Hément asked him, for they must have known his views. Perhaps they thought he would add legitimacy to their meeting, since Etcheverry held arguably the most prestigious post in deaf education in Europe. Or they may have thought that collaboration would bring him some way toward their position. Most likely, they asked him first, knowing that he would refuse, so they could then ask his disgruntled predecessor, Léon Vaïsse.

Vaïsse had tried to steer the Paris school on a middle course. He was fluent in French Sign Language and had helped to launch the New York school on its career of instruction using American Sign Language. But he was as well the first professor in the Paris school to teach the articulation course and the only one who had tried to implement Ordinaire's oralist designs forty years earlier. Vaïsse had also developed a system of visible speech and had published several monographs on articulation, but his efforts after he had become director of the national institution to expand oral teaching beyond an hour a day for select students had been thwarted in several ways. There were not enough teachers to generalize the practice. Moreover, four of the six professors and all the assistants were deaf; they were joined by the hearing professors and the pupils in opposing more oralism. Finally, Vaïsse's superiors in the Ministry of the Interior also denied him their support. In 1861, they had asked the Academy of Sciences to consider the vexed question of the relative roles of sign and speech in the education of the deaf, and it had concluded, in the words of the distinguished scholar Adolphe Franck, who wrote the report, that oral instruction "disturbs, more than it serves the development of relations between the deaf and hearing. Nothing can create speech in a child who has never known it. . . . What is taught him under the name of speech is merely a dangerous and useless sham."[7]

Even so, Vaïsse had continued to press for more speech, eventually precipitating two revolts by faculty and students. Finally, the ministry, perhaps reminded too vividly of Ordinaire's failure, had asked him for his resignation (he was by then seventy-five) and replaced him with Etcheverry, director of the Bordeaux school.[8]

The ministry appointed Vaïsse honorary director, but that could hardly salve his wounded pride. Magnat and Hément knew their man; he accepted their invitation with pleasure. The "congress" opened the last week in September at the Tuileries Palace, with all those I have named attending. Vaïsse's vice-presidents were Councilman Rigault and a certain Emile Grosselin, a stenographer in the Chamber of Deputies whose father had developed a phonetic alphabet, a "reduction" of the letters of French.

Of the twenty-seven teachers attending the meeting, twenty-three of them French, one or two others merit particular notice. The superintendent of schools in Boston was there, representing the Horace Mann School. A dramatic actor by the name of Fourcade was present; some twenty years earlier, he had begun teaching voice to the deaf and aspired, without success, to an appointment at the Paris institution. Instead, he gave normal courses at Bordeaux and Toulouse for the Sisters of Nevers and the Brothers of Saint-Gabriel, who sent representatives to the meeting. Most recently, he had aided a disciple in establishing a little school in Avignon, for which he solicited the Pereires' support, since his own methods, he said, were close to those of their famous ancestor.[9]

I have saved the most important and colorful figure for last. Don Seraphino Balestra, director of the deaf school in Como, near Milan, played a major role in the series of congresses establishing oralism. Balestra was tall, fine-figured, with a Roman face and an eagle eye. Pereire's biographer La Rochelle called him "one of the most passionate apostles of speech." Another oralist who knew him said he resembled "one of the warrior monks of olden times who threw the Christian armies on the shores of Palestine. . . . The Spanish blood that was in his veins gave him brio and Andalusian vigor." Balestra loved the past, particularly its architecture, and taught at the diocesan seminary of Como. "But his excessive application to these studies endangered his mental life." Possibly that is why he was made director of the deaf school, which had been languishing with a score of girls taught by two nuns. Balestra took a normal course at the Paris institution, returned to Como, and brought public attention and funds to his school. Then he visited far-flung European institutions in search of the best method not of educating the deaf but of "restoring them to society," the catch phrase of those who put teaching their own language above all else. "On his return, like Peter the Hermit, he preached a crusade in all the institutions for the deaf in France and Italy along his route. *La parola per la parola* was his text." Said a third oralist who knew him: "He was an ardent propagandist but he lacked science and patience."[10]

As the congress unfolded, a consensus emerged that was surprisingly conservative compared with the position these very same persons would hold as they became increasingly caught up in the oralist tide. Gallaudet claimed the congress advocated the combined system, which is true, but with this important difference from the American understanding of the term: these oralists thought the national oral language should be the vehicle of instruction and that sign was a necessary auxiliary. Balestra fought this eclecticism with all his might, his arms flapping like the blades of a windmill, his body in perpetual motion, his face taking a thousand forms. "Everyone recognizes the superiority of the oral method over the sign method," he said, and added disingenuously, "For the glory of France, choose one of these two doctrines." But he did not prevail. Not then.

The congress members also agreed that the oral method was unsuitable for some of the deaf, for whom the language of instruction must be sign language. These were the pupils, they said, with inadequate intellectual training or capacity. Because the teachers could identify these pupils only by their performance under the oral method, the resolution amounted to advocating sign for those who made no progress with speech. Perhaps Gallaudet was right after all; this policy comes very close to the one adopted by his conference of principals exactly a decade earlier, which he named the "combined system."[11] As oralism spread to growing numbers of institutions, the pupils who proved refractory, hence "retarded," became legion and this clause took on great importance, particularly in government schools, which could not limit admissions.

Since this congress was composed largely of people outside the government-sanctioned system of educating the deaf in three national institutions and numerous regional schools under the Ministry of Interior (Department of Welfare), it is not surprising that all delegates agreed on the desirability of removing schools for the deaf from their present ministry and placing them instead under the Ministry of Public Instruction. But unquestionably, their most important act at this meeting was to plan a second and larger oralist gathering. Hugentobler suggested annual national meetings (he proposed Lyon for the next) and triennial international congresses, save that the next be held in two years. Balestra proposed convening the next congress in Italy, and Vaïsse was appointed honorary president of an organizing committee including Magnat, La Rochelle, and so on—with only one advocate of sign language, the chaplain at Saint-Jacques. Magnat urged a program committee for the Italian meeting; most thought it would be redundant but he insisted and the others conceded. As it turned out, this allowed Magnat to draw up singlehandedly a list of topics for the Italian congress, which he sent to school principals in Europe and America along with a request for written opinions on the issues. Then he wrote a report on the papers that were sent in, summarizing and discussing them while assailing views that left crawl space for the language of the deaf, and distributed his report to all congress delegates on their arrival.

It pleased the members and friends of the Pereire Society, who organized the national meeting at Lyon a year later, to entitle it the First National Conference for Improving the Lot of the Deaf. Houdin was president, Vaïsse, honorary president. As far as I can determine, no deaf people were present. The meeting reaffirmed the eclectic prescription of a year earlier but placed more emphasis, if anything, on the importance of sign language, "which must have a very large part in the education of the deaf," and the resolution added that manual and oral methods, "far from excluding one another, support each other mutually and conduce toward the same end."[12] A second resolution affirmed the legitimacy of the German practice of screening admissions to oral schools.

Abbé Balestra had remained in Paris after the first Pereire reunion in the hope of convincing the ministry to hire him. He devoted eight months and countless visits to this attempt and prepared a report on the conversion of Italian educators to oralism, in which he had played a key role. It seems that up to the time of Gallaudet's tour, most Italian instruction of the deaf had been in their manual language. The first school had been founded in Rome by a disciple of Epée's, the abbé Sylvestri; the second in Genoa by one of Sicard's, Ottavio Assarotti. Then came the school at Siena shortly after Sicard's death, founded and directed for fifty years by the father of Italian education of the deaf, Thomas Pendola.[13] Heavily influenced by the example of Genoa, Pendola's books and practices were predicated on sign language. Next Balestra's own school at Como was established and finally, among the key institutions, the Provincial School for the Poor opened in Milan under Giulio Tarra. Like all the other Italian directors, Balestra had been content to practice the French system, which had become generalized in the wake of Napoleon's armies. Shortly after Gallaudet's visit, however, he received a little brochure entitled *Instruction of the Deaf by the German Method (Method Amman)*, which had been written by David Hirsch, the oralist director at Rotterdam, and sent broadcast to European schools for the deaf. It was this brochure in turn that sent Balestra on his own tour, in the course of which he visited Hirsch and observed his method firsthand.[14] After his return to Como he taught a deaf class totally without sign, and found his efforts successful in a short five months. Then, he goes on to explain, he went around to the other institutions in Italy to convert them. In Milan, Tarra had told Gallaudet that no more than a third of his pupils could profit from speech instruction,[15] but now he resolved that a mixture of methods was prejudicial to his goals and he would follow the prescription of "pure oralism."[16] Signs would be banished, and newcomers housed and taught apart from the old students until all the manually taught students had been graduated.[17] There was a second school for the deaf in Milan, the Royal Institution, destined for the children of wealthy parents who could afford its fees. It, too, converted at about this time.[18] The following year,

Pendola at Siena followed suit. In his seventies when converted to oralism by Balestra, Pendola totally reformed his methods, launched an impassioned oralist journal, and convened the first national congress of Italian educators of the deaf. That meeting, held in Siena five years before the French congress in Lyon, had reached a similar consensus: sign language was essential for the instruction of the deaf initially but should be phased out as the pupils acquired speech and lipreading.

The oralist transformation of the Como and Milan schools triggered that, in turn, of all those in Lombardy and Venetia, while Siena's conversion set the example for all the schools in central and southern Italy. So, by the end of 1871—as Balestra stated in his report to the French minister—Turin, Venice, Bologna, Rome, Naples, Palermo were all teaching in the Italian language. Now with Austria, Switzerland, Belgium, Holland, Norway, and Italy using oral methods, "the world is waiting for France. . . . It will be your glory, M. le Ministre, to instigate this reform by appointing me to the Paris institution." Give me only two months, Balestra begged, and you shall speak with your deaf pupils.

When Balestra heard that the minister had agreed to his proposal in principle, he drew up a plan for the total reform of all deaf education in France—some eighty-five institutions including the parochial schools. But in practice, the minister had something less sweeping in mind. He created a commission and asked Balestra to teach a single demonstration class before them for their evaluation. The abbé appeared as requested and gave the commissioners a lecture on the order of teaching the sounds of French. Then he had some pupils blow out candles. The commission concluded, naturally, that it had too slender a basis to reach any conclusion and recommended an extension of the experimental class, provided it was short. Balestra asked for a fortnight but at the end of that time he asked for four months.

Balestra's importunities led the minister to take several other steps. He sent his inspector-general, Oscar Claveau, on a three-week tour of fifteen oral institutions.[19] Claveau returned only to set out again, this time with the mother superior and one of the sisters in charge of the national institution at Bordeaux (reserved for girls). Claveau had no familiarity with sign language, yet his report turned on that issue. He stated that sign could not be a trustworthy vehicle of instruction because it lacks precision: he claimed, quite mistakenly as it turns out, that a sign by itself does not indicate whether it is a noun or a verb; hence the language has no grammar and grammatical roles can be deduced only from the whole sentence. He went on to explain how Epée tried but failed to remedy this defect with methodical signs.

In Germany, the difficulties in the way of speech have been overcome, Claveau argued. "The schools showing the greatest progress are those where the use of sign is most severely proscribed." The students are taught that people who gesture are inferior to the rest of mankind; the older students then help to repress signing among the younger. It is true that German and Swiss schools select their students, but we are assured that only a small percentage are rejected. Claveau concluded by recommending pure oralism; even if it be at the expense of general education, at least the pupils will have a means of communicating with the rest of society.[20] Clerc's old friend Forestier sent the minister a rebuttal based on fifty years of teaching the deaf: "Sign language is rich in its expressions, extremely simple in its forms; it meets all mental needs; there is no way more direct, certain, and effective to initiate the deaf-mute in the secrets of our [French] language."[21] The rebuttal was ignored.

The minister ordered the Bordeaux school to open as an oral school, just at the time the meeting was taking place in Lyon, and to isolate the old students from the new. After the meeting he met with Magnat, who cited the resolutions of the Paris and Lyon congresses and loudly assailed the reactionary stance of Etcheverry at the head of the Paris school. These developments took place in a period of rising nationalism following the founding of the Third Republic. France was beginning an era of coloniza- tion and diffusion of the French language. The minister ordered that oral French should be the sole language of instruction in all the schools under his control. He fired Etcheverry, replacing him with an otologist, Louis Peyron. Thus he sealed the fate not just of the six hundred pupils in the three national institutions but also of all pupils in the regional and depart- mental schools, and even in those private schools that received state subsidy.[22] Scholarships for pupils attending Forestier's school, for example, were pres- ently cut off.

Finally the moment came, after the fact, to evaluate Balestra's class. Claveau was assigned the task. Apparently the results were unsatisfactory, but excuses were not hard to find. The pupils, drawn from Saint-Jacques, had not been segregated from their signing companions, they had received no oral instruction two days a week, and the trial had been too brief—so said Claveau.[23] An idea of Balestra's difficulties may be had from an account of one classroom incident published in the silent press:[24] "The breath of this priest was extremely repugnant. Overwhelmed by the odor, one articulation pupil stood on his tiptoes, went to the blackboard, seized a piece of chalk, wrote in large letters NO MORE! and retook his place without a sound." Etcheverry, when informed, deprived the whole class of their Sunday out- ing. Balestra requested a longer trial under better conditions but presently the Italian congress planned by the Pereire Society convened in Milan, and no one was interested any longer in Balestra's success or failure.

At the Paris school recently, I saw a poster bearing a sketch of a casket and the words *Milan 1880*. Considering all the present bitterness of the

French deaf toward the Congress of Milan, and all the anger among the
deaf on both sides of the Atlantic just after the congress, I had imagined
a substantial meeting, imposing sets of arguments, a body of findings at odds
with deaf people's steadfast espousal of their manual languages. The proceedings of the congress reveal nothing of the sort. In fact, the meeting was
conceived and conducted as a brief rally by and for opponents of manual
language. Setting aside the speeches of welcome and adieu, and the excur-
sions and visits, we find that the Milan congress amounted to two dozen
hours in which three or four oralists reassured the rest of the rightness of
their actions in the face of troubling evidence to the contrary. Nevertheless,
the meeting at Milan was the single most critical event in driving the languages of the deaf beneath the surface; it is the single most important cause
—more important than hearing loss—of the limited educational achievement of today's deaf men and women, eighty percent of whom, in America,
are engaged in manual or unskilled labor.[25]

Writing from Milan to Harriet Rogers at the Clarke school, Susanna Hull
exulted, "The victory for the cause of pure speech was in great measure
gained, as many were heard to say afterwards, before the actual work of the
congress began."[26] Similarly, Hull's fellow oralist, the headmaster at the
Royal School for Deaf Children, Richard Elliott, reported that the congress
"was mainly a partisan gathering. The machinery to register its decrees on
the lines desired by its promoters had evidently been prepared beforehand
and to me it seemed that the main feature was enthusiasm and fervidly
eloquent advocacy of the 'orale pure' rather than calm deliberation on the
advantages and disadvantages of methods."[27] The Italian promoters, who,
as Balestra explained, had been traveling the "pure oral" route for some
years, had been dismayed by the eclectic resolution of the Paris congress and
were frankly alarmed by the further backsliding at Lyon; this meeting must
not be allowed to fail. The French delegation was of like mind. The minister
had ordained pure oralism and fired the head of the Paris school; the minister's representatives sought vindication by an international congress. The
Pereire Society, like the Ackers group from England, were equally desirous
of ringing acclaim for their position. The location chosen, the makeup of
the organizing committee, the congress schedule and demonstrations, the
composition of the membership, the officers of the meeting—all elements
were artfully orchestrated to produce the desired effect.

In the report that Magnat distributed, dedicated to his employer, Eugène
Pereire, he denies that oral instruction is expensive, that it succeeds only
with the semi-mute, that its product is unnatural-sounding speech, that it
slows mental culture. He ridicules the view that speech is merely an ancillary
skill and an inappropriate vehicle for instruction. He rejects the claim that
the deaf lipread only familiar people well. The advantages of articulation
training, he argues, are that it restores the deaf to society, allows moral and

intellectual development, and proves useful in employment. Moreover, it permits communication with the illiterate, facilitates the acquisition and use of ideas, is better for the lungs, has more precision than sign, makes the pupil the equal of his hearing counterpart, allows spontaneous, rapid, sure, and complete expression of thought, and humanizes the user. Manually taught children are defiant and corruptible. This arises from the disadvantages of sign language. It is doubtful that sign can engender thought. It is concrete. It is not truly connected with feeling and thought. It is a dialect you must learn, not universal, "and this alone condemns it." It sets the deaf person apart, it lacks precision. Its syntax is in conflict with that of the occidental languages and it cannot help in the study of written language. Sign cannot convey number, gender, person, time, nouns, verbs, adverbs, adjectives, he claims. The teacher cannot genuinely communicate with his class in sign; it does not allow him to raise the deaf-mute above his sensations. In sign the deaf cannot link secondary ideas to the principal idea. Since signs strike the senses materially they cannot elicit reasoning, reflection, generalization, and above all abstraction as powerfully as can speech. The sign image takes up more space in the eye than the [labial] image of the spoken word and is not always clearly discernible. The deaf-mute does not perceive his own signs. Signs interfere with manual labor. And on and on.[28]

If the arriving congress-goer had any time remaining after digesting all this, he was urged to attend exhibitions of the achievements of the oral method. Saturday was reserved for the Provincial School for the Poor under Tarra, and Sunday for the Royal Institution under Eliseo Ghislandi. Moreover, all afternoon sessions were canceled to free delegates to visit these schools. It is clear from personal accounts of the congress that the speech and lipreading of the Italian pupils made a great impression on the observers previously uncommitted to oralism. The Italian promoters affirmed this themselves: the conclusions of the meeting were not based on this or that paper or person, they said, but on the facts to be seen in the Italian schools; this is the difference, they claimed proudly, between other conventions and Milan, and this is why some who voted against pure oralism at Lyon were converted in Italy.[29]

Yet there was reason to fear that the delegates were being hoodwinked in the Milan schools. One American observer of the exhibitions reports: "There was evidence of long previous preparation, of severe drilling and personal management to produce the most striking effect. There was an apparently studied absence of definite and all-important special information as each case came up for exhibition. . . . My neighbors, themselves Italian and articulation teachers, informed me that [the best pupils] were not congenitally deaf and had probably mastered speech before entering the institution."[30]

Gallaudet agrees: "I found that many of the pupils exhibited as illustrating what the 'pure oral method' could accomplish with deaf-mutes had in fact learned to speak before losing their hearing."[31] The British headmaster Richard Elliott, although an advocate of oralism, similarly concluded "that everything had been carefully rehearsed beforehand. . . . [The pupils] did answer correctly—in fact, they answered too correctly for there were apparently no mistakes made nor was there any deliberation before the answers were given." Indeed, pupils even began answering questions before they were completed.[32] A few pupils were examined at great length, Gallaudet reported, while others were asked but a single question. Only the Italian teachers were allowed to direct the questions. "No information was given as to the history of any pupil—whether deafness was congenital or acquired, whether speech had developed before hearing was lost or not."[33] From a statistical report on deafness in Italy distributed during the congress, Elliott calculated that fifteen percent of the deaf in the province and eighteen percent nationwide were semi-mute, whereas sixty-three percent at the Royal School and seventy percent at the Provincial School were semi-mute. It certainly seemed likely that these schools were screening admissions and exhibiting primarily students who had learned to speak as every hearing child does.[34]

One observer, from the New York school, found the performances, even those of the semi-mutes, far from satisfactory. Although on the average there were only seven pupils to a teacher at the Milan schools, and sometimes as few as four,[35] this delegate thought the exercises in lipreading "were very nearly a failure." The teachers elaborately mouthed their words "and even then were not understood when off the beaten track"; and Italians unknown to the pupils who attempted to talk with them encountered great difficulty in communicating. He also found the quality of the articulation uneven, "as varied as the pupils."[36] Elliott asked to see the children lipread while an Italian stranger read a passage unknown to them. His request was refused.[37]

While the exhibitions of the "pure oral method" were going on in the Milan schools, James Denison, principal of the Columbian Institution and a deaf educator of many years' experience, observed the pupils awaiting their turn outside. They were signing. "Two or three times a group, noticing the intentness with which I was watching their conversation, abruptly suspended the sign-making part of it. . . . I inquired in signs whether they ever used gestures. The response was a blank mystified look on each face, then a general shaking of heads. But when I reminded them of what I had just observed, they pleaded guilty, with a propitiatory smile, to having partaken of the forbidden fruit of the tree of knowledge."[38] Since signs were used so much outside the classroom, Denison concludes, they might not be entirely unknown inside.

Another exhibition was provided one evening when children from the Royal Institution performed two dramas. The stage was lavishly draped, the scenery effective, the costumes perfect. The parts were recited orally and between acts musical interludes were performed by pupils from schools for the deaf and for the blind. Scripts were provided to the delegates, and Elliott reports that he could follow the parts readily with the words before him.[39] Yet another exhibition involved some thirty graduates of the Milan school, men and women who had become workers, accountants, farmers, fathers and mothers. They were questioned by Abbé Tarra on their professions, events in their lives, plans for the future. One broke into tears in the midst of his discourse. The abbé comforted him and kissed him on both cheeks. The audience applauded and Tarra explained that the speaker was overcome by the thought of an elder brother who was speechless because he had attended school before the oralist reform.[40]

The composition of the membership of the congress was another element ensuring the oralist outcome in advance. Of the 164 delegates, the Italians exceeded a majority by ten and there were fifty-six from France; the committed delegates from these two countries were seven-eighths of the membership. The amity between them went deeper than the desire of each group for language unification in its own country. The armies of Napoleon III had recently fought alongside Italian soldiers against Austria, and the French emperor had supported the Italian king in his struggle for national unity—as more than one delegate mentioned during the congress addresses. One writer quipped that British and French delegates there took German lessons from an Italian priest (the abbé Tarra).[41] The Germans themselves had not been invited, for Prussia had recently trounced France, precipitating the flight of the emperor, the surrender of the French, and the founding of the Third Republic. The Italians would hardly persuade the French by aligning themselves with Germans.

Of the eight British delegates, six were brought by St. John Ackers.[42] Only the American delegation of five was properly accredited (by the Conference of Principals). It included James Denison, the two Gallaudet brothers, the principal of the New York Institution, and a member of his board. All and any persons were welcome at the congress on payment of the fee, with the result that the five American delegates, who represented fifty-one schools and six thousand pupils—more than all the other delegates put together—were outvoted ten to one by congress-goers from the city of Milan alone![43]

Among the French were Claveau, Peyron, and Adolphe Franck (the scholar whose skepticism about oral methods had helped to oust Vaïsse)—all representing the Ministry of the Interior. Houdin represented the rival Ministry of Public Instruction. And there were the Pereire Society group and Houdin's family. There were also eighteen brothers of Saint-Gabriel, several of the whom told Gallaudet that signs "could not be dispensed with in the instruction of deaf-mutes," that "not all deaf-mutes could succeed under the oral method,"[44] and that they intended to say so before the end of the meeting. The first to speak, however, was their leader, Brother Hubert, the inspector of schools for the order. La Rochelle's report to Eugène Pereire tells what happened: "Brother Hubert publicly thanked your family, Mr. President, for the liberality which enabled the brothers of his congregation to be present at Milan in considerable numbers, and closed by declaring himself today unreservedly in favor of the pure oral method."[45] Thereafter, all the brothers voted as a bloc for the pure oral method.

The British delegation included, apart from the Ackers group, a private teacher of the deaf and self-styled psychologist, the Reverend Thomas Arnold. Author of a monumental oralist history of deaf education, he was shortly to become the intellectual leader of his profession in Britain. "Articulate language is superior to sign," Arnold told the congress, "because it is the method employed by nature. Modern science teaches us that what is natural ends up with the upper hand." And: "No doubt signs are often animated and picturesque but they are absolutely inadequate for abstraction." And much more of the same.[46]

The officers of the Milan congress—like the location, organizers, exhibitions, and membership—were chosen to ensure the oralist outcome. The organizers proposed to select Giulio Tarra as the president by acclamation. This rotund abbot in his late fifties, dressed in a black cassock and white collar, was called fervid by his supporters and rabid by his detractors when it came to the language of the deaf minority. For example, in one of his public lectures on the education of the deaf, he said, "Gesture is not the true language of man which suits the dignity of his nature. Gesture, instead of addressing the mind, addresses the imagination and the senses. Moreover, it is not and never will be the language of society. . . . Thus, for us it is an absolute necessity to prohibit that language and to replace it with living speech, the only instrument of human thought."[47] Tarra published his views at Milan in a pamphlet, which he distributed to the congress members. He proposed several honorary presidents: Pereire, Vaïsse, Balestra, Hirsch, and Augusto Zucchi, board president at the Royal School. Two professors at that school and Emile Grosselin, the stenographer, were appointed vice-presidents.

For the agenda of the meeting, the program committee had prepared a list of twenty-six questions. Since no one at the meeting had a method, strictly speaking, of teaching speech or lipreading, the congress could not and did not discuss language-teaching methods. What remained for the agenda were various parameters of education, such as class size, construction of buildings, age of admission and of graduation, the desirability of teacher training, and so on. These items did not fire the imagination of the congress-goers. For most, the burning need was to reaffirm the philosophy underlying their daily endeavors, the replacement of the language of the deaf minority with the national oral language. As Houdin reported to his minister, "The superiority of speech teaching was no longer the question."[48] A comparable modern spectacle might be a congress of European Africanists who knew no African languages reaffirming the necessity of occidental languages in Africa —in the absence of any Africans.

The opening address by Zucchi enjoined the delegates to "remember that living speech is the privilege of man, the sole and certain vehicle of thought, the gift of God, of which it has been truly said, 'Speech is the expression of the soul / As the soul is the expression of divine thought.'"

Magnat was the first delegate to gain the floor and he proceeded to read his monograph, distributed in advance of the congress, with its litany of objections to sign. After twenty minutes, the president cut him off. Franck then rose to deny Magnat's accusation that the French national schools still used sign: for many years they have been using Valade-Gabel's method for teaching French by writing, without sign. Magnat insisted on his right to read his book. The president put it to the assembly, which voted him back into his seat. He retook his place, says one observer, "with utmost indignation, muttering threats of retaliation."[49] There were calls to proceed with the agenda, and countercalls. Finally Balestra took the floor, saying, "Here's a book written in 1855 discussing the incontestable superiority of the oral method. Now those who agree with this opinion can vote yes and those who have another view can vote no." That would dispose of the issue. However, the congress could not come to a close so soon after opening.

Mrs. Ackers (registered as the "mother of a deaf child") read a paper on the advantages of speech over sign for the intellectual development of the deaf child. Critics who claim this is precisely its weakness have judged wrongly, she said: "Certainly we should not compare pupils from pure oral schools who have at most seven years in school . . . with pupils from mimic schools in America who have a longer education and are older when they leave school."

Edward Gallaudet spoke in behalf of the combined system. Speech is important, he said, but no deaf person would change places with a speaking savage or a speaking derelict. Thousands of graduates of the signing schools in Britain, France, and America, "though not in the possession of speech, are living today as educated, intelligent, self-sustaining men and women, happy and prosperous in all the relations of life, useful citizens, grateful for the blessings they have received."[50]

Balestra took the floor again with an impassioned appeal. Arnold said of Balestra that he was a rare man who dwelt apart, for he could find none who would share his ardor. "His gestures, his expressions, his fiery zeal with his vigorous Italian, made us first suspect the presence or absence of something that disturbed his mental balance. But we erred. The man was all there but possessed of a soul whose sympathy was with deaf-mutes. This was his ambition, his mission, and on it he lavished all his genius and affection."[51]

"My friends," Balestra said, "don't vote if you cannot, but when you go home tell what you have seen here. *The deaf-mutes of Italy speak.* We are all children of the one Christ who gave us the example. . . . The minister of Christ must open the mouth of the deaf. . . . I will add that for a Catholic priest the mutes must speak, for we have confession and in the countryside the priest would get everything backwards that the deaf-mute tells him in sign. . . . I beg of you: vote for speech, always speech."

Tarra gave a peroration that took most of two sessions and then was read to the congress again in French by a bilingual colleague. "The kingdom of speech," he began, "is a realm whose queen tolerates no rivals. Speech is jealous and wishes to be the absolute mistress. Like the true mother of the child placed in judgment before Solomon, speech wishes it all for her own —instruction, school, deaf-mute—without sharing; otherwise, she renounces all. . . ."

Said Arnold, "Those who heard him the day he delivered his speech will remember it as one of the brightest days in their lives. His figure, countenance, eye and voice were to many their ideal of the teacher of a deaf-mute." He had never heard so clear and melodious a voice, such convincing reasons. Tarra was short, stooped, plain, of ruddy countenance, "but his eye and look were as tender as a mother's. . . . When I heard Tarra describe his conversion to oralism, shape his reasons, recite his practical proofs, in my heart I exclaimed *Il Maestro*: I, too, was justified. Such a time happens only once in life, but like the star that never sets, it shines on through the journey."

"Let us have no illusions," Tarra continued. "To teach speech successfully we must have courage and with a resolute blow cut cleanly between speech and sign. . . . Who would dare say that these disconnected and crude signs that mechanically reproduce objects and actions are the elements of a language? I know that my pupil has only a few imperfect signs, the rudiments of an edifice that should not exist, a few crumbs of a bread that has no consistency and can never suffice for nourishing his soul, a soul that cries out for a moral and social existence."

The next day, Tarra came to what he called his fundamental argument. "Oral speech is the sole power that can rekindle the light God breathed into man when, giving him a soul in a corporeal body, he gave him also a means of understanding, of conceiving, and of expressing himself. . . . While, on the one hand, mimic signs are not sufficient to express the fullness of thought, on the other they enhance and glorify fantasy and all the faculties of the sense of imagination. . . . The fantastic language of signs exalts the senses and foments the passions, whereas speech elevates the mind much more naturally, with calm, prudence and truth and avoids the danger of exaggerating the sentiment expressed and provoking harmful mental impressions." When a deaf-mute confesses an unjust act in sign, Tarra explained, the sensations accompanying the act are reawakened. For example, when the deaf person confesses in sign language that he has been angry, the detestable passion returns to the sinner, which certainly does not aid his moral reform. In speech on the other hand, the penitent deaf-mute reflects on the evil he has committed and there is nothing to excite the passion again. Tarra ended by defying anyone to define in sign the soul, faith, hope, charity, justice, virtue, the angels, God . . . "At this point the gesture he made," said Denison, "was the unmeaning if not misleading one of pointing with the index finger to the ceiling." He was convinced that the abbé Tarra did not know the language he was rejecting so resolutely. "No shape, no image, no design," Tarra concluded, "can reproduce these ideas. Speech alone, divine itself, is the right way to speak of divine matters. Come to our schools and you will see."

All but the Americans voted for a resolution exalting the dominant oral language and disbarring the sign language whatever the nation:

1. The congress, considering the incontestable superiority of speech over signs, for restoring deaf-mutes to social life and for giving them greater facility in language, declares that the method of articulation should have preference over that of signs in the instruction and education of the deaf and dumb.

2. Considering that the simultaneous use of signs and speech has the disadvantage of injuring speech, lipreading and precision of ideas, the congress declares that the pure oral method ought to be preferred.

In the closing moments of the congress, the academician Adolphe Franck cried from the podium, *"Vive la parole!"* This has been the slogan of hearing educators of the deaf down to the present time. But an American deaf leader has written: "1880 was the year that saw the birth of the infamous Milan resolution that paved the way for foisting upon the deaf everywhere a loathed method; hypocritical in its claims, unnatural in its application, mind-deadening and soul-killing in its ultimate results."[52]

James Denison was the only deaf delegate in this congress on the deaf. In America, however, deaf people representing twenty-one states were gathered in Cincinnati at a meeting about the same size as that in Milan, and held at about the same time. They, too, sought to improve the welfare of deaf people, but they had an entirely different conception of what that was. "The meeting was called the National Convention of Deaf-Mutes," said a deaf leader, "and that's that. If oral magicians, who yank educational rabbits out of silk hats and pearls of speech out of the mouths of those who have never heard, choke over it, why bless 'em!"[53] This group of educators, engineers, businessmen, and so on decided to form a permanent association of the deaf and set about drafting a constitution. Robert P. McGregor, the deaf principal of the Ohio school and then the Colorado school, the heir to Thomas Brown as a platform orator, was elected president. Here is what he had to say about the agenda at Milan. "The ascendancy of the pure oral method has been attained by methods that the deaf, as honest, law-abiding citizens abhor, detest, despise, abominate. . . . Must not that be false which required for its support so much imposture, so much trickery, so much coercion; which belittles, or utterly ignores, the opinions of its own output? . . . In the war of methods the verdict of the educated deaf the whole world over is this: the oral method benefits the *few;* the combined system benefits *all* the deaf. . . . Anyone who upholds the oral method, as an exclusive method, is their enemy."[54]

In the aftermath of Milan, "pure oralism" washed over Europe like a flood tide. Many people and schools were swept up in its advance.[55] There is no single explanation for such tides in human affairs. I have cited the confluence of nationalism, elitism, commercialism, and family pride. Another contributing cause was the educators' desire for total control of their classrooms, which cannot be had if the pupils sign and the teacher knows none. The teacher then becomes the linguistic outcast, the handicapped. Nor can he or she acquire the necessary skill in a year, or even two, any more than an Anglophone teacher can so rapidly prepare himself to teach in French. This understandable reluctance of hearing teachers to master a language radically different from their own continues to have the greatest weight in what are misrepresented as pedagogical decisions. There was a time when teachers of the deaf could not practice without a knowledge of their pupils' primary language. But the vast expansion of schools in Europe and America created more professional positions than there were educators and administrators fluent in sign. Increasingly, people with few ties to the deaf community dominated their education.

The Milan resolutions carry their own self-indictment, for if speech had all the advantages claimed for it and sign all the defects, there would be no need to banish sign from the classroom and the playground, to separate the older children who sign from the younger who do not; speech would be embraced as a matter of course, as it is with the hearing. Sign in class is an unwelcome reminder of another, much easier, route to the deaf child's mind.

The oralist reports of Milan were jubilant. "All discussions have ceased," Tarra wrote, "serious objections have of themselves disappeared, and the long struggle between systems has ended. Never perhaps has a scientific victory been proclaimed with less opposition."[56] Bell cited Milan as proof of natural selection: the oral method was fittest to survive.[57] This decision, he wrote, "has been accepted as final by all subsequent conventions of teachers . . . and most of the sign and combined schools of the continent have since adopted the oral method."[58] Houdin announced victory to his minister and cited Franck's impassioned account from the podium at Milan of how Mohammed entered Mecca, struck the heads off the 360 idols of the Kaaba, and cried, "Begone, useless fakes! The true God has revealed himself."[59]

Franck himself reported to the minister of the interior: "As soon as possible, we must instruct orally all the pupils of our national institutions and not a select group. Speech training should be the general rule, the absolute rule."[60] Yet hadn't Franck's report blocked Vaïsse's oralist reform at Saint-Jacques by calling deaf speech a sham and insisting on the merits of sign? "No," Franck temporized, "with regard to sign I don't have to change my opinion for I realized originally that it was a source of dangerous illusions for the pupil and had the serious drawback of disturbing and confusing his intellect."[61] But what he had written in the Academy of Sciences report originally was: "We cannot prohibit the use of sign, even if that were feasible, without forcing the pupil to struggle violently with himself, without abruptly stopping his intellectual development, disturbing and confusing it."[62] Since Franck had never taught the deaf, knew no sign language or even the manual alphabet, his opinion could not be firmly anchored.[63]

The first Milan resolution advocated oralism over manualism: the language of the classroom was to be the national oral language, not the manual one. Resolution two took the exclusion of sign a step further: it explicitly struck at any compromise in which the oral language was seconded by the manual one; the "pure" oral method was preferred. Yet another resolution explained to the educator how "pure" oralism was to be phased in, and signs out. The new pupils would form a class by themselves, to be instructed in speech. They would be entirely separated from the others, too far advanced to be taught orally, whose education would be completed in sign. Each year a new speaking class would be established; eventually all the pupils who were manually taught would have left. But separation of pupils was only one means of suppressing sign. Surveillance was another. These arrangements not only discouraged the acquisition of sign language by those children who did not already know it, but also ensured that they remained communicatively isolated, submerged as it were, for several years. It deprived them of deaf role models, alienated them from the deaf community.

Here is how one French school applied the Milan resolutions—and, to the best of my knowledge, still does. "The newcomers had a daily regime totally different from the old students, with whom they were not to have any relations whatsoever. To make a sign or even to look at one was to reach for forbidden fruit. Classes, play, meals were separate. . . . Nevertheless, the pupils succeeded in communicating and escaping surveillance, albeit vigilant. When the last pupil taught by sign left the institution, we redoubled our vigilance and tolerated not a single sign."[64] This professor describes the pedagogical measures for suppression in mild terms: the children were told to be ashamed of themselves for signing; rewards were given for not signing all week. But it is easy to imagine that more severe measures were taken. We know that holes were drilled in doors so the staff could detect signing in secret. The National Institution took similar measures, and within a year schools in Caen, Lille, Soissons, and other provincial cities were following the Paris lead.

The Milan resolution on phasing in the replacement of sign meant that deaf professors would be fired seven years later (the average length of studies less one year), and so it came to pass at scores of schools in Europe and America.[65] The National Institution for the Deaf in Paris published a little brochure which was called in the preface, "a touching farewell by the director to the deaf professors who were leaving their posts at the school since as of this date it will no longer have students taught by the old method."

"Ladies and Gentlemen:

"Progress cannot be accomplished, unfortunately, without some sacrifice.

"With the oral method, we will no longer see our pupils leave this school and spread throughout the world to found institutions for the deaf everywhere. It was a beautiful and touching thing to see these migrations of the deaf, called forth first, in the school founded by the abbé de l'Epée, from the shadows of their own ignorance, then to carry the light to their unfortunate fellows in all the countries of Europe and across the seas.

"This school, the oldest of them all, was like a mother church to all those created since 1760 in Europe, America, and Australia; and in nearly all of them the teachers began as pupils here. The oral method does not require hearing to learn speech but it does absolutely require hearing to teach speech. Hereafter, far from hoping to furnish the world with teachers from among our deaf pupils, we can no longer even have the satisfaction of keeping some for ourselves.

"No more graduates like Laurent Clerc, alumnus of this institution, founder of North American education of the deaf, which last year celebrated its centennial. No more like Berthier, who died a few months ago after eighty years in our institution as pupil, professor, and honorary professor. No more men like Messieurs Tessières and Dusuzeau, alongside me here, as professors in the institution where they began as pupils.

"The complete disappearance of mime has yet other sadnesses in store for us. We will have to discharge several teachers, as devoted as they are distinguished, whose only fault is to be deaf. It is not without great heartache—and I speak for all the institution—that we see step down from their chairs men like Tessières, Dusuzeau, and Théobald, like M. Tronc, our devoted writing teacher, like M. Simon, our excellent deputy headmaster.

"I know, deaf colleagues, with what selflessness you accede to this difficult sacrifice. You recognize that the welfare of the pupils is at stake and therefore you raise not a word of complaint in these painful circumstances. May I be allowed not to imitate your silent resignation but to recall aloud the value of the professors that we must lose today.

"It is you, M. Théobald, who, despite the absence of a sense, rendered so much service not only to your class but to the general progress of our teaching. None among your hearing colleagues contributed more to the preparation of our curriculum, of which we may be proud, since it is followed in almost all other French schools for the deaf. . . . Finally, it is you, M. Dusuzeau, who have for so long brought honor to this school. As a student you revealed that intelligence, energy, and perseverance that allow the deaf to acquire instruction, *even with defective methods*, and it is with understandable pride that your teachers saw you become a bachelor of science. Professor, you have repaid one-hundredfold your debt to this institution by giving in turn to the young generations who came after you the knowledge you acquired here. You, too, like M. Théobald, will go into retirement at the young age of forty after hardly twenty years of service.

"Dear colleagues: At the moment you are about to resign your duties as professors there is at least one consolation for us: the Ministry of the Interior has seen fit to appoint you honorary professors and thereby you will feel, I trust, always attached to this institution. . . . When steam navigation replaced sail, did the young captains, proud of the perfect instrument in their hands, have nothing to learn from the old-timers? Of course not. . . . Thus, let us always seek lessons from you, call on your knowledge, refer to your experience, even if we now say, Adieu."[66]

In America, Bell's oralist crusade reduced the number of deaf teachers to a slight fraction of the total, where it remains currently; in the European nations, where the control of education is centralized, the deaf teachers were eliminated to the last man. Soon there would be no need for laws to exclude them, for the reduced intellectual achievements attainable under the new oralist regime effectively prevented the deaf from aspiring to any such career. There is to this day no high school for the deaf in France, and when Gallaudet proposed at Milan a resolution calling for secondary education of the deaf, it was generally considered unrealistic and was dropped.

Milan, as the trail-blazing French anthropologist Bernard Mottez has pointed out, moved the status of speech from a means of education to the end of education itself.[67] If speech is the end, it must of course be taught. Schools were transformed into speech clinics. Tarra, Hull, and other speakers at Milan agreed that the first years of education, as many as necessary, must be devoted to articulation and lipreading, for oral instruction in a subject is futile when the child is unable to understand or reply to the teacher. However, the mediocre results in speaking and reading proved that, as a rule, it would be absurd for a deaf child to aim for lofty educational goals such as a high school degree. There is the occasional exception to this rule: generally, a postlingually deafened child of wealthy (hearing) parents who, like the Hubbards and the Ackers, provide intensive training early and continuously. A recent study by Gallaudet College of the scores of some 17,000 deaf students on the Stanford Achievement Test illustrates how oralism has reduced the educational achievement of the deaf since the days of Laurent Clerc and James Denison. As a benchmark, the achievement of the average hearing seventeen-year-old American student on the SAT is called twelfth-grade level. The achievement of the average deaf seventeen-year-old is sixth-grade level in arithmetic (their best subject), and fourth-grade level in reading ("paragraph meaning").[68]

The situation in France is similar: according to a recent doctoral dissertation by Christian Cuxac, one of a group of young hearing and deaf people who are agitating for reform, "It is virtually impossible in the present oralist context for a profoundly deaf student, or even a severely but prelingually deaf student, to obtain a high school degree."[69] This state of affairs set in rapidly after Milan; by the turn of the century, an inspector-general for the Ministry of the Interior could find that the pupils, "after seven or eight years at the institution, were incapable, not only of speaking, but of writing the teacher's name or even their own. No doubt some of them—not all—could, on graduating, earn a few coins in shoe repair or sewing but this is rather expensive training over eight years in the institution." A dozen years after Milan a teacher at the Paris institution concurred: "Most of our students have such poor intelligence, are so inept at using the few phrases that they want to use, that their impoverished reflection and imagination are expressed only in virtually unintelligible language."[70] A fellow teacher wrote: "The first year our pupils spend at school must be devoted essentially to the study of articulation and lipreading." The second year was devoted to practicing simple sentences, describing tangible objects and events, for "we cannot expect anything more from our pupils, since they do not know enough language to express themselves in other ways. . . . As for abstract nouns we can teach them in the fifth or sixth year as derivations from known adjectives or adverbs. In the sixth year we give them elementary notions of measuring and counting." Students in the sixth year were fifteen years old!

Some years ago on a mission for UNESCO two colleagues and I visited many high schools in English- and French-speaking West Africa, where children were being taught in their second, third, or even fourth language. Teachers there voiced many complaints like those of their counterparts in deaf education. They said that the teaching of French, for example, left little room for instruction in arts and sciences: because the students' poor performance in those subjects was the result of an inadequate command of the language in which they were taught, instruction in that language had to come first, and remain first. Now the deaf student has a predicament similar to that of these African students. Only a few grains of instruction pass through the filter of his poor reading skills and incomprehension of the teacher's language (exacerbated by the necessity to divine it from the movement of his lips). So speech teaching receives top priority and all educational goals are reduced.

As oralism became the rule, teachers and administrators increasingly referred to the cost of educating the deaf, as did the inspector-general decrying the expense of training deaf shoemakers. Thirty years after Milan, the psychologists Binet and Simon conducted the first systematic evaluation of oral education of the deaf by examining the fate of graduates of the Paris and Asnières institutions. "We conclude that the deaf-mutes whom we have examined are not able to carry on a conversation with those around them, but they can understand those they know intimately and be understood by them sufficiently for the satisfaction of their immediate wants, by employing a means of communication composed of words, lipreading, and expressive gestures. . . . People are mistaken about the practical result of the oral method. It seems to us a sort of luxury education, which boosts morale rather than yielding useful and tangible results. It does not enable deaf-mutes to get jobs; it does not permit them to exchange ideas with strangers; it does not allow them even a consecutive conversation with their intimates; and deaf-mutes who have not learned to speak earn their living just as easily as those who have acquired this semblance of speech."[71]

The increased cost of education resulting from the very small classes required if the pupil is to lipread (and receive instruction in speech and lipreading) was but one motive for turning away those students expected to make the least progress under the oral regime. Another was the natural desire of teachers and administrators to favor the population—semi-mutes and semi-deaf, to use Clerc's terms—that would bring them a few pupils who would perform well. The result was that after Milan schools for the deaf were increasingly attended by the least deaf, while the "core" deaf community, deaf children of deaf parents whose maternal language was sign language, were largely excluded. At the Paris institution, for example, admission after Milan was contingent on a medical certificate testifying good sight and aptitude to learn, but also on the finding by a special commission of teachers that the pupil was able to make progress orally. This certainly held the door open to the abuse of admitting the semi-mute and semi-deaf and excluding the rest. Even among those who once heard or still do, many are refractory to oralism; for them the school created a lower division that progressed even more slowly.[72]

What happens to the rejects? The physician of the Paris institution, Dr. Ladreit de Lacharrière, who would head the Paris congress of 1900 that finally sealed the fate of the deaf, affirmed that the rejects were not retarded in the usual sense of the term, they were *diminués*. For them he asked special schools where they could be taught reading and writing and where, "without wasting time trying to teach them to speak," they would be taught in sign language ideas of everyday things, responsibility to oneself and to others, respect, and social discipline. "In these special schools they would be taught manual labor as early as possible." He advocated gardening and field work as the first choice of profession.[73] It is probable that Laurent Clerc, had he attended Saint-Jacques after Milan, would have become a field laborer.

Thus the border between mere deafness and mental debility is determined by fluency in the majority language. Medicine, or more exactly the medico-psychological model, is the shield the oppressor holds in front of himself as he advances. The niggardly inspector-general from the Ministry of the Interior wrote of the Paris institution: "It should begin by purging itself of a dead weight of twenty-five percent composed of the incapable and the semi-retarded. . . . To classify pupils accordingly, which is difficult in only a few cases, all the children should spend two years at the institution, and only after this delay would the retarded clearly recognized as such be sent to an agricultural institution. The idiots and the semi-idiots should be shipped out [*sic*] immediately." He adds: "I am not opposed to teaching the weak-minded, after they are isolated, using the oral method. People can do what they like, provided they do not burden the teachers, who are always very expensive, and provided they keep the general expenses at the lowest possible level."[74]

In the aftermath of Milan, the conception of the deaf as a social class regressed to the view that had prevailed a century earlier, when Epée was beginning his labors: as their poor achievement confirmed, they were defective. "Everyone knows," said our inspector-general, "that the deaf are inferior in all respects. Only professional philanthropists have said they are men like everyone else. . . . Similar to *homo-alalus*, to man without speech in prehistoric times, yet even more retarded since they cannot hear, they pass among like men as their shadows, without hearing them, without understanding them: all human things are foreign to them."[75] The suppression of sign, the firing of deaf faculty, the retrenchment of educational goals, and the medical model of the deaf as defective all conduced to Milan's last catastrophic effect: the infantilizing of deaf young men and women. For the oralist teachers, childishness and docility were desirable qualities in a pupil, as Tarra explains: "The habit of full dependence, which the deaf-mute contracts in catching what is said from the lips and communicating ideas by the orderly, rational, and tranquil means of oral conversation, takes from them that indocile and wild spirit peculiar to those who express themselves by the fantastic and passionate method of gestures, and always renders them more obedient, respectful, affectionate, sincere, and good."[76] The orally taught deaf child of hearing parents generally finds that only his parents can under-stand him, and this aggravates and prolongs his dependence and narrows his circle.

Shortly before his death Vaïsse surveyed all the "reforms" that followed Milan and their consequences and, to the horror of the Pereire Society, published a disavowal, in a major Paris newspaper, of the pure oralist cause associated with his name. The occasion was the publication of La Rochelle's adulatory biography of Jacob Pereire, commissioned by his grandson. In his review of the book, Vaïsse affirmed that Pereire's pedagogical principles—which included dactylology, pantomime, writing, and articulation (but not lipreading)—clearly placed him in the camp of Edward Miner Gallaudet, among the followers of the combined system. "We, who do not believe in the possibility of absolutely excluding sign language in the education of the born deaf, cannot but applaud teachers who, like Pereire, make use of all the means of teaching that nature places at their disposal."[77] Adolphe Franck, too, soon reverted to his original anti-oral position. But these were only two voices, too few, too late. The oralist tide continued to swell.

Three national conferences of hearing educators of the deaf in France contributed to the growth of the oralist movement. The one in Bordeaux not long after Milan resolved in favor of teaching the deaf to perform manual labor, especially in agriculture, and of encouraging them to stay with their families and away from large cities (hence, away from each other).[78] Other resolutions reaffirmed pure oralism and the importance of treating deaf children like the hearing and of encouraging them to mix with the hearing. The next two conferences occurred in Paris a year apart. The first was organized by a renegade group loyal to Pereire. Several deaf professors, now forcibly retired, attended the meeting. Théobald, for example, urged that deaf teachers have a place in a model school for the deaf, one of the items on the agenda, but all the hearing professors there disagreed with his proposal. He also asked to read a paper on the role of the teacher outside the classroom, having ceded the ground inside to his hearing counterparts, but the president ruled the paper out of order and the request stricken from the minutes. Poor M. Théobald also tried to explain the value of ancient history for the curriculum in the deaf school, but his remarks were ignored, somewhat in the way indulgent parents would seek to ignore their child's inopportune remarks, and the group voted for more and earlier instruction in manual skills. Another concern of this meeting was the total eradication of signing, which continued to appear like an obtuse and uninvited guest. "The congress, considering the importance of banishing the use of signs," reads the resolution unanimously adopted, "invites the teacher to allow only oral communication in class, in study hall, and in recreation and to provide his pupils, as they may require them, the necessary oral expressions they lack. It will facilitate his task to group the pupils according to their degree of development."[79]

A national congress the following year was likewise concerned with the large numbers of retarded pupils turning up in the schools since the advent of oralism.[80] For example, Dr. Ladreit de Lacharrière warned, "Children with all the signs of intelligence prove sometimes totally incompetent. After a year in our institutions they have learned nothing." Consequently, the congress voted for the establishment of special classes for the retarded.[81] Another deaf professor, Henri Gaillard, had prepared a paper on the use of sign with the retarded. He was forbidden to read it, but it appears in an appendix to the proceedings. The national conferences were also a battle-ground for the two opposing ministries, Public Instruction and Interior: their representatives maneuvered to elect or defeat certain candidates for office, to insert or delete items on the program, to call or postpone the next meeting, to include or exclude various groups from the voting membership. After each meeting, pamphlets flew in all directions accusing the other side of treachery. On one side of the contest were the private schools serving the upper class, most with fealty to Pereire, who wanted to seize control of the state and parochial institutions, transferring them to the Ministry of Public Instruction. On the other side were the larger group of civil servants and religious and laicized teachers, who feared a loss of perquisites and enroll-ments if they left the aegis of the Ministry of the Interior.[82]

This issue dominated the third international congress, held in Brussels three years after Milan, which had to be aborted because of the strife that it and nationalist sentiment engendered. Milan had been enjoyable for the hearing teachers. It was for many their first conference and their first trip abroad and they wanted to continue holding such meetings. Two hundred and fifty came to Brussels, the largest congress yet. The majority wanted to avoid reopening the question of methods, the more so as the local Belgian president of the meeting avowedly favored the combined system and many local schools followed that method. But the minority also wanted silence, for fear of a reaffirmation of Milan. All agreed to pretend the emperor was wearing clothes. Few other questions were of general interest, although the congress did call for "agricultural asylums" where "the deaf of little intelli-gence, unable to receive the usual instruction, can at least learn a trade." Many delegates desired a resolution affirming the right of every deaf child to an education, and some wanted model schools and teacher-training pro-grams and evaluation. But the clerical majority saw that these were steps along the way to urging that deaf schools come under ministries of public instruction—indeed that was the logical outcome of the hearing-oriented pedagogy since Milan—and they fought bitterly to prevent these questions from reaching the floor. The meeting degenerated into a brawl: speakers were ignored or shouted down, groups met impromptu in the audience, and all this even in the presence of the king of Belgium. His Majesty remarked that teachers of the deaf reminded him of his own parliament, and he left. Little was achieved in the first few days of the meeting, and when the

German delegation proposed Frankfurt as the site of the next congress, the French sent up such an uproar that the chairman was powerless to bring the meeting to order. He finally ended the congress two days early, ordering that his farewell speech be printed in the minutes. As far as I can tell, there were no deaf voting members, but one hard-of-hearing man, a graduate of the Rotterdam school under Hirsch, did speak on instruction in trades, and a deaf artist submitted a memoir in which he called for greater use of sign language. There were no interpreters provided, so I presume there were no deaf people in the audience.[83]

Nevertheless, the educated deaf, taught under the old system in French Sign Language, were not silent. They expressed their views in periodicals addressed to the deaf and in congresses of their own. One particularly frank spokesman for the deaf, L. Limosin, published a description of his classes under Vaïsse: "Sometimes the old man made us speak with our mouths open, sometimes he made us pronounce the expressions written on the board. Then, having uttered that spoken language which we were a thousand leagues from understanding, we asked each other in sign language the meaning of what he made us say. Having vainly queried each other on the matter, we confronted the imperious necessity of asking him for a sign language explanation of what it was all about."[84] The silent press labeled oralism the method of "violence, oppression, obscurantism, charlatanism, which only makes idiots of the poor deaf-mute children," and called Magnat, "the inventor of this torture of the tongue, nose, throat, and eyes called the pure oral method."[85] Claveau and Franck were "reactionaries who throw dust in the eyes of the minister of the interior, exaggerating the so-called advantages of the pure oral method. His first duty is to fire them." Claveau relied on all these congresses "in order to retain his shameful post of murderer of the intelligence and soul of deaf children."[86] Another deaf leader, Victor Chambellan, urged the authorities to "stop tying the hands of the deaf, proscribing that vivid language which alone can restore them to moral life and the bosom of society."[87]

The international congresses of the deaf were launched in reaction to the banishment of their language decreed by the hearing in Milan. The first was held in Paris, on the centennial of Epée's death, under the presidency of Ernest Dusuzeau, one of the deaf professors forced into retirement a few years earlier. The American delegation, twenty-three in all, included a deaf author, a professor at Gallaudet College, two of the faculty of the New York school, the missionary Job Turner, the current president of the National Association of the Deaf, and Edward Miner Gallaudet. In all there were about 150 delegates at the congress.

The first speaker was Thomas Fox (educator, editor, next president of the National Association of the Deaf): "Suppress the language of signs and the deaf man is excluded from all society, even that of his brothers in misfortune; he will be more isolated than ever." O. H. Regensberg (journalist, publisher): "Everywhere we see deaf-mutes associating exclusively among their own society and almost never in that of hearing society. It is natural for the deaf man to seek the society of those . . . who have the same means of communication and approximately the same tastes. I doubt he can ever be forced to change." Victor Chambellan (dean of deaf professors forced into retirement from the Paris school): "At the end of his studies, the young deaf-mute seeks above all the society of other deaf-mutes. That's understandable: those who can communicate with each other, gather with each other. Let us spread our sign language among the hearing. Then the deaf man will be torn from his isolation, the prejudices that victimize him will fall away, sympathetic communication will develop between him and society . . . new progress will be made, and a real service done for humanity." Claudius Forestier (school principal, author): "I was sharply pained to learn that people with no experience have the audacity to propose the interdiction of sign language. This would be to tear it from our very soul since it is a part of our nature, the life of our thoughts. Sign remains the one true means of leading our younger brethren to a knowledge of the national language."

From sign language and the goals and conduct of education, the deaf delegates proceeded to discuss marriage, the teaching profession, deaf gatherings and organizations, law and the deaf. Of all the conclusions on these issues reached by hearing professionals in Paris, Milan, and Brussels, not a single one agreed with the views of the deaf themselves meeting in Paris. Their congress ended with quite a different set of resolutions for promoting their welfare. Here is the first: "The congress proclaims the infallibility of the method of the abbé de l'Epée, which, without excluding the use of speech, recognizes manual language as the most suitable instrument for developing the intellect of the deaf." The congress closed to cries of: "Long live the emancipation of the deaf!"[88]

The second international congress of the deaf was held four years later in Chicago, in connection with a meeting of the National Association of the Deaf. Nearly two thousand deaf men and women from various schools, regions, occupations were present. At the opening banquet, Edward Miner Gallaudet addressed the gathering with a signed discourse on the deaf and the power of their organizations. He called the propagation of oralism disastrous for their education, and said it had gained the upper hand in Italy and France by "accidental means"—a remark greeted with wild applause. "The majority of parents," Gallaudet said, "seem to prefer that their children speak imperfectly than that they acquire intellectual knowledge." All intelligent and fair-minded people who have worked for our cause agree that the language of signs is the most essential element in the complete education of the deaf, even on the oral plan. He gave long and detailed praise of deaf teachers and attacked their exclusion from schools for the deaf. The president of the congress, a deaf chemist, called attention "to the greatest menace confronting the American deaf, pure oralism." French delegates were particularly struck and humiliated (their term) by the participation of many intelligent and charming deaf women; deaf women were still interned in France and were allowed no part in social or political gatherings.

The Chicago congress of the deaf, like its successor in Geneva three years later, in 1896, resolved in favor of the combined system of instruction.[89] The Geneva meeting also called for the rehiring of deaf professors and for an end to the teaching of manual labor in deaf schools. An Italian delegate at Geneva described Italy as "weeping at the sight of so many poor deaf-mutes who leave school speaking like parrots with no understanding of what they are saying," and a German delegate asked if the time had not passed for resolutions and the time had not come for the use of power. It was unclear what more forcible actions could be taken, however. The respective ministries that controlled deaf education listened only to hearing educators. The congress elected an international commission to visit their ambassadors at Bern and present its resolutions. It also planned the next meeting, which, as it turned out, was held in conjunction with the fourth international congress on the education and welfare of the deaf, convened in Paris in 1900 by hearing professors.[90]

When Edward Miner Gallaudet arrived in Paris for this momentous occasion in the history of the deaf, his diary records, he first paid a sentimental visit to the rue Saint-Jacques, where it had all begun over a century earlier. He stood in the courtyard of the national school, and while the statue of the abbé de l'Epée looked benevolently down on him, he imagined his father arriving to attend one of Massieu's classes, he imagined Dr. Itard crossing the courtyard on some urgent errand from the infirmary to Sicard's apartment, he imagined Clerc standing before the gate, bracing himself before striding through on his way to Hartford in the New World. Then Edward wheeled, braced himself for the last great battle of his life (he was sixty-three), and he, too, strode through the gates.

He descended the rue Bonaparte as far as the church of Saint-Germain, where the abbé Sicard had been held during the Reign of Terror, and took the wide boulevard that leads to the Seine and the immense Place de la Concorde. He proceeded along the Right Bank and finally he arrived at the Palace of Congresses. Nine immense bays of glass, two stories high, dominated the façade. They were divided into three groups by two tall pylons on which festoons had been sculpted over a sphere containing a star. Garlands of leaves crowned the bays from one end of the long rectangular building to the other. Edward entered through a wide portal on the façade opposite the Seine. Two enormous halls lay to either side of him and directly ahead, grand stairways that rose majestically with three landings to the second floor. They emptied into a vast gallery running the length of the building, overlooking the Seine on one side, giving access to several congress halls on the other. He made his way along the gallery, checking the signs on each door: "Congress on the Welfare of Deaf-Mutes—Hearing Section"; "—Deaf Section"; "—Joint Opening Session"; he entered the last to find himself at the back of an auditorium that could seat eight hundred. On the platform was the president of the meeting, Dr. Ladreit de Lacharrière, portly and self-important, his face sporting much of the hair that his scalp lacked: bushy eyebrows and mustache, and abundant side-whiskers. He looked down at nearly two hundred hearing delegates, about half in clerical garb, and more than two hundred deaf delegates from all over the Western world.

In a sketch of the president, Alexander Graham Bell described him as a doctor of authority and wealth who came from one of the oldest families of the department of Ardèche. At thirty-four he became chief physician of the Paris institution for the deaf, where he had remained for as many years again; he also founded a French journal of otology.[91]

In the preface to a textbook on speech teaching, Ladreit de Lacharrière later wrote: "The deaf-mute is by nature fickle and improvident, subject to idleness, drunkenness, and debauchery, easily duped and readily corrupted."[92] The faculty of the Paris institution were so aggrieved by his appointment to head the organizing committee, and thus the congress, that teachers from all three national institutions walked out on the planning meetings and boycotted the congress.[93]

A much graver irregularity was the decision, a year before the congress, to separate the deaf from the hearing meeting. The ministerial delegate for all congresses at the exposition stated that he regretted the planning committee's decision; rather than a deaf section and a hearing section, he would have preferred one on teaching and another on welfare. The deaf spokesman, Henri Gaillard, editor of a newspaper for the deaf, warmly agreed with this plan, but Ladreit de Lacharrière refused integrated sessions, arguing that they would be too long and confusion would arise from the near-simultaneous translation of sign to speech and vice versa. Gaillard then proposed a common meeting at the end of the congress merely to debate and vote on the resolutions. The doctor rejected that as well. Then the deaf planners met and decided that their choice was to acquiesce or attempt to disrupt plans for the congress; they chose to acquiesce.[94]

In fact, the president had little choice. The great preponderance of deaf delegates over hearing meant that, in a joint meeting, the deaf could obtain the endorsement of the congress for any resolution on which they were united, and they were united—almost to a man—on the evils of pure oralism, the merits of sign, the wisdom of deaf marriages, the need for deaf teachers. The entire scaffolding of Milan could be torn down! Then, too, even if the hearing delegates had outnumbered the deaf, most of their

EDWARD MINER GALLAUDET

leaders were vehemently opposed to an airing of the wishes of the deaf concerning their own welfare. Consider, for example, the attitude of G. Ferreri, who, with the deaths of Balestra and Tarra, had emerged as the leader of Italian educators of the deaf. In the leading Italian journal on deaf education, Ferreri wrote that he planned to withdraw from the congress if the deaf were allowed into the hearing meetings. "I have always claimed that the deaf, even well instructed, can in no way be put on the same plane with their hearing educators." It is easy to imagine how the infantilizing of many deaf students by Italian oralism gave Ferreri daily evidence for his belief. "Since they lack from earliest childhood," he continued, "the element that shapes intelligence, namely the mother tongue, they always remain inferior in their psychological development even when the most patient and skillful art renders them speech. What can one say of these very deaf who, lacking an education that would give them a clear and exact appreciation of the great gift of speech, persist in considering as a natural language their violent and spasmodic miming, which can at best simply establish their kinship with the famous primates."[95] A professor at Siena put more pithily the representative view of the hearing delegates: "Since when do we consult the patient on the nature of his treatment?"[96]

The opening ceremonies of the congress were held jointly. "Although there are no more adversaries of the oral method," Dr. Ladreit de Lacharrière told his hearing and deaf audience of some four hundred, "we cannot ignore the fact that many are asking why the method hasn't produced everything expected of it." But in public schools, he argued, we do not indict the method if some pupils do not learn to read. We blame the inadequacy of the pupils. Whence he concluded that educators need to make a better selection of their deaf pupils. He held forth as the goal of the congress the establishment of a triage of the deaf, based on intelligence. First, the inferior students would be turned toward agriculture. (Under oralism these would tend to be, as I have told, the core deaf community, deaf at birth or before attaining full mastery of the oral language.) Then, those with mediocre aptitude would be trained for artisanal jobs as at present (shoemaking, woodworking, and the like). Finally, the gifted students should be prepared for higher instruction. (An oral criterion of "gifted" selects the semi-mute and semi-deaf.) Let us be realistic, he said. In the last twenty years I have found this rare, third type of pupil only in the private schools, which are inaccessible to the social class with modest means.

"If the program of the deaf section differs from our own," the president said, "we will have no difficulty showing who has the truth on his side." Many deaf people here were educated, he explained, before the advent of oralism. Their tendency is to isolate themselves from the world of speaking people, and everyone recognizes that they are slowing down the progress we desire for their class. We cannot criticize the use of sign among them "any more than we can criticize those who speak Provençal, Basque, or Breton dialects [sic], but that does not prevent us from reserving for our schools the language of Bossuet, Corneille, and Victor Hugo."97 "But I want to stress," he added, "that we walk hand in hand with the deaf section."

Then came the turn of Ernest Dusuzeau, head of the deaf section, who spoke in French Sign Language and was translated into French. "There have been many congresses aimed at improving our lot," he said, "but none of them has been satisfactory." He asked the audience to join him in homage to Dr. Ladreit de Lacharrière. We have no objection, he explained, to the search for improvements in the oral method. Why would we? Speech is obviously the greatest gift of all gifts for us who do not hear. "We ask only one thing: that our natural language, the language of signs, be not sacrificed for spoken language.

> *"A bird am I!*
> *Behold the wings by which I fly,*
> *Nor, cruel, them to me deny."*

("It is fortunate," wrote Ferreri in his account, "that the great majority of our pupils now understand how short these wings are, how inadequate for the requirements of social life, and how necessary the maintenance of speech is, not to fly high, for the truly deaf will never fly, but to extricate themselves from difficulty in the simplest matters of everyday life.")

Right from the first session of the hearing section on Monday morning, Gallaudet and Bell traded blows. Among others, including Ferreri, they were elected honorary presidents of the meeting, and Bell took the occasion to affirm the growth of oralism in the United States. Gallaudet claimed it was not pure oralism that was growing but rather the combined system of educating the deaf, which was spreading to formerly manual schools. Bell, like Ferreri, agreed with excluding the deaf from the congress deliberations: "It goes without saying that those who are themselves unable to speak are not the proper judges of the value of speech to the deaf." Four oralists were elected as vice-presidents, including the omnipresent Eugène Pereire and Auguste Houdin. Gallaudet rose to call the Milan declarations a great error. He showed how unrepresentative that congress had been, yet "its decisions have been cited for twenty years as if they had the weight of a judgment of the Supreme Court." Now this congress, he said, is no more representative: anyone with ten francs can vote. Milan decided nothing, for the controversy rages. Nor can this congress decide such issues. There should be an open exchange of ideas and the use of friendly persuasion without voting. He read a resolution to that effect and asked the endorsement of the congress. Whereupon Dr. Ladreit de Lacharrière declared—while giving no one else an opportunity to express an opinion, or submitting the proposal to a vote—that the proposition was rejected by the congress, which was forthwith adjourned until the afternoon.

At the start of the second of six sessions, Oscar Claveau, now promoted to inspector of welfare establishments for the French Ministry of the Interior, asked as a point of order for the congress to reaffirm explicitly that the right to vote was reserved to hearing delegates and any speaking deaf. "This principle is no doubt already in the minds of everyone as it is inadmissible to grant the right to vote to people who cannot follow the discussions." He then launched into a long discourse whose purpose was to delete the first question from the agenda of the congress: it asked whether institutions for the deaf were to be considered as schools or as welfare programs. This was the ticklish issue of ministries that Claveau had been beating down successfully for some thirty years. There arose a furious debate in which Claveau was opposed by the president, Ferreri, La Rochelle, and others, but he was the spokesman for the religious establishment, whose delegates were in the majority, and in the end he had his way.

The third session opened with a paper by Gallaudet. He asked to read it to a joint session of the two sections; the leaders of the deaf section supported this request but Dr. Ladreit de Lacharrière demurred. He also earned Gallaudet's ire by cutting off his remarks without previously informing him of a time limit.[98] This was Gallaudet's bitterest and most incisive attack on oralism since he had helped launch it by introducing the combined method in America almost a half-century earlier. He claimed that oralism had not fulfilled its promises and he raised the question of whose testimony should carry the most weight in determining whether it had kept its promises or not. The teachers'? But they are partisan and too familiar with their own pupils' speech to make an accurate judgment. The testimony of friends and acquaintances of the deaf? But they, too, adjust to the poor speech and gestures of the orally taught pupil. The opinions of strangers? Their testimony is more important. But the greatest weight should be given to the views of the deaf themselves. You can imagine how those remarks were greeted by oralist teachers, who had repeatedly excluded the views of the deaf! But even harsher words were to come: Gallaudet raised the question whether oralist educators were defective morally. He stated that they were engaged in a cover-up. It was hardly possible that these teachers were deceiving themselves about the poor fruits of oralism, so it must be that they intended to deceive everyone else. Swiss and German delegates followed him in affirming that oralism has no application to the truly deaf, that it had not kept its promises.

In the afternoon, oralists and their opponents exchanged blows. Claveau appealed for "the same cry that rang out twenty years ago: Long live speech!" Finally Edward Fay, vice-president of Gallaudet College and editor of the *American Annals of the Deaf*, presented a resolution in behalf of the combined system: choose the method to suit the pupil but teach speech to all who can profit. The director of the oral school at Asnières began by reading the conclusions of the Milan congress and then presented a resolution of his own reaffirming pure oralism. When the question was called, the combined system received only seven votes while nearly everyone else voted for the second resolution: "The congress, considering the incontestable superiority of speech over signs for restoring the deaf-mute to society and for giving him a more perfect knowledge of language, declares that it maintains the conclusions of the Milan congress."

The president then read a letter from the deaf section proposing that they present their resolutions for review by the hearing, and vice versa, in a joint session. Ladreit de Lacharrière refused, stating that it would be a waste of time, since there was no easy and useful way for the two sections to meet together. Gallaudet rose trembling with rage: "If I am in the minority of the hearing section, I am in the majority in the section of the deaf, and proud of it. It is inadmissible that you refuse to speak with the deaf. They have as much awareness of their rights, as much discernment, and as much determination as you do! They are the first to be affected by these proceedings, they have the right to be heard. I protest your attitude!"[99]

The last day of the congress opened with a motion by Gallaudet to alter the resolutions to read correctly: it is not the *congress* that considers speech incontestably superior to sign but the *hearing section* that does. The motion was defeated. Gallaudet then proposed a joint final session with the deaf. Refused. He asked permission to read the resolutions of the deaf section. Refused.[100] The final session was devoted to "protecting" the deaf. Ferreri explained that deaf women need asylums after school since they cannot marry and no employment is open to them. But males also need protective organizations, the discussants agreed. Some wanted demands made of the government for shelters and special workshops for school graduates; others saw such resolutions as legitimizing the involvement of ministries of welfare and were opposed. All seemed to have forgotten that oralism was supposed to restore the deaf to society.

Most of the deaf at the congress had been taught that sign was contemptible and should be shunned. Thirteen of the fifteen leaders of the deaf section could speak and had been educated in oral schools. Yet the deaf all communicated in sign language. Likewise, the hearing members had to rely on the language of the deaf, had to find an interpreter, when they wanted to converse with a deaf person. "Nevertheless, these hearing men were too obtuse, too self-satisfied, too blind," wrote an American deaf leader, "to see what consummate fools they were making of themselves."[101] The deaf section debated and resolved on a score of issues, among them the exclusion of the deaf from joint meetings with the hearing section, methods of instruction, art and industrial teaching in the schools, higher education, the deaf as teachers, homes for the aged, results of pure oral teaching, careers and professions for the deaf, and many more. But the first resolution and the one clearly dearest to all hearts was a call for the combined system of education; it was virtually identical to Fay's resolution, which had been rejected almost unanimously by the hearing section, and it was adopted unanimously by the deaf.[102]

James L. Smith, a professor at the Minnesota school, captured the sentiment of the deaf delegates when he cited the Declaration of Independence, affirming, "Government derives its power from the consent of the governed —but not when it comes to the affairs of the deaf." Here there are two congresses, he said, and two conclusions; the governed demand one thing, the governing authority, another. "We protest in vain. Our petitions addressed to governments receive no response, our resolutions at national and international congresses are ignored. . . . If you ask hearing educators how they can act in utter disregard of the wishes of the deaf, they answer that we do not know our own best interest. If that were true, then they have failed in the first objective of education, which is to enable the student to think and judge for himself. . . . In fact, the deaf are in a better position to judge these issues than the hearing. They know what it is to be deaf, they know what it is to have only a single method available for education, they know what it is to be forever blocked in their legitimate demands.

"Let us join together as one," Smith appealed, "to protest these educators who would fix our destiny without consulting us, without hearing us. Here in the greatest republic of the Old World, the delegates from that in the New ask all present to join together to affirm a new declaration of human rights, the right of the deaf to life, liberty, the pursuit of happiness, and the education of their children on a plan they accept. Let us declare to the entire world that the deaf will not be crucified on the cross of a single method."[103]

But the deaf did not have—do not have—the final word. The final word, as always, came from their hearing benefactors. As the new century dawned on deaf education after the Paris meeting, a representative report came from the principal of the Nebraska school, Frank Booth. His credentials as well as his words were symptomatic of the revolution that had taken place since the death of Laurent Clerc. Booth's father, Edmund, was that pioneering deaf journalist and organizer of the first convention of American deaf people whose trials in the West and achievements throughout the land Clerc described so lovingly. The hearing son had become not only principal of one of the largest schools for the deaf but also secretary-treasurer of Bell's American Association to Promote the Teaching of Speech to the Deaf. At the recent Paris congress, Booth wrote in the *Association Review*, "the oral method has been weighed in the balance—and it may be believed weighed conscientiously and with all fairness—and it is not found wanting."

Whereas Milan was a hope, he said, Paris was a conclusion—a verdict after trial. "The action of Paris will have the chief effect . . . to confirm the faith of those who practice . . . oral education of the deaf. . . . The question of methods," he concluded, "is practically retired from the field of discussion."[104]

And the silence fell.

ACKNOWLEDGMENTS

I am grateful to the following libraries for giving me space in which to work, access to their collections, and advice: American School for the Deaf, Hartford, Conn.; Amherst College Library; Archives départementales du Nord, Lille; Archives Nationales, Paris; Bibliothèque Municipale de Lille; Bibliothèque Nationale, Paris; Boston Athenaeum; Boston Public Library; British Museum; Connecticut Historical Society; Connecticut State Library; Clarke School, Northampton, Mass.; Danish School for the Deaf, Copenhagen; E. M. Gallaudet Library, Washington, D.C.; Hartford Public Library; Institut Départemental de Réhabilitation de la Parole et de l'Audition, Lille; Institut National de Jeunes Sourds de Paris; Instituto Nacional de Educação de Surdos, Rio de Janeiro; Lexington School for the Deaf, New York, N.Y.; Library of Congress; Massachusetts State Library; National Library of Brazil; Northeastern University Library; New York Public Library; Pennsylvania School for the Deaf; Smith College Library; Stowe-Day Foundation, Hartford; Watkinson Library, Trinity College; Widener Library, Harvard University; Yale University Libraries; University of Massachusetts—Amherst Library. Photographs were supplied by the Bibliothèque Nationale and the E. M. Gallaudet Library.

Many colleagues and friends made important contributions to this book that I am happy to acknowledge here. The following aided me primarily in conducting research: René Bernard and Christian Cuxac, Institut National de Jeunes Sourds; Louise Dennett, Northeastern University; Alain Dessaints, Institut National de Jeunes Sourds; Fern Edwards and Corrine Hilton, E. M. Gallaudet Library; Robert Hoffmeister, Boston University; Donald Klopfer, Random House; Brian Lancaster, Columbia University; Arlene Markowicz, Institut National de Jeunes Sourds de Paris; Pierre Montagnon, Maire, La Balme–Les Grottes; Nicholas Morris, Boston University; Franklin Philip, Northeastern University; Gary Richards, Boston, Mass.; Jeanne Siraco, Northeastern University; M. Sabino Cruz and Maria de Jesus Silva, Instituto National de las Communication Humana; Peter van den Noort, Boston, Mass.; Lars von der Leith, University of Copenhagen; Christian Wayser, Paris; Dora Weiner, University of California, Los Angeles.

I am indebted for assistance in editing and translation to: Loredana Clementi, Boston, Mass.; José Gabilondo, Harvard University; Jean-Michel Gendre, Boston, Mass.; Scott Gortikov, Boston, Mass.; Thomas Stehling, Boston, Mass.; David Steiger, New York, N.Y.

I was aided in the preparation of the manuscript by: Ronald Butzlaff, Harvard University; James Hough, New York University; Mark Mandel, Northeastern University; Joan Rogers, Boston, Mass.; George Sells, Boston, Mass.; Charles Still, UNESCO.

A sabbatical from Northeastern University and the assistance of its Dean's office, computing center, libraries, and office of sponsored programs made this book possible, as did support of my research on sign language from the Translations Program of the National Endowment for the Humanities, the Linguistics Program of the National Science Foundation, and the National Institute of Neurological and Communicative Disorders and Stroke. Part of this research was conducted while I was on the faculty of the Institut d'Etudes Phonétiques et Linguistiques (Sorbonne).

Ursula Bellugi (Salk Institute), Gil Eastman (Gallaudet College), Edward Klima and Carol Padden (University of California, San Diego), Brian Lancaster (Columbia University), Nicholas Morris (Boston University), Franklin Philip (Northeastern University), Richard Pillard (Boston University), Mordecai Rimor and Judy Shepard-Kegl (Northeastern University), and William Stokoe (Gallaudet College) read the manuscript and made many excellent suggestions.

Finally, I am grateful to my publisher, Jason Epstein, for his early commitment to this work and to my editor, Corona Machemer, for countless valuable contributions to the manuscript.

NOTES

CHAPTER ONE / MY NEW FAMILY

1. Some brief reminiscences about Laurent Clerc in his old age were published in the periodical *Silent World* (Anon., 1871a). Also see Fox (1935, *3* [5]), p. 9; Hotchkiss (1913); F. Clerc (1885).

2. In the late 1860s, Samuel Howe, director of the Perkins School for the Blind, sparked a heated controversy by urging that sign language be prohibited in schools for the deaf. See Massachusetts Board of State Charities (1866, 1867), Howe (1866), Hubbard (1867), Sanborn (1867).

3. Clerc presented this defense of diversity in an address written for delivery on the occasion of a public examination of the pupils of the American Asylum for the Deaf, which he founded with Thomas Gallaudet in 1817 (Clerc, 1818b, pp. 11–12).

4. Clerc wrote an autobiographical sketch which appeared in Henry Barnard's memorial tribute to Thomas Gallaudet (Clerc, 1852).

5. Louis Laurent Marie Clerc, b. La Balme, Dec. 26, 1785. Mother: Marie Françoise Clerc (née Marie Elizabeth Candy), d. Feb. 2, 1825 (Clerc [1852] gives May 1818). Father: Joseph François Clerc, b. 1747, d. La Balme, Apr. 4, 1816. Mayor of La Balme, 1780–1814. Paternal uncle and godfather: Laurent Clerc, businessman in Lyon, m. Louise Monet, Apr. 3, 1794, d. Jan. 22, 1827. Brother: François Clerc, businessman in Lyon. Two sisters. I am deeply indebted to the mayor of La-Balme-Les-Grottes, Pierre Montagnon, for the warm reception he accorded me, for a tour of Clerc's home, recently purchased by the village, and for assistance in searching village records.

6. So states Clerc (1852), but Sicard was in hiding in the Paris suburbs to avoid deportation; see later. L.J.F. Alhoy (1755–1826) was the administrator in his absence, Sept. 1797–Nov. 1799. In the same autobiographical sketch, Clerc states that he entered the school for the deaf at the age of "about 12, that is, in 1797," but school records reported by Karakostas (1981) show he was admitted 1 fructidor an 6 (Aug. 18, 1798).

7. See reminiscences of Jean Massieu by Sicard (1800), Clerc (1849); Itard (1821d), 1842 edition; and Berthier (1873). Esquiros (1847) gives Massieu's name sign.

8. A history of the school building appears in Denis (1896), Chassé (1974), Bernard (1961), and, to a lesser degree, Valette (1867).

9. On Feb. 13, 1794, the National Convention ordered its committees on Alienation and Public Aid to place the deaf in the Seminary of Saint Magloire; the committee ordered the transfer on Mar. 5 and the move took place Apr. 1.

10. Bébian (1817) lists the staff and duties under Sicard's directorship.

11. Peet (1852), Head (1855), Gallaudet (1870), Valette (1867), Du Camp (1877) give some details of the daily schedule. Also see Institution Impériale (1805) and La Rochefoucauld-Liancourt, 1792, cited in Weiner (1982), for contemporary accounts of daily life in the early period.

12. Peet (1852b), pp. 91–93; Karakostas (1981), pp. 128–144.

13. Appears in De Gérando (1827), v. 1, pp. 587–592.

14. Desloges (1779) pp. 13–14.

15. This account is based on Morel's biography (1850b). Apparently the same man is the subject of an anecdote related by Clerc and reported in Chamberlain (1857), p. 69.

16. On the early curriculum see Paulmier (1821).

17. White bread and soup accounted for a third of the food budget in 1810; meat, one-fourth; wine, one-fifth; vegetables, one-sixth. No milk. See Bernard (1980b).

18. Woodbridge (1830), p. 335.

19. Mosaics came to France as a result of Napoleon's Italian campaign, and the ministry created the mosaic shop at the school, for ten deaf pupils to learn the craft, in 1801.

20. The *Journal des Savants* and the *Journal d'Agriculture* according to a report by Prieur (reprinted in Bloch and Tuetey, 1911).

21. I am deeply indebted to M. René Bernard for giving me access to his unpublished study of life in the National Institution for Deaf-Mutes at the start of the nineteenth century (Bernard, 1980c). These vignettes come from that source; the pupils were Clerc's contemporaries but not in the same class. Admissions from 1790 to 1800 are listed in Karakostas (1981).

22. Pain (1828). Clerc (1848) describes a visit to the Refuge.

23. I have used the term "deaf-mute" consistent with the practice during Clerc's lifetime, although it has since fallen into disfavor for reasons examined in this book. More on the abbé Margaron: Karakostas (1981), pp. 120–122.

CHAPTER 2 / THE SHEPHERD AND THE SYMBOL

1. Bébian (1817) states, however, that the pupils never used manual French among themselves, preferring French Sign Language.

2. The visit is described in Institution Impériale (1805) and in Villenave (1893), pp. 335–336.

3. Bouteiller (1956) gives the history of the society. Also see Copans and Jamin (1978).

4. Autobiography of Jean Massieu. Lebouvier Desmortiers (1800) states (p. 252 of the 1829 edition): "Massieu prepared the sketch of his childhood to fulfill a request of Citizen Jauffret who had asked for it. This part was written 30 messidor an 6 [July 18, 1798]. It is all the more accurate as Massieu, in addressing Jauffret, was addressing one of his old friends. This deaf-mute was asked at a public meeting to name the persons most dear to him. He wrote on the blackboard in front of five hundred people, 'My true teacher, Abbé Sicard, the First Consul, and my friend Jauffret.' " The author goes on to say that this history was read at a public meeting 30 pluviôse last (? Feb. 19, 1800) and inspired a lady to send Massieu a letter with questions. The history and the letter were read at a second meeting 5 germinal (? Mar. 26, 1800) and Massieu responded on the spot to questions. A record of the two meetings is to appear, he states, in the first volume of the *Mémoires de la Société des Observateurs de l'Homme*. Lebouvier Desmortiers then presents a summary from memory.

Since Jauffret was the permanent secretary of the Society of Observers of Man, it is not surprising that the autobiography was scheduled to appear in that society's memoirs. These were never published in their entirety, although selections appear in Hervé (1911) and Copans and Jamin (1978). Jauffret published the history but not the questions and answers anonymously (with the assistance of P.A.M. Migier): *La Corbeille des fleurs et le panier de fruits*. *La Corbeille des fleurs* is often given as a citation in later reprintings of the history; however, it does not appear there but is in the second volume, *Le Panier de fruits* (pp. 72–86 of the second ed., 1819, Geneva-Paris [n.p.]).

The document appears next in quotation in Sicard (1808b), appendix, where it is joined by questions and answers, probably the ones to which Lebouvier Desmortiers referred, and the whole is attributed to "Madame V. C." Clerc (1849) identifies her as Mme. Victoria Clo, although the name "Cellier" appears at the end of a reprinting by Sicard (1851). The version in the present work, including both the history and the questions and answers, is a translation of the appendix to Sicard (1808b). Occasional deletions from the earlier Jauffret version (1806) have been reinserted in place. The various publications of this autobiography are as follows: (1) 1806–1807, Jauffret, *La Corbeille des fleurs et le panier de fruits*. (2) 1808b, Sicard, *Théorie des signes*, pp. 625–647. (3) 1819, Jauffret, *Le Panier de fruits*, second ed., pp. 72-86. (4) 1821a, Akerly (transl.), *Elementary exercises*, pp. 329–342. (5) 1826, Bébian, *Journal d'Instruction*, pp. 333–335. (6) 1829, Rodenbach. (7) 1834, Richardin. (8) 1835, Rodenbach. (9) 1849, Clerc (transl.). (10) 1851, Sicard, *Album d'un sourd-muet*, 16 pp. (11) 1873, Berthier, *L'Abbé Sicard*, pp. 146–156. (12) 1976, Lane (transl.), *Wild Boy of Aveyron*, pp. 101–102 (abridged).

About a decade before his death, Massieu wrote another autobiography, which is excerpted in Berthier (1873), who gives as his source "*Le Nord*, 1838, published in that locale," referring to Lille, where Massieu lived and directed a school. Leglay (1838), reporting on the graduation ceremonies at Massieu's school on Aug. 29, 1838, states that Massieu read fragments of his autobiography at the graduation. Apparently, these were published in an issue of the *Revue du Nord* on or near that date and served as Berthier's source. A diligent search in Lille, at the municipal library, the departmental archives, and the Institut départemental de Réhabilitation de la Parole et de l'Audition (successor to Massieu's school), failed to unearth the manuscript autobiography or the relevant issue of the *Revue du Nord*. The national library does not have this newspaper and other municipal libraries in the département du Nord lack the relevant issue. I am pleased to acknowledge the assistance of Franklin Philip in this search. See chapter 9 for more on Massieu's life in Lille.

5. See Fay (1886).

6. Reminiscences of Massieu appear in Sicard (1800), Itard (1821d), consult second edition, Clerc (1849), Berthier (1873).

7. Berthier (1873), p. 145.

8. Sicard (1800), p. x of the 1803 ed. In 1787, a year after opening his school and before Massieu was brought

to his attention, Sicard wrote, "There is nothing more discouraging than the air of stupidity and confusion of these unfortunate beings whose education can begin only with tangible signs and literal representations" (p. 29).

9. Sicard (1808), p. 8. Also see Bernard (1980c), sec. VIII.

10. Sicard's addresses, the question asked of Massieu, and his replies appear in Sicard (1795). Massieu was a teacher in a third sense: he wrote a basic French vocabulary list (Massieu, 1808) that Sicard incorporated in his classes and books, and that was thus a guide for vocabularies in schools in other lands. He also wrote a grammar, which, incomplete, was never published.

11. Report of the committee July 21, 1791 (Bloch and Tuetey, 1911, p. 738).

12. Massieu was named head teaching assistant on Apr. 4, 1790; confirmed by the Constituent Assembly July 21, 1791, National Convention Jan. 7, 1795, and the Ministry of the Interior Sept. 22, 1800.

13. Préseau (1872) says Sicard took the "minor oath" on Aug. 10, 1792, swearing allegiance to "Liberty and Equality," and even contributed 200 livres to the revolutionary tribunal. Weiner (1982) says that Valentin Haüy, director of the School for the Blind, probably denounced him to the commune.

14. Among them was an instructor from his school, Abbé Laurent, according to Berthier (1838b), p. 181, but Massieu's memoirs (cited in Berthier, 1873, p. 169) state that the abbé Laborde, "instituteur adjoint des sourd-muets," was a victim of Sept. 2, 1792. Sicard also encountered a *surveillant* from the school, a M. Labranche (Berthier, 1838b, p. 182).

15. Sicard (1797). The original is quoted in Karakostas (1981), p. 195, from the *Archives Parlementaires*, 31 août 1792, p. 150.

16. Sicard (1797), p. 130.

17. On Sicard's ordeal (1797) also see Tissot (1834); Hué (n.d.); Michaud (1858); Berthier (1838c); Tuetey (1890), v. 5, nos. 182, 183, 213, 214, 1060.

18. Landes (1876), p. 8, reprints a letter from Sicard praising Monnot.

19. Sicard was interrogated by the Revolutionary Surveillance and Safety Committee of the Arsenal Section (the school was at that time in the Celestine monastery on the Right Bank, next to the Armory) in September 1793 (Karakostas, 1981). See Tuetey (1890), v. 10, nos. 528, 534, 554, 555, 745, 747, 1076, 1085; v. 11, no. 165. He was apparently denounced by Valentin Haüy, instructor of the blind; their conflict arose in this way. The National Assembly had ordered the school for the deaf housed in the Celestine monastery (the order of execution was dated Aug. 24, 1790; however, Epée's disciple the abbé Masse had given the pupils classes there beginning six months earlier, in February 1790). See Tuetey (1890) v. 3, no. 463. The blind were ordered to join the deaf on Sept. 28, 1791 (Tuetey, 1890, v. 3, no. 458), but they were separated when the deaf moved to their present quarters on Apr. 1, 1794. See Tuetey (1890), v. 6, nos. 1556–1563. Haüy's culpability is discussed in Karakostas (1981), pp. 75–76; Weiner (1982); l'Esprit (1917).

20. Crisis of 18 fructidor an 5 (Sept. 4, 1797).

21. Sicard's second in command, Louis-François-Joseph Alhoy (1755–1826), took over during his absence: 18 fructidor an 5 to 18 brumaire an 8 (Sept. 4, 1797, to Nov. 9, 1799). When Sicard returned from exile, Alhoy left to become a hospital administrator.

22. Sicard (1800a).

23. Sicard (1800b).

24. Initially, a record of his public exercises (1774), expanded in 1776 and 1784. For English translations, see Arrowsmith (1819) and Epée (1776, 1784).

25. *Ami des Lois*, 21 brumaire an 6 (Nov. 11, 1797).

26. Bouilly (1800b), p. 7.

27. Massieu's memoirs mention these facts. Cited in Berthier (1873), pp. 170–171.

28. Bouilly (1800b), p. 8. Bouilly sent a letter to the editor of the *Courrier des spectacles* (22 frimaire an 7 [Dec. 12, 1798]) to announce his new play. The notice ends: "May the public acclaim my new efforts! May they, above all, demonstrating the great importance of the institution founded by the abbé de l'Epée, incite respect and gratitude for those whom this great man has chosen as the heirs to his genius" (cited in Fournier des Ormes, 1851, p. 232).

29. Bouilly (1800a). First performed Dec. 14, 1799.

30. Nov. 9, 1799.

31. According to Massieu's memoirs, cited in Berthier (1873), p. 171. See Bernard (1941), p. 164.

32. This account follows Bouilly's description: (1835), p. 183ff.

33. Bouilly (1800a), p. 81.

34. Bouilly (1835) mentions Collin d'Harleville.

35. Bouilly (1800b), p. 10. Also in Massieu's memoirs, cited in Berthier (1873), p. 171.

36. 22 nivôse an 8 (Jan. 12, 1800), Berthier (1852a), p. 142.

37. Described in Bouilly (1800b). It took place on 25 nivôse an 8 (Jan. 15, 1800). Two days earlier, Sicard wrote to Bouilly: "Enjoy your triumph, my dear colleague; I am back on the job since yesterday. Your modesty prevents you from claiming your proper share of credit for this victory. It is your play, acclaimed so beautiful, so moving, so absorbing, that put me back in the public eye" (Bouilly, 1800b, p. iii). Bernard (1941, p. 169) points out that (according to Massieu's memoirs, excerpted in Berthier, 1873) Sicard told Massieu he was "becoming free again since the suppression of the Directory." The coup d'état occurred 18 brumaire an 8 (Nov. 9, 1799) and Sicard's interview with Massieu and the legislator who would intervene in his behalf was sometime later that month. But the first showing of Bouilly's play was Dec. 14, 1799, so the play, Bernard argues, could not be responsible for freeing Sicard. However, Sicard's letter to Bouilly (above) and Napoleon's expression of thanks to the playwright for giving him the occasion to free Sicard (Bouilly, 1835, p. 213) suggest that the coup d'état merely allowed Sicard

to move more freely out of his hiding place in the Faubourg Saint-Marceau and Bouilly's play led to his definitive reinstatement as the head of the Paris school.

38. Some description appears in biographies of Sicard by Berthier (1873) and Hué (n.d.); the latter has a sketch.

39. Anon. (1822a).

40. Bouilly (1835), p. 203.

41. Bouilly (1835), p. 213.

CHAPTER 3 / HIGH THEATER

1. Sept. 20, 1742, according to most biographers, but Vaïsse (1844g) says Sept. 28. He was born in Fousseret.

2. Sicard took vows in 1765.

3. Cornié (1903).

4. Berthier (1873) states that the school was created in 1782, but Cornié's exhaustive study (1903) of the school states that courses began Feb. 20, 1786; by the end of that year there were 22 pupils.

5. Sicard (1787a,b, 1789a, 1789b, 1790).

6. "You know very well that in the last two years you haven't given thirty lessons to the pupils," Saint-Sernin wrote to Sicard in 1790. "Massieu should be a daily reminder of what I have done and am capable of doing" (cited in Cornié, 1903, p. 34). For a biographical sketch of Saint-Sernin, see Valade-Gabel (1844). In the program for the public exercises at the Museum on Sept. 12 and 15, 1789, Sicard states that Saint-Sernin is charged with the basic curriculum, including grammar, arithmetic, astronomy, geometry, geography, and metaphysics (!), while he, Sicard, was responsible for religious instruction (Sicard, 1789b). During this period, Sicard was also a corresponding member of the Paris and Toulouse academies and of the Royal Literary Society of Bayeux.

7. Institution Royale des Sourds-Muets de Paris (1836).

8. Peet (1859a), p. 321.

9. Denis (1895a) describes the role of the abbé Masse.

10. Bloch and Tuetey (1911), p. 738, state that the "ancien garde des Sceaux" was a member of the commission to choose Epée's successor, and Valade-Gabel (1844) says that Champion de Cicé became Garde des Sceaux. The former authors give Apr. 6, 1790, as the date on which the commission handed down its selection, but Weiner (1982) and Denis (1895a) state that Sicard was installed as headmaster on Apr. 1, 1790.

11. See Tuetey (1890), v. 3, nos. 459, 464–470. Baker (1842), p. 388, and Vaïsse (1844a) state that "Father Perrenet, an Augustine," was a candidate and Weiner (1982) also gives his name. Tuetey (1890), v. 3, nos. 467, 468, gives Pernay, Salvant, and Sicard. Re: Salvan, see Montaigne (1829), p. 7, 1847 ed.

12. Blanchet (1850), Denis (1895a), and Bloch and Tuetey (1911) give Nov. 21, 1778, as the date. Morel (1846), p. 27, gives Jan. 21, 1778. Baker (1842), p. 388, gives amounts of subsidy. Denis (1895a), p. 246, doubts that the school ever received any money from the king and finds evidence only for some meager subsidies from several bishops. Denis (1895a), p. 8, gives the wording of the king's orders. See Anon. (1785), Amclot (1778).

13. Anon. (1790), p. 4. Cited in Weiner (1982).

14. Chronology: *Mar. 25, 1785*—the king's council assigns the vacant Celestine monastery as a permanent home for Epée's school (Anon., 1785; Weiner, 1982, p. 9). Epée dies Dec. 23, 1789. *Feb. 27, 1790*—the Department of Public Instruction informs the Garde des Sceaux that the abbé Masse has opened a class with Epée's pupils in the Celestine monastery (Tuetey, 1890, v. 3, no. 463). *Feb. 18, 1790*—representatives of the Paris Commune appear before the National Assembly with a request for funds (Bloch and Tuetey, 1911, p. 113, fn. 1; Tuetey, 1890, v. 3, no. 462). *Apr. 6, 1790*—Sicard nominated director (Karakostas, 1981). *May 24, 1790*—the National Assembly sends to its Committee on Mendicity a petition from Sicard (Morel, 1846, p. 27). *Aug. 19, 1790*—Sicard appears before the Committee on Mendicity with four pupils. The Committee suggests Sicard appear before the National Assembly to seek a decree providing funds (Bloch and Tuetey, 1911, p. 114). *Aug. 24, 1790*—Sicard and pupils appear before National Assembly (Tuetey, 1890, v. 3, no. 480), which decrees that the request is referred to the Committee on Mendicity (Bloch and Tuetey, 1911, p. 116, fn. 2; Tuetey, 1890, v. 3, no. 481; Blanchet, 1850, p. 237). *Aug. 26, 1790*—M. Prieur makes an initial report (Bloch and Tuetey, 1911, p. 120). *Sept. 10, 1790*—M. Prieur makes a further report (Bloch and Tuetey, 1911, p. 129). *Oct. 22, 1790*—the committee urges the city of Paris to take steps to rehabilitate the Celestine monastery (Bloch and Tuetey, 1911, p. 153). *Nov. 1, 1790*—Sicard appears before the committee to urge a decree to nationalize the school (Bloch and Tuetey, 1911, p. 162). *Nov. 8, 1790*—the committee repeats its exhortation of the city (Bloch and Tuetey, 1911, p. 176; Tuetey, 1890, v. 3, no. 486). *Nov. 17, 1790*—the committee learns that the city has matched its provisional contribution of 1,200 francs (Bloch and Tuetey, 1911, p. 188). *Jan. 27, 1791*—Sicard appears a second time before the National Assembly (Weiner, 1982, p. 14). *Mar. 21, 1791; Apr. 27, 1791; May 2, 1791; May 19, 1791*—further discussions in committee. *July 21, 1791*—in the name of the Committee on Mendicity and several others, the Prieur report is presented to the National Assembly and voted into law. Sicard addresses the Assembly (Bloch and Tuetey, 1911, pp. 738–757; Tuetey, 1890, v. 3, no. 490). *Sept. 28, 1791*—the National Assembly confirms its decree of July 21, 1791, and adds details with respect to the blind, who are to join the deaf at the Celestine monastery (Bloch and Tuetey, 1911, p. 325; Blanchet, 1850, p. 240). *Oct. 1, 1791*—Legislative Assembly convenes.

15. Further dates in the legislative history of the school: May 12 and 14, 1793, a decree by the Convention nationalizes the school at Bordeaux, provides twenty-four scholarships, envisions that in Paris as a normal school, and plans the creation of six schools in all to serve an estimated 4,000 deaf (Maignet, 1793). Maignet also argues that the Celestine monastery is an unsuitable home for the Paris school; next to the arsenal, it is frequented by workers manufacturing arms. They move about in the building and their presence and materials outside prevent promenades for the deaf. He suggests instead the Saint Magloire monastery, a move which is authorized Feb. 13, 1794, and implemented Apr. 1, 1794. A decree of Jan. 5, 1795, increases scholarships to sixty each in Paris and Bordeaux, and makes children nine to sixteen eligible for five years' schooling (Alhoy, 1795).

16. Tuetey (1890), v. 5, no. 2339, on poor conditions at Celestine monastery.

17. Hermiopolis (1822), p. 5.

18. Decreed Feb. 13, 1794, by the National Convention. Order of execution Mar. 5. The move actually took place Apr. 1, 1794.

19. Institution Impériale des Sourds-Muets (1805).

20. Institution Impériale des Sourds-Muets (1806).

21. Hué (n.d.). After Sicard's death, King Charles X and the dauphin attended the exercises in 1828; Prince Louis Napoleon, President of the Republic, came in 1849 and Emperor Napoleon III in 1866 (Chassé, 1974).

22. Massieu (1815).

23. The size of the crowd is mentioned in Anon., "An account of the institution in Paris for the education of the deaf and dumb," reprinted in Mann (1836). Other articles describing these demonstrations are: Berthier (1838a, 1873), Frank (1804), Institution Impériale (1805, 1806), de Jouy (1813), Kotzebue (1805), Meramia (1815), Meyer (1798, 1802), Michaud (1858), Pain (1828), Paulmier (1831), Weiner (1982).

24. See the *Journal de Paris*, Feb. 22, 1806, cited in Bernard (1952).

25. Lyman (1814), pp. 91–93. Sicard's pupils, no less than his audiences, were subjected to his metaphysical bombast and grammatical theories. The abbé de l'Epée had chastised him a decade earlier: "You struggle and make your pupils struggle needlessly, trying to teach them a science that we never even teach our disciples. . . . By obliging your pupils to acquire at the outset what they should acquire through long use of language, you run the risk of alienating them" (letter reprinted in Berthier, 1873, p. 211). Sicard did not agree; he thought that, chalk in hand, he was endowing the deaf with language "as a mother teaches her hearing child" (Sicard, 1800, p. 9 of the 1803 edition).

26. In 1793 the existing academies of France were suppressed. In 1795, the Institut national des sciences et des arts was established, comprising three classes: sciences physiques et mathématiques; sciences morales et politiques; and littérature et beaux-arts. In 1803 the organization was modified and the Institut divided into four classes: sciences physiques et mathématiques; langue et littérature françaises; histoire et littérature anciennes; and beaux-arts. In 1816 the older designation of "Académie" was revived, with four divisions: Académie française; Académie des inscriptions et belles lettres; Académie des sciences; Académie des beaux-arts. The fifth academy, Académie des sciences morales et politiques, was added in 1832. The Institut has successively had the names: Institut national des sciences et arts (1795); Institut national de France (1803); Institut de France (1806); Institut impérial de France (1811); Institut Royal de France (1814) (Library of Congress, *National Union Catalogue, pre-1956 Imprints*).

The institute had great prestige and influence under Napoleon, a member of the first class, who said he was a follower not of Christ but of the Institut (cited in Copans, 1978). The second class was the stronghold of the ideologists, the materialist psychological school founded by Condillac, and it was they who proposed the contest that De Gérando won. When Napoleon became emperor (1804), he had little sympathy for the revolutionary liberalism that the ideologues represented. Since Condillac's philosophy inspired and guided the Société des Observateurs de l'Homme, it is not surprising that, when the society requested permission to add "impérial" to its name, Napoleon refused and it atrophied and died.

27. Michaud (1858), p. 287.

28. Bigot de Préameneu (1822).

29. The school was founded and Sicard appointed Oct. 30, 1794 (9 brumaire an 3). See Préseau (1812), Hué (n.d.).

30. Nov. 9, 1804 (Weiner, 1982, p. 32). Sicard had a friend from the museum in Bordeaux, André Daniel Laffon de Ladébat (1746–1829), Protestant economist and businessman, who was a high civil servant in the Ministry of the Interior. He also had the trust of the minister himself, Jean-Antoine Chaptal (1756–1832); under the Consulate the former helped rescue him from prison during the Terror. Both probably aided his assignment to the administrative board of the Paris Asylum. (See Weiner, 1982.)

31. 1805–1822, according to Denis (1896), p. 69.

32. 1816. Michaud (1858), p. 287.

33. See Paulmier (1821a, 1834b) and Anon. (1815b) for a description of the celebration.

34. Leroy (1823) gave an oration on Sicard's grave in behalf of the society; this was planned as an annual event.

35. Michaud (1858).

36. 1814. Berthier (1838a), p. 187; Anon. (1822a), p. 20.

37. 1814. Michaud (1858), p. 287; Anon. (1822a), p. 20.

38. In 1818. Michaud (1858), p. 287.

39. According to Weiner (1982), p. 37. Michaud (1858), p. 287, spells it *Wasa* and says the Queen of Sweden awarded it in 1815 or 1816. Berthier (1838a) also spells it *Wasa*.

40. June 1814. Anon. (1822a), p. 21, says the allied princes attended one of Sicard's public exercises. Francis I of Austria did visit on May 11, 1815. Michaud (1858), p. 287, says Alexander gave Sicard the Order of Sainte-Anne and does not mention Saint Vladimir. Sicard was in favor with the Russian court. The empress Maria Feodorovna, mother of Czar Alexander I, founded a little school for the deaf near St. Petersburg which she placed under the direction of a Pole who had studied Epée's system in Vienna, probably under his disciple there, the abbé Storck. At some point, Sicard sent the empress his *Theory of Signs* and she sent him a gift of a ring with a stone worth 30,000 francs. Then she wrote to ask Sicard for an instructor and he sent one of his hearing students, the abbé Jauffret, in 1810. See Landes (1876); De Gérando (1827); Berthier (1873). There was talk of sending Clerc but in the end only one teacher was to go and it was assumed he had to be hearing (Sicard, 1808).

41. Sicard did, however, take the "minor oath" on Aug. 10, 1792 (Préseau, 1872), and he made a personal contribution of 200 livres to the Revolutionary Tribunal two weeks before he was arrested.

42. The exact name is: *Annales réligieuses, politiques et littéraires*. Michaud (1858) p. 286, and Weiner (1982) say that Sicard was arrested under the general proscription of journalists 18 fructidor an V (Sept. 4, 1797) as editor of the *Annales catholiques*.

43. Clerc (1852), p. 107.

44. Berthier (1838a), p. 187.

45. Berthier (1873); Dubois (1894), p. 236.

46. Clerc (1815), Paulmier (1834a), p. 5.

47. Mar. 20, 1815.

48. Berthier (1838a), p. 187, says that Sicard's decline into senility began when he was sixty, in 1802!

49. Berthier (1838a), p. 187. Anon. (1822), p. 21.

50. Anon. (1822a). Berthier (1838a), p. 187, states that Napoleon once had Sicard released from debtor's prison and paid his creditors.

51. Gard reported that Saint-Sernin used the sign language of the deaf to communicate with his pupils and convey the meanings of these sentences. Sicard, however, never used French Sign Language, always chalk, or fingerspelling, or occasionally Epée's methodical signs. See Berthier (1873), p. 12; also Berthier (1838a).

52. Hué (n.d.).

53. The most useful Sicard biographies are: Anon. (1822), Berthier (1873), Hué (n.d.), Michaud (1858), Weiner (1982).

CHAPTER 4 / A TALE BASED ON FACT

1. Bouilly offered to transpose the action elsewhere when threatened with a suit by a retainer of the Solar family but they settled on a mere change of subtitle: from *Faits historiques* (Historical Facts) to *Comédie historique* (Historical Play). The correspondence is described in Fournier des Ormes (1851). For the text of Bouilly's play, see Bouilly (1800). It had 26 performances from 1799 to 1840 at the Comédie-Française, then moved to the Odéon. Berthier and Bélanger counseled actors for performances later in the nineteenth century. See Bernard (1941).

2. Etcheverry (1876b).

3. The boy was actually brought first to Cuvilly and given to a guardian while inquiries were made. After a month, the lieutenant-general of police, on the recommendation of the noble family of Cuvilly, Herault de Séchelles, had the boy brought to Bicêtre. Of many accounts of the Solar story, the most authoritative and detailed is Berthier (1852a).

4. June 13, 1775.

5. Cited in Fournier des Ormes (1851), pp. 189–191. Also appears in Epée (1876).

6. M. Pavillon, prévôt de la mare chaussée de l'Ile-de-France.

7. Initially, in the late 1760s, there were only five or six pupils. Within a decade, however, there were thirty and by the year of Epée's death, 1789, there were over sixty. When there were few pupils, classes were held on the third floor of the house (Epée's brother occupied the second). As their numbers grew, Epée installed a chapel in the spacious rear building that doubled as a classroom. It was torn down in 1876 when the streets were widened to construct the Avenue de l'Opéra (Le Père, 1879, p. 23).

8. See E. Fournier (1877), pp. 169–171, who confirms the schedule of classes. The pensions were directed by M. Chevrot (also spelled Chevrau by some authors) for the boys and Mmes. Cornu, Trumeau, and Lefébure for the girls (Bernard, 1961, p. 30). Perrolle (1782) gives the names of sixteen of Epée's pupils at the boys' pension, including Solar, Didier (also spelled Deydier), Clément de la Pujade. About half the male pupils apparently could respond to sound by bone conduction. Perrolle saw Solar put his fingers in his ears when a very loud noise was made behind him. Pujade could hear bells. In 1777, the ages of the pupils ranged from six to twenty.

9. Epée (1776).

10. Condillac: *Essay on the Origins of Human Knowledge* (1746). *Course of Study for the Prince of Parma* (1775).

11. James Burnet, Lord Monboddo (1773).

12. Prince Doria-Pamphyli; Aug. 13, 1783.

13. See Berthier (1852a), p. 346.

14. Dec. 14, 1784. See Porter (1856a).

15. Joseph II (1741–1791) visited the school on May 7, 1777, and the church May 11, 1777. See Valade-Gabel (1875).

16. Joseph II visit to Epée: see Escoffon (1899), p. 110; Etcheverry (1876a), p. 15; Paganel (1853), p. 283; Arneth (1874), p. 63.

17. Berthier (1852a), p. 68; the letter is translated in Schara (1908).

18. Nov. 24, 1712. Some authors err on this date but Berthier (1852a), p. 336, reproduces the birth certificate.

19. Collège de Quatre Nations, Versailles.

20. The division was by then nearly a century old. The Jesuits were in the ascendancy in France; they persecuted the followers of this heresy, which had begun in Louvain but had spread rapidly throughout much of the French clergy. The Jesuits had the backing of Rome, which condemned Jansenism in four papal bulls (1656, 1665, 1705, and 1713), and the support of the Crown, which, concerned for national unity, ordered all bishops to require their clergy to sign the oath of Pope Alexander VII, contained in the second bull. The king made the first papal bull state law in 1664, and his order to the bishops was issued in 1666. When the Jesuits broke up the Jansenist order at Port Royal, where Pascal, Arnauld, and Nicole had walked and studied, the Jansenists took refuge in Holland and established an independent church, which still exists, with the seat of its episcopate in Utrecht.

21. Bélanger (1886) gives July 13, 1733, as the date of his admission to the bar; Arnaud (1900) gives 1731. It was Msgr. Christophe de Beaumont (1703–1781), known for his love of discipline, the severity of his moral

principles, his harsh criticism of Rousseau's *Emile,* and his intolerance of Jansenism, who refused to admit Epée to the priesthood.

22. Bébian (1819).

23. Bishop Jacques Bénigne Bossuet (b. 1654), nephew of the famous Jacques Bénigne Bossuet (1627–1704), bishop of Meaux, appointed Epée subdeacon of Fouges Mar. 31, 1736; deacon, Sept. 22, 1736; canon of Pougy Mar. 28, 1738; priest, Apr. 5, 1738. (Berthier, 1852a, p. 12).

24. Fauchet (1790), p. 9.

25. Tronson de Coudray was ordered deported to Guiana, along with Sicard and various journalists, in the famous instruction of 18 fructidor. Sicard, as we have seen, went into hiding in the Paris suburbs; Tronson de Coudray died in exile (Clair and Clapier, 1823).

26. The order was issued Apr. 20, 1779.

27. Decision of June 28, 1781.

28. Epée (1776), p. 98. Cited in Bébian (1819), p. 56.

29. Vaïsse (1878) explains that Father Simon Vanin, purveyor of the Fathers of the Christian Doctrine, was affiliated with the Convent of Saint-Julien des Ménétriers (rue Saint-Martin) and not with the monastery under the protection of Saint Charles, which was located in rue des Fossés Saint-Victor. Vanin's pupils, however, lived in the latter street, as Clerc (1816d, p. 33) confirms: the twins "lived opposite the Society of the Fathers of the Christian Doctrine . . . [to which] the abbé de l'Epée had formerly belonged." Father Vanin died Sept. 19, 1759, and Epée's first public demonstration was in 1771, so he met the deaf women in the 1760s. Epée tells us that Vanin had been dead "a rather long time"; thus he began his instruction of the deaf in the late 1760s. However, Sicard (1789b), p. 18, states that Epée began "thirty years ago." Vanin apparently began teaching the deaf in the 1740s. He also taught the distinguished pupil of Pereire, Saboureux de Fontenay, knew Pereire well, and sought his advice.

30. Epée (1776), p. 8.

31. Epée (1776), second letter. Romans 10:17; Saint Augustine continues: A man born deaf is incapable of learning to read, which would lead him to the faith (quoted in Peet, 1851d).

32. Raffon (1794). Cited in Blanchet (1850), pp. 250–253. Perhaps Epée and Sicard failed to recognize the status of French Sign Language in part because the French have always had difficulty in believing in the adequacy of any language other than their own, especially if it was not written. The philosopher and encyclopedist Denis Diderot, a contemporary of Epée, suggested that the study of the French language would reveal the universal principles of thought, since the order of words in the French sentence revealed the order of ideas in the mind (Diderot, 1751). Likewise later, Sicard, criticizing Epée's method for its failure to teach French syntax, wrote: "What kind of sentences could a man write in a foreign language who knew only the meaning of each word without knowing its syntax, above all if he had as a native language only the language of nature, the language of the peoples of Africa, the language of the deaf and dumb. We know the sentences of the Negroes; we can judge those of the deaf and dumb, who are even closer to nature" (Sicard, 1790, pp. 15–16).

33. Condillac (1746), part I, sec. iv, ch. II. This is why Massieu was at pains in his autobiography to tell us that, before receiving Sicard's instruction, "I saw cattle, horses, mules, pigs, dogs, cats, vegetables, houses, fields, grapevines, and after considering all these objects, I remembered them well."

34. Condillac (1775), part I, ch. I.

35. Destutt de Tracy (1798), pp. 238–450; he later retracted this claim: (1803), p. 388 of the 1817 edition.

36. John 20:31.

37. The idea probably came originally from John Locke's *Essay on Human Understanding,* first published in French in 1700, which had a profound influence on Condillac. Locke wrote: "It was necessary that man should find out some external sensible signs, whereof those invisible ideas which his thoughts are made up of, might be known to others. For this purpose nothing was so fit, either for plenty or quickness, as those articulate sounds with which so much ease and variety he found himself able to make. . . . Words . . . came to be made use of by men as the signs of their ideas; not by any natural connexion that there is between particular articulate sounds and certain ideas, for then there would be but one language amongst all men; but by a voluntary imposition whereby such a word is made arbitrarily the mark of such an idea." See Locke (1690), book 3, ch. 2, sec. 1 (v. 2, p. 8, Dover 1959 ed.).

38. Epée (1776), part 1, ch. IV, p. 36.

39. Clerc visited France in 1820, 1835, and 1846. See Clerc (1848). Also see Valade-Gabel's article on the notebooks in Bélanger (1886), pp. 24–30.

40. Epée (1784), pp. 16–17.

41. The abbé Sicard later replaced Epée's Latin constructions with conceptual ones but they were long constructions nonetheless. Slavishly following Condillac's precept of analysis, Sicard concluded that if a peach, for example, is the union of a color, a taste, and a texture, then the sign for a peach must contain the signs for yellow, sweet, fuzzy, and so on. Thus each French word was paired, in his system, not with a sign from French Sign Language, nor even an invented sign, but rather with a lengthy description comprising many signs and even pantomime. This is the great error of Sicard's dictionary, which he published in his *Theory of Signs.* Here, for example, is how Sicard requires the expression of the word "Providence": "Make the signs for all living things, be they vegetable or animal, receiving life and all that preserves it. Depict an immense being, occupying all space, looking down with care and concern on all living things so that none will perish through disregard. Compare this benevolent being with a mother whose heart looks after her son whom she has been forced to send far from home. Represent manually all the daily miracles of the Providence which commands the waters of the sky to moisten the earth, the sun to warm it, man to cultivate it, and which undertakes alone to make the trees fecund and the fields fertile. All of these details require only three signs that convey the high points, and they are: first, the signs of plants and animals, living; second, the Creator granting them, since they lack the essentials of life, all the daily blessings required for their survival; third, that eternal eye discovering all needs, as would a caring mother, leaving

none unsatisfied" (Sicard, 1808b, pp. 217–218). Peet (1859a) contrasts Epée's sign for "believe" (p. 292) with Sicard's (p. 327); Puybonnieux (1846) contrasts French Sign Language HATE with Sicard's prescription (p. 218). In French Sign Language, the concept of "Providence" is conveyed in a single sign, just as it is conveyed by one word in French: the signer holds his hands in front of him (as if pressing against a wall) and nods them twice. Ironically, it was a commonplace to view these signs as defective since they were brief, "reduced" by contrast with pantomime, and thus less pictorial. See De Gérando (1827). Yet the reduced sign is invariably easier to produce, is more regular from one person to the next, allows more rapid conversation, and evokes the associated idea more surely than the pantomimic one chosen by Sicard or Epée.

42. Epée (1784), part III.

43. Cited in Valade-Gabel (1900), p. 101.

44. Cited in Sicard (1800), p. xli, 1803 ed. See also Bébian (1819), pp. 54–56.

45. Critiques of Epée's methods will be found in: Morel (1846), p. 83; Magnat (1896); Peet (1859a); Bébian (1827), pp. 191–207; Sicard (1790); Berthier (1840c), p. 44; (1852), p. 31.

46. See Barnard (1835), p. 389; Peet (1857a), p. 339; Williams (1893), p. 22. The contact between the oral language community and the sign language community, particularly the presence of bilingual speakers, leads to the spontaneous development of varieties of sign language between ASL and manual English (and in France between FSL and manual French). Increasingly, these varieties are called Pidgin Sign English in the United States (Woodward, 1973; Woodward and Markowicz, 1975), although in a helpful discussion of the issue Battison (1978, ch. 3) prefers the term Sign English. On the contemporary French scene, Pidgin Sign French is generally called Français Signé (Moody, 1983), which invites confusion with prescriptive signing systems invented to capture grammatical features of French, including Epée's system of methodical signs.

47. Bernard (1961), p. 30.

48. The reference here is to the Revolution of 1789. There was a second revolution in 1830.

49. See Clerc (1851c), p. 65.

50. Other French disciples (cited in Bernard, 1961, p. 31): Salvan from Riom, Huby from Rouen, Delinière and Dumourier from Le Mans, Dubourg from Toulouse, Ferrand from Chartres, Pernet de Foncine from Epinal, and Masse from Paris. In his dictionary, Epée (1896) states that there were fourteen disciples from France or abroad who came for his lessons. He started work on a kind of dictionary of methodical signs to assist them when they returned to the cities from which they had come. It was finished in 1787 but no funds were available to print it until 1896.

51. See Bélanger (1886), p. 33, for a list.

52. Schara (1908). On May and other disciples, see Scagliotti (1823).

53. Hervás y Panduro (1795), pp. 31, 53, of the 1875 French translation.

54. Daras (1856) gives a useful chronology but seems to be in error on the founding of the Madrid School, which he dates in 1765. See De Gérando (1827), p. 213.

55. On Borg, see Piroux (1843b).

56. Sources on the growth of European schools: Valette (1867); Bélanger (1886); Pitrois (1912); Scagliotti (1823). On the professions of the French deaf in 1835, see Berthier (1852a), p. 240.

57. On the number of schools, the *Association Review*, 1901, p. 397, reports 196 in 1850 and 327 in 1857, virtually all in Europe and America. The *American Annals of the Deaf*, 1869, p. 63, reports 28 American schools for the deaf that year. Talbot (1895) states that there were 115 American teachers of the deaf in 1857, 41 percent of them deaf; McGregor (1893) gives the same percentage. Clarke (1900a) reports 187 American teachers of the deaf in 1870, the same fraction deaf themselves. Thus, in America there were about 6.7 teachers per school. With some 200 schools worldwide, these ratios yield an estimate in line with that attributed here to Clerc; some 550 teachers of the deaf in 1869.

58. Michaud (1858), p. 509: 7,000–12,000 livres. Anon. (1863b): 400 pounds sterling; Baker (1842), p. 383, says 300 livres were about 12 pounds sterling. Bazot (1819), p. 51: 10,000 francs. Berthier (1852a), p. 76: 12,000 livres, corresponding to 7,000 or 8,000 francs. DeLand (1917), p. 44: 3,000 dollars. Valette (1857), p. 21: Epée received 7,000 or 8,000 francs according to his niece, the comtesse de Courcel. H. P. Peet (1859a), p. 295, gives 14,000 livres or 2,600 dollars.

59. The daughter of Louis XIV is buried in Saint Roch, as is the philosopher Holbach and the writer Piron. Bossuet's funeral was held here, as was the baptism of Molière's child. Epée is buried in the chapel named for Saint Nicolas, which belonged to his family. It was violated in 1793 and the lead of his coffin converted to cannon balls to hold off the enemies of the Revolution. In 1838, Epée's remains were recovered and reinterred. In 1841 a monument was placed over the tomb and the following year a statue erected at Versailles (Berthier, 1874).

60. Tronson de Coudray, the eloquent barrister who had successfully defended Cazeaux, became the friend of Jean Nicolas Bouilly and presented him to the bar in 1787, before he began his career as a playwright (Bouilly, 1835, p. 141). References on Solar affair: secondary sources—'A' (1800); 'A' (1964); Bernard (1941); Berthier (1852a); Bouilly (1800a, 1835); Clair and Clapier (1823); Dubief (1891); Dubois (1894); Etcheverry (1876); Fournier des Ormes (1851); Jubinal (1866), contains text of 'A,' 1800); LePère (1879); Marechalle and Constant (1831); Préseau (1872); Rodenbach (1829); primary sources—de la Cretelle (1780); Elie de Beaumont (1779 a,b,c, 1780); Eude (1799); Moreau de Vorme (1799); Moreau de Vorme and Tronson de Coudray (1779); Tronson de Coudray (1779, 1780a,b).

CHAPTER 5 / THE SECRET

1. De Gérando (1827).

2. Beda Venerabilis (733), book V, ch. ii.

3. Rudolph Agricola (1433–1485); Agricola (1528).

4. Jérôme Cardan (1501–1576). Mullet (1971) also calls Cardan an egomaniacal scalawag.

5. John Wilkins (1614–1672).

6. Kenelm Digby (1603–1665); Digby (1644).

7. They implicated rather than named Bonet. See later.

8. Juan Pablo Bonet (1579–1629?); Bonet (1620).

9. George Dalgarno (1626–1687). See: Dalgarno (1680); Anon. (1817); Stewart (1812).

10. Francis Van Helmont (1618–1699).

11. George Sibscota (1670). On the plagiarism, see Guyot and Guyot (1842), p. 483.

12. John Bulwer (1644). Bulwer (1614–1684).

13. La Rochelle (1882) has written the definitive biography of Pereire. A rather more colorful and partisan account comes from Edouard Séguin (1847); both had access to private family documents. There is also a more terse biography by Hément (1875). Also see Coste d'Arnobat (1803) and Bernheim (1981). I have conjectured that Clerc and Marois met.

14. La Rochelle (1822), p. 344.

15. Cited in Valade-Gabel (1839), p. 30; attributed to Deschamps.

16. La Rochelle (1882), pp. 126, 127.

17. She entered Pereire's tutelage May 2, 1756, along with Marie Le Rat Magnitot, also seven.

18. Quoted in Séguin (1847), p. 116.

19. Mar. 15, 1771. She was presented along with Mlle. Le Rat and Me. de la Voute. It is described in Séguin (1847), p. 137.

20. Georges Louis Leclerc de Buffon (1707–1788); his 44-volume *Histoire Naturelle* was published between 1749 and 1804.

21. Jean-Jacques Rousseau (1712–1778).

22. Hément (1875), p. 44.

23. Alphonse Laurent de Blois went to interview Marie Marois when she was eighty in 1829; he was the father of a deaf boy and the author of several books on the education of the deaf. A summary of his interview appears in: Laurent (1831a), pp. 13–16; Institution Royale des Sourds-Muets (1832), no. 3, pp. 240–241. On the use of signs, also see Séguin (1845), p. 336; La Rochelle (1882), p. 49.

24. Séguin (1847), p. 211, quotes a letter from her to this effect.

25. Quoted in Séguin (1847), p. 316.

26. When Pereire's daughter-in-law thought to revive the name and the methods of the great teacher, Marie Marois wrote from Orléans, "The narrow circle in which I have lived until now, and the separation from society which my condition has always imposed and imposes even more so today, are powerful reasons to prevent me from participating in your plan. . . . The years that weigh heavily on me have weakened the skills that my illustrious teacher taught me and, through disuse of his art and method, have left me only a few scanty notions." Quoted in La Rochelle (1882), p. 521.

27. Bonet (1620).

28. Holder (1669).

29. Amman (1692, 1700). Sibscota (1670) was also cited.

30. The post of interpreter to the king was awarded Pereire in 1765.

31. Roth (1932).

32. Apr. 11, 1715. The first Jews admitted legally in France, by ordinance of King Henry II (1549–1559), were called New Christians or Portuguese Jews, but they were not necessarily Portuguese. This and Pereire's ancestry are no doubt responsible for the widespread misattribution of his nationality. He was not Portuguese but Spanish, a matter of some importance, as will appear.

33. La Rochelle (1882), p. 2, cites evidence that Beaumarin was born deaf, and on p. 240 he cites Pereire's affirmation that the deafness was "absolute."

34. Some writers say he owned or operated five large farms, but this is a misunderstanding. The term was applied after 1664 to provinces that had accepted the abolition of internal customs barriers ordered by Colbert.

35. La Rochelle (1882 p. 23), Hément (1875, p. 16), and Pereire's contract with M. d'Etavigny (Séguin, 1847, pp. 23–270) state that his son was born deaf; Pereire (1768, p. 514) says he was "perfectly deaf." Kilian (1885, pp. 9–10) says, however: "We can believe that for Heinicke, Van Helmont and Amman, whoever did not speak was deaf. This explains the speed with which they obtained their results; [they were] not with pupils born deaf but with retarded children, semi-idiots, semi-deaf, like d'Agy [sic] d'Etavigny, a famous pupil of Pereire, a child who had spoken until perhaps the age of nine or ten."

36. At Beaumont-en-Auge.

37. An intimate of the king, and a member of the Royal Academy of Sciences, the duke of Chaulnes, whose duchy lay just thirty kilometers away, went with his sister to the abbey to interview the old monk in writing in 1733. This duke did not meet Pereire for another seventeen years, but when he did he became the most important person in his life for he gave him a pupil (his deaf godson, Saboureux de Fontenay), who became so erudite he astonished France and its king and challenged the abbé de l'Epée. Etienne Defaye (also spelled de Fay) taught at the Abbey of Saint-Jean-d'Amiens. A copy of the original interrogation appears in Séguin (1847), pp. 244–247. Séguin states (p. 248) that Azy d'Etavigny was at this school five years but Cazeaux (1746, cited in Valade-Gabel, 1875, p. 40), a contemporary and more reliable source, says he spent "seven to eight years in the school (from 1735 or 1736 to 1743)."

38. See Denis (1887), who gives as an estimate of his date of birth the year 1670.

39. André (1746), pp. 341–342.

40. Dated June 14, 1746. See Pereire (1747), reprinted in Séguin (1847), pp. 23–27; also La Rochelle (1882), p. 25, gives excerpts. The text says La Rochelle is the site, but that is an error; Pereire was to go to Beaumont-en-Auge and did so.

41. Nov. 22, 1746. Pereire (1747), p. 335, and Séguin, p. 38, list the members present.

42. Bishop of Bayeux, Msgr. Albert de Luynes. The syllabification appears in the report of the commission, Pereire (1747), reprinted in Séguin (1847), p. 38.

43. Pereire arrived at the college on July 13, 1746, and the testimonial was dated May 6, 1747. It is published in Séguin (1847), p. 43ff.

44. Hôtel d'Auvergne, Quai des Augustins.

45. Quoted in La Rochelle (1882), p. 37.

46. Mar. 4, 1749, Hôtel de Bourgogne, rue de Savoie.

47. June 11, 1749. Pereire (1749).

48. Buffon (1749), p. 350; p. 182, 1818 ed.

49. Coste d'Arnobat (1803), who knew Pereire personally, gives the report of the commission, other documents, and a summary list of d'Étavigny's skills.

50. Herder (1785), book 9, ch. 2, p. 233, of the 1800 translation by Churchill.

51. Misspelled Ramires de Cortone.

52. The letter is reprinted in La Rochelle (1882), p. 64ff.

53. In Ganges, near Montpellier. He was born in 1738. Heinicke (1781), p. 25 of the 1968 English translation, mistakenly states that Saboureux was deafened at age eight. All authors and Saboureux himself in his autobiography state he was born deaf (Saboureux de Fontenay, 1764, p. 295). Pereire (1768), p. 511, says he is not profoundly deaf.

54. Saboureux de Fontenay appeared before the Royal Academy of Sciences on Jan. 27, 1751.

55. Seven months after they began, a cleric was sought in Paris who knew some sign language; this casts some doubt about Saboureux's abilities in French, at least at this early stage in his education. Whom should they find but Father Vanin, the very priest who was, at about the same time, teaching the history of the saints to the two deaf sisters that Epée was fatefully to encounter. Incidentally, Saboureux makes it quite clear in his autobiography that Father Vanin used engravings to teach religion, and sign language to explain the engravings and the words printed beneath each. Thus his instruction of the deaf sisters who would become Epée's pupils was no doubt in sign. Both Defaye and Vanin, then, preceded Epée in using sign language to instruct the deaf. Father Vanin and Pereire became friends as well as collaborators, and the priest was later responsible for sending him an additional pupil, named Le Couteux.

56. Lebouvier Desmortiers (1800), p. 226.

57. Epée (1776), I, p. 7; II, pp. 27–28.

58. Diderot (1751).

59. Pereire (1768).

60. Pereire (1768).

61. Saboureux de Fontenay (1779). Deleau proposed a system of phonetic fingerspelling in 1830 which he said originated with Pereire (La Rochelle, 1882, p. 265). Gaussens (1872), pp. 79–80, judges that Pereire's dactylology had 25 handshapes for the letters of the alphabet, 34 shapes for pronunciation of basic sounds, and 22 elements for letters that change pronunciation according to context, for a total of 81 elements. In addition, iconic gestures specified accents, pausing, abbreviations, numbers, etc. Laurent (1831a) claims that the phonetic elements in Pereire's alphabet correspond to syllables. In another letter, explaining the principles of five different methods of teaching the deaf, Saboureux states that the method of Ponce de León and of Pereire was the manual alphabet.

62. Pereire (1768), p. 509.

63. Condillac (1775), introduction, v. 1, p. 406, 1947 ed.

64. Buffon (1749) v. 5, p. 194, 1818 ed.

65. Braille invented his alphabet in 1829. Haüy (1745–1822); Braille (1809–1852); see Weiner (1974).

66. Rousseau (162), book 2, p. 146, 1939 ed.; p. 138, 1979 English translation.

67. Vaïsse, quoted in Congress on Deaf—International—First (1878), pp. 478–479.

68. Desloges (1779a), pp. 31–32. Desloges stated in an interview with Pereire that his publisher, whom Saboureux knew well, was the abbé Copineau, canon of the Church of Saint-Louis-du-Louvre. La Rochelle (1882), p. 408.

69. Quoted in Séguin (1847), p. 217.

70. Quoted in Séguin (1847), p. 224.

71. Others who tried to guess Pereire's secret were Père Y.-M. André (1746) of the Caen academy, who wrote a book about it; Dubois, Marois's confessor (cited in Séguin); Recoing (1823) gives a manual alphabet based on syllables.

72. Epée (1784), p. 159.

73. Harvey Peet, Clerc's colleague and head of the New York Institution for the Deaf and Dumb, is the source for these remarks.

74. Yebra (1593). Melchor Yebra (1524–1586).

75. Petersson (1956).

76. Digby (1644), pp. 307–309, 1645 ed. Also see DeLand (1920).

77. Di Castro (1642), cited in Farrar (1890), p. 41; Saint-Simon (1788) and Morhoff (1732), cited in Denis (1887d). Also see Braddock (1975), pp. 126–128.

78. Louis de Rouvroy, duke of Saint-Simon (1675–1755), wrote celebrated *Mémoires* (1694–1723) about the life of the court. (He was an ancestor of Claude Henri de Saint-Simon, philosopher and economist, who influenced Séguin, among many others.) This passage is cited in Denis (1887d), p. 202. The court of Louis XIV went into mourning for two weeks when the prince of Carignan died. Victor Emmanuel, king of Italy, was his direct descendant.

79. Ramirez de Carrion (1629). De Gérando, possibly on Antonio's authority (1788), says de Carrion was born deaf, and many authors following him have repeated this error. None of de Carrion's contemporaries mention such a thing and his work as an oral teacher of the deaf and secretary to a deaf man make it most unlikely.

80. Alfonso Fernandez de Cordova y Figueroa, Marquis de Priego.

81. Cited in Farrar (1890), p. 39.

82. Many writers—e.g., A. Valade-Gabel (1875)—call Ramirez de Carrion's disciple Pierre de Castro. De Gérando (1827), p. 326, calls him "the first physician of the Duke of Mantua who taught the son of Prince Thomas of Savoy." Farrar (1890) argues that this is a misattribution. Chaves and Soler (1975) state that di Castro's works carried the first name Ezechiele in 1642 and Pietro thereafter.

83. Di Castro (1642), cited in Farrar (1890), p. 41.

84. Cited in Farrar (1890), p. 55. Also related by A. Valade-Gabel (1875, p. 40ff), who seems to have gotten it from Perolle (1782, pp. 24–27), who got it from Epée in person, who got it from a Dr. Sachs of Lewenheim; Sachs (1670).

85. His publisher was Juan Bautista de Morales, cited in Chaves and Soler (1975). Digby never stated that he taught Luis de Velasco, or anyone else, for that matter. Nor did Digby claim Bonet was the de Velascos' teacher, although virtually everyone has taken it for granted, since Bonet was in the Constable's employ and had indeed written a book, which Digby said Luis's teacher had done. Digby also said, however, that the teacher was a priest who was still alive and in the service of the prince of Carignan. Now, neither Bonet nor Ramirez de Carrion was a priest, but only the latter was still alive in 1644, when Digby published; Bonet had died about the time the prince was born, more than a decade earlier.

86. Saint-Simon (1788), cited in Denis (1887d), p. 204. This hypothesis is confirmed by a contemporary of Luis de Velasco's son, Pedro, who became the Spanish ambassador to England. That observer wrote that Pedro's "father, born deaf and mute, had learned to make himself understood, to read, write, etc., along with the prince of Carignan at Madrid, through the efforts of a Spaniard named Emmanuel Ramirez de Carrion." Also note that Braddock (1975), p. 104, says Don Luis (1604–1664) became deaf at age two.

87. Four years before Kenelm Digby's book appeared, the founder and first secretary of the Royal Society, John Wilkins (1614–1672), recorded that one unidentified man had taught the deaf to speak, first by having them write the name of any object he pointed to and "afterwards provoking them to such motions of the tongue as might answer the several words." The teacher had also trained the deaf with sign language. We do not know how Wilkins learned the story and whether he was referring to Ponce de León (1520–1584) or Bonet (1579–1629) or Ramirez de Carrion (1579–?). Wilkins noted "what dialogues of gestures passed between persons born deaf and dumb," by which they communicated "as directly as if they had the benefit of speech." See Mullett (1971), p. 124.

88. Translated in A. Valade-Gabel (1875), p. 51; Peet (1850b), p. 119; and Farrar (1890), p. 28. It was originally unearthed and published by the abbé Feyjóo y Montenegro (also spelled Feijóo), 1753, v. IV, carta 7. The document is dated Aug. 24, 1578. The reference to Aristotle is apparently to his *History of Animals*, book 4, ch. 9, sec. 8, Arnold (1888). p. 5, translates the relevant passage: "Those who are born deaf all become speechless. They have a voice but are destitute of speech." The Creswell 1891 translation (London: Bell, 1891) is: "All that are born dumb and all children utter sounds but have no language." The D. W. Thompson translation (Oxford: Clarendon, 1910) is: "Men that are deaf are in all cases also dumb; that is, they can make vocal sounds but they cannot speak." Hodgson (1953), p. 62, also attributes to Aristotle the statement, "Those who are born deaf all become senseless and incapable of reason." Bender (1970), p. 21, states that this is a mistranslation and gives Peet's (1851d) explanation of the source of the error: "Among the Greeks, the same word *(kophoi)*, denoting primarily dull of mind (like our *dumb*), was used both for the deaf and for the dumb" (p. 106).

89. Castañiza (1583), cited in Hervás y Panduro (1795), v. i, p. 301; Antonio (1788), p. 228; De Gérando (1827), p. 310; and in Farrar (1890), p. 32. On the search for Ponce's manuscript: (1) Guyot and Guyot (1842) state: "According to an annotation made by M. Ramon de la Sagra during a visit to the Institute for the Deaf at Groningen July 9, 1838, there had just been found in the library of a Spanish convent (the monastery of San Salvador at Oña) the original work of Pedro Ponce. See also, Ramon de la Sagra, *Cinque Meses en la America del Norte*, pp. 23–29, P. Ponce, and by the same author *Voyage en Hollande et en Belgique*, Paris, 1839, v. 1, p. 152, where the author says of Ponce's manuscript that Dom Barth. Gallardo had cited it in his circular of Jan. 19, 1838, giving the titles of very precious Spanish works. See Carton, *Le Sourd-Muet et l'Aveugle*, v. 2, 1838, p. 128, which states that M. De Gérando was hoping to receive a copy. According to de la Sagra, Ponce got his idea from the old pantomime dances; Hernandez says from the book written by Beda." (2) Hernández (1814) says Ponce used a manual alphabet. If so, this is consistent with the case that Bonet's methods were taken from Ponce. (3) Leroy (1842), p. 12, says Ponce's manuscript has been found: "They are in the hands of a deputy to the Cortes, a friend of M. Ramon de la Sagra, who has promised a copy to the administration of the Royal School of Paris. (4) Bébian (1826a), p. 126, says Gall cites a passage from Ponce's book communicated by Emmanuel Nuñez de Taboada and "an ecclesiastic whom I know and who stayed in this monastery during the emigration had occasion to see the manuscript." (5) Gall and Spurzheim (1810), v. 1, pp. xxiv–xxvi, publish a letter from Emmanuel Nuñez de Taboada acclaiming Ponce's discovery and citing his contemporaries but without information on the manuscript. (6) Chaves and Soler (1975) give additional details on the unsuccessful search for Ponce's manuscript, and confirm that José Gallardo, deputy and librarian to the Cortes (parliament), had read the book and had a copy made in Seville in 1823 that was lost. The author of *Don Quixote* also seems to be crediting Ponce when he tells of a monk who came to Valladolid and succeeded in making a deaf man hear and speak (Cervantes, 1614, cited in Farrar, 1890, p. 32).

90. Aristotle, book 4, ch. 9, of the 1891 translation.

91. Vallès (1587), p. 78, 1592 ed.

92. Baltasar de Zuniñga, cited in Chaves and Soler (1974).

93. Morales (1575), p. 38, cited in Hervás y Panduro (1795) and Farrar (1890), p. 30.

94. Hervás y Panduro (1795) states that the constable who employed Ponce, Inigo Hernandez de Velasco, was the father of the constable who employed Bonet, Bernardino Hernandez de Velasco. However, Farrar (1890) indicates that he was the grandfather, as does Braddock (1975, p. 103), probably on Farrar's authority; Chaves and Soler (1975) show Farrar correct.

95. El Mudo (1526–1579). See Braddock (1975), pp. 123–126.

96. Code of Justinian, bk. iii, tit. 20, 7; bk. vi, 22, 10; see Arnold (1888), *Manual*, p. 17; Peet (1857).

97. A fellow monk at Oña, Lasso, wrote a treatise for the de Velascos on the aspects of Spanish law that no longer restricted them since they were no longer dumb. See Farrar (1892). Vaïsse (1844b), p. 4. The first de Velasco of record is Pedro Hernandez, count of Haro, whom the Spanish king Henry IV made constable, vice-king in effect, in 1473, although he was not of royal birth. Pedro had two sons; one, the duke of Frias, had no children, so the title of constable passed to the other, Inigo. He had two sons at the dawn of the sixteenth century: Pedro, third constable of Castile, who had no children, and Juan, the marquis of Berlanga by marriage, who had eight, five of them deaf. The two hearing daughters married counts, while a hearing son, Inigo, was tutored at home. The three deaf daughters were sent to convents and the two deaf sons to the monastery of Oña. This not only kept the deaf scions of the family out of sight of society but also prevented them from reproducing. The youngest son, Pedro, was Ponce de León's amazing deaf student who could sing the plainchant with a congregation of monks, keeping time and tune, as one of their number reports; he died when he was twenty. Ponce's education of the oldest son, Francisco, was called "marvelous," "miraculous," "unheard of"; he was "the first deaf-mute in the world who spoke through the ingenuity of man." Before this miracle, however, the title of constable had passed to the only hearing boy, Inigo, from his uncle Pedro, who died in 1557. If Inigo had died or remained childless, the title would have passed to Francisco if he could speak, or out of the family if he could not. But Ponce's pupil was not put to the test, since Inigo had a hearing son, the fifth constable, Juan, who died young. He left two sons, Bernardino, who became the sixth constable and Bonet's employer, and Luis, the deaf pupil of Ramirez de Carrion whom Kenelm Digby announced to an astonished Europe and whom the king named the marquis of Fresno. Once again the family's fortunes potentially hinged on speech: if Bernardino died childless, the title would pass to Luis if, thanks to Ramirez de Carrion, he could speak. Again, the problem did not arise. The title passed to a hearing son of Bernardino and Luis's son Pedro became merely the second marquis of Fresno and ambassador to England.

98. Translated in Farrar (1890), p. 69.

99. Antonio (1788) also suggests Bonet's book was not an original work but based on what he learned in the de Velasco family.

100. Sachs (1670).

101. Coste d'Arnobat (1803), p. 30.

102. Feyjóo y Montenegro (1730).

103. In a letter to Desloges, published in Deschamps (1780), Saboureux cites his prior autobiography (1765); his letter on music in the *Journal de Physique*, July 2, 1773; a sketch of his early ideas published by an anonymous author in a collection, *Antilogie et fragments philosophiques;* and his memoir on meteorology presented to the Royal Academy. Deschamps (1780).

104. Saboureux de Fontenay (1779), p. 35.

105. La Rochelle (1882), p. 406ff. The interview took place on Oct. 31 and Nov. 6, 1779.

106. The *Journal Encyclopédique de Bouillon;* see Anon. (1780). Reprinted in De Gérando (1827), pp. 449–450. Translated in Braddock (1975), p. 46. Desloges was born in 1747 at Le Grand-Pressigny, near La Haye, Tours diocese.

107. Amman (1700), 1873 translation, reprinted 1965, p. 10.

108. He taught speech much as Ponce did, and Bonet described, by showing a letter, teaching the articulatory configuration to sound its "reduced" value, then showing his pupils how to write the letter. However, he also taught lipreading. A few years before publishing his book, Deschamps came to Paris to consult Pereire and afterward kept up a brisk correspondence with the master demutizer. Deschamps (1779).

109. Desloges (1779a), pp. 14–15.

110. Deschamps (1779), p. 32.

111. Anon. (1780).

112. Epée (1896). The plan for the work appears in Epée (1784) but it was published posthumously.

113. Sicard (1808b).

114. De Gérando (1827), p. 590.

115. Desloges (1779a), p. 28. Deschamps (1779), p. xxx.

116. These letters and programs constitute the second part of his 1776 book. The first part is a description of his method and a critique of Pereire's. The work was revised for publication in 1784. Here he drops the attack on Pereire and theologians, and adds some new means of instruction. Appended to the 1784 version are two other "parts": an essay on speech teaching and an account of his dispute with Heinicke. The essay on speech teaching was edited and published separately by Sicard in 1820, along with an introduction and a eulogy by Bébian. In 1827, Bébian reprinted the work in his two-volume course of instruction for the deaf. Arrowsmith translated Epée (1784), including the essay on speech, into English in 1819, and Green did likewise in 1801, reprinted in 1860.

117. Epée (1776), part II, p. 8, (1771 letter).

118. Epée (1784), p. 215 of the 1819 English translation. Likewise in the 1773 letter, "The congenitally deaf can speak as we do when they are taught" (Epée, 1776, part II, p. 56; 1773 letter). Also see: Epée (1776), part

I, p. 55; part II, pp. 24, 57 (1772 and 1773 letters). Epée's pupil Louis Clément de la Pujade recited a Latin discourse of five and a half pages at one of his public exercises (however, Louis could detect the sound of bells, as well as the ticking of a watch placed between his teeth) and at another exercise debated the definition of philosophy with his fellow student Francis Deydier, who accompanied the count of Solar on his journey. Epée also taught another scholar to repeat aloud the twenty-eighth chapter of the Gospel according to Matthew and to recite the morning service on Sunday. The British philosopher Lord Monboddo reports on a visits to Epée's school in 1773: "He had brought some of his scholars a surprising length; and one of them I particularly remember, a girl who spoke so pleasantly I would not have known her to be deaf. On Clément de la Pujade, see Perolle (1782), cited in Valade-Gabel (1875). He could also detect shouting through an ear-trumpet applied to his temple. The discourse is published in Epée (1776), part II, p. 127. On the scholar who recited the gospel: Epée (1784), p. 256 of the 1819 English translation. See the "Notice" in Epée (1774). Also see Burnet (1773), p. 192.

When Abbé Sicard was appointed to the national college for teacher training, he presented a pupil, according to the stenographic record, "who loudly and clearly pronounces the words corresponding to signs that are made to him" (Sicard, 1795, v. 1, p. 252; v. 3, p. 266). This pupil, Peyre, also read aloud Massieu's written answers to questions from the audience. Sicard, almost as transported as his audience, then affirmed that Peyre was better than any of Pereire's pupils. History has not passed down to us the degree of his deafness or his age at onset.

119. Epée (1776), part I, p. 24.

120. Epée (1784), p. 257 of the 1819 (Arrowsmith) translation.

121. Sicard (1795), v. 4, pp. 267–269 (Apr. 10, 1795). On Sicard's low regard for teaching speech to the deaf, also see T. Gallaudet (1818b), p. 132.

122. Epée (1776), part I, p. 33.

123. Epée (1776), part I, pp. 37, 154.

124. Saboureux de Fontenay (1765), p. 428.

125. Cited in La Rochelle (1882), p. 16; Epée (1776), part I, p. 119.

126. Quoted in Epée (1776), part I, p. 119.

127. Pereire, July 7, 1777, cited in Séguin (1847), pp. 154–161.

128. Saboureux de Fontenay (1780).

129. Amman (1700), pp. 8, 10, 1965 ed., 1873 English translation. Johann Conrad Amman (1669–1724), born Schaffhausen, Switzerland.

130. Amman (1700), p. 2, 1965 ed., 1873 English translation.

131. Amman (1700), p. 12, 1965 ed., 1873 English translation.

132. Amman (1692), p. xxvi, 1972 ed., 1694 English translation. Also see letter to John Hudde in Amman (1700), p. xvii ff, 1873 English translation.

133. Amman (1700), p. 52, 1965 ed., 1873 English translation.

134. Amman also knew nothing, he said, of the work of Francis Mercurius, Baron Van Helmont, who had affirmed in print twenty-five years earlier that Hebrew is the natural language of man, that its characters depict the positions of the vocal organs required to make the corresponding sounds, and that with this discovery he had taught a deaf child to lipread in three weeks. The pupil reportedly proceeded on his own to read books, and to learn Hebrew by comparing German and Hebrew translations of the Bible. Consequently, when Van Helmont read Amman's book, he went to see him to explain how he, not Amman, was the first teacher of the deaf. Van Helmont's brother was the famous physician and chemist who discovered carbonic gas and invented the thermometer. Van Helmont (1667).

135. See L. W. Kerger (1704). Reprinted in German with the work of Raphel in 1801. Carton (1847), p. 55, states that De Gérando is in error in affirming that Entmuller taught a deaf-mute. The person who did the teaching was Kerger, who—at Entmuller's request—informed the Academy of Natural Curiosities of his method. The first teachers of the deaf to follow him were in Silesia. L. W. Kerger and his sister acknowledged their debt to Ponce, Bonet, Wallis, as well as Amman, but denied that speech was indispensable to mental culture and preferred to teach written language with the aid of sign. Next, George Raphel (1673–1740), a compatriot of Kerger, a pastor and a Greek scholar with three deaf daughters, published an account of how he taught the eldest to speak, following Amman. Like Kerger, he gave great weight to reading and writing and did not hesitate to communicate with his children in some form of sign language (no doubt, the "home sign" that would develop naturally in a family with several deaf children). See Raphel (1718).

136. Heinicke (1723–1790); Heinicke, 1782, pp. 43–44, of the 1968 English translation. Epée revised his 1776 book in 1784. By then he was under attack from another quarter, Samuel Heinicke. He updated his method, added his essay on teaching speech, presented his dispute with Heinicke. He deleted the material designed to convince theologians and philosophers that the deaf could be educated through sign—that, by the grace of God, was no longer necessary. And as nothing more had been heard from Pereire or Saboureux in the eight years since publication of the first edition, he deleted the critique of them, believing that was no longer necessary either.

137. Heinicke, 1782, p. 42, 1968 English translation.

138. Rae (1848c).

139. Kilian (1885), p. 6.

140. Saboureux de Fontenay (1765), p. 429. The dispute between Heinicke and Epée arose in this way. The Seven Years War found France and Austria on one side and Great Britain and Prussia on the other: Austria was opposed to the rising kingdom of Prussia in a struggle for supremacy in Germany, while the two other powers fought mainly over the new colonies in America. Thus, Joseph II, head of the ruling house of Austria and Holy Roman Emperor, was led by his military alliance with France as well as his ties to its king, his brother-in-law, to turn to the abbé de l'Epée to help him found the first state school for the deaf. As we have seen, he sent him the abbé Storck, who returned to Vienna eight months later and opened a school there. Hearing of this Franco-Austrian alliance in the education of the deaf, the German Heinicke wrote to Storck assailing Epée's methods and praising his own. It was then that Storck volunteered to come see for himself and Heinicke repelled the attack on his secrecy by

demanding his exorbitant fee. (Kilian, 1885, p. 8). When Epée received a copy of Heinicke's letter to Storck, he shot off a rebuttal, which earned him one in turn, to which he replied. After a third and final exchange, Epée approached several scientific academies to arbitrate the dispute and the Zurich Academy accepted.

Heinicke's first letter stated two main objections to Epée and instruction by sign: hearing cannot be replaced by sight; and abstract concepts cannot be taught through written language and methodical signs. In his reply, Epée tells how his pupils have mastered grammar and can write virtually any sentence in French, proving Heinicke's objections invalid. In his reply, Heinicke explains that written words represent sounds; hence they cannot stay in the congenitally deaf man's memory. When they are in front of him he can think of the things to which they refer, but when they are removed, he cannot remember the words. Heinicke's pupils, on the other hand, have learned to articulate, their written language rests on their spoken language, so they can retain it. Epée replied that Heinicke's method was like Pereire's and had the same disadvantage, leaving pupils for more than a year in articulation training, without mental development. The deaf should be taught to speak after they have a knowledge of words and things, not before. This was the case with his pupils, who, without any speech, used more than a thousand French words in a month's classes and discussed matters as abstract as religion. Heinicke's last letter contained the remarks about secrecy quoted earlier; he is not prepared to say any more except that his method is based on articulation, uses some fingerspelling, and taste—not sight—replaces hearing. In his final response, Epée warned that fingerspelling a French word is merely transcribing it and nothing more. He mocks Heinicke's careless claim that "taste replaces hearing"; presumably he meant that he taught his deaf pupils to attend to the sensations of touch in their mouths while they wre articulating.

The Zurich Academy examined pupils trained with Epée's methods by his disciple Ulrich in Zurich and gave the day to Epée, ruling that his pupils transformed written words into signs as hearing people do into speech. Thus, the deaf think not in letters but in signs. This settled matters for Epée, who published a full account in his final work. Storck could not find peace so promptly. The editor of a leading Viennese newspaper rendered his own verdict, in favor of Epée, and Heinicke returned to the attack in a series of twenty letters to the editor. Next Storck was accosted by a professor Nicolai, a member of the Berlin Academy, who asked permission to strike his breast while a deaf pupil chosen at random described the event. The pupil wrote: "Hand lie on heart" and Nicolai, who said he intended to convey the idea of solemnly affirming, went away satisfied that sign could not convey abstract ideas (Berthier, 1840c, p. 70). Probably Nicolai was a poor mimic, who lacked facial expression. In any case, a deaf person would have signed "affirm" (in ASL, probably the sign that can be glossed TRUE-BUSINESS) and that would not have been ambiguous. Nicolai published a book extolling Heinicke and assailing Epée (among other things, he called him "soft in the head"). When Nicolai's critique appeared in the German and French papers, Epée lodged a rebuttal and invited the Berlin Academy to judge who was right, "in the interests of present and future deaf people" (Berthier, 1852a, p. 72; De Gérando, 1827, v. 1, p. 500). Epée's reply appears in the *Journal de Paris* (Epée, 1785). Nicolai sidestepped the debate with Epée, saying he had criticized Storck, not Epée, and Storck should reply; he never did.

Two of Heinicke's contemporaries, German teachers of the deaf, deserve mention for completeness. Benjamin Lasius published a book in Leipzig, three years before Heinicke's school opened there, giving an account of the education of a congenitally deaf young woman. The emphasis was on writing—no speech or fingerspelling, little sign (Lasius, 1775). Johan Arnoldi (1777), a Lutheran minister, taught the son of a Hessian noble, among others. His pupils' sign language and pictures were his main means; he also taught sham speech to pupils who could profit by that instruction. Also see Peet (1859a), Rae (1848c).

141. In 1783. Cited in Blanchet (1850), p. 34.

142. 1788. After the school was temporarily moved to the royal castle Hohenschönhausen, it was converted to a royal institution in 1798, and a site was chosen for it in the city (Hartmann, 1881, p. 131).

143. John Wallis (1616–1703); Wallis (1653).

144. Anthony Wood (sometimes à Wood), 1632–1695, English antiquary. See Wood (1691).

145. John Aubrey (1626–1697). Quoted in Mullett (1971), p. 133. See Aubrey (1696), p. 160, 1949 ed.

146. Letters dated Dec. 30, 1661, May 6, 1662, reproduced in Boyle (1700), pp. 453–455 of the 1772 edition.

147. Wallis letters dated Mar. 14, 1662, not published until July 18, 1670.

148. May 14, 1662. *Journal Book of the Royal Society*, I, pp. 60–61.

149. William Holder (1616–1698). See Holder (1678). Holder's labors had begun in 1659 when Popham was ten. Because the boy's mother had been frightened in pregnancy, Holder explained, his pupil's head was distorted, the passage in the left ear was far too small, that in the right far too large. However, with one end of a taut lute-string between his teeth, the youth could perceive any strong sound. Now Wallis had witnessed the instruction of Popham two years before he accepted Daniel Whaley as a pupil, Holder protested, and his first letter to Dr. Boyle should have mentioned it. Moreover, by the time Wallis wrote his second letter to the Royal Society, making it appear he had endowed Popham with speech, Holder had published two accounts of his prior labors: a letter to the Society, and a book on the elements of speech, one much like Amman's, with claims for the superiority of vocal language, an inventory of its phonetic elements, and practical advice on how to teach (Holder, 1668). The letter (1668) only discusses the boy's hearing but the book (1669) goes into teaching sham speech. Before Holder and Wallis, John Bulwer wrote several books on the nature of gesture (1644, 1648), in which he also discussed Digby's report and advocated schools for the deaf. He did not teach any deaf people nor apparently have any impact on the education of the deaf. In short, it is reasonable to speculate that Wallis knew he was not the first English instructor of the deaf, or even of Popham, but he kept this a secret to glorify his accomplishment.

150. Wallis (1678).

151. Aubrey (1696), v. 1, p. 404. Wood (1691), v. 2, p. 816.

152. Purver (1967).

153. Reported in Purver (1967); Wilkins (1641).

154. Aubrey (1696).

155. Wallis (1696, 1698).

156. Watson (1949). Dalgarno mentions in the introduction to his book that he knew Wallis; Dalgarno (1680). The *Edinburgh Review* (Anon., 1835, p. 416) says Wallis "plundered" Dalgarno. See note 5–182.

157. Defoe (1720).

158. Porter (1848a), p. 182. Abernathy (1959) states that Dalgarno (1680) was the first English writer to advocate a manual alphabet for the deaf and that the two-handed alphabet now in use in Great Britain first appeared in an anonymous work, *Digiti Lingua,* published in London in 1698, and then later figured in Defoe's book (1720).

159. Wallis (1698).

160. De Gérando (1827), p. 313.

161. Hubbard (1891) says Braidwood was "an elocutionist," and Mullet (1971) says "a writing master" but I know of no evidence for these claims.

162. Burnet (1774), book I, ch. XV, pp. 192–194.

163. Stevenson and Guthrie (1949) mention this.

164. Quoted in Watson (1949), p. 23.

165. Herries (1766).

166. Herries (1767).

167. Anon. (1769).

168. Johnson (1775), p. 383. In the same passage, Johnson mentions another oralist, a contemporary of Braidwood, name Henry Baker (1698–1775), who had told him he would soon publish a book on his method. He never did and had no lasting impact. Baker tutored the three deaf children of a London attorney, then opened a school for the wealthy deaf, where he followed Wallis's methods, that is, Ponce-Bonet. He required a one-hundred-pound bond of each pupil not to reveal the secret of his method, married Daniel Defoe's daughter, published erotic rhymes and two books on the microscope, and became a member of the Royal Society. Arnold (1888) discovered Baker's manuscript and discusses its contents. H.P. Peet (1859a) says Baker taught "Lady Inchiquin and her sister."

169. Pennant (1776), pp. 256–258. Edinburgh Institution (1819).

170. Arnot (1779), pp. 425–426.

171. The move occurred in 1783. John died in 1798. Bender (1970, p. 113), apparently on the authority of Hodgson (1953, pp. 143, 148), states that John Braidwood was not Thomas's son but nephew and son-in-law; Watson (1949) also uses the latter term. Syle, however, a reliable source, studied the Braidwood genealogy and calls John Thomas's son (reported in Fay, 1878). Bell's (1918) account of the genealogy is the same as Syle's (but may be based on it). Moreover, Thomas Braidwood Jr. (quoted in T. Gallaudet, 1818c, p. 127) states "Watson was instructed in this art by my grandfather and father" (i.e., Thomas Braidwood and son John).

172. Geikie (1900); Watson (1949), p. 29.

173. Porter (1848a), p. 43. Kinniburgh resigned in 1847 after thirty-six years as headmaster (Watson, 1949, p. 71).

174. About 1814. Thomas died 1825.

175. The timetable of the founding of British schools for the deaf is: London, 1792, Old Kent Road, later moved to Margate; Edinburgh, 1810; Birmingham, 1814; Liverpool, 1825; Manchester, 1825; Exeter, 1827; Doncaster, 1829. The first school to adopt the "German System" was at Yorkshire, 1876. Government support of schools for the deaf came only in 1893 under the Elementary Education Act.

176. The school was founded through the efforts of two Church of England clergy: John Townsend and Henry Cox Mason. It opened with six pupils. See Gilbert (1873) and Townsend (1831). Concerning the cost of tuition at a Braidwood school, Anon. (1822b) gives 100 pounds a year. Townsend (1831), p. 36, and H.P. Peet (1859a), p. 312, speak of a woman who spent 1500 pounds for her deaf child, presumably 300 per year. Geikie (1900) gives 114 dollars a year as the fee charged for instructing his uncle in 1806.

177. Joseph Watson stated that the method of instructing the deaf he learned from his uncle, Thomas Braidwood, was based on John Wallis's letters to the Royal Society (Watson, 1809, p. 23; p. 83ff). Thus, he affirmed, he started by learning signs from his deaf pupils in order to teach them, as Wallis did (Millar, 1827, p. 205). Likewise, a historical sketch published by the Edinburgh school says that Braidwood had applied to the instruction of Charles Shirreff the plan given in the proceedings of the Royal Society "and thus many of the superior classes of society in this country were made acquainted with the possibility of teaching the deaf and dumb to understand written language." Note the words "written language."

178. Cited in Watson (1949), pp. 48–50. Speech gradually dropped from the Braidwood curriculum, according to Charles Baker, quoted in Chamberlain (1867b) and E. Gallaudet (1867), p. 49. The Glasgow school under Duncan Anderson followed Bébian's methods; the Aberdeen school was directed by a disciple of Sicard; the teacher in the Edinburgh Day School for the deaf was deaf himself (Watson, 1949, p. 53). Sign language remained the primary vehicle for the instruction of the deaf in Scotland throughout the nineteenth century. Dugald Stewart (1753–1828), who founded the Scottish common-sense school of philosophy, was a professor at the University of Edinburgh, and he watched Braidwood's school develop in that city (Stewart, 1812, p. 322). Stewart also called from relative obscurity to public attention a Scottish writer on education of the deaf, George Dalgarno (1626?–1687). Dalgarno was eclipsed by Wallis, in part because his book (1680) was confined to principles. He read Digby and Bonet, says he counts Wallis as a friend and may have been the person who communicated Bonet to Wallis. Dalgarno places emphasis on the manual alphabet and written language. He also believed that speech and lipreading could not be mastered sufficiently to be of practical use. Anon. (1835c) presents the case that Wallis also plagiarized Dalgarno (p. 416).

179. Porter (1858a), p. 120.

180. Quoted in Syle (1887), p. 12.

181. Lowe was with Watson from age six to eighteen. He was admitted to the bar in 1829. See Braddock (1975) and H.P. Peet (1859a), p. 312.

182. Fox (1935, 3 [5]), p. 4.

183. Quoted in Anon. (1896), p. 33. Also see Bass and Healy (1949), p. 25.

184. *Association Review*, 1900, 2, 36–42.

185. Green (1783). Credit for the first American publication on the education of the deaf goes to Francis Green; *Boston Magazine* in December 1784 and January 1785 gave reviews of his *Vox Oculis Subjecta*, published in England in 1783. Green's letter of 1781 to Richard Bagley, health officer of the port of New York, did not appear in print in America until 1804. The first work on the education of the deaf actually written and published in America was by William Thornton (1793), who was the first head of the U.S. Patent Office and architect of the first capitol in Washington. A brief sketch of Thornton's life and work by A. G. Bell will be found in the *Association Review*, 1900, 2, 113–118. Bell suggests that Thornton knew of Braidwood's and Epée's schools and methods, since he was graduated from the University of Edinburgh in 1784 and then continued his medical studies in Paris.

186. Cited in Bell (1900a). Also see Bell in Clarke School (1893a), pp. 53–54.

187. Hubbard (1898), p. 5.

CHAPTER 6 / SUCCESS AND FAILURE

1. On Berthier: Bernard (1980a), p. 7. Cuxac (1980), p. 149, states that Berthier "became profoundly deaf before the age of three." Braddock (1976) states that Berthier was deafened "in early childhood," but Paulmier (1834), p. 382, states that his pupil was born deaf. Berthier refers to himself as congenitally deaf *("sourd-muet de naissance")* in *L'Ami des Sourds-Muets* (1840, 2, 143–144). Berthier had two hearing teachers who were also responsible for his successful education, and both were gifted signers. The first was Roch-Ambroise Bébian; the other was Louis Paulmier, the oldest disciple of Sicard, who had attended one of his demonstrations while still an artillery officer, and had seen the light. See Berthier (1873), p. 227, on Paulmier.

2. Paulmier (1834a), p. 382.

3. Denis (1895b), p. 43; Clerc quoted in Chamberlain (1857a). Bernard (1980a), p. 7, gives these dates: Berthier entered 1811, *moniteur*, 1819, *répétiteur*, 1824, professor, 1829.

4. Berthier (1852b), p. 31.

5. Société Universelle des Sourds-Muets, founded 1838. Karakostas (1981) states that the sign language in use in Paris outside the national institution was relatively isolated from, and distinct from, that used within the institution. Some of Berthier's articles recording the struggle of the deaf are: (1836, 40c, 46, 40a); his 1840 rebuttal of Itard (1821d) was published (1852b).

6. First welfare organization of deaf: Société Centrale des Sourds-Muets de Paris.

7. Clerc (1857a). If Berthier was considered Clerc's successor, then Alphonse Lenoir was Massieu's. Likewise a pupil of Bébian, Lenoir was careful, calm, imperturbable, full of great good sense, a beautiful soul, according to his contemporaries. He had a taste for art and was often to be found in the Parisian galleries. He published an interesting collection of brief tales by and about the deaf (Lenoir, 1850).

8. Pélissier (1846a), p. 13. Cuxac (1980), p. 152, mentions Pélissier's bilingualism. Also see Braddock (1975).

9. Pélissier (1856). Brouland (1855) and Lambert (1865) provide illustrative iconographies and Puybonnieux (1846), p. 217, gives some verbal examples of reduced signs. Grosselin and Pélissier published sign vocabulary cards in 1857 that I have been unable to locate. Probably this is an alternate format of Pélissier (1856). See the review of the cards by Valade-Gabel (1859). Other dictionaries of French or American Sign Language prior to the spate in the present decade are, in order of date of preparation, Epée (1896), Sicard (1808), Blanchet (1850) (these are all verbal); Lambert (1865, 1870), Hutton (1900), Long (1918), Michaels (1923), Higgins (1923), Riekehof (1961), Stokoe, Casterline and Croneberg (1965), Oléron (1974).

10. Blanchet (1850) describes Forestier (1810–1891) in these terms. Cuxac (1980), p. 120, fn. 1, states that Forestier was profoundly deaf at birth. In response to Itard's slander of the character of the deaf, Berthier published some of Forestier's letters to show that deaf people have the same kind of emotional reactions as do hearing people.

11. Société Centrale (1842), p. 46.

12. Forestier (1854).

13. Peet (1859), p. 330.

14. R.A. Bébian, born Aug. 4, 1789; died Feb. 24, 1839.

15. Institution Royale des Sourds-Muets (1842): Berthier calls Bébian the only hearing person who really mastered sign. Bébian (1817) states in a letter to Sicard that he learned sign mainly from Laurent Clerc.

16. Sicard cited in Berthier (1873), p. 246ff. Sicard's letter is dated Mar. 1819.

17. Bébian (1817, 1819). On methodical signs and sign systems based on French or English, see: Aléa (1824); Bébian (1820, 1826b, 1834, p. 38); Berthier (1839, p. 7); Bornstein (1973); Burnet (1854, 1855a,b); Clerc (1857b); Cochrane (1871); Gustason et al. (1972); the exchanges between J.A. Jacobs and H.P. Peet; Keep (1871); Markowicz (1975); I.L. Peet (1853, 1868); Reich and Bick (1976); Sicard (1808b); Talbot (1872); Valade-Gabel (1862b); Valentine (1870, 1872).

18. Recounted in Esquiros (1847), p. 411.

19. *Directors* elsewhere in this era who came from Paris institution (+ =deaf): Chazottes, at Toulouse; Piroux, Nancy; Carton, Bruges; Fleury, Saint Petersburg; Riviere, Rodez; Desongnis, Arras; Dessagne "dans le cantal"; Valade, Bordeaux; Massieu+, Lille; Georges+, Mons; Bertrand+, Limoges; Platin+, Pay; *Professors* elsewhere: Clerc+, Hartford; Benjamin+ and Godfrey+, Lille; Ackerman+, Esquermes (near Lille); Maupin+, Besançon; Richardin+, Nancy (Institution Royale des Sourds-Muets, 1839).

20. See Bébian (1826a), p. 164ff.

21. This is substantially Peet's evaluation. (H.P. Peet, 1859a). Bébian's manual (1827) was completed in 1822 but awaited commercial publication for a government subsidy that never came.

22. Bébian (1827a), p. 8.

23. Bébian (1825). The classes that Bébian's system transcribes are movements, handshapes, locations, relative hand positions, and facial expressions. He distinguishes simple, curved, circular, and oblique movement vectors traveling in one of two directions in one of three planes. Eight other forms of movement (e.g., wavelike) and eight movement diacritics (e.g., stressed) are specified—a total of 67 transcriptions. Each movement symbol has a form appropriate to its referent, as do the 26 symbols presented for various head and body locations. Handshape symbols are schematic drawings of the contours of the hand: only two configurations are illustrated but in many orientations for both hands separately, yielding 54 transcriptions. Fourteen symbols are proposed for specifying the position of one hand in relation to the other. Twenty symbols are listed for ten opposing pairs of expressive states (e.g., pleasure-pain). Also see G. Hutton (1869) and J.S. Hutton (1870, 1874).

24. Bébian (1826a).

25. Bébian (1831).

26. Berthier et Lenoir (1830).

27. Bébian (1834).

28. Bébian (1826a), p. 195.

29. De Gérando (1827), p. 572, says "signs of reduction" (i.e., French Sign Language) "are currently the principal means of instruction at the National Institute for the Deaf." Carton (1847), p. 63; Blanchet (1850), p. 158.

30. Barnard (1835), p. 389.

31. New York Institution for Instruction of the Deaf and Dumb, *Reports* (1834), p. 29.

32. Karakostas (1981), p. 112, states that Massieu was accused of soliciting a minor in the Paris woods and that this contributed to his leaving the Paris school. On Massieu's activities after leaving Paris: Rodenbach (1835); Clerc (1849); Leglay (1847); Berthier (1873), p. 162; Lefèbvre (1857?); Kelkun (1888). Massieu's school opened Oct. 1, 1834, promptly received a subsidy from the city council, and gave its first public exhibition in 1836. Scholarships were awarded by the département du Nord beginning 1838. Massieu retired on pension a year later when the brothers of he order Saint-Gabriel took charge of the male pupils, and the sisters of Sagesse took charge of the females. Massieu died July 23, 1846.

33. History has not passed down to us the name of the student whose accident led to Itard's intervention nor the precise day on which it occurred in the year 1799.

34. Bouteiller (1956); Copans and Jamin (1978); Stocking (1964). Sicard was a member of the society, as were the baron De Gérando and another member of the administrative boad at Saint-Jacques, Mathieu Montmorency. In addition to linguists and philosophers there were the first psychiatrist, Philippe Pinel; Baron Georges Cuvier, who founded comparative anatomy; various naturalists; doctors—Itard would become a member; archeologists, historians, more than a dozen explorers, some sixty members in all.

35. To get the wild boy brought to Paris, the abbé Sicard appealed to the minister of the interior, Lucien Bonaparte, Napoleon's brother. At first, Sicard thought he was unsuccessful in his request; he wrote to Baron De Gérando on Feb. 26, 1800: "As I no longer have any hope of getting my savage since a family has been found for him," I can arrange for you and your party to attend one of my demonstrations. He asked for the size of the party, since tickets would be needed. The letter appears in Berthier (1873), appendix.

36. Jean-Marc Itard (1774–1838). See Lane (1976).

37. Itard (1801), p. 134, 1964 ed.

38. Bonnaterre (1800), pp. 256–275.

39. Sicard (1800), p. x, 1803 ed.

40. Porcher (1938), p. 115, says the school physician earned 800 francs a year in 1838. Unskilled labor in the early nineteenth century earned two to three francs a day; the figure is now (1981) about 100. Using this guide to the change in purchasing power, we can estimate that Itard's salary at the end of his career was the equivalent of a current 32,000 francs annually. At a typical exchange rate of five francs to the dollar, this income corresponds to some $6,500 a year.

41. Itard (1801), p. xxiii, 1964 ed.

42. Itard (1808, 1821a).

43. Itard (1801), p. 163, 1964 ed.

44. De Gérando (1848), translated in Lane (1976), p. 144.

45. Itard (1807), p. 229, 1964 ed.

46. De Gérando's letter is dated July 13, 1810, cited in Puybonnieux (1846), p. 145.

47. Virey (1817), p. 269.

48. In 1811 the government proposed sending to Saint-Jacques another youth who had been living in the wild for some years. Sicard and the board were horrified: it would be fruitless for the boy and dangerous for the other pupils. No sense in repeating the experiment with Victor, which had shown the difficulties and even the uselessness of such efforts (Bernard, 1980c, p. 60).

49. Itard (1825). The baron Cuvier went to the Paris school and tried his hand on the remains of yet another former pupil, but equally without success.

50. Luigi Galvani (1737–1798), published in 1791.

51. Cited in Corone (1960).

52. Itard (1821d), p. 342, 1842 ed. "In Itard's time, the principal causes of deafness were hydrocephalus, brain fever, scarlet fever, measles, dentition, convulsions, inflammation of the lungs, colds, smallpox, and whooping cough" (Hodgson, 1953, p. 191). For other related articles on medicine, see: Académie Impériale de Médecine (1853), Ackerknecht (1967), Adelon et al. (1812), Blanchet (1853a), Cartwright (1851), Corone (1960), G.E. Day (1836), Deleau (1826, 1828), Dunglison (1833), Ganière (1964), Houdin (1853), Husson (1833), Itard (1802, 1825, 1826a,b, 1827a,b,c,d, 1829), Lebouvier Desmortiers (1801), Ménière (1853), Volquin (1853).

53. "A host of pupils," wrote Itard's successor, Dr. Ménière, "were subjected to the most painful, barbaric, absurd

and useless treatments." One pupil even had her skull pierced to give sounds more direct access (1853, p. 47). Also see Varjot (1980).

54. Cited in Esquiros (1847), p. 412. Also see Itard's regrets in Hoffbauer (1827), p. 181, and the negative evaluations of later physicians cited in Bernard (1980c), p. 62.

55. Quoted in Houdin (1855), p. 14.

56. Kitto (1848), cited in Batson and Bergman (1976), pp. 170–171, 204.

57. Itard (1821b), p. 212.

58. Itard (1821d).

59. Berthier published a hundred-page book to refute this broadcast defamation (Berthier, 1852b. The refutation was written in 1840.) Bébian also attacked it in the pages of his journal (Bébian, 1826a, p. 14).

60. "Of all the staff at the school, Itard was the most prejudiced against the deaf. . . . He wanted to banish sign language, of which he learned none during thirty years at the institution" (Blanchet, 1850, p. 95).

61. The idea came to him, he recounts in his *Treatise*, when he was invited by the abbé Sicard, in the winter of 1802, to witness some acoustical experiments performed on his pupils. A physicist brought several sound-making instruments of his own invention and generated sounds so piercing that many of the pupils seemed to hear them. Itard suggested that the pupils be blindfolded and told to raise their hands for each sound they could hear. To his amazement, a few more hands went up each time the shrill sound was made. He had the experiment repeated with a softer and duller sound. Fewer hands were raised, of course, but again repeated stimulation of the ear seemed to increase its sensitivity. These results shocked Itard "like a dazzling flash of light that showed me the route I must follow to bring a paralyzed sense to life. . . . Four successive years of caring for and experimenting with a child found in the woods had taught me ways of awakening the sense organs" (Itard, 1821d, pp. 355–356, 1842 ed.).

62. Itard (1827), p. 179.

63. Chesselden (1728); Académie Royale des Sciences (1703).

64. Itard (1808); Halle and Moreau (1808).

65. Hoffbauer (1827), p. 179.

66. Itard (1808), p. 75; (1802), pp. 534–535, no. 6.

67. Among the pupils whom Itard exhibited, the most accomplished speaker was indeed his protégé Allibert, who had the least possibility of signing: entrusted entirely to Itard, who put him in the care of a hearing governess, Allibert was cut off from the signing community (Itard, 1821d, p. 390, 1842 ed.).

68. Husson (1833), p. 138, 1894 ed.

69. Allibert quoted in Ménière (1853), p. 186.

70. Berthier (1852a), p. 85, identifies Eugène Allibert as one of Itard's early speech pupils. Vaïsse (1848b), p. 34, reports his nomination for the post of professor and calls him a rapid and brilliant scholarly success. Itard describes his hearing (1824) and cites him in his will (Petit, 1859). His predilection for signing is discussed in Académie Impériale de Médecine (1853), p. 975, and Ménière (1853), p. 299.

71. Itard (1826), p. 256.

72. Itard (1821d), p. 391, 1842 ed.; Itard (1824), p. 9.

73. Itard (1824), p. 11.

74. Itard (1827c), pp. 181, 190.

75. Itard (1821a), p. 12.

76. Itard (1827c), pp. 202–203.

77. Reported in Berthier (1852b), p. 89.

78. Itard (1826b), pp. 6–8.

79. Gall and Spurzheim (1810, p. 125) also hypothesize a deaf society with these results.

80. Itard (1821d), p. 325, 1842 ed.

81. Itard (1821d), pp. 327–329, 1842 ed. Matters were not that simple. Massieu came from a family of peasants, Clerc from the bourgeoisie. Massieu had Sicard for a teacher but Clerc had Massieu. Comparing his medical files from his first years as resident physician at the institution with those from a period two decades later, Itard found that the earlier pupils were unable to respond properly to written questions such as "Are you completely deaf? Can you hear a little? Were you born deaf?" Similarly, their handwritten explanations of the illnesses for which they came to see Itard were often unintelligible or, worse, misleading. But by the time Itard wrote his *Treatise*, the level of general education was much higher; the knowledge of French, acquired through the mediation of manual French following Sicard's methods, was much greater; and these problems of communication had practically disappeared (Itard, 1821d, p. 330, 1842 ed.). The first inquiry was in 1813, the second in 1831 (Blanchet, 1850, p. 98).

82. Jean-Jacques Virey, a fellow member of the Society of Observers of Man, wrote a natural history of the human species (including a long dissertation on Victor of Aveyron) in which he espoused the prevailing view, which divided the human races into beautiful and white, on the one hand, and ugly and brown or black, on the other (Virey, 1801, v. 1, p. 145). The former are to be found in temperate climes, appropriate for civilized people. Another member of the society noted that the perfect beauty of Apollo and Venus belong to the first category whereas the traits of the Negro are more like those of the orangutan. See Bouteiller (1956). As if the savages themselves realized this similarity, "orangutan" meant "wild man." For the society as for De Gérando, savages, wild children, and the deaf were all debased forms of human life and all equally interesting. I have related how the society brought Victor to Paris, studied him, and failed to see the significance of the things Victor could do well on his own. (Lane, 1976). It heard several communications on sign language, particularly from Sicard and Massieu, and sponsored Sicard's so-called sign dictionary, to allow "communication with the deaf but also primitive peoples" (Copans and Jamin, 1978). (The dictionary could serve for two unrelated groups because it contained

pantomime, not sign.) The society also organized all-day nature walks with lectures in a rustic setting, and on one Sicard appeared among the bushes and harangued the troop on the education of the deaf. Much more could be learned, however, from studying an entire primitive nation than a collection of deaf people or a single wild boy. Thus the society planned a major expedition to Australia, which sailed in October of 1800 with the largest contingent of scientists that had ever embarked. To prepare and guide the scientists on the expedition, the society's distinguished anatomist, Baron Georges Cuvier, wrote a memoir on anatomical differences among the races with instructions on how to collect skulls and other bones and pack them for shipping. De Gérando wrote a counterpart memoir on the behavior of primitive peoples and how to study them. De Gérando was very much in the tradition set down by Condillac, as were Pinel, Itard, indeed the entire Society of Observers and the French Institute. The science of man should use the methods of the natural sciences: the first stage is careful observation, the second comparison, the third induction of general laws. Savages were particularly suitable objects of study because they are subject to fewer modifying influences.

De Gérando begins by explaining that we are so ignorant of other cultures because prior observations were made so improperly. Worst of all, De Gérando says, prior observers failed to learn any of the native tongue, so they could not understand the inhabitants' customs, ceremonies, history, or even what they did with various tools and artifacts. They could not report on the natives' language, and describe the grammatical rules it obeyed, if any. They could learn nothing of the inhabitants' ideas and opinions, unless they learned to communicate with them. "How else could one appreciate their manner of seeing and feeling, [or record] the most secret and essential traits of their character?" What this expedition should do, then, he argued, is to learn Sicard's system of methodical signs for the deaf in order to establish initial communication with the tribes.

83. De Gérando (1800a), p. 163, 1978 ed.

84. De Gérando (1820), p. 8, 1832 English translation.

85. De Gérando (1820), p. 96, 1832 English translation.

86. De Gérando (1800b), p. 460.

87. De Gérando (1800b), pp. 464, 460.

88. Bayle-Mouillard (1846), p. 34; Morel (1843), p. 19.

89. Biographies of De Gérando: Bayle-Mouillard (1846), Beugnot (1842), Boulatignier (1842), Mignet (1854), Morel (1846), Peabody (1861), E. Peet (1851).

90. Quoted in Le Père (1879), p. 60.

91. Bébian (1834), Gondelin May–Sept., 1822.

92. De Gérando (1827), p. 572. Recoing (1829). Valade-Gabel (1894), p. 158ff.

93. Morel was born Dec. 5, 1805; he joined the Paris institution Nov. 19, 1824 at the age of forty-two. He was in charge of Itard's high class (1845) and was to stand in for the director in his absence. Before coming to the Paris school, he was secretary in the government audit office for nineteen years and business manager of the institute for the blind for three years. He founded the *Annales de l'Education des Sourds-Muets et des Aveugles* (1844–1852) and edited the four circulars published by the Peris school between 1827 and 1836. In 1850 Morel was made director of the Bordeaux school for the deaf, succeeding Valade-Gabel, and in 1857 he died at the age of fifty-one. Gineste (1981), p. 326, states that Morel was forty-two when he joined the Paris school in 1824 but this is evidently an error as the eulogy by one of Morel's collaborators at Bordeaux (translated in Porter, 1858b) gives his birthdate as Dec. 5, 1805.

94. Perrier, July 18, 1823–June 29, 1827; Borel, June 30, 1827–Nov. 14, 1831.

95. The Conseil de Perfectionnement had five members: Reynuard, Remusat, E. Ordinaire, F. Cuvier, Feuillet. The administrative board comprised the baron De Gérando, the duke of Doudeauville, peer of France, the count Alexis de Noailles, Minister of State and deputy in the Legislature, Dr. Gueneau de Mussy, director of the National Teacher Training College, Baron Rendu, an attorney general, the count of Breteuil, former prefect and a peer, and Frédéric Cuvier, inspector general of universities. None of them knew anything of the deaf and their language.

96. Dupont (1897), pp. 25–26.

97. Institution Royale des Sourds-Muets (1832), p. 83ff. The closest the new director had ever been to the deaf before was when he visited the Besançon school and tried to give the pupils a few lessons based on what he had seen in Germany. He knew nothing of the sign language he was so opposed to—not even that it had nouns and verbs. "I will provide a new proof," he wrote "both of the sterility of sign language in all that concerns the external world and of its great defects arising from its false and exaggerated claims." The proof had to do with milking cows. "When the sign of milking is for the pupil the sign of milk, what then is the sign for milking? . . . There you see what the richness and power of sign comes down to—for truly, whenever the sign language has the asset of calling a certain object to mind, it always does so by creating the confusion I have illustrated" (Ordinaire, 1836, p. 194). Pélissier's dictionary gives the signs for *lait* (milk) and *traire* (to milk) used at that time, and they were quite different, as they are here in America as well (Pélissier, 1856, plate 3, no. 10, and plate 7, no. 22). "Since these kinds of mimic signs can never have the variety and precision of written language no matter what we do," Ordinaire wrote, "it would be a mistake to give them much use in instructing the deaf" (Ordinaire, 1836, p. 206).

98. The first group had been presented to the Faculty of Medicine in 1808. See Halle and Moreau (1808). This report will be found in Husson (1833), and it is reprinted in the 1842 edition of Itard (1821). Itard's three reports to the administration are: (1821a), (1824), (1826).

99. Bébian (1831), p. 10, says the money, 3,000 francs, was never used, but Houdin (1855), p. 117, Blanchet (1853a), and others say the class was taught by Valade-Gabel, which he seems to confirm (1894, p. 158). Hervaux (1911) gives a biography of Valade-Gabel. See Cornié (1903).

100. This system was called *rotation* but meant adherence. See Puybonnieux (1846), (1857).

101. Bébian (1834).

102. Bébian (1834), pp. 20–21.

103. Institution Royale des Sourds-Muets (1832), p. 257ff. Also see Bébian (1834).

104. Puybonnieux (1843), p. 61.

105. Blanchet (1850), p. lxxii.

106. Bébian (1834).

107. Esquiros (1847); Morel (1843), p. 25; Puybonnieux (1843), p. 61, (1857).

108. Bébian (1834).

109. De Gérando (1827), p. 572.

110. When the abortive attempt at imposing the majority language ended and the avenue of a teaching career was reopened to the deaf, the faculty proposed that unusually gifted pupils be kept on after their six-year course to receive supplementary training and then go on to an apprenticeship with a teacher (Morel, 1845, p. 95). Itard left in his will six scholarships for pupils in this supplementary course, but he specified that it must be conducted in French so that the deaf man can "cease to think in his inherently defective and abbreviated language" (Itard, quoted in Morel, 1845; English translation, Lane, 1976, p. 272). Itard died believing French Sign Language was a truncated form of manual French and not a language in its own right, that it was useful in the early stages of instruction but not at the most advanced levels. Itard bequeathed 8,000 francs for the supplementary course: "an absolute requirement for its implementation ought to be to exclude the use of sign language." In an effort to prepare some students for this enterprise, the articulation class was revived under Puybonnieux and taught intermittently for four years. When Edouard Morel then started Itard's supplementary course, however, he found that it had to be conducted in writing. Clerc visited it not long after and found communication in sign and written French (Clerc, 1848; Esquiros, 1847; Séguin, 1847, p. 318; Académie Impériale de Médecine, 1853, p. 1012).

History of the articulation class: begun in 1828 at Itard's insistence, seconded by the Academy of Medicine, which had reviewed his physiological training of hearing and speech, the class was taught first by J.J. Valade-Gabel. It was canceled in 1832 in the backlash from Ordinaire's attempt to impose total oralism on the school. The class resumed and was taught intermittently by Puybonnieux from 1839 to 1843. With Itard's will endowing an oral high class, the articulation class became essential, was restored by ministerial decree in 1843, and was taught by Vaïsse one hour daily for seven years. In 1850, J.J. Valade-Gabel, having returned to Paris from Bordeaux, took over the class. His son André taught it from 1851 to 1852, when the director doubled class time to two hours daily—as always, for those who showed some profit by it. Then Hector Volquin taught the course (1852–1857), succeeded by André Valade-Gabel. See Dupont (1897); Académie Impériale de Médecine (1853), p. 850. When Clerc visited the articulation class he found it had about a fifth of the students, taught one hour a day by Léon Vaïsse, who told his visitor that "the most promising pupils might at least be able to make themselves understood" (Day, 1845, p. 95). Valade-Gabel, fired from Bordeaux for mysterious reasons, returned to Paris and took over the articulation class. Vaïsse took charge of Itard's supplementary course, where he used sign extensively—he called banishing it "acting like a blind man's teacher who refuses to speak" (Vaïsse, 1854, cited in Petit, 1859, pp. 29–30).

111. Franck (1861); Magnat (1896), p. 75.

112. Blanchet (1856); Magnat in Congress on Deaf—International—First (1878), pp. 409–410; Day and Peet (1861), pp. 99–100. In 1848 Blanchet called the speech of the deaf "the result of constraint and even violence; a temporary achievement, an accident, an anomaly, not the product of knowing how to move the speech organs naturally" (p. 21 of the 1850 ed.). On the other hand, sign language "can reflect and convey all the feelings in man's heart, all the ideas in man's mind" (p. 75).

113. Blanchet (1853a), Houdin (1853), Ménière (1853), Volquin (1853a), Académie Impériale de Médecine (1853).

114. Berthier (1853), p. 2.

115. Quoted in Ménière (1853), p. 186.

116. See Drouot (1911), Franck (1861), p. 13. Dubois's school, founded in 1837, merged with the Paris institution in 1856. He was asked to choose two of his six pupils, who were selected at random from the Paris school, and teach them to speak. In 1849 the pupils were examined by a commission including Blanchet (resident physician at the Paris school) and E. Morel. In 1855, Dubois's father died, the pupils were transferred to the National Institution, and Dubois and his two sisters were given teaching appointments to instruct the classes. In 1859 the female pupils were all transferred to Bordeaux and the three Duboises left the professorial corps to work in families with very young deaf children. See Congress on Deaf—National—French (1881), pp. 165–166.

117. Séguin (1875), p. 62.

118. Vaïsse (1848b). See his biography by Magnat (1885).

119. De Gérando (1839), p. 521.

120. The will is quoted in Petit (1859), pp. 5–9.

121. The French had then, even more than they do now, a single idea of what it was to be a Frenchman. France was the soil in which the Enlightenment flowered, in which democracy took root. Frenchmen spoke French, the language that was the vehicle for the most advanced literature, government, philosophy, and science. The new order had no place for other languages. Shortly after the founding of the new republic the legislature was told: "Federalism and superstition speak Breton; emigration and hate of the republic speak German; the counterrevolution speaks Italian and fanaticism speaks Basque" (Archives Parlementaires, 1ère série, v. 83, p. 715 [Paris: Centre National de la Recherche Scientifique, 1961], quoted in Certeau et al., 1975, p. 11). "Governments do not realize, or do not feel keenly enough," a deputy expostulated, "how much the annihilation of regional speech is necessary for education, the true knowledge of religion, the ready implementation of the law, national happiness and political tranquility" (Grégoire, quoted in Certeau et al., 1975, p. 21). The renowned Encyclopedia defined a patois as "a degenerate tongue such as is spoken in almost all the provinces. . . . The language of France is spoken only in the capital" (Diderot, 1765, p. 992 of the 1778 ed., quoted in Certeau et al., 1975, p. 51). The representatives voted to place a French-speaking schoolteacher in every community where "the inhabitants speak a foreign idiom."

In these circumstances, members of French society who were fundamentally different from the rest had two possibilities—exclusion or assimilation. The mentally ill and retarded were sent outside the city and walled up—

they were called *aliénés*, estranged—and the deaf were excluded in a walled enclosure, a miniature city and farm on top of Mount Sainte-Geneviève. But you could leave the savage state if you could learn to speak French. If you spoke French normally you could leave the asylum for the retarded and mentally ill at La Salpêtrière, you could leave Saint-Jacques, you could go to the schools where the new governing classes were being trained, you could be a person at law, you could marry and have children who spoke French. In the panoply of new branches of knowledge there was even one specially devoted to performing this transformation. It was so new then that it had yet to be baptized but it was the lawful child of the new medicine wed to the philosophy of Condillac, and so it was soon called *la médecine morale*, mental medicine; one of its chief proponents was Jean-Marc Itard. Assimilation or exclusion—Itard was a victim of this antithesis. A doctor, he was charged by his society to alleviate problems that were not medical but rather, in Berthier's terms, "lofty questions of humanity."

The legislature passed a second law requiring French as the exclusive language of all official acts and contracts, even in the private sector (Decree of 2 thermidor an 2). The law was not put into application, however. The abbé Grégoire, a member of the Committee of Public Instruction and possibly the best-known "patriot curate" of postrevolutionary France, presented to the legislature the results of a massive investigation of the diversity of languages in the land; it was entitled *On the Necessity and Means of Destroying the Patois and Universalizing the Use of French.* This fear of linguistic diversity had not diminished in France over eight decades later, even though the new institutions had become secure. In 1864 the Minister of Public Instruction repeated the Grégoire investigation. "Are there schools in your sector where instruction is in the patois?" he wrote to public school inspectors in the provinces. "What can be done to change this state of affairs?" (*Bulletin Administratif du Ministère de l'Instruction Publique*, nouvelle série, 1864, 1, 395–406, quoted in Certeau et al., 1975, p. 270).

The quotation on drapetomania is from Cartwright (1851), cited in Chorover (1979).

CHAPTER 7 / FORTUNE AND MISFORTUNE

1. Strakhovsky (1970).

2. Nicholas Morris of Boston University has kindly prepared the following report on Count Machwitz.

Sometime between 1800 and 1803, Czar Alexander I began an affair with the Princess Marie Antonova Naryshkina, born in Poland as the Princess Czetwertinski and established in Russia as the wife of the wealthy Prince Naryshkin. Alexander had many liaisons before, during, and after his attachment to Naryshkina, but she was to become the one true passion of his life and endure as his mistress until 1822 (Almedingen, 1964, p. 32; Valloton, 1966, p. 288). Florinsky (1967, pp. 631–632), states: "Alexander I, fair, tall and handsome, was slightly lame, having been thrown from his horse in 1794, and early in life he became affected with progressive deafness. . . . This relationship [with Naryshkina] pursued its uneven course until 1819 and resulted in the birth of several children whom Alexander recognized as his own, although he was aware that Mme. Naryshkin had other lovers." According to Almedingen (1964), p. 85, Naryshkina bore Alexander a child in 1803 and "in the summer of 1804 . . . Naryshkina came to her villa at Peterhof and soon the world heard of her second pregnancy." A third child, a girl, was born to this couple in 1808 (Valloton, 1966, p. 288). In a letter dated June 27, 1810, from Alexander to his sister, we learn that yet a fourth child of Alexander and Naryshkina, a girl, had recently died (Alexander, 1975). If Clerc's pupil, Count Alexander Machwitz, was indeed the natural son of Czar Alexander, as Clerc claims, he may well have been Naryshkina's child born in 1803 or the one born in 1804; he would than have been about twelve when Clerc left for America in 1816, which is consistent with the age for studying at the Paris institute and the touching departure scene that Clerc describes. There seems to be no record of other illegitimate children of the czar. Alexander might have embraced as his own a child born to Naryshkina from one of her other liaisons (Gribble, 1931) but those occurred too late for a son to be of school age in 1815, and the boy could not have inherited Alexander's deafness. Brian-Chaninov (1934, p. 298) states, however, that Naryshkina bore the czar only one son, in 1813. From the preceding, we cannot confirm Clerc's claim but neither can we reject it.

3. Landes (1876).

4. Sicard (1808a). Clerc Papers no. 2. The Clerc Papers at the Yale University Library include an incomplete inventory that assigns numbers to letters and other documents in the collection. The abbé Sicard wrote: "I have reflected on Clerc's desire to accompany M. Jauffret and for the reasons Clerc urges I approve of the journey. But I want Clerc to retain his position at our institution and he must therefore request a leave of absence for six months when it appears that he can leave. . . . It will be necessary to keep the greatest secrecy about this trip, even as regards Massieu. Clerc must consult his family. In writing to them, he must not ask leave until Her Majesty the Empress shall have answered my proposal. . . ." Sicard had chosen Jean-Baptiste Jauffret (1771–1828) because he was on intimate terms with his brothers. The oldest was the Bishop of Metz and had edited with Sicard the *Annales Religieuses* for which the abbé had been ordered deported and was forced into hiding. Another brother was the secretary of the Society of Observers of Man and a good friend to Sicard and Massieu. In truth, Jauffret had been head of a secondary school in Paris and did a creditable job heading the school in St. Petersburg, which was installed in a large house on the right bank of the Neva. Czar Alexander gave him the order of Saint Vladimir (which he had given Sicard), and when he died not long after, one of his disciples succeeded him. See Bébian (1826c); Gallaudet (1818d); Anon. (1896), p. 34.

5. Hamilton (1898); Braddock (1975); Clerc (1858a).

6. Clerc (1858a), Braddock (1975).

7. Sicard (1814).

8. Reprinted in Berthier (1873), p. 243.

9. May 20, 1815. Massieu (1815), p. 123.

10. Handbill dated June 16, 1815, in Clerc Papers no. 40, Yale University.

11. Anon. (1822b), p. 394.

12. The second series ran from June 22 to July 3. Since Gallaudet attended lectures on July 8 and 10, these were apparently part of a third series. Root (1941), p. 69, lists some dignitaries; others are cited in Massieu (1815).

13. Massieu (1815).

14. Massieu (1815), pp. 7, 111.

15. Massieu (1815), p. 93. Also in Clerc (1815).

16. A great many are reprinted in Paulmier (1834a), pp. 312–319.

17. Massieu (1815), pp. 9–10.

18. Massieu (1815), p. 171; Clerc (1818b), p. 3.

19. Clerc (1852); T. H. Gallaudet (1818c), July 8, 10. Also in T. Gallaudet (1815g).

20. Berthier (1873), p. 244. Sicard plans to leave London July 25 and to arrive in Paris by the end of the month.

21. Sicard (1816), Clerc Papers no. 17.

22. Bébian (1826d), p. 357. Clerc Papers no. 10, Yale University.

23. Clerc (1816a).

24. Feb. 14, 1816. T. Gallaudet (1818c).

25. Gallaudet (1816n).

26. Gallaudet (1816n).

27. Clerc Papers no. 20 are a record of an English lesson with Mr. Robertson. The date is uncertain. Massieu (1815) also mentions Clerc's English study prior to the London trip.

28. Beecher (1848). See Stevens (1876). The children of Mary Austin Ledyard (1775–1849) and Mason Fitch Cogswell (1761–1830) were: Mary Austin (1801–1868); Elizabeth (1803–1856); Alice (1805–1830); Mason Fitch (1807[9?]–1865); Catherine Ledyard (1811–1882). See note 7-40.

29. When the Gallaudets came to Hartford, they moved to what is now 90 Chapel Street (Crofut, 1937).

30. Pierre Elisée, b. Mauzé (near La Rochelle), settled La Rochelle. Son Thomas, b. circ. 1724, d. circ. 1772, m. 1750 Catherine Edgar, b. 1725, d. 1774. Son Peter Wallace, b. N.Y., Apr. 21, 1756, d. N.Y. May 16, 1843, m. Hartford, Feb. 27, 1787, Jane dtr. Capt. Thos. and Alice (Howard) Hopkins (who d. Oct. 1797 and Apr. 30, 1778, respectively) b. May 8, 1776, Hartford, d. New York, Nov. 20, 1818. Son Thomas Hopkins, b. Philadelphia, Dec. 10, 1787, d. Hartford, Sept. 9, 1851. On the Gallaudet family, see Hayden (1888); E.M. Gallaudet (1888); Boatner (1959a,b); Dexter (1911), v. 5, pp. 149–157.

31. Walker (1884). Strong (1748–1816): Yale (1769), tutor (1772–1773), ordained (1774), chaplain Revolutionary Army, Connecticut Evangelical Magazine (1800–1815), Connecticut Missionary Society (1798–1806).

32. Perkins (1817).

33. By Isaac Watts, cited in Osborn (1928), p. 336.

34. Goodrich (1857), v. 2, p. 118.

35. Larned (1874).

36. Ebeneezer Devotion (1714–1771). James Cogswell was installed Feb. 19, 1772.

37. Dexter (1911); Bacon (1882).

38. S. Cogswell (1790).

39. Root (1941), p. 37.

40. Strong (1807). For Cogswell genealogy, see Jameson (1884): James, July 1746–Nov. 20, 1792; Alice, Dec. 1749–May 9[11?], 1772; Samuel, May 1754–Aug. 24, 1790; Septimus, Aug. 1769–Oct. 1773; Mason Fitch, Sept. 1761–Dec. 10, 1830. See note 7-28.

41. The diary is excerpted and commented upon in Root (1941), pp. 22–33; Bacon (1882); Trumbull (1886), pp. 600–602.

42. The diary records several visits to "Col. Trumbull's," that is, to Joseph Trumbull. Jonathan Trumbull (1740–1809) was Washington's chief of staff, member of congress in 1789, Speaker of the House in 1791, senator in 1794, and then governor in 1798. His brother John (1756–1843) was a famous portrait painter; his brother Joseph (1737–1778) was the first commissary general of the Continental Army; his daughter, Faith, married Daniel Wadsworth. His father, Jonathan (1710–1785), was Connecticut's governor (1769–1783) during the Revolution.

43. Root (1941), p. 36. On Apr. 13, 1800, Mason Fitch Cogswell married Mary Austin, only daughter of Col. Austin and Sarah (Sheldon) Ledyard of Hartford. See Root (1941), Stevens (1876).

44. Root (1941).

45. Beecher (1848).

46. Knight (1838); Sumner and Russell (1890).

47. Cunningham (1942), p. 211. Cogswell (1824).

48. Crofut (1937). Barber (1836).

49. Sheldon (1865).

50. Howard (1943), p. 201, states that in 1793 the Courant serialized a burlesque to rival the Mercury's Echo, called the Versifier, probably by Mason Cogswell.

51. The physician Lemuel Hopkins was chiefly responsible for the Anarchiad, a dozen serialized poems that chanted the dangers and difficulties of the new federation—the most famous political satire of its time. The aide was David Humphreys. John Trumbull, second cousin to the portrait painter, wrote McFingal, satirizing the position of the British loyalists in New England at the outbreak of the revolution. It went through thirty editions and was considered to "set a new tone in American letters" (Trumbull, 1886). Oliver Wolcott became governor. Richard Alsop was a bibliophile, a naturalist and a linguist. Theodore Dwight was Alsop's brother-in-law, a member of Congress, and an editor; he published the Courant for many years and founded the Mirror, known all over the United States for its vigilant and sharp-tongued defense of federalism. Dwight worked with Mason Cogswell and Richard Alsop on the Echo, and a wrote a hymn that was America's national anthem until displaced by the "Star-Spangled Banner." Noah Webster is the remaining member of the later Wits. On Hopkins: Trumbull (1886), p. 601; Parsons (1936). On Barlow: Morgan (1904), v. 2, p. 305; Sheldon (1865); Parsons (1922), p. 36.

52. A friend and sometime collaborator of these later Wits was a third physician, Elihu Smith, who contributed to the *Echo* and published the first American anthology of poetry but died at twenty-seven of yellow fever.

53. Other sources on the Wits: Parsons (1936), Howard (1943), Goodrich (1857), Harrington (1969). John Trumbull (1750–1831), Joel Barlow (1754–1812), Lemuel Hopkins (1750–1801), David Humphreys (1752–1818), Richard Alsop (1761–1815), Theodore Dwight (1764–1846), Mason Cogswell (1761–1830), Timothy Dwight (1752–1817), Elihu Smith (1771–1797), Noah Webster (1758–1843), Oliver Wolcott (1760–1833).

54. Dunglison's dictionary of medical science, published in Boston in 1833, gives "spotted fever" as a synonym for typhus. The term has also been used as a synonym for Rocky Mountain spotted fever and meningococcal meningitis. See North (1811).

55. Mary Cogswell (1814); Hamett Cogswell (1816).

56. Weld (1848), p. 9. The brothers and sisters of Thomas Hopkins Gallaudet (1787–1851): ii, Edgar (1779–1790); iii, Charles (1792–1830); iv and v, ——— and Catherine (b. and d. Dec. 1793, twins); vi, James (1793–1856); vii, William Edgar (1797–1821); viii, Ann Watts (1800–1850); ix, Jane (1801–1835); x, Theodore (1805–1885); xi, Edward (1808–1847); xii, Wallace (1811–1816).

57. Boatner (1959a); Goodrich (1857), v. 2, p. 126; Anon. (1891b).

58. T.H. Gallaudet (1849).

59. Humphrey (1857), pp. 20–23.

60. Yale: Dexter (1911); Morgan (1904), v. 4, p. 237; Steiner (1893). Yale had changed since Mason Cogswell's day, twenty-five years earlier. There were more students, over two hundred, more buildings in Brick Row, two more professors, and a broader curriculum. Benjamin Silliman, the great pioneer in chemistry, had joined the faculty to teach the physical sciences, Jeremiah Day, future president of the college, taught mathematics, and the current president, Timothy Dwight, met with the seniors five days a week to teach theology, logic, and rhetoric. Dwight was a brilliant orator, his form erect and full of dignity, his face beaming with intelligence and virtue, his whole appearance imposing. Students in tall hats and swallow-tailed coats debated before him such topics as: Are novels beneficial? Are theaters beneficial? Both questions received a negative answer under President Dwight.

61. Barnard (1852).

62. E.M. Gallaudet (1888), p. 26ff.

63. Simpson (1859); Sprague (1857), v. 2, pp. 609–615.

64. When Thomas Gallaudet completed his divinity studies and was licensed to preach, in the spring of the following year, he refused an offer from Daniel Webster and others to serve as their pastor in Portsmouth, N. H. He gave poor health as his reason but he devoted much of the ensuing winter to teaching Alice how to read and write, and it seems he sensed another calling. Gallaudet (1818b).

65. Cited in Haight (1930), p. 58.

66. Cited in Haight (1930), p. 111.

67. Sigourney (1851), pp. 252–253.

68. Sigourney (1851), pp. 254–255. Sigourney has run together in her book letters from different periods. The letter beginning (p. 256) "Mr. Gallaudet gone to Paris" must have been written between Mar. and June 1816. The next, after Dec. 25, 1816, when Reverend Strong died. I do not know the date of the New Haven visit (pp. 255–256) or of the final letter here (pp. 256–257).

69. Sigourney (1854), p. 241.

70. Sigourney (1845), p. 239.

71. Sigourney (1866), pp. 222–223.

72. Oct., 1827, Sigourney collection 2, 6. Cited in Wood (1972), p. 166.

73. Russell (1895), p. 218; Trumbull (1886), p. 163; Parsons (1922), p. 71; Dwight (1866); Perkins (1895), p. 199. I am particularly indebted to Wood's insightful article (1972). Charles Sigourney: b. July 21, 1778, m. (1) Jane Carter, who d. Jan. 24, 1818; (2) Lydia Huntley, June 16, 1819. She d. June 10, 1865. He d. Dec. 30, 1854. On Sigourney see also: as educator, Sheldrick (1971); biography by Haight (1930); life in Norwich, Perkins (1895); Sigourney home, Lowell (1870), Osborn (1928); her social circle, Beecher (1865); her poetry, Duyckinck (1856).

74. Sigourney (1851), p. 259.

75. Green (1783); Epée (1784). Gallaudet (1818b) states that Mason Cogswell had read Epée, and the Library of Congress holdings in the Gallaudet collection include a copy of Francis Green's (1801) translation inscribed "To Thomas Hopkins Gallaudet from M.F. Cogswell, July 1, 1817." H. Barnard (1852) was probably mistaken when he wrote that Mason Cogswell consulted Sicard's works initially.

76. Morgan (1904), v. 2, p. 319; v. 3, pp. 43, 391; S. Gilbert (1839).

77. M.F. Cogswell (1811).

78. Mason subsequently wrote to Gilbert, who responded the following spring with expressions of gratitude. "I now feel a strong confidence that before a very distant period we shall have a school established for these unfortunate children—God knows how much it is wanted!" Of his thirteen children, he wrote, five were deaf (one later attended the Hartford school). To remind the clergy of their promise to conduct the census and to excite public interest, he had written an article, which he hoped Mason would give to the publisher of a Hartford newspaper (S. Gilbert, 1812). The article was indeed published in May in the Connecticut *Courant*, which Theodore Dwight then edited. The article is reprinted in *Association Review*, 1901, 3, pp. 134–135.

79. M.F. Cogswell (1812).

80. *Association Review*, 1900, 2, p. 263ff.

81. Reprinted in E.M. Gallaudet (1888).

82. Kimball (1814).

83. Trumbull (1886), p. 602; E.M. Gallaudet (1913).

84. Parsons (1922), p. 109.

85. Trumbull (1886), p. 598. Daniel Buck was, like Woodbridge, a merchant. Major John Caldwell was a ship-builder and legislator and a partner of Daniel's father in the insurance business (Morgan, 1904, v. 4, p. 218). Henry Hudson, a prominent businessman who later became mayor, was there, as was a Mr. Joseph Battel from Norfolk (all others were from Hartford).

86. This quote appears in T.H. Gallaudet (1824a).

87. On Apr. 20, 1815. The meeting was held Apr. 13. Moores (1978), p. 50, describes discrepancies in dates given by various authors for the date of the meeting and of Gallaudet's sailing. Thomas Gallaudet's son and biographer, E. M. Gallaudet (1888), p. 49, gives April 13, 1815, for the meeting, as does Cogswell's biographer (Bartlett, 1899, p. 612). Gallaudet's letters from the ship (1815c,d) show that he got on board May 19, 1815, and that sailing was delayed five or six days. Lewis Weld, the second director of the American Asylum, states that the ship left May 25, 1815, a fact confirmed by E. M. Gallaudet (1888), p. 56. Weld also confirms that Gallaudet agreed to go to France on April 20, 1815 (the date is also given in Gallaudet's journal), but it seems he is in error in stating that the subscribers' meeting took place after that accord, on May 1, rather than before it, on April 13, as E. M. Gallaudet (1888) and Bartlett (1899) would have it. E. M. Gallaudet (1886b) gives March 13 for the meeting and April 25 for the sailing (pp. 131–132); it seems he predated both of the events by one month, an error he corrected in his biography of his father.

88. T.H. Gallaudet (1815c, 1815d).

89. T.H. Gallaudet (1815b). A month later, Gallaudet wrote to Cogswell again (T.H. Gallaudet, 1815e). He was still on board the *Mexico*. He had written another letter to Alice, enclosed, and *Hymn at Sea*, which was sung on board at the worship service. See T.H. Gallaudet (1815a).

90. T.H. Gallaudet (1815f).

91. T.H. Gallaudet (1818c).

92. T.H. Gallaudet (1818g).

93. Cited in Goodrich (1857), v. 2, p. 222.

94. See Humphrey (1857), p. 57. Anon. (1818a) estimates 15,000, half of them children (p. 226).

95. T.H. Gallaudet (1818c). The other primary sources for events in London are Gallaudet's letters in the Library of Congress, in E.M. Gallaudet (1888), and in Humphrey (1857). On the meeting of the trustees, see Anon. (1822b), p. 40; Arrowsmith (1819), p. 14.

96. T.H. Gallaudet (1818c), p. 2.

97. T.H. Gallaudet (1815g). Thomas Gallaudet took up lodging at his brother James's, where he found a letter from Alice Cogswell: A. Cogswell (1815b). Also see A. Cogswell (1815c).

98. T.H. Gallaudet (1818c).

99. Bracketed expressions in "Monday 10th" are quoted from T.H. Gallaudet (1815g).

100. Bell (1918). Mrs. Braidwood had just written to her son John in Virginia: "We were very much surprised and rather alarmed lately by the application of a Mr. Gallaydet [sic]. . . . Having flattered ourselves that you were long 'ere this established . . . we have recommended his making application to you." It is unlikely that John Braidwood received the letter. It is reprinted in the *Association Review*, 1900, 2, 396–397.

101. T.H. Gallaudet (1815i).

102. Thomas described him in a letter to an Andover friend: "There is something most engaging about him. . . . Dignity, benevolence, modesty, nay, child-like simplicity, combined with great ease and elegance and when I saw him, softened almost into tenderness, somewhat like melancholy—and I thought, how would some of our self-conceited, ostentatious, confident, domineering, conversation-engrossing, literary, scrap-puffing, oracular, dog-matical, would-be great folks hide their diminished heads and blush at their petty greatness if they could see the chaste modesty of one of the greatest scholars and philosophers of Europe!" Cited in Humphrey (1857), pp. 45–47. The interview is also mentioned in T.H. Gallaudet (1815j).

103. Stewart (1812).

104. E.M. Gallaudet (1888), pp. 52, 88. T.H. Gallaudet (1815j).

105. Sources on Brace: Gallaudet (1815m), Woodruff (1849), Weld (1837). Also see Howe (1857); Schwartz (1956). On Mitchell: see Stewart (1812) and the biography in Porter (1848b).

106. A. Cogswell (1815e). John Gordon (1816) was on the governing board of the Asylum and James F. Gordon (1818) was its secretary. Gallaudet visited the former, fruitlessly as it turned out. See his letter to Mason Cogswell: T.H. Gallaudet (1815j).

107. Joseph Turner entered the Edinburgh Institution at age twelve in 1811. Further mention of his communicat-ing chiefly by sign appears in the school report for the annual exercise of the following year (Edinburgh Institution, 1817, pp. 55, 65).

108. Hannah More (1745–1833).

109. Zachary Macaulay (1768–1838), editor of the *Christian Observer* (1802–1816) and father of Thomas Babing-ton Macaulay, English historian, invited Thomas to spend Sabbath at his house in Clapham some four miles from town (T.H. Gallaudet, 1816c).

110. Macaulay (1817).

111. Macaulay (1818a). His denial also appears in J.F. Gordon (1818); see T.H. Gallaudet's rebuttal (1818g).

112. Macaulay (1818b). History shortly tested the honesty of these disclaimers. A Dublin physician, C.E.H. Orpen, started a subscription to open a deaf school and applied to Watson for a qualified instructor or permission to send one for training; he was refused. Next he applied to Thomas Braidwood's grandson, then head of the Birmingham institution, "but he would not teach anyone without being well paid and without an engagement not to teach anyone else (as teacher) for some years" (Barnard, 1852, p. 77, 1859 ed.). Finally, Orpen approached Kinniburgh, who decried the fact that the English "still act on the same illiberal plan," but explained that his

bond to them forced him to refuse also (reprinted in Humphrey, 1857, p. 82). So the Dublin school opened with untrained teachers. Shortly, Kinniburgh's bond to London expired and the Dublin principal could finally receive his instruction—on condition that he pay Kinniburgh 750 pounds for three months' tuition and swear never to give instruction to any who might set up a rival institution in Scotland! See Syle (1887), p. 13; Barnard (1852). The restriction was ultimately removed.

113. T.H. Gallaudet (1816e).

114. T.H. Gallaudet (1816f).

115. T.H. Gallaudet (1816g).

116. In T.H. Gallaudet (1818c) Gallaudet says he is to receive daily private lessons from Massieu, but in T.H. Gallaudet (1816n) Massieu proposes that he and Clerc alternate in giving Gallaudet lessons. In T.H. Gallaudet (1818b), he states that he received daily lessons "from Massieu and Clerc." Clerc (1852) says he taught Gallaudet three times a week. Boatner (1959a) and Booth (1881) also mention that Gallaudet took some lessons from Sicard's hearing collaborator, Paulmier.

117. T.H. Gallaudet (1818a).

118. Macaulay (1818c); H. More, cited in E.M. Gallaudet (1888), p. 105.

119. A. Cogswell (1815f).

120. A list of contributors appears in Fusfeld (1922). Also see E.M. Gallaudet (1886a); M. Cogswell and Woodbridge (1815).

121. M.F. Cogswell and Woodbridge (1816a).

122. The second Monday of June, 1816. At the same place, on June 26, by-laws were adopted and officers appointed (Barnard, 1852, p. 130 of the 1859 ed.).

123. T.H. Gallaudet (1816g).

124. Clerc (1852).

125. T.H. Gallaudet (1816h). Gallaudet made his proposal on May 20, 1816, and wrote this letter on May 21.

126. Clerc (1816b).

127. Bébian (1826d), p. 357, says Clerc was paid 500 francs at the Institution. Clerc's contract with Gallaudet states he is to be paid $500. There were five francs to the dollar then as, approximately, now (1981).

128. Clerc (1816b).

129. Sicard (1816).

130. Reprinted in E.M. Gallaudet (1888), p. 97.

131. T.H. Gallaudet (1816l). Translated and excerpted in Lane (1976), pp. 216–217. A Mr. Upson, a friend of Mason's and Wilder's trading partner in America, introduced Gallaudet and Wilder (T.H. Gallaudet, 1816h). Gallaudet went to see Sicard in Paris bearing a letter of introduction from Zachary Macaulay and he was accompanied by S.V.S. Wilder, who was known to Sicard. It was Wilder who, on the illness of the American ambassador, represented the United States at Napoleon's marriage to the daughter of Francis I, emperor of Austria. Wilder was president of the American Tract Society and fond of broadcasting Bibles throughout France. See Root (1941).

132. Sicard (1817). On Gallaudet's goodbye to Paulmier, see E. Booth (1881). Gallaudet's letter of thanks to Paulmier is reprinted in Paulmier (1834a), pp. 339–340.

133. T.H. Gallaudet (1816b). The letter is in: A. Cogswell (1816a). The pupil Gallaudet came to know best at Kinniburgh's school was Helen Hall. He wrote about her (1816d) to Mason Cogswell, urged Helen to write to Alice, which she did (T.H. Gallaudet, 1816b), and Helen's father wrote to Mason enclosing another exchange between their daughters (J. Hall, 1816).

134. T.H. Gallaudet (1816i).

135. The passport issued to Clerc for return from his second trip to France in 1835 is among the Clerc Papers no. 21 bis, Yale University Library. Clerc lists the date of his departure as June 18, 1816 (Clerc Papers no. 67).

CHAPTER 8 / SPREADING THE WORD

1. Clerc (1816c).

2. Locke (1690), book 3, ch. 2, sec. 1 (v. 2, p. 8, Dover 1959 ed.).

3. Macaulay's letter of Nov. 7, 1818 (reprinted in E. M. Gallaudet, 1888, p. 106), states: "The luminous account you gave me of the superiority of the French mode of instruction over the deaf and dumb you will have already seen in the pages of the *Christian Observer*."

4. "B" (1818).

5. As Thomas sailed toward America, Alice wrote a brief essay on his homecoming in Lydia Sigourney's class: "Mr. Gallaudet gone to Paris.—Come back with Mr. Clerc—Teach deaf and dumb, new words, new signs. —Oh, beautiful.—I very afraid wind blow hard on Ocean—turn over ship.—Alice very afraid.—Mr. Gallaudet will pray God to keep, not drown.—Wind blow right way.—I very glad." Reprinted in Sigourney (1851), p. 256.

6. Anon. (1818b).

7. "B" (1819).

8. T.H. Gallaudet (1819a).

9. Arrowsmith (1819), p. 85.

10. Arrowsmith (1824), p. 487.

11. Anon. (1822b).

12. Rémi Valade published a grammar of French Sign Language: Valade, Y.L. Rémi (1854b). Also see: Lane and

Grosjean (1980), Klima and Bellugi (1979). The discussion of fallacies was inspired by Markowicz (1977), and see Baker and Padden (1978). For other articles on sign language before 1900, see: Anon (1863, 1865); Akerly (1824); F.A.P. Barnard (1834, 1835); Bébian (1817, 1825, 1826a,b); Bell (1898); Berthier (1852b); F.W. Booth (1902, 1905a,b, 1909); Caldwell (1912); Cary (1851); Chambellan (1887); Critchley (1939); Crouter (1894); De Gérando (1827); Fay (1892); Francis (1859); Frishberg (1975); Fusfeld (1958); T.H. Gallaudet (1859); George (1890); Haerne (1875); G. Hutton (1869); J.S. Hutton (1870, 1874); Keep (1857, 1869, 1871a,b); Kinney (1859); Knowlson (1965); Kroeber (1958); Lambert (1865); H. Lane (1976, 1978a, 1980); Markowicz (1977); Mottez (1975); New York Institution (1838), p. 21, (1845); H.P. Peet (1851b, 1867); I.L. Peet (1887); Porter (1846); Rambosson (1853); Sibscota (1670); Sicard (1808); Stokoe (1960); Syle (1873a), p. 158; Turner (1859); Tylor (1865); Vaïsse (1854); Valade (1854a,b); Weeks (1890); Wilkins (1694); Williams (1898); Woodbridge (1830); Woodward (1973, 1976, 1978a); Woodward and Erting (1975); Woodward and De Santis (1977).

13. T.H. Gallaudet (1816j) wrote to Mason Cogswell on sighting land. Clerc gives this date (Clerc Papers, no. 67). For Clerc's impressions of New York, see Clerc (1852), pp. 110–111.

14. The letter by Nathaniel Moore is reprinted in E.M. Gallaudet (1888), pp. 112–115.

15. T.H. Gallaudet (1816k).

16. American School (1816c).

17. The letter is reprinted in the *Association Review*, 1902, 4, 20–21.

18. Also with Dr. Edward Miller. Samuel Latham Mitchill (1764–1831), often misspelled Mitchell. The letter is reprinted in the *Association Review*, 1900, 2, 66–68. It was written in 1781, published in 1804.

19. See: Bell in the *Association Review*, 1901, 3, 439–451; Sommers (1835).

20. Currier (1893), p. 10.

21. Samuel Hopkins, b. 1721, grad. Yale 1741. Edwards was then 39 and Timothy Dwight's mother, 8. See Hopkins (1854).

22. Cited in Grant (1978). Twain came to Hartford in January 1868, and again in June 1869, but did not settle there until 1871 (Boatner, 1959a, p. 117). Clerc gives the date of his arrival in Hartford as August 22, 1816 (Clerc Papers no. 67). Rugoff (1981), p. 568, states that in the 1850s Hartford had the highest per capita income in the United States.

23. See Clerc (1816c), p. 13.

24. Boston: arrived Sept. 4, 1816. Lectures to men at Boston Atheneum Sept. 7 and 9, to women at New Court House Sept. 10. See Clerc (1852) for texts. Clerc (1816d) is a copy of the coverage in *Boston Intelligencer* on Sept. 14 and *Columbian Centinel* Sept. 18. Barnard (1852), p. 154, 1859 ed., lists contributors by city.

25. M.F. Cogswell (1816b).

26. Salem: address Sept. 24, 1816. Clerc (1816d) recopies coverage in the *Salem Gazette* for Sept. 27, including text of address. New Haven: address on Oct. 18. Clerc (1816d) recopies coverage in the *Connecticut Journal* for Oct. 22, including text of address and questions and answers. Also cited in *Courant*: Anon. (1816).

27. M. Cogswell (1816c).

28. T.H. Gallaudet (1816m).

29. New York: M.F. Cogswell (1816d).

30. New York: M.F. Cogswell (1816e). This third meeting took place on Monday, Nov. 4, in the mayor's office and the fourth on Dec. 6 (New York Institution *Reports*, 1816).

31. Albany: M.F. Cogswell (1816f). They left New York City on Wednesday, Nov. 6, and arrived Albany Thursday, Nov. 7. Address on Saturday, Nov. 9. Clerc (1816d) copies coverage in the *Albany Daily Advertiser* for Tuesday, Nov. 12, including the text of the address and questions and answers.

32. M.F. Cogswell (1816g).

33. Currier (1893), p. 10; New York Institution *Reports* (1816), p. 429 of the 1901 reprinting. New York City: the group left Albany on Monday, Nov. 18, and arrived in New York the following day (M.F. Cogswell, 1816h,i). Mason Cogswell went directly to the post office and found a letter from Alice: "My very most dear Pappa—I think and I afraid you never come back here Hartford. I want you here all family . . .

"I want see Mr. Clerc I want see signs very many Mr. Clerc tell signs I love very much see signs Mr. Clerc same very beautiful signs Mr. Gallaudet . . .

"How many days before you come back here in Hartford,—My mama and my Sisters and My Brother all family says me give love you very much give you,—My very most Dear Papa very kind and I love you very much much I give kiss you, Most affectionate Daughter, Alice Cogswell" (A. Cogswell, 1816b).

34. Hallam (1816). Hallam's letter indicates that Mason had written to Braidwood a second time in the fall of 1816, enclosing his letter with one to Hallam.

35. Bell *Association Review*, 1905, 7, 50.

36. Bell *Association Review*, 1901, 3, 430.

37. American School (1816c).

38. Philadelphia: Gallaudet and Clerc left New York on Friday, Nov. 23 (Cogswell, 1816i). The address was on Saturday, Dec. 7 (Clerc, 1816d). The latter source copies coverage in the Philadelphia *Gazette* for Dec. 11, including the text of Clerc's address and questions and answers. Also reprinted in Clerc (1817a). The meeting is also reported in the *Courant* on Dec. 24; see Clerc (1816e).

39. American School (1816); Gard (1816).

40. Burlington. Clerc Papers no. 66: Notice from Burlington Dec. 16; Clerc and Gallaudet will demonstrate the extraordinary success that has attended the education of the deaf and dumb in France—come to the Academy (T.H. Gallaudet, 1816m). Clerc and Gallaudet returned to New York by way of Burlington, N.J. A town meeting was held with the ex-governor presiding: they made a favorable impression. The largest subscription was $500 from the good father Boudinet and the smallest from a little girl who gave fifty cents anonymously. Boudinet urged

them to call for a subscription on Joseph Bonaparte, the ex-king of Spain, who had retired to the United States after Waterloo. They waited a day at Bordentown to see him but he did not return from a trip, so they left him a letter and a subscription paper, fruitlessly, as it turned out.

41. New York: Clerc (1817b); New York Institution *Reports* (1817); A. Cogswell (1816c). The fifth meeting took place on Jan. 14, 1817. The fifth report of the N.Y. Institution states that there were ten wards by the time of a sixth meeting on Jan. 23, 1817. The census tolled 66 deaf and dumb residents of the city, seven wards reporting, population of 120,000. Reprinted in *Association Review*, 1905, 7, 65–70. H.P. Peet (1852c), p. 7, states that the population was 100,000. Alice wrote from Hartford (A. Cogswell, 1816c).

42. M.F. Cogswell (1817a,b,c).

43. E.M. Gallaudet (1888), p. 118.

44. Turner (1870); Barnard (1852), p. 21 of the 1859 ed. Clerc gives the opening date of the school in the City Hotel as April 17, 1817 (Clerc Papers no. 67).

45. Barnard (1852); Dutton (1852), p. 426; Booth (1881); Sprague (1857); Rae (1854).

46. T.H. Gallaudet (1818a).

47. E.M. Gallaudet (1886a), p. 426.

48. Boatner (1959a).

49. Morgan (1904), v. 3, p. 151; Dooey (1938); Waldo (1818). Boatner (1959a) states that Morgan's coffeehouse was opened by Joseph Morgan, grandfather of J. Pierpont Morgan.

50. Lane (1978b); Goodrich (1857), v. 2, p. 127.

51. Many authors mistakenly give the second home of the asylum, on Prospect Street, as its first. However, Stansbury (1817a) described the school on Main Street while living there and Weld (1848), the second principal, confirmed this. Also see Russell (1895); Barnard (1852), p. 194, 1859 ed.

52. W. Turner (1853b).

53. Dillingham (1816).

54. S. Gilbert (1812, 1816).

55. Backus had taught at the Central New York Asylum, founded in 1822. Mr. William Reid went to the New York Institution to prepare himself for its direction. In 1832, Peet went there and proposed a merger, which was declined. In 1836, the legislature forced the merger and Backus acquired the *Radii* (Fox, 1932).

56. Cited in Braddock (1975), p. 5. His example was followed by Edmund Booth, editor of the *Eureka*, and by James George (1825–1876), editor of the *Richmond* (Ky.) *Messenger*, acquired 1861.

57. A. Cogswell (1817).

58. T.H. Gallaudet (1818b); Root (1941), p. 71.

59. Clerc (1818b). J. Williams (1893a) states that, of the first 100 pupils, 28 came from 23 families, in which there were 48 other deaf. In this group, one-half were born deaf, another third were prelingually deafened. Their average age was eighteen. The average stay grew gradually; by 1835 the minimum was five years. Names and statistics appear in the 71st report of the American School.

60. J. Williams (1893a).

61. J. Turner (1885); Anon. (1871a).

62. New York Institution *Reports* (1838); H.P. Peet (1857a).

63. Stone (1867), p. 27; J. Williams (1893); Peet (1857), p. 359; Moores (1978), p. 214.

64. Williams (1882), p. 56. Also see the second report of the American School.

65. Barnard (1852); Barber (1836); Woodbridge (1830).

66. T.H. Gallaudet (1821a).

67. Cited in E.M. Gallaudet (1888), p. 121. And an early report from the school states that its original design was to make it "the gate to heaven for those poor lambs of the flock who have hitherto been wandering in the paths of ignorance, like sheep without a shepherd" (third report of the American School, cited in E.A. Fay, 1917a).

68. Barnard (1852); Peet (1852); J. Harrington (1852); Conference of Executives (1888).

69. E.M. Gallaudet (1888), p. 123.

70. Root (1941), p. 71; Syle (1887), p. 18; a sketch appears p. 22. The building was at 15, later renumbered 48, Prospect Street. Clerc (1825); in 1818 there were 115 scholars.

71. De Witt Clinton was an admirer of Mitchill's, according to Gross (1861). The histories of the New York Institution in Currier (1893) and the school's fifth report do not contain an accurate record of the meetings leading up to its incorporation. These were: (1) at Rev. Stanford's home; (2) at Tammany Hall; (3) at the mayor's office, Nov. 4, 1816, Mason Cogswell attending; (4) at the mayor's office, call for census, Dec. 6, 1816, Laurent Clerc present (Clerc, 1817b); (5) at the mayor's office, report on census, Jan. 14, 1817; (6) at the mayor's office, report on constitution, Jan. 23, 1817 (see *Association Review*, 1901, 3, 438); (7) a meeting leading to petition to the legislature for Act of Incorporation, submitted Apr. 15, 1817; (8) first board meeting, May 22, 1817.

72. Stansbury (1817b). Several of the female pupils urged Clerc to chat with them after school in the ladies' sitting room. He felt it an innocent request he should endeavor to grant since their chief business at the asylum was to acquire language and his language was the foundation for all their improvement. Mrs. Stansbury considered that the young ladies were in her charge, that Clerc was too attentive to them, and that he must not join them in the sitting room (T.H. Gallaudet, 1817b,c). After this and many other incidents, Thomas Gallaudet asked the board to request the Stansburys' resignation. This they did, but the superintendent argued that there were no grounds for dissatisfaction and that if Thomas "could not get along with him," as he was reported to have said, then Thomas did not have to board in the house, he could board elsewhere. The matter was left there and Stansbury crowed in a letter to his brother that he had "defeated the machinations of a malignant enemy" (Stansbury, 1817c).

73. Currier (1893).

74. Clerc (1818a).

75. Superintendents in this era at the American Asylum: Stansbury (1817–1818); Samuel Whittlesey (1818–1824). Title changed to Steward: H. Peet (1824–1881); W.W. Turner (1831–1847). See Barnard (1852).

76. W.C. Woodbridge was hired Dec. 4, 1817. See T.H. Gallaudet (1818b). Alcott (1861) gives a biography.

77. T.H. Gallaudet (1817d).

78. Barnard (1852), p. 75, 1859 ed. Stone (1867) gives a garbled account of names and dates. Barnard has the facts straight. It is ironic that a few years earlier Woodbridge had received a pressing invitation from the Birmingham school to succeed its director, Thomas Braidwood, who had died. They wanted someone from Hartford since they wished to supplant sham speech with education through sign language; when Woodbridge refused because of his health, they hired a Swiss Protestant who was a follower of Epée's method.

79. W. Turner (1853b); Braddock (1975).

80. Braddock (1975). Whiton and Loring were assistants in 1825 and instructors beginning in 1826.

81. E. Booth (1881); F. Booth (1905c).

82. F. Booth (1905c); Sagra (1837), p. 444; Braddock (1975).

83. E. Booth (1953). Booth, his wife, and his brother-in-law had the pleasure of finding themselves denoted in the census of 1840 as "deaf, dumb, blind, idiotic, insane, and colored." The reason this entry was made for Anamosa was that the returns of the census were grossly perverted in the interests of slavery, to create the impression that a far greater proportion of the free blacks of the North suffered from various physical infirmities than the slaves of the South. (The French Annals of Public Health then cited these false census results, among others, as proving that blacks tend to marry relatives and have defective offspring. See Fay, 1876, p. 207.) According to H.P. Peet (1852c), quite the reverse was true: a lower incidence of deafness among blacks than among whites in the North. Figuier (1863), p. 339, cites the fake census figures from Iowa and concludes: "In the colored population, in which slavery facilitates consanguineous and even incestuous union, the proportion of deaf-mutes was ninety-one times higher than in the white population, protected by civil, moral, and religious law." For more on tampering with the 1840 census to safeguard slavery, see Jarvis (1855).

84. Clerc (1852), p. 114; Turner (1870); E.M. Gallaudet (1888), p. 132; Carlin (1885). Thomas Gallaudet found Clerc's absence a further burden (T.H. Gallaudet, 1818c, p. 132).

85. Root (1941); E.M. Gallaudet (1886a, b, 1888); Weld (1848). The application to Congress was Jan. 25, 1819; the board voted thanks on Mar. 19, and petitioned the General Assembly for a change in name in May 1819. About a year after the school opened, Clerc took forty-two pupils to Center Church, where he gave an address and conducted a public examination before the governor and both houses of the legislature (Clerc, 1818b).

86. Sicard (1817).

87. Contract dated Apr. 25, 1820. Clerc Papers.

88. E.M. Gallaudet (1888), p. 130; Moores (1978), p. 76, also mentions the salary inequity.

89. E. Booth (1881).

90. Sicard (1820).

91. Chester (1820); Root (1941), p. 89.

92. T.H. Gallaudet (1821b); G.O. Fay (1899); Burnet (1835); Barber (1836), p. 32.

93. Carlin [n.d.], p. 2. Crofut (1937).

94. Williams (1882).

95. Stone (1866).

96. Barnard (1852), p. 92, 1859 ed.

97. T.H. Gallaudet (1824a); Stone (1867), p. 23; Anon. (1824).

98. Morse (1933), p. 176.

99. Anon. (1835a).

100. Report of the New York Institution for 1843, cited in Barnard (1852), p. 92, 1859 ed. Also see Clarke Institution (1893a), p. 15.

101. H.P. Peet (1857a).

102. Cited in Bell, Association Review, 7, 53–60.

103. Akerly (1821a); F.A.P. Barnard (1834). Akerly then wrote to Cogswell stating that Stansbury had persuaded them Hartford was ill-disposed toward them, even jealous, but now that he was gone, there could be a rapprochement. He enclosed a copy of a textbook he had written to replace Watson's. Mason Cogswell answered huffily that their success placed them above jealousy; Hartford had been ill-disposed to the New York school in view of the way they began, the principal they chose, and their mode of instruction (Akerly, 1821b; M.F. Cogswell, 1821).

104. Currier (1893); H.P. Peet (1857a); N.Y. State Senate (1827).

105. Clerc (1827); the school replied in its ninth report.

106. New York State Department of Public Instruction (1828).

107. H.P. Peet: Part I, 1845b; Part II, 1849b; Part III, 1850a.

108. Fay et al. (1873); Jones (1922). Harvey Prindle Peet (1794–1873).

109. Vaïsse had come to Saint-Jacques as instructor in training, on the recommendation of the duke of Doudeauville, directly from school in Versailles when he was nineteen. In a year he was placed in charge of the entering class and in three he was sent to New York, where he worked with Harvey Peet for six years. When he returned to Paris, he took over Itard's supplementary class of instruction (for the most advanced students). Itard had

specified in his will that it was to be taught orally but Vaïsse realized that was impossible, so he used sign, but he did start a little articulation class: one hour a day for those who could profit. "It is only by means of signs that we can put the deaf man in possession of another language," he wrote, "and instill in him the various branches of knowledge" (Vaïsse, 1848b, p. 10). Vaïsse visited the oralist schools in Switzerland and Germany that had so impressed Ordinaire, and he criticized them roundly. He found that children were expelled for lack of speech, that only a few pupils could be assigned to each teacher, that general education and training in trades were preempted by speech training. "It is above all with the intermediary of gestures, and often only by this means," he wrote, "that we can make enter into the deaf pupil's intelligence by eye what enters ordinary pupils' intelligence by ear" (Vaïsse, 1844b, p. 650). But he believed that articulation was an important complement and wrote monographs on how to teach speech (Vaïsse, 1838, 1853). Also see Magnat (1885) and Gineste (1981).

110. Anon. (1831); Anon. (1832a). Peet convened the first Convention of American Instructors of the Deaf in 1850.

111. F. Booth (1905c), p. 229; Wilson and Fiske (1888); F.A.P. Barnard (1912); Davenport (1939).

112. Keep (1880), p. 59. Also see J. Williams (1882); I.L. Peet (1875); E.M. Gallaudet (1884).

113. Bartlett (1853); Moores (1978), p. 190.

114. Bartlett's most famous pupil was Henry Winter Syle, the first deaf American to become an Episcopal priest. After losing his hearing from scarlet fever when he was six, Syle enrolled in Bartlett's school, then the American Asylum, next at Cambridge University, and finally he received master's degrees from Yale and Trinity. To be ordained, he had to pass a rigorous examination in history, philosophy, church doctrine, and classical languages, and to overcome the prejudices of his time. Fortunately, his bishop thought it as appropriate to ordain a deaf man to teach in sign as an Indian to preach in Cherokee. See Gannon (1981), pp. 181–183; Davidson (1890).

115. Patterson (1877).

116. See Moores (1978), p. 52; Gerson (1978).

117. Gerson (1978); Pennsylvania Institution *Reports* (1821, 1822).

118. Pennsylvania Institution *Reports* (1822), pp. 7–9.

119. Clerc (1823); Weld (1826); Pennsylvania Institution (1823); Foster (1876).

120. Abraham Hutton (1798–1870); Wilson and Fiske (1888); Barclay (1870).

121. H.P. Peet (1851d).

122. Pyatt (1868).

123. Clerc quoted in Pyatt (1868).

124. Albert Newsam (1809–1864); Wilson and Fiske (1888).

125. Carlin (1867).

126. John Carlin (1818–1891); Domich (1939); Braddock (1975); Wilson and Fiske (1888); E.M. Gallaudet (1884).

127. Carlin (1847).

128. Burnet (1835).

129. Nack (1827).

130. Braddock (1975), p. 7; Gallaher (1898), p. 18; Anon. 1894. On publications by deaf authors, see also: Ballin (1930), Batson and Bergman (1976), E. Booth (1953), Calkins (1924), Eastman (1974), E.M. Gallaudet (1873, 1884), Gannon (1981), L. Jacobs (1974), Kitto (1848, 1856), E.J. Mann (1836), Nack (1827), Panara, Denis and McFarlane (1960), Remy (1893), Sandham (1812), Spradley and Spradley (1978), Syle (1873b), Tidyman (1974).

131. Pélissier (1844). Clerc brought this volume with him when he returned from France in 1847 (Braddock, 1975, p. 49).

132. Beauchamp (1970).

133. McClure (1923).

134. H. Peet (1870).

135. Fosdick (1893); Jacobs (1852).

136. A key to the controversy over methodical signs: Jacobs (1853); Burnet (1854); Jacobs (1855a); Burnet (1855a); Jacobs (1855b); Burnet (1855b); Jacobs (1855c), (1856); Burnet (1856); Jacobs (1857); Peet (1858); Jacobs (1858); Burnet and Porter (1858); Peet (1859b); Jacobs (1859); Peet (1859c); Talbot (1872). Burnet (1835), p. 100.
     When Jacobs got to Danville, Mitchill resigned, returned to New York. He married the deaf assistant matron at the New York School, Mary Rose, then became head at Canajoharie, but he died in the year that Peet went there to propose a merger (H. Peet, 1853a). His widow later married the first deaf teacher at the New York School —a skillful native signer—Nathan Totten. They went to teach at the North Carolina school and then at the Illinois school when it opened—and there Totten died at the early age of thirty-five, leaving a twice-bereaved widow. Jacobs's school thrived until the Civil War, for Kentucky became one of the battlegrounds, held by one side, then the other. Parents were afraid to send their children to a school far from home in a war area. Jacobs's son, William, and his nephew entered the Union army, from which William—handsome, intelligent, lovable, destined to succeed his father—did not return. Kentucky was also the site of an early oral school (1844–1854) founded by a Baptist minister, who came from Virginia in 1818. At one point he returned there to consult with Rev. Kirkpatrick, Braidwood's associate in Manchester. When he died, the project ended (McClure, 1899).

137. Stone (1853b); E.M. Gallaudet (1886b).

138. Willard, Danfort E. Ball, Clarissa Morse. See Burnet (1835), p. 107.

139. H. Peet (1853b).

140. 1863–1866; a teacher was promoted: G.L. Weed. Then G.O. Fay took over the direction (1866–1880). See Patterson (1893). Stone died in Hartford in 1870 from the blow of a locomotive.

141. Castleman (1852).

142. Bass and Healy (1949).

143. Doyle (1893).

144. Hallam (1818).

145. Bell, *Association Review*, 1900, 2, 257–519; Bell (1918). Stone (1866), p. 19.

146. A note on enrollments. In 1852, Barnard estimated that 3,000 pupils had been educated in schools for the deaf since 1817. The year before, 1,100 were enrolled in 13 schools with the sponsorship of 23 states. He estimated the whole number of deaf in the United States at 10,000, the number of school age, 3,000, and thus a delinquency rate of two-thirds. In 1867, Stone reported that some 1,500 pupils had graduated from the American Asylum alone and 130 teachers were exercising their profession. In 1857, Peet gives the size of the New York school at 315 enrollments, Hartford, 200, Paris, 180, Groningen, 180.

147. The first Convention of American Instructors of the Deaf (CAID) was held in 1850. One-fourth came from Hartford. The *American Annals of the Deaf* was launched in 1847 by the American Asylum and then undertaken by CAID (H.P. Peet, 1859a).

148. Sagra (1837), p. 442. Barnard (1852), p. 100, 1859 ed.

149. Quebec school founded 1831, Mexico City school, 1865. For descriptions of schools for the deaf, consult the index under the name of the school and the city in which it was located. For articles describing several schools, see: Anon. (1853), Ackers (1874), M.E. Adams (1896), Addison (1908), Banerji (1897), H. Barnard (1878), Bébian (1826a,c,d), Chapin (1846), E.P. Clarke (1900a), Clerc (1848), Daras (1853a), G. Day (1845), G. Day and Peet (1861), H.E. Day et al. (1928), Ely (1854), Fay (1886), Ferreri (1908), Fornari (1904), E.M. Gallaudet (1867a,b, 1876, 1897), Greenwood (1839), Hansen (1908), Haycock (1923), Heidsiek (1899, 1900), Hitz (1907), Hobart (1899), Laishley (1885), E.J. Mann (1836), Palluy (1829), H.P. Peet (1852b), Peet and Campbell (1849), Porter (1846), Rae (1852), Rogers (1873), Ryerson (1868), Sagra (1839), Valade-Gabel (1875), Volta Bureau (1902), Watteville (1845), Weld (1845), Wilkinson (1893a,b), Yale (1883).

CHAPTER 9 / CONCERNING WOMEN

1. Quoted in Braddock (1975).

2. Quoted in Root (1941), pp. 75–76.

3. Cogswell genealogy in Root (1941), p. 115ff; Jameson (1884), pp. 244–246, 402–404. Weld left Hartford to succeed Clerc at Philadelphia only to return to succeed Thomas Gallaudet on his retirement. He and Mary Austin Cogswell had five children, the first named after Mason, the last after Alice. Alice's second sister, Elizabeth, married a Hartford judge, grandson of the governor of the Plymouth Colony, had two children, and was commissioned major and surgeon in the Union army. Alice's youngest sister, Catherine Ledyard, married a Presbyterian minister who helped to found the theological seminary at Princeton; they had seven children.

4. Morse (1933); Sumner and Russell (1890).

5. Sumner and Russell (1890).

6. Perkins (1895); Beecher (1848). The Beechers and the Cogswells were friendly; see Rugoff (1981), p. 103.

7. The Sigourney poem appears in Beecher (1848) and in Holycross (1913), p. 61, with an extract of an accompanying letter. Beecher implies that it was she who was by Alice's side throughout her final illness. It is likely, but unconfirmed, that Clerc was also present.

8. A. Cogswell (1816c). The Gallaudet letters were T.H. Gallaudet (1815k), (1816c). He also wrote a report for Stewart; T.H. Gallaudet (1815m).

9. Primary sources on Julia Brace: Weld (1837), L.H. Woodruff (1849), Burnet (1835).

10. Blackstone quoted in Howe (1857), p. 386.

11. Mrs. Laurent Clerc (née Eliza Crocker) (1792–1880). They had six children, three boys and three girls. See T.F. Fox (1935, 3 [5]).

12. Osborn (1928); Russell (1895).

13. Moeller (1909), p. 318.

14. Clerc (1858b).

15. Fay (1898), p. 14; Clerc (1852); Clerc Papers no. 42.

16. Turner (1868).

17. Weld (1848); Turner (1848); D. Peet (1856).

18. Bemiss (1858); Fay (1898), p. 106; Morris (1861).

19. Fay (1898); Moores (1978), p. 81ff; Fraser (1976).

20. Turner (1848), p. 32; Morris (1861); Fay (1898), pp. 18, 102, 134. Turner also stated (1868), "Every consideration of philanthropy as well as the interests of congenitally deaf persons themselves should induce their teachers and friends to urge upon them the impropriety of such intermarriages" (p. 96). Bell cites this quote in his *Memoir* (1883b) and in Bell (1890a). Turner is here speaking of marriages between two congenitally deaf persons. From a sample of 740 persons who visited the American Asylum over some years and provided familial information, Turner counted 24 families with both parents congenitally deaf; in nine of these, there were one or more deaf-mutes, an incidence he labeled three-fifths. Of course, his sample would tend to include families that had deaf children. Fay (1898, p. 134) found in a sample of 3,000 marriages with one or both partners deaf that 335 had both partners congenitally deaf and one-fourth of these had deaf children. The incidence is about the same, whatever the deafness of the parents, if both have deaf relatives. For more on this topic see chapter 11.

21. T.H. Gallaudet (1847).

22. Nash and Nash (1981), p. 24.

23. See several studies reviewed in Mindel and Vernon (1971).

24. Mindel and Vernon (1971), p. 96.

25. Paulmier (1834a), p. 381.

26. Barclay (1870), p. 30.

27. Berthier (1842b). Also discussed in H.P. Peet (1857b), p. 38, and H.P. Peet (1867), 11, p. 254. Berthier (1837a, 1840b). See, further, the case reported by Piroux (1842d), also discussed in H.P. Peet (1857b), p. 41. Anon. (1869b) describes a sign language wedding in New York. On the law and the deaf before 1900, see: Anon (1838, 1839, 1840, 1861), Bébian (1826a,e,f, 1827b,c), Bélanger (1901a,b,c), Berthier (1837a, 1838c, 1840b, 1842a,b), Breton de la Martinière (1800), Chambeyron (1838), Chazal (1893, 1894), Clerc (1858a), Deming (1854), Desessarts (1773), Fay (1912), Forestier (1838a), E.M. Gallaudet (1872), Itard (1827c), Morel (1838), H.P. Peet (1857b, 1867), Piroux (1838a,b,c, 1839a,b,e, 1840a,b, 1841a,b, 1842a,c,d,e,f,g), Puybonnieux (1856, 1858b, 1859), Seiss (1887), Tillinghast (1902), Vaïsse (1844a), Van Bastelaer (1890), Vive (1796).

28. Genealogy in Hall (1883), p. 17. Also see Griswold (1933, 1938).

29. T.H. Gallaudet (1818d). Also see Conference of Executives (1888), p. 72; and S. Fowler (1818).

30. Anon. (1913). Rev. T. Gallaudet (1857).

31. Draper (1877); Barclay (1870), p. 26, also lists members of the Gallaudet family.

32. Stokes (1914); Dexter (1911), v. 5, pp. 749–757.

33. Dutton (1852).

34. Rae (1851); Barnard (1852), p. 95.

35. Chamberlain (1869a). Bell (1883b), ch. 4, traces deafness in this family in detail.

36. Quoted in Braddock (1975), p. 6. Also see Chamberlain (1886).

37. Braddock (1975), p. 59; Groce (1980, 1981); Huntington (1981); Poole (1983). On other island deaf communities, see Washabaugh (1979, 1981).

38. Rae (1851); Turner (1870); Syle (1887), p. 28.

39. Convention of Deaf-Mutes (1853).

40. Anon. (1895) says Chamberlain (1832–1895) was deafened at age eight.

41. New England Gallaudet Association (1854).

42. Chamberlain (1857a,b, 1858).

43. Flournoy et al. (1856). For a note on the Flournoy family, see Association Review, 1900, 2, p. 499, fn. 1.

44. Itard (1821d), p. 331 of the 1842 ed.

45. Richardin (1834).

46. Rae et al. (1854); Pyatt (1868), p. 84.

47. E.M. Gallaudet (1907a).

48. H.P. Peet (1852a, 1851a); Carlin (1853); Draper (1900); Columbian Institution (1864).

49. Boatner (1959b); Columbian Institution (1870).

50. E.M. Gallaudet (1912a).

51. E.M. Gallaudet (1907a), p. 35.

52. Draper (1872). The graduates in the first class became a principal of the Western Pennsylvania School for the Deaf, the principal examiner of the U.S. Patent Office, and a professor at the National Deaf-Mute College. The name was changed to Gallaudet College in 1894 in honor of Thomas Hopkins Gallaudet. See Atwood (1964), Gallaudet College Alumni Association (1964). On the first graduation, see Chamberlain (1869c) and Clymer (1869).

53. E.M. Gallaudet (1912a).

54. E. Booth (1881); Draper (1877); Boatner (1959a).

55. F.J. Clerc (1885).

56. Turner (1870).

57. Lewis Weld (1796–1853). Turner (1854); Barclay (1870), p. 34; Pyatt (1868), pp. 27–31.

58. Williams (1887); J.W. Jones (1922).

59. Clerc Papers no. 30; Porter (1858). Clerc retired in May 1858 (Clerc Papers no. 67). Clerc (1858b) gives the exact date: April 28, 1858.

60. Chamberlain (1869b).

CHAPTER 10 / A DANGEROUS INCURSION

1. Massieu (1815), p. 171. Likewise, Harvey Peet, his son Isaac, and Gilbert Gamage found, on a trip to France, that they could communicate with Vaïsse's pupils. At the end of the trip, Harvey Peet's son Isaac conveyed a detailed account of the tour to the pupils at Saint-Jacques, as verified by the essays they wrote out afterward. Perhaps this is not surprising considering that French Sign Language is the parent of American; Peet indeed confirms that they had the most success in manual communication in France, somewhat more difficulty in Italy and Switzerland (H.P. Peet, 1852b, p. 143; Braddock, 1975, pp. 17–19; Barclay, 1870, p. 13). Similarly, Reverend Stansbury recounted to his colleagues in New York that when he visited St. Petersburg, he told a short story in sign and the pupils wrote it correctly on their slates. The founders of that school, you may recall, spoke French Sign Language. A Chinese young man passing through Hartford who knew no English was brought to Clerc one day though he knew no Chinese. Clerc learned many interesting facts about his origins, his parents, his former pursuits, his residence in the U.S. and his ideas concerning God and a future state. After a while, his informant caught on and

started using a lot of pantomime himself (Reported in T.H. Gallaudet, 1819a, p. 648; Humphrey, 1857, p. 147). Lewis Weld had a similar experience with another Chinese man in Philadelphia (Barclay, 1870, p. 13).

2. Thomas Gallaudet took an interest in the problem of the slaves. Because of him, a Moorish prince sold into slavery in this country was manumitted and returned to Africa with his family (Stone, 1869, p. 107; Boatner, 1959a,b; Anon., 1891b; Rae, 1854; T.H. Gallaudet, 1828b).

3. ASL and Indian signs similar: Porter (1846), p. 505; T.H. Gallaudet (1820d); Akerly (1824); James (1823).

4. Huet secured the support of the emperor Dom Pedro II in 1855; the emperor created a governing board for the school, which opened Jan. 1, 1856. I am indebted to the Instituto Nacional de Educação de Surdos for giving me access to their library. The *Grande Encyclopédie Delta Larousse*, published in Rio de Janeiro in 1978, states that E. Huet's brother, Adolphe Huet, founded the sister institution in Mexico City, but Mexican documents provide no evidence for this.

5. I am deeply indebted to Professor Maria de Jesus Silva and Professor Sabino Cruz of the Instituto National de las Communication Humana, Mexico DF, for the warm reception accorded me. Dr. Cruz provided much useful information on Edward Huet, who was apparently at the Paris Institution in the same era as Clerc. There is, however, no proof that they corresponded after Clerc went to America, Huet to Brazil, then Mexico.

6. Cited in Heath (1972), whose treatment of the language situation in Mexico has been very helpful to me.

7. Cited in Heath (1972), p. 83.

8. These issues are discussed in Grosjean (1982).

9. New York Institution, Twelfth Report, 1828, pp. 13–14.

10. American Asylum, Annual Report for 1836.

11. J.W. Howe (1876), p. 115.

12. Schwartz (1956), pp. 5, 156.

13. It moved to South Boston and changed its name to Perkins Institution and Massachusetts Asylum for the Blind in 1829 (Winsor, 1881, p. 273).

14. Winsor (1881); Sanborn (1891), p. 126; Schwartz (1956), p. 52; H. Barnard (1862); Noyes (1911). Also see: Haüy (1786). Haüy (1745–1822). I am full of admiration for Weiner's masterly detective work and skillful synthesis in describing the lives of Haüy and Sicard and their relations: (1974, 1977). H. Barnard (1862) reports Fisher's Parisian studies and goal of emulating Haüy.

15. Hall (1881), p. 243, states that Laura Bridgman was deafened at age twenty-six months.

16. Richards (1936); Sanborn (1891), p. 146; Schwartz (1956), p. 67; Laura Dewey Bridgman was born Dec. 21, 1829. Howe had visited Julia Brace in 1834. Laura's parents brought her to Howe's institution on October 4, 1837. For more on the deaf and blind, consult index under Brace, Bridgman, Keller, Mitchell; and: Bébian (1826), v. 1, pp. 55, 102, v. 2, pp. 1, 12; Berthier (1837b); Burnet (1835), pp. 120–143; Forestier (1838b); Fuller (1892); Howe (1873, 1875); I.L. Peet (1851); Porter (1848b); W.R. Scott (1844), p. 27; Stone (1867), p. 35; Wade (1900); Weiner (1974); Winsor (1881); Woodruff (1849).

17. Howe (1909), p. 54.

18. Richards (1936); Howe (1857).

19. Howe (1857), p. 376.

20. Howe (1875).

21. Quoted in Noyes (1911), p. 762.

22. Dickens (1898), pp. 33–52.

23. Hall (1881), pp. 237–276.

24. Howe (1873); Richards (1936), p. 90.

25. Stone (1867), p. 35.

26. Caswell, deafened at age three, was born in 1829 and went to Perkins at age twelve. Lucy Reed, born 1827, deafened at age three, arrived at age fourteen. Caswell learned some hundred nouns and a few adjectives. Reed learned less, became a seamstress.

27. Howe's report, written in 1842, reprinted in Howe (1873), p. 4.

28. Howe (1909), p. 55.

29. Richards (1936), p. 4.

30. Cited in Schwartz (1956), p. 73.

31. Fenner and Fishburn (1968), p. 54. On Mann, see Downs (1974) and Tharp (1953).

32. Quoted in Schwartz (1956), p. 98.

33. Massachusetts House of Representatives (1843); Schwartz (1956), p. 276ff. The two children were Frank and Susan Worcester. "Neither of them ever spoke a word nor, to my knowledge, ever attempted to speak." See Rogers et al. (1912), p. 421; Schwartz (1956), p. 276ff. Several authors say Howe taught deaf pupils but this is an error. See Rogers et al. (1912).

34. Tharp (1953), p. 196; Massachusetts Senate Joint Special Committee (1867), p. 321.

35. Messerli (1972), p. 393.

36. Downs (1974), p. 96.

37. Mann (1844a), pp. 75, 79, 81.

38. Webster (1789), p. 171.

39. Kilian (1885), p. 13. Hodgson (1953) states (p. 138) that on Heinicke's death his widow and son-in-law, Reich, "carried on at Weissenfels." Later he refers to the "institution at Weissenfels which had been created by Samuel Heinicke" (p. 215). Likewise, Bender (1970), possibly on Hodgson's authority, refers to Hill's entering, in 1830,

"the old Heinicke institute at Weissenfels" (p. 132). However, all other sources, including several German ones (see Hoffman, 1901; Rae, 1848c; Arnold, 1888; Kilian, 1885) and Bender herself (1970, p. 103), concur that Heinicke was called to Leipzig by Frederick Augustus, prince of Saxony, to found a school for the deaf, which began in 1778 with nine pupils. Heinicke's immediate successors at Leipzig were his widow and son-in-law, Eschke (d. 1811), according to Kilian (1885), who were succeeded in turn by Petschke (d. 1822) and Reich. There is no disagreement that Hill went to the school in Weissenfels in 1830. Day (1845) states that it was founded in 1829 (p. 191) and confirms that Reich was director at Leipzig (pp. 107, 123), not Weissenfels.

40. Jäger (1830).

41. Hill was trained by Eschke's successor and former collaborator, Ludwig Grasshoff, who became director with permission of Heinicke's family after Eschke's death.

42. Frederick Moritz Hill (1805–1874).

43. Johann Baptiste Graser (1766–1841).

44. Hill (1858), translated in Gordon (1885a), p. 126. Weld (1845), p. 85, and Day and H.P. Peet (1861), p. 99, also give negative reports.

45. Day (1845), p. 99.

46. Howe written 1842, reprinted in Howe (1873), p. 4. On the trip, also see Richards (1936), p. 135.

47. H.P. Peet (1867), p. 230.

48. Turner relates these events in the Conference of American Instructors of the Deaf (1850), pp. 141–143; as does Porter (1846), p. 505. The case came up during the hearings of the Massachusetts Senate Joint Special Committee (1867) and a letter from Whipple appears in the appendix to those hearings. Further details will be found in Clarke School (1893a), pp. 27 and 31–32.

49. T.H. Gallaudet (1844). Letter to Mann.

50. I regret that a quote from this unsigned article was mistakenly attributed to Woodbridge rather than Peet in Lane (1980a), p. 144. See H.P. Peet (1844a).

51. Mann (1844b).

52. Weld (1845); Day (1845); H.P. Peet (1852b); Day and Peet (1861).

53. Quoted in Massachusetts Senate Joint Special Committee (1867), p. 75.

54. Stone (1866), p. 21, reports that, in 1845, a professor Dahlerup, having visited several schools in Germany, urged the Copenhagen institution to adopt the German method, but the rest of the faculty refused and the school continued on the French system.

55. Haug quoted in Morel et al. (1849).

56. Weld (1845), p. 188.

57. Letter from Morel to Weld quoted p. 72 of Massachusetts Senate Joint Special Committee (1867).

58. See Kilian (1885), p. 23.

59. Morel, Haug, and Wagner (1849), p. 58. Negative reports on German oralism: Day (1845); E.M. Gallaudet (1867b); Morel, Haug, and Wagner (1849); Vaïsse (1848b); Weld (1845).

60. Quoted in Day (1845), p. 112.

61. Hill, cited in E.M. Gallaudet (1867b), p. 29. Day cited in Puybonnieux (1846), p. 193: "Speech is not a general means of instruction, even in Germany." O.F. Kruse affirms that most schools conducted on the German plan —those in Berlin, Dresden, Vienna, Prague, Augsburg, Munich, Bern, and Basel—use sign "constantly"; only Weissenfels, Leipzig, and Zurich are excepted (quoted in Académie Impériale de Médecine, 1853, p. 865). In England, articulation gradually sank in prestige after Braidwood's death at the turn of the century. By mid-century, only his original school, relocated in London, was teaching speech and lipreading and then only as a complement and by means of sign language. See the 1844 report of the London Asylum, cited in Porter (1848a), p. 42. Also see Farrar (1923), pp. 71, 74; Syle (1874), p. 736; Day (1845), p. 90. Likewise Swiss, Italian, and Belgian schools were conducting their instruction of the deaf in sign language: Swiss (Syle, 1874, p. 736), Italian (ibid,; Volquin, 1853a), Belgian (Blanchet, 1851, p. 14). In America, the signing society evolved rapidly up to Clerc's time: Syle (1874), gives forty institutions, averaging 115 pupils, five hearing teachers and three deaf.

62. Peet (1868a).

63. American Asylum 29th Report (1845) and 39th Report (1855).

64. American Asylum 43rd Report (1859).

65. Chamberlain (1888b).

66. Anon. (1868b).

67. New York Institution (1847), 28th Report, for the year 1846; Syle (1873), p. 151. For Mann's self-defense, see Mann (1865), p. 290.

68. Massachusetts Board of State Charities (1866), pp. lii–lviii.

69. DeLand (1912b), p. 518, implies that Howe was also behind a petition to the Senate in 1861 that led to a resolve to explore state education of the deaf; the initiative was killed in the House (Massachusetts Senate Committee on Education, 1861).

70. Massachusetts House of Representatives Joint Special Committee (1863a, b).

71. Sanborn (1891), p. 228; DeLand (1908), ch. 16; Yale (1931), p. 63.

72. DeLand (1908), ch. 14; Bruce (1973b), p. 83. Gardiner Greene Hubbard (1822–1897). Hubbard was the son of a Massachusetts Supreme Court justice with ancestry reaching back to the *Mayflower*. His paternal grandfather was a prosperous merchant, his maternal grandfather one of the wealthiest men in Boston. Hubbard went to Dartmouth, then to Harvard Law School; he married the daughter of a rich New York banker and settled in Cambridge. Hubbard was a resourceful man and a promoter. He wanted quicker transit between his home in Cambridge and his law office in Boston, considered others would, too, and organized the first street railway outside

of New York City. He also created the Cambridge Gas and Light Company. He was a patent lawyer much interested in the promise of telegraphy. The Hubbards lost their first child, a son, to illness, then came five daughters, the last dying in infancy.

73. DeLand (1908), p. 63; Yale (1923).

74. Bruce (1973b), p. 87.

75. Rogers et al. (1912).

76. Dudley: DeLand (1908), ch. 15.

77. Conference of Executives (1868), pp. 70, 72, 75.

78. Massachusetts Senate Committee on Public Charitable Institutions (1864). Initial report Apr. 12, 1864; final report May 11, Senate document 287.

79. Yale (1910).

80. DeLand (1908), ch. 14.

81. Bruce (1973b), p. 90. Henry Lippitt became governor of Rhode Island in 1875. DeLand (1912b).

82. Rogers et al. (1911); Lippitt (1947), pp. 35–40.

83. DeLand (1908), p. 126.

84. Henderson (1939); Bruce (1973b), p. 66; the three other participants at Mrs. Lamson's home, Nov. 7, 1865, were John D. Philbrick, Henry M. Dexter, and James C. Dunn.

85. To offset the high tuition, Hubbard raised a subscription of one thousand dollars: Henry Lippitt contributed, as did the Honorable Thomas Talbot, who was a member of the Massachusetts Governor's Council (1864–1869) and Harriet Rogers's brother-in-law. Talbot's fellow council member, the Honorable Francis Bird, considered the most powerful politician in the state then, also gave. Talbot was lieutenant governor, 1872; governor, 1872 and 1878–1880.

86. Porter (1871).

87. Stone (1866).

88. Howe (1866).

89. Massachusetts Board of State Charities (1866), p. lviii.

90. Howe (1875). Keep (1866, 1867).

91. DeLand (1908), ch. 11; Sanborn (1891), p. 306.

92. Schwartz (1956), p. 280.

93. Massachusetts Senate Joint Special Committee (1867), pp. 1–2.

94. Sanborn (1912), p. 583.

95. Sanborn (1867a,b). Sanborn pursued the campaign with an anonymous article published in the *North American Review* and in the *Nation*. In it he gives a highly selective history of the oral education of the deaf, culminating in support for the plan currently before the legislature. He repeats the arguments for oralism—dispersion and economy—and implies that Harriet Rogers's school would be the beneficiary of the state funds if the legislation were passed. Also see: Burnet (1867); Chamberlain (1867a,b); Carlin (1867).

96. Massachusetts Board of State Charities (1867), pp. liii–lxxiv.

97. Massachusetts Board of State Charities (1867), p. 173.

98. Rogers et al. (1912)

99. DeLand (1908), p. 63; Rogers et al. (1912); Sanborn (1912), p. 580. Josiah Quincy Jr. was mayor of Boston from 1846 to 1849. His father, Josiah Quincy, was called the "great mayor" (1823–1829). The son also served seven years in the state senate, where he was president in 1843 and 1844, while his father was president of Harvard College.

100. DeLand (1908), p. 60.

101. Hubbard (1898).

102. Massachusetts Senate Committee on Education (1861). DeLand (1912b), p. 518, implies that Howe was also behind this initiative. Smith and some other deaf persons from Boston submitted a petition six years earlier to the Senate Committee on Education with the same proposal Howe and Hubbard subsequently made to the legislature. His friendship with the two Boston potentates undoubtedly goes back some way.

103. Richards (1928), p. 128; Howe (1868); Elliott and Hall (1903), p. 24.

104. Massachusetts Senate Joint Special Committee (1867), pp. 197, 200.

105. Massachusetts Senate Joint Special Committee (1867), pp. 205, 206.

106. DeLand (1908), p. 69; Rogers et al. (1912); Leonard (1918).

107. Ch. 311, Act of 1867.

108. Schunhoff (1957), p. 16. The Clarke Institution opened Oct. 1, 1867. At his death, John Clarke's property was valued at $200,000. He had originally planned to bequeath his estate to the Clarke school but he was so dissatisfied with the arrangement under which the school rented property from Lewis Dudley that he later reduced the award to $120,000 and made it contingent on the school's never purchasing its facilities from Dudley. It appears that Dudley both championed the cause of the school before the legislature and received personal gain thereby (Chamberlain, 1869e).

109. DeLand (1908), p. 60.

110. Bruce (1973b), p. 80; Bell (1872a).

111. DeLand (1908), pp. 80–81.

112. Clarke School *Report* (1882).

113. This account of the trip is based on E.M. Gallaudet's diary (1867a) and published report (1867b).

114. On the failure of the Blanchet plan: E.M. Gallaudet (1867b), p. 44; Varjot (1980); and its German counterpart, the Graser plan: Weld (1845), p. 80ff; G.E. Day (1845), p. 99ff; Day and Peet (1861), pp. 99–100 of the abridged version; Day (1861); J.C. Gordon in National Education Association (1885).

115. Conference of Executives (1868), p. 77.

116. Massachusetts Board of State Charities (1868), p. lxxi.

117. E.M. Gallaudet (1868b), p. 47.

118. Alexander Graham Bell Association (1892c), p. 299.

119. Although Carlin ridiculed them in the silent press. See Carlin (1868a,b), Anon. (1868d).

120. Sanborn (1869); Lane (1980a), p. 148.

121. Clarke School (1893). The school was first gathered in 1864 under Bernard Engelsmann.

122. DeLand (1908), p. 160; Hubbard (1898); Rogers et al. (1912), p. 476.

123. The name was changed to the Horace Mann School in 1877. It opened with nine pupils, Nov. 10, 1869 (Greene, 1893).

124. Cited in Bruce (1973b), p. 58.

125. Root (1941), p. 68. A memorial plaque has also been placed in the town hall at La-Balme-Les-Grottes. Obituaries: Chamberlain (1869d), Bartlett (1869).

CHAPTER 11 / THE DENIAL

1. See Currier (1912); Mc Gregor (1896), pp. 44–45.

2. Fay (1913a).

3. Veditz (1907a), p. 16.

4. Addressing the Third Convention of Articulation Teachers, June 1884. Quoted in DeLand (1922a), v. 24, p. 418.

5. Quoted in Bruce (1973b), p. 154.

6. Quoted in Waite (1961), p. 141.

7. Bell (1884), p. 52.

8. Lane and Grosjean (1980); Klima and Bellugi (1979).

9. National Education Association (1885), p. 9.

10. According to his biographer: Bruce (1973b), p. 382; (1973a), p. 148. Bruce's scholarly and comprehensive biography of Bell, although somewhat partisan to its subject, is enormously valuable for the student of deaf history.

11. National Education Association (1885), p. 21.

12. Conference of Executives (1884), p. 178.

13. Bell (1894b), p. 21.

14. Bell (1884), p. 39. Also Bell (1872a), p. 166: "All intelligent deaf-mutes acquire the power of mechanical speech."

15. Quoted in Bruce (1973b), p. 369.

16. See Mackenzie (1928).

17. Osborne (1943), p. 17; Bruce (1973b), p. 61; Watson (1913), p. 9.

18. Quoted in Bruce (1973b), p. 161.

19. Anon. (1869a). See the retirement petition, Clerc Papers no. 30; Sept. 4, 1856.

20. Bruce (1974), p. 3. L. Grosvenor (1950), p. 44.

21. Quoted in Bruce (1973b), p. 379. Also see Fairchild (1923), p. 196.

22. Mackenzie (1928).

23. Quoted in Bruce (1973b), p. 309.

24. Quoted in Bruce (1973b), p. 308.

25. Quoted in Bruce (1973b), p. 323.

26. Ballin (1930), p. 66; Bruce (1973b), p. 321.

27. Quoted in Bruce (1973b), p. 380.

28. Bell (1906–08).

29. National Education Association (1885), p. 62.

30. Bell (1910b).

31. Mayne (1929); Bruce (1973b).

32. Bruce (1973b), p. 14.

33. Curry (1906). Alexander Melville Bell (1819–1905).

34. Hitz (1905), p. 423.

35. Other sources on Alexander Melville Bell: DeLand (1908), p. 189; Bruce (1973b), p. 19; Mackenzie (1928).

36. Quoted in Bruce (1973b), p. 33.

37. Deland (1908), p. 193.

38. Hull (1865); Deland (1915).

39. Henderson (1939).

40. Bruce (1974), p. 4.

41. Bruce (1973b), p. 80.

42. DeLand (1908), p. 200.

43. Bell (1894b); Winefield (1981), p. 55.

44. Bell (1872b).

45. Schunhoff (1957), p. 26.

46. Bell (1883a); Waite (1961).

47. DeLand (1922); Murphy (1954).

48. Waite (1961), p. 49.

49. Bruce (1973b), pp. 90, 100.

50. Nearly fifty years later, Mabel discovered in some family papers that she had suffered a hearing loss when she was five and had never lost her ability to speak. She had always believed she was deafened younger and had lost all speech. Had the truth been known before the fall when she first met Bell, he might have had less faith in the possibilities of teaching articulation and lipreading. As a model of deaf people Mabel misled him in other ways as well, since she was not only a native speaker of English but also bookish, rich, and averse to other deaf people. Winefield (1981), p. 169.

51. Bruce (1973b), p. 257.

52. M.H. Bell (1908).

53. Initially, there was a great demand for teachers trained in Visible Speech and Bell organized a convention, held in Worcester: Bruce (1973b), p. 100. First Convention of Articulation Teachers, Worcester, Jan. 1874. Concerning the failure of Visible Speech at Clarke: Yale (1927c); Yale (1931), pp. 56–58. Hubbard and Rogers were more optimistic at first, however: Fay (1874), pp. 176–177.

54. American Asylum Fifty-seventh Report; Fay (1874), p. 179.

55. Bender (1970), p. 158; Séguin (1880), p. 81; Bruce (1973), p. 77.

56. Congress on Deaf—International—Second (1880), p. 89. See the critique by Greenberger (1874).

57. Bell (1888); Jenkins (1890b).

58. Moores (1978), p. 267, 1982 edition.

59. Mitchell (1971b), p. 350; Moores (1978), p. 71, 1982 edition.

60. DeLand (1908), pp. 164, 201.

61. Yale (1931), p. 69ff.

62. Gordon (1892a), nos. 21,567 and 21,570; DeLand (1922a), ch. 25, p. 37.

63. Conference of Executives (1884), p. 158.

64. Quoted in Bruce (1973b), pp. 181, 183.

65. Bruce (1973b) discusses the exact wording.

66. E.M. Gallaudet (1907a), pp. 105–106. For a sketch of Draper's career, see Boatner (1959a), p. 77.

67. Bruce (1973b), p. 197. Also see Field (1878), Osborne (1943), DeLand (1908, 1922), Watson (1913, 1926).

68. Hofstadter (1944).

69. Bell (1914).

70. Bell (1891c).

71. See the helpful discussion in Bruce (1973b), ch. 31.

72. American Genetic Association (1906), p. 11; Jordan (1908), p. 201.

73. Bell (1923); Woods (1923).

74. Bell (1920), p. 341. On restriction of immigration by racially biased intelligence testing, see Chorover's brilliant book (1979) on social control; American Genetic Association (1912a), p. 1; Henderson (1909), p. 227; Goddard (1917), p. 271.

75. Bell (1906–8); Bruce (1973b), p. 413.

76. Bell (1910c).

77. Fay (1916b), p. 283.

78. A.G. Bell to David Fairchild, Nov. 23, 1908, Bell papers, Library of Congress. Quoted in Winefield (1981), p. 184.

79. Bell (1884), p. 66.

80. Bell (1883b). Read to the National Academy of Sciences, Nov. 13, 1883.

81. DeLand (1912a).

82. Quoted in DeLand (1922a), ch. 24, p. 415.

83. R.H. Johnson (1918), p. 6.

84. Ballin (1930), p. 74.

85. Olivier and George (1893).

86. Bell (1888), p. 184.

87. Quoted in Mitchell (1971b), p. 355. Also see Fay (1916b).

88. Veditz (1907a). National Association of the Deaf Proceedings (1907).

89. Bell et al. (1908b).

90. American Genetic Association (1912), p. 3.

91. Haller (1963), p. 133.

92. Chamberlain (1888a,b).

93. Olivier and George (1893).

94. Seliney (1888a,b). The vice-president of the National Deaf-Mute College, Edward Fay, undertook a more complete and detailed study of family deafness with financial support from Bell; it is considered the soundest study of heredity in the nineteenth century. Fay found that deaf people generally have hearing children: only 9.7 percent of deaf marriages did not, and only 8.6 percent of the children from deaf marriages were themselves deaf. There was no greater likelihood of a deaf child if both parents were deaf than if only one was. Fay also found that marriages among the deaf were happier than mixed marriages, less likely to end in divorce or separation. And banishing sign and residential schools apparently would not help avoid deaf intermarriage, because about three out of four deaf marriages involved two deaf partners, no matter whether the partners had gone to residential schools teaching in sign or residential schools exclusively oral or oral day schools. The shared friends, the shared struggle, and the shared language were no doubt responsible for these figures (Fay, 1898).

95. Bell (1906–8).

96. Fraser (1976); Brown et al. (1967).

97. Lloyd (1968).

98. Bell (1891c); also see Bell (1908a, 1916). See the exchange between Bell and Gillett: Gillett (1890a,b, 1891); Bell (1890b); E.M. Gallaudet (1890); Fay (1884, 1885).

99. Cited in Bruce (1973b), p. 399. Bell was abashed: Cited in Winefield (1981), p. 202.

100. Arrowsmith (1819). The translation appears to be the same one that was published in 1801 and reprinted in 1860 in the *American Annals of the Deaf*, where it is attributed to F. Green. Also see: Bartlett (1853).

101. Wisconsin Phonological Institute (1893). On Bell and day schools, also see: DeLand (1922a), p. 361; Bruce (1973b); Bell (1883c, 1885a,b,d, 1894a, 1897a,b); Watson (1949), p. 156. On day schools, see: Anon. (1826b), p. 750; Anon. (1896), pp. 49–50; Bartlett (1853); Bingham (1899); DeLand (1908), pp. 156–7, 174, 266–9; Gordon (1885a,b); Jack (1907); Jones (1918), p. 194; Moeller (1909), p. 319; Moores (1978); National Education Association (1885); Odegard (1939); Rae (1854), p. 37ff; Spencer (1893); Ward (1936); Wesselius (1901); Williams (1885); Wisconsin Phonological Institute (1894).

102. National Education Association (1885).

103. Way and Whipple (1891). This outcome also owed much to a deaf woman, Miss Daisy Way. Deafened at age five, she had studied in an oral school, received instruction from a private articulation teacher and her mother, entered the public schools in Iowa, graduated from high school there, and gone to business school in Milwaukee. The WPI arranged for her to meet many legislators, and to urge the day-school movement on them. Her fluent speech, intelligence, and grace captivated the legislators and paved the way for Bell's campaign—although the law in question would not give other deaf children Daisy Way's experience of coeducation with the hearing, which was agreed by all sides to be generally impossible.

104. Wisconsin Phonological Institute (1894).

105. Quoted in Bruce (1973b), p. 395.

106. Bruce (1973b), p. 394; DeLand (1908), p. 120.

107. Draper (1904).

108. Bruce (1973b), p. 395; Ballin (1930), p. 74.

109. Wesselius (1901).

110. Bingham (1899).

111. Fay (1913a).

112. Ballin (1930); also see Anon. (1826b, 1896); Fay (1886); Carlin in Rae (1854), p. 37.

113. Bell quoted in DeLand (1922a), ch. 25, p. 94.

114. Bell quoted in DeLand (1922a), ch. 25, p. 147.

115. Conference of Executives (1884), p. 178.

116. Boatner (1959), p. 106.

117. Ackers (1874).

118. Quoted in Fay (1889).

119. Elliott (1911).

120. E.M. Gallaudet Gallaudet (1895c,d). Edward Gallaudet favored a deaf person's taking a hearing spouse, on the model of his mother (Anon. 1890c).

121. Fay (1887); E.M. Gallaudet (1907a).

122. J.C. Gordon (1892a).

123. Royal Commission (1886), p. lxiii.

124. E.M. Gallaudet (1895c,d). Note that the plan recommended by the Conference of Principals starts the education of most deaf children with a failure, which hardly seems psychologically or pedagagically sound. The commission was not interested in ending the age-old British practice of refusing education to deaf children for lack of sufficient charitable contributions; while it was meeting, nearly half the applicants to the London school, for example, were refused admission. Instead of recommending public education of deaf children, which many schoolmasters feared would deprive them of their lucrative private pupils, the commission proposed an annual government grant of fifty dollars per pupil. Bray (1893).

125. A.G. Bell Association (1884a), p. 132.

126. DeLand (1919); McClure (1950).

127. G. McClure (1961), p. 105.

128. DeLand (1913), Bruce (1973b, 1974). The name of the association was changed in 1956 to the Alexander Graham Bell Association.

129. E.M. Gallaudet (1894a,b); Convention of American Instructors of the Deaf (1893).

130. E.M. Gallaudet (1895c).

131. Eyewitness description by McClure (1950).

132. E.B. Boatner (1946); Drake (1940), Gannon (1981), p. 19.

133. For biographies of deaf teachers see Gallaher (1898); of the 148 biographical sketches about a third appear under the professional rubric "teacher"; also see Braddock (1975), Panara and Panara (1984). More on teachers and teacher training prior to 1900: Bell (1884, 1885a, b, 1891a,b), Boatner (1946), E.P. Clarke (1900a,b), Conference of Executives (1884), Dobyns (1893), Drake (1940), Draper (1899), Ferreri (1908), E.M. Gallaudet (1891, a,b, 1892b, 1909), Gannon (1981), Gordon (1892a,b), P. Hall (1908), Harris (1933), Javal (1887), Jones (1918), Lane (1980b), Ligot (1893), Logan (1877), McGregor (1893), Moores (1982), Newman (1971), H.P. Peet (1853b), I.L. Peet (1893a), Talbot (1895), Thollon (1907), Tillinghast (1908, 1909, 1917a), Tyler (1856), Veditz (1893), Volquin (1856).

134. B. Talbot (1895).

135. McClure (1950); Boatner (1959), p. 131.

136. Quoted in Winefield (1981), p. 114.

137. Bell and E.M. Gallaudet (1891a), Committee on Appropriations, Jan. 27, 1891.

138. E.M. Gallaudet (1891d); address to the Minnesota School for the Deaf. Also see E.M. Gallaudet (1907a), p. 160.

139. E.M. Gallaudet (1891c); Gordon (1892d).

140. Quoted in Winefield (1981), p. 94.

141. A.G. Bell Association (1910); DeLand (1908), p. 94.

142. E.P. Clarke (1900b); E.M. Gallaudet (1891a); Fay (1899).

143. E.P. Clarke (1900a); Moores (1978), p. 22, 1982 edition.

144. E.M. Gallaudet and Hall (1909), pp. 46, 48.

145. Ballin (1930).

146. Grosjean (1982).

147. Newman (1971). The quoted remarks have been abridged.

148. Lane and Grosjean (1980); Bellugi and Studdert-Kennedy (1980).

149. Klima and Bellugi (1979).

150. Bellugi and Studdert-Kennedy (1980).

151. Bell (1884). Also M.H. Bell (1895), p. 167.

CHAPTER 12 / THE INCURABLE DEAFNESS

1. Jacob Rodrigues Pereire (sometimes spelled Pereira) (1715–1780) had two sons, Jacob-Emile (b. 1800) and Isaac (b. 1806); they became railroad barons and financiers. Their friend and relative Olinde Rodrigues converted them to the theory of social regeneration preached by Saint-Simon. Both were elected deputies to the National Assembly. Isaac's son Eugène (b. 1831), trained as an engineer, entered family banking concerns and was elected deputy to the National Assembly in 1863. Beau de Loménie (1963), pp. 166–168; Vapereau (1893), v. 2, p. 1232; Hoefer (1863), pp. 574–575.

2. The Pereire school opened Aug. 15, 1875, with nine pupils. Magnat (1882a, 1896); La Rochelle (1882), p. 557, (1886), p. 4; Hément (1885a); Hément and Magnat (1881); Royal Commission (1886), number 483.

3. Dubois's school opened 1837, joined the national institution 1856, separated 1868. Saint-Hippolyte-du-Fort founded 1856. Hugentobler was in charge of the Geneva school, founded by Renz in 1866, from 1869 to 1872.

4. I am indebted for this observation and many more, which I have signaled where they occur, to the brilliant doctoral dissertation of Christian Cuxac (1980).

5. Magnat (1882b).

6. Etcheverry (1876a).

7. Franck (1861a).

8. In 1872. Lane (1976); Séguin (1875), pp. 6162.

9. La Rochelle (1882), p. 553; Fay (1879a).

10. La Rochelle (1882), p. 561; Arnold (1888), p. 428; Druot (1911).

11. Congress on Deaf—International—First (1878). The resolutions concerning method are translated in Gordon (1900).

12. I am indebted to Cuxac (1980) for this observation. Congress on Deaf—National (1879).

13. Banchi (1891).

14. Arnold (1888).

15. E.M. Gallaudet (1867b), p. 36.

16. Farrar (1923).

17. Royal Commission (1886), numbers 455, 482. Anon. (1895) states that the Hirsch pamphlet also directly affected Tarra's practices and that the founder of his school, Count Taverna, wrote Hirsch in Aug. 1868.

18. Cesare Castiglione, the head of the administrative board at the Royal Institute of Milan, also went to Germany and Switzerland about this time and published his findings on return. On Dec. 28, 1869, the minister of public instruction, C. Correnti, ordered "pure oralism" at his school. However, the director was apparently opposed and simply extended articulation training.

19. With T. Denis. See Denis (1886).

20. Claveau (1880).

21. Forestier (1880).

22. Denis (1882); Magnat (1896), p. 80.

23. Denis (1887c), pp. 81, 104.

24. Limosin (1886a), p. 68.

25. Cited in Mindel and Vernon (1971), p. 102; also see Schein and Delk (1974).

26. Hull (1880).

27. Elliott (1911), p. 241. But see Marchio's (1881) and Hull's (1881) defense of the fairness of the meeting, and Gallaudet's rebuttal (1881e).

28. Magnat (1880), p. 84.

29. Marchio (1881).

30. Denison (1881), p. 45.

31. E.M. Gallaudet (1881f).

32. Elliott (1882, 1911)

33. E.M. Gallaudet (1881c).

34. Elliott (1882), p. 155. One writer claimed that Tarra rejected nineteen out of twenty applicants, but he vigorously denied the charge (Tarra, 1883b).

35. I.L. Peet in New York Institution (1881), p. 68.

36. Stoddard and Gallaudet (1881), p. 117.

37. Elliott (1882).

38. Denison (1881), p. 4.

39. Peet (1881); Elliott (1911).

40. Franck (1880), p. 29; Elliott (1911). Facchini and Rimondo (1981). Tarra (1878), p. 103.

41. Hodgson (1953), p. 232. Fay (1880b).

42. Fay (1881a,c).

43. E.M. Gallaudet (1881c).

44. E.M. Gallaudet (1881c), p. 8.

45. La Rochelle (1880), p. 16; Congress on Deaf—International—Second (1880a), p. 155; Fay (1881b).

46. Congress on Deaf—International—Second (1880a), p. 78.

47. Tarra translated in Vaïsse (1881b). Also see Dubranle (1889). Speaking of Tarra's school, a few doors down the same street, Ghislandi, head of the Royal School, said "the contest is warm between the purists and non-purists; I am of the latter who agree with the congress of Siena." Quoted in Séguin (1880), p. 77ff.

48. Houdin (1881a); I.L. Peet (1881).

49. Denison (1881).

50. E.M. Gallaudet (1881d), p. 57.

51. Arnold (1888), p. 428.

52. Veditz (1933).

53. Veditz (1933). The meeting was held in Cincinnati, August 25–27, 1880.

54. McGregor in Holycross (1913); Gannon (1981); Veditz (1933).

55. Buxton (1883), pp. 44–47.

56. Tarra (1883a).

57. Cited in Winefield (1981), p. 206.

58. Bell (1896a), p. 12.

59. Houdin (1881a); Fay (1881d).

60. Franck (1880), p. 30.

61. Congress on Deaf—International—Second (1880a), p. 200.

62. Franck (1861), p. 24.

63. Limosin (1886b).

64. Quoted in Cuxac (1980).

65. Dubranle (1889). Drouot (1911), p. 177; Vaïsse (1881a). Elliott (1911), p. 303. Currier (1894).

66. Javal (1887).

67. Mottez (1975).

68. Gentile (1973). Reported in Moores (1978), p. 297, 1982 edition; also see Mindel and Vernon (1971), pp. 87–105, for a discussion of earlier studies.

69. Cuxac (1980). Also see Moody (1983): "We must have the courage to recognize and affirm that the deaf today in France are massively and profoundly undereducated." The untiring labors of a few Americans in Paris to engender

a renaissance of French Sign Language—notably the interpreter-dramatist William Moody and his collaborators, and the sociolinguist Harry Markowicz, go some way in repaying to France the vast debt of signing Americans.

70. Quoted in Cuxac (1980), pp. 263–265. The cost per pupil was estimated at 15,000 francs.

71. Binet and Simon (1910), pp. 24, 30.

72. Deltour (1892).

73. Ladreit de Lacharrière (1894).

74. Cited in Cuxac (1980), pp. 259–260.

75. Cited in Cuxac (1980), pp. 255–256.

76. Tarra (1878), p. 104ff. Also see Tarra in Congress on Deaf—International—Second (1880a), p. 100.

77. Vaïsse (1883). I want particularly to thank Brian Lancaster for his skillful search for the original French article at the Bibliothèque Nationale with only scanty information as a guide.

78. Congress on Deaf—National—French (1881).

79. Congress on Deaf—National—French (1884).

80. This meeting also considered itself the Third National Conference but was, in fact, the fourth. Held 1885.

81. Congress on Deaf—National—French (1885), p. 89.

82. La Rochelle (1886).

83. Congress on Deaf—International—Third (1883ab); Hodgson (1953), p. 245. Elliott (1911), p. 417; La Rochelle (1884).

84. Limosin (1886a), p. 32.

85. Limosin (1886d, 1885a).

86. Limosin (1885b).

87. Chambellan (1884), p. 18.

88. Congress of Deaf—International—First (1889).

89. Congress of Deaf—International—Second (1893a,b).

90. Congress of Deaf—International—Third (1896).

91. Bell (1900c).

92. Ladreit de Lacharrière in Goguillot (1889), pp. 19–21. Also see E.M. Gallaudet (1907a), p. 171.

93. E.M. Gallaudet (1907a), p. 171; Congress on Deaf—International—Fourth (1900a), p. 222.

94. Congress on Deaf—International—Fourth (1900b), p. xiv. Deaf section. For an exchange with a deaf leader, see Ladreit de Lacharrière (1899a,b); Camplo (1899).

95. Congress on Deaf—International—Fourth (1900a).

96. Quoted in Cuxac (1980), p. 7bis; p. 13, 1983 edition.

97. Congress on Deaf—International—Fourth (1900a), p. 6; Ladreit de Lacharrière (1900c).

98. E.M. Gallaudet (1900d).

99. Congress on Deaf—International—Fourth (1900a), p. 114.

100. E.M. Gallaudet (1900d), p. 420.

101. McGregor quoted in Holycross (1913).

102. Congress on Deaf—International—Fourth (1901b,d).

103. Congress on Deaf—International—Fourth (1900b), pp. 332–336.

104. F.W. Booth (1900a).

BIBLIOGRAPHY

With a Guide for the Student of Deaf History

Excellent library collections on American and French deaf history prior to 1900 are found in the Edward Miner Gallaudet Library and the Volta Bureau (both in Washington, D.C.) and the library of the French national school for the deaf (Institut National de Jeunes Sourds de Paris). The Boston Public Library, the Library of Congress, and the French national library (Bibliothèque Nationale) contain many works concerning the deaf not in the specialized collections. The comprehensive National Union Catalogue (pre-1956 imprints) can be found in most university libraries, which can arrange to borrow the works listed there. Books published before the turn of the century in the collection of the Bibliothèque Nationale are listed in its author catalogue, and these works may be ordered in microform from Clearwater Publishing Co. (1995 Broadway, New York, N.Y. 10023). Works by anonymous French authors can sometimes be found in the catalogue with the aid of a guide by Barbier (1822), which unmasks them. French documents published between September 22, 1792, and December 31, 1805, are often dated according to the republican calendar, and a table of equivalences to the Roman calendar is a valuable tool.

An indispensable bibliography on European deaf history was published by Guyot (1842) and updated in part by Alings (1883), based on the collection at the Groningen school for the deaf. Bibliographies of the collection at the Paris school will be found in Peyron (1883), Bélanger (1889), and Bernard (1940). Gallaudet College has published a dictionary catalogue to its collection (1970). Other specialized bibliographies, brief but helpful, are: Cary (1846), Porter (1848), Fay (1879b), Fay (1897b), Victoria University (1932), Austin (1975), and Fleischer (1978).

Two early textbooks on the education of the deaf provide extensive bibliographies, although their sources are generally restricted to works by and about hearing people: Arnold (1888) and De Gérando (1827). Texts by Best (1943), Hodgson (1953), and Bender (1970) come later but treat historical matters more briefly, In this category I favor the more recent and balanced treatment in Moores (1982) and Moody (1983).

Reference works on deaf history that I often consulted were Braddock's superb collection of biographical sketches, *Notable Deaf Persons* (1975), Fay's compendious *Histories of American Schools for the Deaf* (1893), and Gannon's recent survey of the American deaf heritage (1981), the only such work that extends up to the present. Berthier's classic biographies of Epée (1852) and Sicard (1873) and their pupils serve as reference works for the French history. His essay on deaf history is among the valuable French documents translated by Philip (1984).

Periodicals are the most important source of information on deaf history and foremost among these are the *American Annals of the Deaf.* This periodical began publication at the American Asylum in 1847, edited by L. Rae, who was succeeded in 1854 by S. Porter. The Convention of American Instructors of the Deaf published the *Annals* beginning in 1850. Publication was suspended in 1861 and resumed in 1868 under L. Pratt, who was succeeded by E. A. Fay (1870–1920). The nineteenth-century *Annals* are a treasure trove of informed and articulate reflections on issues of concern to the deaf—historical, philosophical, psychological, and educational. Alas, the *Annals* did not retain this character in the present century, but ready access to a bound collection complete from 1847 to 1900 is invaluable. The *Annals* published subject and author indices for volumes 1–30 (1885), 31–50 (1905), and 1–100 (1955). Fellendorf (1977) gives a selective bibliography for the *Annals*, 1847–1946, and the *Volta Review*, 1899–1976 (see below). The Convention of American Instructors of the Deaf publishes annual *Proceedings* (1850–), whose early numbers contain many articles of historical merit, often reprinted in the *Annals*, and a valuable record of debates. Much the same may be said of the Conference of Executives of American Schools for the Deaf. (Fauth and Fauth [1950] have prepared a bibliography and guide to the meetings of the convention.)

The *Proceedings* of the Alexander Graham Bell Association (1891–) and its periodical, the *Volta Review* (1899–), chronicle, especially, efforts to teach speech and speechreading to the deaf. The *Proceedings* of the triennial meetings of the National Association of the Deaf (1880–) are an essential source of information on the American deaf community in the last century. Most of these periodicals are available from University Microfilms (Ann Arbor, Michigan). The Readex Microprint series, in most library collections, includes many early American newspapers (1704–1820), imprints (1639–1800, 1801–1819), and an index to early American periodicals (1730–1860), which the student can supplement with Poole's Index (1802–1906). However, the Readex microform is illegible and it is impossible to make a readable photocopy. The early annual *Reports* from the first two schools for the deaf in the United States, the American School (formerly Connecticut Asylum, then American Asylum, 1817–) and the New York School (formerly New York Institution for the Instruction of the Deaf and Dumb, 1819–), provide much valuable original material. The contemporary periodical *Sign Language Studies* contains articles of historical interest as well as studies of the structure and communication of modern deaf communities in the United States and abroad.

On the French scene, the counterpart to the *American Annals* is the *Revue générale de l'enseignement des sourds-muets* (1899–), published by the Paris school. There were a score of other periodicals concerning the deaf in the last century, many short-lived; most appear in the bibliography to the present work. Major French periodicals concerning the deaf, published during the first half of the nineteenth century were: Bébian's *Journal de l'instruction des sourds-muets et des aveugles* (1826–1827); the four *Circulaires* published by the Institution Royale des Sourds-Muets in 1827, 1829, 1832, and 1836; Piroux's *L'Ami des sourds-muets* (1838–1843); Morel's *Annales de l'éducation des sourds-muets et des aveugles* (1844–1850); Abbé Daras's *Bienfaiteur des sourds-muets et des aveugles;* and *L'Impartial,* edited by Puybonnieux and Volquin (1856–1859). The Paris school and the French national library have reasonably good collections. The proceedings of the national congresses on the education of the deaf (in 1879, 1881, 1884, and 1885) are an important source of information on developments in France.

Of particular value for documenting events in deaf history occurring late in the nineteenth century are the proceedings of the several international congresses held by the deaf and by hearing educators. Here is a summary list by title: (1) Congrès international des sourds-muets—Paris, 1889; Chicago, 1893; Geneva, 1896; Paris, 1912. (2) International Conference on the Education of the Deaf—Edinburgh, 1907. (3) International Congress of the Deaf—St. Louis, 1904. (4) International Congress on the Education of the Deaf—Paris, 1878; Milan, 1880; Paris, 1883; Paris, 1900; Liège, 1905; London, 1925; West Trenton, 1933. (5) World's Congress of the Deaf—Chicago, 1893; Colorado Springs, 1910; Paris, 1912. Thus there were international congresses of the deaf in 1889, 1893, 1896, 1900 (deaf section, hearing congress), 1904, 1910, and 1912; and on the deaf in 1878, 1880, 1883, 1900, 1905, 1907, 1925, and 1933.

The nineteenth-century "silent press" (newspapers and magazines addressed primarily to a deaf audience) presents many more problems for the researcher, and a microform collection of publications in widely scattered libraries is sorely needed. Syle (1873b), Cloud (1925), Best (1943), and Gannon (1981) provide partial lists and some can be located with the aid of Gregory (1937).

Mentioned earlier in the present work were Backus's *Radii* (1837–1846) and Chamberlain's *Gallaudet Guide and Deaf-Mute Companion* (1860–1865). The *Silent Worker*, which began in 1888 (volume 1 was called the *Deaf-Mute Times*) and ceased in 1929 (revived 1948; renamed *Deaf American*, 1964), is available from University Microfilms. Another major publication is the *Deaf-Mute's Journal*, founded 1872; the name was changed to *New York Journal of the Deaf* and it ceased publication in 1951. There were several other short-lived publications and many of the residential schools published their own newspapers in the last century (see Gannon, 1981); the collections are widely scattered.

The same lamentable state of affairs exists in France. (For a partial list of the French silent press, see Remy, 1893.) A contemporary French periodical containing articles by and about the renascent deaf community in France is *Coup d'Oeil;* its pages are inspiring and informative. (It is published by the Maison des Sciences de L'Homme, 64 Boulevard Raspail, Paris 75006.) Fiction and poetry by deaf authors are often valuable to the historian as well, since they occasionally provide facts and they always reveal attitudes and values. I particularly recommend Ballin (1930), Kitto (1848), and the selections in Gallaudet (1884), and Batson and Bergman (1976).

I have referred extensively to three sets of personal papers: the Clerc and Cogswell papers at Yale University and the Gallaudet papers at the Library of Congress. All are available on microfilm, which can be purchased from the source collection, and the last may also be consulted at the E. M. Gallaudet Library, which has prepared a useful inventory. The personal papers of Bell and Howe have been so thoroughly perused by Bruce (1973b) and Schwartz (1956) respectively that I found it unnecessary for the present purpose to consult the originals in all but a few instances. Only a few personal papers of Epée, Sicard, and Haüy have been preserved and these are in the French national archives; Wiener's articles provide an excellent starting point (1970, 1974, 1977, 1982). Pertinent official French documents are catalogued (and indexed) in Bloch and Tuetey (1911).

◆

Anonymous. William Holder's "Elements of Speech." *Philosophical Transactions*, 1669, *(47)*, 958–959.

Anonymous. Review of Amman's "Traité de la parole." In: *Mémoires pour l'histoire des sciences commencées à Trévoux.* Paris: 1748. P. 154, art. 8. Reprinted: Coste d'Arnobat (1803), pp. 52–56.

Anonymous. [On Braidwood.] *Scots Magazine*, 1769, *31*, 342–343.

Anonymous. To the publisher of the Pennsylvania Magazine. *Pennsylvania Magazine*, 1776, *2*, 73–76.

Anonymous. [Discussion of] "Observations d'un sourd et muet" [by P. Desloges]. *Journal Encylopédique*, 1780, *1*, 446–465.

Anonymous. *Arrêt du conseil d'état du roi qui ordonne que l'établissement formé pour l'instruction des sourds et muets par le sieur abbé de l'Epée sera incessamment et irrévocablement placé et fondé dans la partie des bâtiments des Célestins de Paris . . . 25 mars 1785.* Paris: Imprimerie Royale, 1785.

Anonymous. *Adresse des représentants de la commune de Paris à l'Assemblée Nationale sur la formation d'un établissement national en faveur des sourds et muets.* Paris: Lottin, 1790.

Anonymous. American Asylum for the Deaf and Dumb. [Essay on the proposed establishment of the asylum.] *Literary and Philosophical Repertory*, 1815, *2*, 291–293. (a)

Anonymous. The deaf and dumb and blind [at the Royal Institute of Paris]. *Literary and Philosophical Repertory*, 1815, *2*, 152–153. (b)

Anonymous. [Clerc presented to the Connecticut Legislature.] *Connecticut Courant*, 1816, *52 (2700)*, 22 Oct.

Anonymous. Dalgarno. *Encyclopaedia Britannica.* Supplement to the 4th, 5th, and 6th editions. Edinburgh: Archibald, Constable, 1817. Vol. 3, p. 466. (a)

Anonymous. [Opening of Connecticut Asylum.] *Connecticut Courant*, 1817, *53 (2730)*, 20 May. (b).

Anonymous. London. In: Brewster, D. (ed.). *The American Edition of the Edinburgh Encyclopedia.* Philadelphia: Parker, 1818. Pp. 208–231. (a)

Anonymous. [Reply to "Expediency of Teaching the Deaf and Dumb to Speak."] *Christian Observer*, 1818, *17*, 787–791. Reprinted: *Volta Review*, 1903, *5*, 374–378. (b)

Anonymous. Jean Massieu. *Biographie des hommes vivants.* Paris: Michaud, 1818. (c)

Anonymous. Connecticut Asylum for the Deaf and Dumb. *Christian Observer*, 1819, *18*, 64–65. (a)

Anonymous. Review of Gallaudet's sermons. *Christian Spectator*, 1819, *1*, 27–36. (b)

Anonymous. Notice sur M. l'Abbé Sicard. *L'Ami de la religion et du roi*, 1822, *32*, 17–23. (a)

Anonymous. Art. VI. [On] "The Art of Instructing the Infant Deaf and Dumb" by John Pauncefort Arrowsmith. *Quarterly Review (London)*, 1822, *26 (52)*, 391–405. Reprinted from: *Monthly Review*, 1821, *95*, 32–41. (b)

Anonymous. American Asylum for Deaf and Dumb. *Christian Observer*, 1824, *24*, 719.

Anonymous. American Asylum for the Deaf and Dumb. *American Journal of Education*, 1826, *1*, 631–632. (a)

Anonymous. On the instruction of deaf mutes. *Christian Observer*, 1826, *26*, 749–756. (b)

Anonymous. Massieu. *Galerie historique des contemporains.* Third edition. Le Mans: Le Roux, 1827. Pp. 16–17. (a)

Anonymous. Jean-Marc Itard, ses fonctions, ses écrits. *Mercure de France au XIXème siècle*, 1827, *19*, 15 Dec., 497–499. (b)

Anonymous. Les sourds-muets. *Nouveau tableau de Paris.* Paris: Pillet, 1828. Vol. 2, pp. 340–354.

Anonymous. Deaf and dumb institutions. *American Annals of Education*, series 3, 1830, *1 (part 1)*, 409–413.

Anonymous. New York deaf and dumb asylum. *Monthly Repository and Library of Entertaining Knowledge*, 1831, *1*, 231–232.

Anonymous. New York Asylum for the Deaf and Dumb. *American Annals of Education*, series 3, 1832, *2*, 396–397. (a)

Anonymous. Article 4. Instruction of the deaf and dumb. *American Annals of Education*, series 3, 1832, *2*, 25–35. (b)

Anonymous. Instruction of the deaf and dumb. *Knight's Penny Magazine*, 1832, 24 Apr., 27. (c)

Anonymous. Article 9. Educating the deaf and dumb . . . *Monthly Review*, 1834, *134*, 378–383. (a)

Anonymous. Education of the deaf and dumb. *American Annals of Education*, series 3, 1834, *4*, 53–58. (b)

Anonymous. The American Asylum for the Deaf and Dumb at Hartford, Connecticut. *American Magazine*, 1835, 145–147. (a)

Anonymous. The works of George Dalgarno of Aberdeen. *Edinburgh Review*, 1835, *61 (124)*, 407–417. (b)

Anonymous. An account of the institution in Paris for the education of deaf and dumb. In: Mann (1836), pp. 232–241.

Anonymous. The abbé de l'Epée and the deaf and dumb. *Knight's Penny Magazine*, 1837, 29 July, 286–288. (a)

Anonymous. Bulletin bibliographique. Journaux, revues et écrits périodiques publiés dans le département du Nord. *Revue du Nord*, 1837, *2*. (b)

Anonymous. Cour d'assises du Puy-de-Dôme (Riom). Audience du 22 novembre [1838]. Vols domestiques—sourd-muet accusé. *Gazette des tribunaux*, 1838, *4 (4130)*, 6 Dec., 127–128.

Anonymous. Cour d'assises des Deux-Sèvres (Niort). Audience du 31 janvier, 1839. Tentative d'assassinat par un sourd-muet sur sa tante et sur trois enfants. *Gazette des tribunaux*, 1839, *5*, 12 Feb. 372.

Anonymous. Tribune correctionnelle de la Seine. Audience du 9 avril [1840]. *Gazette des tribunaux*, 1840, *6*, 10 Apr., 560.

Anonymous. [On the] Seventh Annual Report of the Secretary of the Board of Education, Massachusetts. *New Jerusalem Magazine*, 1844, *17*, 287–296.

Anonymous. Education of the deaf and dumb. *American Whig Review*, 1846, *3*, 497–516.

Anonymous. Presentation of silver plate to Messrs. Gallaudet and Clerc. In: American School for the Deaf, Reports, (1851), 23–44. Reprinted: Rae (1851).

Anonymous. Education des sourds-muets en France. *Bienfaiteur des sourds-muets et des aveugles*, 1853, *1*, 103–115.

Anonymous. Revue des méthodes. Etudes sur la pantomime classique. *Bienfaiteur des sourds-muets et des aveugles*, 1854, *2*, 246–255, 273–279.

Anonymous. Land of silence. *Edinburgh Review*, 1855, *102*, 116–147.

Anonymous. Trial of an uneducated deaf-mute for murder in North Carolina. *American Annals of the Deaf*, 1861, *13*, 35–52.

Anonymous. Sign Language. *Chamber's Journal* (Edinburgh), 1863, *39*, 273–275. (a)

Anonymous. How the deaf-mutes were cared for by L'Epée and Sicard. *American Annals of the Deaf*, 1928, *73*, 366–377, 458–468. Reprinted from: Wesleyan Sunday School Magazine, 1863. (b)

Anonymous. Gesture language and word language. *Intellectual Observer*, 1865, *7*, 451–456.

Anonymous. Proceedings of the American Social Science Association (New York, N.Y., 19–21 November). *National Deaf-Mute Gazette*, 1868, *2 (13)*, 3–6. (a)

Anonymous. Correspondence. *National Deaf-Mute Gazette*, 1868, *2 (20)*, 11–12. (b)

Anonymous. John Smith on Laurent Clerc. *National Deaf-Mute Gazette*, 1868, *2 (17)*, 15. (c)

Anonymous. Reply to Mr. Carlin's letter. *National Deaf-Mute Gazette*, 1868, *2 (20)*, 13. (d)

Anonymous. A Golden Wedding. *Connecticut Courant*, 11 May, 1869. (a) Reprinted: Chamberlain (1869b).

Anonymous. A pantomimic wedding. *Deaf-Mute's Friend*, 1869, *1*, 333–334. (b)

Anonymous. Reminiscences of Laurent Clerc. *Silent World*, 1871, *1*, 5–6. (a)

Anonymous. The Clerc Memorial. *Silent World*, 1871, *1*, 9–11. (b)

Anonymous. The national deaf-mute college at Washington. *Old and New Magazine*, 1872, 492–497.

Anonymous. Making the dumb to speak. *Chamber's Journal* (Edinburgh), 1874, *51*, 595–597.

Anonymous. Education of the deaf. *Littell's Living Age*, 1879, *140*, 125–128. (a)

Anonymous. The young deaf and dumb at lessons. *All the Year*, 1879, *22*, 371–377. (b)

Anonymous. The Brussels convention. *American Annals of the Deaf*, 1883, *28*, 254–262. (a)

Anonymous. *Hartford Illustrated*. Gardner, Mass.: Lithotype Printing, 1883. (b)

Anonymous. [Eleventh anniversary of the founding of the Mission of Deaf-Mutes.] *New York Daily Tribune*, 3 Dec. 1883, 4. (c)

Anonymous. The silent schools of Kendall Green. *Harper's New Monthly Magazine*, 1884, *69*, 181–187.

Anonymous. [Debate on oralism.] *Courrier français des sourds-muets*, 1887, *3*, 51–53, 75–77, 123–125; 1888, *4*, 3–7, 35–37, 51–54, 67–69, 82–85. (a)

Anonymous. Aux détracteurs de la mimique. *Courrier français des sourds-muets*, 1887, *3*, 41–43, 64–66, 77–79. (b)

Anonymous. Art. 3. [On the] Report of the Royal Commission on the Blind, the Deaf and Dumb of the United Kingdom. *Quarterly Review* (London), 1890, *170*, 59–79. (a)

Anonymous. Le Dictionnaire Larousse et les sourds-muets. *Revue internationale de l'enseignement des sourds-muets*, 1890, *6*, 59–61. (b)

Anonymous. An able paper by Dr. E. M. Gallaudet on matrimony among the deaf. *Silent Worker*, 1890, *4 (27)*, 2. Dec. 25. (c)

Anonymous. Ephémérides de la surdi-mutité en France. *Revue française de l'éducation des sourds-muets*, 1890, *6*, 149–150; 1891, *7*, 53–55. (d)

Anonymous. Petition to the German emperor. *Blätter für Taubstummenbildung*, 1891. Translated in: *American Annals of the Deaf*, 1892, *37*, 173. (a)

Anonymous. Life and Light, unpublished manuscript, 1891, E. M. Gallaudet Papers, Library of Congress. (b)

Anonymous. Howard Glyndon. *Silent Worker*, 1894, *6*, 1.

Anonymous. La méthode orale en Italie. *Revue internationale de l'enseignement des sourds-muets*, 1895, *11*, 111–112. (a)

Anonymous. William Martin Chamberlain. *Silent Worker*, 1895, *7 (7)*, 1. (b)

Anonymous. American Annals of the Deaf. *Silent Worker*, 1895, *8 (2)*, 2. (c)

Anonymous. Some notable benefactors of the deaf in America. In: Alexander Graham Bell Association, Proceedings, (1896), 28–59.

Anonymous. Les contemporains sourds-muets: Eugène Née. *Le sourd-muet illustré*, 1899, *3 (30)*, 1. (a)

Anonymous. Amos G. Draper. *Silent Worker*, 1899, *12 (2)*, 2. (b)

Anonymous. John Burton Hotchkiss. *Silent Worker*, 1900, *12 (6)*, 2.

Anonymous. *A Memorial Tribute to the Rev. Thomas Gallaudet*. New York: Fanwood Press, 1902.

Anonymous. The institution press: the sign language under discussion again. *Association Review*, 1905, *7*, 449–452.

Anonymous. *Catalogue général des manuscrits des bibliothèques publiques de France*. Paris: Plon, 1909. (a)

Anonymous. Méthode des signes ou méthode orale? MM. Binet et Simon défendent la première mais l'Ecole Nationale des Sourds-Muets est partisan de la seconde. M. Druot en donne les raisons. *L'Eclair*, 1909, Dec. (b)

Anonymous. The institution press: how can we reduce signs to a minimum? A sign language exhibit. *Association Review*, 1909, *11*, 198–204. (c)

Anonymous. *Some Candid Opinions of the Sign Language by Orally Educated Deaf Persons, Educators and School Superintendents*. Boston: Schulz, 1910.

Anonymous. To honor the memory of Mrs. Thomas H. Gallaudet. *Hartford Courant*, 1913, Apr. 1.

Anonymous. The census of the deaf and dumb: 1910. *Volta Review*, 1915, *17*, 371–378.

Anonymous. Notes and letters [anti-sign]. *Volta Review*, 1921, *23*, 45,47.

Anonymous. Fowler homestead. [1936?] Gallaudet Papers, Library of Congress.

"A." Cause célèbre. Affaire du petit sourd et muet de l'Abbé de l'Epée. *Décade Philosophique*, 1800, *(23)*, 284–294.

"A." L'Abbé de l'Epée et le pseudo-Comte de Solar. *Journal français d'otorinolaringologie*, 1964, *13*, 114–124.

Abernathy, E. An historical sketch of the manual alphabets. *American Annals of the Deaf*, 1959, *104*, 232–240.

Abrantes, L. *Histoire des salons de Paris*. Brussels: 1838. Vol. 3, pp. 339, 341.

Académie des Sciences Morales et Politiques de Paris. *Mémoires de l'Institut National des Sciences et Arts . . . Sciences Morales et Politiques*. Paris: Baudouin, 1796–1803.

Académie Impériale de Médecine. Rapport sur la surdi-mutité. *Bulletin de l'Académie de Médecine*, 1852–3, *18*, 656–1018.

Académie Royale de Sciences. Mémoire [sur un sourd-muet de Chartres]. *Histoire et mémoires de l'Académie Royale des Sciences*, 1703, *17*, 18–19. Reprinted: Coste d'Arnobat (1803), 56–58. English translation: Templeman, E. *Curious Remarks and Observations in Physics*. London: Davis, 1753. Pp. 24–25.

Ackerknecht, E. *Medicine at the Paris Hospital; 1794–1848*. Baltimore: Johns Hopkins, 1967.

Ackers, B. St. John. Letter on his visit to institutions for the deaf and dumb in America and Europe. In: Clarke Institution for Deaf-Mutes, Reports, (1874), 12–22.

———. The causes of deafness. *American Annals of the Deaf*, 1878, *23*, 10–17.

———. Historical notes on the education of the deaf. *Royal Historical Society London Transactions*, 1880, *8*, 163–171.

Ackers, Mrs. B. St. John. Notes on the International Congress for the Study of Questions on the Education and Assistance of Deaf-Mutes—Paris, 6–8 August 1900. Hearing section. *Association Review*, 1900, *2*, 438–445.

Adam de Boisgontier. L'Abbé de l'Epée. Etude biographique. *Musée des familles*, 1859, Feb., 137–140.

Adams, J. T. *The Founding of New England*. Boston: Little, Brown, 1949.

Adams, L. Condillac and the principle of identity. *New Englander*, 1876, *35*, 440–466.

Adams, M. E. Two schools across the water. *American Annals of the Deaf*, 1896, *41*, 380–390.

———. Miss Fuller's retirement. *Volta Review*, 1910, *12*, 361–362. (a)

———. Oralism in oral schools. *American Annals of the Deaf*, 1910, *55*, 379–385. (b)

———. A few memories of Alexander Graham Bell. *American Annals of the Deaf*, 1929, *74*, 467–479.

Adams, T. *Report* [on the] *New York Institution for the Instruction of the Deaf and Dumb*. New York: New York Institution for the Instruction of the Deaf and Dumb, 1913.

Addison, W.H. Report on a visit to some of the American schools for the deaf. *Association Review*, 1908, *10*, 64–80.

Adelon, N. P., et al. *Dictionnaire des sciences médicales*. Paris: Panckoucke, 1812–1822.

Adkins, N. F. *Index to Early American Periodicals, 1730–1860*. New York: Readex Microprint, 1976.

Agricola, R. *De inuentione dialectica libri tres*. Paris: Simonem Colinaeum, 1529.

Akerly, S. *Elementary Exercises for the Deaf and Dumb*. New York: E. Conrad, 1821. (a)

———. Letter to Mason Cogswell [28 Aug. 1821]. *Association Review*, 1902, *4*, 38–39. (b)

———. *Observations and Correspondence on the Nature and Cure of Deafness*. New York: Conrad, 1821. (c)

———. Observations on the language of signs. *American Journal of Science*, 1824, *8*, 348–358.

———. Deaf and dumb. *American Journal of Education*, 1826, *1*, 432. (a)

———. *Address delivered at Washington Hall on 30 May 1826, as introductory to the exercises of the pupils of the N.Y. Institution for the Instruction of the Deaf and Dumb*. New York: E. Conrad, 1826. (b)

Alcott, W. A. William Channing Woodbridge. *American Journal of Education*, 1858, *5*, 51–64. Reprinted: Barnard (1861), 268–280.

Aléa, J. M. *Eloge de l'Abbé de l'Epée ou essai des avantages du système des signes méthodiques appliqué à l'instruction générale élémentaire*. Translated from Spanish by M. P. Paris: Rosa, 1824.

Alexander I. *Scenes of Russian Court Life, Being the Correspondence of Alexander I with His Sister, Catherine*. Translated by H. Havelock. London: Jarrolds, 1915.

Alexander Graham Bell Association. Proceedings of the first convention of articulation teachers of the deaf and dumb. *American Annals of the Deaf*, 1874, *19*, 91–100. (a)

———. Proceedings of the second convention of articulation teachers of the deaf and dumb. *American Annals of the Deaf*, 1874, 217–219. (b)

———. Proceedings of the third convention of articulation teachers of the deaf and dumb. *The Voice* [*Werner's Magazine*], 1884, 129–134. (a)

———. The third convention of American articulation teachers. *American Annals of the Deaf*, 1884, *29*, 237–267. (b)

————. *Proceedings of the Summer Meeting.* First–Fifth. Rochester: Alexander Graham Bell Association, 1891–1896.

————. [First meeting of the board of directors of the] American Association to Promote the Teaching of Speech to the Deaf. *American Annals of the Deaf,* 1891, *36,* 222–224. (a)

————. First summer meeting of the American Association to Promote the Teaching of Speech to the Deaf. *American Annals of the Deaf,* 1891, *36,* 274–282. (b)

————. The second summer meeting of the American Association to Promote the Teaching of Speech to the Deaf. *American Annals of the Deaf,* 1892, *37,* 292–295. (a)

————. Business meeting. In: Alexander Graham Bell Association, Proceedings (1892), 149–155. (b)

————. [Methods of instructing the deaf.] In: Alexander Graham Bell Association, Proceedings (1892), 287–308. (c)

————. Reports from Abroad. In: Alexander Graham Bell Association, Proceedings (1894), 1–18, 25–31.

————. Reports on oral instruction in American schools. In: Alexander Graham Bell Association, Proceedings (1896), 238–257.

————. *Circulars of Information 3,4,5,6: International Reports of Schools for the Deaf.* Washington, D.C.: Gibson, 1896, 1897, 1898, 1902.

————. *Statistics of Speech Teaching in American Schools for the Deaf for the Year 1901.* Philadelphia: Institution for the Deaf and Dumb, 1901.

————. *Some Opinions of the Oral Method Expressed by Graduates of the Oral Method.* Washington, D.C.: Alexander Graham Bell Association, 1932.

————. *A Century of Oral Education in the United States, 1867–1967. Proceedings of the International Conference on Oral Education of the Deaf, Northampton and New York: 1967.* Washington, D.C.: Alexander Graham Bell Association, 1967.

Alhoy, L.F.J. Les sourds et muets de naissance sont admis à la barre. *Gazette nationale ou le moniteur universel,* 1795, *(108),* 7 Jan., 447–448.

————. *De L'Education des sourds et muets de naissance.* Paris: Imprimerie des Associés, 1800.

————. *Promenade poétique dans les hospices de Paris.* Paris: Trouvé, 1826.

Alings, A.W. *Catalogus bibliothecae guyotianae.* Groningen: Hoitsema, 1883.

Almedingen, M.E. *The Emperor Alexander I.* New York: Vanguard, 1964.

Amclot, [?]. *Arrêt du conseil d'état du roi, concernant l'éducation et l'enseignement des sourds et muets. 21 novembre 1778.* Paris: Imprimerie Royale, 1778.

American Association to Promote the Teaching of Speech to the Deaf. See: Alexander Graham Bell Association.

American Asylum. See: American School for the Deaf.

American Breeders' Association. See: American Genetic Association.

American Genetic Association. *Annual Report, American Breeders' Association.* Washington, D.C.: American Breeders' Association, 1905–1912.

American Genetic Association. A business salutation. *Proceedings of the American Breeders' Association,* 1905, *1,* 8–11.

American Genetic Association, Eugenics Section. Committee on Eugenics. *Proceedings of the American Breeders' Association,* 1906, *2,* 11.

American Genetic Association, Eugenics Section. . . . *American Sterilization Laws. Preliminary report of the committee of the eugenics section of the American Breeders' Association to study and to report on the best practical means for cutting off the defective germ plasm in the human population.* London: Eugenics Educational Society [1912]. (a)

American Genetic Association, Eugenics Section. General questionnaire . . . Committee to study and report on the best practical means of cutting off the defective germ plasm in the human population. . . . Unpublished manuscript, Department of Labor Library, Washington, D.C. [1912?]. (b)

American Instructors of the Deaf. See: Convention of American Instructors of the Deaf.

American Journal of Education. *Analytical Index to Barnard's American Journal of Education.* Washington, D.C.: Government Printing Office, 1892. Johnson reprint, 1970.

American School for the Deaf. *Reports.* Hartford: Hudson, 1817–1899.

————. List of subscribers to the fund to send Gallaudet to Europe [1815]. Unpublished manuscript, American School for the Deaf, Hartford. Reprinted: Fusfeld (1922).

————. Newspaper articles relating to the founding of the American School [1816]. *Association Review,* 1901, *3,* 341–343. (a)

————. Extracts from the early reports of the Hartford school showing the attitude of the school toward speech teaching [1816]. *Association Review,* 1902, *4,* 139–151. (b)

————. Gleanings from the Philadelphia newspapers of 1816. *Association Review,* 1902, *4,* 439–454. (c)

————. *A Brief History of the American Asylum at Hartford.* Hartford: Case, Lockwood and Brainard, 1893.

American Stockbreeders' Association. See: American Genetic Association.

Amman, J. C. *Surdus Loquens.* Amsterdam: Wetstenium, 1692. English translation: *The Talking Deaf Man.* London: Hawkins, 1694. Reprinted: Menston, Yorkshire: Scholar Press, 1972.

————. *Dissertatio de Loquela.* Amsterdam: J. Wolters, 1700. French translation: *Dissertation sur la parole.* In: Deschamps, C. F. *Cours élémentaire d'éducation des sourds et muets.* Paris: Debure, 1779. Pp. 207–362. English translation: *A Dissertation on Speech.* London: Sampson, 1873. Reprinted: Amsterdam: North Holland, 1965.

Anagnos, M. *Education of the Blind. Historical Sketch.* Boston: Rand, 1882.

André, Y. M. Discours ou divination sur la manière dont on peut apprendre à parler aux muets. [Address to the Caen Academy, 22 Nov. 1746.] In: *Oeuvres.* Paris: Ganeau, 1766.

Andres, J. P. Dell'origine et della vicende dell'arte d'insegnar a parlare ai sordi-muti. Vienna, 1793.

Anger, [?]. Critique de la théorie des signes par Sicard. *Journal général de France,* 1817, *17 (951).*

Antonio, N. *Bibliotheca Hispana Nova.* Madrid: Ibarra, 1788. Vol. 1, pp. 354, 754; vol. 2, p. 228.

Appleton's Cyclopedia of American Biography. See: Wilson, J. G., and Fiske, J.

Aristotle. *History of Animals.* [355 B.C.] Translated by R. Cresswell. London: Bell, 1891.

Arnaud, C. L'Abbé de l'Epée et son oeuvre. *Revue générale de l'enseignement des sourds-muets,* 1900, *2,* 33–40; *3,* 57–67. Reprinted: Paris: Imprimerie d'ouvriers, 1900.

Arneth, A. von. *Marie Antoinette. Correspondance secrète entre Marie-Thérèse et le comte de Mercy-d'Argenteau.* Paris: Firmin Didot, 1874.

Arnold, T. *Education of Deaf-Mutes, a Manual for Teachers.* London: Wertheimer and Lea, 1888. Revised: Farrar (1923).

———. *The Education of the Deaf and Dumb.* London: Stock, 1879. Revised edition: *Education of the Deaf: A Manual for Teachers.* London: National College of Teachers of the Deaf, 1923.

Arnoldi, J.L.F. *Praktische Unterweissung Taub-Stumme Personnen Reden und Schreiben zu Lehren.* Giessen: 1777.

Arnot, H. *History of Edinburgh.* Murray, 1779.

Arrowsmith, J. P. *The Art of Instructing the Infant Deaf and Dumb.* London: Taylor and Hessey, 1819.

———. On teaching the deaf and dumb to articulate. *Christian Observer,* 1824, *24,* 487–493.

Association of Masters of the Public Schools. *Remarks on the Seventh Annual Report of Horace Mann.* Boston: Little, Brown, 1844.

———. *Rejoinder to the "Reply" of Horace Mann.* Boston: Little, Brown, 1845.

Atwood, A.W. *Gallaudet College, Its First One Hundred Years.* Lancaster: Intelligencer, 1964.

Aubrey, J. *Aubrey's Brief Lives.* [Manuscript, 1696.] London: Secker and Warburg, 1949.

Augustinus, A. *Collected Works.* Edinburgh: Clark, 1871–76.

Austin, G. *Bibliography: Deafness.* Silver Spring: National Association of the Deaf, 1975.

Ausubel, H. *Historians and Their Craft.* New York: Columbia University Press, 1950.

Ayres, J. A. Lucius H. Woodruff. *American Annals of the Deaf,* 1853, *5,* 45–48.

"B" [Gallaudet, T.H.]. Expediency of teaching the deaf and dumb to articulate. *Christian Observer,* 1818, *17,* 514–517. Reprinted: *Association Review,* 1903, *5,* 369–374.

"B" [Gallaudet, T.H.]. On teaching the deaf and dumb to articulate. *Christian Observer,* 1819, *18,* 29–30.

Bachaumont, L. P. *Mémoires secrets.* Paris: Brissat, 1830.

Bacon, L. Old times in Connecticut. *New Englander,* 1882, *41,* 1–31.

Bairati, E. *La Belle Epoque: Fifteen Euphoric Years of European History.* New York: Morrow, 1978.

Baker, C. On the education of the deaf and dumb. *Penny Cyclopedia,* 1837, *507.* Reprinted: Baker, C. *Contributions to the Education of the Deaf and Dumb.* London: 1843. Pp. 101–170.

———. *Contributions to Publications of the Society for the Diffusion of Useful Knowledge and the Central Society of Education.* London: author, 1842.

Baker, C., and Battison, R. *Sign Language and the Deaf Community.* Silver Spring: National Association of the Deaf, 1980.

Baker, C., and Padden, C. *American Sign Language: A Look at Its History, Structure, and Community.* Silver Spring: T.J. Publishers, 1978.

Ballesteros, J. M. *Instrucción de Sordomudos.* Madrid: 1845.

Ballin, A. *A Deaf-Mute Howls.* Los Angeles: Grafton, 1930.

Bally, V. F. *"Mimographie" par Bébian.* Paris: Regnoux, 1826.

Banchi, V. *Tomaso Pendola e il suo istituto. Notizie Storiche.* Siena: Bernardino, 1891.

Banerji, J. N. *A Visit to the Institutions for the Deaf and Dumb (and the Blind) in England, Ireland and America.* Calcutta: Bose, 1897.

Barber, J. W. *Connecticut Historical Collections.* New Haven: Barber, 1836. Reprinted: Hartford: Hartford Architecture Conservancy, 1976.

Barbier, A. *Dictionnaire des ouvrages anonymes.* Paris: Barroes, 1822–1827.

Barclay, J. J. *An Address Commemorative of the Virtues and Services of Abraham B. Hutton.* Philadelphia: Pennsylvania Institution for the Deaf and Dumb, 1870.

Barnard, F. A. P. Education of the deaf and dumb. *North American Review,* 1834, *38,* 307–357.

———. Existing state of the art of instructing the deaf and dumb. *Literary and Theological Review,* 1835, *2,* 367–398.

———. Instruction for the deaf and dumb. *Quarterly Christian Spectator,* 1837, *9,* 521–553.

———. The difficulties of the deaf and dumb in the acquisition of language. *American Annals of the Deaf,* 1870, *15,* 161–165.

———. Autobiographical sketch. *Mississippi Historical Society Publications,* 1912, *12,* 107–121.

Barnard, H. *Tribute to Gallaudet. A Discourse in Commemoration of the Life, Character and Services of the Rev.*

T. H. Gallaudet, with an appendix. Hartford: Brockett and Hutchinson, 1852. Reprinted: *Common School Journal,* 1852, 6, 1–220; *American Annals of the Deaf,* 1852, 4, 81–136. Abridged: *American Journal of Education and College Review,* 1855, 1, 417–420; Barnard (1861), 96–118.

———. *Educational Biography.* New York: Brownell, 1861. (a)

———. Memoir of H. P. Peet. In: Barnard (1861), 231–248. Revised: Fay, E. A. (1873). (b)

———. Horace Mann. In: Barnard (1861), 365–404. (c)

———. Frederick A. P. Barnard. In: Barnard (1861), 496–524. (d)

———. Samuel Gridley Howe. *American Journal of Education,* 1862, 11, 389–399.

———. See: Commissioner of Education (1876).

———. Schools for the deaf and dumb. *American Journal of Education,* 1878, 29, cxlii–cxlvi, 115, 586–589.

———. Deaf and Dumb. *Johnson's New Universal Cyclopedia.* New York: Johnson, 1884. Pp. 1279–1281.

Barns, C. R. The aggressions of Alexander. In: National Association of the Deaf, Proceedings, (1916), 99–101.

Barrett, M. Ten days with the deaf and dumb. *New Monthly Magazine,* 1873, 47, 496–506.

Bartlett, D. Family education for young deaf-mute children. *American Annals of the Deaf,* 1853, 5, 32–35.

———. *Language Addressed to the Different Senses.* Hartford: Case, Lockwood, 1865.

———. A sermon on the death of Laurent Clerc. *Deaf-Mute's Journal,* 1869, 1, 238–239; 244.

Bartlett, E. S. Extracts from the diary of Dr. Mason Fitch Cogswell. *Connecticut Magazine,* 1899, 5, 532–537; 562–569; 606–614. Excerpted from: Bacon (1882).

Bass, R. A., and Healy, J. E. *History of the Education of the Deaf in Virginia.* Staunton: Virginia School for the Deaf and Blind, 1949.

Batson, T.W., and Bergman, E. *The Deaf Experience.* Second edition. South Waterford: Merriam-Eddy, 1976.

Bayle-Mouillard, J. B. *Eloge de Joseph-Marie Baron de Gérando.* Paris: Renouard, 1846.

Bazot, E. F. *Eloge historique de l'Abbé de l'Epée.* Paris: Barba, 1819. Second edition, also 1819, includes letter from Paulmier; third edition, corrected and enlarged (without Paulmier letter), 1821.

Beard, C.A. Written history as an act of faith. *American Historical Review,* 1934, 39, 219–231.

———. That noble dream. *American Historical Review,* 1936, 41, 74–87.

Beau de Loménie, E. *Les Responsabilités des dynasties bourgeoises en France.* Paris: Denoël, 1963.

Beauchamp, J.B. The Kentucky School, the first state-supported school. *Deaf American,* 1970, 15–18.

Bébian, R. A. *Essai sur les sourds-muets et sur le langage naturel, ou Introduction à une classification naturelle des idées avec leur signes propres.* Paris: Dentu, 1817. English translation: Philip (1984).

———. *Eloge de Charles-Michel de l'Epée.* Paris: Dentu, 1819. Reprinted: Sicard (1820). Excerpts translated in: Rae (1848a); Holycross (1913).

———. *Mimographie ou essai d'écriture mimique.* Paris: Colas, 1825.

———. *Journal de l'instruction des sourds-muets et des aveugles rédigé par M. Bébian.* Paris: Institution Spéciale des Sourds-Muets, 1826–1827. (a)

———. Suite de l'examen des diverses méthodes employées pour l'instruction des sourds-muets: école de l'Abbé Sicard. *Journal de l'instruction des sourds-muets et des aveugles,* 1826, 1, 320–335; 2, 22–53. (b)

———. Notice sur l'Institution Impériale des Sourds-Muets de Saint-Petersbourg. *Journal de l'instruction des sourds-muets et des aveugles,* 1826, 1, 91–95. (c)

———. Instruction des sourds-muets aux Etats-Unis. *Journal de l'instruction des sourds-muets et des aveugles,* 1826, 1, 356–364. (d)

———. Sourd-Muet accusé de rébellion et de violence contre les agents de l'autorité. *Journal de l'instruction des sourds-muets et des aveugles,* 1826, 1, 39–42. (e)

———. Cours d'assises de Paris, audience du 6 juillet 1826; vol commis par un sourd-muet. *Journal de l'instruction des sourds-muets et des aveugles,* 1826, 1, 42–46. (f)

———. *Manuel d'enseignement pratique des sourds-muets.* Paris: Méquignon, 1827. (a)

———. Affaire du sourd-muet Filleron. Cours d'Assises de la Seine, séance du août, 1827. *Journal de l'instruction des sourds-muets et des aveugles,* 1827, 2, 53–84. (b)

———. Affaire du sourd-muet Sauron. *Journal de l'instruction des sourds-muets et des aveugles,* 1827, 2, 85–95. (c)

———. De l'enseignement des sourds-muets. *Journal de l'instruction publique,* 1828, 70–79. (a)

———. Opérations intellectuelles du sourd-muet. *Journal de l'instruction publique,* 1828, 242–253. (b)

———. *Education des sourds muets, mise à la portée des instituteurs et de tous les parents; cours d'instruction élémentaire dans une suite d'exercices gradués, expliqués par des figures. Principes.* Paris: Béthune, 1831.

———. *Examen critique de la nouvelle organisation de l'enseignement dans l'Institution Royale des Sourds-Muets de Paris.* Paris: Treuttel et Wurtz, 1834.

Becker, C. L. *Detachment and the Writing of History.* Ithaca: Cornell University Press, 1958.

Beda Venerabilis. *Historia Ecclesiastica Gentis Anglorum.* [Manuscript, 733.] English translation: Stapleton, T. *The History of the Church of England.* Antwerp: Laet, 1565.

Beecher, C. E. Reminiscences. *Christian Keepsake,* 1848, 11, 262–282. Excerpted: *Common School Journal,* 1852, 6, 65–70.; Barnard, H. (1852).

———. Mrs. Lydia H. Sigourney. *Hours at Home,* 1865, 1, 559–561.

———. *Educational Reminiscences and Suggestions.* New York: Ford, 1874.

Beecher, L. *Autobiography.* New York: Harper, 1866.

Beers, H. A. *The Connecticut Wits and Other Essays.* New Haven: Yale University Press, 1843.

Bejarano, E. *L'Espagne et les sourds-muets.* Madrid: 1905.

Bélanger, A. *Historique des méthodes à l'Institution Nationale des Sourds-Muets de Paris.* Paris: Pelluard, 1883.

————. *Etude bibliographique et iconographique sur l'Abbé de l'Epée.* Paris: Ritti, 1886.

————. *Enseignement des sourds-muets. Bibliographie générale.* Paris: E. Bélanger, 1889.

————. De la nécessité d'un interprète. *Revue générale de l'enseignement des sourds-muets,* 1901, *3,* 54–58. (a)

————. Un sourd-muet devant la justice française. *Revue générale de l'enseignement des sourds-muets,* 1901, *3,* 35–39. (b)

————. Le sourd-muet devant la loi française: ses droits, ses devoirs. *Revue générale de l'enseignement des sourds-muets,* 1901, *3,* 100–108. (c)

————. Le language des sourds-muets. *Revue générale de l'enseignement des sourds-muets,* 1906, *8,* 93–99.

Bell, A. G. Articulation for Deaf Mutes. In: Conference of Executives of American Schools for the Deaf, Proceedings, (1872), 152–177. (a)

————. Visible speech as a means of communicating articulation to deaf-mutes. *American Annals of the Deaf,* 1872, *17,* 1–21. (b)

————. Upon a method of teaching language to a very young congenitally deaf child. *American Annals of the Deaf,* 1883, *28,* 124–139. (a)

————. *Memoir Upon the Formation of a Deaf Variety of the Human Race.* New Haven: National Academy of Sciences, 1883. (b)

————. Hearing without ears. Dr. Alexander Graham Bell's latest invention—his school for deaf mutes in Washington. *Washington Evening Star,* 31 Oct. 1883. (c)

————. The education of deaf-mutes. *New York Daily Tribune,* Dec. 23, 1883. (d)

————. Fallacies concerning the deaf. *American Annals of the Deaf,* 1884, *29,* 32–69. Reprinted: Washington, D.C.: Gibson, 1884.

————. The Wisconsin bill relating to the instruction of deaf mutes. *Science,* 1885, *5 (118),* 375. (a)

————. Deaf-Mute instruction in relation to the work of the public schools. National Education Association, Proceedings, (1885), 8–21. (b)

————. Is there a correlation between defects of the senses? *Science,* 1885, *5 (106),* 127–129. (c)

————. Teaching deaf children. Mr. Alexander Graham Bell explains his methods and his plans. *Washington Evening Star,* 8 Oct. 1885. (d)

————. Education of deaf children: evidence of E. M. Gallaudet and A. G. Bell . . . [1886] In: Gordon (1892a).

————. *Marriage of Deaf-Mutes.* Baddeck: Island Reporter, 1887. Reprinted from *National Deaf-Mute Gazette.*

————. *Facts and Opinions Relating to the Deaf, from America.* London: Spottiswoode, 1888.

————. Professor A. Graham Bell's studies of the deaf. *Science,* 1890, *16 (396),* 135–136. (a)

————. Deaf Mutes [reply]. *Science,* 1890, *16 (412),* 358–359. (b)

————. Teaching the deaf and dumb. Statement of Professor Alexander Graham Bell. Address to Conference Committee of Congress on Appropriations, 27 Jan. 1891. Washington, D.C.: Volta Bureau. (a)

————. Deaf mute instruction. *Science,* 1891, *17 (420),* 105. (b)

————. Marriage. *Science,* 1891, *17 (424),* 160–163. Reprinted: *Silent World,* 1891, *5 (6),* 1, 4; *Marriage: An Address to the Deaf.* Third edition. Washington, D.C.: Sanders, 1898. (c)

————. [History of the American Association to Promote the Teaching of Speech to the Deaf.] In: Alexander Graham Bell Association, Proceedings, (1891), 1–24. (d)

————. See: Clarke School (1893a).

————. Presidential address. In: Alexander Graham Bell Association, Proceedings, (1893). (a)

————. Upon the classification of methods of instructing the deaf. In: Conference of Executives of American Schools for the Deaf, Proceedings, (1893), 86–98. (b)

————. *Address Upon the Condition of Articulation Teaching in American Schools for the Deaf.* Boston: Sawyer, 1893. (c)

————. *Improvement of the Wisconsin System of Education for Deaf-Mutes.* Milwaukee: Wisconsin Phonological Institute, 1894. (a)

————. *Utility of Signs.* Philadelphia: Pennsylvania Institution, 1894. (b)

————. Valedictory. In: Alexander Graham Bell Association, Proceedings, (1894), 11–30. (c)

————. *Growth of the Oral Method of Instructing the Deaf.* Boston: Rockwell and Churchill, 1896. (a)

————. *Methods of Instructing the Deaf and Dumb in the Means of Communication in the United States. Statistics Compiled from the American Annals of the Deaf.* Washington, D.C.: Gibson, 1896. (b)

————. Education of the deaf. In: National Education Association, Proceedings, (1897), 96–104. (a)

————. *A Few Thoughts Concerning Parents Associations.* Washington, D.C.: Sanders, 1897. (b)

————. *The Mystic Oral School: An Argument in Its Favor.* Washington, D.C.: Gibson, 1897. (c)

————. *Methods of Instructing the Deaf in the United States Compiled from the American Annals of the Deaf.* Washington, D.C.: Gibson, 1898. (a)

————. *The Question of Sign Language and the Utility of Signs in the Instruction of the Deaf.* Washington, D.C.: Sanders, 1898. Excerpted: *Volta Review,* 1915, *17,* 13–18. (b)

————. Address of the President. *Association Review*, 1899, *1*, 67–106.

————. Historical notes concerning the teaching of speech to the deaf. *Association Review*, 1900, *2*, 33–68, 113–115, 257–272, 385–409, 489–519; 1901, *3*, 131–140, 329–357, 428–452; 1902, *4*, 19–41, 139–151, 439–454; 1903, *5*, 369–378; 1905, *7*, 49–70.

————. *A Philanthropist of the Last Century Identified as a Boston Man*. Worcester: Hamilton, 1900. (a)

————. Sketch of the life of Francis Green, with extracts from his unpublished autobiography. *Association Review*, 1900, *2*, 119–126. (b)

————. The International Congress. *Association Review*, 1900, *2*, 424–437. (c)

————. *The Mechanism of Speech; Lectures Delivered Before the American Association to Promote the Teaching of Speech to the Deaf*. New York: Funk and Wagnall, 1906.

————. Special Report upon the deaf based on the returns of the twelfth census. *Association Review*, 1906, *8*, 351–370, 442–469; 1907, *9*, 336–356, 427–444, 533–545; 1908, *10*, 36–47, 138–147, 240–255, 349–364, 455–464, table.

————. *A Few Thoughts Concerning Eugenics*. Washington, D.C.: Judd and Detweiler, 1908. Reprinted: *Association Review*, 1908, *10*, 166–173.

————. Eugenics. *Proceedings of the American Breeders' Association*, 1909, *5*, 218–220.

————. Dr. Bell's reply to the National Association of the Deaf resolutions. *Volta Review*, 1910, *12*, 60–61. (a)

————. Notes of early life. *Volta Review*, 1910, *12*, 155–160. (b)

————. A census of the able-bodied. *Volta Review*, 1910, *12*, 403–406. (c)

————. Growth of the American Association to Promote the Teaching of Speech to the Deaf. *Volta Review*, 1912, *14*, 245–250. (a)

————. Statement relative to work on the census of the deaf. *Volta Review*, 1912, *14*, 522–526. (b)

————. Reminiscences of early days of speech-teaching. *Volta Review*, 1912, *14*, 579–581. (c)

————. How to improve the race. *Journal of Heredity*, 1914, *5(1)*, 1–7.

————. Graphical studies of marriages of the deaf. *Volta Review*, 1916, *18*, 468–478.

————. *The Growth of the Oral Method in America*. Northampton: Clarke School, 1917.

————. John Braidwood in America. *American Annals of the Deaf*, 1918, *63*, 459–463.

————. *Who Shall Inherit Long Life?* Washington, D.C.: Judd and Detweiler, 1919.

————. Is race suicide possible? *Journal of Heredity*, 1920, *11*, 339–341.

————. Saving the six-nippled breed. Mr. Bell's last contribution to science, with an introduction by Mrs. Bell. *Journal of Heredity*, 1923, *14*, 99–111.

————. The Association and its purposes. [Excerpts from earlier publications.] *Volta Review*, 1940, *42*, 622–625. (a)

————. *Calendar of Correspondence in Volta Bureau*. Washington, D.C.: Historical Records Survey, 1940. (b)

Bell, A. G., Gordon, J. C., and Clarke, F.D. Report of the committee on the hearing of the deaf. *American annals of the Deaf*, 1885, *30*, 59–63.

Bell, A. G., Smith, J. L., and Jordan, D. S. Legislative interference with marriages of the deaf. *Association Review*, 1908, *10*, 227–228.

Bell, D. C., and Bell, A. M. *Bell's Standard Elocutionist*. London: Simpkin, Marshal, 1871.

Bell, E. M., et al. Dedication of Gardiner Greene Hubbard Hall, Clarke School. *Volta Review*, 1913, *14*, 745–749.

Bell, M. H. The subtle art of speechreading. *Atlantic Monthly*, 1895, *75*, 164–172.

————. *The Story of the Rise of the Oral Method in America as Told in the Writings of the Late Honorable Gardiner G. Hubbard*. Washington, D.C.: W.F. Roberts, 1898.

————. What the Melville Bell symbols mean to me. *Association Review*, 1908, *10*, 308–311.

Bellugi, U., and Studdert-Kennedy, M. *Signed and Spoken Language: Biological Constraints on Linguistic Form*. Deerfield Beach: Verlag Chemie, 1980.

Bemiss, S. *Report on the Influence of Marriages of Consanguinity*. Philadelphia: Collins, 1858.

Bender, R. E. *The Conquest of Deafness*. Cleveland: Case Western Reserve University Press, 1970.

Benjamin. See: Guillemont, F. L.

Bentley, K. Dr. Bell's legacy to parents of deaf children. *Volta Review*, 1969, *71*, 145–147.

————. Alexander Graham Bell and Volta Bureau. *Volta Review*, 1970, *72*, 144–152.

Bernard, R. See: Institution Nationale des Sourds-Muets de Paris (1941).

————. Le séminaire Saint-Magloire, Les Oratoriens, et L'Institut des Sourds-Muets. *Société historique, archéologique, et artistique des 5e, 13e, 14e arrondissements*, 1 June 1940, 2–4.

————. *Surdité . . . dans le théâtre français*. Paris: Rodstein, 1941.

————. Présentation d'élèves du temps de Sicard. *Revue générale de l'enseignement des déficients auditifs*, 1952, *44*, 1–3.

————. L'Institut National de Jeunes Sourds de Paris. Résumé historique. *Revue générale de l'enseignement des sourds-muets*, 1961, *53*, 29–32, 47–68.

————. Autour du sauvage de l'Aveyron. *Revue générale de l'enseignement des déficients auditifs*, 1974, *66*, 82–89.

————. Un dossier sur Victor, le Sauvage de l'Aveyron, à l'Institution des Sourds-Muets de Paris. *Bulletin d'audiophonologie*, 1977, *7 (5)*, 33–68. (a)

————. Un siècle de thèses à l'Institution des Sourds-Muets de Paris (1860–1959). *Bulletin d'audiophonologie,* 1977, *7 (5),* 69–97. (b)

————. Boursiers de 1802—1ère partie. *Bulletin d'audiophonologie,* 1977, *7 (5),* 99–110. (c)

————. Un siècle de thèses (1860–1959). *Bulletin d'audiophonologie,* 1977, *7 (5),* 111–131. (d)

————. Des dossiers des boursiers d'antan à l'Institution des Sourds-Muets de Paris. Unpublished manuscript, Institut National des Jeunes Sourds de Paris, 1980. (a)

————. Des hospices contre l'Institut Royal des Sourds-Muets. *Revue générale de l'enseignement des déficients auditifs,* 1980, *72,* 144–149. (b)

————. Variétés: Boursiers de 1802 à l'Institut National des Sourds-Muets de Paris. Unpublished manuscript, Institut National des Jeunes Sourds de Paris, 1980. (c)

————. Les cours normaux pour la formation des maîtres des sourds-muets en France au XIXe siècle. *Bulletin d'audiophonologie,* 1980, *11,* 2. (d)

Bernheim, R. N. Jacob Rodrigues Pereire. In: *Seventh World Congress of Jewish Studies, 1977.* Jerusalem: World Union of Jewish Studies, 1981. Pp. 57–66.

Berry, G. Deafness in the United States, a statistical review. *Volta Review,* 1938, *40,* 69–71, 120.

Berthier, F. Histoire de l'éducation des sourds-muets. *Journal de l'Institut Historique de Paris,* 1836–7, *4/5,* 97–115. Reprinted: *Histoire et statistique de l'éducation des sourds-muets.* Paris: F. Berthier, 1836.

————. Lettre sur les difficultés au mariage des sourds-muets. *Le Sourd-Muet et l'aveugle,* 1837, *1,* 190–195. (a)

————. Letter to the editor of *Le Temps. Le Sourd-Muet et l'aveugle,* 1837, *1,* 49–54. (b)

————. Sicard. In: *Dictionnaire de la conversation et de la lecture.* Paris: Belin-Mandar, 1838. Vol. 49, pp. 181–188. (a)

————. Muet. In: *Dictionnaire de la conversation et de la lecture.* Paris: Belin-Mandar, 1838. Vol. 39, pp. 163–169. Reprinted: *L'Ami des sourds-muets,* 1842, *5,* 122–128. (b)

————. Les sourds-muets devant les tribunaux civils et criminels. *Le Droit (Journal général des tribunaux),* 1838, *3 (943),* 3639–3640. Reprinted: *L'Ami des sourds-muets,* 1839, *1,* 35–40. (c)

————. Notice sur la vie et les ouvrages d'Auguste Bébian. Paris: J. Ledoyen, 1839.

————. Communication sur le rôle important qu'a joué la mimique chez les peuples anciens et celui auquel elle pourrait être appelée chez les modernes. In: *Congrès Historique réuni à Paris septembre-octobre 1839.* Paris: H. L. Delloye, 1840. Pp. 97–117. (a)

————. Lettre à M. le rédacteur de *l'Univers. L'Ami des sourds-muets,* 1840, *2,* 143–144. (b)

————. Les Sourds-Muets avant et depuis l'abbé de l'Epée. Paris: J. Ledoyen, 1840. English translation: Philip (1984). (c)

————. Correspondance. Lettre au rédacteur. *L'Ami des sourds-muets,* 1842, *4,* 109–110. (a)

————. A M. le rédacteur du journal *Le Commerce. L'Ami des sourds-muets,* 1842, *4,* 142–144. Reprinted from *Le Commerce,* 14 Sept. 1842. (b)

————. Discours prononcé le 12 août 1842. In: Institution Royale des Sourds-Muets de Paris, *Distribution solonelle des prix.* Paris: Institution Royale des Sourds-Muets, 1842. (c)

————, et al. Les sourds-muets au XIXe siècle. Paris: Institution Royale des Sourds-Muets, 1846.

————. Discours prononcé en langage mimique. Paris: Institution Royale des Sourds-Muets, 1849.

————. L'Abbé de l'Epée. Paris: Michel Lévy frères, 1852. (a)

————. Sur l'Opinion de feu le Dr. Itard. Paris: Michel Lévy frères, 1852. (b)

————. Observations sur la mimique considérée dans ses rapports avec l'enseignement des sourds-muets. A M. le Président et à Messieurs les Membres de l'Académie Impériale de Médecine. Paris: Martinet, 1853.

————. L'Abbé de l'Epée. Paris: Paul Durocq, 1870.

————. L'Abbé Sicard. Paris: C. Douniol, 1873.

————. Un mot sur le buste de l'Abbé de l'Epée à l'Eglise Saint-Roch, à Paris, et sa statue à Versailles. Paris: Donaud, 1874.

————. Sourds-Muets. In: *L'Encyclopédie du XIXe siècle.* Paris: Cosson, 1844.

Berthier, F., and Lenoir, A. Les sourds-muets vont réclamer du Roi Louis Philippe leur ci-devant instituteur Bébian. *Sentinelle du Peuple,* 1830, *(3),* Nov. 14, 1–2.

Best, H. *The Deaf Mute Population of the United States, 1920. A Statistical Analysis of the Data Obtained at the Fourteenth Decennial Census.* Washington, D.C.: Government Printing Office, 1928.

————. *Deafness and the Deaf in the United States.* New York: Macmillan, 1943.

Beugnot, A. *Eloge funèbre du Baron de Gérando.* Paris: Crapelet, 1842.

Bibliothèque Nationale. *Catalogue Général des Livres Imprimés. Auteurs.* Paris: Imprimerie Nationale, 1897.

Bigot de Préameneu. Réponse au discours de M. l'Evêque d'Hermiopolis. In: Hermiopolis, *Discours prononcé dans la séance publique tenue par l'Académie Française pour la réception de M. l'Evêque d'Hermiopolis le 28 novembre 1822.* Paris: Firmin Didot, 1822.

Binet, A., and Simon, T. Peut-on enseigner la parole aux sourds-muets? *L'Année psychologique,* 1909, *15,* 373–396. English translation: An investigation concerning the value of the oral method. *American Annals of the Deaf,* 1910, *55,* 4–33.

Bingham, K. All along the line. In: National Education Association, Proceedings, (1899), 1165–1171.

Bishop, W. H. Impressions of deaf mute instruction in Paris. *American Annals of the Deaf,* 1889, *34,* 272–285.

Blanchet, A. L. *La Surdi-Mutité.* Paris: Labé, 1850.

————. *Premier rapport à M. le Ministre de l'Intérieur sur l'enseignement et le développement de la parole dans les établissements des sourds-muets belges et allemands.* Paris: Labbé, 1851.

————. *Rapport de l'Académie Impériale à M. le Ministre de l'Intérieur sur un mémoire relatif à l'enseignement de la parole aux sourds-muets.* Paris: Maulde et Renou, 1853. (a)

————. Historique de la question du langage dans l'éducation des sourds-muets. *La Lancette française,* 1853, *26,* 211. (b)

————. *Moyens de généraliser l'éducation des sourds-muets . . . sans les séparer de la famille et des parlants.* Paris: Labé, 1856.

————. *Manuel pour l'enseignement des sourds-muets dans les écoles primaires sans les séparer de la famille et des entendants-parlants et moyens de les doter de la parole.* Paris: Hachette, 1866.

Bloch, C., and Tuetey, A. (eds.). *Procès-verbaux et rapports du Comité de Mendicité de la Constituante, 1790–1791.* Paris: Imprimerie Nationale, 1911.

Boatner, E. B. *Deaf Teachers of the Deaf.* Hartford: American School, 1946.

————. A half century of progress in the New England schools. The American School for the Deaf. *Volta Review,* 1939, *41,* 485–488.

Boatner, M. *Gallaudet the Builder: The Physical Aspects of His Work in Washington.* Washington, D.C.: Gallaudet College, 1951.

————. The Washington life of Edward Miner Gallaudet. *American Annals of the Deaf,* 1955, *100,* 313–318.

————. Vocational education under the Gallaudets. *American Annals of the Deaf,* 1957, *102,* 300–311.

————. *The Voice of the Deaf.* Washington, D.C.: Public Affairs Press, 1959. (a)

————. The Gallaudet Papers. *Library of Congress, Quarterly Journal of Recent Acquisitions,* 1959, *17,* 1–12. (b)

————. Contributions of the late Amos Kendall. Unpublished manuscript, E. M. Gallaudet Library, Washington, D.C., 196[?].

Bonet, J. P. *Reducción de las Letras y Arte para Enseñar à Ablar los Mudos.* Madrid: Abarca de Angulo, 1620. English translation: *Simplification of the Letters of the Alphabet and Method of Teaching Deaf-Mutes to Speak. Translated from the original Spanish by H. N. Dixon, with an historical introduction by A. Farrar.* Harrogate: A. Farrar, 1890.

Bonnaterre, P.J. *Notice historique sur le saurvage de Averyron.* Paris: Panckovcke, 1800. Reprinted: Anonymous, *Histoire naturelle de l'homme,* 2nd ed. Paris: Armand-Aubrée, 1834.

Bonnefoy, G. *Les Questions d'éducation et d'assistance de sourds-muets au congrès international de Paris de 1900.* Paris: Institut de Bibliographie, 1901.

Booth, E. Miss Martineau and deaf-mutes. *American Annals of the Deaf,* 1877, *22,* 80–83.

———— Thomas Hopkins Gallaudet. *Iowa Institution Hawkeye,* 1881. Reprinted: *American Era,* 1943, *30,* 23–25. Excerpted: *American Annals of the Deaf,* 1881, *26,* 200–201.

———— *Edmund Booth, Forty-niner, the Life Story of a Deaf Pioneer.* Stockton: San Joaquin Pioneer and Historical Society, 1953.

Booth, F. W. The sign language: its use and abuse in the school-room. In: Convention of American Instructors of the Deaf, Proceedings (1893), 58–63.

———— The Association magazine. *Association Review,* 1899, *1,* 1–5.

———— Editorial. *Association Review,* 1900, *2,* 451–452. (a)

———— Discovery of an early instance of instruction of a deaf-mute in America. *Association Review,* 1900, *2,* 527–533. (b)

———— Editorial: the passing of the sign method. *Association Review,* 1902, *4,* 188–190.

———— The degeneracy of the sign language and its doom. *Association Review,* 1905, *7,* 198–199. (a)

———— Editorial Comment: The passing of the sign method. *Association Review,* 1905, *7,* 449–452. (b)

———— Edmund Booth: A life sketch. *Association Review,* 1905, *7,* 225–237. (c)

————. Natural signs and the sign language. *Association Review,* 1909, *11,* 164–166.

Bornstein, H. A description of some current sign systems designed to represent English. *American Annals of the Deaf,* 1973, *118,* 454–463.

Boselli, C. A. *Au congrès international de 1880.* Genoa: Sourds-Muets, 1880.

Boudin, J. C., et al. *Le français par l'usage: enseignement synthétique de la langue aux sourds-muets.* Paris: F. Nathan, 1906.

Bouilly, J. N. *L'Abbé de l'Epée, comédie historique en cinq actes et en prose.* Paris: André, 1800. English translation: London: Longman and Rees, 1801; Hartford: Goodrich, 1818; London: Hamilton, Adams, 1870. (a)

————. *Rentrée du Citoyen Sicard à l'Institution Nationale des Sourds-Muets.* Paris: Dupont, 1800. (b)

————. *Mes récapitulations. Deuxième époque: 1791–1812.* Paris: Janet, 1835.

Boulatignier, S. J. *Notice nécrologique de M. le Baron de Gérando.* Paris: Thunot, 1842.

Boundinet, E. Letter to Mason Fitch Cogswell, 12 November 1818, from Burlington. Cogswell Papers, Yale University.

Bourneville, D. M. (ed.). *Rapports et mémoires sur le sauvage de l'Aveyron, l'idiotie et la surdi-mutité, par Itard.* Paris: F. Alcan, 1894.

Bourse, [Chanoine]. *Les institutions de sourds-muets en Italie et le congrès de Milan.* Citeaux, Côte d'or: Institut de Saint-Médard-les-Soissons, 1880.

Bousquet, J.B.E. *Eloge historique, J. M. Itard. Mémoires de l'Académie de Médecine,* 1840, *8,* 1–18.

Bouteiller, M. La Société des Observateurs de l'Homme. *Bulletin de la Société d'Anthropologie*, 1956, 7, 448–465.

Boyle, R. *The Works of Robert Boyle*. London: Phillips, 1700.

Braddock, G. C. *Notable Deaf Persons*. Washington, D.C.: Gallaudet College Alumni Association, 1975.

Braidwood, J. [Plans to open deaf school.] *Weekly Register*, 1812, 2, supplement, 21 March, 53. Reprinted: *Association Review*, 1900, 2, 402–404.

Bray, R. E. The Royal Commission of Great Britain: its work and results. In: Congress of Deaf—International —Second (1893), 255–264.

Breteuil, [?]. *Arrêt du Conseil d'État du roi, qui ordonne que l'établissement formé pour l'instruction des sourds et muets par le sieur Abbé de l'Epée sera incessamment et irrévocablement placé et fondé dans la partie des bâtiments des Célestins à Paris, à ce désignée, par le sieur Lemoine de Couson, architecte . . . 25 mars 1785*. Paris: Imprimerie Royale, 1785.

Breton de la Martinière, J.B.J. *Procès de François Duval sourd et muet de naissance accusé de vol avec effraction*. Paris: Deseunl, 1800.

Brian-Chaninov, N. *Alexandre Ier*. Paris: Grasset, 1934.

Brigham, C. S. *History and Bibliography of American Newspapers, 1610–1820*. Worcester: American Antiquarian Society, 1947.

Brooks, V. W. *The Flowering of New England, 1815–1865*. New York: Dutton, 1936.

Brouland, J. *Explication d'un dictionnaire des signes du langage mimique*. Paris: Imprimerie de l'Institution Impériale des Sourds-Muets, 1855.

Brown, K. S., Hopkins, L. A., and Hudgins, R. B. Causes of childhood deafness. In: Alexander Graham Bell Association, Proceedings, (1967), 77–107.

Brown, T. In memory of Laurent Clerc: unveiling of the bust and monument. *Silent World*, 1874, 4, 3–8.

Bruce, R. V. Excerpts from "Bell: Alexander Graham Bell and the Conquest of Solitude." *Volta Review*, 1973, 75, 146–154. (a).

———. *Bell, Alexander Graham Bell and the Conquest of Solitude*. Boston: Little, Brown, 1973. (b)

———. *Alexander Graham Bell, Teacher of the Deaf*. Northampton: Clarke School, 1974.

Bruhier d' Ablaincourt, J. J. Lettre sur les sourds et muets. In: *Caprices d'imagination*. Paris: Briasson, 1740. Pp. 167–179.

Buffalo, C. L. L. (Chief). *How to Talk in the Indian Sign Language*. Akron: Goodrich Rubber Company, 1930.

Buffon, G. L. *Histoire naturelle de l'homme*. Paris: Imprimerie Royale, 1749. Reprinted: Buffon, G. L. *Oeuvres complètes*. Paris: Rapet, 1818. Vol. 5.

Buisson, S. *Les sourds-muets en France*. Paris: Guillaumin, 1903.

Bulwer, J. *Chirologia: or the Natural Language of the Hand. Composed of the speaking motions and discoursing gestures thereof. Whereunto is added Chironomia: or the art of manual rhetoricke etc. by J.B. Gent Philochiroso-phus*. London: Gent, 1644.

———. *Philocophus: or the Deafe and Dumbe Man's Friend*. London: Moseley: 1648.

Burlingame, R. *Out of Silence into Sound: The Life of Alexander Graham Bell*. New York: Macmillan, 1964.

Burnet, J. (Lord Monboddo). *Of the Origin and Progress of Language*. London: Caddell, 1773. Second edition: 1774.

Burnet, J. R. *Tales of the Deaf and Dumb*. Newark: Olds, 1835.

———. Deaf and dumb. *American Biblical Repository*, second series, 1842, 8, 269–309.

———. The necessity of methodical signs considered. Further experiments. *American Annals of the Deaf*, 1854, 7, 1–14.

———. Colloquial signs versus methodical signs. *American Annals of the Deaf*, 1855, 7, 133–157. (a)

———. Misapprehensions corrected. *American Annals of the Deaf*, 1855, 8, 45–55. (b)

———. The case of Laura Bridgman. *American Annals of the Deaf*, 1856, 8, 159–172.

———. *Memoir of Dudley Peet, M.D., Professor in the New York Institution for the Deaf and Dumb*. New York: author, 1863.

———. On G. G. Hubbard's pamphlet, "The Education of Deaf-Mutes, Shall It Be by Signs or by Articulation?" *National Deaf-Mute Gazette*, 1867, 1 (8), 3–5.

Burnet, J. R., and Porter, S. Under what forms do deaf-mutes apprehend words? *American Annals of the Deaf*, 1858, 10, 228–241.

Burton, R. F. *The City of the Saints, and across the Rocky Mountains to California*. London: Longman, 1861. Reprinted: New York: Knopf, 1963.

Buxton, D. Notes of progress in the education of the deaf. *American Annals of the Deaf*, 1883, 28, 37–47.

Caldwell, W. A. The sign language. *Volta Review*, 1912, 14, 316.

Calkins, E. E. *Louder Please. Autobiography of a Deaf Man*. Boston: Atlantic Monthly Press, 1924.

Cameron, K. W. *Research Keys . . . Indexes of the Christian Examiner and the North American Review*. Hartford: Transcendental Books, 1967.

Camplo, J. Les congrès et l'orale. *Journal des sourds-muets*, 1899, 5, 447–449.

Cardano, G. . . . *Quo continentur Opuscula Miscellanea ex Fragmentis et Paralipomensis*. Lugduni: Huguetan et Ravaud, 1663.

Carlin, J. Reminiscences on the Life of Laurent Clerc. [n.d.] Clerc Papers no. 34a, Yale University.

————. The mute's lament. *American Annals of the Deaf*, 1847, *1*, 15–16.

————. Advantages and disadvantages of the use of signs. *American Annals of the Deaf*, 1852, *4*, 49–57.

————. On the mechanical and professional occupations of deaf-mute graduates. In: Convention of American Instructors of the Deaf, Proceedings (1853), 200–214.

————. A reply to Mr. Chamberlain. *National Deaf-Mute Gazette*, 1867, *1 (9)*, 10–11.

————. Professor Gallaudet's resolution. *National Deaf-Mute Gazette*, 1868, *2 (19)*, 14. (a)

————. Mr. Carlin's reply to the above. *National Deaf-Mute Gazette*, 1868, *2 (20)*, 13–15. (b)

Carr, J. *Stranger in France*. Brattleboro: Thomas, 1806.

Carton, C. L. Des signes dans l'éducation des sourds-muets. *Le Sourd-Muet et l'aveugle*, 1837, *1*, 247–256. (a)

————. Revue: "Essai sur l'éducation" par Ordinaire at "Histoire et statistique de l'éducation des sourds-muets" par Berthier. *Le Sourd-Muet et l'aveugle*, 1837, *1*, 26–31. (b)

————. [Comparison of blindness and deafness.] *Le Sourd-Muet et l'aveugle*, 1837, *1*, 45–54. (c)

————. Liste chronologique des ouvrages publiés sur les sourds-muets et leur instruction avant l'Abbé de l'Epée. In: *Annuaire*. Bruges: Institut des Sourds-Muets et des Aveugles, 1841. Pp. 41–56.

————. *De l'education des sourds-muets*. Brussels: Hayez, 1846.

————. *Mémoire [sur les] sourds-muets*. Brussels: Hayez, 1847.

———— *L'Instruction des sourds-muets*. Brussels: Goemaere, 1856.

Cartwright, S.A. Report on the diseases and physical peculiarities of the Negro race. *New Orleans Medical and Surgical Journal*, 1851, 709–712.

Cary, J. A. Catalogue of books and other publications relating to the deaf and dumb added to the library of the institution. In: New York Institution for the Instruction of the Deaf and Dumb, Reports (1846), 85–103.

————. Deaf-Mute idioms. In: Convention of American Instructors of the Deaf, Proceedings (1851), 103–113.

Castañiza, J. *Vida de San Benito*. Salamanca: 1583.

Castex, A. Jean Itard; notes sur sa vie et son oeuvre. *Bulletin d'Oto-rhino-laryngologie*, 1919–1920, *18*, 239–253.

Castle, D. L. "Misinformation" among advocates of non-oral methodologies. *American Annals of the Deaf*, 1970, *115*, 666–667.

Castleman, T. T. Obituary notice of Rev. J. D. Tyler. *American Annals of the Deaf*, 1852, *4*, 173–178.

Caulfield, S.F.A. Deaf-Mutes and the new system of visible speech. *Victoria Magazine*, 1873, *21*, 193–200.

Cazeaux, [?]. [Address on Pereire.] *Procès Verbaux de l'Académie Royale des Belles-Lettres de Caen*, 1746, séance du 22 novembre.

Celliez. See: Sicard, R. A. C. (1851).

Census, Bureau of (U.S. Dept. of Commerce). *Deaf-Mutes in the United States. Analysis of the Census of 1910*. Washington, D.C.: U.S. Government Printing Office, 1918.

Certeau, M., Julia, D., and Revel, J. *Une politique de la langue. La Révolution Française et les patois: l'Enquête de Grégoire*. Paris: Gaillard, 1975.

Chambellan, V. G. *De l'importance incontestable du langage mimique dans l'enseignement des sourds-muets de naissance*. Paris: author, 1884.

————. *Quelques mots sur la vulgarisation du langage des signes*. Paris: auteur, 1887.

———— (ed). See: Congress of Deaf—International—First (1889).

————. Oralism in France. In: National Association of the Deaf, Proceedings (1893), 218–230.

Chamberlain, W. M. Proceedings of the convention of the New England Gallaudet Association of Deaf-Mutes. Summary of address by L. Clerc. *American Annals of the Deaf*, 1857, *9*, 65–87. (a)

————. Proceedings of the Board of Managers of the New England Gallaudet Association of Deaf-Mutes. *American Annals of the Deaf*, 1857, *9*, 236–243. (b)

————. Proceedings of the Third Convention of the New England Gallaudet Association of Deaf-Mutes. *American Annals of the Deaf*, 1858, *10*, 205–219.

————. Reply to Mr. Carlin. *National Deaf-Mute Gazette*, 1867, *1 (8)*, 10–11. (a)

————. Editorial [on Stone/Hubbard controversy]. *National Deaf-Mute Gazette*, 1867, *1 (11)*, 8–9. (b)

————. Life and adventures of William B. Swett. *Deaf-Mute's Friend*, 1869, *1*, 33–36, 65–71, 129–133, 161–164, 225–230, 289–292, 321–324, 353–358. (a)

————. A golden wedding. *Deaf Mute's Friend*, 1869, *1*, 170–172. Reprinted from: Anon. (1869a). (b)

————. The deaf-mute college. *Deaf-Mute's Friend*, 1869, *1*, 193–197. (c)

————. Obituary of Laurent Clerc. *Deaf-Mute's Friend*, 1869, *1*, 216–217. (d)

————. A liberal bequest. *Deaf-Mute's Friend*, 1869, *1*, 235. (e)

————. Miscellaneous. *American Annals of the Deaf*, 1875, *20, 54*.

————. Thomas Brown. *American Annals of the Deaf*, 1886, *31*, 204–210.

————. The "animus." *American Annals of the Deaf*, 1888, *33*, 133–137. (a)

————. My experience and conclusions as a lip-reader. In: Empire State Association of Deaf-Mutes, *Proceedings of the Twelfth Convention*. Rome, N.Y.: Register, 1888. Pp. 18–27. (b)

Chambeyron, [?]. Relation d'une tentative de vol qui aurait été exercée sur une sourde-muette. *Annales d'hygiène publique et de médecine légale*, 1838, *20*, 94–98.

Chapin, W. *Report on Benevolent Institutions of Great Britain and Paris*. Columbus: Scott, 1846.

Charbonnier, [?]. Réponse au Dictionnaire Larousse. *Revue internationale de l'enseignement des sourds-muets*, 1890, *6*, 82–84.

Chasen, B., and Zuckerman, W. The effects of total communication and oralism on deaf third-grade rubella students. *American Annals of the Deaf*, 1976, *121*, 394–404.

Chassé, J. L'Institut National de Jeunes Sourds de Paris—hier at aujourd'hui. *Revue générale de l'enseignement des déficients auditifs*, 1974, *66*, 90–103.

Chaves, T. L., and Soler, J. L. Pedro Ponce de León, first teacher of the deaf. *Sign Language Studies*, 1974, *5*, 48–63.

————. Manuel Ramirez de Carrion (1579–1652) and his secret method of teaching the deaf. *Sign Language Studies*, 1975, *8*, 235–248.

Chazal, J. *Un Grand Complot*. Paris: author, 1893.

————. *Un Tribunal sourd-muet*. Paris: author, 1894.

————. A Dijon. *Le Sourd-Muet illustré*, 1898, *2 (18)*, 2–3; *(19)*, 1–2.

Chesselden, W. An account of some observations made by a young gentleman who was born blind, or lost his sight so early, that he had no remembrance of ever having seen, and was couched between 13 and 14 years of age. *Philosophical Transactions of the Royal Society*, 1728, *35*, 447–450. No. 402.

Chester, C. Letter to Clerc, 1820. Clerc Papers no. 46, Yale University.

Chevalier, A. Recherches historiques sur l'enseignement des sourds-muets. Pereire et l'abbé de l'Epée. *Le Correspondant*, 1883, 934–942.

Chittenden, R. L. On the benefits conferred upon the deaf mute by the usual course of instruction. In: Convention of American Instructors of the Deaf, Proceedings (1853), 175–183.

Chorover, S. *From Genesis to Genocide*. Cambridge, Mass.: M.I.T. Press, 1979.

Clair, [?], and Clapier, A. Notice sur Tronson du Coudray. *Le Barreau français: collection des chefs-d'oeuvre de l'éloquence judiciaire en France*. Paris: Panckoucke, 1823. Pp. 167–172.

Clark, A. S. John Robinson Keep. *American Annals of the Deaf*, 1885, *30*, 69–81.

Clark, G. L. *A History of Connecticut*. New York: Putnam, 1914.

Clark, W. P. *The Indian Sign Language; with brief explanatory notes on the gestures taught deaf-mutes in our institutions*. Philadelphia: Hamersley, 1885.

Clarke, E. P. An analysis of the schools and instructors of the deaf in the United States. *American Annals of the Deaf*, 1900, *45*, 228–236. (a)

————. The training of teachers of the deaf in the United States. *American Annals of the Deaf*, 1900, *45*, 345–367. (b)

Clarke, F. D. The use of the sign language. In: Convention of American Instructors of the Deaf, Proceedings (1890), 171–186.

Clarke Institution. See: Clarke School.

Clarke School. Annual Reports, 1868–.

————. *Teaching the Deaf by Articulation as Pursued in the Clarke Institution for Deaf Children*. Boston: Wright and Potter, 1876.

————. *Addresses Delivered at the Twenty-fifth Anniversary of the Opening of the Clarke Institution*. Northampton: Gazette, 1893. Excerpted: Fay, E.A. (1893). (a)

————. Outline of first year's work at the Clarke Institution. In: Alexander Graham Bell Association, Proceedings (1893), 287–295. (b)

————. *Clarke School and Its Alumni, 1867–1947*. Northampton: Clarke School, 1947.

Claveau, O. *L'Enseignement de la parole dans les institutions des sourds-muets. Rapport à M. le Ministre de l'Intérieur et des Cultes*. Paris: Imprimerie Nationale, 1880.

————. *De la parole comme objet et comme moyen d'enseignement dans les institutions de sourds-muets, rapport à M. le Ministre de l'Intérieur*. Paris: Imprimerie Nationale, 1881.

————. Introduction. L'Enseignement de la parole aux sourds-muets. In: Meyer, G. H., *Organes de la parole et leur emploi pour la formation des sons du langage*. Translated from the German by O. Claveau. Paris: Bibliothéque Scientifique, 1885.

————. *Rapport au Ministre de l'Intérieur sur les résultats des examens pour la délivrance des certificats d'aptitude concernant l'enseignement des sourds-muets élèves boursiers des départements ou des communes, et sur l'état de l'enseignement dans les institutions de sourds-muets de France*. Paris: Imprimerie des journaux officiels, 1886. (a)

————. Sourds-Muets. *Dictionnaire de pédagogie et d'instruction primaire*. Paris: 1886. (b)

————. *Un Progrès inattendu*. Paris: Revue française de l'éducation des sourds-muets, 1891.

Claveau, O., Le Guay, G., and Rousseau, H. *Rapport sur les travaux de Congrès de Bruxelles pour l'amélioration du sort des sourds-muets et sur les institutions des sourds-muets de la Belgique et de la Hollande, présenté à M. Waldeck-Rousseau, Ministre de l'Intérieur*. Paris: Imprimerie des journaux officiels, 1884.

Clerc, F. J. (Rev.). [Description of his father, 1885.] Clerc Papers no. 41, Yale University Library. Excerpted: Anonymous (1896).

Clerc, L. [Petition to the directors for increased pay, 1812.] Clerc Papers no. 10, Yale University. (a)

————. [Letter to M. L'Abbé Sicard on his birthday, 1812.] Clerc Papers no. 6, Yale University. (b)

————. [Response to the young Marquise de ————, 1815.] Clerc Papers no. 40, Yale University.

————. [Petition to the directors for better food, May 10, 1816.] Clerc Papers no. 9, Yale University. (a)

————. [Written conversation on Clerc's request to Sicard to go to the U.S., 1816.] Clerc Papers no. 15, 16. Yale University. (b)

————. *The Diary of Laurent Clerc's Voyage from France to America in 1816.* Hartford: American School for the Deaf, 1952. Reprinted from: Clerc Papers no. 68, Yale University. (c)

————. [Transcribed clippings on his fund-raising: September–November 1816.] Clerc Papers no. 69, Yale University. (d)

————. [Fund-raising address in Philadelphia.] *Connecticut Courant,* 1816, *52 (2709),* 24 Dec. (e)

————. [Arrival in U.S. and address.] *The Portfolio,* 1817, *3,* 84–89. (a)

————. Letter to Mason Fitch Cogswell, 14 Jan. 1817, from New York. Clerc Papers no. 57, Yale University. (b)

————. Letter to Mason Fitch Cogswell, 7 May 1818, from Hartford. Reprinted: *Association Review,* 1902, *4,* 32–34. (a)

————. [*Address to the Connecticut Legislature, 28 May 1818.*] Hartford: Hudson, 1818. (b)

————. Letter to Rev. Mr. Wainwright. *North American Review,* 1818, *7,* 132-136. (c)

————. Preface. In: Bouilly, J. N. *Deaf and Dumb or the Abbé de l'Epée.* Translated from the French of M. Bouilly. Hartford: Goodrich, 1818. (d)

————. American Asylum contract, 25 Apr. 1820. Clerc Papers no. 50, Yale University.

————. Letter to the Directors of the Pennsylvania Institution for the Deaf and Dumb, 22 Apr. 1822. Reprinted: Pennsylvania Institution for the Deaf and Dumb, *Second Annual Report.* Philadelphia: Fry, 1823. Pp. 9–12.

————. The origin of the establishment of the American Asylum at Hartford, Connecticut, for the Instruction of the Deaf and Dumb, with a short sketch of kindred institutions throughout the United States of America. Unpublished manuscript, American School for the Deaf, Hartford, 1825.

————. Letter to the Honorable John Spencer of the Senate, February 1827. Clerc Papers no. 36, Yale University.

————. Letter to F.A.P. Barnard on psychology of sign, 1835. Clerc Papers no. 38, Yale University.

————. Visits to some of the schools for the deaf and dumb in France and England. *American Annals of the Deaf,* 1848, *1,* 62–66, 113–120, 170–176.

————. Jean Massieu. *American Annals of the Deaf,* 1849, *2,* 84–89, 203–217. Excerpted: Holycross (1913).

————. Oration on receiving a testimonial from the deaf, 1850. In: Rae (1851), 56–59.

————. Address at funeral of Rev. T. H. Gallaudet at Hartford, 12 Sept. 1851. Excerpted: Convention of Deaf-Mutes (1853). (a)

————. Address on accepting silver pitcher. In: Rae (1851). (b)

————. Some hints to teachers of the deaf and dumb. In: Convention of American Instructors of the Deaf, Proceedings (1851), 64–75. (c)

————. [Autobiography.] In: Barnard, H. (1852), 106–116.

————. Oration at the dedication of a monument to T. H. Gallaudet. In: Rae (1854), 23–26.

————. Address to the New England Gallaudet Association. In: Chamberlain (1857a).

————. [A defense of manual English.] In: Keep, J. R. The mode of learning the sign language. Convention of American Instructors of the Deaf, Proceedings (1857), 151–152. (b)

————. Notice of the late St. George Randolph—with other reminiscences. *American Annals of the Deaf,* 1858, *10,* 51–54. (a)

————. Retirement of Mr. Clerc. *American Annals of the Deaf,* 1858, *10,* 181–183. (b)

————. Address. In: Columbian Institution, *Inauguration of the College for the Deaf and Dumb at Washington, D.C., 28 June 1864.* Washington, D.C.: Pearson, 1864. Pp. 41–43.

Cloud, J. H. Address. National Association of the Deaf, Proceedings (1925). Reprinted: *Silent Worker,* 1925, *37,* 201–205.

Clymer, [?]. Letter from Washington. *Deaf-Mute's Friend,* 1869, *1,* 218–221.

Cochefer, J. Histoire des sociétés des sourds-muets jusqu'à nos jours. *L'Echo de la Société d'Appui Fraternel de Sourds-Muets de France,* 1889, *1,* (2), 6–7; (3), 7–8; (5), 7; (6), 7–8; (8), (9), 7–8; (10), 7–8; (11), 7–8.

Cochrane, W. Methodical signs instead of colloquial. *American Annals of the Deaf,* 1871, *16,* 11–17.

Cogswell, A. [Essay on the return of peace in 1815.] Reprinted: Sigourney (1851), 249. Excerpted: Root (1941), 72. (a)

————. Letter to T. H. Gallaudet, 6 July 1815. Gallaudet Papers, Library of Congress. (b)

————. Letter to T.H. Gallaudet, 14 Aug. 1815. Gallaudet Papers, Library of Congress. (c)

————. Letter to Lydia Huntley, 30 Aug. 1815. Gallaudet Papers, Library of Congress. (d)

————. Letter to T.H. Gallaudet, 11 Oct. 1815. Reprinted: Gallaudet, E. M. (1888), 86–88. (e)

————. Letter to T. H. Gallaudet, 13 Dec. 1815. Gallaudet Papers, Library of Congress. Reprinted: Fay, E. A. (1913b), 232–233. (f)

————. Letter to T. H. Gallaudet, Apr. 1816. Gallaudet Papers, Library of Congress. Reprinted: Fay, E. A. (1913b), 233–234.(a)

————. Letter to Mason Fitch Cogswell, 17 Nov. 1816. Gallaudet Papers, Library of Congress. (b)

————. Letter to T. H. Gallaudet, 27 Dec. 1816. Gallaudet Papers, Library of Congress. Reprinted: Fay, E.A. (1913b), 234–235. (c)

————. Letter to Sophia and Parnel Fowler, Sept. 1817. Gallaudet Papers, Library of Congress.

————. Letter to Laurent Clerc, 1819. Clerc Papers no. 43, Yale University.

————. On the death of Sarah Colt, 1821. Reprinted: Root (1941), 75–76.

Cogswell, H. Letter to Mason Fitch Cogswell, 10 Mar. 1816. Cogswell Papers, Yale University.

Cogswell, M. A. Letter to Mason Fitch Cogswell from Guilford in response to his letter of 24 Aug. 1814. Cogswell Papers, Yale University.

Cogswell, M. F. [Diary, 1788.] Reprinted: Bacon (1882). Excerpted: Bartlett (1899); Root (1942).

————. Sketch of the history of the weather and diseases at Hartford, in Connecticut, during the winter and spring of 1798. *Medical Repository*, 1799, *2*, 299–301.

————. Letter to the Rev. Abel Flint, 18 June 1811. Reprinted: *Association Review*, 1901, *3*, 131–132.

————. Letter to John Braidwood, 20 Apr. 1812. Cogswell Papers, Yale University. Reprinted: Root (1941), 66–67.

————. List of subscribers to defray Gallaudet's expense in Europe, 1 May 1815. Reprinted: *Association Review*, 1901, *3*, 329–331.

————. Letter to Mary Cogswell, 7 Sept. 1816, from Boston. Cogswell Papers, Yale University. Reprinted: *Association Review*, 1901, *3*, 348. (b)

————. Letter to Mary Cogswell, 30 Oct. 1816, from New Haven. Cogswell Papers, Yale University. Reprinted: *Association Review*, 1901, *3*, 349; Root (1941), 80–81. (c)

————. Letter to Mary Cogswell, 4 Nov. 1816, from New York. Cogswell Papers, Yale University. Reprinted: *Association Review*, 1901, *3*, 350; Root (1941), 81–82. (d)

————. Letter to Mary Cogswell, 6 Nov. 1816, from New York. Cogswell Papers, Yale University. Reprinted: *Association Review*, 1901, *3*, 351; Root (1941), 82–83. (e)

————. Letter to Mary Cogswell, 10 Nov. 1816, from Albany. Cogswell Papers, Yale University. Reprinted: *Association Review*, 1901, *3*, 352–354; Root (1941), 83–84. (f)

————. Letter to Mary Cogswell, 17 Nov. 1816, from Albany. Cogswell Papers, Yale University. Reprinted: *Association Review*, 1901, *3*, 354–356; Root (1941), 84–85. (g)

————. Letter to Alice Cogswell, 20 Nov. 1816, from New York. Cogswell Papers, Yale University. Reprinted: *Association Review*, *3*, 356; Root (1941), 85–86. (h)

————. Letter to Mary Cogswell, 21 Nov. 1816, from New York. Cogswell Papers, Yale University. Reprinted: *Association Review*, 1901, *3*, 356. (i)

————. Letter to S. Akerly, 15 Oct. 1821. Reprinted: *Association Review*, 1902, *4*, 39–41.

————. Account of an operation for the extirpation of a tumor in which a ligature was applied to the carotid artery. *New England Journal of Medicine and Surgery*, 1824, *13*, 357–360.

Cogswell, M.F., and Wadsworth, D. Deaf and Dumb Asylum. *Connecticut Mirror*, 24 Mar. 1817. Reprinted: *Association Review*, 1902, *4*, 23. (a)

————. [Course of instruction to begin at Connecticut Asylum.] *Connecticut Courant*, 1817, *53 (2722)*, 25 Mar. (b)

————. Deaf and Dumb Asylum. *American Mercury*, 1817, *(1710)*, 8 Apr. (c)

Cogswell, M. F., and Woodbridge, W. Petition to the Honorable General Assembly of the State of Connecticut [1816]. Reprinted: *Association Review*, 1901, *3*, 137–138.

Cogswell, S. Letter to Rev. James Cogswell, 13 May 1790. Cogswell Papers, Yale University.

Colombat, M. *Méthode rationnelle d'articulation à l'usage des institutions de sourds-muets (école française)*. Paris: P. Asselin, 1875.

Columbian Institution for the Deaf and Dumb. *Annual Reports*. Washington, D.C.: 1857/58–.

————. *Inauguration of the College for the Deaf and Dumb at Washington, D.C., 28 June 1864*. Washington, D.C.: Pearson, 1864.

————. *Proceedings of the Board of Directors . . . and Eulogistic of the Late Hon. Amos Kendall*. Washington, D.C.: Gibson, 1870.

————. A message to all interested in promoting the education of the deaf in Europe. *American Annals of the Deaf*, 1897, *42*, 273–281.

Commissioner of Education. Report for 1880 [*sic*]. *American Journal of Education*, 1876, *25*, lx–lxii, clxvii–clxxiii, ccii, 744–749, 874–875.

————. Report for 1877. *American Journal of Education*, 1878, *29*, cxlii–cxlvi, 115, 586–589.

Condillac, E. B. (abbé de). *Essai sur l'origine des connaissances humaines*. Amsterdam: Mortier, 1746. Reprinted: Condillac (1947). English translation: Philip (1982).

————. *Traité des sensations*, Paris: Debure, 1754. Reprinted: Condillac (1947). English translation: Carr, G. *Condillac's Treatise on the Sensations*. Los Angeles: University of California, 1930; Philip (1982).

————. *Cours d'étude pour l'instruction du prince de Parme*. Parma: Imprimerie Royale, 1775. Reprinted: Condillac (1947).

————. *La logique*. Paris: l'Esprit et Debure, 1780. Reprinted: Condillac (1947). 1948. English translation: Philip (1982).

————. *Oeuvres philosophiques*. Paris: Presses Universitaires de France, 1947–48.

Conference of Executives of American Schools for the Deaf. *Proceedings of the Conference of Superintendents and Principals of American Schools for the Deaf*. [Various]: 1868–1913.

————. Report of the committee on classification of methods of instructing the deaf. *American Annals of the Deaf*, 1893, *38*, 291–414.

Congress of Deaf—International—First (1889). Chambellan, V. (ed.). *Compte-rendu. Congrès international des sourds-muets.* Paris: Association Amicale des Sourds-Muets de France, 1890.

Congress of Deaf—International—Second (1893). World's Congress of the Deaf. *Proceedings of the World's Congress of the Deaf and the Report of the Fourth Convention of the National Association of the Deaf.* Chicago: National Association of the Deaf, 1893. (a)

————. *Congrès international des sourds-muets. Chicago 1893. Compte-rendu.* Paris: Journal des Sourds-Muets, 1893. (b)

Congress of Deaf—International—Third (1896). Gaillard, H. (ed.). Le troisième congrès international des sourds-muets. *Journal des sourds-muets,* 1896, *2,* 294–297. Reprinted: Paris: Journal des Sourds-Muets, 1898.

Congress of Deaf—International—Fourth (1904). The international congress and the seventh convention of the National Association of the Deaf. *American Annals of the Deaf,* 1904, *49,* 343–348. (a)

————. *Proceedings of the World's Congress of the Deaf and the Report of the Seventh Convention of the National Association of the Deaf.* Fort Smith: 1904. (b)

Congress of Deaf—International—Fifth (1910). The World's Congress of the Deaf. *American Annals of the Deaf,* 1910, *55,* 395–411. (a)

————. *Proceedings of the Ninth Convention of the National Association of the Deaf and the Third World's Congress of the Deaf.* Los Angeles: Philocophus press, 1912 [?]. (b)

Congress of Deaf—International—Sixth (1912). Gaillard, H. (ed.). *Troisième congrès international des sourds-muets tenu à la Sorbonne à Paris les 1er et 2 août 1912.* Paris: 35 rue de Montreuil, 1913.

Congress of Deaf—National—France (1893). *Compte-rendu, Congrès de sourds-muets tenu à Aix-les-Bains le 24 septembre 1893.* Montpellier: Fabre, 1894.

Congress of Deaf—National—France (1911). *Deuxième Congrès national pour l'amélioration du sort des sourds-muets organisé par l'Union Nationale des Sociétés de Sourds-Muets à Roubaix, les 13, 14, et 15 août 1911 . . . Compte-rendu des travaux.* Roubaix: Imprimerie du journal, 1911.

Congress of Deaf—National—Germany (1875). See: Etcheverry (1876).

Congress on Deaf—Instructors (1893). *Proceedings of the World's Congress of Instructors of the Deaf.* Washington, D.C.: American Annals of the Deaf, 1893.

Congress on Deaf—International—First (1878). *Compte-rendu . . . Congrès universel pour l'amélioration du sort des aveugles et des sourds-muets.* Paris: Imprimerie Nationale, 1879.

Congress on Deaf—International—Second (1880). *Compte-rendu . . . Congrès international pour l'amélioration du sort des sourds-muets.* Rome: Botta, 1881. (a)

————. Kinsey, A. (ed.). *Report of the Proceedings . . .* London: Allen, 1880. (b)

————. *Gli istituti e le scuole dei sordomuti in Italia. Risultati dell'inchiesta statistica ordinata dal comitato locale per Congresso internazionale dei maestri sordomuti.* Rome: Elzeviriana, 1880. (c)

Congress on Deaf—International—Third (1883). Van Schelle, L. (ed.). *Résumé analytique des travaux du troisième congrès international pour l'amélioration du sort des sourds-muets, tenu à Bruxelles du 13 au 18 août 1883 précédé d'un aperçu sur l'origine des congrès internationaux pour l'amélioration du sort des sourds-muets et des résolutions prises par les congrès de Paris et Milan.* Brussels: F. Hayez, 1883. (a)

————. *Compte-rendu . . . Congrès international pour l'amélioration du sort des sourds-muets.* Brussels: F. Hayez, 1883. (b)

Congress on Deaf—International—Fourth (1900). The Paris Congress [first circular]. *American Annals of the Deaf,* 1899, 470–472.

————. Ladreit de Lacharrière, L. (ed.). *Exposition universelle de 1900. Congrès international pour l'étude des questions d'éducation et d'assistance des sourds-muets tenu les 6, 7, et 8 août 1900, au Palais des Congrès de l'Exposition. Compte-rendu des travaux de la section des entendants.* Paris: Imprimerie d'Ouvriers Sourds-Muets, 1900. (a)

————. Gaillard, H., and Jeanvoine, H. (eds.). *Congrès international pour l'étude des questions d'éducation et d'assistance des sourds-muets (section des sourds-muets). Compte-rendu des débats et relations diverses.* Paris: Imprimerie d'Ouvriers Sourds-Muets, 1900. (b)

————. *Exposition universelle de 1900. Congrès international pour l'étude des questions d'éducation et d'assistance des sourds-muets, tenu à Paris du 6 au 8 août 1900. Relation des travaux de l'Educazione dei Sordomuti* [G.C. Ferreri, ed.], *traduit par J. Auffray . . . Suivi des procès verbaux sommaires par le Dr. Martha.* Asnières: Institut Départemental de Sourds-Muets et de Sourdes-Muettes, 1901. *Relation* reprinted: Martha, A., and Gaillard, H. Paris: Imprimerie nationale, 1901. (c)

————. Resolutions adopted by the hearing section of the Paris Congress of 1900. *American Annals of the Deaf,* 1901, *46,* 329–331. (d)

————. Resolutions adopted by the deaf section of the Paris Congress of 1900. *Association Review,* 1901, *3,* 43–50. (e)

————. Resolutions adopted by the deaf section of the Paris Congress of 1900. *American Annals of the Deaf,* 1901, *46,* 108–111. (f)

Congress on Deaf—International—Fifth (1905). *Compte-rendu . . . Congrès international pour l'amélioration du sort des sourds-muets.* Liège: Société de secours mutuels des sourds-muets de l'arrondissement de Liège, 1905.

Congress on Deaf—International—Sixth (1907). *International Conference on the Education of the Deaf, Proceedings.* Edinburgh: Darien Press, 1907.

Congress on Deaf—National—French (1879). Hugentobler, J. (ed.).. Compte-rendu du congrès de Lyon. *Revue internationale de l'enseignement des sourds-muets,* 1885, *1,* 188–195, 222–226.

Congress on Deaf—National—French (1881). *Congrès national pour l'amélioration du sort des sourds-muets.*

Congrès de Bordeaux tenu du 8 au 14 août 1881 . . . *Comptes-rendus analytiques des séances.* Bordeaux: Durand, 1882.

Congress on Deaf—National—French (1884). *Congrès national pour l'amélioration du sort des sourds-muets. Congrès de Paris tenu du 15 au 20 septembre 1884.* Paris: Avenue du Villiers 84, 1885.

Congress on Deaf—National—French (1885). *Troisième* [sic] *congrès national pour l'amélioration du sort des sourds-muets. Congrès de Paris tenu du 4 au 6 août 1885. Comptes-rendus analytiques des séances.* Paris: Ritti, 1886. (a)

————. Riom, L. (ed.). *Troisième* [sic] *Congrès national des instituteurs des sourds-muets tenu à Paris les 4, 5, 6 août 1885. Revue internationale de l'enseignement des sourds-muets,* 1885, *1,* 129–151. (b)

Connolly, E. E. The Horace Mann School yesterday, today and tomorrow. *Volta Review,* 1967, *69,* 138–146.

Connor, L. *Speech for the Deaf Child: Knowledge and Use.* Washington, D.C.: A.G. Bell Association, 1971.

Convention of American Instructors of the Deaf. *Proceedings.* Hartford [etc.]: 1850–.

————. The proposed union of the Convention and the Association. *American Annals of the Deaf,* 1893, *39,* 47–51.

————. [Obituaries of] Rev. Thomas Gallaudet, Philip Goode Gillet, Dr. Joseph C. Gordon. In: *Proceedings* (1906), 180–182.

Convention of Deaf Mutes. *Monument to Thomas H. Gallaudet. Proceedings. 23–24 February 1853.* Montpellier: Walton, 1853.

Copans, J., and Jamin, J. *Aux Origines de l'anthropologie française: les mémoires de la Société des Observateurs de l'Homme en l'an VIII.* Paris: Le Sycomore, 1978.

Cope, E. D. Letter to the Editor. *Science,* 1890, *16 (398),* 163.

Copenhagen Institution for Deaf Mutes. Jensen, O. C. (ed.). *Katalog Over Bibliotheket.* Copenhagen: [n.p.], 1910.

Cornié, A. *Etude sur l'Institution Nationale des Sourdes-Muettes de Bordeaux, 1786–1903.* Bordeaux: Pech, 1903.

Corone, A. Contribution à l'histoire de la sonde d'Itard. *Histoire de la Médecine,* 1960, *10,* 41–42.

Coste d'Arnobat, C. P. *Essai sur de prétendues découvertes nouvelles, dont la plupart sont agées de plusieurs siècles.* Paris: Patris, 1803.

Cox, T. F. The combined system and the oral method in their relation to the education of deaf-mutes. *American Annals of the Deaf,* 1910, *55,* 401–403.

Cresson, M. F. *Journey into Fame: The Life of Daniel Chester French.* Cambridge, Mass.: Harvard University Press, 1947.

Cretelle, [?]. *Plaidoyer . . . dans l'affaire du Sr. Cazeaux, étudiant en droit à l'Université de Toulouse, et de Joseph, soi-disant Comte de Solar.* Toulouse: Desclassan, 1780.

Critchley, M. *The Language of Gesture.* London: Arnold, 1939.

Crofut, F. *Guide to the History and Historical Sites of Connecticut.* New Haven: Yale, 1937.

Crouter, A.L.E. Instruction of the deaf. *Science,* 1891, *17 (423),* 141–142.

————. History of oral work in the Pennsylvania Institution. In: Alexander Graham Bell Association, *Proceedings* (1892), 273–284.

————. Statistics of articulation work in America. Convention of American Instructors of the Deaf, *Proceedings* (1893), 284–289.

————. La décadence des signes en Amérique. *Revue internationale de l'enseignement des sourds-muets,* 1894, *10,* 180.

————. Changes of method in the Pennsylvania Institution. *American Annals of the Deaf,* 1901, *46,* 62–68.

————. A visit to the Clarke School in 1875. *Association Review,* 1906, *8,* 194–198. (a)

————. The address of the president before the seventh summer meeting. *Association Review,* 1906, *8,* 301–317. Reprinted: *Association Review,* 1907, *9,* 110–126. Excerpted: *American Annals of the Deaf,* 1906, *51,* 320–327. (b)

————. Speech problems in combined system schools. In: Convention of American Instructors of the Deaf, *Proceedings* (1915), 111–120.

Cunningham, C. E. *Timothy Dwight.* New York: Macmillan, 1942.

Currier, E. H. A history of the New York Institution for the Instruction of the Deaf and Dumb. In: Fay, E. A. (1893).

————. *The History of Articulation Teaching in the New York Institution.* New York: New York Institution, 1894. Reprinted: Alexander Graham Bell Association, *Proceedings* [1894], 16–34.

————. *The Deaf: "By their fruits ye shall know them."* New York: New York Institution for the Instruction of the Deaf, 1912.

Curry, S. S. *Alexander Melville Bell (Some Memories). With fragments from a pupil's notebook.* Boston: School of Expression, 1906.

Curtis, J. H. *An Essay on the Deaf and Dumb.* London: Longman, 1829.

Cuxac, C. *L'Education des sourds en France depuis l'abbé de l'Epée.* Doctorat du troisième cycle, Université de Paris V, 1980. Revised: *Le Langage des Sourds.* Paris: Payot, 1983.

"D." The deaf and dumb. *Analectic Magazine,* 1820, *1,* 419–431.

Dalgarno, G. *Ars Signorum Vulgo Character Philosophica.* London: Hayes, 1661.

————. *Didascalocophus.* Oxford: 1680. Reprinted: *American Annals of the Deaf,* 1857, *9,* 14–64.

Danger, O. The mixed method and the pure oral method in Germany. *Association Review,* 1901, *3,* 411–417.

Daras (l'abbé). Les trois écoles. *Bienfaiteur des sourds-muets et des aveugles*, 1853, *1*, 43–53. (a)

———. L'Education des sourds-muets. France. Esquisse du progrès. *Bienfaiteur des sourds-muets et des aveugles*, 1853, *1*, 103–115. (b)

———. Mimique. *Bienfaiteur des sourds-muets et des aveugles*, 1853, *1*, 144–145. (c)

———. Coup d'oeil universel sur les origines de l'art [d'éducation des sourds-muets]. *Bienfaiteur des sourds-muets et des aveugles*, 1856, *4*, 6–15; 19–32.

Davenport, C. B. Biographical memoir of F.A.P. Barnard. *National Aacademy of Sciences Biographical Memoirs*, 1939, *20*, 259–272.

Davidson, S.G. Henry Winter Syle. *American Annals of the Deaf*, 1890, *35*, 71–75.

———. The orally taught deaf after graduation. In: Convention of America Instructors of the Deaf, Proceedings (1893), 180–185.

———. The relation of language to mental development and of speech to language teaching. *Association Review*, 1899, *1*, 129–139.

———. The comparison of methods. *American Annals of the Deaf*, 1901, *46*, 324–337.

———. The American oral method. *Association Review*, 1906, *8*, 95–100.

Day, G. E. On the late efforts in France and other parts of Europe to restore the deaf and dumb to hearing. *American Journal of Science and Arts*, 1836, *30*, 301–323.

———. *Report on the Institutions for the Deaf and Dumb in Central and Western Europe in the year 1844 to the Board of Directors of the New York Institution.* Albany: Carroll and Cook, 1845.

Day, G., and Peet, H. *Report of the Select Committee on Articulation, Dr. Peet's letter on Instructions to Dr. Day, and Dr. Day's Report on the Institutions for the Deaf and Dumb in Holland, with an account of a visit to a class of M. Dubois in Paris, and a statement of the results of teaching articulation in Great Britain.* In: New York Institution, Reports (1861), 55–93. Abridged: *American Annals of the Deaf*, 1861, *13*, 86–109.

Day, H. E., Fusfeld, I. S., and Pinter, R. (eds.). *A Survey of American Schools for the Deaf, 1924–1925.* Washington, D.C.: National Research Council, 1928.

Defoe, D. *The Life and Strange Surprising Adventures of Robinson Crusoe.* London: Taylor, 1719.

———. *Life and Adventures of Mr. Duncan Campbell.* London: Curll, 1720.

De Gérando, J. M. *Des signes et de l'art de penser.* Paris: Goujon, 1800. (a)

———. *Considérations sur les diverses méthodes à suivre dans l'observation des peuples sauvages.* Paris: Société des Observateurs de l'Homme, 1800. Reprinted: Copans, J., and Jamin, J. (eds.). *Aux origines de l'anthropologie française.* Paris: Le Sycomore, 1978. English translation: Moore, F.C.T. *The Observation of Savage People.* Berkeley: University of California Press, 1969. (b)

———. *De la génération des connaissances humaines.* Berlin: Decker, 1802.

———. *Le Visiteur du pauvre.* Paris: Calas, 1820. Revised: *De la bienfaisance publique.* Paris: J. Renouard, 1839. English translation: Peabody, E. *The Visitor of the Poor.* Boston: Hilliard, Gray, Little and Wilkins, 1832.

———. *De l'education des sourds-muets de naissance.* Paris: Mequignon, 1827.

———. Considérations sur le Sauvage de l'Aveyron: Ecrit posthume de M. de Gérando. *Annales de l'education des sourds-muets et des aveugles*, 1848, *5*, 110–114.

DeGering, E. *Gallaudet, Friend of the Deaf.* New York: McKay, 1964.

Dejean, M. La méthode orale pure. Est-elle applicable à tous les sourds-muets? *Revue générale de l'enseignement de sourds-muets*, 1899, *1*, 133–137.

DeLand, F. World benefactions of Alexander Graham Bell. *Association Review*, 1905, *7*, 167–171. (a)

———. The real romance of the telephone, or why deaf children need no longer be dumb. *Association Review*, 1905, *7*, 306–326, 389–399; 1906, *8*, 1–27, 120–135, 205–222, 329–344, 406–427; 1907, *9*, 324–335, 401–419, 505–520; 1908, *10*, 1–35, 233–239, 343–348, 449–454; 1909, *11*, 1–12. Reprinted: *Dumb No Longer; Romance of the Telephone.* Washington, D.C.: Volta Bureau, 1908.

———. Marriages of the deaf. *Volta Review*, 1912, *14*, 186–189. (a)

———. Tribute to Mr. Henry Lippitt. *Volta Review*, 1912, *14*, 516–522. (b)

———. Volta Bureau. *Volta Review*, 1913, *14*, 605–621.

———. An early use of the Melville Bell symbols with the deaf. *Volta Review*, 1915, *17*, 487–489.

———. The speech method? Or Sicard's method? *Volta Review*, 1916, *18*, 113–114.

———. The abbé de l'Epée. *Volta Review*, 1917, *19*, 40–45.

———. Is the combined method a social and economic menace? *Volta Review*, 1918, *20*, 412.

———. Working in behalf of deaf children (Or how, when, and why the American Association to Promote the Teaching of Speech to the Deaf was organized). *Volta Review*, 1919, *21*, 523–530, 581–585, 663–669, 701–702.

———. Pedro Ponce De León (born 1520). Juan Pablo Bonet (author, 1620). *Volta Review*, 1920, *22*, 391–421.

———. An ever-continuing memorial. *Volta Review*, 1922, *24*, 351–363, 413–422, 465–471; *25*, 34–39, 90–99, 145–152, 190–197. (a)

———. Address at the New Home School for Little Deaf Children, Kensington, Md., 1922. Reprinted: *Volta Review*, 1972, *74*, 145–149. (b)

———. The telephone, the radiophone, the graphophone, the music record, and modern lip-reading. *Volta Review*, 1924, *26*, 251–253.

———. Alexander Graham Bell's benefactions to aid the hard-of-hearing adult. *Volta Review*, 1928, *30*, 440–442.

————. *The Story of Lip-Reading.* Washington, D.C.: Alexander Graham Bell Association, 1931. Revised edition: 1968.

Deleau, N. Première [2ème, 3ème] lettres. *Journal de l'instruction des sourds-muets et des aveugles,* 1826, *1,* 222–231; 263–276; 276–297.

————. *Assertions de M. Itard sur le traitement des sourds-muets.* Paris: Fournier, 1828.

————. *Exposé d'une nouvelle dactylologie alphabétique et syllabique.* Cambrai: Hurez, 1830.

Deltour, F. L'Institution Nationale des Sourds-Muets de Paris. *Revue des deux mondes,* 1892, *111,* 174–207.

Deming, [?]. Remarks [at the completion of the Gallaudet monument]. In: Rae (1854).

De Minimis [pseud.]. Précautions contre les signes. *Revue internationale de l'enseignement des sourds-muets,* 1885–86, *1,* 91–93.

Denis, T. *Les Institutions nationales des sourds-muets et le Ministre de l'Intérieur.* Paris: Berger-Levrault, 1882.

————. *L'Enseignement de la parole aux sourds-muets.* Paris: Berger-Levrault, 1886.

————. Etude sur les débuts, les progrès et le couronnement de l'oeuvre de l'abbé de l'Epée. In: Bélanger (1886).

————. The first instructor of the deaf in France. *American Annals of the Deaf,* 1887, *32,* 113–118. (a)

————. *Les Conseils généraux et les institutions de sourds-muets.* Paris: Berger-Levrault, 1887. (b)

————. Causerie, l'abbé Balestra. *Revue française de l'éducation des sourds-muets,* 1887, *3,* 5–12, 29–36, 77–82, 101–105. (c)

————. L'Instituteur du Prince de Carignan. *Revue française de l'éducation des Sourds-Muets,* 1887, *3,* 197–204. (d)

————. L'Abbé Masse. Successeur immédiat de l'abbé de l'Epée. *Revue française de l'éducation des sourds-muets,* 1895, *10,* 244–252, 263–266. (a)

————. Ferdinand Berthier, homme de lettres. In: Denis, T. *Etudes variées concernant les sourds-muets.* Paris: Imprimerie de la Revue Française, 1895. Pp. 43–48. (b)

————. *Notice sur l'Institution Nationale de Sourds-Muets de Paris depuis son origine jusqu'à nos jours (1760–1896).* Paris: Typographie de l'Institution Nationale, 1896.

————. *Catalogue sommaire du musée universel des sourds-muets.* Paris: Imprimerie de l'Institution Nationale, 1897.

Denison, J. The memory of Laurent Clerc. *American Annals of the Deaf,* 1874, *19,* 238–244.

————. Impressions of the Milan Convention. *American Annals of the Deaf,* 1881, *26,* 41–50.

Derby, I. *The History of the First School of Deaf-Mutes of America.* South Weymouth: Derby, 1883.

Deschamps, C. F. *Lettre à M. De S———, capitaine de cavalerie, sur l'institution des sourds et muets.* London and Paris: J. Valade, 1777.

————. *Cours élémentaire d'éducation des sourds et muets.* Paris: Debure, 1779.

————. *Lettre à M. de Bellisle . . . pour servir de réponse aux Observations d'un sourd et muet sur "Un Cours élémentaire d'éducation des sourds et muets."* [n.p.l.]: [author?], 1780.

————. *De la manière de suppléer aux oreilles par les yeux, pour servir de suite au "Cours élémentaire d'éducation des sourds-muets."* Paris: Debure, 1783.

Desclapières, L. Une visite aux sourds-muets parlants. *Le Figaro,* 15 Aug. 1883.

Desessarts, N. *Causes célèbres et intéressantes de toutes les cours souveraines du royaume, avec les jugements qui les ont décidées.* Paris: Simon, 1773.

Desloges, P. *Observations d'un sourd et muet sur "Un Cours élémentaire d'éducation des sourds et muets," publié en 1779 par M. l'abbé Deschamps.* Amsterdam and Paris: B. Morin, 1779. English translation: Philip (1984). (a)

————. Lettre à M. le Marquis de Condorcet. *Mercure de France,* 18 Dec. 1779. (b)

————. Lettre à M. Bellisle . . . en réponse à celle que lui a écrite à M. l'abbé Deschamps au sujet des observations de M. Desloges. *Journal encyclopédique,* 1780, *6,* 125–132.

Destutt de Tracy, A.L.C. Mémoire sur la faculté de penser. *Mémoires de l'Institut National des Sciences et Arts pour l'an IV de la République. Sciences Morales et Politiques.* Paris: Baudouin, 1798. Vol. 1, pp. 283–450.

————. *Elémens d'idéologie. Seconde Partie: Grammaire.* Paris: Courcier, 1803.

Dexter, F.B. *Biographical Sketches of the Graduates of Yale College with Annals of the College History.* New York: Holt, 1911.

————. *Student Life at Yale College under the First President Dwight (1795–1817).* Worcester: The Society, 1918.

Dicarlo, L.M. Much ado about the obvious. *Volta Review,* 1966, *68,* 269–273.

Dickens, C. *American Notes.* London: Chapman and Hall, 1898.

Didaskalos [pseud.]. Schools for the deaf and dumb. *The Nation,* 1867, *4,* 339–340.

Diderot, D. Lettre sur les sourds et muets [1751]. In: *Oeuvres complètes.* Paris: Garnier, 1875. Vol. 1, pp. 349–428. Reprinted: *Diderot Studies,* 1965, *7.*

————. *Encyclopédie ou dictionnaire raisonné des sciences, arts et métiers.* Neuchâtel: Faulche, 1765. Surdité: Vol. 15, pp. 686–687.

Digby, K. *Two treatises: in the one of which the Nature of Bodies, in the other, the Nature of Man's soul, is looked into: in a way of discovery of the Immortality of Reasonable Souls.* Paris: Blaizot, 1644.

Dillingham, N. Letter to Mason Fitch Cogswell, 26 Aug. 1816, from Lexington. Cogswell Papers, Yale University.

Dix, J. Extracts from the report of the Superintendent of Common Schools, on the education of the deaf and dumb. In: New York Institution for the Instruction of the Deaf and Dumb, Reports (1836), 68–71.

Dobyns, J.R. Deaf-Mutes as teachers. In: Convention of American Instructors of the Deaf, Proceedings (1893), 78–80.

Doctor, P.V. A brief history of the education of the deaf in the U.S. Unpublished manuscript, E. M. Gallaudet Library, Washington, D.C., 19[?].

———. Biographical sources on the teaching of speech to the deaf in the United States, 1815–1868. Unpublished manuscript, E. M. Gallaudet Library, Washington, D.C., 195[?].

———. Thirty-second meeting of the Convention of American Instructors of the Deaf. *American Annals of the Deaf*, 1941, *46*, 299–349.

———. *Amos Kendall.* A paper read at the Palaver Club in Washington D.C. Unpublished manuscript, E. M. Gallaudet Library, Washington, D.C., 1949.

———. *Amos Kendall, Nineteenth-Century Humanitarian.* Washington, D.C.: Gallaudet College, 1957.

———. A guide to literature in journals, proceedings, indexes and abstracts on the education and welfare of the deaf. *American Annals of the Deaf*, 1951, *96*, 432–446.

———. *A Deaf Boy Grows Up in the U.S.A.* Washington, D.C.: Gallaudet College, 1958.

———. *The History of the Conference of Executives of American Schools for the Deaf, 1868–1968.* Washington, D.C.: [n.p.], 1968.

Domich, H. *John Carlin. A Biographical Sketch.* Washington, D.C.: Gallaudet College Press, 1939.

Dooey, M. H. Famous visitors and distinguished guests of Hartford, 1645–1936. M.A. Thesis, Trinity College, 1938.

Douard, F. A propos de l'article rédigé par M. Franck qu'a publié la *Revue française des sourds-muets. Défense des sourds-muets*, 1886, *2*, 94–95.

———. A propos de l'affaire Dreyfus. *Journal des sourds-muets*. 1899, *5*, 332–333.

Dougherty, G. T. Opening address. In: National Association of the Deaf, Proceedings (1893), 14–20.

Downs, R. P. *Horace Mann: Champion of Public Schools.* New York: Twayne, 1974.

———. *Henry Barnard.* Boston: Twayne, 1977.

Doyle, T. S. The Virginia Institution for the Education of the Deaf and Dumb (and of the Blind). In: Fay, E. A. (1893).

Drake, H. D. The deaf teacher of the deaf. *American Annals of the Deaf*, 1940, *85*, 148–152.

Draper, A. G. The silent college at Washington. *Scribner's Monthly*, 1872, *3*, 727–733.

———. *Sophia Gallaudet. American Annals of the Deaf*, 1877, *22*, 170–183. Reprinted: Pamphlet, Gallaudet Papers, Library of Congress, 1877.

———. Dr. Bell's "Memoir" and criticisms upon it. *American Annals of the Deaf*, 1888, *33*, 37–43.

———. *Report of Professor Draper on the International Congress of Deaf-Mutes at Paris* [1889]. Washington, D.C.: Government Printing Office, 1890. (a)

———. Notes on the meeting of the deaf at Paris [1889.] *American Annals of the Deaf*, 1890, *35*, 30–33. (b)

———. Some results of College work. In: Columbian Institution for the Deaf and Dumb, Reports (1890), 12–17. (c)

———. The attitude of the adult deaf towards pure oralism. *American Annals of the Deaf*, 1895, *40*, 44–54.

———. The future of the deaf in America. In: National Association of the Deaf, Proceedings (1896), 15–22.

———. Oral work by deaf teachers—manual work by oral teachers. In: Convention of American Instructors of the Deaf, Proceedings (1899), 122–128.

———. *History of the College. Alumni Association of Gallaudet College Minutes and Proceedings, Meetings 1889–1899.* Grinell: Waring, 1900.

———. The deaf section of the Paris Congress of 1900. *American Annals of the Deaf*, 1901, *46*, 218–223.

———. Thomas Gallaudet. *American Annals of the Deaf*, 1902, *47*, 393–403.

———. The education of the deaf in America. In: National Association of the Deaf, Proceedings (1904), 22–38.

Driggs, F. M. Progress in the education of the deaf. In: Convention of American Instructors of the Deaf, Proceedings, (1930), 6–10.

Drouot, E. The Binet investigation of the oral method. *American Annals of the Deaf*, 1910, *55*, 307–324.

———. Historique de l'enseignement de la parole aux sourds-muets en France. *Bulletin international de l'enseignement des sourds-muets*, 1911, *2*, 153–180.

Dubief, E. *L'Abbé de l'Epée et l'éducation des sourds-muets.* Paris: Cerf, 1891.

Dublar, L. J. *Mutisme sténographique . . . et réfutation du système actuel des signes et de la mimographie de l'abbé de l'Epée.* Paris: Delaunay, 1835.

Dubois, B. *Dactyologie, ou art de converser au moyen des doigts, par l'abbé de l'Epée . . . suivi de notes explicatives.* Paris: author, 1867.

———. 176ème anniversaire de la naissance de l'abbé de l'Epée. Comptes-rendus des banquets consacrés à le célébrer. *Journal des sourds-muets*, 1888, *1*, 131–144; *2*, 3–15.

———. A propos du sourd-muet Joseph, dit le comte de Solar [et] de Napoléon Ier. *Revue internationale de l'enseignement des sourds-muets*, 1894, *9*, 235–237.

Dubranle, A. Mort de l'abbé J. Tarra. *Revue internationale*, 1889, *5*, 97–100.

Dubranle, A., and Dupont, M. *Esquisse historique et court exposé de la méthode suivie pour l'instruction des sourds-muets par l'abbé Tarra.* Paris: Delgrave, 1883.

Du Camp, M. L'Enseignement exceptionnel: l'institution des sourds-muets. *Revue des deux mondes*, 2ème période, 1873, 55–77. Reprinted: *Paris, ses organes, ses fonctions, sa vie dans la seconde moitié du 19ème siècle.* Paris: Hachette, 1869–1875. Vol. 5, ch. 26. English translation: The National Institution for the Deaf and Dumb at Paris. *American Annals of the Deaf*, 1877, *22*, 1–19, 74–80.

Dudesert, P. D. *Mémoires sur l'éducation des sourds-muets.* Caen: 1827.

Dudley, D.C. The sign language: its use and abuse in the school-room. In: Convention of American Instructors of the Deaf, Proceedings (1893), 66–70.

Dufau, P.A. Epée. In: *Dictionnaire de la conversation et de la lecture.* Paris: Berlin Mandar, 1838. Pp. 453–456.

Dufo de Germane. Encore le Dictionnaire Larousse. *Revue internationale de l'enseignement des sourds-muets*, 1890, *6*, 100–102.

Dunbar, M.W. On the language of signs among certain North American Indians. *American Philosophical Transactions*, 1804, *6*, 1–8.

Dunglison, R. *A New Dictionary of Medical Science and Literature* . . . Boston: Charles-Bowen, 1833.

Dupont, M. *La Voix du sourd.* Paris: Plon, 1882.

——. *La Lecture des lèvres, palliatif de la surdité.* Paris: V. Goupy et Jourdan, 1884.

—— (ed.). See: Kilian (1885).

——. *Communications faites au congrès de Paris.* Geneva: Taponnier and Studer, 1885. (a)

——. *L'Institution Nationale des Sourds-Muets au congrès de Paris, Septembre 1884.* Paris: G. Pelluard, 1885. (b)

——. *L'Enseignement de la parole à l'Institution Nationale des Sourds-Muets de Paris.* Paris: Carré, 1897.

——. *Ministère de l'Intérieur. Institution Nationale des Sourds-Muets de Paris. L'Enseignement auriculaire. Rapports.* Paris: Plon, Nourrit, 1889.

——. La question des méthodes. *Revue générale de l'enseignement des sourds-muets*, 1900, *2*, 6–13.

Duport, L.F. *Loi relative à M. l'abbé de l'Epée et à son établissement en faveur des sourds-muets. Donnée à Paris le 29 juillet 1791.* Paris: Imprimerie Royale, 1791.

Dutton, S.W.S. "The Lost Senses" by John Kitto. *North British Review*, 1847, *6*, 331–364.

——. Rev. T. H. Gallaudet and deaf-mute instruction. *New Englander*, 1852, *10*, 415–432.

Duvignau, R. *A propos de sourds-muets. Considérations historiques sur l'éducation et l'instruction préparatoires du jeune sourd-muet.* Paris: Schanck, 1897.

——. Quelques vues sur la méthode. *Revue générale des sourds-muets*, 1899, *1*, 189–195.

Duyckinck, E. A., and Duyckinck, G. L. *Encyclopedia of American Literature.* New York: Scribner, 1856.

Dwight, T. (1752–1817). *Dwight's Travels in New England and New York.* New Haven: T. Dwight, 1821. Reprinted: Knowles, K. (ed.). *Travels in New England: based on Timothy Dwight's Travels in New England and New York.* Barre: Crown, 1977. Reprinted: Solomon, B. M. (ed.). Cambridge Mass.: Harvard, 1969.

——. *Memoirs.* Glasgow: Chalmers and Collins, 1822.

Dwight, T. (1828–1896). Mrs. Sigourney. *New Englander*, 1866, *25*, 330–358.

D'Yvoi, P. La mimique considérée comme une langue universelle. *L'Impartial*, 1859, *4*, 16–25.

Eastman, G. *Sign Me Alice.* Washington, D.C.: Gallaudet College, 1974.

Edinburgh Institution. *Report of the Institution for the Support and Education of Deaf and Dumb Children.* Edinburgh: [n.p.], 1817.

——. Report. *Christian Observer*, 1819, *18*, 259–260.

——. *An Historical Sketch of the Rise and Present State of the Edinburgh Deaf and Dumb Institution.* Edinburgh: Shaw, 1835.

Elie de Beaumont, J.B.J. *Mémoire et réponse à M. l'abbé de l'Epée pour le Sieur Cazeaux, accusé d'avoir supprimé la personne et l'état du Comte de Solar.* Paris: Cellot, 1779. (a)

——. *Réponse de M. Elie de Beaumont aux lettres de M. l'abbé de l'Epée.* Paris: Jorry, 1779. (b)

——. *Vue générale de l'affaire du soi-disant Comte de Solar.* Paris: Demonville, 1780.

Elliott, M. H., and Hall, F. H. *Laura Bridgman.* Boston: Little Brown, 1903.

Elliott, R. Speech for the deaf. *American Annals of the Deaf*, 1869, *14*, 129–145.

——. The Milan Congress and the future of the education of the deaf and dumb. *American Annals of the Deaf*, 1882, *27*, 146–158.

——. The proper adjustment of methods in the education of the deaf. In: Convention of American Instructors of the Deaf, Proceedings (1893), 98–102.

——. Reminiscences of a retired educator. *Volta Review*, 1911, *13*, 240–244, 303–306, 358–361, 416–419, 478–482, 534–536.

Ely, A. W. Education of the deaf and dumb in Europe and America. *Debows Review*, 1854, *17*, 435–451.

Ely, E. S. *A contrast between Calvinism and Hopkinsianism.* New York: Whiting, 1811.

England, J. *Of Educating the Deaf and Dumb.* Montrose: Smith, 1819.

Englesman, B. Deaf-mutism: its pathology, causes and treatment. *Medical Record*, 1888, *34*, 534.

——. Deaf mutes and their instruction. *Science*, 1890, *16 (402)*, 218–221. (a)

——. The education of the deaf. *Science*, 1890, *16 (409)*, 317. (b)

————. The education of the deaf. *Science*, 1891, *17 (416)*, 51.

Epée, C. M. (abbé de l'). *Exercice de sourds et muets qui se fera le jeudi 2 juillet 1772, chez M. l'abbé de l'Epée, rue des Moulins, Butte St.-Roch, depuis trois heures jusqu'à sept*. Paris: L. Cellot, 1772.

————. *Exercice de sourds et muets, qui se fera le 6 août 1773, chez M. l'abbé de l'Epée*. Paris: Grangé, 1773.

————. *Institution des sourds et muets ou recueil des exercices soutenus par les sourds et muets pendant les années 1771, 1772, 1773, 1774 . . .* Paris: Butard, 1774. Reprinted: Epée (1776).

————. *Institution des Sourds-Muets par la voie des signes méthodiques*. Paris: Nyon, 1776. Revised: Epée (1784). English translation (excerpts): *American Annals of the Deaf*, 1861, *13*, 8–29.

————. *La véritable manière d'instruire les sourds-muets, confirmée par une longue expérience*. Paris: Nyon, 1784. Reprinted: Epée (1788); (Part II): *L'Art d'enseigner à parler aux sourds-muets de naissance*, Sicard (1820); English translations: Arrowsmith (1819); Green, F. (transl.), *The Method of Educating the Deaf and Dumb Confirmed by Long Experience*. London: Cooke, 1801. Reprinted: (Parts I and II) *American Annals of the Deaf*, 1860, *12*, 1–132; Philip (1984; abridged).

————. Lettre de l'instituteur des sourds et muets de Paris à MM. de l'Académie de Berlin, et lettre du même à M. Nicolay savant critique de Berlin. *Journal de Paris*, 1785, *147*, 27 May, 604–605.

————. Muets et sourds. In: *Encyclopédie méthodique des arts et métiers*. Paris: Panckoucke, 1788. Pp. 275–313.

————. Histoire abrégée de tout ce qui concerne le jeune Solar. *Bulletin de la Société Centrale d'Education et d'Assistance pour les Sourds-Muets en France*, 1876, *3*, 84–88.

————. *Dictionnaire des sourds-muets, publié d'après le manuscrit original et précédé d'une préface par le Dr. J.A.A. Rattel*. Paris: Baillière, 1896.

Escoffon, A. *L'Abbé de l'Epée* Paris: Tolra and Simonet, 1899.

Esquiros, A. Les Sourds-Muets. In: *Paris au XIX siècle*. Paris: Imprimerie Unis, 1847. Vol. 2, pp. 391–492.

Etcheverry, M. Copie d'un manuscrit de l'abbé de l'Epée. See: Epée, C. M. (1876).

————. *Les Sourds-Muets en France et en Allemagne*. Paris: Delgrave, 1876. (a)

————. Histoire d'un tableau. *Bulletin de la Société Centrale d'Education et d'Assistance pour les Sourds-Muets en France*, 1876, *3*, 13–22, 25–31. (b)

————. *Statue de l'abbé de l'Epée, oeuvre de Félix Martin. Compte-Rendu de la séance d'inauguration. Notice biographique, documents divers*. See: le Père, E. C. P. (1879).

Eude, J.F. *Rapport du procès Solar, fait le 5 juin 1792 et jours suivants . . . sur l'appel de la sentence définitive rendue au Chatelet de Paris le 8 juin, 1781*. Paris: 1799.

Facchini, M. [Historical reflections on the oral method and sign language in Italy.] In: Volterra, V. (ed.). *I Segni Come Parole*. Turin: Boringieri, 1981.

Facchini, M., and Rimondini, P. [Encounters and collisions between otologists and deaf educators in the 1800s.] Unpublished paper, Conference on Nonverbal Communication, C.N.R., Rome, 1981.

Fairchild, D. Alexander Graham Bell: Some characters of his greatness. *Journal of Heredity*, 1923, *13*, 195–199.

————. *The World Was My Garden*. New York: Scribner, 1938.

Farrar, A. Introduction. In: Bonet, J.P. *Simplification of the Letters of the Alphabet . . . Translated from the original Spanish by H. N. Dixon*. Harrogate: A. Farrar, 1890.

————. A sixteenth-century treatise. *American Annals of the Deaf*, 1892, *37*, 195–205.

————. *Arnold on the Education of the Deaf: A Manual for Teachers. Revised and rewritten by A. Farrar*. London: National College of Teachers of the Deaf, 1923.

Fauchet, C. *Oraison funèbre de Charles-Michel de L'Epée*. Paris: Lottin, 1790.

Fauth, B. L., and Fauth, W. W. A study of the proceedings of the Convention of American Instructors of the Deaf. *American Annals of the Deaf*, 1950, *95*, 280–314.

Fay, A.C. The teaching of speech in the Hartford School. In: Alexander Graham Bell Association, Proceedings (1894), 1–11.

Fay, E.A. Memorial of Harvey Prindle Peet. *American Annals of the Deaf*, 1873, *18*, 69–121.

————. Visible speech. *American Annals of the Deaf*, 1874, *19*, 176–182.

————. Consanguineous marriages as a cause of deaf-mutism. *American Annals of the Deaf*, 1876, *21*, 204–218.

————. The Braidwood family. *American Annals of the Deaf*, 1878, *23*, 64–65.

————. Miscellaneous. *American Annals of the Deaf*, 1879, 24, 56–57. (a)

————. Works relating to the deaf and dumb in the libraries of American institutions for the deaf and dumb. *American Annals of the Deaf*, 1879, *24*, 133–178. (b)

————. The Lyons convention. *American Annals of the Deaf*, 1880, *25*, 101–102. (a)

————. Miscellaneous. *American Annals of the Deaf*, 1880, *25*, 293–295. (b)

————. Notices of publications. *American Annals of the Deaf*, 1881, *26*, 75–76. (a)

————. [E. Pereire and the Frères Saint-Gabriel.] *American Annals of the Deaf*, 1881, *26*, 163–164. (b)

————. A protest. *American Annals of the Deaf*, 1881, *26*, 138–139. (c)

————. Notices of publications. *American Annals of the Deaf*, 1881, *26*, 192–193. (d)

————. Discussion by the American Academy of Sciences concerning the formation of a deaf variety of the human race. *American Annals of the Deaf*, 1884, *29*, 70–77.

————. Notices of publications: Bell, Alexander Graham. "Memoir upon the Formation of a Deaf Variety of the Human Race." *American Annals of the Deaf*, 1885, *30*, 155–162.

————. Deaf-Mutes. In: Buck, A. H. (ed.). *Reference Handbook of the Medical Sciences*. New York: William Wood, 1886. Pp. 363–386. Reprinted: *American Annals of the Deaf*, 1888, *33*, 199–216, 241–259.

————. President Gallaudet's mission to England. *American Annals of the Deaf*, 1887, *32*, 20–31.

————. The education of the deaf and dumb. *New Castle Daily Journal*, 10 Dec. 1889.

————. The instruction of the deaf. *Science*, 1891, *17 (421)*, 122.

————. Abusive language by signs. *American Annals of the Deaf*, 1892, *37*, 311–312.

————. School statistics of the deaf. In: Convention of American Instructors of the Deaf, Proceedings (1893), 269–283.

————. *Histories of American Schools for the Deaf, 1817–1893*. Washington, D.C.: Volta Bureau, 1893.

————. An inquiry concerning the results of marriages of the deaf in America. *American Annals of the Deaf*, 1897, *42*, 96–107. (a)

————. Bibliography of marriages of the deaf. *American Annals of the Deaf*, 1897, *42*, 237–256. (b)

————. *Marriages of the Deaf in America*. Washington, D.C.: Volta Bureau, 1898.

————. Miscellaneous. [Some criticisms of Bell's "Methods of instructing the deaf in the United States."] *American Annals of the Deaf*, 1899, *44*, 132–134.

————. Our international congress. *American Annals of the Deaf*, 1900, *45*, 324–328. (a)

————. The Paris congress of 1900. *American Annals of the Deaf*, 1900, *45*, 404–416. (b)

————. How can the term "charitable" be applied to the education of any children? National Educational Association, Proceedings (1903), 1007–1013.

————. President Gallaudet's retirement. *Volta Review*, 1910, *12*, 194–198.

————. What did Lucretius say? *American Annals of the Deaf*, 1912, *57*, 213–214.

————. Progress in the education of the deaf. In: U.S. Bureau of Education, *Report*. Washington, D.C.: Government Printing Office, 1913. Vol. 1, pp. 453–469. Reprinted: Washington, D.C.: Government Printing Office, 1914. (a)

————. Letters of Thomas Hopkins Gallaudet and Alice Cogswell. *American Annals of the Deaf*, 1913, *58*, 227–235. (b)

————. Progress in the education of the deaf. *Volta Review*, 1916, *18*, 71–76. (a)

————. Miscellaneous. Marriages of the deaf. *American Annals of the Deaf*, 1916, *61*, 283–284. (b)

————. The centennial of the American School at Hartford. *American Annals of the Deaf*, 1917, *62*, 370–382. (a)

————. Notices of publications: Bell, A. G. "Graphical Studies of Marriages of the Deaf." *American Annals of the Deaf*, 1917, *62*, 473–483. (b)

Fay, G.O. The methods of deaf-mute education. *American Annals of the Deaf*, 1873, *18*, 13–22.

————. The Ohio Institution for the Education of the Deaf and Dumb since 1853. *American Annals of the Deaf*, 1877, *22*, 167–170.

————. The sign language: the basis of instruction for deaf-mutes. *American Annals of the Deaf*, 1882, *27*, 208–211.

————. The education and care of the deaf. In: National Conference of Charities and Correction, Proceedings (1886), 215.

————. The relation of Hartford to the education of the deaf. *American Annals of the Deaf*, 1899, *44*, 419–435.

Fellendorf, G. W. 75 years of excitement. *Volta Review*, 1976, *78*, 100–103.

————. *Bibliography on Deafness: Volta Review, 1899–1976; American Annals of the Deaf, 1874–1976*. Revised edition. Washington, D.C.: Alexander Graham Bell Association for the Deaf, 1977.

Fenner, M.S., and Fishburn, E.C. *Pioneer American Educators*. Washington, D.C.: Horace Mann Fund, N.E.A., 1944, 1968.

Ferlus, [?]. Epitre à M. L'abbé Sicard. *Journal encyclopédique ou universel*, 1789, *2*, 103–110.

Ferreri, G. C. See: Congress on Deaf—International—Fourth (1900c).

————. The oral method: its fitness for the deaf. *Association Review*, 1902, *4*, 344–353. (a)

————. Another word about the battle of methods. *American Annals of the Deaf*, 1902, *47*, 30–44. (b)

————. The congresses of the deaf held at Liège, Belgium, 1905. *Association Review*, 1906, *8*, 59–63.

————. The American institutions for the education of the deaf. Chapter XIV. Hellen Keller. *Association Review*, 1907, *9*, 521–532.

————. *The American Institutions for the Education of the Deaf*. Philadelphia: Pennsylvania Institution, 1908.

————. Mistaken investigations concerning the value of the oral method. *American Annals of the Deaf*, 1910, *55*, 34–38.

Feyjóo y Montenegro, B. [On the invention of the art of teaching speech to mutes.] In: *Teatro critico universal*. Madrid: Mojados, 1730. Fifth edition: Madrid, 1923. Vol. 4, pp. 417–419. French translation: Coste d'Arnobat (1803), 26–32.

————. *Cartas eruditas y curiosas*. Madrid: 1753.

Field, K. *The History of Bell's Telephone*. London: Electric Telephone Company, 1878.

Figuier, L. G. Méthode à la portée des instituteurs primaires pour enseigner aux sourds-muets la langue française sans l'intermédiaire du langage des signes. In: Figuier, L. *L'Année Scientifique*. Paris: Hachette, 1858. Pp. 258–263.

———. Du danger des mariages consanguins. In: Figuier, L. *L'Année Scientifique*. Paris: Hachette, 1863. Pp. 338–344.

———. L'Education des sourds-muets (méthode Houdin). In: Figuier, L. *L'Année Scientifique*. Paris: Hachette, 1865. Pp. 408–410.

Fitzgerald, E. M. *Signs and Pure Oralism*. Circular of information no. 3. Silver Spring: National Association of the Deaf, [n.d.].

Fleischer, L. Sign language bibliography. Unpublished manuscript, California State University at Northridge, 1978.

Florinsky, M. T. *Russia: A History and an Interpretation*. New York: Macmillan, 1967.

Flournoy, J. J., et al. Scheme for a commonwealth of the deaf and dumb. *American Annals of the Deaf*, 1856, *8*, 118–125; 1858, *10*, 40–45, 72–90.

Fontanes, [?]. "Cours d'instruction d'un sourd-muet" par R. A. Sicard. *Spectateur du Nord (Hambourg)*, 1800, *13*, 178–184.

[Fontenay, L.A. de]. *Antilogie et fragments philosophiques ou collection . . .* Paris: Vincent, 1774.

Forestier, C. [Les Sourds-muets et la loi.] *L'Ami des sourds-muets*, 1838, *1*, 123–124. (a)

———. Correspondance. [Aveugles et sourds-muets comparés.] *L'Ami des sourds-muets*, 1838, *1*, 150–155. (b)

———. *Cours complet*. Paris: Hachette, 1854.

———. *Lettre á M. le Ministre de L'Intérieur au sujet du Rapport du M. Claveau, Inspecteur Général des Etablissements de Bienfaisance, sur l'enseignement de la parole dans les institutions des sourds-muets*. Lyon: Pitrat, 1880.

———. *Parallèle entre l'instruction des sourds-muets par le langage des signes et leur enseignement par l'articulation artificielle, suivi de quelques observations sur la méthode du célèbre Pereire et sur les résolutions qu'a votées contre l'enseignement par le langage des signes le congrès international tenu à Milan du 6 au 12 septembre 1880*. Lyon: Pitrat, 1883.

Fornari, P. American institutions for the deaf. *Association Review*, 1904, *6*, 1–8.

Fosdick, C. P. A short history of the Kentucky School for the Deaf. In Fay, E. A. (1893).

———. *A Centennial History of the Kentucky School for the Deaf*. Danville: Kentucky Standard, 1923.

Foster, J. History of the Pennsylvania Institution. *American Annals of the Deaf*, 1876, *21*, 171–178.

Fournier, E. *Physiologie et instruction du sourd-muet*. Paris: Delahaye, 1868.

———. *Histoire de la Butte des Moulins*. Paris: Henry et Lepin, 1877.

Fournier des Ormes. Le Comte de Solar. *Revue de Paris*, 1851, *12*, 181–244.

Fowler, C. C. *History of the Fowlers*. Batavia: 1950.

Fowler, C. W. *History of the Weld family*. Middletown: Pelton and King, 1879.

Fowler, S. Letter to T. H. Gallaudet, 3 April 1818. Gallaudet College Archives, Washington, D.C., 1818.

Fox, M. A. La Haute Education des sourds-muets aux Etats-Unis d'Amérique. In: Congress on Deaf—International—Fourth (1900), 371–377.

Fox, T. F. The social status of the deaf in the United States. In: National Association of the Deaf, Proceedings (1904), 132–139. Reprinted: *American Annals of the Deaf*, 1904, *49*, 369–378.

———. The New York Institution for the Deaf. *Fanwood Journal*, 1932, *1*, (2) 1–2; (3) 1–2; (4) 1–2; (5) 1–2; (6) 1–3; 1933, *1*, (7) 1–2; (8) 1–3; (9) 1–2; (10) 1–3; (11) 1–3; (12) 1–5; (13) 1–6, 19–24.

———. Summary of the education of the deaf. *Fanwood Journal*, 1933, *1*, (10) 13–14; (11) 13–14; (12) 5–6; 1934, *2*, (1) 9–11; (2) 4–5; (3) 3–4; (4) 6–7; (5) 5–6; (11) 5–6; (12) 5–6; 1935, *3*, (1) 10–12; (2) 9–10; (3) 3–5; (4) 4–5; (5) 1–9.

Francis, J. M. The difficulties of a beginner in a sign language. In: Convention of American Instructors of the Deaf, Proceedings (1859), 101–120.

Franck, A. *Rapport à S.E.M. le Ministre par une commission de l'Institut*. Paris: [n.p.], 1861. Reprinted: *Revue européenne*, 1861, 15 July, 257–294.

———. Conférence au théâtre de la Porte Saint-Martin sur l'abbé de l'Epée. See: Le Père, E.C.P. (1879), 29–39.

———. *Rapport au Ministre de L'Intérieur sur le congrès international réunie à Milan du 6 au 12 septembre* [1880] *pour l'amélioration du sort des sourds-muets . . .* Paris: Wittersheim, 1880.

———. La parole du sourd-muet. *Revue française des sourds-muets*, 1886, *2*, 56–59.

Frank, J. *Reise nach Paris, London, und einem grossen Theile des übrigen Englands und Schottlands in Beziehung auf Spitäler, Versorgungshäuser, übrige Armen-Institute, medizinishe Lehrenstalten und Gefängnisse*. Vienna: Camesianische Buchhandlung, 1804.

Fraser, G. R. *The Causes of Profound Deafness in Childhood*. Baltimore: Johns Hopkins University Press, 1976.

Frishberg, N. Arbitrariness and iconicity: historical change in American Sign Language. *Language*, 1975, *51*, 696–719.

Fuller, S. How Helen Keller was taught to speak. In Alexander Graham Bell Association, Proceedings, (1891), 183–197.

Fusfeld, I. S. The subscription of May 1, 1815. *American Annals of the Deaf*, 1922, *67*, 92.

———. How the deaf communicate—manual language. *American Annals of the Deaf*, 1958, *103*, 264–282.

Gaillard, H. A review of the contemporary deaf-mute world—consequences which flow from it. In: Congress of Deaf—International—Second (1893a), 173–176.

———. *Le Sourd-Muet à l'ouvrage en France. Carrières et professions*. Paris: author, 1894.

——. (ed.). See: Congress of Deaf—International—Third (1896).

——. *Vie sociale des sourds-muets. Carrières et professions des sourds-muets, Mémoire lu au congrès international des sourds-muets.* Paris: Imprimerie d'Ouvriers Sourds-Muets, 1900. (a)

——. *L'Enseignement des sourds-muets. La vraie méthode. Mémoire lu au Congrès International des Sourds-Muets* Paris: Imprimerie d'Ouvriers Sourds-Muets, 1900. (b)

——. *La Situation des sourds-muets en France au début du XX siècle.* Paris: Bureau de *L'Echo des Sourds-Muets,* 1904. English translation: The condition of the deaf in France. In: National Association of the Deaf, Proceedings, (1904), 105–116.

——. De mieux en mieux. *Revue des sourds-muets,* 1907, *1,* 161–162.

——. *Remise en question de l'enseignement des sourds-muets. Réplique à une brochure de feu le Dr. Albert Regnard.* Marseille: Albert Vendrevert, 1911.

——. (ed.). See: Congress of Deaf—International—Sixth (1912).

——. *Bi-centenaire de l'abbé de l'Epée. Compte-rendu des fêtes du bi-centenaire.* Paris: 35 rue de Montreuil, Album, 1913.

——. *Bienfaiteur des sourds-muets et des aveugles et exploiteurs des sourds-muets. Le cas du Pasteur Vigier. Conférence mimée le 1er mars 1914 á l'Assemblée de l'Avenir silencieux.* Niort: Th. Martin, 1915.

——. *Essai d'histoire de l'enseignement des sourds-muets.* Asnières: P. Scagliola, 1916.

Gaillard, H., and Jeanvoine, H. (eds.). See: Congress on Deaf—International—Fourth (1900b).

Gall, F. J., and Spurzheim, G. *Anatomie et physiologie du système nerveux en général et du cerveau en particulier.* Paris: F. Schoell, 1810.

Gallaher, J. E. *Representative Deaf Persons of the United States.* Chicago: Gallaher, 1898. Second edition [further biographies], Grinnell: Waring, 1903.

Gallaudet College. *Announcement of Deaf-Mute College.* Washington, D.C.: 1866.

——. *Dictionary Catalogue on Deafness and the Deaf.* Boston: Hall, 1970.

——. *Gallaudet College Almanac.* Washington, D.C.: Gallaudet College Alumni Association, 1974.

——. *Deafpride Papers: Perspectives and Options.* Washington, D.C.: Deafpride, 1976.

——. See also: Columbian Institution.

Gallaudet College Alumni Association. *Our Heritage: Gallaudet College Centennial 1864–1964.* Washington, D.C.: Graphic Arts Press, 1964.

Gallaudet, E. M. Book II. Travels Abroad 1867. Unpublished manuscript, Gallaudet Papers, Library of Congress. (a)

——. Report of the president on the systems of deaf-mute instruction pursued in Europe. In: Columbian Institution for the Deaf and Dumb, Reports (1867), 10–55. (b)

——. American and European systems of deaf-mute instruction compared. *National Deaf-Mute Gazette,* 1868, *2 (15),* 3–7. Reprinted: *New Englander,* 1868, *27,* 1–11. (a)

——. The American system of deaf-mute instruction—its incidental defects and their remedies. *American Annals of the Deaf,* 1868, *13,* 147–170. (b)

——. A day in the Imperial Institution for Deaf-Mutes in Paris. *American Annals of the Deaf,* 1870, *15,* 129–132.

——. Is sign language used to excess in teaching deaf-mutes? *American Annals of the Deaf,* 1871, *16,* 26–33.

——. Congress and the deaf and dumb. *Silent World,* 1872, *2,* (4) 1; (7) 3–4; (8) 4–5; (?) 5.

——. Deaf-Mute conventions, associations and newspapers. *American Annals of the Deaf,* 1873, *18,* 200–207.

——. Results of the articulation teaching at Northampton. *American Annals of the Deaf,* 1874, *19,* 136–145. (a)

——. The deaf-mute college at Washington. *American Journal of Social Science,* 1874, *6,* 160–163. (b)

——. Deaf-mutism. *International Review,* 1875, *2,* 471–487.

——. *Deaf-mute Instruction as Represented in the Vienna Exhibition of 1873.* Washington, D.C.: Government Printing Office, 1875. Reprinted: *American Annals of the Deaf,* 1876, *21,* 17–19.

——. Deaf-mutism. In: Convention of American Instructors of the Deaf, Proceedings (1876), 144–146.

——. The education of the deaf. *London Times,* 2 Oct. 1880. P. 7. (a)

——. International Convention of Instructors of the Deaf and Dumb at Milan, Italy. In: Columbian Institution for the Deaf and Dumb, Reports (1880), 5–7. (b)

——. How shall the deaf be educated? *International Review,* 1881, *11,* 503–516. (a)

——. International Convention of Instructors of Deaf-Mutes at Milan. *Education,* 1881, *1,* 279–285. (b)

——. The Milan Convention. *American Annals of the Deaf,* 1881, *26,* 1–16. (c)

——. Remarks on the combined system. *American Annals of the Deaf,* 1881, *26,* 56–59. (d)

——. Letter to the editor. *American Annals of the Deaf,* 1881, *26,* 133–135. (e)

——. Rejoinder to Padre Marchio. *American Annals of the Deaf,* 1881, *26,* 164–167. (f)

——. President Garfield's connection with the deaf-mute college. *American Annals of the Deaf,* 1882, *27,* 1–12.

——. The poetry of the deaf. *American Annals of the Deaf,* 1884, *29,* 200–222.

——. The American Asylum. In: Trumbull, J. H. *The Memorial History of Hartford County, Connecticut 1633–1884.* Boston: Osgood, 1886. (a)

————. History of the education of the deaf in the United States. *American Annals of the Deaf*, 1886, *31*, 130–147. Reprinted from: *The Encyclopedia Americana (supplement to the Encyclopaedia Britannica)*. Philadelphia: J. M. Stoddart, 1883. Pp. 131–146. (b)

————. The value of the sign language to the deaf. *American Annals of the Deaf*, 1887, *32*, 141–147.

————. *Life of Thomas Hopkins Gallaudet*. New York: Holt, 1888.

————. The intermarriage of the deaf. *Science*, 1890, *16 (408)*, 296–299.

————. Teaching the deaf and dumb. Statement of Dr. Edward M. Gallaudet, President of the Columbian Institution for the Deaf and Dumb. Address to Conference Committee of Congress on Appropriations, 27 Jan. 1891. Washington, D.C.: Government Printing Office, 1891. (a)

————. A new departure in deaf-mute education. *Science*, 1891, *17 (423)*, 143. (b)

————. College correspondence. *(Minnesota School for the Deaf) Companion*, 7 Mar. 1891, 3. (c)

————. *The Combined System of Educating the Deaf*. Washington, D.C.: Gibson Brothers, 1891. (d)

————. Values in the education of the deaf. *Educational Review*, 1892, *4*, 16–26. (a)

————. Our profession. *American Annals of the Deaf*, 1892, *37*, 1–9. (b)

————. Remarks at graduation exercises of the American School for the Deaf at Hartford. *Deaf-Mute's Journal*, 1892, *23*, 8 Sept. (c)

————. The ideal school for the deaf. *American Annals of the Deaf*, 1892, *37*, 280–285. (d)

————. The proper adjustment of methods in the education of the deaf. In: Convention of American Instructors of the Deaf, Proceedings (1893), 90–97. (a)

————. The education of the deaf, its opportunities and its perils. In: Congress of Deaf—International—Second (1893), 25–27. (b)

————. A few words from the college at Washington. In: Conference of Executives of American Schools for the Deaf, Proceedings (1893), 116–123. (c)

————. What constitutes success in oral teaching? In: Alexander Graham Bell Association, Proceedings (1893), 139–148. (d)

————. A suggestion to members of the Convention. *American Annals of the Deaf*, 1894, *39*, 125–129. (a)

————. The overture from the Convention to the Association. *American Annals of the Deaf*, 1894, *39*, 232–240. (b)

————. The tongue of the dumb shall sing. Paper read before the Anthropological Society. Unpublished manuscript, Gallaudet College Archives, Washington, D.C., 1895. (a)

————. The education of deaf-mutes; an interesting statement by the president of the college. *New York Evening Post*, 1895, 24 Apr. (b)

————. Some incidents in the progress of deaf-mute education in America. In: Convention of American Instructors of the Deaf, Proceedings (1895), 40–56. (c)

————. What is the combined system? *American Annals of the Deaf*, 1895, *40*, 30–35. (d)

————. The deaf and dumb. Paper read at Social Science Convention at Saratoga. *Portland, Oregon, Evening Express*, 1896, 14 Feb. (a)

————. Is an oral college needed? *American Annals of the Deaf*, 1896, *41*, 163–170. (b)

————. [European tour, 1897.] Unpublished diary, Gallaudet Papers, Library of Congress.

————. The deaf and their possibilities. In: National Education Association, Proceedings (1898), 208–214. (a)

————. Some important corrections. *American Annals of the Deaf*, 1898, *43*, 7–15. (b)

————. Must the sign-language go? *American Annals of the Deaf*, 1899, *44*, 221–229.

————. *What Is Speech Worth to the Deaf?* Washington, D.C.: Gallaudet College, 1900. (a)

————. The Paris Congress. *Association Review*, 1900, *2*, 478–480. (b)

————. The International Congress of 1900. *American Annals of the Deaf*, 1900, *45*, 244–249. (c)

————. Echoes of the Paris Congress of 1900. *American Annals of the Deaf*, 1900, *45*, 416–426. (d)

————. President's address [manualism versus oralism]. In: Convention of American Instructors for the Deaf, Proceedings (1902), 41–57, 78–81. (a)

————. Address of E. M. Gallaudet to the Wisconsin School Fiftieth Anniversary. Unpublished manuscript, Gallaudet College Archives, Washington, D.C., 1902. (b)

————. A message to the Congress of the Deaf. In: Congress of Deaf—International—Fourth (1904), 11–14. Reprinted: *American Annals of the Deaf*, 1904, *49*, 349–352.

————. Address of the president. *American Annals of the Deaf*, 1905, *50*, 345–351.

————. A correction [concerning the history of Gallaudet College]. *Association Review*, 1906, *8*, 241–242. (a)

————. Address of the President [manualism versus oralism]. In: Convention of American Instructors of the Deaf, Proceedings (1906), 28–31, 66–74. (b)

————. History of the college for the deaf. Unpublished manuscript, E. M. Gallaudet Library, Washington, D.C., 1907. (a)

————. Address to the Eighth Convention of the National Association of the Deaf. In: National Association of the Deaf, Proceedings (1907), 17–20. (b)

————. The descendants of T. H. Gallaudet and Sophia Fowler. Unpublished manuscript, Gallaudet Papers, Library of Congress, 1910.

————. A history of the Columbia Institution for the Deaf and Dumb. *Records of the Columbia Historical Society*, 1912, *15*, 1–22. (a)

———. President Gallaudet's address [manualism versus oralism]. In: Convention of American Instructors of the Deaf, Proceedings (1912), 38–41. (b)

———. Recent changes in the education of the deaf in America and Europe. Notes for an address to the educational club at Hartford, 18 Oct. 1912. Unpublished manuscript, Connecticut State Library, 1912. (c)

———. A forgotten Hartford philanthropist. Unpublished manuscript, Connecticut State Library, 1912. (d)

———. Rose Terry Cooke. Unpublished manuscript, E. M. Gallaudet Library, Washington, D.C., 1913.

Gallaudet, E.M., and Hall, P. The normal department of Gallaudet College [and sign in instruction]. In: Convention of American Instructors of the Deaf, Proceedings (1909), 38–56.

Gallaudet, Sophia Fowler. See: Fowler, S.

Gallaudet, T. H. Hymn at sea. Unpublished manuscript, Gallaudet Papers, Library of Congress, 1815. (a)

———. Letter to Alice Cogswell, 14 May 1815, from New York. Reprinted: Humphrey (1857), p. 31. (b)

———. Letter to Mason Cogswell, 19 May 1815, from New York. Gallaudet Papers, Library of Congress. (c)

———. Letter to Ward Woodbridge, 23 May 1815, from New York. Gallaudet Papers, Library of Congress. (d)

———. Letter to [?] and Alice Cogswell, 24 June 1815, from ship Mexico. Gallaudet Papers, Library of Congress. Note to Alice Cogswell reprinted: Fay, E. A. (1913b), 227–228. (e)

———. Letter to Ward Woodbridge, 10 July 1815, from London. Reprinted: Humphrey (1857), 31–33. (f)

———. Letter to Mason Cogswell, 11 July 1815, from London. Gallaudet Papers, Library of Congress. (g)

———. Letter to Alice Cogswell, 15 Aug. 1815, from London. Reprinted: Humphrey (1857), 41–43. (h)

———. Letter to Mason Cogswell, 15 Aug. 1815, from London. Reprinted: Gallaudet, E. M. (1888), 60–75. (i)

———. Letter to Mason Cogswell, 22 Sept. 1815, from Edinburgh. Reprinted: Gallaudet, E. M. (1888), 76–81. Excerpted: Humphrey (1857), 51–52. (j)

———. Letter to W. Woodbridge, 30 Sept. 1815, from Edinburgh. Reprinted: Humphrey (1857), 44–45. (k)

———. Letter to W. Woodbridge, 6 Dec. 1815, from Edinburgh. Reprinted: Humphrey (1857), 50–51. Excerpted: Gallaudet, E. M. (1888), 82–84. (l)

———. Letter to Dugald Stewart, 26 Sept. 1815, at Edinburgh. Excerpted: Gallaudet, E. M. (1888), 88–92. (m)

———. [American Asylum.] Connecticut Mirror, 22 May 1815. (n)

———. Letter to Mason Cogswell, 11 Jan. 1816, from Edinburgh. Reprinted: Humphrey (1857), 48–49. (a)

———. Letter to Alice Cogswell, 22 Jan. 1816, from Edinburgh. Gallaudet Papers, Library of Congress. Reprinted: Fay, E. A. (1913b), 228–230; Humphrey (1857), 43. (b)

———. Letter to Mason Cogswell, 5[?] Feb. 1816, from Edinburgh. Reprinted: Humphrey (1857), 53–54. (c)

———. Letter to Mason Cogswell, 21 Feb. 1816, from London. Gallaudet Papers, Library of Congress. (d)

———. Letter to D. Wadsworth, 14 Mar. 1816, from Paris. Gallaudet Papers, Library of Congress. Excerpted: Humphrey (1857), 60 [mislabeled addressee, Woodbridge]. (e)

———. Letter to Alice Cogswell, 24 Mar. 1816, from Paris. Gallaudet Papers, Library of Congress. Reprinted: Lane (1976), 244–245; Fay, E. A. (1913b), 230–231. Excerpted: Humphrey (1857), 62–63. (f)

———. Letter to Mason Cogswell, 11 Apr. 1816, from Paris. Gallaudet Papers, Library of Congress. Excerpted: Humphrey (1857), 63–64. (g)

———. Letter to Abbé R. A. Sicard, 21 May 1816, in Paris. Reprinted: Gallaudet, E. M. (1888), 94–97. (h)

———. Letter to Mason Cogswell, 17 June 1816, from Le Havre. Reprinted: Root (1941), 69; Association Review, 1901, 3, 336–337. (i)

———. Letter to Mason Cogswell, 8 Aug. 1816, from the ship Mary Augusta. Reprinted: Association Review, 1901, 3, 337. (j)

———. Letter to Mason Cogswell, 15 Aug. 1816, from New York. Reprinted: Root (1941), 70; Association Review, 1901, 3, 339. (k)

———. Contract between Gallaudet and Clerc [1816]. Gallaudet Papers, Library of Congress. Abridged translation: American Annals of the Deaf, 1879, 24, 115–117; Lane (1976). (l)

———. Letter to Mason Cogswell, 18 Dec. 1816, from New Brunswick. Gallaudet Papers, Library of Congress. (m)

———. [Notes to L. Clerc and J. Massieu in a café.] Gallaudet Papers, Library of Congress, 1816. (n)

———. A Sermon Delivered at the Opening of the Connecticut Asylum . . . 20 April 1817, in the Brick Church in Hartford. Hartford: Hudson, 1817. (a)

———. Letter to N. Terry, [?] Sept. 1817, at Hartford. Gallaudet Papers, Library of Congress. (b)

———. Letter to the Board of the Connecticut Asylum, 4 Sept. 1817. Reprinted: Gallaudet, E. M. (1888), 124; Association Review, 1902, 2, 29–31. (c)

———. Copy of a conversation between L. Clerc and W. C. Woodbridge held 19 Oct. 1817. Gallaudet Papers, Library of Congress. (d)

———. Discourses on Various Points of Christian Faith. London: Ellerton, 1818; Hatchard, 1818; Hartford: Goodrich, 1818. (a)

———. Intelligence and remarks regarding the Institution at Hartford for Instructing the Deaf and Dumb. North American Review, 1818, 7, 127–137. (b)

———. A journal of some occurrences in my life which have a relation to the instruction of the deaf and dumb [1818]. Unpublished manuscript, Gallaudet Papers, Library of Congress. Excerpted: Barnard (1852), 117–130. (c)

———. Letter to [?], 25 Jan. 1818, from Hartford. [History of deaf education.] Gallaudet Papers, Library of Congress. (d)

——. Letter to the Board of Directors of the American Asylum, 3 Aug. 1818, at Hartford. Unpublished manuscript, American School for the Deaf, Hartford. (e)

——. Letter to Mason Cogswell, 29 Aug. 1818, from Ballston. Cogswell Papers, Yale University. (f)

——. To the editor of the Christian Instructor. *(Edinburgh) Christian Instructor*, 1818, *17*, 166–168. (g)

——. On teaching the deaf and dumb. *Christian Observer*, 1819, *18*, 646–650, 784–787. (a)

——. *An Address Delivered at a Meeting for Prayer, with Reference to the Sandwich Mission, in the Brick Church in Hartford, 11 Oct. 1819.* Hartford: Lincoln, 1819. (b)

——. *A Discourse Delivered at the Annual Meeting of the Hartford Evangelical Tract Society. Hartford, 5 January 1820.* Hartford: 1820. (a)

——. Letter to Mason Cogswell, 18 Sept. 1820. Cogswell Papers, Yale University. (b)

——. Letter to T. Chalmers, 20 Sept. 1820, from New York. Reprinted: Humphrey (1857), 97–99. (c)

——. Sermon, 16 Mar. 1821. Unpublished manuscript, American School for the Deaf, Hartford, 1821. (a)

——. *A Discourse Delivered at the Dedication of the American Asylum, 22 May 1821.* Hartford: Hudson, 1821. (b)

——. *Sermon on Duty and Advantages of According Instruction to the Deaf and Dumb.* Portland: Mirror Office (A. Stanley), 1824. Reprinted: Humphrey (1857), 130–146. (a)

——. Jesus, I turn to thee. 24 Jan. 1824. Unpublished manuscript, Watkinson Library, Trinity College, Hartford. (b)

——. The language of signs auxiliary to the Christian missionary. *Christian Observer*, 1826, *26*, 592–600. Reprinted: *Literary and Theological Review*, 1834, *1*, 200–213. (a)

——. Oral language and the language of signs. *Christian Observer*, 1826, *26*, 464–470, 525–533. (b)

——. A marriage hymn. [On the wedding of Lewis Weld and Mary A. Cogswell.] 7 May 1828. Unpublished manuscript, Weld Family Papers, Connecticut State Library. (a)

——. *A Statement with regard to the Moorish Prince, Abduhl Rahhakman. Published by order of the committee appointed to solicit subscriptions in New York to aid in redeeming the family of the prince from slavery.* New York: Fanshaw, 1828. (b)

——. Letter to Lewis Weld, 9 June 1829, from Hartford. Gallaudet Papers, Library of Congress.

——. Letter to Lewis Weld, 18 May 1830, from Hartford. Gallaudet Papers, Library of Congress. (a)

——. Philosophy of language. *American Annals of Education*, series 3, 1830, *1* (part 1), (70)–(77), 117–123, 157–160. (b)

——. Language of infancy. *American Annals of Education*, series 3, 1831, *1* (part 2), 99–102, 321–323; *2*, 185–190.

——. Recollections of the deaf and dumb. *American Annals of Education*, series 3, 1838, *8*, 3–11. Reprinted: *American Annals of the Deaf*, 1849, *2*, 54–59.

——. On attention. *American Annals of Education*, series 3, 1839, *9*, 111–113, 173–176.

——. Letter to H. Mann, 13 May 1844, from Hartford. Gallaudet Papers, Library of Congress. Reprinted: Barclay (1870), 25–27.

——. Letter to Rev. T. Gallaudet, 6 May 1845, from Hartford. Gallaudet Papers, Library of Congress.

——. On the natural language of the deaf and its value and uses in the instruction of the deaf and dumb. *American Annals of the Deaf*, 1847, *1*, 79–93. Reprinted: Humphrey (1857), 170–197.

——. Reminiscences of deaf-mute instruction. *American Annals of the Deaf*, 1849, *2*, 90–96.

——. My former pupils and friends. (Address delivered before a memorable gathering of the deaf at Hartford, 1850.) In: Anonymous (1851), 34. (a)

——. [Obituary.] *New York Times*, 1851, *1 (1)*, 18 Sept.

Gallaudet, T. (Rev.) Recollections of my father. Unpublished manuscript, Watkinson Library, Trinity College, Hartford, 1851[?].

——. On articulation and reading on the lips. In: Convention of American Instructors of the Deaf, Proceedings (1853), 238–247.

——. Entries in Rev. T. Gallaudet's journal after the death of his father and letter 28 July 1857. Unpublished manuscript, Watkinson Library, Trinity College, Hartford.

——. Methods of perfecting the sign language. In: Convention of American Instructors of the Deaf, Proceedings (1859), 189–213.

——. Report on the Milan Congress. In: Peet, I.L. (1880). Excerpted: Clarke School (1893a), 23.

——. The language of deaf-mutes. *New York Daily Tribune*, Dec. 3, 1883, 5.

——. The moral and religious condition of the deaf after leaving school. In: Convention of American Instructors of the Deaf, Proceedings (1893), 240–243.

Ganière, P. *L'Académie de Médecine*. Paris: Maloine, 1964.

Gannon, J. R. *Deaf Heritage. A Narrative History of Deaf America.* Silver Spring: National Association of the Deaf, 1981.

Gard, F. Letter to L. Clerc, 11 May 1811. Clerc Papers no. 2, Yale University Library.

——. Letter to [Dr. S. Mitchill?] from Bordeaux, April 1816. Reprinted: *Association Review*, 1902, *4*, 21–22.

Gardiner, M. The story of visible speech. *Volta Review*, 1910, *12*, 99–102.

Garnett, C.B., Jr. *The World of Silence: A New Venture in Philosophy.* New York: Greenwich Books, 1967.

Gaussens, E. *Etude sur les sourds-muets.* Bordeaux: Coderc, 1872.

——. *Etude sur les principaux instituteurs des sourds-muets et leurs méthodes.* Bordeaux: Coderc, 1877.

Geer, E. *Hartford City Directory for 1866.* Hartford: [n.p.], 1866.

Geikie, A. [John] Braidwood in the Edinburgh Institution (1810). *Association Review*, 1900, 2, 407–408.

General Association of Connecticut. Minutes of the meeting held in Farmington, Connecticut, June 1811. Reprinted: *Association Review*, 1901, 3, 132.

——. Minute of meeting held at Sharon, Connecticut, 17 June 1812. Reprinted: *Association Review*, 1901, 3, 136.

Gentile, A. Further studies in achievement testing hearing-impaired students. In: Gallaudet College, Office of Demographic Studies (ed.), *Annual Survey of Hearing-Impaired Children and Youth.* Washington, D.C.: Gallaudet College, 1973.

George, D. W. Signs and fingerspelling. *American Annals of the Deaf*, 1890, 35, 115–117.

——. Recent occurrences among the deaf of France. In: National Association of the Deaf, Proceedings (1896), 27–30.

Gerson, L. The Pennsylvania School for the Deaf 1820–1892, with a focus on David G. Seixas. Unpublished manuscript, Boston University, Department of Special Education, 1978.

Gilbert, S. Journal or chronicle of Sylvester Gilbert of Hebron. Unpublished manuscript, Connecticut State Library, Hartford, [n.d.].

——. Letter to Mason Cogswell, Mar. 1812, from Hebron. Cogswell Papers, Yale University. Reprinted: *Association Review*, 1901, 3, 133–136.

——. Letter to Mason Cogswell, 18 July 1816, from Hebron. Cogswell Papers, Yale University. Reprinted: *Association Review*, 1901, 3, 138–139.

——. Biographical sketch of the Honorable Sylvester Gilbert prepared by himself. Unpublished manuscript, Connecticut State Library, [1839].

Gilbert, W. Deaf and dumb asylum. *Good Words*, 1873, 14, 252–256.

Gillet, H.S. The mode of teaching language. In: Convention of American Instructors of the Deaf, Proceedings (1851), 12–20.

Gillett, P.G. Deaf-Mutes. *Science*, 1890, 16 (404), 248–249. (a)

——. The intermarriage of the deaf and their education. *Science*, 1890, 16 (412), 353–357. (b)

——. Dr. Gillett to Mr. Bell. The controversy over the marrying of deaf-mutes. *Silent Worker*, 1890, 4, 1,4. Nov. 27. (c)

——. Deaf mutes—their intermarriage and offspring. *Science*, 1891, 17 (417), 57–60.

——. Inaugural Address. In: Alexander Graham Bell Association, Proceedings (1894), 31–40.

Gineste, T. *Victor de L'Aveyron.* Paris: Le Sycomore, 1981.

Giovanni, O. De la nécessité et des moyens de combattre la tradition des signes conventionnels. *Revue internationale de l'enseignement des sourds-muets*, 1887, 3, 172–176, 195–199, 227–231, 306–309.

"G.M." Est-ce la faillite d'une méthode? *L'Eclair*, 26 Nov. 1909.

Goddard, H. Mental tests and the immigrant. *Journal of Delinquency*, 1917, 2, 243–277.

Goguillot, L. *Comment on fait parler les sourds-muets. Précédé d'une préface par M. le Dr. Ladreit de Lacharrière.* Paris: Masson, 1889.

Goldstein, M. A. The Society of Progressive Oral Advocates: its origin and purposes. *Volta Review*, 1917, 19, 443–447. Excerpted: *Volta Review*, 1976, 78, 140–143.

Goldstein, M. A. An acoustic method. *Volta Review*, 1920, 22, 716–719.

Goodrich, S.G. *Recollections of a Lifetime.* New York: Miller, Otran, and Mulligan, 1857. Reprinted: Detroit: Gale Research, 1967.

Gordon, J. Dumb and Deaf. In: Brewster, D. (ed.). *The American Edition of the New Edinburgh Encyclopedia.* Philadelphia: Parker, 1816. Vol. 8, part 1, pp. 1–15. Reprinted: 1832.

Gordon, J.C. Deaf-mutes and the public schools from 1815 to today. *American Annals of the Deaf*, 1885, 31, 121–143. Excerpted from: National Education Association (1885). (a)

——. Hints to parents. *American Annals of the Deaf*, 1885, 30, 241–250. (b)

——. Notes on manual spelling. *American Annals of the Deaf*, 1886, 31, 53–60.

—— (ed.). *Education of Deaf Children. Evidence of E. M. Gallaudet and A. G. Bell presented to the Royal Commission of the United Kingdom on the Condition of the Blind, the Deaf and the Dumb.* Washington, D.C.: Volta Bureau, 1892. (a)

——. Progress of speech teaching. In: Gordon (1892c), xxvi–l. (b)

——. *Notes and Observations upon the Education of the Deaf, with a revised index to "Education of Deaf Children."* Washington, D.C.: Volta Bureau, 1892. (c)

——. The new departure at Kendall Green. *American Annals of the Deaf*, 1892, 37, 121–127. (d)

——. Oral work in schools using the combined system. In: Convention of American Instructors of the Deaf, Proceedings (1893), 139–143.

——. *Address Upon the Occasion of the Opening of the First Meeting of the Oral Section of the Convention of American Instructors of the Deaf, 4 July 1895.* Washington, D.C.: Volta Bureau, 1895.

——. *The Difference between the Two Systems of Teaching Deaf-Mute Children the English Language.* Washington, D.C.: Sanders, 1898.

——. Resolutions relating to speech teaching: 1868–1900. *Association Review*, 1900, 2, 520–526.

[Gordon, J.F.]. To the editor of the Christian Instructor. (Edinburgh) *Christian Instructor*, 1818, *16*, 32–34.

Gosse, (l'abbé). *Prières et instructions à l'usage des sourds-muets de naissance.* Tournay: 1805.

Gosselin, L. *L'Impénétrable Secret du sourd-muet mort et vivant.* Paris: Perrin, 1929.

Gouin, [?]. Letter to Clerc dissuading him from going to America. Clerc Papers no. 19, Yale University, 1816.

Graff, E. Tapage perdu. *Echo de la Société d'Appui Fraternel des Sourds-Muets de France*, 1889, *1*, (4) 5–6; (5) 4–5.

Grant, M. H. *In and About Hartford: Tours and Tales.* Hartford: Connecticut Historical Society, 1978.

[Green, F.]. On teaching the deaf to understand language and the dumb to speak. Letter to Richard Bagley, Health Officer of New York, 1781. Reprinted: *Medical Repository*, 1804, *2*, 73–75; *Association Review*, 1900, *2*, 66–68; Arnold (1888), 96–97.

——. *Vox Oculis Subjecta. A dissertation on the . . . art of imparting speech . . . to the naturally deaf and . . . dumb, with a particular account of the Academy of Messrs. Braidwood . . . by a parent.* London: B. White, 1783. Excerpted: *A New Edition of "Vox Oculis Subjecta," Part I.* London: 1873; reprinted: Boston: Parents' Education Association for Deaf Children, 1897.

[——]. To the reverend the Clergy in the State of Massachusetts. *New England Palladium*, 1803, *21 (23)*, 1–2. 14 Oct. Reprinted: Green, S. (1861).

[——(transl.)]. Extracts from the "Institution des sourds et muets" of the Abbé de l'Epée. *American Annals of the Deaf*, 1861, *13*, 8–29.

Green, S. The earliest advocate of the education of deaf-mutes in America. *American Annals of the Deaf*, 1861, *13*, 1–8.

Greenberger, D. Visible speech as a means of communicating articulation to deaf-mutes. A reply to Mr. A. G. Bell's article in the Annals. *American Annals of the Deaf*, 1874, *19*, 65–74.

——. Articulation. *American Annals of the Deaf*, 1876, *21*, 183–190.

——. Methods of teaching articulation. In: Conference of Executives of American Schools for the Deaf, Proceedings (1880), 117–130.

——. Articulation teaching in Italy. *American Annals of the Deaf*, 1881, *26*, 50–56, 112–129.

Greene, D. The Institution for the Improved Instruction of Deaf-Mutes. In: Fay, E. A. (1893), vol. 2, ch. 26.

Greenwood, F. P. De La Sagra's five months in the United States. *Christian Examiner*, 1839, *25*, 72–85.

Grégoire, E. *Un centenaire. (Centenaire de la mort de l'abbé de l'Epée).* Paris: Carre, 1889. Reprinted: *Gazette des Sourds-Muets*, 1891, *1*, (7), (8); *2*, (1) 3–9; (8) 115–120.

Grégoire, H. *Rapport sur la nécessité et les moyens d'anéantir les patois et d'universaliser l'usage de la langue française.* Paris: Comité d'Instruction Publique, 1794. Reprinted: de Certeau, M., Julia, D., and Revel, J. *Une Politique de la langue: La Révolution française et les patois.* Paris: Gallimard, 1975. Pp. 300–317.

Grégoire, L. *Dictionnaire encyclopédique d'histoire, de biographie, de mythologie et de géographie.* Paris: Garnier frères, 1871.

Gregory, W. *American Newspapers 1821–1936. A Union List.* New York: Wilson, 1937.

——. *International Congresses and Conferences 1840–1937. A Union List of Their Publications Available in Libraries of the U.S. and Canada.* New York: Krauss Reprint, 1967.

Gribble, F. *The Life and Times of Alexander I of Russia.* New York: Dutton, 1931.

Grimley, T. The deaf and the dumb. *Irish Quarterly Review*, 1859, *8*, 1285–1324.

Griswold, M. H. The Fowlers of Moose Hill. *The Shore Line Times*, 9 Nov. 1933.

——. *Yester-years of Guilford.* Guilford: Shore Line Times Publishing Company, 1938.

Groce, N. Everyone here spoke sign language. *Natural History*, 1980, *89 (6)*, 10–16.

——. The island's hereditary deaf: a lesson in understanding. *Dukes County Intelligencer*, 1981, *22 (3)*, 83–95.

Gross, S. D. *Lives of Eminent American Physicians and Surgeons of the Nineteenth Century.* Philadelphia, Lindsay, 1861.

Grosselin, A., and Pélissier, P. *Cartes mimo-mnémoniques.* Paris: Borrani, 1861.

Grosvenor, E.M.B. My father, Volta Bureau, and the Association. *Volta Review*, 1950, *52*, 112–114.

——. My father, Alexander Graham Bell. *Volta Review*, 1951, *53*, 349, 386–388.

——. Mrs. Alexander Graham Bell—a reminiscence. *Volta Review*, 1957, *59*, 299–305.

——. Dr. Bell, pioneer of a new era. *Volta Review*, 1958, *60*, 110–111, 141.

——. A Bell bibliography. *Volta Review*, 1960, *62*, 111–112, 139.

Grosvenor, L. My grandfather Bell. *The New Yorker*, 11 Nov. 1950, 44–48.

Grosvenor, M.B. Memories of my grandfather. *Volta Review*, 1940, *42*, 621–622.

Guillemont, F.L. *Histoire du sourd-muet Benjamin à l'Institution Royale des Sourds-Muets à Paris, écrite par lui-même.* Paris: Borrani, 1838.

——. Discours que devait prononcer M. Benjamin, Professeur sourd-muet, à la distribution des prix aux élèves de l'institution dirigée par M. Massieu. *L'Ami des sourds-muets*, 1839–40, *2*, 13–15. Reprinted: Cambrai: Lesne-Daloin, [n.d.].

Guilleminault, G. *La Belle Epoque.* Paris: DeNoël, 1957.

Gustason, G., Pfetzing, D., and Zawolkow, E. *Signing Exact English.* Rossmoor: Modern Signs Press, 1972.

Guyot, C., and Guyot, R.T. *Liste Littéraire Philocophe . . . ou catalogue d'étude de ce qui a été publié jusqu'à nos jours sur les sourds-muets.* Groningen: J. Oomkens, 1842. Reprinted: Amsterdam: B.M. Israel, 1967.

Hadley, L.F. *A List of the Primary Gestures in Indian Sign talk.* Andarko: author, 1887.

————. *A Lesson in Sign Talk.* Fort Smith: [n.p.], 1890

————. *Indian Sign Talk.* Chicago: Baker, 1893.

Haerne, D.P.A. de. *De l'enseignement spécial des sourds-muets, considéré dans les méthodes principales, d'après la tradition et le progrès.* Brussels: Devaux, 1865.

————. The natural language of signs. *American Annals of the Deaf,* 1875, *20,* 73–87, 137–153, 216–228; *21,* 11–16.

Haight, G. *Mrs. Sigourney, the Sweet Singer of Hartford.* New Haven: Yale University Press, 1930.

Halevy, L. *L'Enseignement des sourds-muets. L'Abbé Sicard et Massieu, son élève. L'Abbé de l'Epée. Amman et Jacob Pereire. Suivi de L'Eloquence du Geste ou la partie d'échecs de Diderot au Café Procope.* Paris: A. Ghio, 1877.

Hall, B. *Travels in North America in the Years 1827–1828.* Edinburgh: Cadell, 1829.

Hall, D.B. *Halls of New England.* Albany: Munsell, 1883.

Hall, G.S. Laura Bridgman. In: *Aspects of German Culture.* Boston: Osgood, 1881. Pp. 237–276.

Hall, J. Letter to M.F. Cogswell, 15 June 1816, from Thornly Park (Scotland). Cogswell Papers, Yale University.

Hall, P.R. Language Contact in the U.S.S.R.: Some prospects for language maintenance among Soviet minority language groups. Unpublished doctoral dissertation, Georgetown University, Washington, D.C., 1974.

Hall, P. The normal department of Gallaudet College [and the use of sign language]. *American Annals of the Deaf,* 1908, *53,* 293–308.

————. Our debt to the American School for the Deaf. *American Annals of the Deaf,* 1923, *68,* 217–225.

Hallam, E. Letter to M. F. Cogswell, 6 Oct. 1816. Cogswell Papers, Connecticut Historical Society. Reprinted: *Association Review,* 1900, *2,* 408–409.

————. Letter to M.F. Cogswell, 10 Mar. 1818, from Richmond. Cogswell Papers, Yale University. Reprinted: *Association Review,* 1900, *2,* 517–518.

Halle, J.N. and Moreau, J.L. Rapports sur deux mémoires relatifs aux moyens de rendre l'ouïe aux sourds-muets (présentés à la Société de l'Ecole de Médecine de Paris par M. Itard). *Gazette nationale ou le Moniteur universel,* 1808, *36 (211),* 8 Aug. 874–875, 878.

Haller, M. *Eugenics: Hereditarian Attitudes in American Thought.* New Brunswick: Rutgers University Press, 1963.

Hamilton, S.M. *Writings of James Monroe.* New York: Putnam, 1898.

Hammond, H.C. The use and abuse of signs in the school room. In: Convention of American Instructors of the Deaf, Proceedings (1893), 63–66.

Hansen, A. A visit to American schools for the deaf. *Association Review,* 1908, *10,* 48–63.

————. The basis of the Binet-Simon inquiry. *Volta Review,* 1910, *12,* 190–193.

————. The Clarke School. *Volta Review,* 1912, *14,* 31–40.

Hanson, O. The question of methods in Sweden. *American Annals of the Deaf,* 1891, *36,* 292–295.

————. The term "charitable" as applied in our schools and other misconceptions concerning the deaf. In: Congress of Deaf—International—Second (1893), 268–270.

————. How the National Association may be made more useful. In: National Association of the Deaf, Proceedings (1900), 17–20.

————. The sign languages in American Schools. *Association Review,* 1901, *3,* 223–226; 1902, *4,* 129–131; 1903, *5,* 195–196; 1904, *6,* 150–151; 1905, *7,* 327–328; 1906, *8,* 162–163; 1907, *9,* 384; 1908, *10,* 282.

————. Comparative statistics of methods of educating the deaf in the United States. *American Annals of the Deaf,* 1902, *47,* 349–357.

————. *Oral Teaching of the Deaf: Reply to an Address by Dr. Carroll G. Pearse, President, National Education Association.* Circular of information no. 7. Silver Spring: National Association of the Deaf, 1912.

Hardy, W.G. *Bell Resounding.* Northampton: Clarke School, 1976.

Harrington, J. Thomas Hopkins Gallaudet. *Christian Examiner,* 1852, *53,* 105–114.

Harrington, K. *Richard Alsop. A Hartford Wit.* Middletown: Wesleyan, 1969.

Harris, G.I. The value of the deaf teacher. In: Convention of American Instructors of the Deaf, Proceedings (1933), 117–121.

Hartmann, A. *Deafmutism and the Education of Deaf Mutes by Lipreading and Articulation.* Translated and enlarged by James P. Cassels. London: Baillière, 1881.

Haug, L. De l'enseignement de la parole et de son application à tous les sourds-muets, parallèle entre la méthode allemande at la méthode française (Discours prononcé à la conférence de Pforzheim, 5 octobre 1847). *Annales de l'éducation des sourds-muets et des aveugles,* 1848, *5,* 161–179. English translation: American School for the Deaf, Reports (1849), 33–64.

Haüy, V. *Essai sur l'éducation des aveugles.* Paris: [n.p.], 1786. English translation: Blacklock, T. *Essay on the Education of the Blind.* Edinburgh: [n.p.], 1793.

Havstad, L.A. How the deaf converse with each other in Norway. *American Annals of the Deaf,* 1892, *37,* 113–118.

Hay, J., Homes, M., and Montgomery, G. Bicultural adaptation and survival: the experience of the first two years of the Scottish workshop with the deaf. Paper presented to the VIII World Congress of the World Federation of the Deaf, Varna, Bulgaria, 26 June 1979. Edinburgh University, Department of Psychology, 1979.

Haycock, G.S. *The Education of the Deaf in America.* Stoke, England: [n.p.], 1923.

Hayden, H.E. The Gallaudets of New Rochelle, New York. *New York Genealogical and Biographical Record*, 1888, *19*, 118–121.

Head, F. Institution Nationale des Sourds-Muets. In: *A Faggot of French Sticks*. London: Murray, 1855. Vol. 2, pp. 129–140. Excerpted: *American Annals of the Deaf*, 1852, *4*, 252–258.

Heath, S. *Telling Tongues: Language Policy in Mexico*. New York: Teachers College Press, 1972.

Heidsiek, J. The results of the oral method in Germany. *American Annals of the Deaf*, 1887, *32*, 104–113.

———. The situation in Germany. *American Annals of the Deaf*, 1891, *36*, 267–270.

———. The education of the deaf in the United States. Report of a visit and a further contribution to the question of methods. *American Annals of the Deaf*, 1899, *44*, 177–210, 32–358, 439–455; 1900, *45*, 16–26.

———. *Report of a Visit to American Schools for the Deaf*. Translated by G. Veditz. Rochester: Western New York Institution for the Deaf, 1900.

Heinicke, S. *Controverse entre l'abbé de l'Epée et Samuel Heinicke au sujet de la véritable manière d'instruire les sourds-muets*. Paris: Pelluard, 1881.

———. *The Exchange of Letters between Samuel Heinicke and Abbé Charles Michel de l'Epée*. Annotated by C.B. Garnett, Jr. New York: Vantage Press, 1968.

Helmont, F.M. van. See: Van Helmont, F.M.

Hément, F. *Jacob Rodrigues Pereire, premier instituteur des sourds-muets en France*. Paris: Didier, 1875.

———. *Conférence sur l'enseignement des sourds-muets par la parole (méthode J.R. Pereire)*. Paris: Imprimerie Nationale, 1879.

———. *Rapport sur le congrès national à Bordeaux du 8 au 14 août 1881*. Paris: Imprimerie Nationale, 1882.

———. *Sur la transmission des caractères et des aptitudes à propos de quelques observations faites chez les sourds-muets*. Orléans: Girardot, 1885. (a)

———. *Rapport à M. le Ministre de l'Instruction Publique et des Beaux Arts sur le congrès international tenu à Bruxelles du 13 au 20 août 1883 pour l'amélioration du sort des sourds-muets*. Paris: Gauthiers-Villars, 1885. (b)

Hément, F., and Magnat, M. *Réponses à un article de M. l'abbé Marchio publié dans le journal "Dell'educazione dei sordo-muti" en mars 1881 á Sienne (Italie)*. Paris: E. Rinuy, 1881.

Henderson, C.R. Practical eugenics. *Proceedings of the American Breeders' Association*, 1909, *5*, 223–227.

Henderson, J.M. A half-century of progress in the New England Schools—III. The Horace Mann School for the Deaf. *Volta Review*, 1939, *41*, 627–630.

Hermiopolis, [L'Evêque d']. *Discours prononcés dans la séance publique tenue par l'Académie Française, pour la réception de M. l'Evêque d'Hermiopolis le 28 novembre, 1822*. Paris: Firmin Didot, 1822.

Hernández, T. *Discursio pronunciado en la apertura del Real Colegio de Surdo-Mudos*. Madrid: Sancha, 1814.

———. *Discursio pronunciado al principiar los éxamenes públicos des los alumnos del real colegio de sordo-mudos la tarde del 17 de octobre de 1816*. Madrid: Sancha, 1816.

[Herries, J.]. To the author. *Scots Magazine*, 1766, *28*, 31.

[———] [On Braidwood.] *Scots Magazine*, 1767, *29*, 421.

[———] To the author. *Scots Magazine*, 1769, *31*, 342–343.

———. *The Elements of Speech*. London: Dilly, 1773.

Hervás y Panduro, L. *Escuela española de sordo-mudos . . .* Madrid: Villalpando, 1795. French translation: Valade-Gabel (1875).

Hervaux, V. Etude sur J.-J. Valade-Gabel. *Bulletin international de l'enseignement des sourds-muets*, 1911, *3*, 281–310.

Hervé, G. Le Sauvage de l'Aveyron devant les Observateurs de l'Homme. *Revue d'anthropologie*, 1911, *21*, 383–398, 441–454.

Hickernell, W.F. Eugenics and the United States census. *Volta Review*, 1912, *13*, 399–402.

Higgins, D.D. *How to Talk to the Deaf*. Saint Louis: Higgins, 1923. Second edition: Chicago: Paluch, 1942.

Higgins, F.C. The education of the deaf—the book mart, being a list of books on the deaf, speech and speech reading, the language of signs, etc., now in print. *American Annals of the Deaf*, 1947, *92*, 151–168; 1950, *95*, 315–349.

Hilaire, T.R.P. *Discours sur la parole et les sourds-muets*. Currière: Imprimerie de l'Ecole des Sourds-Muets, 1887.

Hirsch, D. *L'Enseignement des sourds-muets d'après la méthode allemande*. Rotterdam: Wyt, 1868.

Hirsch, D. *Le Troisième Congrès International pour l'Amélioration du Sort des Sourds-Muets, tenu à Bruxelles, considéré en rapport avec l'Institution des Sourds-Muets à Rotterdam*. Rotterdam: Van Meurs and Stufkens, 1884.

Hitz, J. Dr. A. Graham Bell's private experimental school. In: Fay, E.A. (1893).

———. Dr. Joseph Claybaugh Gordon. *Association Review*, 1903, *5*, 213–227.

———. Alexander Melville Bell. *Association Review*, 1905, *7*, 421–439.

———. The progress of speech work in foreign schools. *Association Review*, 1907, *9*, 272–280.

Hobart, K.F. Visits to foreign schools. In: Convention of American Instructors of the Deaf, Proceedings (1899), 161–163.

Hodgson, E.A. [Eulogy of President Garfield.] In: Columbian Institution for the Deaf and Dumb, Reports (1883), 7–9.

———. *Benefits of Education to the Deaf*. New York: Fanwood Press, 1917.

Hodgson, K.W. *The Deaf and Their Problems*. London: Watts, 1953.

Hoefer, F. *Nouvelle Biographie générale*. Paris: Didot, 1863.

Hoffbauer, J.C. *Médecine Légale relative aux aliénés et aux sourds-muets*. Translated from the German by A.M. Chambeyron. Paris: Baillière, 1827.

Hoffman, H. The education of deaf-mutes in Germany at the end of the nineteenth century. *Association Review*, 1901, *3*, 1–10.

Hofstadter, R. *Social Darwinism in American Thought, 1860–1915*. Philadelphia: University of Pennsylvania Press, 1944.

Holder, W. An account of an experiment concerning deafness. *Philosophical Transactions*, 1668, *(35)*, 18 May, 665–668.

———. *Elements of Speech, with an appendix concerning persons that are deaf and dumb*. London: Martyn, 1669. Reprinted: Mengston: Scholar Press, 1967.

———. *A Supplement to the Philosophical Transactions of July 1670. Some Reflections on Dr. Wallis, His Letter There Inserted*. London: Brome, 1678.

Holycross, E.I. *The Abbé de l'Epée and Other Early Teachers of the Deaf*. Columbus: I. Holycross, 1913.

Hopkins, S. *Works. With a memoir by E. A. Park*. Boston: Doctrinal Tract and Books Society, 1854.

Horace Mann School for the Deaf. *One Hundredth Anniversary*. Boston: School Committee, 1969.

Hotchkiss, J. B. Articulation for semi-mutes. *American Annals of the Deaf*, 1870, *15*, 136–149.

———. Jared Ayres. *American Annals of the Deaf*, 1886, *31*, 210–215.

———. Memories of old Hartford. Film. Silver Spring: National Association of the Deaf, 1913.

Houdin, A. *Société générale d'assistance et de prévoyance pour les sourds-muets de France . . . Compte-rendu des travaux et de la situation de la Société*. Paris: Le fondateur, 1852.

———. Académie Impériale de Médecine. *Question de la surdi-mutité. Bienfaiteur des sourds-muets et des aveugles des sourds-muets*, 1853, *1*, 71–79; 1854, *2*, 130–141, 188–200; 1855, *3*, 57–134. Revised: *De la surdi-mutité; examen critique et raisonné de la discussion soulevée à l'Académie Impériale de Médecine de Paris, séances des 19 et 26 avril . . . 1853 sur cinq questions*. Paris: Lubé, 1855.

———. *La parole rendue aux sourds-muets* Paris: Asselin, 1865.

———. De la parole articulée dans l'enseignement des sourds-muets. *Bulletin de la Société Centrale d'Education et d'Assistance*, 1874, *1*, 18–20, 46–49, 65–70, 94–98; 1875, *2*, 36–42, 63–67, 85–89; 1876, *3*, 42–44, 52–54.

———. *L'Enseignement des sourds-muets en 1874. L'Enseignement mimique et de la parole articulée. La Vérité sur ces deux enseignements et sur l'état des progrès accomplis*. Paris: Douniol, 1874.

———. *Congrès international de Milan, Rapport sur les mémoires envoyés en réponse à la première et à la deuxième question spéciale du programme*. Paris: author, 1880.

———. *Rapport sur le congrès international des maîtres des sourds-muets à Milan en 1880*. Paris: Imprimerie Nationale, 1881. (a)

———. *Allocutions et discours prononcés aux congrès nationaux de Lyon et de Bordeaux pour l'amélioration du sort des sourds-muets, et au congrès international de Milan*. Paris: Imprimerie de Chaix, 1881. (b)

———. *Congrès national de Bordeaux pour l'amélioration du sort des sourds-muets . . . Rapport de statistique présenté en séance le . . . 11 août 1881*. Bordeaux: Féret et fils, 1882.

———. *Congrès international de Bruxelles*. Brussels: F. Hayez, 1883.

Howard, J.C. Methods of deaf-mute instruction. In: Convention of American Instructors of the Deaf, Proceedings (1915), 44–46.

Howard, L. *The Connecticut Wits*. Chicago: University of Chicago Press, 1943.

Howard, P.E. *The Life Story of Henry Clay Trumbull*. Philadelphia: Sunday School Times, 1905.

Howe, J.W. *Memoir of Dr. Samuel Gridley Howe*. Boston: Wright, 1876. (a)

———. *The Massachusetts Philanthropist*. Boston: Rand, 1876. (b)

Howe, S.G. Letter to Charles Sumner, 12 June 1844. Howe Papers, Houghton Library, Harvard University. (a)

———. Letter to Horace Mann, 9 Oct. 1844. Howe Papers, Houghton Library, Harvard University. (b)

———. Laura Bridgman. *American Journal of Education*, 1857, *4*, 383–400.

———. *Remarks Upon the Education of Deaf-Mutes, in Defence of the Doctrines of the Second Annual Report of the Massachusetts Board of State Charities, and in Reply to the Charges of Rev. Collins Stone, Principal of the American Asylum at Hartford*. Boston: Walker, Fuller, 1866.

———. Letter in regard to certain changes to be made at the Perkins Institution. April 12, 1868. Boston: Perkins Institution, 1868.

———. *Laura Bridgman*. Boston: South Boston Inquirer, 1873.

———. Laura Bridgman. *American Annals of the Deaf*, 1875, *20*, 100–110.

———. *Letters and Journals (edited by Laura E. Richards with notes by F.B. Sanborn)*. Boston: Estes, 1909.

———. See also: Massachusetts Board of State Charities (1866); Massachusetts State Senate Joint Special Committee on the Education of Deaf-Mutes (1867).

Hubbard, G. G. *The Education of Deaf Mutes; Shall It Be by Signs or by Articulation?* Boston: Williams, 1867.

———. Report of President Hubbard of the Clarke Institution for Deaf-Mutes to Hon. J. White, Secretary of the Massachusetts Board of Education. *National Deaf-Mute Gazette*, 1868, *2 (17)*, 10–12.

———. The origin of the Clarke Institution. *American Annals of the Deaf*, 1876, *21*, 178–183.

———. Response to Gallaudet. *American Annals of the Deaf*, 1884, *29*, 64–67.

———. Introduction of the articulating system for the deaf in America. *Science*, 1890, *16 (411)*, 337–340.

———. History of the education of the deaf. In: Alexander Graham Bell Association, Proceedings (1891), 89–101.

———. The founding and early history of the Clarke Institution. In: Clarke School for the Deaf, Reports (1893), 1–8.

———. *The Story of the Rise of the Oral Method in America, as told in the Writings of the late Hon. Gardiner G. Hubbard.* Bell, M.H. (ed.). Washington, D.C.: Roberts, 1898.

Hubbard, G. G., and Gallaudet, E.M. The action of the joint committee on the union of the Convention and the Association. *American Annals of the Deaf*, 1895, *40*, 153–158.

Hubbard, T., et al. Letter to Mrs. M.F. Cogswell [1830] from New Haven. Cogswell Papers, Yale University.

Hubert-Valleroux, M.E. *Des Sourds-Muets et des aveugles. Mémoire sur l'état actuel des institutions à leur usage et sur les réformes à y apporter.* Paris: Masson, 1852.

———. *De l'assistance sociale, ce qu'elle a été, ce qu'elle est, ce qu'elle devrait être.* Paris: Guillaumin, 1855.

Hué, G. *Abbé Sicard.* Paris: 5 rue Bayard, 1908.

Hugentobler, J. *Quelques mots sur la méthode d'articulation dans l'enseignement des sourds-muets.* Lyon: Georg, 1874.

———. *Du Sourd-Muet de naissance.* Neuchâtel: Bulletin Continental, 1876. (a)

———. *Cours d'articulation.* Paris and Lyon: Delgrave, 1876. (b)

———. *L'Enseignement du sourd-muet d'après la méthode orale.* Lyon: Association Typographique, 1882.

———. *Compte-rendu du Congrès de Lyon.* See: Congress on Deaf—National—French (1879).

———. *Des Moyens d'empêcher les communications par signes au début de l'enseignement.* Paris: Ritti, 1886.

———. *L'Education intellectuelle et professionelle du sourd-muet intelligent et de l'enfant sourd-muet arriéré, au point de vue des deux méthodes, méthode orale pure et méthode mixte, Congrès d'Assistance tenu du 26 juin au 3 juillet 1894 à Lyon.* Lyon: P. Legendre, 1894.

———. Reorganization of the education of the deaf in France. *Association Review*, 1905, *7*, 172–174.

Hull, S.E. *The Education of the Deaf and Dumb Practically Considered.* London: [n.p.], 1865.

Hull, S. Letter to Miss Rogers on the international congress held at Milan. In: Clarke School for the Deaf, Reports (1880), 35–43. Reprinted: *Education*, 1881, *1*, 286–293.

———. The International Congress: a reply. *American Annals of the Deaf*, 1881, *26*, 93–98.

Humphrey, H. *The Life and Labors of the Rev. T. H. Gallaudet.* New York: Carter, 1857.

Hunt, W. *American Biographical Sketchbook.* New York: Cornish, Lamport and Company, 1848.

Huntington, E.L. Lydia Sigourney. In: *Eminent Women of the Age.* Hartford: Betts, 1869. Pp. 85–101.

Huntington, G. Chilmark's deaf: valued citizens. *Dukes County Intelligencer*, 1981, *22 (3)*, 98–102.

Husson, H.M. De L'Education physiologique du sens auditif chez les sourds-muets. *Mémoires de l'Académie Royale de Médecine*, 1833, *2*, 178–196. Reprinted: *Transactions Médicales: Journal de Médecine*, 1833, *12*, 249; Itard, J.M.G. *Traité des maladies de l'oreille et de l'audition.* Second edition. Paris: Méquignon-Marvis fils, 1842; Bourneville, D.M. (ed.). *Rapports et mémoires sur le sauvage de l'Aveyron, l'idiotie et la surdi-mutité par Itard.* Paris: F. Alcan, 1894. Excerpted: *Journal général de médecine*, 1828, *103*, 391–398.

Hutton, G. Specimens of a dictionary of natural signs for the deaf and dumb. Unpublished manuscript, Volta Bureau, Washington, D.C., [1855?].

———. The practicality and advantages of writing and printing natural signs. *American Annals of the Deaf*, 1869, *14*, 157–182.

Hutton, J.S. [Importance of sign and sign transcription.] In: Convention of American Instructors of the Deaf, Proceedings (1870), 208–225.

———. Posthumous papers of the late George Hutton. *American Annals of the Deaf*, 1874, *19*, 205–216; 1875, *20*, 91–99; 1876, *21*, 30–47.

Institution Impériale des Sourds-Muets de Paris. *Notice historique de ce qui s'est passé à l'institution des sourds-muets, et à celle des aveugles-nés, les jours où S.S. le pape Pie VII a bien voulu visiter ces deux institutions.* Paris: Imprimerie des Sourds-Muets, 1805.

———. *Exercice publique des sourds-muets de naissance en présence de son éminence M. le cardinal Belloy, Archevêque de Paris et tout son clergé . . . le 8 juillet 1806.* Paris: Imprimerie des Sourds-Muets, 1806.

———. Programme général de l'enseignement des sourds-muets adopté . . . 22 juillet 1837. *Annales de l'éducation des sourds-muets et des aveugles*, 1844, *1*, 129–144, 193–208.

Institution Nationale des Sourds-Muets de Paris. *Arrêté du 23 juillet 1888 déterminant les conditions et programmes des concours et examens pour le recrutement et l'avancement du personnel enseignant des institutions nationales de sourds-muets.* Paris: Atelier de Typographie de l'Institution, 1888.

———. Report to Volta Bureau. In: Volta Bureau, Circular of information number 5. Washington, D.C.: Gibson, 1898. Pp. 6–7.

———. Bernard, R. (ed.). *Catalogue de la Bibliothèque de l'Institution Nationale des Sourds-Muets de Paris; ouvrages en langue française entrés jusqu'en 1940: auteurs.* Paris: L. Rodstein, 1941.

Institution Royale des Sourds-Muets de Paris. *Première circulaire.* Paris: Plassan, 1827.

———. *Deuxième circulaire.* Paris: Imprimerie Royal, 1829.

———. *Troisième circulaire.* Paris: Imprimerie Royal, 1832.

———. *Quatrième circulaire.* Paris: Imprimerie Royal, 1836.

———. Discours du Président à la distribution des prix. 1838–1839. *L'Ami des sourds-muets*, 1839–40, *2*, 40–46.

————. Discours à la distribution des prix pour l'année 1839–40. *L'Ami des sourds-muets*, 1839–40, *3*, 8–13.

————. Discours du Président à la distribution des prix, 13 août 1842. *L'Ami des sourds-muets*, 1842–3, *5*, 24–29.

————. *Mémoire adressé à M. le Ministre de l'Intérieur par les professeurs de l'Institution Royale des Sourds-Muets de Paris sur la nécessité de transférer les écoles de sourds-muets au Ministre de l'Instruction Publique*. Paris: Fain et Thunot, 1847.

Itard, J.M.G. *De L'Education d'un homme sauvage ou des premiers développements physiques et moraux du jeune sauvage de l'Aveyron*. Paris: Gouyon, 1801. Reprinted: Bourneville (1894); Itard (1821d, second edition); Malson (1964). English translations: Nogent, *An Historical Account of the Discovery and Education of a Savage Man, or the first Developments, Physical and Moral, of the Young Savage Caught in the Woods near Aveyron in the Year 1798*. London: Phillips, 1802; Humphrey, G., and Humphrey, M. *The Wild Boy of Aveyron*. New York: Appleton-Century-Crofts, 1932; (excerpts) Lane (1976).

————. *Rapport sur la vaccine, fait aux administrateurs de l'Institution Nationale des Sourds-Muets*. Paris: Imprimerie des Sourds-Muets de Naissance, [1801?].

————. Notes. In: Willich, A.F. *Hygiène domestique ou l'art de conserver la santé et de prolonger la vie*. Vol. 2. Paris: Ducauroy, 1802. Pp. 511–599.

————. *Rapport fait à S.E. le Ministre de l'Intérieur sur les nouveaux développements et l'état actuel du sauvage de l'Aveyron*. Paris: Imprimerie Impériale, 1807. Reprinted: Bourneville (1894); Itard (1821d, second edition); Malson (1964). English translations: Humphrey, G., and Humphrey, M. *The Wild Boy of Aveyron*. New York: Appleton-Century-Crofts, 1932; Malson (1964); (excerpts) Lane (1976).

————. Extraits de deux mémoires présentés à la Société . . . Mémoire sur les moyens de rendre l'ouïe aux sourds-muets . . . Mémoire sur les moyens de rendre la parole aux sourds-muets. *Bulletin de l'Ecole de Médecine de Paris*, 1808, *1*, 72–79.

————. Rapport fait à MM. les administrateurs de l'Institution des Sourds-Muets, sur ceux d'entre les élèves qui, étant doués de quelque degré d'audition, seraient susceptibles d'apprendre à parler et à entendre. *Journal universel des sciences médicales*, 1821, *22*, 5–17. (a)

————. Sourd. In: Adelon (1821), vol. 52, pp. 210–215. (b)

————. Surdité. In: Adelon (1821), vol. 53, pp. 461–506. (c)

————. *Traité des maladies de l'oreille et de l'audition*. Paris: Méquignon-Marvis, 1821. Second edition: Paris: Méquignon-Marvis fils, 1842. (d)

————. *Deuxième rapport fait en 1824 sur nos sourds-muets incomplets à l'occasion de la jeune Goddart*. Unpublished manuscript, Archives de l'Institution Nationale des Sourds-Muets, Paris, 1824.

————. *Rapport de M. Itard fait à l'administration le 8 juillet 1825*. Unpublished manuscript, Archives de l'Institution Nationale des Sourds-Muets. Paris, 1825. Reprinted: Premier rapport . . . sur divers traitements contre la surdi-mutité. *Revue médicale française et étrangère et journal de clinique*, 1827, *3*, 27–38.

————. Lettres sur les sourds-muets qui entendent et qui parlent. *Journal d'instruction des sourds-muets et des aveugles*, 1826, *1*, 208–231, 253–263. Reprinted (Third letter): *Lettre aux rédacteurs du "Globe" sur les sourds-muets qui entendent et qui parlent*. Paris: Guiraudet, [1829]. (a)

————. *Troisième rapport, contenant un premier aperçu sur la méthode d'instruction à donner à ceux des sourds-muets qui sont doués jusqu'à un certain point des facultés auditives et orales (7 juillet 1826)*. Unpublished manuscript, Archives de l'Institution Nationale des Sourds-Muets. Paris, 1826. (b)

————. Deuxième rapport . . . sur divers traitements contre la surdi-mutité. *Revue médicale française et étrangère et journal de clinique*, 1827, *3*, 189–200. (a)

————. Troisième rapport. *Revue médicale française et étrangère et journal de clinique*, 1827, *3*, 200–210. (b)

————. Notes. In: Hoffbauer, J.C. *Médecine Légale relative aux aliénés et aux sourds-muets*. Paris: Baillière, 1827, Pp. 176–230. (c)

————. Traitement de la surdité de naissance par les injections dans l'oreille moyenne. *Journal général de médecine*, 1827, *100*, 222–226. (d)

————. Mémoire sur le mutisme produit par la lésion des fonctions intellectuelles. *Mémoires de l'Académie Royale de Médecine*, 1828, *1*, 1–18. Reprinted: Bourneville (1894); Itard (1821, second edition).

————. Sur l'usage et la forme des cornets acoustiques. *Journal général de médecine*, 1829, *106*, 284–288.

————. Sur un mémoire intitulé "Recherches sur la surdi-mutité, considérée particulièrement sous le rapport de ses causes et de son traitement" (par Gairal). *Mémoires de l'Académie Royale de Médecine*, 1836, *5*, 525–552. English translation: On the surgical treatment of deafness. In: *Dunglison's American Medical Library*. Philadelphia: Waldre, 1838. Pp. 75–92.

————. Testament. *Bulletin de l'Académie de Médecine*, 1839, *3*, 924–926.

Jack, F.M. Why Wisconsin believes in public day schools for the deaf. In: National Education Association, Proceedings (1907), 986–990.

Jacobs, J.A. *Lessons for the Deaf and Dumb*. Lexington: Todd, 1834.

————. Relative to the establishment of new institutions. In: Convention of American Instructors of the Deaf and Dumb, Proceedings (1851), 136–138.

————. The Kentucky Institution for the Deaf and Dumb. *American Annals of the Deaf*, 1852, *4*, 237–244.

————. On the disuse of natural signs in the instruction of deaf mutes. *American Annals of the Deaf*, 1853, *5*, 95–110.

————. On the disuse of colloquial signs in the instruction of the deaf and dumb, and the necessity of general signs following the order of the words. *American Annals of the Deaf*, 1855, *7*, 69–81. (a).

————. The philosophy of signs in the instruction of deaf mutes. *American Annals of the Deaf,* 1855, *7,* 197–228. (b)

————. Mechanical, alias methodical signs. *American Annals of the Deaf,* 1855, *8,* 93–104. (c)

————. The methodical signs for *and* and the verb *to be. American Annals of the Deaf,* 1856, *8,* 185–187.

————. Preface to an unpublished work. *American Annals of the Deaf,* 1857, *9,* 129–139.

————. A sufficient admission—words the representatives of signs—signs in the order of words. *American Annals of the Deaf,* 1858, *10,* 219–227.

————. The relation of written words to signs, the same as their relation to spoken words. *American Annals of the Deaf,* 1859, *11,* 65–78.

Jacobs, L. *A Deaf Adult Speaks Out* [1974]. Second edition. Washington, D.C.: Gallaudet College Press, 1980.

Jäger, V. *Über die Behandlung welche Blinden und Taubstummen Kindern zu Theil werden sollten.* Stuttgart: [n.p.], 1830.

James, E. *Report of an expedition from Pittsburg to the Rocky Mountains, performed in the years 1819, 1820 . . . under the command of Major S. H. Long.* London: 1823. Reprinted: Cleveland: A. H. Clark, 1905. Excerpted: James, E. The Indian language of signs. *American Annals of the Deaf,* 1852, *4,* 157–172.

Jameson, E.O. *Cogswells in America.* Boston: Mudge, 1884.

Jamet, P.F. *Mémoires sur l'instruction des sourds-muets.* Third edition. Paris: Poussielgue, 1832.

Jarvis, E. *Insanity and Idiocy in Massachusetts. Report of the Commission on Lunacy, 1855.* Cambridge, Mass.: Harvard University Press, 1971.

Jauffret, L.F. *La Corbeille de fleurs et le panier de fruits.* Paris: Perlet, 1806–1807. Second edition: *Le Panier de fruits.* Geneva-Paris: 1819.

Javal, E. [Adieu aux professeurs sourds.] *Revue internationale de l'enseignement des sourds-muets,* 1887, *3,* 285–287.

Jeanvoine, H. Les sourds-muets et la parole. *Journal des sourds-muets,* 1902, *8,* 163–165.

————. The moral, intellectual, industrial, and social status of the deaf in France. In: Congress of Deaf—International—Fourth (1904), 89–99.

Jenkins, R.C. *Henry Barnard.* Hartford: Hartford State Teachers Association, 1937.

Jenkins, W.G. The scientific testimony of "Facts and Opinions." *Science,* 1890, *16 (393),* 85–88. (a)

————. Professor A.G. Bell's studies on the deaf. *Science,* 1890, *16 (395),* 117–119. (b)

————. Dr. A.G. Bell's studies on the deaf. *Science,* 1890, *16 (398),* 163. (c)

————. Oral work in schools using the combined system. In: Convention of American Instructors of the Deaf, Proceedings (1893), 134–138.

Jenks, H.F. The deaf hear, the dumb speak. *Monthly Religious Magazine,* 1873, *50,* 125–134.

Johnson, R.H. The marriage of the deaf. *Jewish Deaf,* 1918, 5–6.

Johnson, R.O. State of Indiana Institution for the Education of the Deaf. In: Fay, E.A. (1893).

Johnson, S. *A Journey to the Western Islands of Scotland.* London: Strahaw and Cadell, 1775. Reprinted: *Johnson's Journey to the Western Islands.* Boston: Houghton Mifflin, 1965.

Jones, J.W. One hundred years of history in the education of the deaf in America and its present status. In: Convention of American Instructors of the Deaf, Proceedings (1918), 181–199.

————. The first triumvirate among educators of the deaf in the United States. *American Annals of the Deaf,* 1922, *67,* 193–203.

Jones, W.G. The importance of signs. In: Convention of American Instructors of the Deaf, Proceedings (1890), 108–111.

Jordan, D.S. Committee on Eugenics. *Proceedings of the American Breeders' Association,* 1909, *5,* 217–218.

Jordan, I.K., Gustason, G., and Rosen, R. Current communication trends at programs for the deaf. *American Annals of the Deaf,* 1976, *12,* 527–532.

————. An update on current communication trends at programs for the deaf. *American Annals of the Deaf,* 1979, *124,* 350–357.

de Jouy, E. *L'Hermite de la chaussée d'Antin.* Paris: Pillet, 1813–1814. English translation (excerpted): *Portfolio,* 1817, *3,* 122–127; *American Annals of the Deaf,* 1859, *11,* 78–84.

Jubinal, A. *Le Sourd-Muet de l'abbé de l'Epée.* St. Germain: Toinon, [1866].

Karacostas, A. L'Institution Nationale des Sourds-Muets de Paris de 1790 à 1800. Doctoral dissertation, Université de Paris V, Faculté de Médecine Cochin Port-Royal, 1981.

Keating B. *The Flamboyant Mr. Colt and His Deadly Six-Shooter.* New York: Doubleday, 1978.

Keep, J. R. On the best method of teaching language to the higher classes in our institutions for the deaf and dumb. In: Convention of American Instructors of the Deaf, Proceedings (1853), 15–35.

————. The mode of learning the sign language. In: Convention of American Instructors of the Deaf, Proceedings (1857), 133–153.

———— *Remarks on the Theories of Dr. Samuel Howe Respecting the Education of Deaf-Mutes as set forth in the Second Report of the Board of State Charities.* [Boston?]: [n.p.], 1866.

————. Signs in deaf-mute education. *New Englander,* 1867, *26,* 506–524.

————. How should deaf-mute children learn verbal language? *American Annals of the Deaf,* 1870, *15,* 26–37.

————. Natural signs—shall they be abandoned? *American Annals of the Deaf,* 1871, *16,* 17–25. (a)

————. The sign language. *New Englander*, 1871, *30*, 203–214. Reprinted: *American Annals of the Deaf*, 1871, *16*, 221–234. (b)

————. David Ely Bartlett. *American Annals of the Deaf*, 1880, *25*, 53–67.

Keep, J.R., and Hubbard, G.G. [Exchange of letters on] the language of signs. *American Annals of the Deaf*, 1869, *14*, 89–95.

Kelkun, C. *Au Jour le jour. Chroniques sur Lille*. Lille: Nouveliste, 1888.

Keller, H.A. *The World I Live In*. New York: Century, 1908.

————. *The Story of My Life*. Garden City: Doubleday, 1954.

Kendall, A. *Autobiography*. New York: Smith, 1949.

Kerger, L. W. *Littera ad Ettmullerum de cura surdorum mutorumque*. 1704. German translation in: Raphel (1801).

————. De surdomutorum cura lignitio. In: Academiae Caesareo-Leopoldino, *Naturae curiosorum Ephemerides: centuria 1 & 2*. Frankfurt: 1712. Appendix, p. 233.

Kilian, C. *Historique de l'enseignement des sourds-muets en Allemagne*. Paris: Pelluard, 1885.

Kimball, E. Letter to M.F. Cogswell, 4 Jan. 1814, from Salem. Cogswell Papers, Yale University.

Kinney, R. H. A few thoughts on the universality and power of the language of signs. In: Convention of American Instructors of the Deaf, Proceedings (1859), 85–98.

Kinsey, A. A. *The Education of the Deaf on the German system*. London: Allen, 1879.

————. (ed.). See: Congress on Deaf—International—Second (1880).

————. *On the Education of the Deaf*. London: [n.p.], 1880.

————. *How Far Is the German System Practiced in the Institutions for the Deaf and Dumb in the United Kingdom?* London: Allen, 1881.

Kitto, J. *The Lost Senses*. Edinburgh: Oliphant, 1848.

————. *Memoirs of John Kitto*. Edinburgh: Oliphant, 1856.

Klima, E., and Bellugi, U. *The Signs of Language*. Cambridge Mass.: Harvard University Press, 1979.

Kloss, H. "Abstand" languages and "Ausbau" languages. *Anthropological Linguistics*, 1967, 9 (7), 29–41. (a)

————. Bilingualism and nationalism. *Journal of Social Issues*, 1967, *23*, 39–47. (b)

Knight, J. Introductory lecture. *Yale Medical Institution*, 1838, 13–19. Reprinted: Tribute to M. F. Cogswell. In: Williams, S.W. (ed.). *American Medical Biography*. Greenfield: Merriam, 1845. Pp. 100–109.

Knowlson, J. R. The idea of gesture as a universal language in the 17th and 18th centuries. *Journal of the History of Ideas*, 1965, 495–508.

Kotzebue, A. F. von. Institut des sourds-muets. In: *Souvenirs de Paris en 1804*. Translated from the German, Second edition. Paris: Barba, 1805. Vol. 2, pp. 209–215.

Kroeber, A. L. Sign language inquiry. *International Journal of American Linguistics*, 1958, *24*, 1–19. Reprinted with: Mallery (1881), 1972 edition.

Kruse, O. F. *Essai sur la conciliation des méthodes d'enseignement des sourds-muets*. Translated from German by de Haerne. Bruges: Beyaert, 1871.

————. The combined method of instructing the deaf and dumb. *American Annals of the Deaf*, 1872, *17*, 197–256.

Ladreit de Lacharrière, J.F. Assistance des sourds-muets adultes. *Revue internationale de l'enseignement des sourds-muets*, 1894, *10*, 322–331.

————. A propos du congrès des sourds-muets de 1900. *Journal des sourds-muets*, 1899, *5*, 367–368. (a)

————. Congrès international de 1900. *Journal des sourds-muets*, 1899, *5*, 370–371. (b)

————. Address of Dr. Ladreit de Lacharrière, chairman of organization of the Paris Congress. Section of hearing persons. *Association Review*, 1900, *2*, 463–470. (c)

Ladreit de Lacharrière, J. F., and Bélanger, A. (eds.). See: Congress on Deaf—National—French (1885).

Lagier, V. Méthodes et effets de méthodes. *Journal des sourds-muets*, 1869, *2*, 322–323.

Laishley, R. *Report upon State Education in Great Britain, France, Switzerland, Italy, Germany, Belgium and the United States*. London: Judd, 1885.

Lallemand, L. *Histoire de la charité. Tome 4. Les temps modernes. Europe*. Paris: Picard, 1912.

Lambert, L.M. *Le langage de la physionomie et du geste*. Paris: J. Lecoffre, 1865.

————. Les sourds-muets reçus aux Tuileries par LL. MM. l'Empereur, l'Impératrice, et le Prince Impérial. *Le Conseiller des sourds-muets*, 1866, *2*, 7–8.

————. Méthode d'instruction des sourds-muets adultes. *Le Conseiller des sourds-muets*, 1870, 6, 69–83, 167–174.

Lambert, W.E. A social psychology of bilingualism. *Journal of Social Issues*, 1967, *23 (2)*, 91–109.

Lampson, E.R. Mason Fitch Cogswell. *Yale Journal of Biology and Medicine*, 1930, *3*, 4–9.

Lamson, M. *Life and Education of Laura Dewey Bridgman, the Deaf, Dumb and Blind Girl*. Boston: New England Publishing, 1878.

Lance, Chief Long. *Indian Sign Language*. Akron: B.F. Goodrich, 1930.

Landes, J. *De la réorganisation de l'enseignement de l'institution des Sourds-Muets de Paris*. Paris: Boucquin, 1860.

————. *Une Lettre de L'Impératrice Marie Théodorowna de Russie à L'abbé Sicard et autres documents inédits*. Sarlat: Michelet, 1876.

Lane, H. *The Wild Boy of Aveyron*. Cambridge, Mass.: Harvard University Press, 1976. French translation: Paris, Payot, 1979.

―――. Notes for a psycho-history of American Sign Language. In: National Association of the Deaf, *Proceedings of the National Symposium on Sign Language Research and Teaching*. Silver Spring: National Association of the Deaf, 1977. Pp. 105–114. Reprinted: *Deaf American*, 1977, *30*, 3–7.

―――. My name is Laurent Clerc. In: National Association of the Deaf, *Proceedings of the National Symposium on Sign Language Research and Teaching*. Silver Spring: National Association of the Deaf, 1978. Pp. 327–334.

―――. A chronology of the oppression of sign language in France and the United States. In: Lane, H., and Grosjean, F. (1980), 119–161. French translation: *Langages*, 1980, *56*, 92–124. (a)

―――. Jean Massieu and deaf teachers of the deaf. Address to the National Symposium on Sign Language Research and Teaching, Boston, October 1980. (b)

Lane, H., and Battison, R. The role of oral language in the evolution of manual language. In: Gerver, D., and Sinaiko, W. (eds). *Language Interpretation and Communication*. New York: Plenum, 1978. Pp. 57–80. (a)

Lane, H., and Grosjean, F. *Recent Perspectives on American Sign Language*. Hillsdale: Lawrence Erlbaum Associates, 1980. French translation: *Langages*, 1980, *56*.

Lane, H.S. Thoughts on oral advocacy today . . . with memories of the Society of Oral Advocates. *Volta Review*, 1976, *78*, 136–140.

Larned, E.D. *History of Windham County*. Worcester: C. Hamilton, 1874–1880.

―――. *Historical Gleanings in Windham County, Connecticut*. Providence: Preston and Rounds, 1899.

La Rochelle, E. *Congrès de Milan pour L'amélioration du sort des sourds-muets en 1880*. Paris: M. Saint-Jorre, 1880.

―――. *Jacob-Rodrigues Pereire, premier instituteur des sourds-muets en France: sa view et ses travaux*. Paris: P. Dupont, 1882.

―――. *Le Ministère de l'Intérieur et l'éducation des sourds-muets*. Paris: Saint-Jorre, 1883.

―――. *Congrès international, Bruxelles, 1883, sourds-muets. Réponse à M. Claveau à propos de son rapport au Ministre de l'Intérieur*. Paris: Saint-Jorre, 1884.

―――. *Congrès administratif français de 1885 dans L'intérêt des sourds-muets. Examen critique*. Paris: Saint-Jorre, 1886.

Lash, J.P. *Helen and Teacher*. New York: Merloyd Lawrence, 1980.

Lasius, O.B. *Ausführliche Nachricht*. Leipsig: Weygand, 1775.

Lasso, [?]. *Tratado legal sobre los mudos*. [Manuscript, 1550.] Madrid: Nuñez, 1919.

Laurent, A. *Mémoire sur l'éducation des sourds-muets, à MM. les membres du conseil d'administration de l'Institution Royale des Sourds-Muets de Paris*. Blois: Dézairs, 1831. (a)

―――. *La Parole rendue aux sourds-muets*. Paris: Johanneau, 1831. (b)

Lazare, F. *Dictionnaire administratif et historique des rues de Paris*. Paris: Lazare, 1844.

Lebos, P. (ed.). *France. Dictionnaire encyclopédique*. Paris: Didot, 1840–1845.

Lebouvier Desmortiers, U.R.T. *Mémoire ou considérations sur les sourds-muets de naissance . . .* Paris: Buisson, 1800.

Le Cat, J.B. *Traité des sensations et des passions générales et des sens en particulier*. Paris: Valat La Chapelle, 1767.

Lefèbvre, G. *The French Revolution*. New York: Columbia University Press, 1969.

Lefèbvre, H. Les Aveugles et les sourds-muets. Institution de Ronchin-Lez-Lille. Unpublished manuscript, Bibliothèque Municipale de Lille. [185?].

Leglay, A.J. [Commencement at Massieu's school for the deaf.] *L'Echo du Nord, (241)*, 29 Aug. 1838.

―――. Massieu. [Funeral oration.] In: *Annuaire statistique du département du Nord*. Lille: 1847. Pp. 444–448.

Leglay, J. Massieu. In: *Biographie universelle . . .* Paris: Gaume, 1856. Vol. 9, p. 106.

Legouvé, E. Bouilly et l'abbé de l'Epée. *Revue des cours littéraires*, 1870, *(13)*, 193–200.

Legrand, A. Mariages des sourds-muets en Amérique. *Revue générale de l'enseignement des sourds-muets*, 1900, *2*, 41–45.

―――. Biographie de Massieu. *Revue générale de l'enseignement des sourds-muets*, 1911, *13 (2))*, 21–26.

Lenoir, A. *Dactylologie ou langage des doigts . . .* Paris: 20 rue M. le Prince, 1848.

―――. *Faits divers*. Paris: 15 rue Racine, 1850.

Lenôtre. See: Gosselin, L. (1929).

Leonard, E.C. The fiftieth anniversary of the founding of the Clarke School, Northampton, Mass. *Volta Review*, 1918, *20*, 45–65.

Le Père, E.C.P. *Statue de l'abbé de l'Epée. Compte-rendu de la séance d'inauguration présidée le 14 mai 1879, dans la salle des exercices de l'Institution Nationale des Sourds-Muets de Paris, par M. Le Père*. Paris: Boucquin, 1879.

Leroy, F. *Discours prononcé aux distributions des prix de l'Institution Royale des Sourds-Muets de Bordeaux, 1839–1841, accompagné de notes historiques*. Bordeaux: H. Faye, 1842.

Leroy, M. *Discours funèbre prononcé au cimetière de l'Est, en présence et au nom de la Société Grammaticale, sur la tombe de l'abbé Sicard, le 11 mai 1823, jour anniversaire de sa mort. Suivi des adieux gesticulés par Berthier, sourd-muet de naissance, au nom de ses compagnons d'infortune*. Paris: Herhan, 1823.

L'Esprit, R.A.M. L'abbé Sicard, second instituteur des sourds-muets. *Le Magasin pittoresque*, 1917, 1 August, 232–236. (a)

————. L'Abbé Sicard et Haüy. *Revue générale de l'enseignement des sourds-muets*, 1917, *18(10)*, 157–160.

Ligot, J. The deaf as teachers and teaching as a profession for the deaf. In: Congress of Deaf—International—Second (1893), 159–162.

————. Deux opinions. *Journal des sourds-muets*, 1895, *1*, 340–341.

————. Une réponse forcée. *Journal des sourds-muets*, 1896, *2*, 338–340.

Limosin, L. Les drôleries du congrès international de Bruxelles. *Défense des sourds-muets*, 1885, *1*, 58–60. (a)

————. Notice biographique sur J. Piroux. *Défense des sourds-muets*, 1885, *1*, 60–62. (b)

————. La fête de l'abbé de l'Epée. *Défense des sourds-muets*, 1885, *1*, 63–64. (c)

————. Encore les drôleries du congrès national des instituteurs des sourds-muets de Paris. *Défense des sourds-muets*, 1885, *1*, 65–69. (d)

————. Pourquoi garder le silence à la distribution des prix dans l'Institution des Sourds-Muets de Paris cette année. *Défense des sourds-muets*, 1885, *1*, 75–76. (e)

————. A la future ligue des sourds-muets, pour la défense de leur école mère instituée par décrets de l'assemblée constituante (loi des 21 et 29 juillet 1791). *Défense des sourds-muets*, 1885, *1*, 83–86. (f)

————. Les enfants sourds-muets réduits à essuyer les haleines puantes des Chevaliers de l'Articulation. *Défense des sourds-muets*, 1886, *2*, 31–33, 43–45, 55–57, 67–69. (a)

————. Sus à Franck fanatisé par la méthode allemande d'articulation. *Défense des sourds-muets*, 1886, *2*, 79–81. (b)

————. Un peu d'attention s'il vous plaît, MM. Franck et Cie. *Défense des sourds-muets*, 1886, *2*, 105–106. (c)

————. Les vautours du Prométhée des sourds-muets. *Défense des sourds-muets*, 1886, *2*, 127–129. (d)

Lippitt, M.A. *I Married a New Englander*. Boston: Chapman, 1947.

Lloyd, G. *International Research Seminar on the Vocational Rehabilitation of Deaf Persons*. Washington, D.C.: Social and Rehabilitation Service, DHEW, 1968.

Locke, J. *An Essay Concerning Human Understanding*. London: Th. Basset, 1690. Reprinted: New York: Dover, 1959.

Logan, J.H. The necessity of a training school for teachers of the deaf. *American Annals of the Deaf*, 1877, *22*, 89–92.

Long, J.S. *The Sign Language: A Manual of Signs*. Iowa City: Athens Press, 1918.

Long, S.H. *Expedition to the Rocky Mountains*. See: James, E.

Longueville, T. *Life of Sir Kenelm Digby*. London: Longmans, Green, 1896.

Lorenzana, F. *Cartas pastorales y edictos*. Mexico: Hogal, 1770. Translated in: Heath (1972).

Lowell, J.R. A Virginian in New England thirty-five years ago. *Atlantic Monthly*, 1870, *26*, 739–748. Excerpted: *American Annals of the Deaf*, 1872, *17*, 64.

Lunde, A.S. *Occupational Conditions Among the Deaf; a Report on a National Survey*. Washington, D.C.: Gallaudet, 1959.

Lyman, T. *A Few Weeks in Paris*. Boston: Eliot, 1814.

[Macaulay, Z.]. United States Asylum for the deaf and dumb. *Christian Observer*, 1817, *16*, 822–823.

[————]. Answers to correspondents. *Christian Observer*, 1818, *17*, 68. (a)

[————]. Answers to correspondents. *Christian Observer*, 1818, *17*, 132. (b)

————. Review of Gallaudet's "Discourses." *Christian Observer*, 1818, *17*, 456–470. (c)

Mackenzie, C. *Alexander Graham Bell, the Man Who Contracted Space*. New York: Houghton Mifflin, 1928. Reprinted: Freeport: Books for Libraries Press, 1971.

Magnat, M. *Cours d'articulation*. Paris: Sandoz, 1874.

————. *Méthode Jacob-Rodrigues-Pereire appliquée . . . à l'enseignement du premier âge*. Paris: Fishbacher et Sandoz, 1876.

————. *Méthode et procédés, plan d'études (Congrès international de Paris, 1878)*. Geneva: Taponnier and Studer, 1879.

————. *Organisation des écoles de sourds-muets. Etudes d'un des rapporteurs du comité d'organisation du congrès international de Milan en 1880*. Geneva: Tapponier and Studer, 1880.

————. *De l'Impossibilité de l'enseignement des sourds-muets dans l'école primaire. Réponse à M. Grosselin*. Paris: author, 1882. (a)

————. *Historique de la fondation des congrès pour l'amélioration du sort des sourds-muets*. Paris: author, 1882. (b)

————. Biographie: Léon Vaïsse. *Revue internationale de l'enseignement des sourds-muets*, 1885, *1*, 240–244.

————. Historical sketch of the teaching of deaf-mutes in France. In: Alexander Graham Bell Association, Proceedings (1896), 66–81.

Maignet, E. *Rapport et projet de décret sur l'origine des établissements pour les sourds-muets indigents*. Paris: Imprimerie Nationale, 1793.

Mallery, G. *A Collection of Gesture Signs and Signals of the North American Indians with some Comparisons*. Washington, D.C.: Smithsonian Institution, 1880. Reprinted: Umiker-Sebeok and Sebeok (1978). (a)

————. *Introduction to the Study of Sign Language Among the North American Indians as Illustrating the Gesture Speech of Mankind*. Washington, D.C.: Bureau of American Ethnology, 1880. Reprinted: Umiker-Sebeok and Sebeok (1978). (b)

———. The sign language of the North American Indians. In: American Association for the Advancement of Science, Proceedings (1879), 493–519. Reprinted: *American Annals of the Deaf*, 1880, *25*, 1–19. (c)

———. *Sign Language among North American Indians Compared with that among other Peoples and Deaf-Mutes*. Washington, D.C.: Bureau of American Ethnology, 1881. Reprinted: The Hague: Mouton, 1972.

———. The gesture speech of man. American Association for the Advancement of Science, Proceedings (1882), 283–313. Excerpted: *American Annals of the Deaf*, 1881, *27*, 69. Reprinted: Umiker-Sebeok and Sebeok (1978).

Malson, L. (ed.). *Les Enfants sauvages*. Paris: Union Générale d'Editions, 1964. English translation: *Wolf Child*. New York: Monthly Review Press, 1972.

Manceron, C. *Les Hommes de la liberté: I. Les Vingt Ans du roi*. Paris: Lafont, 1972. English translation: *Twilight of the Old Order*. New York: Knopf, 1977.

Mann, E.J. *The Deaf and Dumb; or a Collection of Articles Relating to the Condition of Deaf Mutes, their Education, and the Principal Asylums Devoted to their Instruction*. Boston: Hitchcock, 1836.

Mann, H. Seventh annual report of the secretary of the [Massachusetts] Board of Education. *Common School Journal*, 1844, *6*, 65–196. (a)

———. Letter to S.G. Howe, 19 Oct. 1844. Mann Papers, Massachusetts Historical Society. (b)

———. *Reply to the "Remarks" of Thirty-one Boston Schoolmasters on the Seventh Annual Report of the Secretary of the Massachusetts Board of Education*. Boston: Fowle, 1844. (c)

———. *Answer to the "Rejoinder" of Twenty-nine Boston Schoolmasters, Part of Thirty-one Who Published "Remarks" on the Seventh Annual Report of the Secretary of the Massachusetts Board of Education*. Boston: Fowle and Capen, 1845.

———. *Report of an Educational Tour in Germany and Parts of Great Britain and Ireland*. London: Simpkin, 1846.

———. *The Life and Works of Horace Mann*. Boston: Walker Fuller, 1865.

———. *Horace Mann and the Crisis in Education*. Fuller, L. (ed.). Antioch: Antioch Press, 1965.

Mann, M., and Peet, H.P. Exchange of letters on teaching the deaf and dumb to speak. *Herald of Health*, 1868, *11*, 230; *12*, 77–80, 230.

Mann, M.T. *Life of Horace Mann*. Boston: Small, 1888. Reprinted: Washington, D.C.: National Education Association, 1937.

Mantel, I. *L'Otologie à Paris au debut du 19e siècle*. Zurich: Jures-Verlag, 1965.

Marchio, Padre. A reply to Dr. Gallaudet (Abridged from the Italian). *American Annals of the Deaf*, 1881, *26*, 130–132, 160–164.

Marcy, R.B. *The Prairie Traveler*. New York: Harper, 1859. Reprinted: Williamstown: Corner House Publishers, 1968.

Marechalle, A.M., et Constant, L.C.L. *L'Abbé de l'Epée ou le muet de Toulouse, pièce historique*. Paris: Breaute, 1831.

Marichelle, H. Bouches closes entr'ouvertes. "Que M. Binet vienne voir nos élèves." *L'Eclair*, December 1909.

Markowicz, H. L'Epée's methodical signs revisited. In: Williams, C.M. (ed.). *Proceedings of the Second Gallaudet Symposium on Research in Deafness: Language and Communication Research Problems*. Washington, D.C.: Gallaudet Press, 1975. Pp. 73–78.

———. *American Sign Language: Fact and Fancy*. Washington, D.C.: Gallaudet College, 1977.

———. *La communauté des sourds-muets en tant que minorité linguistique*. *Coup d'Oeil*, 1980, *24*, supplement.

Maroger, D. *Catherine II, impératrice de Russie. Mémoires de Catherine II écrits par elle-même*. Paris: Hachette, 1953.

Martha, A., and Gaillard, H. See: Congress on Deaf—International—Fourth (1900).

Martineau, H. Letter to the deaf. *Tait's Edinburgh Magazine*, 1834, *1*, 174–179.

———. *Retrospect of Western Travel*. New York: Harper, 1838.

Massachusetts Board of State Charities. *Annual Reports*, 1–15. Boston: Wright and Potter, 1863/64–1877/78.

Massachusetts House of Representatives. Committee on Public Charitable Institutions. *Report on Deaf and Dumb*. House Document 66. 1843.

Massachusetts House of Representatives, Joint Special Committee. Draft Report. Unpublished manuscript, 1863. (a)

———. Report on the Creation of a Board of State Charities. House Document 277, April 20, 1863. (b)

Massachusetts Senate, Committee on Education. Committee report on the petition of Amos Smith Jr. . . . Senate Document 133. 1861.

Massachusetts Senate, Committee on Public Charitable Institutions. Report on bill to incorporate Massachusetts school for deaf-mutes, April 12, 1864. Senate Documents 170, 171, 172. Final Report, May 11, 1864, Senate Document 287.

Massachusetts Senate Joint Special Committee on the Education of Deaf-Mutes. *Report on Deaf-Mute Education in Massachusetts*. Senate Document 265. 27 May 1867. Boston: Wright and Potter, 1867.

Massachusetts State Legislature. Census of deaf and dumb persons. Manuscript, State Archives. 1817.

Massieu, J. Vers de J. Massieu, sourd et muet de naissance à MM. les Francs-Maçons de la loge de Bordeaux, qui le font élever à leurs frais, à l'école des sourds-muets de Paris, par Ferlus, interprète de Massieu. *Journal encyclopédique*, 1790, September, 275.

———. *Nomenclature ou tableau général des noms, des adjectifs énonciatifs* . . . Paris: 1808.

———. *Recueil des définitions et réponses de Massieu et Clerc . . .* London: Cox and Bayle, 1815.

Massieu, J.B. *Rapport et projet de décret sur l'établissement d'une école de sourds-muets en la ville de Bordeaux.* [Paris]: Imprimé par l'ordre de la Convention Nationale, [1793].

Maudit, M. Les sourds-muets et la méthode orale. In: Congress on Deaf—International—Fourth (1900), 57–90.

———. *L'Education des sourds-muets.* Paris: Hachette, 1900.

Mayne, R.E. The Bell family and English speech. *Volta Review,* 1929, *31,* 453–456.

McClure, G. The first oral school west of the Alleghanies. *American Annals of the Deaf,* 1899, *44,* 359–363.

———. The first State School for the deaf. *American Annals of the Deaf,* 1923, *68,* 97–120.

———. Dr. Edward Gallaudet as I remember him. *Just Once a Month,* 1949, *29,* 1–3, 12–16.

———. Letter to Maxine Tull Boatner, 1950. Gallaudet Papers, Library of Congress.

———. The history of LPF. In: Convention of American Instructors of the Deaf, Proceedings (1961), 103–108.

McClure, W. Historical perspectives in the education of the deaf. In: Griffith, J. (ed.). *Persons with Hearing Loss.* Springfield: Charles Thomas, 1969. Pp. 3–30.

McClure, W.J. The controversy over methods. *Silent Worker,* 1954, *66,* 13–15.

McConnell, A. *Tsar Alexander I: Paternalistic Reformer.* Arlington Heights: AHM Publishing, 1970.

McGregor, R.P. Oration [on history of deaf education in the U.S.]. In: National Association of the Deaf, Proceedings (1890), 21–31.

———. Deaf teachers. In: Congress of Deaf—International—Second (1893), 163–166.

———. The proscription of signs. In: National Association of the Deaf, Proceedings (1896), 43–47.

———. The social side of oralism. *American Annals of the Deaf,* 1910, *55,* 403–405.

———. Introduction. In: Holycross, E. (1913), 5–9.

McIntire, T. Indiana Institution for the Deaf and Dumb. *American Annals of the Deaf,* 1854, *6,* 142–161.

Meadow, K. Early manual communication in relation to the deaf child's intellectual, social and communicative functioning. *American Annals of the Deaf,* 1968, *113,* 29–41.

Meding, H.L. *Manuel du Paris médical: recueil des renseignements historiques, statistiques, administratifs et scientifiques sur les hôpitaux et hospices civils et militaires.* Paris: Baillière, 1853.

Meltzer, M. *A Light in the Dark: The Life of Samuel Gridley Howe.* New York: Crowell, 1964.

Menard de la Groye, F.R.P. *Rapport fait sur une pétition du Citoyen Alhoy, premier instituteur et chef de l'Ecole Nationale des Sourds-Muets de Paris, tendant à faire adopter un moyen simple et facile pour assurer l'existence de cette école, et pour en conserver et créer d'autres également précieuses à l'humanité.* Paris: Imprimerie Nationale, 1800.

Ménière, P. *De la guérison de la surdi-mutité et de l'éducation des sourds-muets. Exposé de la discussion qui a eu lieu à l'Académie Impériale de Médecine, avec notes critiques.* Paris: Baillière, 1853.

Meramia, [pseud.]. Letter to the editor [on Sicard's instruction]. *Christian Observer,* 1815, 371–372.

Mercier, L.S. *Mon bonnet de nuit.* Neuchâtel: Société typographique, 1784.

Mersch, [?]. Le Combat pour le mime. *La France des sourds-muets,* 1904, *2,* 173–175.

Messerli, J. *Horace Mann: A Biography.* New York: Knopf, 1972.

Metzger, D. A.M. Eugène Née. "Les heures graves". *Journal des sourds-muets,* 1900, *6,* 135–137. (a)

———. Nouvelle Lettre à M. Née. *Journal des sourds-muets,* 1900, *6,* 185–190. (b)

Meyer, F.J.L. *Briefe aus der Hauptstadt und dem innern Frankreichs.* Hamburg: [n.p.], 1798. Second edition: Tübingen: Cotta, 1802.

Michaels, J. *Handbook of Sign Language.* Atlanta: Home Mission, 1923.

Michaud, J.F. (ed.). *Biographie universelle.* Paris: Desplaces, 1858.

Mignet, F.A. *Institut Impérial de France. Notice historique sur la vie et les travaux de M. le Baron de Gérando.* Paris: Firmin Didot, 1854.

Millar, D. (ed.). *Encyclopaedia Edinensis or Dictionary of Arts, Sciences, and Literature.* Edinburgh: Anderson, 1827.

Milner, A.C. *Newspaper indexes. A location and subject guide for researchers.* Scarecrow Press, 1979.

Mindel, E., and Vernon, M. *They Grow in Silence.* Silver Spring: National Association of the Deaf, 1971.

Miner, T. *Typhus Syncopalis, Sinking Typhus, or the Spotted Fever of New England.* Middletown, Conn.: author, 1825.

Mises, R., and Gineste, T. Le statut fait à l'enfant malade mental, la place de la controverse entre Pinel et Itard. 150ème anniversaire de la mort de Pinel. *Annales médico-psychologiques,* 1976, *134,* 73–80.

Mitchell, S.H. An examination of selected factors related to the economic status of the deaf population. Unpublished doctoral dissertation, American University, 1971. (a)

———. The haunting influence of Alexander Graham Bell. *American Annals of the Deaf,* 1971, *116,* 349–356. (b)

Moeller, F.A. The education of the deaf and dumb. In: Herberman, A.C., et al. (eds.). *Catholic Encyclopedia.* New York: Gilmary, 1909. Vol. 5, pp. 315–321.

Monboddo, Lord. See: Burnet, J.

Montaigne, Abbé. *Recherches sur les connaissances intellectuelles des sourds-muets.* Paris: Le Clere, 1829.

Montague, H. A man who loved deaf children. *Volta Review,* 1938, *40,* 74–77, 116.

———. Mr. Bell's private school. *Volta Review,* 1940, *42,* 324–326, 395.

Montgomery, G. *The Integration and Disintegration of the Deaf in Society.* Edinburgh: Scottish Workshop Publications, 1981.

———— (ed.). See: Hay, J.

Montgomery, I. The practical value of articulation. *American Annals of the Deaf,* 1870, *15,* 133–136.

Montorgueil, G. La faillite d'une méthode. Les sourds-muets éduqués comprennent-ils la parole? *L'Eclair,* 25 Nov. 1909.

Moody, W. *Introduction à l'histoire et à la grammaire de la langue des signes. Entre les mains des sourds.* Paris: International Visual Theater, 1983.

Moore, W. Letter to M. F. Cogswell, 4 Sept. 1816, from New York. Cogswell Papers, Yale University.

Moores, D. Oral versus manual. "Old prejudices die hard but die they must." *American Annals of the Deaf,* 1970, *115,* 667–669.

————. *Educating the Deaf.* Boston: Houghton Mifflin, 1978. Second edition: 1982.

Morales, A. de. Pedro Ponce. In: *Las Antigüedades de las ciudades de España.* En casa de Iuan Ihigues de Lequerica: Alcalà de Henares, 1575. P. 38. French translation: Forestier (1883), 85–86.

Moravia, S. *Il tramonto dell'Illuminismo. Filosofia e politica nella società francese 1770–1810.* Bari: Laterza, 1968.

Moreau de Vormes, J.A.A. *Lettre à M. l'abbé de l'Epée.* Paris: Knappen, 1779.

Moreau de Vormes, J.A.A., and Tronson du Coudray, E. *Consultation d'anciens avocats au Parlement.* Paris: Knappen, 1779.

Morel, E. *Notice biographique sur l'abbé de l'Epée.* Paris: Renouard, 1833.

————. Sourds-Muets. Question pénale. *Gazette des Tribunaux,* 1838, *4 (4135),* 12 December, 148. Reprinted: *L'Ami des sourds-muets,* 1838–9, *1,* 21–22.

————. Discours 14 août 1843. In: Institution Royale des Sourds-Muets. *Discours et distribution des prix.* Paris: Imprimerie des sourds-muets, 1843. Pp. 1–28.

————. Introduction. *Annales de l'éducation des sourds-muets et des aveugles,* 1844, *1,* 1–27.

————. Notice biographique sur le Dr. Itard. *Annales de l'éducation des sourds-muets et des aveugles,* 1845, *2,* 84–99. English translation: Peet, E. Biographical sketch of Dr. Itard. *American Annals of the Deaf,* 1853, *5,* 110–124.

————. De l'organisation générale de l'éducation des sourds-muets en France. *Annales de l'éducation des sourds-muets et des aveugles,* 1846, *3,* 21–32, 105–116; 1847, *4,* 51–70; 1850, *7,* 81–100, 161–178.

————. Observations sur les deux mémoires précédents [Haug; Wagner]. *Annales de l'éducation des sourds-muets et des aveugles,* 1848, *5,* 185–212. English translation: Morel et al. (1849).

————. Un sourd-muet contemporain de l'abbé de l'Epée. *Annales de l'éducation des sourds-muets et des aveugles,* 1850, *7,* 225–229.

Morel, E., Haug, L., and Wagner, [?]. Appendix. Instruction in articulation. The German and French methods compared. In: American School for the Deaf, Reports (1849), 33–64.

Morel, O. *Essai sur la vie et les travaux de Marie-Joseph Baron de Gérando.* Paris: Renouard, 1846. English translation of excerpts: Peet, E. (1851).

Morgan, F. (ed.). *Connecticut as a Colony and as a State.* Hartford: Publishing Society of Connecticut, 1904.

Morgan, J.S. *Noah Webster.* New York: Mason-Charter, 1975.

Morris, O. Consanguineous marriages and their results in respect to deaf-dumbness. *American Annals of the Deaf,* 1861, *13,* 29–34.

Morris, O.W. Deafness and diseases of the ear. In: Convention of American Instructors of the Deaf, Proceedings (1853), 215–237.

Morse, J. *A Neglected Period of Connecticut's History. 1818–1850.* New Haven: Yale University Press, 1933.

Mottez, B. *A Propos d'une langue stigmatisée, la langue des signes.* Paris: Ecole des Hautes Etudes en Sciences Sociales, 1975.

Mulholland, A. (ed.). *Oral Education Today and Tomorrow.* Washington, D.C.: Alexander Graham Bell Association, 1981.

Mullet, C.F. Arte to make the dumb to speak, the deafe to hear. *Journal of the History of Medicine and Allied Sciences,* 1971, *26,* 123–149.

Murphy, A. Dr. Bell and Boston University. *Volta Review,* 1954, *56,* 249–250.

Nack, J. *The Legend of the Rock and Other Poems.* New York: Conrad, 1827.

Nash, J.E., and Nash, A. *Deafness in Society.* Lexington: Lexington Books, 1981.

National Association of the Deaf. *Proceedings of the Triennial Convention.* [various]: 1880–.

————. *Superintendents Defend the Sign Language.* Circular of information no. 4. Silver Spring: National Association of the Deaf, [n.d.].

————. General remarks. In: National Association of the Deaf, Proceedings (1893), 274–282.

————. Resolutions of the World's Congress of the Deaf. *Volta Review,* 1910, *12,* 53.

————. [Resolutions on sign language.] In: Convention of American Instructors of the Deaf, Proceedings (1912), 133–134.

————. *Methods of Educating the Deaf and Opinions about the Sign Language by Educators of the Deaf, by Orally-Educated Deaf and Others Competent to Speak on the Subject.* Circular of information no. 9. Seattle: Root and Christenson, 1914.

National Conference on Charities and Correction. *A Guide to the Study of Charities and Correction by means* of the Proceedings of the National Conference of Charities and Correction using 34 volumes, 1874–1907. (A. Johnson, ed.). Washington, D.C.: National Conference of Charities and Correction, 1908.

National Education Association. Proceedings of Meeting held in the Senate Chamber, Madison, Wisconsin, 16 July 1884, to Consider the Subject of Deaf-Mute Instruction in Relation to the Work of Public Schools. Washington, D.C.: Gibson, 1885.

Navarro Tomàs, T. Juan Pablo Bonet. Barcelona: Imprenta de la Casa de Curitat, 1920.

Née, E. Les Sourds-Muets et les anthropologues. Paris: Imprimerie des Sourds-Muets, 1898.

――――. La cité du rêve. Exposition de 1900. Pour les sourds-muets. Journal des sourds-muets, 1900, 6, 87–90. (a)

――――. Les heures graves. Journal des sourds-muets, 1900, 6, 121–122. (b)

――――. A M. D. Metzger. "Les heures graves." Journal des sourds-muets, 1900, 6, 149–153. (c)

Nelson, W. Headmaster's Report of a Visit of Inquiry to Schools for the Deaf and Dumb in the United States of America. Manchester: Sever, 1903.

New England Gallaudet Association of Deaf Mutes. Proceedings of the Constitution Committee. Bradford: Inquirer, 1854. Reprinted: Chamberlain (1857).

Newman, L. As a deaf teacher sees it. Deaf American, 1971, 23, 11–12.

New York Institution for the Improved Instruction of Deaf-Mutes. See: Greene, D. (1893).

New York Institution for the Instruction of the Deaf and Dumb. Annual Reports. 1818–. Albany: [various], 1819–1925.

――――. Proceedings of various meetings concerned with the founding of the New York School and associated correspondence [1816]. Association Review, 1901, 3, 428–452.

――――. Report of the committee to ascertain the number of deaf and dumb in New York, read at the fifth meeting of citizens held January 14, 1817. Reprinted: Association Review, 1901, 3, 433–437.

――――. Extracts from the early reports of the New York Institution showing the attitude of the school toward speech teaching. Association Review, 1905, 7, 49–70.

――――. Report of the Committee on Instruction. In: New York Institution for the Instruction of the Deaf and Dumb, Reports (1846), 99–105.

――――. Commemorative Exercises and a Recital of the Steps which led to the Founding . . . 100th Anniversary. New York: New York Institution for the Instruction of the Deaf and Dumb, 1917.

New York State, Central New York School for the Deaf, Canajoharie. Central Asylum for the Instruction of the Deaf and Dumb. Annual Reports to the Legislature of the State of New York. Canajoharie: 1824–1836, 1–13.

New York State, Central New York School for the Deaf, Rome. Annual Report. Rome: 1873/4–.

New York State Department of Public Instruction. Report of the Secretary of State in Relation to the Instruction of the Deaf and Dumb in the City of New York. Made to the Senate April 14, 1828. Albany: Croswell and Van Benthuysen, 1828.

――――. Annual Report of the Superintendent of Common Schools of New York on the Central Asylum and the New York Institution. Albany: Croswell, 1830.

――――. Annual Report of the Superintendent of Common Schools in Relation to the Instruction of the Deaf and Dumb. Albany: Croswell, 1836.

New York State Senate Committee on Literature. [Report of Mr. Spencer on "an act to provide for the building of an asylum for the deaf and dumb in the City of New York."] New York Senate Journal, 1827, 50th session, 5 March, 301–305.

Nordin, F. Report on the Paris Congress. Association Review, 1901, 3, 106–118.

North, E. A Treatise on a Malignant Epidemic Commonly Called Spotted Fever. New York: Swords, 1811.

Noyes, F.K. The servant of humanity. The life of Samuel Gridley Howe. Volta Review, 1911, 12, 755–765.

O'Connor, C. Some modern trends in education of the deaf. Volta Review, 1945, 47, 197–200, 248.

――――. "That the deaf may speak." Address of the President. Volta Review, 1952, 54, 418–420, 466.

Odegard, B. A History of the State Board of Control of Wisconsin and the State Institutions. Madison: State Board, 1939.

Oléron, P. Eléments de répertoire du langage gestuel des sourds-muets. Paris: C.N.R.S., 1974.

Olivier, J. Une question à M. Franck. Défense des sourds-muets, 1886, 2, 104–105.

Olivier, J., and George, D.W. Should the deaf marry the deaf? In: Congress of Deaf—International—Second (1893), 110–115.

Olmedilla y Puig, J. Pedro Ponce de León. El primero que enseñó à hablar à los sordo-mudos. Madrid: 1912.

Olmsted, D. Timothy Dwight as a teacher. In: Barnard, H. (1861), 78–96.

Orcutt, A.W. The orally taught deaf after leaving school. In: Convention of American Instructors of the Deaf, Proceedings (1893), 185–190.

Ordinaire, D. Institut Royal des Sourds-Muets de Paris. Discours prononcé à la distribution des prix, août 1835. Paris: Gratiot, 1835.

――――. Essai sur l'éducation, et spécialement sur celle du sourd-muet. Paris: Hachette, 1836.

Orpen, C.E.H. Utility of speech to the deaf. Christian Observer, 1827, 27, 82–90.

――――. Anecdotes and Annals of the Deaf and Dumb. Second edition. London: Tims, 1836.

Osborn, N.G. (ed.). History of Connecticut. New York: States Historical Company, 1928.

Osborne, H.S. Biographical memoir of Alexander Graham Bell, 1847–1922. National Academy of Sciences Biographical Memoirs, 1943, 23, 1–19.

Owrid, H.L. Studies in manual communication with hearing impaired children. *Volta Review*, 1971, *73*, 428–438.

Padden, C., and Markowicz, H. Cultural conflicts between hearing and deaf communities. In: Crammatte, F.B., and Crammatte, A.B. (eds.). *VII World's Congress of the World Federation of the Deaf*. Silver Spring: National Association of the Deaf, 1976. Pp. 407–411.

Paganel, C. *L'Histoire de Joseph II*. Paris: Plon, 1853.

[Pain, J.M.]. *Nouveaux tableaux de Paris ou observations* . . . Paris: Pillet, 1828.

Palluy, [?]. Statistique des institutions des sourds-muets en France et à l'étranger. *Revue de Paris*, 1829, *6*, 36–50.

Panara, R., Denis, T.B., and McFarlane, J.H. (eds.). *The Silent Muse: An Anthology of Prose and Poetry by the Deaf*. Toronto: Gallaudet College Alumni Association, 1960.

Panara, R., and Panara, J. *Great Deaf Americans*. Silver Spring, Md.: T. J. Publishers, 1984.

Paris. Exposition Universelle, 1900. *Exhibition Paris, 1900. A Practical Guide*. London: Heinemann, 1900. (a)

————. *Le Livre d'or de l'exposition de 1900*. Paris: Cornély, 1900. (b)

————. *L'Exposition de Paris [1900]. Encyclopédie du siècle*. Paris: Librairie Illustrée Montgredien et Cie., 1900. (c)

————. [Picard, A.]. *Exposition universelle internationale de 1900 à Paris. Rapport général administratif et technique*. Paris: Imprimerie Nationale, 1902–3. (d)

Parker, E.P. *History of the Second Church, Hartford*. Hartford: Belknap, 1892.

Parkin, J.H. *Bell and Baldwin*. Toronto: University of Toronto Press, 1964.

Parsons, F. *Friendly Club and Other Portraits*. Hartford: Edwin Valentine Mitchell, 1922.

————. *The Hartford Wits*. Hartford: Privately printed, 1936.

Patterson, R. Fisher Ames Spofford. *American Annals of the Deaf*, 1877, *22*, 215–219.

————. History of the Ohio Institution for the Education of the Deaf and Dumb. In: Fay, E.A. (1893).

Paulmier, L.P. Lettre à M. Bazot. In: Bazot (1819), 33–73.

————. La Fête de M. l'abbé Sicard. *L'Abeille*, 1821, *4*, 474–479. (a)

————. Aperçu du plan d'éducation des sourds-muets. Paris: Angeclo, 1821. (b)

————. Nécrologie de l'Abbé Sicard. *Revue encyclopédique*, 1822, *14*, 454–455.

————. L'Abbé de l'Epée. In: Anonymous, *Galerie française ou collection des portraits des hommes et des femmes célèbres*. Paris: Didot, 1821–23. Vol. 3, pp. 335–341.

————. Une Séance des sourds-muets. In: Anonymous, *Paris ou le livre des cent et un*. Paris: Ladvocat, 1831–1834. Vol. 3, pp. 245–272.

————. *Le Sourd-Muet.*. Paris: Imprimerie d'Angeclo, 1834. (a)

————. *Institut Royal des Sourds-Muets de Naissance. Une Fête de l'abbé Sicard*. Paris: Gratiot, 1834. (b)

————. *Considérations sur l'instruction des sourds-muets*. Paris: Institut Royal des Sourds-Muets, 1844.

Peabody, E.P. De Gérando. *North American Review*, 1861, *92*, 391–415.

Peet, D. The remote and paradoxical causes of deafness. *American Annals of the Deaf*, 1856, *8*, 129–158.

Peet, E. Sketch of the life of Baron De Gérando. In: Convention of American Instructors of the Deaf, Proceedings, (1851), 114–123. Reprinted: *American Annals of the Deaf*, 1852, *4*, 178–187.

Peet, H.P. [On sign language and deaf education.] In: New York Institution for the Instruction of the Deaf and Dumb, Reports (1841), 13–39.

————. [On the] "Seventh Annual Report of the Secretary of the Massachusetts Board of Education." *North American Review*, 1844, *59*, 329–352. (a)

————. *A Vocabulary and Elementary Lessons for the Deaf and Dumb*. New York: Day, 1844. (b)

————. Report of Mr. Peet's tour through central and western New York with a select number of his deaf and dumb pupils in the months of July and August 1844. In: New York Institution for the Instruction of the Deaf and Dumb, Reports (1845), 62–78. (a)

————. *Course of Instruction for the Deaf and Dumb*. Part I. New York: Egbert, Hovey and King, 1845. (b)

————. [On the importance of sign language in educating the deaf.] Report of the President. In: New York Institution for the Instruction of the Deaf and Dumb, Reports (1846), 5–32.

————. Letter to Samuel Gridley Howe, 17 Jan. 1847. Howe Papers, Houghton Library, Harvard University. (a)

————. *Address Delivered at the New York Institution for the Instruction of the Deaf and Dumb, 2 December 1846. With an appendix containing the proceedings at the dedication of the chapel*. New York: Egbert, Hovey and King, 1847. (b)

————. *Address Delivered at Commons Hall at Raleigh, on the occasion of laying the cornerstone of the North Carolina Institution for the Instruction of the Deaf and Dumb, 14 April 1848*. New York: Egbert, Hovey and King, 1848.

————. *Course of Instruction for the Deaf and Dumb*. Part II. New York: Egbert, Hovey and King, 1849.

————. *Course of Instruction for the Deaf and Dumb*. Part III. New York: Egbert, Hovey and King, 1850. (a)

————. Analysis of Bonet's treatise on the art of teaching the dumb to speak. *American Annals of the Deaf*, 1850, *3*, 200–211. (b)

————. Proceedings of the Second Convention of American Instructors of the Deaf and Dumb. *American Annals of the Deaf*, 1851, *4*, 1–41. (a)

————. Elements of the language of signs. In: Convention of American Instructors of the Deaf, Proceedings (1851), 193–208. Reprinted: *American Annals of the Deaf*, 1853, *5*, 83–95. (b)

————. Course of instruction for the deaf and dumb. In: Convention of American Instructors of the Deaf, Proceedings (1851), 38–63. (c)

————. Memoir on the origin and early history of the art of instructing the deaf and dumb. *American Annals of the Deaf*, 1851, *3*, 126–160. (d)

————. *Report on the Education of the Deaf and Dumb in the Higher Branches of Learning.* New York: J. Egbert, 1852. (a)

————. Report on European institutions for the instruction of the deaf and dumb. In: New York Institution for the Instruction of the Deaf and Dumb, Reports (1852), 83–317. (b)

————. *Statistics of the Deaf and Dumb. A paper read before the Medical Society of the State of New York, 25 June 1852.* New York: Egbert, 1852. (c)

————. Tribute to the memory of the late Thomas Gallaudet. *American Annals of the Deaf*, 1852, *5*, 65–77. (d)

————. Necrology. Nathan M. Totten. *American Annals of the Deaf*, 1853, *5*, 35–40. (a)

————. The personal character of the teacher considered in reference to the influence of his example on the character of his pupils. In: Convention of American Instructors of the Deaf, Proceedings (1853), 184–199. (b)

————. J. Adison Cary. *American Annals of the Deaf*, 1853, *5*, 48–52. (c)

————. Letter to Samuel Gridley Howe, 28 Mar. 1853. Howe Papers, Houghton Library, Harvard University. (d)

————. Notions of the deaf and dumb before instruction, especially in regard to religious subjects. *American Annals of the Deaf*, 1855, *8*, 1–44.

————. New York Institution for the Deaf and Dumb. *Journal of Education*, 1857, *3*, 346–365. Excerpted: *American Annals of the Deaf*, 1857, *9*, 168–183. (a)

————. *Legal Rights and Responsibilities of the Deaf and Dumb.* Richmond: Wynne, 1857. (b)

————. Signs unnecessary as the "representation of words." *American Annals of the Deaf*, 1858, *10*, 129–136.

————. Memoir on the history of the art of instructing the deaf and dumb—second period. In: Convention of American Instructors of the Deaf, Proceedings (1859), 277–341. (a)

————. Words not representative of signs but ideas. *American Annals of the Deaf*, 1859, *11*, 1–8. (b)

————. Review of the arguments of Mr. Jacobs on methodical signs. *American Annals of the Deaf*, 1859, *11*, 129–142. (c)

————. See also: Day and Peet (1861).

————. The deaf and dumb. *Herald of Health*, 1867, *10*, 17–23, 72–77, 105–108, 228–234, 281–284; 1868, *11*, 61–64, 108–112, 220–224, 254–255; 1868, *12*, 12–16, 110–112.

————. Signs versus articulation. Paper read at the Social Science Convention in New York. *National Deaf-Mute Gazette*, 1868, *2 (14)*, 3–9. (a)

————. Deaf-Mute instruction. *Hours at Home*, 1868, *6*, 237–246. (b)

————. Notes of a visit to the Clarke Institution. *American Annals of the Deaf*, 1869, *14*, 82–88.

————. Necrology [L. Clerc, A. Jacobs, A. Hutton.] *American Annals of the Deaf*, 1870, *15*, 245–248.

Peet, H.P., and Campbell, W.W. Mr. Peet's letter of instruction to Mr. Campbell and Mr. Campbell's report on teaching articulation in the British Isles. In: New York Institution for the Instruction of the Deaf and Dumb, Reports (1849), 86–89.

Peet, I.L. James Edward Meystre. In: Convention of American Instructors of the Deaf, Proceedings (1851), 169–192.

————. The use of grammatical symbols in the instruction of the deaf and dumb. In: Convention of American Instructors of the Deaf, Proceedings (1853), 263–288.

————. Initial signs. *American Annals of the Deaf*, 1868, *13*, 171–184.

————. John Robertson Burnet. *American Annals of the Deaf*, 1875, *20*, 55–72.

————. The greatest good to the greatest number. *American Annals of the Deaf*, 1878, *23*, 151–157.

————. Report of the principal. In: New York Institution for the Instruction of the Deaf and Dumb, Reports (1881), 46–72.

————. The combined system of education. In: Convention of American Instructors of the Deaf, Proceedings (1887), 152–189.

————. Thomas Hopkins Gallaudet. *American Annals of the Deaf*, 1887, *33*, 43–54. Reprinted: Conference of Executives of American Schools for the Deaf, Proceedings (1888).

————. The influence of the life and work of the abbé de l'Epée. *American Annals of the Deaf*, 1890, *35*, 133–150. (a)

————. The relation of the sign language to the education of the deaf. In: Convention of American Instructors of the Deaf, Proceedings (1890), 100–108. (b)

————. Deaf-Mutes as teachers. In: Convention of American Instructors of the Deaf, Proceedings (1893), 70–77. (a)

————. A method of teaching articulation to every pupil. *American Annals of the Deaf*, 1893, *38*, 281–291. (b)

Peet, W.B. The education of the deaf and dumb. *Scribner's*, 1892, *12*, 463–474.

Pélissier, P. Lettre au rédacteur. *L'Ami des sourds-muets*, 1839–40, *2*, 119–120.

————. *Poésies d'un sourd-muet.* Paris: Gosselin, 1844.

———— (ed.). *Les Sourds-Muets aux XIXeme siècle.* Paris: Bautruche, 1846. (a)

————. *Discours prononcé en langage mimique . . . 11 août, 1846.* Paris: Imprimerie de Lottin de St. Germain, 1846. (b)

————. *Discours prononcé en langage mimique . . . le 10 août 1853.* Paris: Baucquin, 1853.

————. *L'Enseignement primaire des sourds-muets à la portée de tout le monde, avec une iconographie des signes.* Paris: Dupont, 1856.

Pendola, T. *Aux Membres du congrès international de Milan, pour l'amélioration du sort des sourds-muets.* Siena: Imprimerie des Sourds-Muets, 1880.

Pennant, T. *A Tour in Scotland . . . in 1772.* London: White, 1776.

Pennsylvania Institution for the Deaf and Dumb. *Reports.* Philadelphia: [various], 1822–.

————. *Documents in Relation to the Dismissal of David G. Seixas . . .* Philadelphia: Pennsylvania Institution for the Deaf and Dumb, 1822.

Pereire, J.R. Discours de M. Pereire [22 Nov. 1746, to the Royal Academy of Belles-Lettres of Caen]. *Suite de la clef ou journal historique sur les matières du temps,* 1747, *62,* 332–338. Reprinted: La Rochelle (1882), 29–31.

————. *Mémoire que M. Pereire a lu dans la séance de l'Académie Royale des Sciences du 11 juin 1749 et dans lequel en présentant à cette compagnie un jeune sourd et muet de naissance, il expose avec quel succès il lui a appris à parler.* Paris: 1749. Reprinted: Coste d'Arnobat (1803), 58–73. English translation: Akerly (1821a).

————. *Lettre de M. Pereire à M. Remond de St. Albine.* [1750]. Reprinted: Coste d'Arnobat (1803), 73–76. English translation: Akerly (1821a).

————. *Observations sur les sourds-muets et sur quelques endroits du Mémoire de M. Ernaud . . .* [1768]. In: *Mémoires de mathématique et de physique présentés à l'Académie Royale des Sciences par divers savants.* Paris: Imprimerie Royale, 1750–1786. Vol. 5, pp. 500–530.

Perez de Urbel, J. *Fray Pedro Ponce de León y el origen del arte de enseñar à hablar a los mudos.* Madrid: Editorial Obras Selectas, 1973.

Périni, C. Discours [on Abbé Tarra]. *Revue internationale de l'enseignement des sourds-muets,* 1890, *6,* 79–82.

Perkins, M.E. *Old Houses of the Ancient Town of Norwich 1660–1800.* Norwich: Bulletin, 1895.

Perkins, N. *A Sermon Delivered at the Interment of the Reverend Nathan Strong, D.D., who died December 25, 1816 aged 68 . . .* Hartford: Goodman, 1817.

Perkins Institution and Massachusetts School for the Blind. *Annual Reports.* Boston: 1833–1923.

Perrolle, E. *Dissertation anatomico-acoustique contenant: (1) des expériences qui font connaître une propriété qu'ont presque toutes les parties externes de la tête et quelques-unes du col de sentir et propager le son par le toucher, (2) un essai d'expériences fait à Paris en 1777 sur des sourds-muets de M. l'abbé de l'Epée.* Paris: Méquignon, 1782.

Perry, C. Time allowed for the public schooling of deaf as compared with hearing children, and how to make the most of it. National Educational Association, Proceedings (1899), 1157–1162.

Pestalozzi, J.H. *Wie Gertrud Ihre Kinder Lehrt . . .* Leipzig: P. Reclam, [1801]. English translation: Holland, L.E., and Turner, F.C. *How Gertrude Teaches Her Children.* London: Remax House, 1966.

Peters, S. *A General History of Connecticut.* London: author, 1781.

Petersson, R.T. *Sir Kenelm Digby.* Cambridge, Mass.: Harvard University Press, 1956.

Petit, J. *Mémoire à l'appui d'une demande en concession de terres en Algérie.* Digne: Vial, 1859.

Pettengill, B.D. The sign language. *American Annals of the Deaf,* 1873, *18,* 1–12.

Pettingell, J.H. What the Bible says of the deaf and dumb. *American Annals of the Deaf,* 1881, *26,* 226–238.

Peyron, L., and Bélanger, A. *Catalogue de la bibliothèque de l'Institution Nationale des Sourds-Muets de Paris, Première partie.* Paris: Pelluard, 1883.

Philip, F. *Major Philosophical Works of Etienne Bonnot, Abbé de Condillac.* Hillsdale, N.J.: Lawrence Erlbaum Associates, 1982.

Philip, F., and Lane, H. *The Deaf Experience: Classics in Language and Education.* Cambridge, Mass.: Harvard University Press, 1984.

Pilet, E. The Federation of Societies of the Deaf in France. In: Congress of the Deaf—International—Fourth (1904), 101–104.

Piroux, J. *Le Vocabulaire des sourds-muets (partie iconographique). 1ère livraison contenant 500 noms appellatifs, de la langue usuelle, interprétés par un pareil nombre de figures correspondantes.* Nancy: Grimblot, 1830.

————. *Théorie philosophique de l'enseignement des sourds-muets. Discours.* Paris: Hachette, 1831.

————. Législation. *L'Ami des sourds-muets,* 1838–39, *1,* 5–6. (1838a)

————. Nouvelles. *L'Ami des sourds-muets,* 1838–39, *1,* 10–13. (1838b)

————. Nouvelles. *L'Ami des sourds-muets,* 1838–39, *1,* 31–32. (1838c)

————. Nouvelles. Coups et blessures par un sourd-muet. *L'Ami des sourds-muets,* 1838–39, *1,* 46–48. (1839a)

————. Nouvelles. *L'Ami des sourds-muets,* 1838–39, *1,* 54–59. (1839b)

————. Nouvelles. *L'Ami des sourds-muets,* 1838–39, *1,* 74. (1839c)

————. Tableau statistique des sourds-muets dans chaque pays du monde, et tableau statistique des institutions de sourds-muets en France. *L'Ami des sourds-muets,* 1838–39, *1,* 147–148. (1839d)

————. *L'Ami des sourds-muets,* 1839–40, *2,* 23–26. (1839e)

————. Législation. *L'Ami des sourds-muets,* 1839–40, *2,* 72–74. (1840a)

————. Variétés. Plaintes par un sourd-muet contre un sourd-muet. Voies de fait. Débats à l'aide de la mimique. *L'Ami des sourds-muets,* 1839–40, *2,* 89–93. (1840b)

――――. Tableaux statistiques des institutions de sourds-muets en Europe. *L'Ami des sourds-muets,* 1839–40, *2,* 148. (1840c)

――――. Législation. *L'Ami des sourds-muets,* 1840–41, *3,* 50–51. (1841a)

――――. Variétés. Travaux de la Société Centrale des Sourds-Muets de Paris; lettres de Forestier sur les sourds-muets devant la loi. *L'Ami des sourds-muets,* 1840–41, *3,* 56–63. (1841b)

――――. [Review of] "Les Sourds-Muets avant et depuis l'Abbé de l'Epée." *L'Ami des sourds-muets,* 1840–41, *3,* 122–24. (1841c)

――――. Résumé chronologique des opinions des savants sur les sourds-muets et des travaux de leurs instituteurs. *L'Ami des sourds-muets,* 1840–41, *3,* 134–140. (1841d)

――――. Nouvelles. *L'Ami des sourds-muets,* 1841–42, *4,* 47. (1842a)

――――. Résumé des travaux de la Société Centrale. *L'Ami des sourds-muets,* 1841–42, *4,* 58. (1842b)

――――. Législation. Chambre des Députés. Séance du samedi 9 avril. Exposé par F. Berthier. *L'Ami des sourds-muets,* 1841–42, *4,* 73–74. (1842c)

――――. Nouvelles. Opposition au mariage entre un sourd-muet et une sourde-muette. *L'Ami des sourds-muets,* 1841–42, *4,* 110–112. (1842d)

――――. Double assassinat commis par un sourd-muet. *L'Ami des sourds-muets,* 1841–42, *4,* 144–145. (1842e)

――――. Nouvelles. *L'Ami des sourds-muets,* 1842–43, *5,* 9–12. (1842f)

――――. Variétés. *L'Ami des sourds-muets,* 1842–43, *5,* 17–23. (1842g)

――――. Examen approfondi de l'ouvrage de l'abbé de l'Epée. *L'Ami des sourds-muets,* 1842–43, *5,* 33–45, 65–72, 97–108. (1843a)

――――. Notice sur Pierre-Aron Borg. *L'Ami des sourds-muets,* 1842–43, *5,* 72. (1843b)

――――. *Mémoire.* Paris: Hachette, 1850. (a)

――――. *Solution des principales questions relatives aux sourds-muets considérés en eux-mêmes et dans la société.* Paris: Hachette, 1850. (b)

――――. *Réflexions sur l'enseignement des sourds-muets à propos des discussions devant l'Académie Impériale de Médecine.* Nancy: Institution des Sourds-Muets, 1852.

――――. De la parole pour le sourd-muet. *L'Impartial,* 1856, *1,* 97–110, 129–136, 161–167, 193–201.

――――. *Examen comparatif de toutes les méthodes inventées pour l'instruction des sourds-muets.* Nancy: Institution des Sourds-Muets, 1861.

――――. *Dissertation sur la question de savoir si la méthode allemande est préférable à la méthode française.* Nancy: Institution des Sourds-Muets, 1867.

Pitrois, Y. *La Vie de l'abbé de l'Epée, racontée aux sourds-muets.* St-Etienne: Imprimerie des Sourds-Muets, [1912].

――――. The national institution for the deaf in Paris. *Volta Review,* 1913, *14,* 710–718.

Pool, I. de Sola (ed.). *The Social Impact of the Telephone.* Cambridge, Mass.: M.I.T. Press, 1977.

Poole, J. A preliminary description of Martha's Vineyard Sign Language; its origins and influence upon American Sign Language. Unpublished paper, Boston University School of Education.

Porcher, A. Itard. *Revue générale de l'enseignement des sourds-muets,* 1938, *39 (9),* 113–124; 1938, *39 (10),* 129–132; 1939, *40,* 1–6.

Porter, S. Education of the deaf and dumb. *American Review,* 1846, *3,* 497–516.

――――. Bibliographical. *American Annals of the Deaf,* 1848, *1,* 33–44, 181–193, 229–237; 1849, *2,* 39–51, 112–123, 243–250. (a)

――――. Particulars concerning James Mitchell. *American Annals of the Deaf,* 1848, *1,* 234–237, 246–258. (b)

――――. Scrofula among the deaf and dumb. In: Convention of American Instructors of the Deaf, Proceedings (1851), 145–168.

――――. Report of the committee on statistics, of a plan of registration. In: Convention of American Instructors of the Deaf, Proceedings (1853), 86–120.

――――. John Quincy Adams and the Abbé de l'Epée. *American Annals of the Deaf,* 1856, *8,* 248–249. (a)

――――. Charles Fox and his deaf mute son. *American Annals of the Deaf,* 1856, *8,* 249–250. (b)

――――. The deaf-mute Lord Seaforth—anecdotes. *American Annals of the Deaf,* 1858, *10,* 118–123. (a)

――――. The late Edward Morel. *American Annals of the Deaf,* 1858, *10,* 55–59. (b)

――――. Retirement of Mr. Clerc. *American Annals of the Deaf,* 1858, *10,* 181–183. (c)

――――. Book notices. De Gérando. *American Annals of the Deaf,* 1861, *13,* 122–125.

――――. The late Reverend Collins Stone. *American Annals of the Deaf,* 1871, *16,* 124–142.

――――. Is thought possible without language? *Princeton Review,* 1881, series 4, *7,* 104–128.

Porter, S.H. The suppression of signs by force. *American Annals of the Deaf,* 1893, *39,* 169–178.

Préseau, V.C. Abbé de l'Epée. Abbé Sicard. In: *Les Grandes Figures nationales et les héros du peuple.* Paris: Didier, 1872. Vol. 2, 79–101, 103–111.

Prickett, H.T., and Hunt, J.T. Education of the deaf—the next ten years. *American Annals of the Deaf,* 1977, *122,* 365–381.

Prieur, [?]. Rapport sur l'établissement de l'institution des sourds-muets de naissance, fait au nom des Comités de l'Extinction de la Mendicité, de l'Aliénation des Biens Nationaux, des Finances et de Constitution. [1790.] Reprinted: Bloch and Tuetey (1911), 736–745.

Purcell, R. *Connecticut in Transition. 1775–1818.* Middletown: Wesleyan University Press, 1963.

Purver, M. *The Royal Society: Conception and Creation.* London: Routledge, 1967.

Puybonnieux, J.B. *La parole enseignée aux sourds-muets sans le secours de l'oreille.* Paris: Kuglemann, 1843.

———. *Mutisme et surdité.* Paris: Baillière, 1846.

———. De la capacité légale des sourds-muets. *L'Impartial,* 1856, *1,* 40–49.

———. La rotation à l'institution impériale. *L'Impartial,* 1857, *2,* 253–271.

———. Biographie: l'abbé de l'Epée. *L'Impartial,* 1858, *3,* 239–249. (a)

———. Des interprètes pour les sourds-muets. *L'Impartial,* 1858, *3,* 231–238. (b)

———. Un accusé sourd et muet. *L'Impartial,* 1859, *4,* 25–28.

Pyatt, J. *Memoir of Albert Newsam.* Philadelphia: [n.p.], 1868.

Quigley, S.P. *The Education of Deaf Children.* Baltimore: University Park Press, 1982.

Rae, L. The Abbé de l'Epée. *American Annals of the Deaf,* 1848, *1,* 69–76. (a)

———. Historical sketch of the instruction of the deaf and dumb before the time of de l'Epée. *American Annals of the Deaf,* 1848, *1,* 197–208. (b)

———. A monument to Heinicke. *American Annals of the Deaf,* 1848, *1,* 166–170. (c)

———. Presentation of silver plate to Messrs. Gallaudet and Clerc. *American Annals of the Deaf,* 1851, *3,* 41–64. Reprinted from: Anonymous (1851).

———. Dr. Peet's European tour. *American Annals of the Deaf,* 1852, *4,* 243–252.

———. Higher education for the deaf and dumb. *American Annals of the Deaf,* 1852, *4,* 259–261; 1853, *5,* 56–59.

———. The philosophical basis of language. In: Convention of American Instructors of the Deaf, Proceedings (1853), 155–174. (a)

———. On the proper use of signs in the instruction of the deaf and dumb. *American Annals of the Deaf,* 1853, *5,* 21–31. (b)

Rae, L., et al. Ceremonies at the completion of the Gallaudet Monument. *American Annals of the Deaf,* 1854, *7,* 19–54.

Raffron, [?]. *Convention Nationale. Observations sur les établissements proposés par les Comités de Secours et d'Instruction Publique en faveur des sourds-muets.* Paris: 1794. Reprinted: Blanchet (1850), vol. 2, pp. 250–253.

Rambosson, J.P. *Langue universelle: Langage mimique.* Paris: Garnier, 1853.

Ramirez de Carrion, M. *Maravillas de la naturaleza.* Montella: Francisco Garcia, 1629.

Rancurel, G. De la suppression des signes dans les institutions des sourds-muets. *Revue internationale de l'enseignement des sourds-muets,* 1890, *6,* 46–51.

Ranier, J., Altshuler, K., and Kallmann, F. (eds.). *Family and Mental Health Problems in a Deaf Population.* New York: New York State Psychiatric Institute. Second edition. Columbia University Press, 1969.

Raphel, G. *Die Kunst Taube und Stumme Reden zu Lehren.* Lüneburg: 1718.

Raymond, H. Questions de méthode. *Revue générale de l'enseignement des sourds-muets,* 1899, *1,* 184–189.

Recoing, J.B. *Le Sourd-Muet dactylogique.* Paris: Venet, 1823.

———. *Le Sourd-Muet entendant par les yeux.* Paris: Raret, 1829.

Reich, P.A., and Bick, M. An empirical investigation of some claims made in support of visible English. *American Annals of the Deaf,* 1976, *121,* 573–577.

Reinhardt, A.C., et al. Schools where deaf children talk and talk and where no use is made of the sign language or the finger alphabet. *Volta Review,* 1918, *20,* 476–484.

Reiter, F.H. A half century of progress in the New England schools. II. *Volta Review,* 1939, *41,* 562–565, 601.

Remy, H. Newspapers for the deaf in France. In: Congress of the Deaf—International—Second (1893), 85–86.

Rémy-Valade, Y.L. See: Valade, Y.L. Rémi.

Rey de la Croix. *Le Philanthrope chrétien; ou Eloge de l'abbé de l'Epée.* Beziers: Fuzier, 1822.

Richard, T.E., Triandis, E.C., and Patterson, C.H. Indices of employer prejudice toward disabled applicants. *Journal of Applied Psychology,* 1963, *47,* 52–55.

Richardin, C.J. *Réflexions sur l'état moral des sourds-muets sans instruction sur celui des sourds-muets qu'on instruit.* Paris: Hachette, 1834.

Richards, L.E. *Laura Bridgman: The Story of an Opened Door.* New York: Appleton, 1928.

———. *Samuel Gridley Howe.* New York: Appleton, 1936.

Riche, M. Essai sur la vie de l'abbé de l'Epée. *Rapports généraux de la Société Philanthropique de Paris,* 1792, *1,* 39–70.

Riekehof, L.L. *The American Sign Language.* Indianapolis: Shaneyfelt, 1961.

Roberts, L. Heredity and intermarriage: factors in deaf-mutism. *Volta Review,* 1912, *14,* 184–186.

Robertson, J. [Letter to Clerc commending him on his English and correcting it.] Clerc Papers no. 20, Yale University.

Robinson, W. The advisability of entire separation of manual and oral pupils. In: Convention of American Instructors of the Deaf, Proceedings (1899), 163–168.

Rodenbach, A. *Coup d'oeil d'un aveugle sur les sourds-muets.* Brussels: Hauman, 1829.

———. *Les Aveugles et les sourds-muets: histoire, instruction, éducation, biographie.* Brussels: Slingeneyer, 1835.

Rogers, H.B. Visit to European institutions. In: Clarke Institution for Deaf-Mutes, Reports (1873), Part II, 25–36.

―――. Early experiences in teaching the deaf to speak. In: Alexander Graham Bell Association, Proceedings (1896), 60–65.

Rogers, H.B., Sanborn, F.B., and Richards, L.E. Dr. S. G. Howe's connection with oral work. *Volta Review*, 1911, *13*, 420–422.

Rogers, H.B., True, M.H., Fuller, S., and Fay, E. Reminiscences of early days of speech teaching. *Volta Review*, 1912, *14*, 469–479.

Roget, P. Deaf and Dumb. In: *Encyclopaedia Britannica*. Supplement to the 4th, 5th, and 6th editions. Edinburgh: Archibald, Constable, 1817. Vol. 3, pp. 467–483.

Root, G.M. (ed.). *Father and Daughter: The Cogswell Papers*. West Hartford: American School for the Deaf, 1941.

Rosen, G. The philosophy of ideology and the emergence of modern medicine in France. *Bulletin of the History of Medicine*, 1946, *20*, 328–339.

Roth, C. *A History of the Marranos*. Philadelphia: Jewish Publication Society of America, 1932.

Rousseau, J.J. *Emile, ou De L'Education*. The Hague: Néaulme, 1762. Reprinted: Paris: Garnier, 1939. English translation: Bloom, A. *Emile, or On Education*. New York: Basic Books, 1979.

Royal Commission on the Blind, the Deaf and the Dumb, &c. *Report*. London: H.M. Stationery Office, 1886. Abridged: J.C. Gordon (1892a).

Rugoff, M. *The Beechers*. New York: Harper and Row, 1981.

Russell, G.W. *Early Medicine and Early Medicine Men in Connecticut*. Hartford: author, 1892.

―――. *Contributions to the History of Christ Church, Hartford*. Hartford: Belknap and Warfield, 1895.

Russel, W.O. *A Treatise on Crimes*. London: Butterworth, 1819.

Ryerson, A.E. *Report on Institutions in Europe and America for the Deaf and Dumb*. Toronto: Telegraph, 1868.

Saboureux de Fontenay. Lettre de M. Saboureux-de-Fontenay, sourd et muet de naissance, à Mlle. ***. Versailles, Le 26 décembre 1764. Suite de la clef ou Journal historique sur les matières du temps [Journal du Verdun], 1765, 98, 284–298, 361–372. English translation: Philip (1984).

―――. Letter to M. Desloges 10 Oct. 1779. In: Deschamps (1780), 35–37.

―――. Letter to l'Abbé Deschamps 6 Jan. 1780. In: Deschamps (1780), 43–44.

Sachs, P. J. Miscellanea curiosa Ephemeridium medico-physicarum Germanicarum. *Academiae Naturae Curiosum*. Leipzig: [n. p.], 1670.

Sagra, R. de la. *Voyage en Hollande, en Belgique* . . . Paris: Bertrand, 1839.

―――. *Cinq Mois aux Etats-Unis de l'Amérique du Nord, depuis le 29 avril jusqu'au 23 septembre 1835; journal de voyage* . . . traduit de l'Espagnol par René Baissas. Paris: Levrault, 1837.

―――. Lettre à M. Piroux. *L'Ami des sourds-muets*, 1841–2, 4, 12–14.

Saint-Simon (Louis de Rouvroy, Duc de). *Mémoires*. Paris: Buisson, 1788.

Sanborn, F.B. Schools for the deaf and dumb. *The Nation*, 1867, *4*, 249–250. (a)

―――. Deaf-Mute education. *North American Review*, 1867, *104*, 512–531. (b)

―――. [On the] Tenth Annual Report of the Columbian Institution for the Deaf and Dumb, for the year ending June 30, 1867. *North American Review*, 1868, *107*, 334–337.

―――. [On the] Eleventh Annual Report of the Columbian Institution for the Deaf and Dumb, for the year ending June 30, 1868. *North American Review*, 1869, *109*, 287–289.

―――. *Dr. S. G. Howe:* New York: Funk and Wagnall's, 1891.

―――. See: Clarke School (1893), 9–34.

―――. *Recollections of Seventy Years*. Boston: Badger, 1909.

―――. [Founding of the Clarke School.] *Volta Review*, 1912, *14*, 581–584.

Sandham, E. *Deaf and Dumb*. Philadelphia: Peirce, 1812.

Sayce, A.H. Sign language among the American Indians. *Nature*, 1880, *22*, 93–94.

Scagliotti, G.B. *Cenni storici sulle istituzioni de' surdi-muti* . . . Turin: Imprimerie Royale, 1823.

Schara, J.S. The great extension of the manual method in Europe in the last century owing to the influence of Emperor Joseph II. *Association Review*, 1908, *10*, 272–273.

Schein, J.D., and Delk, M. *The Deaf Population in the United States*. Silver Spring: National Association of the Deaf, 1974.

Schmael, O. Samuel Heinicke and the education of the deaf. *Volta Review*, 1970, *72*, 237–241.

Schunhoff, H.F. *The Teaching of Speech and by Speech in Public Residential Schools for the Deaf in the United States 1815–1955*. Romney: West Virginia School for the Deaf and the Blind, 1957.

Schwartz, H. *Samuel Gridley Howe: Social Reformer, 1801–1876*. Cambridge, Mass.: Harvard University Press, 1956.

Scott, J. *A Visit to Paris in 1814* . . . Philadelphia: Parker, 1816. (a)

―――. *Paris Revisited in 1815*. Third edition. London: Longman, 1816. (b)

Scott, W.R. *The Deaf and Dumb: Their Position in Society and the Principles of their Education*. London: Graham, 1844.

Séguin, E. *Jacob-Rodrigues Pereire. Notice sur sa vie et ses travaux et analyse raisonnée de sa méthode*. Paris: Baillière, Guyot et Scribe, 1847. Reprinted (Part II): *Rééducation Orthophonique*, 1980, 18 (115).

―――. *Report on Education 1875*. Second edition. Milwaukee: Doerflinger, 1880. Reprinted: Delmar: Scholars Facsimile, 1976.

Seigel, J.P. The Enlightenment and the evolution of a language of signs in France and England. *Journal of the History of Ideas*, 1969, *30*, 96–115.

Seiss, J.A. *Children of Silence: or the Story of the Deaf.* Philadelphia: Porter and Coates, 1887.

Seliney, F.L. President's address. In: Empire State Association of Deaf Mutes. *Proceedings of the Twelfth Convention.* Rome: Register, 1888. Pp. 5–9. (a)

——. [Review of] Bell, Alexander Graham. "Memoir upon the formation of a deaf variety of the human race." *American Annals of the Deaf*, 1888, *33*, 129–133. (b)

Seton, E.T. *Sign Talk.* Garden City: Doubleday, 1918.

Sexton, S. Deafness and education. *New York Daily Tribune*, Nov. 26, 1883, 3.

Sheldon, F. The Pleiades of Connecticut. *Atlantic Monthly*, 1865, *15*, 187–201.

Sheldrick, H. (ed.). *Pioneer Women Teachers of Connecticut.* Winsted: Connecticut Delta Kappa Gamma Society, 1971.

Sibscota, G. *The Deaf and Dumb Man's Discourse* . . . London: H. Bruges for W. Cook, 1670. Reprinted (Sections II and III): *American Annals of the Deaf*, 1859, *11*, 98–111.

Sicard, R.A.C. Discours de clôture prononcé le 15 septembre. In: *Recueil des ouvrages du Musée de Bordeaux. Année 1787.* Bordeaux: Racle, 1787. Pp. 344–365. (a)

——. Essai sur l'art d'instruire les sourds-muets de naissance. In: *Recueil des ouvrages du Musée de Bordeaux. Année 1787.* Bordeaux: Racle, 1787. Pp. 27–61. (b)

—— *Exercices que soutiendront les sourds et muets de naissance les 12 et 15 septembre 1789 dans la salle du Musée de Bordeaux* . . . Bordeaux: Racle, 1789. (a)

—— *Mémoire sur l'art d'instruire les sourds et muets de naissance* . . . Bordeaux: Racle, 1789. (b)

——. *Second Mémoire sur l'art d'instruire les sourds et muets de naissance.* Paris: Knapen, 1790.

——. Relation adressée par M. l'abbé Sicard, instituteur des sourds et muets à un de ses amis sur les dangers qu'il a courus les 2 et 3 septembre 1792. *Annales Religieuses*, 1797, *1*, 13–72. Reprinted: Jourgniac-Saint-Médard, F. *Relation historique sur les journées des 2 et 3 septembre 1792.* Paris: Bertrand, 1806; Serieys, A. *La Mort de Robespierre.* Paris: Monory, 1801. English translation (excerpts): Rae, L. The great peril of Sicard. *American Annals of the Deaf*, 1848, *1*, 16–24; Lane (1976).

——. Métaphysique. Chapitre préliminaire d'un ouvrage sur l'art d'instruire les sourds-muets, par le C. Sicard, instituteur des sourds-muets de naissance. *Magasin encyclopédique*, 1795, *3*, 30–50. (a)

——. L'Art de la parole. In: Anonymous (ed.). *Séances des Ecoles Normales.* Paris: L. Reynier, 1795. Vol. 1, pp. 115–137, 244–265, 336–358; vol. 3, pp. 138–145; vol. 4, pp. 263–271. (b)

——. Sur la nécessité d'instruire les sourds-muets. *Magasin encyclopédique*, 1796, *2*, 32–56. (a)

——. *Catéchisme ou instruction chrétienne à l'usage des sourds-muets.* Paris: Institution Nationale des Sourds-Muets, 1796. (b)

——. *Manuel de l'enfance.* Paris: Le Clère, 1797.

——. *Eléments de grammaire générale.* Paris: Bourlotton, 1799. Third edition, enlarged. Paris: Deterville, 1808.

——. *Cours d'instruction d'un sourd-muet de naissance.* Paris: Le Clère, 1800. Second edition: Paris: Le Clère, 1803. English translation (abridged): Philip (1984).

——. *Journée chrétienne d'un sourd-muet, ou exercice pour la messe* . . . Paris: [n.p.], 1803.

——. *Discours prononcé dans la séance publique tenue par la classe de la langue et de la littérature française de l'Institut de France . . . en réponse au discours de réception de S.E. Mgr. le Cardinal Maury, prononcé le 6 mai 1807.* Third edition. Avignon: Séguin frères, 1807.

——. [Note on Clerc's desire to go to Russia.] 1808. Clerc Papers no. 2, Yale University. (a)

——. *Théorie des signes pour l'instruction des sourds-muets . . . Suivie d'une notice sur l'enfance de Massieu.* Paris: Imprimerie de l'Institution des Sourds-Muets, 1808. (b)

——. Sur la nécessité d'instruire les sourds-muets de naissance et sur les premiers moyens de communication avec ces infortunés. In: *Bibliothèque académique.* Paris: Delacour, 1811. Vol. 4, pp. 240–274.

——. [Letter to a friend on Napoleon's exile to Elba, the Bourbon monarchy, Alexander of Russia, etc.] Clerc Papers no. 40a, Yale University, 1814.

——. [Notice of his demonstrations in England.] Clerc Papers no. 40, Yale University, 1815.

——. Letter to Bishop Cheverus, 16 June 1816, from Paris. Clerc Papers no. 17, Yale University, 1816.

——. Letter to L. Clerc in Hartford, 26 August 1817. Clerc Papers no. 14, Yale University, 1817.

——. [Written conversation on Clerc's visit to Paris in 1820.] Clerc Papers no. 27, Yale University, 1820.

——. (ed.). *L'Art d'enseigner à parler aux sourds-muets de naissance, par l'abbé de l'Epée, précédé de l'éloge historique de l'abbé de l'Epée, par Bébian.* Paris: Dentu, 1820. Reprinted: Bébian (1827). English translation: Arrowsmith (1801). (a)

——. Avant-Propos. In: Sicard (1820). (b)

——. *Album d'un sourd-muet. Notice sur l'enfance de Massieu, sourd-muet.* Lons-le-Saunier: Imprimerie de Courbet, 1851.

——. Lettre à son beau-frère. *Bulletin de la Société Centrale d'Education et d'Assistance*, 1876, *2*, 95–96. Reprinted: Landes (1876).

Sigourney, L.H. *Memoir of Phoebe P. Hammond, a pupil in the American Asylum at Hartford.* New York: Sleight and Van Norden, 1833.

——. Prayers of the deaf and dumb. In: *Scenes in My Native Land.* Boston: Munroe, 1845. Pp. 239–245.

——. *Letters to my Pupils.* Second edition. New York: Carter, 1851.

————. The marriage of the deaf and dumb. In: *Select Poems*. Eleventh edition. Philadelphia: Parry and McMillan, 1854.

————. *Letters of Life*. New York: Appleton, 1866.

Simpson, H. Thomas Gallaudet. In: *Lives of Eminent Philadelphians*. Philadelphia: Brotherhood, 1859. Pp. 387–389.

Sklar, K. *Catharine Beecher, a Study in American Domesticity*. New Haven: Yale University Press, 1973.

Smith, E.A. *The Life and Letters of Nathaniel Smith*. New Haven: Yale University Press, 1914.

Smith, J.L. A comment on comparison of methods at Mount Airy. *American Annals of the Deaf*, 1901, *46*, 224–231.

————. The abuse of the sign language. *American Annals of the Deaf*, 1902, *47*, 157–182.

————. Gallaudet day. In: Congress of the Deaf—International—Fourth (1904), 7–10.

Smith, T.C. The writing of American history in America from 1884 to 1934. *American Historical Review*, 1935, *50*, 439–449.

Snyckers, M. *Le Sourd parlant*. Paris: [n.p.], 1886.

Société Centrale des Sourds-Muets de Paris. *Banquets des sourds-muets réunis pour fêter les anniversaires de la naissance de l'abbé de l'Epée*. Paris: Ledoyen, 1842.

Society of Progressive Oral Advocates. Proceedings. *Volta Review*, 1919, *21*, 95–101, 171–172.

Sommers, C.G. *Memoir of Reverend John Stanford*. New York: Swords, Stanford, 1835. Excerpted: *Association Review*, 1901, *3*, 439, 450–452.

Sparrow, R. Method of articulation teaching in the Clarke Institution. In: Alexander Graham Bell Association, Proceedings (1891), 285–296.

Spencer, R.C. The Wisconsin System of Public Day Schools. In: Fay, E.A. (1893).

Spradley, T.S., and Spradley, J.P. *Deaf Like Me*. New York: Random House, 1978.

Sprague, W.B. James Cogswell. In: *Annals of the American Pulpit*. New York: Carter, 1857. Vol. 1, pp. 445–448. (a)

————. Thomas Hopkins Gallaudet. In: *Annals of the American Pulpit*. New York: Carter, 1857. Vol. 2, pp. 609–615. (b)

Stansbury, A.O. [Letter to his brother Arthur in New York, 12 July 1817.] Reprinted: *Association Review*, 1902, *4*, 26–28. (a)

————. [Letter to his brother Arthur in New York, 3 August 1817.] Reprinted: *Association Review*, 1902, *4*, 28–29. (b)

————. [Letter to his brother Arthur in New York, 17 Sept. 1817.] Reprinted: *Association Review*, 1902, *4*, 31–32. (c)

————. [Quotations from his letters after he became superintendent of the New York Institution. 1818–1820.] Reprinted: *Association Review*, 1902, *4*, 37–38.

Steiner, B.C. *The History of Education in Connecticut*. Washington, D.C.: U.S. Government Printing Office, 1893.

————. *History of Guilford and Madison*. Guilford: Guilford Free Library, 1975.

————. *Life of Henry Barnard*. Washington, D.C.: U.S. Government Printing Office, 1919.

Steppuhn, [?]. Germany's present position on signs. *Volta Review*, 1911, *12*, 648–651. (a)

————. Our present attitude with respect to the sign language. *American Annals of the Deaf*, 1911, *56*, 127–142. (b)

Stevens, J.A. The Family of Ledyard, descendants of John Ledyard in two generations. *New York Genealogical and Biographical Record*, 1876, *7*, 10–13.

Stevenson, O.J. *The Talking Wire: The Story of Alexander Graham Bell*. New York: Messner, 1947.

Stevenson, R.S., and Guthrie, D. *A History of Otolaryngology*. Baltimore: Williams and Wilkins, 1949.

Stewart, D. Some accounts of a boy born blind and deaf. *Transactions of the Royal Society of Edinburgh*, 1812, *7*, 39. Reprinted: *The Works of Dugald Stewart*. Cambridge: Hillard and Brown, 1829. Vol. 3, pp. 287–355.

Stocking, G. French anthropology in 1800. *Isis*, 1964, *55(2)*, 134–150.

Stoddard, G.A., and Gallaudet, T. (Rev.). Reports of the Commissioners of the Board of Directors of the New York Institution for the Instruction of the Deaf and Dumb to the International Conference for the Amelioration of the Condition of Deaf-Mutes, held in Milan, September 1880. In: New York Institution for the Instruction of the Deaf and Dumb, Reports, (1881), 117–123.

Stokes, A.P. *Memorials of Eminent Yale Men*. New Haven: Yale University Press, 1914.

Stokoe, W.C. Sign language structure. *Studies in Linguistics*, occasional papers, 1960, *8*.

Stokoe, W.C., Casterline, D.C., and Croneberg, C.G. *A Dictionary of American Sign Language*. Washington, D.C.: Gallaudet College Press, 1965. Second edition: Silver Spring, Md.: Linstok, 1976.

Stokoe, W.C., Russell, B.H., and Padden, C. An elite group in deaf society. *Sign Language Studies*, 1976, *12*, 189–210.

Stone, C. Articulation as a medium for the instruction of the deaf and dumb. *American Annals of the Deaf*, 1849, *2*, 105–112, 232–242.

————. On the use of methodical signs. In: Convention of American Instructors of the Deaf, Proceedings (1851), 87–102.

————. On the difficulties encountered by the deaf and dumb in learning language. In: Convention of American Instructors of the Deaf, Proceedings (1853), 121–154. (a)

————. The Ohio Institution for the Deaf and Dumb. *American Annals of the Deaf*, 1853, *5*, 221–237. (b)

————. Report of the Principal. In: American School for the Deaf, Reports (1866), 11–39.

————. Report of the Principal. In: American School for the Deaf, Reports (1867), 30.

————. Address upon the history and methods of deaf-mute instruction. *American Annals of the Deaf*, 1869, *14*, 95–121.

Storrs, R.S. Articulation in deaf-mute instruction. *American Annals of the Deaf*, 1882, *27*, 160–162.

————. Deaf-mutes and the oral method. *American Annals of the Deaf*, 1883, *28*, 145–167.

Strauss, P. *Paris ignoré*. Paris: Imprimeries Réunies, 1885 [?].

————. *Conseil supérieur de l'assistance publique. Rapport sur l'Institution Nationale des Sourds-Muets. Annexe à la séance du 15 juillet 1895*. Paris: Imprimerie Melbun, 1895.

Strong, N. *A Funeral Sermon Delivered at Hartford, 6 January 1807, at the funeral of Reverend James Cogswell*. Hartford: Hudson and Goodwin, 1807.

Stuckless, E.R., and Birch, J.W. The influence of early manual communication on the linguistic development of deaf children. *American Annals of the Deaf*, 1966, *111*, 452–460, 499–504.

Sumner, G., and Russell, G.W. *Sketches [and reminiscences] of Physicians in Hartford in 1820*. Hartford: Case, Lockwood and Brainard, 1890.

Sutermeister, E. Is the sign language a necessity called forth by nature and circumstances? *Association Review*, 1908, *10*, 365–380.

Syle, H.W. A summary of the recorded researches and opinions of H. P. Peet. *American Annals of the Deaf*, 1873, *18*, 133–162, 213–241. (a)

————. Societies and periodicals for the deaf. *American Annals of the Deaf*, 1873, *18*, 255–262. (b)

————. Deaf and dumb. In: *American Encyclopedia*. New revised edition. New York: Appleton, 1874. Vol. 5, pp. 727–741.

————. *A Retrospect of the Education of the Deaf*. Philadelphia: Cullingworth, 1886.

————. *Biographical Sketch of Thomas Hopkins Gallaudet*. Philadelphia: Cullingworth, 1887.

Talbot, B. Changes in our profession. *American Annals of the Deaf*, 1895, *40*, 173–186.

Talbot, C.H. The Kentucky Institution and methodical signs. *American Annals of the Deaf*, 1872, *17*, 137–157.

Talma, C. (Vanhove). *Etudes sur l'art théâtral*. Paris: Feret, 1836.

Tarra, G. The teaching of articulation in Italy. *American Annals of the Deaf*, 1878, *23*, 99–106.

————. Resolutions of the Milan Convention. *American Annals of the Deaf*, 1881, *26*, 64–65.

————. *The Pure Oral Method, the Best for the Teaching of all Deaf Children*. [Translations from the writings of Guilio Tarra.] London: Allen, 1883. (a)

————. *Esquisse historique et court exposé de la méthode suivie pour l'instruction des sourds-muets de la paroisse et du diocèse de Milan*. [Translated from the Italian by Dubranle, M., and Dupont, M.] Paris: Delgrave, 1883. (b)

Taylor, H. The importance of a right beginning. National Educational Association, Proceedings (1899), 1162–1165.

————. Oralism in combined schools. *Association Review*, 1909, *11*, 332–347.

————. Oralism in schools. *Volta Review*, 1910, *12*, 349–353. Reprinted: *American Annals of the Deaf*, 1910, *55*, 379–385.

————. The President's address. *Volta Review*, 1925, *27*, 2–5.

————. Caroline Ardelia Yale. *Volta Review*, 1933, *35*, 415–417, 436–437.

————, et al. Alexander Graham Bell memorial session. *Volta Review*, 1925, *27*, 61–65.

Taylor, W.E. Shall speaking pupils receive instruction in sign classes? In: Convention of American Instructors of the Deaf, Proceedings (1890), 293–301.

Taylor, W., and Taylor, I. The education of physically handicapped children in France. *Exceptional Children*, 1959, *26 (2)*, 75–81.

Terry, N. Letter to Mason Fitch Cogswell, 28 Dec. 1817, from Washington, D.C. Cogswell Papers, Yale University.

Tharp, L.H. *Until Victory: Horace Mann and Mary Peabody*. Boston: Little, Brown, 1953.

Thollon, B. *La méthode orale pour l'instruction des sourds-muets, ni méthode mixte, ni méthode orale pure*. Paris: Institution des Sourds-Muets, 1905.

————. *Faut-il des maîtres spéciaux pour instruire les sourds-muets?* Paris: Institution des Sourds-Muets, 1907.

————. Present condition of the instruction of the deaf in France. *American Annals of the Deaf*, 1912, *57*, 6–22.

————. Le problème de l'éducation des sourds-muets. *Revue anthropologique*, 1913, *23*, 89–97.

————. *Cours normal pour la formation des professeurs de sourds-muets*. Montreal: Institution des Sourds-Muets, 1935–37.

Thompson, E.S. The speech habit in the deaf. In: Convention of American Instructors of the Deaf, Proceedings (1893), 143–147.

Thoms, H. The medical institution of Yale College and the Connecticut State Medical Library. *Connecticut Medicine*, 1960, *24*, 546–551.

Thornton, W. Memoir on teaching language to deaf and dumb. *Transactions of the American Philosophical Society*, 1793, *3*, 310–319.

Tidyman, E. *Dummy*. Boston: Little, Brown, 1974.

Tiffany, O. Life and Labors of Thomas Hopkins Gallaudet. *North American Review*, 1858, *87*, 517–532.

Tillinghast, J.A. The social status of the deaf in the past. *American Annals of the Deaf*, 1902, *47*, 147–156.

———. Reflections of an ex-educator of the deaf. *American Annals of the Deaf*, 1908, *53*, 421–438; 1909, *54*, 7–23, 237–253; 1910, *55*, 245–254, 462–473.

———. What is failure in oral education? In: Convention of American Instructors of the Deaf, Proceedings (1909), 57–69.

———. The drift of opinion as to pure oral departments in combined system schools. *Volta Review*, 1917, *19*, 1–3. (a)

———. The oral method of education of the deaf. *Volta Review*, 1917, *19*, 457–462. (b)

Tissot, P.F. *Histoire complète de la Révolution Française*. Paris: [n.p.], 1834.

Tomkins, W. *Indian Sign Language*. New York: Dover, 1969.

Toussaint, N.J.B. *De la nécessité des signes pour la formation des idées et de divers sujets de la philosophie morale*. Stuttgart and Tübingen: Cotta, 1827.

Townsend, J. *Memoirs of Reverend John Townsend*. Boston: Cracker and Brewster, 1831.

Toynbee, J. *The Deaf and Dumb: Their Condition, Education, and Medical Treatment*. London: Churchill, 1858.

Trask, C. Articulation and lip reading. *American Annals of the Deaf*, 1869, *14*, 146–156.

Tronson de Coudray, E. *Plaidoyer prononcé à l'audience du 2 mars et à l'audience du 9 mars*. Paris: Jorry, 1779.

———. *Plaidoyers pour le Sieur Cazeaux*. Paris: Knapen, 1780. (a)

———. *Second plaidoyer pour le Sieur Cazeaux*. Paris: Knapen, 1780. (b)

Trumbull, J.H. *The Memorial History of Hartford County, Connecticut 1633–1884*. Boston: Osgood, 1886.

Tucker, W.J. A half-century of progress at the New England schools. IV. The Mystic Oral School. *Volta Review*, 1939, *41*, 682–684.

Tuetey, A. *Répertoire général des sources manuscrites de l'histoire de Paris pendant la Révolution Française*. Paris: Imprimerie Nouvelle, 1890.

Turcan, J. La parole du sourd-muet, écrite par M. F. *Défense des sourds-muets*, 1886, *2*, 69–71.

Turner, J. Reminiscences on the life of Laurent Clerc. Clerc Papers no. 34b, Yale University, 1885.

Turner, W. Causes of deafness. *American Annals of the Deaf*, 1848, *1*, 25–32.

———. Course of instruction. *American Annals of the Deaf*, 1849, *2*, 97–104.

———. High school for the deaf and dumb. In: Convention of American Instructors of the Deaf, Proceedings (1851), 21–37.

———. On the teaching of grammar to the deaf and dumb. In: Convention of American Instructors of the Deaf, Proceedings (1853), 248–262. (a)

———. George H. Loring. *American Annals of the Deaf*, 1853, *5*, 40–45. (b)

———. Biographical notice of Lewis Weld, Esq., late principal of the American Asylumn. *American Annals of the Deaf*, 1854, *6*, 184–192.

———. On the deaf-mute language. In: Convention of American Instructors of the Deaf, Proceedings (1859), 177–185.

———. Hereditary deafness. In: Conference of Executives of American Schools for the Deaf, Proceedings (1868), 91–96.

———. Laurent Clerc. *American Annals of the Deaf*, 1870, *15*, 14–25.

Tyler, J. D. [Letter on Braidwood's Virginia school, enclosing Col. Bolling's letter.] *Southern Churchman*, 4 March 1842.

Tyler, W.E. Qualifications demanded in an instructor of the deaf and dumb. *American Annals of the Deaf*, 1856, *8*, 202–206.

Tylor, E.B. *Researches into the Early History of Mankind and the Development of Civilization*. London: Murray, 1865.

Umiker-Sebeok, D.J., and Sebeok, T.A. *Aboriginal Sign Languages of the Americas and Australia*. New York: Plenum, 1979.

Vaïsse, L. *Le Mécanisme de la parole mis à la portée des sourds-muets de naissance*. Paris: Institution Royale, 1838.

———. *Essai d'une grammaire symbolique à l'usage des sourds-muets*. Paris: Desportes, 1839.

———. *Essai historique sur la condition sociale et l'éducation des sourds-muets en France*. Paris: Didot, 1844. (a)

———. *Les Sourds-Muets et leur éducation*. Paris: Didot, 1844. (b)

———. Sourds-Muets. In: Lebos, P. (1844), 529–534. (c)

———. Clerc. In: Lebos, P. (1844), 207. (d)

———. L'Epée. In: Lebos, P. (1844), 176–177. (e)

———. Massieu. In: Lebos, P. (ed.) (1844), 674. (f)

———. Sicard. In: Lebos, P. (ed.) (1844), 489. (g)

———. Discours prononcé à la distribution des prix de l'Institut Royal des Sourds-Muets de Paris le 11 août 1847. *Annales de l'éducation des sourds-muets et des aveugles*, 1848, *5*, 49–80. Revision: Vaïsse, L. (1848b).

———. *Des conditions dans lesquelles s'entreprend et des moyens par lesquels s'accomplit l'instruction des sourds de naissance*. Paris: Hachette, 1848. (b)

————. *De l'écriture* . . . Paris: Firmin Didot, 1848. (c)

————. *De la parole considérée au double point de vue de la physiologie et de la grammaire*. Paris: Didot, 1853.

————. *De la pantomime comme langage naturel et moyen d'instruction des sourds-muets*. Paris: Hachette, 1854.

————. *Histoire et principes de l'art d'instruire les sourds-muets*. Paris: Hachette, 1865.

————. *Principes de l'enseignement de la parole aux sourds de naissance*. Paris: Hachette, 1870.

————. *Simples Réflexions sur quelques questions de détail* . . . Paris: Hachette, 1872. English translation (abridged): Practical suggestions relating to the instruction of the deaf and dumb. *American Annals of the Deaf*, 1874, *19*, 10–20.

————. Saboureux de Fontenay and his instructor Pereire. *American Annals of the Deaf*, 1878, *23*, 37–40. (a)

————. *Un Document retrouvé et quelques faits établis concernant l'histoire de l'éducation des sourds-muets en France*. Rodez: Ratery, 1878. English translation: *American Annals of the Deaf*, 1879, *24*, 80–90. (b)

————. The International Convention of 1880. *American Annals of the Deaf*, 1880, *25*, 151–157.

————, L. Un premier résultat du Congrès International de Milan. *Conseiller-Messager des sourds-muets*, 1881, *4*, supplement, 1–4. (a)

————. La méthode italienne. *Conseiller-Messager des sourds-muets*, 1881, supplement (9–12), (1) juin-octobre. (b)

————. Jacob-Rodrigues Pereire. *Le Courrier du soir*, 1882, *5 (1478)*, 15 avril, 3. Reprinted: *American Annals of the Deaf*, 1883, *28*, 221–226.

Valade, Y.L. Rémi. *Essai sur les mesures législatives à provoquer pour étendre à tous les sourds-muets de la France le bienfait de l'éducation* . . . Bordeaux: H. Faye, 1845.

————. *Etudes sur la lexicologie et la grammaire du langage naturel des signes*. Paris: Ladrange, 1854. Reprinted: Hong Kong: Editions Langages Croises, Chiu Ming Publishing, 1982. (a)

————. *Essai sur la grammaire du langage naturel des signes à l'usage des sourds-muets*. Paris: Roret, 1854. (b)

————. *De quelques préjugés relatifs aux sourds-muets de naissance, discours prononcé à la distribution des prix de l'Institution Impériale des Sourds-Muets de Paris, le 9 août 1856*. Paris: Boucquin, 1856.

————. *De l'origine du langage et de l'influence que les signes naturels ont exercée sur sa formation* . . . *Discours prononcé à la distribution solennelle des prix* [de l'Institution des Sourds-Muets de Paris]. Paris: Boucquin, 1866. Reprinted: *American Annals of the Deaf*, 1873, *18*, 27–41.

Valade-Gabel, A. *Histoire de l'art d'apprendre aux sourds-muets la langue écrite et la langue parlée*. Paris: Delgrave, 1875. Translation of: Hervas y Panduro (1795).

————. *Etude sur l'école espagnole des sourds-muets de Laurent Hervas y Panduro*. Grasse: Imbert, 1897.

Valade-Gabel, J.J. *De l'insuffisance du temps accordé aux sourds-muets pour leur instruction et des moyens d'y remédier*. Bordeaux: Lavigne, [n.d.].

————. *De la conduite à tenir avec les sourds-muets après leur sortie de l'école*. Bordeaux: Lavigne, [n.d.].

————. Extrait d'une lettre de M. Valade-Gabel. *Le Sourd-Muet et l'aveugle*, 1837, *1*, 256–262.

————. *Premier Mémoire sur cette question: Quel rôle l'articulation sur les lèvres doivent-elles jouer dans l'enseignement des sourds-muets?* Bordeaux: Gazay, 1839.

————. *Deuxième Mémoire sur cette question: Quel rôle l'articulation et la lecture sur les lèvres doivent-elles jouer dans l'enseignement des sourds-muets?* Paris-Bordeaux: Concierges des Institutions Royales, [n.d.]

————. *Notice sur la vie et les travaux de Jean Saint-Sernin, premier instituteur en chef de l'Institution Royale des Sourds-Muets de Bordeaux* . . . Bordeaux: Lavigne, 1844.

————. *Pereire et de l'Epée. Discours prononcé à la distribution des prix de l'Institution Nationale des Sourds-Muets de Bordeaux, le 25 août 1848*. Bordeaux: Durand, 1848.

————. Notice sur un ouvrage inédit de l'abbé de l'Epée. 1852. In: Bélanger, A. (1886).

————. *A M. le Président et à Messieurs les Membres de l'Académie Impériale de Médecine*. [*Lettre sur l'éducation des sourds-muets*.] Paris: Thunot, 1853. (a)

————. *Nouvelles Etrennes de l'enfance, petites lectures illustrées à l'usage des salles d'asiles*. Paris: author, 1853. (b)

————. Cartes mimo-mnémoniques de MM. Grosselin et Pélissier. *L'Impartial*, 1859, *2*, 165–171; 1860, *3*, 116–124.

————. *L'Enfant ne saurait-il apprendre à parler sans l'intervention des signes! Réponse à un examen critique du rapport de M. Franck, membre de l'Institut, sur la méthode intuitive pour enseigner la langue française aux sourds-muets*. Paris: Corbeil, imprimerie de Crété, 1862. (a)

————. *Des signes méthodiques et des signes réguliers, réponse aux observations publiées au sujet du rapport de M. Franck, membre de l'Institut, sur les méthodes d'enseignement en usage pour instruire les sourds-muets*. Paris: Corbeil, imprimerie de Crété, 1862. (b)

————. *Guide des instituteurs primaires pour commencer l'éducation des sourds-muets*. Paris: Dezobry, 1863.

————. *De la situation des écoles de sourds-muets non subventionnées par l'Etat*. Bordeaux: G. Gounouilhou, 1875. English translation: *American Annals of the Deaf*, 1879, *24*, 229–252.

————. *La Parole enseignée au sourd-muet, cours de phonomimie professé par J.J. Valade-Gabel, recueilli et publié par A. Valade-Gabel*. Paris: C. Delagrave, 1878.

————. *Lettres, notes et rapports de J.J. Valade-Gabel* . . . [*avec une introduction d'André Valade-Gabel*]. Grasse: E. Imbert, 1894.

————. *Méthode intuitive de J.J. Valade-Gabel pour enseigner la langue française aux sourds-muets, publiée par A. Valade-Gabel*. Grasse: E. Imbert, 1900.

Valade-Gabel, J.J., and Valade-Gabel, A. *Plan d'études. Programme de l'enseignement pour les écoles subventionnées par l'Etat.* Paris: C. Delagrave, 1879.

Valade-Gabel, J.J., and Valade-Gabel, T. *Méthode à la portée des instituteurs primaires pour enseigner aux sourds-muets la langue française sans l'intermédiaire du langage des signes.* Paris: Dezobry et Magdeleine, 1857.

Valade-Gabel, P.A. *L'Abbé de l'Epée à Villereau.* Reims: Cercle Abbé de l'Epée, 1903.

Valentine, E.G. The proper order of signs. In: Convention of American Instructors of the Deaf, Proceedings (1870), 44–80.

———. Shall we abandon the English order? *American Annals of the Deaf*, 1872, *17*, 33–47.

Valette, Marquis de la. *Les Etablissements généraux de bienfaisance placés sous le patronage de l'Impératrice. Monographies.* Paris: Imprimerie Impériale, 1867.

Valette, J. *Les Sourds-Muets avant, pendant, et après leur instruction, réponses aux questions ordinaires.* Toulouse: Gibrac, 1855.

———. *Vie de l'abbé de l'Epée.* Toulouse: Troyes, 1857.

———. *Origine de l'enseignement des sourds-muets en France.* Toulouse: Pradel, 1862.

Vallès, F. *De Sacra Philosophia.* Turin: Nicolai Beuilaqual, 1587.

Valloton, H. *Le Tsar Alexandre I.* Paris: Berger-Levrault, 1966.

Van Allen, H. A brief history of the Pennsylvania Institution for the Deaf and Dumb. In: Fay, E.A. (1893).

Van Bastealer, [?]. De l'état légal du sourd-muet. *Revue internationale de l'enseignement des Sourds-Muets*, 1890, *6*, 97–100, 134–140, 168–171, 214–219.

Van Helmont, F.M. *Alphabeti vere naturalis Hebraici brevissima delineatio quae simul methodum suppeditat juxta quam, qui surdi nati sunt, sic informari possunt, ut non alios saltem loquentes intelligant, sed et ipsi ad sermonis usum perveniant.* Sulzbaci: A. Lichtenthaleri, 1667.

———. *The Spirit of Diseases; or Diseases of the Spirit.* London: Hawkins, 1694.

Van Nostrand, J. On the cultivation of sign language as a means of mental improvement to the deaf and dumb. In: Convention of American Instructors of the Deaf, Proceedings (1853), 39–112.

Van Schelle, L. See: Congress on the Deaf—International—Third (1883).

Vapereau, G. *Dictionnaire universel des contemporains.* Paris: Hachette, 1893.

Varjot, B. *Approche de quelques aspects de la vie sociale des sourds-muets et de leur instruction au milieu du XIXème siècle, vus au travers de l'Impartial.* Thèse, Ecole Nationale de la Santé Publique, Rennes, 1980.

Vauchelet, [?]. Bébian. *Le Colonial (Guadeloupe)*, 1911, 17, 24, 31 May, 14 June.

Veditz, G.W. The state of deaf mute education in America. In: Congress of the Deaf—International—Second (1893), 177–190. (a)

———. Deaf-mutes as teachers. In: Convention of American Instructors of the Deaf, Proceedings (1893), 81–83. (b)

———. Recent events among the deaf of Germany. In: National Association of the Deaf, Proceedings (1896), 22–27.

———. President's address. In: National Association of the Deaf, Proceedings (1907), 12–16. (a)

———. The future of the American deaf. In: National Association of the Deaf, Proceedings (1907), 24–28. (b)

———. Miscellaneous: Why not reverse the process? *American Annals of the Deaf*, 1910, *55*, 206–207. (a)

———. President's address. World Congress of the Deaf. *American Annals of the Deaf*, 1910, *55*, 396–398. (b)

———. Preservation of sign language. Film. Silver Spring: National Association of the Deaf, 1913.

———. The genesis of the National Association. *Deaf-Mutes Journal*, 1933, *62 (22)*, 1 June, 1.

Vernon, M., and Koh, S. Early manual communication and deaf children's achievement. *American Annals of the Deaf*, 1970, *115*, 527–536.

———. Effects of oral preschool compared to early manual communication on education and communication in deaf children. *American Annals of the Deaf*, 1971, *116*, 569–574.

Victoria University of Manchester, Library for Deaf Education. *An Annotated Catalog of Books on the Education of the Deaf . . . Collected by A. Farrar.* Stoke-on-Trent: Hill and Ainsworth, 1932.

Villenave, M.G.T. Journal intime 1804–1805. *Revue retrospective*, 1893, *8*, 289–336.

Virey, J.J. *Histoire naturelle du genre humain. (Avec une dissertation sur le sauvage de l'Aveyron).* Paris: Dufart, 1801.

———. "Homme, homme des bois, homme sauvage." In: *Nouveau dictionnaire d'histoire naturelle.* Nouvelle édition, Vol. 15. Paris: Déterville, 1817.

Vivé, P. *Cause célèbre; sourd-muet de naissance convaincu d'avoir contrefait des assignats . . . défendu par Pierre Vivé.* Paris: Morin, 1796.

Volquin, H. *Surdi-mutité. Exposé de quelques faits relatifs à la question pendant devant l'Académie Impériale de Médecine.* Paris: Chalvet, 1853. (a)

———. Etude historique sur l'Institution Impériale des Sourds-Muets de Paris. *Bienfaiteur des sourds-muets et des aveugles*, 1853, *1*, 69–71. (b)

———. *Essai sur les moyens de donner gratuitement aux sourds-muets l'éducation intellectuelle et agricole.* Paris: Chalvet, 1854.

———. *L'Art d'instruire les sourds-muets mis à la portée de tous les instituteurs primaires par un instituteur.* Paris: Hachette, 1856.

———. Des conditions exigées pour devenir en France instituteur des sourds-muets. *L'Impartial*, 1857, 2, 119–123, 141–147.

———. The Central Society of Education and Aid for Deaf Mutes in France, and anniversary festival of deaf-mutes in Paris. *American Annals of the Deaf*, 1857, 9, 153–163.

Volta Bureau. *International Reports of Schools for the Deaf.* Washington, D.C.: Gibson, 1902.

Volta Review. Statistics of speech teaching in American schools for the deaf. 1899, *1*, 84–106, 1900, 2, 298–315; 1901, *3*, 156–160, 280–297; 1902, 4, 134–138, 292–311; 1903, *5*, 190–194, 300–316; 1904, 6, 270–281; 1905, 7, 282–293; 1906, 8, 270–283; 1907, 9, 370–383; 1908, *10*, 290–302; 1909, *11*, 234–246; 1910, *12*, 246–258; 1911, *13*, 104–116; 1912, *14*, 108–121; 681–683; 1913, *15*, 92–103; 1914, *16*, 79–81; 310–322; 1915, *17*, 190–202; 1916, *18*, 200–213; 1917, *19*, 240–252; 1918, *20*, 368–381; 1919, *21*, 392–405; 1920, *22*, 362–375.

Wade, W. A list of deaf-blind persons in the United States and Canada. *American Annals of the Deaf*, 1900, *45*, 317–324.

Wagner, [?]. De la méthode allemande et de la méthode française. *Annales de l'éducation des sourds-muets et des aveugles*, 1848, *5*, 180–185. Translated: Morel (1849).

Waite, H.E. *Make a Joyful Sound: The Romance of Mabel Hubbard and Alexander Graham Bell.* Philadelphia: Macrae Smith, 1961.

Waldo, S.P. *The Tour of James Monroe, President, in 1817.* Hartford: Bolles, 1818.

Walker, G.L. *History of the First Church in Hartford, 1633–1883.* Hartford: Brown and Gross, 1884.

Walker, W. *Ten New England Leaders.* Boston: Silver, Burdett, 1901.

Wallis, J. *Grammatica Linguae Anglicanae.* Oxford: Robinson, 1653. English translation: Greenwood, J. *An Essay Towards a Practical English Grammar.* London: Beltes-Worter, 1729.

Wallis, J. Letters to Mr. Robert Boyle, 30 December 1661 and May 1662. In: Boyle, R. *Works of Robert Boyle.* London: Phillips, 1700.

———. Letter to the Honorable Robert E. Boyle, March 1662. *Philosophical Transactions of the Royal Society*, 1670, *(61)*, Supplement, 18 July, 1087–1099. Excerpted: *American Annals of the Deaf*, 1850, *3*, 227–233.

———. *A Defence of the Royal Society and the Philosophical Transactions Particularly Those for July 1670 in Answer to the Cavils of Dr. W. Holder by way of letter to Wm. Lord Viscount Brouncker.* London: Thomas Moore, 1678.

———. Letter from John Wallis to Thomas Beverly on the education of deaf-mutes. 30 September 1698. Reprinted: *Mathematical Works of John Wallis.* Oxford: 1693. Vol. 3, p. 696; *Philosophical Transactions of the Royal Society*, 1698, *20*, 353–360; (excerpted) Green (1783), 96–113; Arnold (1888), 42–44. French translation: Bébian (1817), 137–149.

———. [Autobiographical letter to Thomas Smith.] In: T. Haerne (ed.). *Peter Langtoft's Chronicle.* Oxford: At the Theatre, 1725. Reprinted: *Works of Thomas Haerne.* London: Bagster, 1810. Vols. 3, 4, pp. clxi–clxx.

Walsh, T.A. The battle of methods. *American Annals of the Deaf*, 1901, *46*, 508–518.

———. The battle of methods—a rejoinder. *American Annals of the Deaf*, 1902, *47*, 196–203.

Ward, L. Handicapped children in our public schools. *Wisconsin Journal of Education*, 1936, 329.

Waring, E. *The Deaf in the Past and Present Times.* Grinnell: E.S. Waring, 1896.

Washabaugh, W. Hearing and deaf signers on Providence Island. *Sign Language Studies*, 1979, *24*, 191–214.

———. The deaf of Grand Cayman, British West Indies. *Sign Language Studies*, 1981, *31*, 117–132.

Watson, J. *Instruction of the Deaf and Dumb.* London: Darton and Harvey, 1809.

Watson, T.A. *The Birth and Babyhood of the Telephone.* New York: American Telegraph and Telephone, 1913.

———. *Exploring Life.* New York: Appleton, 1926.

Watson, T.J. The History of Deaf Education in Scotland from 1760–1939. Doctoral dissertation, University of Edinburgh, 1949.

Watteville du Grab, A. de. Etat actuel des établissements consacrés aux sourds-muets en France. *Annales de l'éducation des sourds-muets et des aveugles*, 1845, *2*, 99–110.

———. *Statistique des établissements de bienfaisance. Rapport sur les sourds-muets . . .* Paris: Imprimerie Impériale, 1861.

Way, D., and Whipple, Z. The Whipple Method. *American Annals of the Deaf*, 1891, *36*, 283–291.

Webster, N. *Dissertations on the English Language.* Boston: Thomas, 1789.

Weeks, W.H. The purity of the sign language. In: National Association of the Deaf, Proceedings (1890), 57–59.

Weiner, D. Le droit de l'homme à la santé—une belle idée devant l'Assemblée Constituante, 1790–1791. *Clio Medica*, 1970, *5*, 210–223.

———. The blind man and the French Revolution. *Bulletin of the History of Medicine*, 1974, *48*, 60–89.

———. Les handicapés et la révolution française. *Aspects de la médecine sociale*, 1977, *6*, 43–53.

———. The deaf-mute and the French Revolution. Unpublished manuscript, School of Medicine, University of California, Los Angeles, 1982.

Weld, L. *Fifth Annual Report to the Legislature by the Pennsylvannia Institution for the Deaf and Dumb, together with an address by Lewis Weld.* Philadelphia: Fry, 1826.

———. *An Address Delivered in the Capitol, in Washington city, February 16, 1828, at an Exhibition of Three of the Pupils of the Pennsylvannia Institution for the Education of the Deaf and Dumb.* Washington, D.C.: Way and Gideon, 1828.

———. *Tenth Annual Report to the Legislature by the Pennsylvannia Institution for the Deaf and Dumb.* Philadelphia: Kite, 1830.

————. Julia Brace. In: American School for the Deaf, Reports (1837), 14–33.

————. [Report of visit to institution for the deaf and dumb in Europe.] In: American School for the Deaf, Reports (1845), 25–123.

————. History of the American Asylum. *American Annals of the Deaf*, 1848, *1*, 7–14. Excerpted: Barnard (1852).

————. Suggestions on certain varieties of the language of signs as used in the instruction of the deaf and dumb. In: Convention of American Instructors of the Deaf, Proceedings (1851), 77–86.

Wentz, C.C. The utility of signs. *American Annals of the Deaf*, 1893, *28*, 124–134.

Wesselius, S. The law and the day school for the deaf. National Education Association, Proceedings (1901), 870–876.

West, L. The Sign Language Analyses. Unpublished doctoral dissertation, Indiana University, 1960.

Westervelt, Z.F. Articulation. In: Convention of American Instructors of the Deaf, Proceedings (1879), 241–267.

————. The disuse of signs. In: Convention of American Instructors of the Deaf, Proceedings (1897), 165–183.

————. The American vernacular method. *American Annals of the Deaf*, 1889, *34*, 191–208.

————. The colloquial use of English by the deaf. In: Convention of American Instructors of the Deaf, Proceedings (1890), 112–119.

————. Dr. G.O. Fay's "week at Rochester." *American Annals of the Deaf*, 1890, *35*, 41–44.

————. American Association to Promote the Teaching of Speech to the Deaf. *American Annals of the Deaf*, 1891, *36*, 222–224.

————. How signs disappeared from the Rochester School. *American Annals of the Deaf*, 1901, *46*, 102–107.

Wheeler, F.R. Growth of American Schools for the deaf. *American Annals of the Deaf*, 1920, *65*, 367–378.

White, H.C. Spelling versus signs. *American Annals of the Deaf*, 1890, *35*, 111–114.

Wied-Neuwied, M. *Maximilian, Prince of Weid's Travels in the Interior of North America.* Cleveland: A.H. Clark, 1906.

Wilkins, J. *Mercury or the Secret and Swift Messenger.* London: Norton, 1641.

Wilkinson, W. The development of speech and of the sign language. *American Annals of the Deaf*, 1881, *26*, 167–178.

————. European notes. *American Annals of the Deaf*, 1893, *38*, 38–44. (a)

————. Visit to schools for the deaf in Europe with special reference to the results obtained by the oral method. In: Conference of Executives of American Schools for the Deaf, Proceedings (1893), 137–140. (b)

————. Isaac Lewis Peet. *American Annals of the Deaf*, 1899, *44*, 77–83.

Williams, J. The "pure oral" and the American system compared. *American Annals of the Deaf*, 1881, *26*, 239–244.

————. What deaf-mute education in the United States owes to the American Asylum and its early instructors. In: Convention of American Instructors of the Deaf, Proceedings (1882), 54–61.

————. Discussion of "Deaf-mute instruction in relation to the work of the public schools" by A.G. Bell. In: National Education Association (1885).

————. William Wolcott Turner. *American Annals of the Deaf*, 1887, *32*, 209–217.

————. A correction. *American Annals of the Deaf*, 1891, *36*, 116–120. (a)

————. Hereditary deafness: a study. *Science*, 1891, *17 (418)*, 76–77. (b)

————. A brief history of the American Asylum at Hartford. In: Fay, E.A. (1893), 1–30. (a)

————. A general view of the education of the deaf in the United States. In: Convention of American Instructors of the Deaf, Proceedings (1893), 9–17. (b)

————. What influence have signs on the manner and morals of the deaf? In: Convention of American Instructors of the Deaf, Proceedings (1899), 257.

Williams, L.L. The medical examination of mentally defective aliens: its scope and limitations. *American Journal of Insanity*, 1914, *71 (2)*, 257–268.

Williams, S.W. Mason Cogswell. In: *American Medical Biography.* Greenfield, Mass.: Merriam, 1844. Pp. 100–109.

Willis, N.P. *American Scenery.* London: 1839. Reprinted: Barre: Imprint Society, 1971.

Wilson, J. G., and Fiske, J. *Appleton's Cyclopedia of American Biography.* New York: Appleton, 1888. Reprinted: Detroit: Gale, 1968.

Winefield, R. Bell, Gallaudet and the Sign Language Debate. Unpublished doctoral dissertation, Harvard University School of Education, 1981.

Winsor, J. (ed.). *Memorial History of Boston.* Boston: Osgood, 1881.

Wisconsin Phonological Institute. History of the Wisconsin System of Public Day Schools. In: Fay, E.A. (1893).

————. *Improvement of the Wisconsin System of Education for Deaf-mutes.* Milwaukee: Wisconsin Phonological Institute, 1894.

Wood, A. *Anthenae Oxoniencenses.* London: Bennet, 1691–1692.

Wood, A.D. Mrs. Sigourney and the sensibility of the inner space. *New England Quarterly*, 1972, *45 (2)*, 163–181.

Woodbridge, W.C. Deaf and Dumb. In: *Encyclopedia Americana.* Philadelphia: Lea and Carey, 1829–33. Vol. 4 [1830], pp. 329–337.

Woodruff, C.E. Prevention of degeneration the only practical eugenics. *Proceedings of the American Breeders' Association,* 1907, *3,* 247–252.

Woodruff, L.H. Julia Brace. *American Annals of the Deaf,* 1849, *2,* 65–74.

Woods, F.A. A review of reviews: Of Madison Grant's "Passing of the Great Race." *Journal of Heredity,* 1923, *14,* 93–95.

Woodward, J. Some characteristics of Pidgin Sign English. *Sign Language Studies,* 1973, *3,* 39–46.

————. Signs of change: Historical variation in American Sign Language. *Sign Language Studies,* 1976, *10,* 81–94. (a)

————. Attitudes toward deaf people on Providence Island: a preliminary survey. *Sign Language Studies,* 1978, *18,* 49–68. (b)

————. Historical bases of American Sign Language. In: Siple, P. (ed.). *Understanding Language Through Sign Language Research.* New York: Academic Press, 1978. (a)

————. Some sociolinguistic problems in the implementation of a bilingual education for deaf students. In: *Proceedings of the National Symposium on Sign Language Research and Teaching.* Silver Spring: National Association of the Deaf, 1978. Pp. 183–203. (b)

Woodward, J., and De Santis, S. Negative incorporation in French and American Sign Language. *Language in Society,* 1977, *6,* 379–388.

Woodward, J., and Erting, C. Synchronic variation and historical change in American Sign Language. *Language Sciences,* 1975, *37,* 9–12.

World's Congress of Instructors of the Deaf. *Proceedings of the World's Congress of Instructors of the Deaf and of the Thirteenth Convention of American Instructors of the Deaf.* See: Convention of American Instructors of the Deaf, Proceedings (1893).

Wright, J.D. The true product of the oral method. *Volta Review,* 1912, *14,* 312–313.

"X." Deaf and dumb. *Christian Observer,* 1824, *24,* 423.

"X, Y." Notice historique sur l'Institut Royal des Sourds-Muets de Milan. *Revue internationale de l'enseignement des sourds-muets,* 1886, *1,* 309–311; 1886, *2,* 115–119.

Yale, C.A. A report on the Third International Congress for the amelioration of the condition of deaf-mutes, and on European schools visited. Appendix A in: Clarke Institution, Reports (1883), 55–81.

————. History and development of articulation teaching in America. In: Alexander Graham Bell Association, Proceedings (1892), 173–182.

————. See: Clarke School (1893).

————. The beginning of speech teaching. *Volta Review,* 1910, *12,* 481–482.

————. Dr. Bell's connection with the Clarke School. *Volta Review,* 1922, *24,* 364–365.

————. Mabel Hubbard Bell—1859–1923. *Volta Review,* 1923, *25,* 107–110.

————. Extracts from the school journal of Miss Rogers. *Volta Review,* 1927, *29,* 199–204. (a)

————. Further glimpses of the early work of Miss Rogers. *Volta Review,* 1927, *29,* 361–363. (b)

————. Dr. Bell's early experiments in giving speech to the deaf. *Volta Review,* 1927, *29,* 293–295. (c)

————. *Years of Building. Memories of a Pioneer in a Special Field of Education.* New York: Dial Press, 1931.

Yater, V. *Mainstreaming of Children with Hearing Loss.* Springfield: Thomas, 1977.

Yebra, M. *Libro Llamado Refugium Infirmorum.* Madrid: Luis Sanchez, 1593.

"Z,A." Plan for instructing the deaf and dumb. *Christian Observer,* 1824, *24,* 226–229.

INDEX

A

Abbé de l'Epée, The (Bouilly), 28, 42–57,
    345, 422
    central figure in, 42–44
    Christian religion in, 56–57
    effect of, 28, 42
    famous scene of, 44–45
    see also Joseph, alleged count of Solar;
    Solar affair
abolitionists, 282, 286–87, 295
abstract concepts:
    deaf as incapable of comprehending, 38,
    47, 78, 91–92
    in sign language, 59, 99, 209, 212,
    374–76
Academy of Medicine, French, 139, 150,
    152–53
Adams, John Quincy, 47, 247
Africans, 282, 399–400
Agricola (Rudolph Bauer), 68
agricultural asylums, 402–3

Akerly, Benjamin A., 239
Akerly, Samuel, 221, 230, 239–40, 247
Albany Advertiser, 220
Aléa, J. M. d', 64
Alexander I, czar of Russia, 155–56, 437
Alexander Graham Bell Association, *see*
    American Association to Promote the
    Teaching of Speech to the Deaf
Alhoy, Louis François, 417, 419
Allibert, Eugène, 138–39, 153, 305, 434
American Annals of the Deaf, 274, 349,
    446, 458
American Association to Promote the
    Teaching of Speech to the Deaf, 368–
    69, 413
American Asylum, *see* Hartford school
American Breeders' Association, 355,
    358–59
American Colonization Society, 274n
American Sign Language, 212–13, 226–27,
    243–44, 373
    abbreviation and regularization of, 226–
    28, 281–82

About the Author

A specialist in the psychology of language and linguistics, HARLAN LANE received his B.A. and M.A. from Columbia University and his Ph.D. under B. F. Skinner at Harvard University in 1960. For several years he was professor of psychology at the University of Michigan, where he was also the director of the Center for Research on Language and Language Behavior. He was then visiting professor at the Sorbonne in Paris for five years and received there his state doctorate in linguistics. After returning to the United States, he served as visiting professor in the department of linguistics at the University of California, San Diego. He is now professor of psychology at Northeastern University, and director of Northeastern's extensive research program on the American Sign Language of the Deaf.

In addition to numerous articles, Dr. Lane is the author of *The Wild Boy of Aveyron*, a highly acclaimed study of the life of a feral child and the foundations of special education, and co-author (with Richard Pillard) of *The Wild Boy of Burundi*, on the psychological catastrophes of childhood. He is editor of *The Deaf Experience*, readings in translation on the history of the deaf, and co-editor (with François Grosjean) of *Recent Perspectives on American Sign Language*, a survey of contemporary scholarship concerning the language of the deaf.